To Helen,
Wishing you a
Christmas and a
New Year. Fr...

PENGUIN BOOKS
THE HINDU NATIONALIST M

Christophe Jaffrelot is a research fellow of the Centre National de la Recherche Scientifique and member of the Centre d'Études et de Recherches Internationales at the Fondation Nationale des Sciences Politiques in Paris. He teaches South Asian politics at the Institut d'Études Politiques in Paris.

Christmas 2000.

CHRISTOPHE JAFFRELOT

The
Hindu Nationalist
Movement
and
Indian Politics

1925 to the 1990s

Strategies of Identity-Building,
Implantation and Mobilisation
(*with special reference to Central India*)

PENGUIN BOOKS

Penguin Books India (P) Ltd., 11 Community Centre, Panchsheel Park, New Delhi 110 017, India
Penguin Books Ltd., 27 Wrights Lane, London W8 5TZ, UK
Penguin Putnam Inc., 375 Hudson Street, New York, NY 10014, USA
Penguin Books Australia Ltd., Ringwood, Victoria, Australia
Penguin Books Canada Ltd., 10 Alcorn Avenue, Suite 300, Toronto, Ontario M4V 3B2, Canada
Penguin Books (NZ) Ltd., 182-190 Wairau Road, Auckland 10, New Zealand

First published as *Les nationalistes hindous* by Presses de la Fondation Nationale des Sciences Politiques, Paris © 1993
First published in the United Kingdom by C. Hurst & Co. (Publishers) Ltd. London
English translation and updating © C. Hurst & Co. (Publishers) Ltd. 1996

Published in Viking by Penguin Books India in association with C. Hurst & Co. (Publishers) Ltd. 1996
Published by Penguin Books India 1999

10 9 8 7 6 5 4 3 2

For Matthieu

ACKNOWLEDGEMENTS

This book is based on the second part of my Ph.D. thesis[1] which was written in 1987-91 under the guidance of Jean Leca, whose help was especially useful in shaping the theoretical framework of the study, and of Bruce Graham, to whom I largely owe my quest for accuracy in addition to much information.

The present edition draws from a French book[2] which has been considerably amended, enlarged and updated. I tried to adapt it for the English-reading public, among whom are a greater number of people familiar with India than there are in France. Secondly, the French version has been brought up to date, which led me to add a fifth part.

Besides my attempt at constructing a model of Hindu nationalist strategies, one specific feature of this book is the concern it shows for the relations between the national and local levels based on my fieldwork in Madhya Pradesh (central India). I thank Jean-Luc Chambard, the Diwan family and Mr N. Rajan as well as the successive directors of the Alliance Française in Bhopal Alain Passagne, Vincent Despagnet and Roger Thévenot for their help while I was conducting research in that state between 1988 and 1995.

This work benefited from the assistance of Chandra Ranade in the transcription of the Hindi interviews I conducted in Delhi and Madhya Pradesh and from the advice of Dr Naheed Ahmad, Alice Thorner and Lorraine Kennedy. Most of my trips to India in connection with this work have been supported financially by the Centre d'Etudes et de Recherches Internationales (Fondation Nationale des Sciences Politiques) whose then director, Jean-Luc Domenach, has always been most helpful. The active work of translation was a co-operative effort, in which Christopher Hurst and Michael Dwyer, the directors of the originating publisher, C. Hurst & Co., played a vital part.

Naturally the book's shortcomings are mine alone.

Finally, this book would not have been possible without the support of my wife, Christine.

1 'Des nationalistes en quête d'une nation. Les partis nationalistes hindous au XXème siècle', Ph.D. thesis, Institut d'Etudes Politiques, Paris, 1991.
2 *Les nationalistes hindous – Idéologie, implantation et mobilisation des années 1920 aux années 1990*, Paris: Presses de la Fondation Nationale des Sciences Politiques, 1993.

CONTENTS

Part V. THE EARLY 1990s: HOW TO CONQUER AND RETAIN POWER

MAPS

TABLES

ILLUSTRATION

ABBREVIATIONS

ABKM	Akhil Bharatiya Kendriya Mandal (executive committee of the RSS)
ABVP	Akhil Bharatiya Vidyarhi Parishad
AMU	Aligarh Muslim University
ARIPP	*Annual Register of Indian Political Parties*
BHEL	Bharat Heavy Electricals Limited
BHU	Benares Hindu University
BJP	Bharatiya Janata Party
BJYM	Bharatiya Janata Yuva Morcha
BLD	Bharatiya Lok Dal
BMAC	Babri Masjid Action Committee
BMCC	Babri Masjid Coordination Committee
BMS	Bharatiya Mazdoor Sangh
BSF	Border Security Force
CPI	Communist Party of India
CPI(M)	Communist Party of India (Marxist)
CRPF	Central Reserve Police Force
DAV College	Dayanand Anglo-Vedic College
EPW	*Economic and Political Weekly*
HM	Hindu Mahasabha
IAR	*Indian Annual Register*
IAS	Indian Administrative Service
IJPS	*The Indian Journal of Political Science*
INTUC	Indian National Trade Union Congress
IOLR	India Office Library and Records (London)
ITC	Instructors' Training Camp
JP	Janata Party
JS	Jana Sangh
JSAIGC	Jana Sangh All India General Council
JSCWC	Jana Sangh Central Working Committee
LSS	Lok Sangharsh Samiti
MAS	*Modern Asian Studies*
MISA	Maintenance of Internal Security Act
MLA	Member of Legislative Assembly

MP	Member of Parliament
NAI	National Archives of India (New Delhi)
NMML	Nehru Memorial Museum and Library
OTC	Officers' Training Camp
PAC	Provincial Army Constabulary (Uttar Pradesh Police)
PSP	Praja Socialist Party
RFSP	*Revue Francaise de Science Politique*
RRP	Ram Rajya Parishad
RSS	Rashtriya Swayamsevak Sangh
SGPC	Shiromani Gurudwara Prabhandak Committee
SP	Socialist Party
SSP	Samyukta Socialist Party
SVD	Samyukta Vidhayak Dal
VHP	Vishwa Hindu Parishad
VKA	Vanavasi Kalyan Ashram

GLOSSARY

dharna	sit-in
gherao	a form of protest that involves surrounding an individual in order to prevent him leaving a building or another location
Gram Raj Abhiyan	campaign for village autonomy
Gurukul	the place where a guru teaches the *Vedas* to brahmacharis
jagirdar	a chief or noble to whom local land revenues and other policing or judicial functions were assigned in the colonial and pre-colonial period
kar sevak	a volunteer who took part in the movement to build a temple at Ayodhya
Hindu Sangathan	a movement launched in the 1920s with the aim of uniting Hindu society by transcending divisions of caste and sect
Hindu Rashtra	the Hindu nation
kisan	peasant
Mandi Samiti	local market committee in charge of regulating the purchase and sale of notified agricultural produce
panchayat	local representative committee elected by several villages
Pandit	a learned Brahmin
pith	monastery
pracharak	propagandist and full-time RSS worker
Ram Shila Pujan	the cult of the bricks with which the Ram temple at Ayodhya was to be built (also used as a means of fund-raising)
Rin Mukti	lit. liberation from debt
sadhu	world renouncer, ascetic Hindu
Sangathan Mantri	organising secretary of the Jana Sangh and later the BJP
sanghchalak	a leading citizen acting as a local patron of the RSS
sarpanch	head of a *panchayat*
sarsanghchalak	chief of the RSS
satyagraha	non-violent protest
shakha	local branch of the RSS
tehsil	sub-division of a district
swayamsevak	a RSS volunteer
zamindar	lit. a possessor of land; formerly a revenue farmer recognised as a landlord by the British Raj

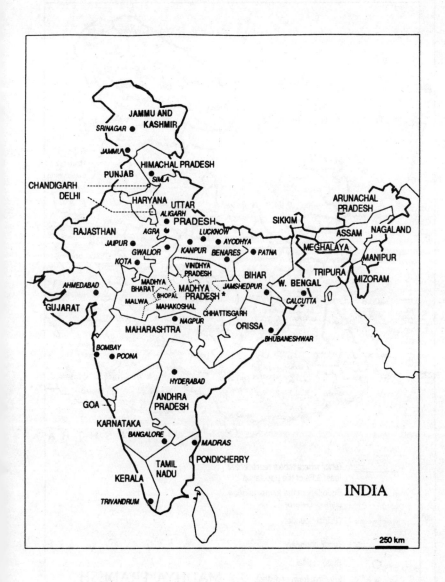

INDIA

250 km

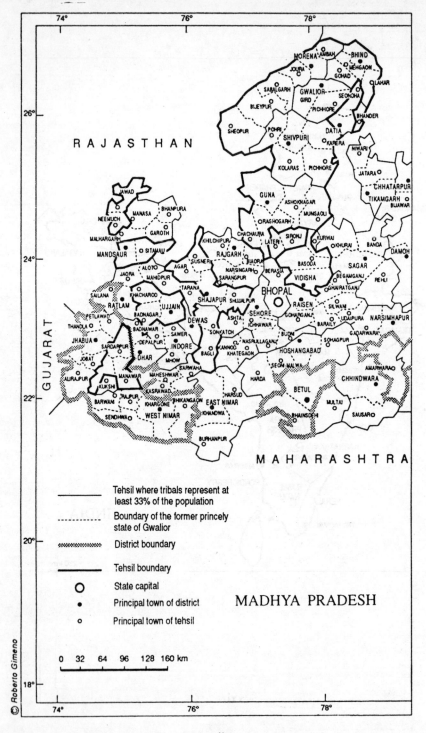

Tehsil where tribals represent at least 33% of the population

Boundary of the former princely state of Gwalior

District boundary

Tehsil boundary

State capital

Principal town of district

Principal town of tehsil

MADHYA PRADESH

0   32   64   96   128   160 km

© Roberto Gimeno

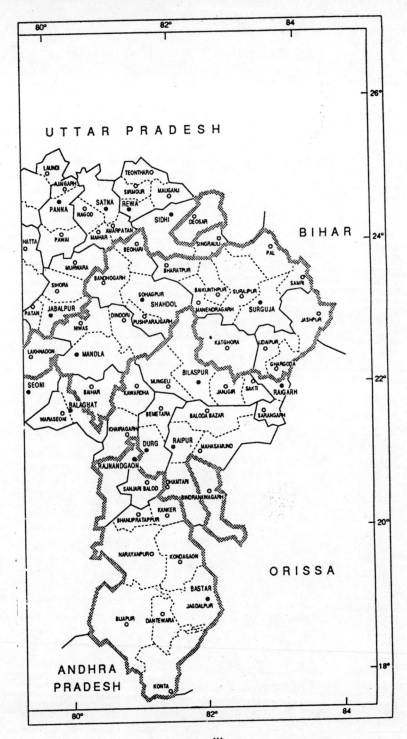

INTRODUCTION

In the late 1980s and early 1990s India witnessed an unprecedented rise in militant Hinduism. This phenomenon is a challenging one for social scientists in so far as the essential characteristics of Hinduism scarcely lend themselves to a closed and monolithic radicalism of the type associated with Muslim, Jewish or Christian 'fundamentalisms'. In fact, Hinduism is distinguished by a socio-cultural differentiation and a capacity for integration which hardly seem compatible with the expression of a militant collective consciousness.

The culture of the low castes incorporates forms of worship and practices which differ from those of the high castes – most notably the Brahmins – who derive their authority from Sanskrit texts; hence the notions of Sanskritised Hinduism and popular Hinduism. At first sight it would seem as if one is dealing with a classic duality between a Great Tradition and a Little Tradition. In the Hindu case, however, this schema is complicated by the lack of unity in the Great Tradition.[2] S.C. Dube underlines this point:

Sanskritic sources provide not one model but many models, some of them involving even fundamentally opposed ideals. What we call Hindu philosophy is not just one school of thought, it is a compendium of many systems of thought, recognizing and advocating many divergent images of society and many different schemes of values.[3]

The Great Tradition of Hinduism, although it sanctions a rigorous orthopraxy embodied in the caste system, does not in fact contain an orthodoxy. This peculiarity results primarily from the lack of any 'Book' which can truly be said to serve as a common reference-point. As Renou points out, 'religious books can be described as books written for the use

---

[1] One uses these concepts in the sense expounded by R. Redfield in 'The natural history of folk society', *Social Forces*, 30 (3), March 1953, p. 228.

[2] Hence the methodological crisis of M. Singer when he attempted to apply Redfield's categories to India (*When a great tradition modernizes*, London: Pall Mall Press, 1972, p. 82).

[3] S.C. Dube, 'The study of complex cultures' in T.K.N. Unnithan, I. Deva and Y. Singh (eds), *Towards a sociology of cultures in India*, New Delhi: Prentice-Hall, 1965, p. 423.

1

of a sect.'[4] Thus the Hinduism of the Great Tradition appears as a 'conglomeration of sects',[5] known as a *sampradaya* (from the Sanskrit *samprada*, to transmit); indeed the essence of the sect lies in 'the uninterrupted transmission from one master to another'[6] of the message of the founding *guru*, which itself derives from a revelation. On the other hand, a Hindu sect may also take the form of a *panth* (way), where the founder is not considered as having been the recipient of a divine revelation. Isolated from one another, these sects are also rivals to the extent that they compete for the patronage of the powerful and for the pre-eminence of their particular teachings. This sectarian logic can lead to an analysis of Hinduism not as a religion but as a juxtaposition of religions[7] which possesses little in the way of a formal structure.

The main current of Hinduism – if not the only one – which became formalised in a way that approximates to an 'ecclesiastical structure'[8] was that of Shankara. This ascetic reformer of the eighth century responded to the spread of Buddhism by establishing monasteries (*math*) in the four corners of India – Sringeri in the south, Dwarka in the west, Badri in the north and Puri in the east – at the head of which were placed *shankaracharyas*, ordained to exercise a spiritual authority comparable to that of the Buddhist clergy.

The development of a collective Hindu consciousness was inhibited not only by the extreme social and religious differentiation within Hinduism but also by a tendency to discount the importance of the Other and therefore to ignore the need for solidarity in the face of that Other. Hinduism has always recognised the existence of 'aliens' and 'barbarians' (*mlecchas*). But such groups were made the object of discrimination, not on the basis of ethnic criteria but because they did not conform to the prescribed rituals of which the Brahmins were the guardians. Once this obstacle had been removed there was no longer a barrier preventing their socio-cultural integration.[9] In this process the internal logic of the caste system reveals its capacity for assimilation: in so far as the hierarchy

[4]   L. Renou, *Religions of Ancient India*, New Delhi: Munshiram Manoharlal, 1972 (2nd edn), p. 50.

[5]   R. Thapar, 'Imagined religious communities? Ancient history and the modern search for a Hindu identity', *Modern Asian Studies* (henceforth *MAS*), 23 (2), 1989, p. 216.

[6]   C. Clémentin-Ohja, *La divinité conquise – carrière d'une sainte*, Nanterre: Société d'ethnologie, 1990, p. 19.

[7]   See H. von Stienencron, 'Hinduism: On the proper use of a deceptive term' in G.D. Sontheimer and H. Kulke (eds), *Hinduism reconsidered*, New Delhi: Manohar, 1989, p. 20.

[8]   R. Thapar, 'Syndicated moksha?', *Seminar*, Sept. 1985, p. 17; see also p. 20.

[9]   R. Thapar, *Ancient Indian history*, New Delhi: Orient Longman, 1978, pp. 165, 169 and 173. See also A. Purasher, 'Attitudes towards the *Mleccha* in early northern India—up to c.A.D. 600', *The Indian Historical Review* 9 (1-2), July 1982–Jan. 1983, pp. 1-30.

represents a system of gradation based on the notion of ritual purity, everyone can find a place in it, below the Brahmins, according to his degree of conformity with the exalted values personified by Brahmins.[10] Thus it was that invaders such as the Huns found themselves classed as Kshatriyas (warriors), observing the ritual practices prescribed for these castes and recognising the authority of the Brahmins.

Paradoxically, the ability to integrate newcomers also reflected an inability to recognise the Other as such. Brahminical texts assume that the indigenous social order has a homologous relationship to the cosmic order, the Dharma; and it is the preservation of this relationship in equilibrium which tends to demand the assimilation of foreign elements into the social system. The same texts describe this society as endowed with a language and territory that have unique attributes and thus enable the rites necessary to perpetuate the Dharmic order to be performed. Sanskrit is that language *par excellence*, and other languages are seen as, at best, degraded forms of it. In parallel to this, North India – Aryavarta – is considered to be the land where the rites necessary for the maintenance of Dharma are fulfilled. These concepts underpin a specific Indian traditional 'xenology' that reflects the Brahminical world view and once again disregards the Other:

The Indocentrism developed in 'orthodox' Hindu thought transcends by far what is ordinarily called 'ethnocentrism'. It is not simply an unquestioned perspective or bias, but a sophisticated theoretical structure of self-universalization and self-isolation. Seen from within this complex, highly differentiated structure, the *mlecchas* are nothing but a faint and distant phenomenon at the horizon of the indigenous tradition. They do not possess an 'otherness' against which one's own identity could be asserted or in which it could be reflected.[11]

This belief in a privileged connection between India and Dharma underlies the logic of the social system of the *varnas*, which consists of Brahmins (priests and men of learning), Kshatriyas (warriors), Vaishyas (merchants and artisans) and Shudras (the servile castes). In a foundation myth of the Vedas – the basis of the Brahminical Great Tradition – these *varnas* are described as owing their origin to the sacrificial dismemberment of the cosmic Primeval Man, the Virat Purusha, when the Brahmin proceeded from his mouth, the Kshatriya from his arms, the Vaishya from his thighs, and the Shudra from his feet.[12] This division of the social structure into four parts reflects the belief in a correspondence between

[10]   L. Dumont, *Homo hierarchicus*, Paris: Gallimard, 1966, p. 242.

[11]   W. Halbfass, *India and Europe – An essay in understanding*, Albany: State University of New York Press, 1988, p. 187.

[12]   *Hymnes spéculatifs du Veda*, notes and translation by L. Renou, Paris: Gallimard/Unesco, 1956, p. 89.

Hindu society and the totality of the cosmic order, a correspondence which hampers the development of a distinct identity. Nothing outside it can have any meaning or be worthy of interest.[13] In the absence of 'them', there cannot be 'we' and 'us'. This worldview, in association with the capacity for integration possessed by the caste system, illustrate the combination of 'inclusivism' and 'hierarchization' described by Paul Hacker as specific to Hindu civilization. This twofold process consists in 'claiming for, and thus including in, one's own religion what really belongs to an alien sect' and 'in affiliating the foreign with what is one's own by way of subordination.'[14] Commenting upon this definition, which complements his notion of 'Indian traditional xenology', Halbfass adds: 'The other, the foreign is not seen as something that could be added to, or combined with, one's own system; instead, it is something a priori contained in it;'[15] or, as we shall see later, which one may *demand to become so*. Thus the dual phenomenon of 'inclusivism' and 'hierarchization' combined with the extreme differentiation within Hindu society to prevent the emergence of a collective identity.

The term 'Hindu' originally derived from the name Indus and was used successively by the Achaemenids, the Greeks and the Muslims to denote the population living beyond that river.[16] However it was not appropriated by the people who themselves bore this designation nor did they use it themselves till the medieval period.[17] According to Romila Thapar, this 'first step towards the crystallisation of what we today call Hinduism was born in the consciousness of being the amorphous, undefined, subordinate, other.'[18]

This development has to be seen in conjunction with the penetration of the subcontinent by Muslim invaders, who were the first to put up a sustained resistance to the capacity of the indigenous culture for assimilation. For example, to be integrated into the Kshatriya *varna* Muslim leaders would have been obliged to recognise the natural superiority of the Brahmins; in fact they refused to give up the practices required by Islam and indeed were prepared in certain circumstances to clash with the

---

[13] The surprise of a Persian savant of the eleventh century when faced with the Brahmins' indifference to his science is well illustrated in E.S. Sachau (ed.), *Alberuni's India*, Lahore: Govt. of West Pakistan, 1962, pp. 26-7.

[14] Hacker, quoted in W. Halbfass, *India and Europe*, op. cit., pp. 404-5.

[15] Ibid., p. 411.

[16] R.E. Frykenberg, 'The emergence of modern Hinduism as a concept and as an institution: a reappraisal with special reference to South India' in G.D. Sontheimer and H. Kulke (eds), *Hinduism reconsidered*, op. cit., p. 30.

[17] See, for instance, J.T. O'Connell, 'The word "Hindu" in Gaudiya Vaishnava texts, *Journal of the American Oriental Society*, 93 (3), 1973, pp. 340-44.

[18] R. Thapar, 'Syndicated moksha?' op. cit., p. 17.

Hindus, as over cow slaughter.[19] Such antagonism was to contribute to the emergence of a 'Hindu' consciousness.

A 'Hindu' consciousness apparently found its principal expression in the seventeenth and eighteenth centuries in the empire of Shivaji and then in the Maratha confederation. In 1720 Brahmins took over the latter kingdom, in which they had formerly served as chief ministers (Peshwas – a name they retained when they became the ruling dynasty) and military chiefs. These two political institutions were formed in Maharashtra in opposition to the Mughal empire and in the name of Dharma;[20] the slaughter of cows, which the Muslims sometimes offered as a sacrifice, was thus forbidden there. But the conquests of the Marathas in the direction of the Gangetic plain 'did not imply the existence of a sense of religious war based on ethnic or communal consciousness'.[21] They resulted from a motivation that was ritual in character – to restore to the Hindus certain holy places, like Varanasi, which were revered throughout India as a whole. In fact, as Christopher Bayly emphasises, it is almost impossible to detect the presence of any communal identity before 1860.

Our contention is that the establishment and later expansion of the militant Hindu movement are indeed modern phenomena which took place despite the original characteristics of Hinduism: the extreme differentiation of its socio-cultural foundations, its 'inclusivism' and 'traditional Indian xenology'. This hypothesis implies that the 'primordialist' explanation, according to which this form of collective political identity originates directly in received cultural elements such as religion and language, will not be discussed here since it does not represent a relevant framework.[22] However it is not our intention to imply that such elements play no role in the formation of nationalist identities; they do indeed do so, but only after passing through a process of reinterpretation.

In the first chapter we analyse this process largely in the context of the theory of ethnic nationalism evolved by Anthony Smith, which is applied to the Arya Samaj, the Hindu Mahasabha and the Rashtriya Swayamsevak Sangh. Our objective, then, is to show that even though Hindu nationalism

---

[19] On the antagonism between Hindus and Muslims in terms of conflicting value-systems see L. Dumont, 'Nationalisme et "communalisme"', Appendix D to *Homo Hierarchicus*, op. cit., pp. 382-3.

[20] However they do not represent nationalist constructions, as argued by Jayant Lele, nationalism being a later development (J. Lele, 'The two faces of nationalism: On the revolutionary potential of tradition' in J. Dafny and A. Akiwowo (eds), *National and ethnic movements*, London: Sage, 1980, p. 78).

[21] C.A. Bayly, 'The pre-history of "Communalism"? Religious conflict in India 1700-1800', *MAS*, 19 (2), 1985, p. 187.

[22] For a critical review of these theories, see C. Jaffrelot, 'Les modèles explicatifs de l'émergence des nations et du nationalisme' in G. Delannoi and P.A. Taguieff (eds), *Théories du nationalisme*, Paris: Kimé, 1991, pp. 139-77.

was constructed as an ideology between the 1870s and 1920s, largely to vindicate the traditional world-view of the upper castes, and in so doing incorporated traditional elements such as 'Indian traditional xenology', it introduced 'modern' features that were totally foreign to Hinduism. In fact, it relied on the invention of a tradition which can be described as a strategy of stigmatisation and emulation.[23] These terms refer to a process of cultural reorganisation launched in reaction to external threats, real and/or imagined, in the form of proselytisation by Christian missionaries, the impact of British rule and the militancy of the Muslim minority. Such a process implied a defensive stigmatisation of these Others, but it also represented a strategic emulation; it redefined Hindu identity in opposition to these 'threatening Others' while – under the pretext of drawing inspiration from a so-called Vedic 'Golden Age' – assimilating those cultural features of the Others which were regarded as prestigious and efficacious in order to regain self-esteem and resist the Others more effectively.

Chapter 2 seeks to show how, after Partition, this strategy of identity-building served as the basis for an instrumentalist strategy consisting in ethno-religious mobilisation through the manipulation of Hindu symbols such as the 'birthplace' of Ram in Ayodhya and the exploitation of communal issues such as the forced exodus of Hindus from Pakistan in 1950. This strategy alone does not have the power to forge a Hindu nationalist identity, as the most radical theoreticians of instrumentalism might claim. However, it appears to be the most efficient means of communicating to the masses the ideological Hindu identity evolved through the strategy of stigmatisation and emulation and closely associated with a tiny élite, since it was largely influenced by Brahminical values. Attempts at ethno-religious mobilisation by the Hindu Mahasabha in the late 1940s and early 1950s were countered by Nehru's government in the name of secularism. Thus it appeared that the implementation of the instrumentalist strategy depended on a more favourable political context. In fact, despite its efforts, the Hindu nationalist movement remained a minor political force throughout the 1950s in comparison to the Indian National Congress. This party succeeded in marginalising the Hindu Mahasabha and the Jana Sangh not only because of Nehru's firm secularism at the Centre but also because its local leaders, at least in the

---

[23] This expression is more appropriate in dealing with Hindu nationalism than 'strategic syncretism', which I used in a similar context ('Hindu nationalism: strategic syncretism in ideology building', *Economic and Political Weekly* (hereafter *EPW*), 20 March 1993, pp. 517-24). In fact, the latter expression was especially relevant in the case of socio-religious reform movements such as the Brahmo Samaj which attempted to evolve a cultural synthesis.

Hindi belt, often manifested Hindu traditionalist attitudes which deprived the Hindu nationalists of part of their *raison d'être*.

Chapter 3 is devoted to a third Hindu nationalist strategy: implantation at the local level and, more precisely, the techniques of party-building. In contrast with the Hindu Mahasabha, the RSS always gave priority to the development of a solid network of activists. From 1951 onwards, its first political front, the Jana Sangh, implemented a strategy of party-building which similarly depended on the formation of such a network rather than on the use of notables and powerful local politicians. Such a phenomenon has to be studied at the local level. The state of Madhya Pradesh, where the Jana Sangh established strong pockets of influence relatively early on, appeared to be a profitable area for this kind of case-study. Thus the material gleaned from Madhya Pradesh is distributed throughout the chapters dealing with Hindu nationalism in the wider sense, in order to examine how the Hindu nationalist party-building strategy evolved in the long term and to explain the interaction between the local and national levels of Hindu nationalist politics. Our analysis reveals that the main division within the Jana Sangh and the party which succeeded it, the Bharatiya Janata Party, was not one of opposing factions competing for power but of local cadres who were prompt to mobilise against the national leadership. The party-building pattern based on RSS-trained activists served as a constraint on the all-India leaders who were criticised by the grassroots when they attempted to moderate their policies in order to win political allies. Thus an important aspect of our study will be precisely to analyse the way Hindu nationalist strategies influence each other.

While concentrating on the case of Madhya Pradesh we shall take note of the role of the Hindu nationalist movement within the larger Indian context, at least in electoral terms. To a great extent this political force remained confined to the Hindi belt, at least till the mid-1990s. That it did so was largely due to the stress it put on a Sanskritised culture, an upper-caste (largely Brahminical) ethos which was more prevalent in North India and an anti-Muslim attitude to which South India was less receptive given the greater integration of Islam in this region. The uneven implantation of the Hindu nationalist movement in geographical terms naturally challenged its claim of representing the identity of the nation. This claim was also called into question by its narrow social base. Up to the 1980s, in effect, Hindu nationalism recruited most of its supporters among the urban upper caste middle class and the landed élite of North India.

This twofold weakness – in geographical as well as social terms – made it necessary to supplement the strategy of implantation based on the appeal of activists by a strategy of ethno-religious mobilisation which could provide the Jana Sangh with a mass following by conferring on the party a dimension of popular Hinduism. In the 1960s the desirability of implementing a strategy of mobilisation was grasped by the Jana Sangh's leaders who, till then, had concentrated on organisational matters, leaving the instrumentalisation of ethno-religious symbols to the Hindu Mahasabha.

These three strategies – the formation of an ideological identity through a strategy of stigmatisation and emulation that capitalised on feelings of vulnerability, the instrumentalist strategy of ethno-religious mobilisation, and a specific pattern of local implantation – assumed a definite shape between the 1920s and the 1950s and were the main elements in the Hindu nationalist quest for power. The principal object of this study is to analyse how they interacted and evolved, and why they failed for so long to make an impact. These problems are studied in the second, third and fourth parts of the book.

Our hypothesis is that the implementation of these strategies required the existence of special conditions which only came into being in the 1980s. The strengthening and diffusion of Hindu nationalist identity were predicated on the perception of a 'threatening Other', while the application of the instrumentalist strategy was affected by two critical factors. The first of these, the dissemination of ideological issues and symbols with the aim of arousing and sustaining an ethno-religious mobilisation, implied the development of a solid network of activists and religious figures able to provide reliable support and a 'moral' guarantee for the Hindu nationalist movement. The second, and most important, was the political context, which either helped or hindered the application of the instrumentalist strategy. In fact this strategy was largely conditioned by the situation prevailing in the political arena, as our review of post-Independence Indian history will enable us to demonstrate.

While the first part of the book analyses the emergence of our three Hindu nationalist strategies in chronological order, the following parts examine the ways in which they were implemented in the 1960s, 1970s and 1980s. These strategies at first failed to make an impact because of the way the Congress dominated the political system, a situation which led the Hindu nationalist leaders to dilute their original approach in the 1960s and 1970s.

In the 1960s, the time-frame for the second part of the book, there was little reason for Hindus to feel vulnerable, while the policies initiated by Nehru and largely adopted by his daughter Indira Gandhi prevented the Hindu nationalist movement from developing a successful strategy of ethno-religious mobilisation. Secularism and socio-economic development were established as two norms of the régime. Thus the Hindu nationalists had no option but to tone down their communal themes and develop an interest in more legitimate ones, such as socio-economic issues. At the same time they relinquished their exclusive reliance on a network of activists and tried to build up their influence by co-opting notables and princes and forging alliances with the mainstream opposition parties. By the late 1960s it appeared that the Jana Sangh was oscillating between two sets of strategies in terms of ideology, mobilisation of support and implantation. The original combination, based on militant Hindu nationalism, the instrumentalisation of ethno-religious symbols and the reliance on RSS-trained activists, was increasingly replaced by moderate strategies that allowed for an understanding to be reached with Hindu traditionalists or other allies, an emphasis on socio-economic or other issues considered to be non-communal and the co-option of an increasing number of more or less committed politicians and notables.

The dilution of the Hindu nationalists' original strategies accelerated during the 1970s, the period reviewed in the third part of the book. The 'JP movement' and then the Emergency enabled the Jana Sangh to become integrated in the Janata Party. The party leadership then developed an alternative strategy (which S.P. Mookerjee, the first president of the Jana Sangh, had already envisaged), namely of forging closer links with the old Hindu traditionalist wing of the Congress. It failed, for a number of reasons, which are analysed in Chapter 8. Many Hindu nationalist activists, regionally and nationally, were not prepared to abandon the ideology and style of the Jana Sangh, while in the political sphere some of the latter's coalition partners objected to the communalism of the ex-Jana Sanghis, either because of their sincere commitment to secularism or for reasons of self-interest.

By the early 1980s the failure of the Hindu nationalist leaders to integrate their movement in a larger structure had left it isolated. However, the wider political context was then more favourable and enabled them to return to their original combination of strategies. The militancy – proselytising and separatist – of certain minorities evoked a new feeling of vulnerability within Hinduism, and many religious leaders responded to it by joining the Hindu nationalist movement. In addition, secularism and socio-economic development were supplanted by entirely different values in the nation's political discourse, and the Congress itself appealed to ethno-religious sentiments. These changing parameters largely account for the Hindu nationalist movement's decision to return to its original approach: namely, bringing its activist network to the forefront and implementing its strategy of ethno-religious mobilisation by taking up the Babri Masjid-Ramjanmabhoomi issue. This agitation was a major reason for the Hindu nationalists' electoral successes in 1989 and 1991.

The fifth part of this study employs the original model but also amends it to analyse the new situation which arose in the 1990s, when the Hindu nationalist movement for the first time acquired widespread popularity through a strategy of ethno-religious mobilisation. The motives of its new supporters turned out to be diverse and difficult to reconcile. Instrumentalist techniques even appeared to be self-contradictory, since the violent means employed by activists – especially during and after the demolition of the mosque in Ayodhya in 1992 – alienated a number of potential or actual supporters who disapproved of such extreme moves or who, on the contrary, lost interest in the Hindu mobilisation once Muslims had been 'taught a lesson'. The Sangathanist party-building pattern was another Hindu nationalist strategy which lost some of its efficacy in the 1990s because of the increasing indiscipline of the BJP, at least in Madhya Pradesh. This development was largely due to the accession to power of the party, an event which necessitated the addition of one variable to our model: performance in office.

From 1993 onwards, the BJP's leaders redirected the party towards a more moderate strategy by downplaying communal issues and emphasising, in a populist perspective, socio-economic questions and the problem of corruption. In 1995 this strategy enabled it further to strengthen its electoral support in western India, where the Congress (I) was weakened by the decay of its organisation and by its growing unpopularity.

Thus this work analyses the way in which the Hindu nationalist movement oscillated between two sets of strategies. The moderate combination relied on an ideological rapprochement with Hindu traditionalists, mobilisation on socio-economic, populist issues and co-option of notables while the radical combination was based on a strategy of identity-building through the stigmatisation and emulation of the Other, ethno-religious mobilisation and the development of a network of activists. In our model, the oscillations between these two sets of strategies depended on several factors: the Hindu feeling of vulnerability that was aroused by the actions of the minorities, the attitude of the Congress party and the mainstream opposition (i.e. the political context), and the role of the activist network and religious leaders of the Hindu nationalist movement.

While the leaders of the Jana Sangh and then the BJP, displaying a more pragmatic approach, tended to be attracted by the moderate combination, the party cadres, the RSS and at a latter stage the Vishwa Hindu Parishad, showed a strong attachment to doctrinal purity and the radical combination as a whole. This tension became an increasingly important variable in explaining the general development of the Hindu nationalist movement's strategy.

Part I. THREE HINDU NATIONALIST STRATEGIES

1

STIGMATISING AND EMULATING 'THREATENING OTHERS' – THE FORMATION OF HINDU NATIONALISM

Hindu nationalism was constructed as an ideology between the 1870s and the 1920s. Although we shall concentrate in this chapter on the period beginning in 1920, when this doctrine crystallised, it is important to trace its antecedents, especially since a similar pattern is observable from the late nineteenth century onwards.

Hindu nationalism derives from socio-religious movements initiated by high caste Hindus, such as the Arya Samaj. This organisation, founded in 1875, was to a large extent set up in reaction against the British colonial state and Christian missions. Its primary concern was to maintain the basic elements of the traditional social order and culture of the Hindus while adapting that tradition to take account of certain aspects of western society. This endeavour implied both the stigmatisation and the emulation of those who threatened Hindu society. At the same time, the tension between cultural preservation and modernisation was solved through the invention of a distant Golden Age which was both indigenous and in accord with modern values. The idea of the Golden Age was to become one of the cornerstones of Hindu nationalism.

In the 1920s certain Hindu ideologues felt threatened by the mobilisation of Muslims in the Khilafat movement. The strategy of simultaneous stigmatisation and emulation of the Other through reference to an invented tradition was revived, notably by the Hindu Mahasabha and the Rashtriya Sawayamsevak Sangh. The ethnic nationalism which thus developed was largely influenced by western examples, as we can see in the writings of V.D. Savarkar and M.S. Golwalkar. This was also the case with the Hindu nationalist organisations, which developed from the 1920s onwards.

However, this borrowing of ideas and organisational principles from their opponents was presented by the Hindu nationalists as if they were engaged in the process of reviving neglected traditions, and indeed some elements of their strategy were derived from indigenous beliefs.

The Hindu nationalist ideology, even though it cannot be compared directly to Italian fascism or German national socialism, envisaged the organisation of the whole of society as a means of producing a new kind of people.

This first chapter is primarily concerned to explain how the Hindu nationalists developed their idea of Hindu identity over several decades. At the same time, it analyses the way in which this enterprise explained the limited but steady growth of the Hindu nationalist movement – especially the RSS. By 1947 this organisation had become a pan-Indian one even though its strongholds remained confined to North India.

The genesis of Hindu nationalism

Today's ideological constructions, as Clifford Geertz has shown, must be studied primarily as reactions to modernisation along Western lines, a process which leads to 'disorientation'. They are based on reinterpreting traditional cultural features in order to preserve them while at the same time giving them fresh meaning, and from this point of view they are 'symbolic strategies'.[1] In this perspective, ideology is defined by Lloyd Fallers as 'that part of culture which is actively concerned with the establishment and defence of patterns of belief and value. Ideology is thus the apologetic part of culture.'[2] It is intended mainly to create a sense of national self-esteem. This approach is not 'primordialist' because culture is not considered here as a static 'given'[3] but as subject to reinterpretation. However, neither Geertz nor Fallers places sufficient emphasis on the social background of the reinterpreters who shape ideologies.[4] This factor

[1]   C. Geertz, *The interpretation of culture*, New York: Basic Books, 1973, p. 230. Geertz's views on ideology as a cultural system are set out on pp. 219-20.

[2]   L.A. Fallers, 'Ideology and culture in Uganda nationalism', *American Anthropologist*, 63 (4) Aug. 1961, p. 677.

[3]   As was the case in another important article by Geertz, 'The integrative revolution – Primordial sentiments and civil politics in the new states' in C. Geertz (ed.), *Old societies and new states*, Glencoe, Ill.: The Free Press, 1963, pp. 105-7.

[4]   Geertz contents himself with writing that 'the patterns of belief and value defended may be, of course, those of a socially subordinate group, as well as those of a socially dominant one, and the "apology" therefore for reform or revolution' (*The interpretation of culture*, op. cit., p. 231 fn.). Fallers recognises that 'ideologies only develop and become dominant when there are groups within society capable of, and interested in, promoting them' but he pays more attention to the social position of these groups than to their cultural framework ('Ideology and culture', op. cit., pp. 683-4). This is possibly due to

deserves greater attention because the major aim of these leaders is to adjust the outward expression of their discourse in order to preserve *what they consider* to be the basic values and identity of society. Their choices are determined by both their cultural framework and social status; thus Hindu nationalism, as we shall see, largely reflects the Brahminical view of the high caste reformers who shaped its ideology.

In this perspective, the explanatory model of Anthony Smith for the emergence of ethnic nationalism proves very useful. According to Smith, ethnic nationalisms start from 'a recognisable cultural unit', their primary concern being to 'to ensure the survival of the group's cultural identity'. By contrast, 'territorial nationalisms start from an imposed entity and possess no common and distinctive cultural identity to protect'.[5] This typology overlaps considerably with the classic opposition between ethnic and universalist nationalisms, the former type being epitomised by Germany and the latter by France.

Dealing with ethnic nationalism, Smith analyses the impact of European modernity on the wider world as having caused a sense of backwardness and decline among colonised and dominated peoples, from which a certain élite stratum, chiefly comprising the intelligentsia, then set about reforming their traditions. Subsequently their main concern was to endow that renewed tradition with the sanction of a theoretical 'Golden Age', an ideological reinterpretation of the past, perfectly fashioned in order to meet the challenge of the West. This historicist construction is the cornerstone of nationalism since it allows peoples threatened by European modernity to regain their self-respect by appropriating the strong points of the aggressor – an ambivalence insisted upon by Plamenatz.[6] It is a schema that fits the case in point to a remarkable degree.

The Arya Samaj and 'Arya nationalism'

In India, the confrontation with an aggressive modernity took place in the course of European penetration and eventual colonisation. The

---

the characteristics of African cultures, which are relatively undifferentiated; in this context it may be relevant to look at society as a whole as a cultural unit, but it is not possible to deal with India in the same way.

5   For Smith 'that does not make them social-class or coalition-type movements against alien oppressors. The rub lies in the perception of the rulers as "aliens". The main aim is to take over the alien's political machinery and adopt his administrative unit as the basis of the projected nation' (A.D. Smith, *Theories of Nationalism*, London: Duckworth, 1971, p. 217).

6   Ibid., see the final chapter; and J. Plamenatz, 'Two types of nationalism' in E. Kamenka (ed.), *Nationalism: the nature and evolution of an idea*, London: Edward Arnold, 1973, pp. 34ff.

bureaucratic structure consequently installed came to be dominated by utilitarian concepts, while after 1813 Christian missions were established on a greatly increased scale. These two different types of institution shared an aversion to Hinduism, with its idolatrous polytheism and caste system – the very antithesis of individualist values. Such beliefs and practices were regularly denigrated. Reforms undertaken by the administration – certain Hindu customs were abolished by law – were complemented by the proselytising and educational activities of the missionaries.

As a response to this threat a number of high-caste Hindus, mostly Brahmins, undertook to reform their society and its religious practices in order to adapt them to Western modernity while preserving the core of Hindu tradition, which they defined mainly in Brahminical terms. The two approaches proceeded in tandem but in varying proportions, determined by the specific character of the different reform movements. The Arya Samaj represents the militant strand from which, in particular, Hindu nationalism would spring forth. Its founder, Swami Dayananda (1824-83), accepted Western criticisms in so far as they related to forms of worship and to the social system, but he argued that in the Vedic era Hinduism had been free from the blemishes for which it was now being condemned. According to Dayananda, in that period the deity was worshipped in the form of an abstract Absolute – something the Arya Samaj ritual tried to restore – and, above all, no system of hereditary endogamous castes, the *jatis*, was admitted. Society recognised only *varnas*, in which children were to be classified by their preceptors or *gurus* according to their individual qualities.[7]

This reasoning was of course much influenced by the writings of the European Orientalists,[8] but Dayananda's used them selectively, thus illustrating the 'construction of a tradition'. Rajni Kothari characterises this process as an effort to legitimise the imitation of Western ideas and practices by presenting them as analogous to elements of indigenous tradition or indeed to have been virtually contained therein since ancient times.[9] Thus in Dayananda's writings a tradition which is clearly hierar-

---

[7]   Dayananda (Swami), *The light of truth*, transl. by G.P. Upadhyaya, Allahabad: Dr Ratna Kumari Svadhyaya Sansthana, 1981, p. 113. According to Dayananda, 'The fixture of the *varna* according to merits and actions should take place at the age of sixteenth year of girls and twenty-fifth year of boys.'

[8]   Dayananda was acquainted with Max Müller's translation of the Veda for instance (J.T.F. Jordens, *Dayananda Saraswati – His life and ideas*, Delhi: Oxford University Press, 1978, p. 56).

[9]   R. Kothari, 'Tradition and modernity revisited', *Government and Opposition*, Summer 1968, pp. 273-93. It seems to me that Kothari's view differs slightly from Hobsbawm's 'invention of tradition' because Hobsbawm puts the emphasis on the capacity of this process to establish fictitious continuity and does not study the disruptive, modern influences from outside. This difference is probably due to the fact that he deals mostly

chical and Brahminical is simultaneously reformed and defended. In fact, the *varnas*, which are described in the Vedas as the original, ideal social system, in no way imply the existence of the values of individualism, e.g. personal merit, as Dayananda claimed.[10] In Vedic writings, as in subsequent Brahminical texts, degrees of ritual purity constituted major criteria in determining social hierarchy.

By means of this reinterpretation of tradition Swami Dayananda pursued three objectives. First, he rejected the social system (by which he meant *jati*), which had been represented as backward by British observers and urged that it be replaced by the 'traditional' *varna* system, emphasising its compatibility with the individualistic values of the Europeans. In this way he helped Hindus to regain their self-esteem. Second, he favoured a degree of Western-inspired social reform in his repudiation of caste, which in his view was prejudicial to social cohesion. While he criticised the way the Indian intelligentsia 'copied' European dress and manners, he admits that 'The Europeans are very dutiful and well disciplined' and that 'These qualifications and deeds have contributed to their advancement...' "[11] Dayananda calls on Hindus to ignore superficial aspects of European culture but to emulate its basic values. Third, his reinterpretation enabled him to rehabilitate a social system of ritual hierarchy, in the guise of a so-called ancestral *varna* system. Even though he considered the Brahmins to be responsible for the development of superstitions and the decline of Hindu society, the alternative social model he proposed was based largely on the traditional – mainly Brahminical – world view, as his recommendation relating to the strict endogamy of the *varnas* indicates. He considered, in an organicist perspective, that such an arrangement 'will maintain the integrity of each *varna* as well as good relations'.[12]

The Arya Samaj illustrates the process analysed by Geertz and Fallers in that it evolved an ideology capable of vindicating a threatened identity. But two characteristics of this construction, that are not necessarily

---

with Europe, where the modernisation process originated. (E. Hobsbawm, 'Introduction: Inventing traditions' in E. Hobsbawm and T. Ranger (eds), *The invention of tradition*, Cambridge University Press, 1983, pp. 1-14).

[10] B.K. Smith, *Classifying the universe – The ancient varna system and the origins of caste*, Oxford University Press, 1994, p. 28.

[11] Dayananda (Swami), *The light of truth*, op. cit., p. 484.

[12] The development is very similar to the one that took place simultaneously, according to Sumit Sarkar, in Bengal through the promotion by Hindu reformers of the concept of '*[a] dhikari-bedoi* (literally, differential rights, claims or powers) [which] conveyed the notion of each *Jati* and *sampraday* (caste and sect) having its own rituals and beliefs in a unified but hierarchically differentiated structure within which each knows its appropriate place' ('Indian nationalism and the politics of Hindutva' in D. Ludden (ed.), *Making India Hindu: Modernity, nationalism and majoritarian Communalism* (University of Pennsylvenia Press, forthcoming).

implied by the theoretical mode, must be emphasised. First, one of the most ardently defended pillars of what is perceived by the Arya Samaj as the Hindu cultural equilibrium is a form of social hierarchy. Obviously the choice of such a priority reflected the dominant role of high caste Hindus in the organisation. Second, the defence of what is defined as Hindu identity implies a paradoxical imitation of the Other. This phenomenon was evident in the attempt by the Arya Samaj to assimilate the dominant cultural traits of the Europeans – such as certain individualistic values – which were thought to explain their strength. The strategy was to assume a new dimension when Swami Dayananda's followers introduced *shuddhi*, a conversion procedure. Hitherto this term had described a purification ritual undertaken by individuals belonging to high castes who had suffered pollution from an impure contact. Since Hinduism lacked conversion techniques, the Arya Samaj reinterpreted this ritual as a means of countering Christian proselytism by imitating its conversion practices.[13]

These practices of the Arya Samaj became incorporated into a logic of cultural reform which could be termed a strategy of emulation. They contain a mimetic dimension, in so far as they imply a reform of Hinduism inspired by the values of its Western opponents. However, this imitation entails a strategy of assimilating those cultural traits which give the opponent his superiority and prestige in order to resist him more effectively, while pretending to discover such traits in one's own 'original civilisation'.

This circuitous means of creating a Golden Age was of crucial importance in that it established ethnic pride. The Aryans of the Vedic era are described as a chosen people to whom 'the formless God revealed perfect knowledge of the Veda'. Some time after the Creation, they came down from Tibet into Aryavarta – a virgin territory between the Himalayas and Vindhya mountains, the Indus and the Brahmaputra – and then became the 'sovereign lords of the earth', whose inhabitants they instructed in Sanskrit, the 'mother of all languages',[14] before falling into a decadent state characterised by the basest superstitions and idolatry. It is possible to detect here an ideological framework partly inherited or borrowing selectively from the ancient world view of the Hindus, which, as mentioned above on the basis of Halbfass's work, assigned pride of place to territory, language and social structure.

The ethnic pride inherent in Arya Samajist ideology was combined with an open stigmatisation of the Others, whom the Arya Samaj none-

---

[13] I have developed this point in 'Les (re)conversions à l'hindouisme (1885-1990). Politisation et diffusion d'une "invention de la tradition"', *Archives de Sciences Sociales des Religions*, 87, 1994, pp. 73-98.

[14] Cf. *The light of truth*, op. cit., pp. 248, 277-9 and 341-5.

theless emulated principally in order to resist them more efficiently. Dayananda devoted the last two chapters of *The light of truth* to a critical study of the Bible and the Koran. He jeers at the idolatry of the Old Testament[15] and scoffs at the weaknesses of the Prophet ('that God is not omniscient'[16]). A few years later, in Bengal, Swami Vivekananda reacted to the deprecating British attitude towards Hindus in a similar fashion. He strongly criticised western materialism in comparison to the spiritual superiority of the Vedanta.[17] By the turn of the century, leaders of the socio-religious reform movements often attacked the Europeans in India in such a manner.

However, we are interested less in this stigmatisation, expressed in general terms, than in that underlying the process of emulation; there is indeed a discourse stigmatising the Other *because* of the threat he poses to the Hindus, and which stimulates the imitation of those cultural traits deemed to be the source of his strength and effectiveness. We shall concentrate on this aspect of stigmatisation in the sections dealing with Hindu nationalism.

The Arya Samaj of Dayananda was not, however, a proponent of *Hindu* nationalism. Its members, up to the beginning of the twentieth century, preferred to stress their specificity with relation to Hinduism, which was described as a degraded form of the Vedic religion. In 1891 the leadership of the movement in the Punjab called on its members to declare themselves as 'Aryas' and not as Hindus at the time of the census.[18] However its ideological characteristics were such that it became one of the first crucibles of Hindu nationalism.[19]

The Hindu Sabha movement

At the turn of the century the principal Indian leaders with Hindu leanings were Bal Gangadhar Tilak in Maharashtra and Aurobindo Ghose in

[15] See, for instance, ibid., p. 623.

[16] Ibid., p. 681.

[17] See K.P. Gupta, 'Religious evolution and social change in India: a study of the Ramakrishna mission Movement' *Contributions to Indian Sociology*, 8, 1974, pp. 25-50.

[18] K. Jones, 'Religious identity and the Indian census' in N.G. Barrier (ed.), *The census in British India*, New Delhi: Manohar, 1981, p. 87.

[19] As an organisation, the Arya Samaj served two principal functions. Its religious dimension, based on the promotion of a ritual reduced to essentials without the worship of idols, had seen its emergence as a simple supplementary Hindu sect of which Dayananda was the *guru*, while its ideology was quickly developed within a small urban intelligentsia which became self-perpetuating as it evolved a specific educational purpose, of which the main component was the revealingly named Dayananda Anglo-Vedic College in Lahore (Punjab). (K. Jones, *Arya Dharm: Hindu consciousness in 19th–century Punjab*, Berkeley: University of California Press, 1976, pp. 67ff.).

Bengal. But neither of them created a Hindu organisation inside or outside the Congress, and instead remained within the party as 'extremists'. In contrast, a specific Hindu movement, the Hindu Sabha, was formed in Punjab by the end of the first decade of the century.

Of all the Indian provinces the Punjab was the most receptive to Dayananda's message. Local Arya Samajists initiated the Hindu Sabha when the pro-Muslim bias of the British administration, which was anxious to assure itself of support among the minorities, was gradually translated into the granting of various important concessions, one of which was the setting-up of separate electorates in 1909. This kind of discrimination awakened in certain Hindus, especially within the Arya Samaj, a feeling of vulnerability, which even took the radical form of an inferiority complex. Lal Chand, a lawyer who headed the main educational institution of the Arya Samaj, the Dayananda Anglo-Vedic College at Lahore, from 1884 till 1904, wrote a series of articles in 1909 which are highly revealing on this point:

Mohammedans have Constantinople behind their back, not to speak of other Mohammedan independent States with which more or less British statesmanship have to deal.[...] British statesmen, therefore, not only desire to conciliate Muslim opinion, but are seriously nervous lest they should give any offence to it.[20]

This analysis underpins the foundation by Arya Samajists of a Hindu Sabha (Hindu Association) in the Punjab by the end of the first decade of this century. Soon after, in the 1911 census, the Arya Samajists of the Punjab declared themselves to be not 'Aryas', as they had previously, but 'Hindus', a highly significant development.[21]

The Hindu Sabha displayed a proto-Hindu nationalism, as testified by a speech by one of its leaders who was also a prominent Arya Samajist, Lala Lajpat Rai, before the first Punjab Provincial Hindu Conference held at Lahore on 21 and 22 October 1909:

It may be that the Hindus by themselves cannot form themselves into a nation in the modern sense of the term, but that is only a play on words. Modern nations are political units. A political unit ordinarily includes all the peoples who live under one common political system and form a State [...] That is the sense in which the expression is used in connection with the body called the 'Indian National Congress' [...] But that is not the only sense in which it is or can be used. In fact, the German word 'Nation' did not necessarily signify a political nation or a State. In that language it connoted what is generally conveyed by the English expression 'people' implying a community possessing a certain civilisation and culture. Using

[20]. Lal Chand, *Self-abnegation in politics*, Lahore: Central Yuvak Sabha, 1938, p. 1.

[21] For more details, see my 'The genesis and development of Hindu nationalism in the Punjab: from the Arya Samaj to the Hindu Sabha (1875-1910)', *Indo-British Review*, 21 (1), pp. 3-40.

it in that sense, there can be no doubt that Hindus are a 'nation' in themselves, because they represent a type of civilisation all their own.[22]

These words refer explicitly to the opposition between ethnic and universalist or territorial nationalism. Lal Chand expressed the same idea in crude terms when he wrote that 'patriotism ought to be communal and not merely geographical'.[23] Influenced by English universalist concepts, the Congress party defined the Indian nation as in effect consisting of all individuals, of all communities, living within the frontiers of the British-Indian realm. This aroused the misgivings of some militant Hindus, such as certain Arya Samajists, who were much more in sympathy with German definitions giving an ethnic basis for nationalism.

The Punjab Hindu Sabha, like its counterpart in the United Provinces (modern Uttar Pradesh) and the Hindu Mahasabha (lit. Great Hindu Association) – the national confederation which had been formed in 1915 – worked to provide a collective defence of the socio-political interests of Hindus.[24] It initially functioned as a pressure group within Congress, concerned to influence the party leadership to contest Muslim demands for increased access in the shape of quotas for the administration and the elective assemblies. The Hindu Mahasabha acquired a more clearly Hindu nationalist orientation in the 1920s, at the end of a new cycle of stigmatisation and emulation of 'threatening Others'.

The Hindu Sangathan movement: stereotypes of the Muslim and the Hindu inferiority complex

In this instance the process was precipitated by a mobilisation on the part of the Muslims. The peace negotiations following the end of the First World War led to fears among them that the Caliphate, hitherto embodied in the person of the Ottoman Sultan, would be suppressed. As a result, in 1919 a number of eminent Muslims launched a 'Khilafat movement' against the British, who were playing a leading role in those negotiations. Many *ulemas* stimulated and sustained the mobilisation in their community through their sermons and the proclamation of a *fatwa*.[25] This mobilisation degenerated in some instances into anti-Hindu riots. In 1921, during a peasant rising against landlords on the Malabar coast of Kerala,

---

22 Cited in G.V. Ketkar, 'The All India Hindu Mahasabha' *Indian Annual Register*, 1941, vol. 1, Calcutta, p. 277.

23 Lal Chand, *Self-abnegation*, op. cit., p. 103.

24 See the excellent synthesis by R. Gordon, 'The Hindu Mahasabha and the Indian National Congress, 1915 to 1926', *MAS*, 9, 2 (1975), pp. 145-203.

25 G. Minault, *The Khilafat movement: Religious symbolism and political mobilization in India*, New York: Columbia University Press, 1982, pp. 121-9.

the Mapillas – descendants of Arab merchants who had settled there from the eighth century onwards – established a *Khilafat* king and attacked Hindus, some of whom were converted by force.[26] These violent episodes marked the beginning of a cycle of inter-communal riots, especially in North India,[27] which culminated in the reinforcing of a sense of inferiority among the majority community. The leaders of the Hindu Mahasabha relaunched their organisation within the framework of a movement they called Hindu Sangathan (Hindu Organisation or Unity), on a firmer ideological base than before, while still pursuing a strategy of stigmatisation and emulation.

Once again it was a matter of resisting an external threat by borrowing the traits which endowed its instigators with strength – always under the pretext of a return to the Vedic Golden Age. This aspect emerged clearly in a report on the Malabar riot written by Balkrishna Shivram Moonje, a former aide of Tilak, who had become the leader of the Hindu Sabha in Nagpur.[28] In this work, which we will discuss as a paradigmatic text in the Weberian sense, Moonje explained Hindu inferiority in unambiguous sociological terms:

The Hindus are divided into so many water-tight compartments, each having a social culture and life of its own that there is hardly any association between them in the wider field of social activities and amenities of the community as a whole [...]; so that if one section happens to come in conflict with the Mahomedans, the other sections hardly ever consider it worth their while to run to its help. [...] The Mahomedans, on the other hand, form one organic community, religiously well-organised and disciplined so that any injury done to any part of the community anywhere is felt as keenly all through out.

Such a contrast, in which the cohesion of the Other is naturally exaggerated, suggests a remedy with strongly imitative elements:

If the Chaturvarna [the system of the four orders], which is a distinctive feature of the Aryan civilisation in the world, is to be maintained and to prosper as I believe it should, and yet union and solidarity is to be evolved, it must give up its system of water-tight compartments of caste and bring about a real organic unity between the four sections of the society which can be done by again bringing into vogue the system of marriage of what are called the Anuloma and Pratiloma Paddhati as provided in our Dharmashastras with a view to bind the four sections of the society

[26] R.L. Hardgrave Jr., 'The Mapilla rebellion, 1921: Peasant revolt in Malabar', *MAS*, 11 (1), 1977, p. 82 and C. Wood, *The Moplah rebellion and its genesis*, New Delhi: People's Publishing House, 1987.

[27] D. Page, *Prelude to Partition: The Indian Muslims and the Imperial System of Control*, New Delhi: Oxford University Press, 1982, p. 74.

[28] *Dharmaveer Dr. Moonje*, Nagpur: Dharmaveer Dr Moonje Janmashatabdi Samaroh Samiti dvara Sampadit, 1972, pp. 32 and 66.

in blood connections and thus bring about organic unity out of the very diversity of sociological functions allotted to these four original varna or castes.[29]

Here are all the elements of the strategy of emulation: an awareness of the (generally exaggerated) aggressiveness displayed by the Other arouses vulnerability and a desire for reform justified by reference to the Vedic Golden Age. In fact, Moonje's invocation of Vedic marriage 'custom' (*paddhati*) reinterprets neatly the *Dharmashastras*; these texts indeed refer to the existence of *anuloma* marriages (lit. 'in the direction of the hair'), where the man is of a caste superior to that of his wife, and those which are *pratiloma* ('against the direction of the hair'), where the hierarchical relationship is reversed, but without in any way justifying marriages that transgress the principle of caste endogamy.[30] But for a Hindu nationalist theorist the mere mention of these practices in texts as prestigious as the *Dharmashastras* is enough to legitimise an innovation that his project demands: the promotion of a sociological model suitable for reinforcing the Hindu community by adopting some of the socio-cultural strengths of the aggressor – under the pretext of a return to the prestigious Vedic era. This diversion into a fictitious version of history allows for the legitimisation of the caste system in an amended form.

The Hindu nationalist eulogy of the *varna* system must also be interpreted in the social context of the majoritarian community itself: in Maharashtra in the 1920s there arose an anti-Brahmin movement and then an agitation of Untouchables led by Dr Ambedkar. Hence the attempt by high caste reformers to promote hierarchical but prestigious social models such as the *varna* system. One of the declared objectives of the Hindu Sangathan movement was the integration of Untouchables into Hindu society with a view to dissuading them from converting to another religion.[31] In 1923 the Hindu Mahasabha voted in favour of resolutions calling for Untouchables to enjoy full access to roads, schools, wells and even temples.[32] However this egalitarianism was presented in an 'organicist' model of society in which social hierarchy was merely relaxed through a reinterpretation of the *varna* system. This hierarchical model remained in effect a mainstay of identity, and the caste system was to be reformed largely in order to legitimise it.

Concerning religion, Moonje expressed anxiety in his report over

---

[29] 'Forcible conversions in Malabar, – Dr Moonje's Report', Nagpur, Aug. 4, 1923, Moonje papers, Sub File 12 (1922-3) NMML (section of mss.), p. 16.

[30] I am most grateful to Charles Malamoud for this information.

[31] This motive also underlied the extension of the *shuddhi* movement to Untouchables as articles by Lajpat Rai testify (see, for instance, 'The depressed classes', in D. Swaroop (ed.), *Politics of conversion*, New Delhi: Deendayal Research Institute, 1986, p. 302).

[32] *Indian Annual Register*, 1923, vol. 1, p. 139.

...the absence of a common meeting place in the Hindu polity for the castes from the highest to the lowest on perfectly equal terms, just as the Mahommedan has in his Masjid [...] [where Muslims] vividly visualise and imbibe the feeling of oneness and the identity of their social and religious interests. It is there in these Masjids that the organic unity is thus manufactured in the heterogeneous mass that goes to make the Mahommedan community of India. Where is such an Institution among the Hindus? [...] Cannot our temples be made to serve the purpose which the Masjid does for the Mahommedan?[33]

Swami Shraddhananda, a Punjabi Arya Samajist who had embraced renunciation as a way of life, developed this proposition in his work *Hindu Sangathan – Saviour of the Dying Race* (1926), in which he drew up a programme of action theoretically intended for the Hindu Mahasabha:

The first step I propose is to build one Hindu Rashtra Mandir [temple of the Hindu nation] in every city and important town, with a compound which could contain an audience of 25,000 and a hall in which *Katha* [prose selections] from Bhagavad Gita, the Upanishads and the great epics Ramayana and Mahabharata could be daily recited. The Rashtra Mandir will be in charge of the local Hindu Sabha which will manage to have Akharas [places for physical exercise] for wrestling and *gatka*, etc. in the same compound. While the sectarian Hindu temples are dominated by their own individual deities, the Catholic Hindu Mandir would be devoted to the worship of the three mother-spirits the Gau-mata [the cow-mother], the Saraswati [goddess of knowledge]-mata and the Bhumi-mata [motherland]. [...] Let a lifelike map of Mother-Bharat [India] be constructed in a prominent place, giving all its characteristics in vivid-colours so that every child of the Matri-Bhumi [earth-mother] may daily bow before the Mother and renew his pledge to restore her to the ancient pinnacle of glory from which she has fallen.[34]

Such temples were needed, according to Shraddhananda, to rival the capacity of mosques like the Jama Masjid in Delhi, which he estimated could hold 25-30,000 people. Jugal Kishor Birla (elder brother of the Marwari industrialist Ghanshyam Das Birla), who was close to the Hindu Mahasabha,[35] financed the construction of such temples, one of which was erected in 1936 in Delhi alongside the head office of the Hindu Mahasabha itself. Savarkar himself had a 'pan-Hindu' temple built at Ratnagiri in 1931.[36] These projects were clearly aimed at reinforcing Hindu society with the social and religious cohesion which it lacked in comparison with

---

[33] 'Forcible conversions in Malabar', op. cit., p. 24.

[34] Shraddhananda Sanyasi, *Hindu Sangathan – Saviour of the dying race*, Delhi: Arjun Press, 1926, pp. 140-1.

[35] He represented the Hindu Sabha of Marwar at the annual session of the Hindu Mahasabha in 1923 (*Amrita Bazar Patrika* in Home Political Department, 1924. Deposit, File no. 198 (NAI)).

[36] D. Keer, *Veer Savarkar*, Bombay: Popular Prakashan, 1988, p. 184.

its adversaries, a movement that also took the form of attempts to endow Hinduism with the characteristics of a 'church'.

Thus the Hindu nationalists became increasingly aware of the need for a kind of ecclesiastical structure in the wake of the conflicts aroused by their attempts to engender reform, as in the case of the *shuddhi* movement, which had antagonised many Sanatanists or orthodox Hindus.[37] Such divisions highlighted the need for greater cohesion within the Hindu camp. The leader-writer of *Mahratta*, a 'Tilakite' journal with which Moonje had close contacts, described this aim as 'to bring out a new Smriti';[38] or, in other words, to rewrite the 'tradition', the essentials of which were transmitted by the *Dharmashastras*.

In order to achieve this renewal, *Mahratta* appealed to the only embryonic religious authority which existed, namely the leaders of the different sects. A religious figure who appeared to be particularly receptive to the appeals of the Hindu nationalists was Dr Kurtkoti, the *Shankaracharya* of Karweer Pith, a dissident Maharashtrian branch of the *math* of Sringeri.[39] Dr Kurtkoti, a Sanskrit scholar whose dissertation had been accepted by the Oriental University of Washington,[40] shared the ideology of the Hindu Mahasabha and did his utmost to create an institution which would exercise a spiritual authority within Hinduism. In 1920 he founded the Maharashtra Hindu Dharma Parishad as a forum at 'whose annual conference all categories of Hindus [were] represented and brought to him legal disputes to settle: the rank of intermediate castes whose exact status was contested, the position of the Untouchables...'[41]

Kurtkoti willingly responded to appeals from *Mahratta* that the *Shankaracharyas* should do 'their duty' by issuing 'a decree giving authority for freedom to readmit other converts [not only those converted by force] who express a wish to return to the bosom of Hinduism.'[42] This decree aroused universal surprise since orthodox Hindus were usually hostile to the re-integration into the fold of their religion of persons whose conversion, in their eyes, implied a high degree of impurity. Kurtkoti seemed to be consciously imitating the *ulemas*. Shocked by the involvement of the latter in the Khilafat movement, he went further and threatened to invite 'Acharyas [a title given to certain Hindu sages and philosophers]...[to]

---

[37] Sanatanist leaders objected in particular to the social advancement of Untouchables or reintegration of converts within Hinduism by means of the ritual of *shuddhi*.

[38] *Mahratta*, 19, Aug. 1923, p. 398.

[39] J. Lütt, 'The shankaracharya of Puri', in A. Eschmann *et al.* (eds), *The cult of Jagannath and the regional tradition of Orissa*, New Delhi: Manohar, 1978, p. 416.

[40] I. Prakash, *A review of the history and works of the Hindu Mahasabha and the Hindu Sangathan movement*, New Delhi: Akhil Charatiya Hindu Mahasabha, 1938, p. 344.

[41] *Mahratta*, 18 Dec. 1921, p. 590.

[42] Ibid., 2. Nov. 1921, p. 470.

formulate their own injunction against the fatwas.'[43] In addition, he supported not only the indissoluble bond between politics and religion but also the idea, which had barely any connection with Hinduism, that the spread of a religion was conditional upon self-government.[44] Kurtkoti thus entered the political arena, more or less in the fashion of the *ulemas*. By presiding over the annual festival organised by the Tilakites to commemorate the coronation of Shivaji,[45] by establishing his own commemoration of the Hindu empire of Vijayanagar, by entrusting the report on the Malabar situation to Moonje,[46] and by taking an active part – notably with his articles in *Mahratta* – in giving fresh impetus to the Hindu Mahasabha, Kurtkoti showed that he was prepared to defend Hinduism by assuming an active spiritual authority in politics. This intervention by a religious leader in the political sphere was in keeping with the strategy of emulation which provided the basis for the Hindu Sangathan movement as a whole.

As is evident in Moonje's report, the process of identity-building crystallised in reaction to a Hindu sense of inferiority or vulnerability which was directly related to stereotypes of the Others (the Muslims and the British). The cohesion attributed to the Muslim community was grossly exaggerated.[47] Most of these stereotypes were not new, but had taken shape between about 1890 and 1910. As early as 1909, U.N. Mukherji had codified some of these images in a series of articles serialised in the *Bengalee* and published under the title, 'Hindus, a dying race'. He had calculated from census reports that within the next 420 years Hindus would disappear because of their steady decline in numbers in comparison to Muslims and Christians. As P.K. Datta demonstrates, the contrasting demographic trends of these two communities were associated with cultural features in Mukherji's writings. The Hindus were weak, notably because of their division into castes, whereas 'social classes in England were bonded in the same feelings on common occasions such as those provided by sports, defence requirements and church activities, an ability that accounted for the overwhelming organisational power their society possess. Islam too had produced a sense of commonness through masjid congregations.'[48]

---

[43] Ibid., 29 Oct. 1922, p. 502.

[44] Ibid., 3 Dec. 1922, p. 556.

[45] Ibid., 26 June 1921, p. 1.

[46] Ibid., 26 Mar. 1922, p. 156.

[47] On the socio-cultural differentiation of Indian Muslims, see M. Gaborieau, 'Hiérarchie sociale et mouvements de réforme chez les musulmans du sous-continent indien', *Social Compass*, 33 (2-3), 1983, pp. 241ff.

[48] P.K. Datta, ' "Dying Hindus" – Production of Hindu communal common sense in early 20th century Bengal', *EPW*, 19 June 1993, p. 1307. Mukherji wrote, for instance: 'The

Many of these stereotypes had been introduced by the British themselves, from the colonisation of Bengal onward,[49] and had since been reiterated. In 1912, the Assistant Director of the Intelligence Bureau wrote in a report: 'The Muhammedan is always a potential fanatic' whereas the Hindu was described as being 'in a deplorable state of physical weakness.'[50] In the 1920s, in the wake of the Khilafat movement these stereotypes coalesced within an emerging Hindu nationalist identity. In fact the idea of the Hindus as a 'dying race' was borrowed by Shraddhananda from Mukherji, whom he had met in 1909. The important lesson of this process for our study lies in what P.K. Datta calls 'the production of Hindu communal common sense', a process through which these stereotypes tend to form a routinised discourse that stresses the need for a Hindu nationalist reaction.

Savarkar and *Hindutva* ethnic nationalism

As Pandey has convincingly argued, the ideology of Hindu nationalism was first codified in the 1920s within a context notable for 'what was perceived as a quite new and threatening level of Muslim organisation, preparedness and militancy'.[51] More instrumental than anyone else in bringing about this qualitative leap was another Maharashtrian Brahmin, Vinayak Damodar Savarkar, the former head of a terrorist group and a future president of the Hindu Mahasabha (1937-42). His work *Hindutva: Who is a Hindu?*, first published at Nagpur in 1923, is a basic text for nationalist 'Hinduness' (the generally accepted translation of 'Hindutva').

This work perfectly illustrates the mechanisms of Hindu nationalist identity-building through the stigmatisation and emulation of 'threatening Others'. Savarkar wrote the book in 1922 while in prison in Ratnagiri. There, he had come in contact with Khilafatist Pathans who, according to Keer, 'rioted and the Hindu prisoners were saved as they were forewarned by Savarkar'.[52] His book rests on the assumption that Hindus are vulnerable in comparison to or *vis-à-vis* 'Pan-isms' such as pan-Islamism:

---

superiority of the [...] Mohammedans is entirely due to their religious revival and systematic moral training' under the direction of the mollahs (cited in ibid.)

[49] For details, see P. Spear, *The Nabobs*, Calcutta: Rupa, 1991 (1963), pp. 195-201, and M. Hasan, 'The myth of unity: colonial and national narratives' in D. Ludden (ed.), *Making India Hindu*, op. cit.

[50] Cited in P.C. Bamford, *Histories of the non-cooperation and Khilafat movements*, New Delhi: K.K. Books, 1985 (1925), p. 111.

[51] G. Pandey, 'Which of us are Hindus?' in G. Pandey (ed.), *Hindus and others – The question of identity in India today*, New Delhi: Viking, 1993, p. 244.

[52] D. Keer, *Veer Savarkar*, op. cit., p. 161.

O Hindus, consolidate and strengthen Hindu nationality; not to give wanton offence to any of our non-Hindu compatriots, in fact to any one in the world but in just and urgent defence of our race and land; to render it impossible for others to betray her or to subject her to unprovoked attack by any of those 'Pan- isms' that are struggling forth from continent to continent.[53]

The 'threatening Others' are stigmatised either because of their divided loyalties ('Mecca to [the Indian Muslims] is a sterner reality than Delhi or Agra')[54] or because of their low level of civilisation as measured by their lack of nationalist virtues.[55] Nevertheless, Savarkar discovered nationalism in his study of the 'threatening Others' and especially in his study of nationalist movements in Europe. When he was a young revolutionary in Maharashtra he was inclined to model himself on Mazzini, while the secret society, Abhinav Bharat (Modern India), which he founded in 1904, was probably intended to resemble Mazzini's Young Italy organisation. After settling down in England in 1906 he read Mazzini's political writings and his autobiography, which he translated into Marathi and sent to India for publication.[56] In his introduction to this study, he likened Garibaldi to Shivaji and Mazzini to Shivaji's *guru*, Ramdas.[57] These comparisons are significant in two respects; they are intended not only to assert the heroic stature of Shivaji and Ramdas but also to imply that the virtues which they exemplified are also the virtues of the leading Italian nationalists. This technique of matching European models of action can also be seen in *Hindutva* where Savarkar declares: 'I read the life of Mazzini and I exclaim "How patriotic *they* are!" I read the life of a Madhvacharya [founder of a Vaishnavite sect] and exclaim, "How patriotic *we* are!"'[58] Such sentiments suggest that Savarkar learnt what nationalism was from western experiments and then tried to apply this imported concept to his own country, a process that relied on a new construction of tradition.

Savarkar's main argument in *Hindutva* is that the Aryans who settled in India at the dawn of history already formed a nation now embodied in the Hindus. Their *Hindutva*, according to him, rests on three pillars: geographical unity, racial features and a common culture. Savarkar mini-

---

[53] V.D. Savarkar, *Hindutva: Who is a Hindu?*, Bombay: S.S. Savarkar, 1969, p. 140. Naturally, this statement about Hindu vulnerability is made in the last pages of the book.

[54] Ibid., p. 135.

[55] Ibid., p. 134.

[56] According to Savarkar's biographer, 'Savarkar's Mazzini was the first book to enjoy an uncommon popularity in Maharashtra' (D. Keer, *Veer Savarkar*, op. cit., p. 34).

[57] E. Fasana, 'From Hindutva to Hindu Rashtra: the social and political thought of Vinayak Damodar Savarkar (1883-1966)', paper presented at the 13th European conference of modern South Asian studies (Toulouse, 30 Sept.-3 Oct. 1994).

[58] V.D. Savarkar, *Hindutva*, op. cit., p. 94.

mises the importance of religious criteria in the definition of a Hindu by claiming that Hinduism was only one of the attributes of 'Hinduness'.[59] This stand reflects the fact that, like most of the ethno-religious nationalists, Savarkar was not himself a believer[60] but rather an ideologue. It can also be explained as an attempt to deal with the extreme religious differentiation within Hindu society, a fact that militated against his plans to fashion a homogenous community. The Hindutva of Savarkar was conceived primarily as an ethnic community possessing a territory and sharing the same racial and cultural characteristics, three attributes which stemmed from the mythical reconstruction of the Vedic Golden Age.

The notion of territory was at the heart of Savarkar's ideological construct but not in the same way as in the universalist conceptions of nationalism; for Savarkar, the territory of India cannot be dissociated from Hindu culture and the Hindu people. In his eyes, Hindus are pre-eminently the descendants of the 'intrepid Aryans [who] made it [the subcontinent] their home and lighted their first sacrificial fire on the bank of the [...] Indus',[61] a river which he considers to be the western border of the Hindu nation. The fact that Aryans first settled on the banks of the Indus is of course yet to be proved, but Savarkar finds the accumulation of such a tradition most useful. His view that the Indus was the frontier of the Hindu nation is part of a broader reinterpretation of the word 'Hindu' or 'Sindhu', the letters 'h' and 's' being interchangeable in Sanskrit:

Sindhu in Sanskrit does not only mean the Indus but also the sea – which girdles the southern peninsula – so that this one word Sindhu points out almost all frontiers of the land at a single stroke[...]and so the epithet Sindhustan calls up the image of our whole Motherland: the land that is between Sindhu and Sindhu – from the Indus to the Sea.[62]

For Savarkar a Hindu was therefore an inhabitant of the zone between the rivers, the seas and the Himalayas, 'so strongly entrenched that no other country in the world is so perfectly designed by the fingers of nature as a geographical unit'.[63] This was why, in the Vedic era, the first Aryans developed there 'the sense of unity of a people' and even a 'sense of nationality'.[64] Here we perceive an ethnic logic: the enclosed character of

---

[59] According to Savarkar, 'a man can be as truly a Hindu as any without believing in the Vedas as an independent religious authority' (ibid., p. 81).

[60] D. Keer, *Veer Savarkar*, op. cit., p. 201. On that point see the typology evolved by Ashis Nandy ('An anti-secularist manifesto', *Seminar*, Oct. 1985, p. 15).

[61] V.D. Savarkar, *Hindutva*, op. cit., pp. 4-5.

[62] Ibid., p. 32.

[63] Ibid., p. 82.

[64] Ibid., p. 5

Hindustan is described as the factor that determines the social unity of a population marked by intermarriage.

Savarkar emphasises that his is not a territorial conception of nationalism as the stress he laid on geographical unity might have suggested:

> The Hindus are not merely the citizens of the Indian state because they are united not only by the bonds of the love they bear to a common motherland but also by the bonds of a common blood. They are not only a nation but race-jati. The word jati, derived from the root Jan, to produce, means a brotherhood, a race determined by a common origin, possessing a common blood. All Hindus claim to have in their veins the blood of the mighty race incorporated with and descended from the Vedic fathers.[65]

In other words, Savarkar rejects any form of nation state based on an abstract social contract and thereby comprising individualised citizens dwelling within the country's administrative frontiers. In contrast with this universalist and territorial pattern of nationalism he emphasises the ethnic and racial substance of the Hindu nation. He argues – as Moonje did – that caste has not barred 'the common flow of blood into our race' because of the *anuloma* and *pratiloma* marriages. This racial argument of Savarkar's reflects the influence of the European writers from whom he derived his intellectual nourishment. He was well acquainted with the works of Herbert Spencer, Charles Darwin, Ernst Haeckel and Thomas H. Huxley whose writings had helped to foster the idea of ethnicity in the scientific and political fields.[66]

The emphasis placed on the racial criterion minimises the importance of internal divisions in Hindu society by assuming the existence of an invisible but potent binding factor, that of blood. However, this reasoning does not lead to an absolute rejection of the 'Other'. In fact the notion of racial purity is absent from Savarkar's ideology. His historical account of the formation of the 'Hindu people' rests on the assumption that Aryans and indigenous populations intermingled when the former entered India,[67] and he calls on foreigners who aspire to become Hindus to marry Hindus and have Hindu children:

> [...] any convert of non-Hindu parentage to Hindutva can be a Hindu, if *bona fide*, he or she adopts our land as his or her country and marries a Hindu, thus coming to love our country as a real Fatherland, and adopts our culture and thus adores our land as the Punyabhu [sacred land]. The children of such a union as that would, other things being equal, be most emphatically Hindus.'[68]

[65] Ibid., pp. 84-5.
[66] V.D. Savarkar, *My transportation for life*, Bombay: Veer Savarkar Prakashan, 1984, pp. 269-70. He refers to 'the law of evolution that lays down the iron command' in *Hindutva*, op.cit., (p. 38).
[67] Ibid., p. 11.
[68] Ibid., p. 130.

Savarkar even contests the idea of racial plurality:

After all there is throughout this world, so far as man is concerned but a single race, the human race kept alive by one common blood, the human blood.[69]

Pandey suggest in his study of *Hindutva* that 'for Savarkar, as well as for other Hindu nationalists of the 1920s and 1930s [...] the Muslims and Christians who lived in India, and had lived in most cases as long as the Hindus, had a place in the country, albeit probably a subordinate one, as "citizens" ("Bharatiya" or "Indian").'[70] Savarkar, for instance, admits that Sister Nivedita (an Irish woman who became a disciple of Swami Vivekananda) should be recognised as a Hindu.[71] Doubtless the Christians and Muslims represented for Savarkar an Otherness of a threatening nature, but by defining them as Hindus by race who became converts only a few generations ago, Savarkar suggests that they could be reintegrated into Hindu society; moreover the descendants of the invaders from Central and Western Asia were invited to become assimilated in the same way as their predecessors, the Huns or other Shakas, had been. An anonymous 'Savarkarite'[72] made an appeal in these terms to the Muslims several years later:

You behave as if you are living in a country with which you have no concern, just as travellers live in a wayside inn for a few days and go away.[...] Once you begin to have that natural feeling of human beings, that love of the dear Motherland, that moment we will take you into our fold and christen you Kshatriyas, without in any way going against the important teaching of the holy prophet.[...] After all Religion is a personal one and a man who wears a dress and calls himself a Muslim does not become one if he does not behave according to the broad tenets of Islam. Hence dear Brethren – most of you were Hindus once and just because you have changed your religion you cannot become foreigners – call yourself proudly Kshatriyas and begin to act like Kshatriyas.[...] I tell you that once you call yourself Kshatriyas, that moment the Hindu-Moslems problem will vanish like mists before the powerful sun. Come on brothers, become Kshatriyas.[73]

That Hindu nationalists were determined to impose their view of integration reflects certain features of Hindu 'inclusivism' and 'traditional Indian xenology' in which there is a refusal, according, respectively, to Hacker and Halbfass, to accept or even imagine the existence of an Other

[69] Ibid., p. 90.

[70] G. Pandey 'Which of us are Hindus?', op. cit., p. 251.

[71] V.D. Savarkar, *Hindutva*, op. cit., p. 131.

[72] I have been able to identify this anonymous author thanks to one of his letters to Savarkar. (Savarkar papers NMML Reel no. 1, File no. 5. Letter of S.R. Narayana Ayyar to Savarkar, 16 May 1938.)

[73] An obscure Hindu, *Grave danger to the Hindus*, K.C. Bhalla Harbinger, Puthujara (Malabar), 1940, pp. 75-6.

beyond the indigenous socio-cultural system.[74] This legacy, as well as the absence of a eugenic programme in Savarkar's writings, suggest that his racism is not really of a biological kind but is one of domination. Taguieff's distinction between the racism of domination and the racism of extermination can be usefully introduced at this point. The former follows an 'inegalitarian logic which places the relation to the Other on a hierarchical scale [...] whose principle is accepted' while the latter follows 'an identitarian logic which refuses any comparison with the Other and [...] can only lead to an aspiration to purity through the elimination of the only source of impurity, the Other.'[75] Savarkar did not put great stress on racial purity for his racism of domination was deeply influenced by the rationale of the caste system; minorities are required to assimilate, but at a subordinate rank, at least below the Brahmins.[76]

The use of 'jati' to translate 'race' is highly revealing in this perspective. In the Brahminical world view *jatis* are species (human, animal and vegetal) which occupy different ranks in the universe in conformity with the Dharma (universal law). Human species are integrated in a hierarchical social order, the caste system.[77] Thus, the translation of 'race' by 'jati' implies that each 'race-jati' is part of a cosmic totality and, more precisely, of the caste-based hierarchy of human society. Some *jatis* may occupy a very low position, but they are nonetheless part of the system. As Romila Thapar and Aloka Parasher pointed out (see pp. 2-3), the *mlecchas* were discriminated against because they did not observe cultural rules recommended by the Dharma, not because of their racial characteristics. The frontier between the Aryas and the *mlecchas* was a relatively open one precisely because the notion of human *jatis* is based not on biological but on cultural criteria. Thus it is very difficult to conceive of a Hindu race – in biological terms – as opposed to other races. There can only be one Hindu culture defining rituals and social rules implemented by a certain human community in which different *jatis* co-exist in a hierarchical relationship. A biological ideology of race is therefore difficult to con-

---

[74] C. Ram-Prasad argues convincingly that 'the generality of the essential Hindu doctrine of inclusivism can be used to further the cause of the ideologue, which is to ensure that the Hindu identity as he conceives it is preserved and propagated.' ('Hindutva ideology: extracting the fundamentals', *Contemporary South Asia*, 2 (3), 1993, p. 294).

[75] P.A. Taguieff, *La force du préjugé – Essai sur le racisme et ses doubles*, Paris: La Découverte, 1988, pp. 166-8 and 174.

[76] This argument has been developed in C. Jaffrelot, 'The idea of the Hindu race in the writings of the Hindu nationalist ideologues in the 1920s-1930s: a concept between two cultures' in P. Robb (ed.), *The idea of race in South Asia*, New Delhi: Oxford University Press, 1995.

[77] O. Herrenschmidt, *Les meilleurs dieux sont hindous*, Paris: L'Age d'homme, 1989, pp. 252-6.

struct in the Hindu context, but a racism of domination by the upper castes appears natural.

The third criterion of Hindutva – a 'common culture' – as defined by Savarkar stems directly from the crucial importance of rituals, social rules and language in Hinduism:

Hindus are bound together not only by the tie of the love we bear to a common fatherland and by the common blood that courses through our veins and keeps our hearts throbbing and our affections warm, but also by the tie of the common homage we pay to our great civilization – our Hindu culture, which could not be better rendered than by the word Sanskriti suggestive as it is of that language, Sanskrit, which has been the chosen means of expression and preservation of that culture, of all that was best and worth-preserving in the history of our race.[78]

Sanskrit is falsely cited by Sarvarkar as the common reference-point for all Indian languages and, in accordance with classical Brahminical texts, as 'language par excellence'.[79] Thenceforward, every political programme reflecting Hindu nationalist ideology called for recognition of Sanskrit or Hindi – the vernacular language closest to it – as the national language. Besides language, 'common laws and rites', such as religious festivals, were cited as criteria of Hindutva by Savarkar; according to him, Christians and Muslims of India were not part of the nation because of their differences in cultural terms:

Mohammedan or Christian communities possess all the essential qualifications of Hindutva but one and all that is that they do not look upon India as their holyland.[80]

On the same page Savarkar explains this criterion in cultural and religious terms:

Their holyland is far off in Arabia and Palestine. Their mythology and Godmen, ideas and heroes are not the children of this soil. Consequently their names and their outlook smack of foreign origin. Their love is divided.[81]

This characterisation of Christianity and Islam leads Savarkar to write that, when the Muslims penetrated in India, 'the conflict of life and death began'.[82] However, this conflict had a positive effect since 'Nothing makes conscious of itself so much as a conflict with non-self'.[83]

In sum, Savarkar's notion of Hindutva rests on cultural criteria rather than on a racial theory and is accordingly in tune with the traditional

[78] V.D. Savarkar, *Hindutva*, op. cit., p. 92.
[79] Ibid., p. 95.
[80] Ibid., p. 113.
[81] Ibid., p. 113.
[82] Ibid., p. 42.
[83] Ibid., p. 43.

Brahminical world view; but at the same time it represents an ethnic nationalism which borrows much from western theories. In the book he wrote about his period of detention in the Andamans between 1911 and 1921, he refers to Bluntschli's *The theory of the State* as a study which he had not only read but also used when teaching his fellow prisoners.[84] Bluntschli was an exponent of German ethnic nationalism, and his writings influenced many Hindu nationalists, including Golwalkar. Savarkar's attachment to this kind of nationalism suggests that he was a zealot in the sense defined by Ashis Nandy, i.e.

[...] one who has internalised the 'defeat' of his religion or culture in the hands of the modern world and [...] who believes that that defeat can be avenged only when the peripheral faiths or ethnicities have internalised the technology of victory of the western man and decided to fight under the flag of their own faiths.[85]

Hindutva marks the internalisation of the notion of ethnic nationalism, a very important element of this 'technology of victory'. This process does not imply that such nationalism was simply borrowed from the West, as diffusionist theorists would have us believe.[86] We are still using here the theoretical frameworks of Geertz, Fallers and especially Anthony Smith, out of which the notion of strategic emulation emerged. Savarkar drew inspiration from Western architects of ethnic nationalism, in the same way that Moonje or Shraddhananda encouraged the imitation of cultural features of the 'threatening Others' in order to fortify Hindus. It is true, however, that Hindutva marked a qualitative change in Hindu nationalism, aspects of which had previously been combined in a loose ideology but which had now acquired a more systematic exposition.

Besides his influence as a writer, Savarkar won respect among Hindu nationalists by his public activities; his period as president of the Hindu Mahasabha brought added prestige to that body, but the fact remained that neither its organisation nor its personnel were suited to the demanding tasks of party-building which it faced.

The Mahasabha formed a pressure group within Congress but recruited its supporters above all among conservative notables and princes; a representative of the ideologically aware intelligentsia such as Moonje, (a Brahmin who was an opthalmologist by profession) thus benefited from the influence and financial support of the heirs to the old kingdom of Nagpur, the Bhonsle maharajahs, whose royal house was

---

[84] V.D. Savarkar, *My transportation for life*, op. cit., pp. 271-2.

[85] A. Nandy, 'An anti-secular manifesto', op. cit., p. 19.

[86] See, for instance, H. Kohn, *A history of nationalism in the East*, London: G. Routledge, 1929; and L. Snyder, *Varieties of nationalism: a comparative study*, New York: Holt, Rinehart and Winston, 1976. p. 113. For an elaborate criticism of the diffusionist approach, see A.D. Smith, *Theories of nationalism*, op. cit., pp. 35-6.

dis-established in 1818, and of an important Nagpur landowner, M.G. Chitnavis.[87] Such a relationship between the intelligentsia and their patrons has been identified by Christopher Bayly as one of the means by which the Congress developed up to the early part of the twentieth century.[88] However the Congress intelligentsia was later freed from the control of notables in part because of the constitutional reforms of 1909 and 1919, which enabled it to appeal to a wider audience. The Hindu Mahasabha, being unable to follow this path, remained highly dependent on the influence of notables whose conservatism and factionalism hampered the development of the organisation.[89] Excluded from Congress in 1937 on account of its communalism, it did not come to be truly represented in elective institutions until Independence. This divorce between the Hindu Mahasabha and Congress was not, however, complete in so far as the pillars of the former preferred to remain in the latter. A prominent example of this duality was Madan Mohan Malaviya, founder of the Benares Hindu University (BHU), whose faction, firmly implanted in the United Provinces (where it rivalled that of the Nehrus), represented the durability of a Hindu traditionalist current within Congress.

While the Hindu Mahasabha experienced an early decline, the RSS developed steadily and was to become the principal standard-bearer of Hindu nationalist ideology. In fact this organisation, which was formed by Hedgewar after he had read *Hindutva* and had been further stimulated by a visit to Savarkar,[90] was deeply influenced by the latter's conception of the nation.

The RSS: a Hindu nationalist sect

The Rashtriya Swayamsevak Sangh (RSS – Association of National Volunteers) was founded at Nagpur in 1925 by Keshav Baliram Hedgewar, who had received his political initiation from Moonje. The latter had sent him to Calcutta in 1910 to pursue his medical studies and – unofficially– to learn terrorist techniques from the Bengali secret societies. He thus made his way into the inner circle of Anushilan Samiti (Society of Practice), to which only an elect few had access. On returning to Nagpur in 1915, he followed Moonje into the Congress while continuing with his

[87] I. Prakash, *A review of the history and work of the Hindu Mahasabha and the Hindu Sangathan movement*, op. cit., p. 246; and S.P. Sen (ed.), *Dictionary of National Biography*, vol. I, Calcutta: Institute of Historical Studies, 1973, p. 316.

[88] C. Bayly, 'Patrons and clients in northern India', *MAS*, 7(3), 1973, pp. 349-88.

[89] For more details on this point, see C. Jaffrelot, 'Des nationalistes en quête d'une nation', op. cit., pp. 404-35.

[90] Hedgewar met Savarkar in March 1925 and started the RSS at the time of Dasahara in September 1925. (D. Keer, *Veer Savarkar*, op. cit., p. 170.)

anti-British activities via the Kranti Dal (Party of the Revolution).[91] The British intensified their repression during the First World War, provoking in the ranks of the Dal the indiscipline which Hedgewar diagnosed as the main weakness of the freedom movement. This analysis extended also to Congress where the factional divisions and the Gandhian method of 'non-co-operation' seemed to him to make that party unsuited for the task of emancipating India from British rule.[92] According to Walter Andersen and Shridhar Damle, from his youth Hedgewar had been 'disturbed that a small group of colonial administrators could rule a vast country like India with such ease'.[93] In addition to this foreign domination there was also the 'threat' from the Muslims. The Nagpur riots of 1923 had a profound effect on Hedgewar.[94] The same circumstances, which had already given new life to the Hindu Mahasabha, awoke feelings of vulnerability in Hedgewar and among certain Hindu circles.[95]

This was the catalyst for a reactivation of the strategy of stigmatisation and emulation. At first glance the mimetic dimension of the RSS is easy to identify since one feature of its volunteers' uniform, the khaki shorts, had been borrowed from the British police.[96] Obviously the para-military style of the RSS reflects an attempt to introduce in Hindu society the cohesion and strength of the 'aggressors', because Hindus are seen as weak and divided. But the borrowed features of the RSS coexist with more authentically Hindu elements. This composite nature probably explains why Andersen and Damle have emphasised some ritualised aspects of the RSS's discipline in terms of character-building,[97] while others have described it as a fascist movement.[98] The notion of strategic emulation probably offers one means of reconciling these conflicting interpretations because it enables us to see how the assimilation of cultural and political features of the Other, such as European forms of extreme nationalism, occurred under the guise of a reinterpretation of traditional institutions

[91] B.V. Deshpande and S.R. Ramaswamy, *Dr Hedgewar, the epoch-maker*, Bangalore: Sahitya Sindhu, 1981, p. 24.

[92] D.V. Kelkar, 'The RSS', *Economic Weekly*, 4 Feb. 1950, p. 134.

[93] W. Andersen and S. Damle, *The brotherhood in saffron: The Rashtriya Swayamsevak Sangh and Hindu revivalism*, New Delhi: Vistaar Publications, 1987, p. 34.

[94] D.V. Kelkar, 'The RSS', art. cit., p. 133.

[95] Moonje, the founder of the Hindu Sabha of Nagpur in 1923, which Hedgewar joined, admitted that there were only 20,000 Muslim inhabitants in the town out of a total of 150,000, but inspite of that fact he said: 'we feel insecure' (cited in W. Andersen and S. Damle, *The brotherhood in saffron*, op. cit., p. 33).

[96] D. Gold, 'Organized Hinduisms: from vedic truth to Hindu nation' in M.E. Martin and R. Scott Appleby (eds), *Fundamentalisms observed*, University of Chicago Press, 1991, p. 577. D. Gold says he owes this insight to Ashis Nandy.

[97] See, for instance, *The brotherhood in saffron*, op. cit., p. 91.

[98] See, for instance, S. Sarkar, 'The fascism of Sangh parivar', *EPW*, 30 Jan. 1993, p. 163.

and values, namely the *akhara*, asceticism and the Hindu sect. Hence our characterisation of the RSS as a Hindu nationalist sect.[99]

The sectarian crucible of the Hindu nation

The RSS took on several features of the Indian terrorist societies, including a military style of training recruits and a certain religiosity. However these features were also reminiscent of older institutions such as the *akharas* and, at another remove, of the Hindu sect.

An ideological akhara. From its inception, the basic unit of the RSS has been the *shakha* (local branch), which, in the beginning, had a close affinity to the *akharas*. The term *akhara* designates a place where the young men of a locality gather daily for body-building, exercise and sports – mainly wrestling and weight-lifting. In this guise the *akhara* retains a ritual dimension – even a spiritual one. It includes a temple – when not attached to one – that is generally dedicated to Hanuman (the monkey god allied to Ram in the *Ramayana*, where he embodies strength); it is placed under the authority of a *guru* who instructs the members of the *akhara* in physical and mental discipline, giving them a certain balance (*sanyam*) that also implies abstinence. Members of an *akhara* are recruited from all social milieux and develop a strong collective attachment to it.[100]

Before this model was reinterpreted by the RSS, many nationalists had already derived inspiration from it – ideologically and organisationally. The clearest such case was that of the Bengali secret societies, with which Hedgewar was so familiar. These organisations often practised martial exercises with a religious overtone which found particular expression in the initiation ceremony: the members of the Anushilan Samiti took an oath of allegiance to the organisation before an image of Kali, with the *Bhagavad Gita* in one hand and a revolver in the other,[101] the presence of the goddess serving as a reminder that the movement drew its ethic of violence partly from the ritual of the Shakta sect. Furthermore, the

---

[99] It should be noted that the Hindi translation for communalism, *sampradayikta*, which is more common than *jativad*, literally means sectarianism.

[100] This discussion is based on ch. 5 of N. Kumar's work on Varanasi, *The artisans of Benaras – Popular culture and identity – 1880-1986*, Princeton University Press, 1988. This is valid for the whole of North India, and the author emphasises that it has been produced by a synthesis of numerous regional influences, notably from Maharashtra. S. Freitag notes that 'The pervasiveness of the akhara in structuring popular activities suggests that its organizational characteristics should be taken very seriously'. (S. Freitag, *Collective action and community: The public arena and the emergence of communalism in North India*, New Delhi: Oxford University Press, 1990, p. 121.)

[101] U. Mukherjee, *Two great revolutionaries: R.B. Bose and J.N. Mukherjee*, Calcutta: Firma K.L. Mukhopadhyay, 1966, p. 17.

structure of these terrorist groups, whose basic cell was a group centred around a *dada* (lit. 'big brother'), reproduced an important Hindu notion, namely the *guru-shishya* (master-disciple) relationship, where 'the disciple must render his total loyalty, devotion and respect to his teacher'.[102] The spiritual dimension of the Anushilan Samiti emerges from its very name since *anushilan* designates 'the fullest development of all faculties, physical and mental'.[103] Its members 'kept up, as a means of self-discipline and preparation, the practice of physical culture and of sports such as lathi-play; this was often bound up with religious vows and with a cult of austerity and sexual abstinence drawn from the Hindu tradition of Brahmacharya.'[104]

Not only terrorist societies but also Congress itself drew inspiration from the traditional *akhara* to develop *prabhat pheris* (drilling in groups, held each morning) that resembled *akhara* processions. These *prabhat pheris*, whose participants sometimes wore uniform and carried batons, were called upon to strengthen the Indian nation both physically and spiritually in the struggle for emancipation.[105] It was in this same spirit that the *akharas* multiplied, especially between 1890-1910 and particularly in Bengal and Maharashtra, the two regions where, together with the Punjab, the extremist current flowed strongest and the terrorist societies were most active. In the 1920s the Hindu Mahasabha called for an increase in the number of *akharas* to protect Hindus in the context of the Khilafat movement. In his presidential address in 1923, M.M. Malaviya recommended the building in each village and *mohalla* (urban quarter) of a small Hanuman temple and an *akhara*.[106] Lajpat Rai, as president of the Hindu Mahasabha in 1925, added the formation of 'gymnasiums' to his movement's programme.[107]

[102] L. A. Gordon, *Bengal: The nationalist movement, 1876-1940*, New York: Columbia University Press, 1974, p. 142.

[103] J. Rosselli, 'The self-image of effeteness: physical education and nationalism in nineteenth century Bengal', *Past and Present*, 86, 1980, p. 130.

[104] Ibid. The revolutionaries were directly inspired by B.C. Chatterji's Bengali novel, *Ananda math* (*The monastery of Felicity*), where the author related in an exaggerated fashion the struggle which ascetic warriors (*nagas*) waged in the eighteenth century against Muslim power in Bengal. This historical episode was described as a battle on behalf of the Goddess-Motherland of a 'community of sons' who formed a 'sect of worshippers' under the authority of a *guru*; these 'sons' had temporarily renounced the world 'in order to cultivate those qualities' which made the English so strong, and in particular to learn the art of combat; at the time of their initiation, they abandoned their families and all caste distinctions. (B.C. Chatterji, trans. and intro. by F. Bhattacharya, *Le monastère de la félicité*, Paris: Publications Orientalistes de France, 1985, pp. 47, 62, 72, and 87-9).

[105] See S. Freitag, *Collective action and community*, op. cit., pp.122 and 225.

[106] Parmanand, *Mahamana Madan Mohan Malaviya*, Benares Hindu University, 1985, p. 624.

[107] *Indian Quarterly Register*, 1925, vol. I, p. 381.

Both the political *akharas* and, subsequently, the RSS were distinguished from the traditional model by their ideological character and style of physical exercise. Physical training and wrestling between individuals gave way to games between opposing teams. This change reflected the influence of the British, for whom 'the development of a healthy body was not as important as playing games of conflict'.[108] For Joseph Alter the *shakha*'s physical training is 'unambiguously Western' because 'even stave training and other kinds of "Indian exercise"are regimented according to western standards of cadence, formation and discipline'[109] V.M. Sirsikar, who joined the RSS in 1933 at Nagpur, mentions that the Sunday parade was accompanied by a band playing English music (the orders for the drill were in English) and 'most of its practices [...] had been borrowed from the University Training Corps.'[110] Again, this phenomenon proceeded from the desire to imitate the cultural traits to which, it was considered, the British rulers owed their strength. As it was, the physical force of the latter had very quickly bred an inferiority complex among the Hindu intelligentsia, whom the British often regarded as puny and effeminate. Here was a clear example of the strategic emulation of which the RSS would be the inheritor. In the case of this organisation, however, the process was deeper and more complex.

In the *shakhas* of the RSS, as in the first political *akharas* or in the terrorist societies, participants trained in drill with the *lathi* (a long bamboo stave) and played team games such as *kabaddi*.[111] Members – *swayamsevaks* – were selected in small numbers from among the youths attending the *shakha*. They then pledged to consecrate themselves to the RSS 'with [their] whole body, heart and money, for in it lies the betterment of Hindus and the country'.[112] This pledge was uttered before an effigy of Hanuman, who was already the presiding figure in the *akharas* of the region, where he was known as Maruti. Moreover, in the early years

---

[108] J. Masselos, 'Spare time and recreation: changing behaviour patterns in Bombay at the turn of the nineteenth century', *South Asia*, 2 (1), June 1984, p. 48.

[109] J. Alter, 'Somatic nationalism: Indian wrestling and militant Hinduism", *MAS*, 28 (3) (1994), p. 567. On this point and for more on the allure of violence see S.H. Deshpande, 'My days in the RSS', *Quest*, 96, July 1975, pp. 19-30.

[110] V.M. Sirsikar, 'My years in the RSS' in E. Zelliot and M. Berntsen (eds.), *The experience of Hindusim*, New York: State University of New York Press, 1988, p. 133.

[111] Sirsikar emphasises that the 'games and calisthenics were especially appealing because, except for the drill they were all Indian' (Ibid. p. 192).

[112] The life oath was inaugurated in 1928. 'I pledge this day that I will remain a member of the Rashtriya Swayamsevak Sangh throughout my life; I shall carry out unhesitatingly any order given by the Sangh. I shall go for work wherever required. Whatever defects of the Sangh I shall come to know, I will never disclose them before any person not connected with the Sangh, even at the cost of my life'. (Cited in W. Andersen, 'The Rashtriya Swayamsevak Sangh I: Early concerns', *EPW*, 11 March 1972, p. 593.)

swayamsevaks were enjoined to remain in their *akharas*, which multiplied in reaction to rioting, and to attend *shakhas* only once or twice a week for political education.[113] Vasant Rao Oke, a Chitpavan Brahmin from Nagpur who joined the RSS in 1927 and was later to occupy high office in the organisation, remembers having been attracted to the movement because of the similarity of the atmosphere he found in the *shakhas* and in the *akhara* where he practised every morning: 'I was attracted because I had a natural inclination to have a good physique, a healthy body, a healthy mind and healthy ideals'.[114] Nana Deshmukh, another Maharashtrian Brahmin, who joined the RSS in 1929 in Akola and later became a leading figure in the Jana Sangh, points out that he had been going to an *akhara*, as had most Maharashtrian males, since childhood, but differentiates the two: '*Akhara* is for physical strength, *shakha* for the national cause. [...] Programmes may be the same but the objectives make the difference. [...] Dr Hedgewar said "Go to the *akharas*, but come to the *shakhas* also." ',[115] *Akharas* concentrated on physical fitness and *shakhas* on cultivation of the mind. The physical and intellectual dimensions were gradually integrated as *shakhas* became a daily occurrence: meetings were held either in the morning or evening and lasted for about one hour.

The resemblance of the RSS to the *akhara* is only formal, given the ideological overtone of the former.[116] However, it tended to raise

---

[113] K.R. Malkani, *The RSS story*, New Delhi: Impex India, 1980, p. 15, and W. Andersen and S. Damle, *The brotherhood in saffron*, op. cit., pp. 34-5. The number of *akharas* in Nagpur division jumped during the mid-1920s from 230 to 570 (ibid.)

[114] Interview with V.R. Oke, 12 Aug. 1992, New Delhi. Even though this kind of motivation seems to be rare nowadays, I came across a similar case at Ujjain where an MLA from the BJP, who, interestingly, was from the Jain community which is known for its non-violent ideals, said that he was attending alternately the *shakha* and his *akhara* (interview with Parast Chand Jain, 26 August 1992, Ujjain).

[115] Interview with N. Deshmukh, 25 Feb. 1994, New Delhi. Before the foundation of the RSS, Hedgewar had already urged young men to attend the courses of physical training organised by a friend of his, Martand Rao Jog, who had just retired from the army. He came to the playground to hold talks (C.P. Bhirshikar, *Shri Bhaiyaji Dani*, Lucknow: Lokahit Prakashan, [n.d.] (Hindi), p. 10.

[116] J. Alter, an authority on the *akhara*, has recently pointed out that even though certain similarities exist between the *akhara* and the *shakha*, one should not exaggerate them: 'In both arenas young men are taught self-control and physical fitness. Personal strength is regarded in both systems as an individualistic form of national strength. The focus on Hanuman as an icon of strength and self-sacrifice is found in both wrestling and RSS circles. Indeed, there are undoubtedly some wrestlers who find much to commend in the militant ideology of Hindu chauvinism [...] Nevertheless, and despite formal parallels, I found that those wrestlers who followed a strict regimen of daily training felt a great deal of ambivalence and some outright hostility towards RSS ideals' (J.S. Alter, *The wrestler's body: ideology and identity in North India*, Berkeley: University of California Press, 1992, p. 261). Indeed, there is at least one major difference between *akharas* and *shakhas*, namely the fact that the former accept Muslim as well as Hindu members.

Hedgewar, as its founder, to the status of a *guru*, so much so that from 1927 he subjected his young recruits to weekly sessions of *baudhik* (ideological education) consisting of simple questions to the novices concerning the Hindu nation, its history and heroes, especially Shivaji. Hedgewar nevertheless refused, as he said repeatedly, to become one of the numerous *gurus* who sow divisions in Hinduism, and it was only in 1929 that he took the title of *sarsanghchalak* (supreme leader), a decision that is analysed below. The true *guru* to whom he demanded that obeisance be paid was the saffron flag of Shivaji, the Bhagwa Dwaj. Even today, the daily session of the *shakhas* opens with the volunteers saluting the flag. They are also called upon to render to it each year a guru dakshina which is supposed to finance the movement, and is so named in reference to the traditional offering made by a pupil to his master in recognition of his teaching.

This ceremony occurs in a cycle of six annual festivals which often coincides with those observed in Hindu society, and which Hedgewar inscribed in the ritual calendar of his movement: Varsha Pratipada (the Hindu new year), Shivajirajyarohonastava (the coronation of Shivaji), guru dakshina, Raksha Bandhan (a North Indian festival in which sisters tie ribbons round the wrists of their brothers to remind them of their duty as protectors, a ritual which the RSS has re-interpreted in such a way that the leader of the *shakha* ties a ribbon around the pole of the saffron flag, after which *swayamsevaks* carry out this ritual for one another as a mark of brotherhood), Dasahara (when *swayamsevaks* pay homage to arms) and Makarsankraman (celebrated at the moment when the sun enters Capricorn – in January – to promote the forces of prosperity).

The first public task assigned to the RSS by its founder included a religious element in so far as it was to protect pilgrims against the rapacity of Muslim fakirs and Brahmin priests at the great festival of Ramanavami (celebrating the birth of Ram) held at Ramtek (near Nagpur) in 1926.[117] However its dominant mission, as an ideological *akhara*, was clearly directed against Muslims, as the events of 1927 in Nagpur reveal. RSS volunteers were involved in a riot during the procession of Mahalakshmi (the festival of Lakshmi, goddess of prosperity),[118] while Hedgewar's be-

---

However, an important point lies in the formal parallels mentioned by Alter because they enabled the RSS to attract young people as if the *shakhas* were modern versions of the *akharas*. E.A. Mann notes that 'The RSS are strong patrons of many Aligarh *akharas* (though not all *akharas* are patronised by the RSS), where drills and organised fights (*shakhas*) are held' (*Boundaries and identities: Muslims, works and status in Aligarh*, New Delhi: Sage, 1992, p. 175).

[117] W. Andersen and S. Damle, *The brotherhood in saffron*, op. cit., p. 35.

[118] On this episode, see T. Basu, P. Datta, S. Sarkar, T. Sarkar and S. Sen, *Khaki shorts and saffron flags*, New Delhi: Orient Longman, 1993, p. 19.

haviour during the festival of Ganesh that same year was very revealing, as shown by V.R. Oke's testimony:

In 1927, there were riots in Nagpur. Hindus were defensive. [In the past] Muslims stopped the Ganesh processions when they passed before a mosque with music. However, in 1927 Dr Hedgewar came in front of the procession, from the beginning, on the mosque road till the tank while beating the drums. Because of him all the others also came along beating the drums. They had the courage then. I took Dr Hedgewar as a challenge against injustice.[119]

The part played by the RSS in such Hindu-Muslim confrontations illustrates its role as an ideological *akhara*, prepared for conflict. It moved in this direction at a time when many *akharas* were beginning to attract violent elements in Indian society.[120] Thus the growth of the RSS in its formative years was probably due largely to its status as a martial body reinterpreting the traditional *akhara*, as so many political groupings from the Bengali secret societies to the Hindu Mahasabha had already done.

The world-renouncer as an activist.   As well as its ritual aspect, the resemblence of the RSS to a religious institution is a function of its emphasis on the merits of renunciation and its social characteristics. In 1927 Hedgewar organised an Officers' Training Camp (OTC) with the task of forming a corps of *pracharaks* (lit. 'preachers')[121] to constitute the backbone of the RSS. Hedgewar called on the *pracharaks* to 'become sadhus first.'[122] Following his example, even today these cadres renounce their professions and generally remain celibate in order to devote themselves to the mission of regenerating the Hindu community. They live an austere life of total devotion to the cause, one which professes to be a form of *karma yoga*, the yoga of action.[123] While *karma yoga* is expounded in the *Bhagavad Gita*, where it is described as a matter of inner sacrifice (action, even when it is violent, can constitute a means of renunciation when it is undertaken without regard to personal advantage and in the

---

[119] Interview with V.R. Oke corroborated in Moonje papers (P. Bacchetta, 'Different choices/different voices: the Rashtra Swayamsevak Sangh, the Rashtra Sevika Samiti and their respective conceptions of the "Hindu nation" in K. Jayawardena (ed.) *Woman and communalism in South Asia*, forthcoming.

[120] On the evolution of the *akharas* of Jaipur and their involvement in communal riots, see S. Mayaram, 'Communal violence in Jaipur', *EPW*, 13 Nov. 1993, p. 2529.

[121] B.V. Deshpande and S.R. Ramaswamy, *Dr Hedgewar, the epoch- maker*, op. cit., pp. 90 and 95. The OTCs, the all-India gathering which took place at Nagpur once a year, would follow three years' training including, at an initial stage, two Instructors' Training Camps (ITCs) organised regionally.

[122] Cited in M.S. Golwalkar, *Bunch of thoughts*, Bangalore: Jagarana Prakashana, 1980, p. 368.

[123] For more details, See W. Andersen and S. Damle, *The brotherhood in saffron*, op. cit., p. 82.

service of Dharma), Hedgewar embraced this doctrine after it had been re-interpreted by militant nationalists, such as Aurobindo, who were close to the Bengali secret societies.[124] In the RSS, one of the usual ways of honouring *pracharaks* when they die has been to designate them as Karma Yogis,[125] following the model established by Hedgewar.

Hedgewar, more or less against his wishes, was recognised as a *guru* by his disciples[126] (his mausoleum is still a place of pilgrimage for members of the RSS).[127] Madhav Sadashiv Golwalkar, designated by Hedgewar as his successor shortly before his death in 1940, was unquestionably regarded as a *guru* by members of the RSS.[128] He had joined the RSS in 1931 after a visit by Hedgewar to the Benares Hindu University, where he taught zoology. On the campus his beard, long hair and simple robe had earned him the nickname of 'Guruji'. In 1937 a religious calling

[124] This extremist leader had a *naga* chief as his guru. (L. Gordon, *Bengal: The nationalist movement, 1876-1940*, op. cit., p. 111). He had translated *The Monastery of Felicity* into English and published it in his journal, *Karma Yogin*, in 1909 (G.E. Monod-Herzen, *Sri Aurobindo*, Pondicherry: Shri Aurobindo Ashram, 1954, p. 46). He saw in *karma yoga* a means of legitimising violence as a form of sacrifice. This activist interpretation is also found in the writings of other extremist leaders such as Lajpat Rai (*The message of the Bhagavad Gita*, Allahabad: 1908) and Tilak (*Srimad Bhagavagita – Rahasya or Karma Yoga Shastra*, Poona: 1965). In its early form such discipline was mainly reputed to bring about self-mastery in the spiritual realm.

[125] See, for example, the cases of Babasaheb Apte (P.G. Sahasrabuddhe, *Karmayogi Babasaheb Apte*, Nagpur: P. Phejpurker, [n.d.] (Hindi)) and Eknath Ranade ('Karma Yogi Eknath Ranade' (*Organiser*, 19 Sept. 1982, p. 14)). In 1995, Moropant Pingle, a Chitpavan Brahmin (like the other two) who had joined the RSS in the 1930s was presented 'as one of that select group described as *deva durlabh* (rare spiritual person) within the RSS (*Organiser*, 16 Apr. 1995).

[126] W. Andersen and S. Damle, *The brotherhood in saffron*, op. cit., pp. 37 and 80.

[127] This mausoleum, named 'Smriti Mandir' (the temple of memory of tradition) was inaugurated in 1962 by Golwalkar, who defended his 'idolatry' of Hedgewar by attributing to him 'superhuman qualities' in his speech (16 Apr. 1962, p. 11). Since the mausoleum attracted a growing number of pilgrims, it soon became necessary to add living accommodation (ibid., 24 Feb. 1973, p. 1), of which a second stage was completed in 1985 to house cadres taking part in the training camps in Nagpur (ibid., 24 March 1985, p. 13). In 1994 a Keshav Smriti Bhavan was built by the RSS on the site of Hedgewar's ancestral family home in Andhra Pradesh and an image installed in it (ibid., 22 May 1994).

[128] Indeed, Golwalkar described the RSS as a sect in the compilation of his writings and speeches that was published in the mid-1960s: 'in our various sects, each individual has a definite emblem in keeping with his particular sect. He dresses and adorns himself in a particular manner, recites a particular mantra and follows a particular code of discipline [...] We too have evolved a technique, an emblem, a 'mantra' and a code of discipline in keeping with our ideal of a unified and disciplined national life. The great and inspiring emblem that we have chosen is the immortal Bhagwa Dwaj which brings before our eyes the living image of our ancient, sacred and integrated national life in all its pristine purity and entirely crossing all superficial barriers of province, sect, creed, caste, language and custom' (M.S. Golwalkar, *Bunch of thoughts*, op. cit, p. 514).

led him to enter an *ashram* in Bengal.[129] The death of his *guru* the same year brought him back to his home in Nagpur.[130] A Bengali *pracharak* explained that 'emotionally [he] had associated that slender bearded face with the highest ideals of purity and abstinence.'[131] He tended to be regarded as a genuine *guru* by the *swayamsevaks*, as is made clear by a poem recited on his sixty-first birthday in the presence of some twenty RSS cadres representing different provinces:

> *Oh Guru, you are the defender of the over-all welfare of the Hindus.*
> *You know what is best for them.*
> *Throughout the year you exert yourself all over the country, without respite.*
> *You give us the light of your knowledge, and captivate our hearts.*[132]

Many *pracharaks* also came to be regarded as *gurus* by the *swayamsevaks* of the *shakhas* which they directed.[133] RSS members who were brought into the movement in 1928-9 by Babasaheb Apte, a Chitpavan Brahmin and one of Hedgewar's first *pracharaks* at Nagpur, remembered him as a master, one whose preaching and recitation of poetry – namely that of Savarkar – revealed a 'new world' to them.[134] Certain Hindu traditionalist leaders were even honoured as *gurus*, against their wishes, by young *swayamsevaks* whose relationship to authority could have no basis other than that between master and disciple.[135]

Rather than their 'knowledge', it was their renunciatory discipline and, more precisely, their disinterestedness which afforded *pracharaks* prestige. This prestige is still evident today, as in this testimony of a *swayamsevak* from Bhopal:

---

[129] On Golwalkar's religious aspirations, see some of his letters translated in English in R. Kohli, *Political ideas of M.S. Golwalkar*, New Delhi: Deep and Deep, 1993, p. 2.

[130] Some *pracharaks* had similar experiences. Babasaheb Kasture, for instance, whose brother was a *sadhu*, relinquished his post of *pracharak* in order to become a *sadhu* for some time (interview with Babasaheb Kasture, 21 Feb. 1994, New Delhi). Swami Prakashanand, a Vishwa Hindu Parishad *sadhu* had previously been an RSS *pracharak*.

[131] H.N. Pandit, *The end of a dream*, New Delhi: All India Sampradayikta Virodhi Committee, 1947, p. 17.

[132] *Organiser*, 15 Mar. 1967, p. 16.

[133] A RSS man in Bhopal introduced another visitor to the author as his 'guru'. This was M.R. Moonje, a *pracharak* whom he had met as a *swayamsevak* in the 1930s (interview with Y.R. Meghawale, 12 Oct. 1991, Bhopal).

[134] Yadav Rao [Joshi], 'An old Swayamsevak recalls Babasaheb Apte', *Organiser*, 2 Sept. 1972, p. 5.

[135] Mauli Chandra Sharma, who belonged to the traditionalist wing of Congress before joining the Jana Sangh in 1951 was imprisoned with *swayamsevaks* during the Kashmir Andolam in 1953. The RSS men sharing his cell expressed their desire to recognise him as their *guru* after he had begun to pass the time by teaching them political theory. It was in this way that he learned the significance of the 'guru-shishya' relationship in the culture of the RSS (Oral History Transcript, Accession no. 327, NMML, p. 206, Hindi).

See that person, who has dedicated his life for the national work, a *pracharak*. *Pracharak* what selfishness will he have? Because he does not want anything. Throughout he has sacrificed himself, money, life, and everything. So, whatever he thinks, he will make clearway. He thinks of you, he thinks of me and that may be in a true picture. Nothing in mind because he has not more affection for you, less affection for me. Nothing like that comes in his mind.[136]

An appeal to the values of renunciation certainly has little justification in this context, since the *pracharaks* are seeking salvation not for themselves but for their nation, and go about achieving this end in the most worldly way possible. Their status is thus seen as provisional and conditioned by this aim, as one of them revealed:

A *pracharak* must be a bachelor because to take care of a family divides loyalty and responsibility. Therefore, though we feel it is not the normal process, yet we have to stick to it for an interim period, until society develops and becomes a nation in the category of world power, in terms of extension, philosophy, science, technique, military strength, etc.[137]

At this stage, we can analyse Hedgewar's call to his followers to become *sadhus* from two points of view. First, it can be seen as a practical move to persuade *pracharaks* to devote all their time and energy to the cause of Hindu nationalism; second, the emphasis on asceticism enabled him to introduce some features of the Hindu sect in the RSS. In a penetrating essay, Gold argues that while the RSS, like the Arya Samaj, differs from 'traditional Hindu sectarian lineages', it has adapted 'traditional ideas of guruhood and wed[ded] it to a larger leadership organization that has acquired a sanctity of its own'.[138] A similar approach underlies our analysis of the RSS as a nationalist 'sect', and the polysemy of the word 'sect' in the Indian context – as well as the inverted commas – must be re-emphasised; it resembles a Hindu sect because it is a closed and dogmatic organisation, but also because of its sociological profile.

In Hinduism, the element of renunciation is opposed to the world of castes in so far as the first represents the domain of the individual and the second forms a holistic system in which the individual has no real place.[139] Hinduism had a notion of individualism, but only in an other-worldly sense. In this perspective, the sect, defined by Dumont as 'a religious

---

[136] Interview with P.P. Bapat, 28 Nov. 1989, Bhopal.

[137] Interview with Acharya Giriraj Kishore, 9 Nov. 1990, New Delhi. This conception of 'active renunciation' as a temporary suspension of the natural order of things for the sake of defending Hinduism in the world had already been at the heart of Chatterji's *The Monastery of Felicity*.

[138] D. Gold, 'Organized Hinduisms', op. cit., p. 563.

[139] L. Dumont, 'Le renoncement dans les religions de l'Inde', *Homo Hierarchicus*, op. cit., Appendix B, p. 336.

grouping constituted primarily by renouncers', 'has the power to recruit irrespective of caste'[140] precisely because the person who has chosen the path of renunciation and is initiated into the sect becomes an individual removed from the everyday world and detached from his social status. M.S.A. Rao emphasises the egalitarian values of the sect, which are inherent in its individualistic dimension[141] even though the lack of concern for the principles underlying the caste system is far from complete.[142]

Since the explicit purpose of the RSS is to unite Hindus, above and beyond caste divisions, in a nationalist perspective, the RSS finds in the Hindu sect a sociological model for the nation. Indeed the sect offers the only system within Hindu society where an egalitarian form of individualism can be observed. What we have here is analogous to the system of values which allows for the emergence of the nation, an entity characterised in sociological terms by the allegiance which it receives from each of its constituent units. Marcel Mauss describes this phenomenon as a moral integration in which no other elements come between the nation and the individual.[143] The building of such a nation of Hindus was the main aim of Hedgewar. In his last speech, made in 1940, he described the RSS as 'the Hindu Rashtra in miniature'[144] precisely because he regarded it as a kind of egalitarian, alternative version of society, a great 'family' or fraternity.[145]

With the RSS, a further stage had been reached in the building of the Hindu nationalist movement, the medium again being the emulation of otherwise stigmatised foreign models. Savarkar had codified the ideology of 'Hindutva' after borrowing its ethnic nationalism from the West. Hedgewar undertook to implement it by providing Hindu nationalism with a social model of the Hindu nation and more immediately with a solid organisation. In this context he emulated Western individualistic values under the pretext of reinterpreting the other-worldly individualism inherent in the Hindu tradition of asceticism. Thus the religious and more

---

[140] Ibid., p. 238.

[141] M.S.A. Rao, 'Some subjective orientations in understanding Indian social reality' in R. Kumar (ed.), *Philosophical theory and social reality*, New Delhi: Allied Publishers, 1984, p. 165.

[142] In the 1960s, B.D. Tripathi found that 73.2% of the 500 *sadhus* he interviewed came from 'twice born' castes whereas 26.8% were Shudras (*Sadhus of India: The sociological view*, Bombay: Popular Prakashan, 1978, p. 84); 63.4% of them strongly supported the caste system (ibid., p. 169). The upper caste bias of Hindu sects is found, in a similar manner, within the RSS, as we shall show below.

[143] M. Mauss, 'La nation' in *Oeuvres*, Paris: Minuit, 1969, vol. 3, p. 588.

[144] Cited in B.V. Deshpande and S.R. Ramaswamy, *Dr Hedgewar, the epoch-maker*, op.cit., p. 188.

[145] J.A. Curran, Jr., *Militant Hinduism in Indian politics: A study of the RSS*, Institute of Pacific Relations, 1951, p. 11.

precisely sectarian appearance of the RSS can probably be explained by the fact that Hedgewar and Golwalkar found in the institutions associated with asceticism a means of developing the sociological structure of an egalitarian, united nation.

RSS Brahminism and its social contradictions

According to K.R. Malkani, at the first Officers' Training Camp, the practice of having meals in common, irrespective of caste, unnerved some Brahmins, who were uneasy about sitting together with low caste Hindus, but Hedgewar insisted that the practice be maintained. The same author further claims that in 1934, after visiting a camp at Wardha in Maharashtra, Gandhi was impressed by the fact that Untouchables were living with the high castes.[146] However, the egalitarian nature of the RSS was contradicted by other features of the movement, and for a long time it was associated with the high castes. The organisation had been founded and developed by Maharashtrian Brahmins – Hedgewar came from a Telugu Brahmin family long resident in Nagpur and Golwalkar was a Karhada Brahmin – and all the early *swayamsevaks* were Brahmins. In his diary, Moonje – himself a Deshastha Brahmin – referred to RSS members as 'Brahmin youths' or 'Brahmin lads'.[147]

While the RSS was conceived primarily as an egalitarian vanguard of the Hindu Rashtra, its leaders' view of the ideal society continued to be based on the *varna* system. In 1938 Golwalkar wrote: 'it is none of the so called drawbacks of the Hindu social order, which prevents us from regaining our ancient glory'.[148] The RSS appears here as an egalitarian, nationalist sect that enshrines what will become the crucible of the Hindu Rashtra *in the long term*, whereas its immediate task seems to be to recover a lost hierarchical social structure.[149]

The RSS attracted many Maharashtrian Brahmins because it embodied their particular culture, one characterised by a combination of Brahminical and martial values.[150] Historically these castes had fulfilled Kshatriya

---

[146] K.R. Malkani, *RSS story*, op.cit., p. 25.

[147] Cited in P. Bacchetta, 'Hindu nationalist women as ideologists: Rashtriya Swayamsevak Sangh, Rashtra Sevika Samiti, and their respective projects for a Hindu nation' in K. Jayawardena (ed.), *Women, gender and fundamentalism in South Asia*, New Delhi: Kali for Women, forthcoming.

[148] M.S. Golwalkar, *We, or our nationhood defined*, Nagpur: Bharat publications, 1939, p. 63.

[149] This point will be developed in chapter 3 when the RSS's attempts to change society via its affiliated unions and political parties will be analysed.

[150] The Brahmins of Maharashtra were thus familiar with the *akharas* (Interview with N. Deshmukh, and W. Andersen and S. Damle *The brotherhood in saffron*, op. cit., p. 35).

functions, in particular by serving in the armies of Shivaji. Ram Das, Shivaji's Brahmin counsellor, whom Hedgewar looked upon as his exemplar, was a good representative of this mixture of asceticism appropriate to his caste and martial valour. In reaction to Muslim expansion, he founded monasteries which included *akharas* dedicated to Hanuman.[151] Such values were the basis for the rejection of Gandhi's political style and programme in many Maharashtrian circles.

In the early 1920s, soon after Gandhi took over the Congress, *Mahratta* published editorials – some of them by the *Shankaracharya* of Karweer Pith – criticising the introduction of the principle of *ahimsa* (nonviolence) in the Congress programme.[152] Furthermore, Gandhi antagonised many of the Maharashtrian Brahmins who joined the RSS because his Hinduism, largely influenced by *bhakti*, excluded many Brahminical values. Finally, Gandhi was resented by high caste Hindus because he posed a real danger to their social position. His mobilisation of the lower strata of society 'threatened to alter the basic characteristic of Indian society by making its cultural periphery its centre'.[153] Here, according to Nandy, lay one of the main reasons why Nathuram Godse decided to kill Gandhi. This Chitpavan Brahmin felt all the more insecure because his socio-economic status was very precarious whereas Marathas and Gujarati Banyas were emerging as the new upwardly mobile groups of Maharashtra.

The first RSS leaders were themselves Brahmins belonging to the middle class or even lower middle class. Hedgewar's family maintained their traditional vocation – the teaching of the Vedas – until 1853, when the Nagpur state came under British rule. Then the disappearance of the Maharajah of Bhonsle's patronage forced them to become priests, a less prestigious occupation, and Hedgewar – who lost his parents when he was young – was brought up in poverty. Golwalkar's father was originally a clerk in the Post and Telegraph Department; subsequently he taught in government schools.[154] Umakant (alias Babasaheb) Apte, who became a *pracharak* in 1927, even before the word was used (he was called

---

[151] R.I. Cashman, *The myth of the Lokamanya*, Berkeley: University of California Press, 1975, p. 15.

[152] See, for example, the *Mahratta*, 29 Oct. 1922, p. 502. Twenty-three years later, Moonje wrote to Gandhi that he had no choice but to reject the latter's non-violence because the Hindu Mahasabha was for 'violence organised and disciplined on modern scientific lines' and opposed the *charkha* (spinning wheel) because 'it emasculates manliness' (Moonje papers, NMML (mss. section), letter of 10 Sept. 1945). As Nandy points out, Gandhi's 'femininity' was a major factor explaining the hostility of the Hindu nationalists (A. Nandy, *At the edge of psychology: essays in politics and culture*, Delhi: Oxford University Press, 1980, p. 78).

[153] Ibid., p. 76.

[154] W. Andersen, 'The Rashtriya Swayamsevak Sangh – I', op. cit., pp. 591 and 594.

parivrajak, 'wandering ascetic'), came from a modest Chitpavan family (his father was a schoolmaster of limited means). He embraced the same career but resigned soon after to become a typist in Nagpur.[155] When it established itself in the Hindi belt the RSS was again in a position to recruit cadres from high-caste young men from the middle classes. For example, Deendayal Upadhyaya, who joined the RSS in Kanpur in 1937, belonged to a Brahmin family which had often found employment in the lower grades of the staff of the railways (both his maternal grandfather and father were stationmasters).[156]

However, some of the first *swayamsevaks* came from élite families. Prabhakar Balwant Dani, who joined the RSS as early as 1925, shortly after its formation, and became one of its principal leaders, was the son of a rich landord from Umred in Nagpur district.[157] In the Hindi belt, too, the RSS attracted recruits from the upper middle class. Rajendra Singh, who was recruited to the RSS in Allahabad in 1942 and at the time of writing was *sarsanghchalak,* was the son of the Chief Engineer of the Public Works Department of the United Provinces.[158]

Although there is insufficient data available to carry out a statistical analysis of the social origins of the early RSS leaders, the cases we know of lead us to conclude that, with some exceptions, most of them came from middle-class Brahmin families.

The pervasiveness of the Brahminical ethic in the ideology and practices of the RSS was probably the main reason why it failed to attract support from the low castes. The Sanskritized Hindu culture which the RSS championed was that of the high tradition, and even its techniques bore the marks of Brahminical culture. Anxious to refashion the Hindu character to make it nationalist, Hedgewar believed that work to this end carried out in the *shakhas* should be inspired by the notion of the Hindu *samskars.* A senior *pracharak* explains that, for the RSS: 'Samskar means that you improve yourself under many respects. If by hearing something, by seeing good things or by doing good things, you progress, then these are *samskars.*'[159]

This loose definition – reiterated by many RSS activists for whom *samskars* never referred to the 'rites associated with the transitional phases of life', as suggested by Andersen and Damle[160] – is drawn from

[155] P.G. Sahasrabuddhe, *Karmayogi Babasaheb Apte,* op. cit., p. 20, and Dvitya Puchpa, *Sanghninva mein visayit,* Lucknow: Lokahit Prakashan, 1992, p. 13 (Hindi).

[156] D.B. Thengadi, *Pandit Deendayal Upadhyaya – Ideology and perception,* Part I: *An inquest,* New Delhi: Suruchi Prakashan, 1988, p. 7.

[157] C.P. Bhishikar, *Shri Bhaiyaji Dani,* op. cit., p. 6.

[158] Madan Lal Khurana, who worked under him in Allahabad, emphasises that Rajendra Singh came from a 'very big family, very educated' (interview with M.L. Khurana, 8 Dec. 1990, New Delhi).

[159] Interview with G. Prabhakar, 7 Oct. 1991, Delhi.

ne of the meanings of *samskar*. In this context the term designates all the good influences which can be exerted in the formation of character, especially on children.[161] At the elementary level, to recommend a healthy lifestyle and good habits, for example, was a way of bestowing the benefits of *samskar*. Such discipline was of course observed particularly among Brahmins, whose status in itself implied respect for these values. By using these techniques, Hedgewar ran the risk of attracting to the *shakhas* mainly members of high castes who hoped to enhance their status by strengthening their *samskars*.

Research in Madhya Pradesh revealed that this danger became a reality since a very large number of high-caste members cited the role of *samskars* as their main motive for joining the RSS. At Shivpuri, a district town 120 km. south of Gwalior, a Banya (a member of a merchant caste), the – son of a *zamindar* (landholder), said that he had entered the RSS because his *samskars* had disintegrated, in particular because he had begun to smoke and drink. The *baudhik pramukh* (chief ideologue) of the *shakha* at Shivpuri described the *samskars* of the RSS just as one would normally define those of Hindu society:

The *samskars* of the RSS consist, for example, in rendering proper respect to older people and making one's home a palace where all can meet. And we try progressively to give children this outlook because in the RSS family there is no bad language, no quarrels. One learns to be polite and to address one's elders with respect. Before starting work or eating one says a prayer.

He added that the *swayamsevak* in his *shakha* were from high castes and the best families.[162] This social composition was logical in so far as the level of discipline implied by these *samskars* is familiar to such people and is an ethical model for their milieu. Here, the RSS shares features with the boy-scout movement; it is seen to impart good manners and to fortify the physique of youths from the upper stratum of society, whose occupa-

---

[160] W. Andersen and S. Damle, *The brotherhood in saffron*, op. cit., p. 83.

[161] L. Kapani, *La notion de samskara*, vol. 1, Paris: de Boccard, 1992, p. 43. In his afterword to U.R. Ananta Murthy's book, A.K. Ramanujan emphasises the polysemy of the word *samskar* which, in the context of the book, designates funeral rites but also a transformation of the individual and especially a typically refined Brahminical upbringing (*Samskar – A rite for a dead man*, Oxford University Press, 1992 (1976), pp. 139-47). Kim Marriot convincingly suggested that 'sanskritisation' should be replaced by 'samskarization' in the sociology of India since, in this process, 'from the point of view of participants, the high-status and ritually pure forms of behavior adopted are truly "samskars" ("impressions" or "alterations of substance"), which change them in fundamental ways' (personal communication to P. Lutgendorf, *The life of a text–Performing the Ramcharitmanas of Tulsidas*, Berkeley: University of California Press, 1991, p. 434).

[162] Interviews conducted on 28 Oct. 1991 at Shivpuri.

tions do not usually require physical strength.[163] Indeed, upper-caste youths may value membership of a *shakha* simply because of the opportunity which it provides for exercise; this is particularly the case with young Banyas, who may be expected to spend working days sitting in the family store. Even though their number has been increasing since the inception of the RSS, there are still very few low caste people in the organisation and their numbers appear to diminish as they rise in the hierarchy.[164] Only a very small proportion have ever become *pracharaks*, a category in which Brahmins – especially those from Maharashtra – have always been over-represented. Andersen and Damle convincingly attribute the appeal of the RSS to the low castes of North India in part to the process of Sanskritisation.[165] One of the few *swayamsevaks* from the Scheduled Castes who was interviewed for the purposes of this study, Satyanarayan Jatiya, illustrates this phenomenon. On the one hand, he emphasised the similarity between the projects of the RSS and those undertaken by Ambedkar, the Untouchable leader who campaigned for the abolition of caste;[166] on the other hand, he stressed that he had been determined to learn Sanskrit and that he belonged to associations of Sanskritists.[167]

---

[163] In Madhya Pradesh, after the ban of the RSS in 1948-9 and the related wave of arrests, despairing fathers – with Brahmin and Banya names – wrote to the Congress leaders to explain that their sons – often in their early twenties and working as teachers or traders–had joined the RSS only to compensate for their physical weakness (Madhya Pradesh Congress Committee papers, F. 82 NMML – section of mss.). The over-representation of Banyas in the RSS also seems due to the fact that, according to D.R. Goyal, who was a full-time RSS worker in Punjab before taking part in the Sampradayikta Virodhi Committee (see below) – 'in a village, the RSS man who wants to set up a *shakha* will first contact the shopkeeper' (interview in *Communalism Combat*, Oct. 1994, p.7).

[164] Among the ten *swayamsevaks* from the *shakhas* of Vikram Mandal in Delhi who had attended an Instructors' Training Camp (ITC), only one was a member of the Scheduled Castes while the majority were Banyas (personal interviews, 11 Oct. 1991).

[165] W. Andersen and S. Damle, *The brotherhood in saffron*, op. cit., pp. 45 and 102. See also W. Andersen and M.K. Saini, 'The Basti Julahan by-election', *Indian Journal of Political Science*, 30 (July-Sept. 1969, pp. 260-76).

[166] 'I praise Ambedkar's work. Equality amongst all, Fraternity, Justice. Such were the goals of Dr Ambedkar [...] He had the ideas but we are putting them into practice in the RSS, because there is no caste and no religion there. The only religion is Bharat Mata and we want to serve the nation.' (Interview with S. Jatiya, 3 Dec. 1990, Ujjain). Another Scheduled Caste *swayamsevak*, Kalka Dass, whose father allegedly had been close to Ambedkar, expressed similar views (interview, 23 Nov. 1990, New Delhi).

[167] Jatiya is secretary of the Sansadiya Sanskrit Parishad, based in Delhi. In 1977 he took the oath in the Vidhan Sabha in Sanskrit and in 1991 he made a speech against the budget in the Lok Sabha in versified Hindi (*Speeches on Budget 1991-92*, New Delhi: BJP (n.d.) pp. 60-9).

Although the predominantly Brahminical culture of the RSS certainly attracted low caste Hindus, the organisation could not rely on this appeal alone in its efforts to expand rapidly within this subaltern stratum of Hindu society. Important aspects of the RSS's ideology seemed therefore to contradict its ambition of building an encompassing Hindu Rashtra. We shall see below that the RSS resorted to instrumentalist techniques of ethno-religious mobilisation – in which its Brahminism was diluted – to overcome this handicap.

From its inception the RSS acted within the logic of a strategy of stigmatisation and emulation in the manner of the Arya Samaj and the Hindu Mahasabha. Founded, like these predecessors, to defend Hindus against 'threatening others', the RSS immediately set itself the task, as did the earlier organisations, of inscribing in Hindu society the values identified as the basis of the strength of the British and the Muslims. This mimetic movement was concerned above all with the principle of national solidarity seen as characteristic of the British and contrasting strongly with the social fragmentation of Hinduism. From the Hindu nationalist point of view Muslims fulfilled the role of 'threatening Others' while the British colonialists represented the Other to be emulated. In fact, the RSS followed Savarkar in importing from the West the notion of ethnic nationalism, but in contrast with Savarkar, who accepted a different political agenda when he joined the Hindu Mahasabha, Hedgewar took on the task of giving a social content to the Hindu Rashtra he wished to create. Emulation of a foreign model of nationhood proceeded under the guise of a reinterpretation of a quintessentially Hindu institution, the sect, which offered a familiar framework into which to introduce nationalistic values. This was possible because the Hindu sect defined itself not only by its exclusive doctrine, but also by a form of individualism inherent in the idea of nation; and because India possessed a tradition of martial arts – epitomised by the *akharas* – which had already been reinterpreted, since the end of the nineteenth century, as a role model for the defence of Hinduism. Our analysis has concentrated up till now on the indigenous dimension of the RSS. It is now necessary to analyse its ideology in a broader perspective.

An ideology of the ethnic nation rather than of the race or the state

The fascistic dimension of the RSS is suggested by its paramilitary style. In 1926 Hedgewar introduced a uniform – consisting of khaki shorts, khaki (later white) shirts and black forage caps – which had already been partly adopted by the corps of volunteers which he set up at the 1920 session of Congress at Nagpur. The *shakhas* also observed strict discipline symbolised by the detailed code of regulations for the daily assembly and dismissal of the company of *swayamsevaks* and by their behaviour when saluting the flag: the 'volunteers' stood to attention, with the right hand held at chest level, palm downwards, head bowed; they were arrayed in ranks in order of age. On some occasions, such as the festival of Dasahara, they marched in step through the streets holding their *lathis* to demonstrate the strength of the movement. These elements suggest that the RSS should be regarded as 'an Indian version of fascism'.[168] As far as the formative years of the RSS are concerned,[169] this expression is especially relevant if it implies that while the RSS belongs, with European fascism, to a general category of anti-liberal movements, it also represents a specifically Indian phenomenon which is not simply a reproduction of European fascism.[170] The RSS had already assumed its final form by the time of the first contacts between the Hindu nationalists and the European fascists, and neither Hedgewar nor Golwalkar developed a theory of the state and the race, a crucial element in fascism and Nazism.

The first contacts between the Hindu nationalists and the European fascists took place in the 1930s. During his stay in Europe for the Round Table Conference of 1930, Moonje was able to visit Italy to 'see the work of the Ballila movement' and where he also met Mussolini.[171] In 1934 a 'close relationship' was established between the Italian Institute for the Middle and Far East (a state-sponsored institution) and the Vice-Chancellor of the University of Calcutta, S.P. Mookerjee, who was to join the Hindu Mahasabha in 1938.[172] In October 1938, shortly after the Munich agreement, Savarkar wrote approvingly of the occupation of the Sudetenland by Germany on the grounds that its inhabitants shared 'common blood and common language with the Germans'.[173] In the late 1930s, both *Hindu Outlook* and *Mahratta* praised Franco, Mussolini and Hitler.[174]

---

[168] Nehru quoted in *Link*, 24 May 1970, p. 15.

[169] Even though this chapter incorporates quotes from recent interviews, it deals with the pre-independence RSS. These citations aim at documenting long-term trends but, of course, the organisation has changed over time. In the late 1980s and early 1990s, it developed a strategy of aggressive street mobilisation which recalled the European fascisms (see S. Sarkar, 'The fascism of the Sangh Parivar', op. cit., p. 163.)

[170] This hypothesis has been explored by Achin Vanaik in a more theoretical and comparative perspective ('Situating threat of Hindu nationalism', *EPW*, 9 July 1994, pp. 1729-48).

[171] *Dharmaveer Dr B.S. Moonje Commemoration Volume*, Nagpur: Birth Centenary Celebration Committee, 1972, pp. 25 and 68-9.

[172] M. Prayer, 'Italian fascist régime and nationalist India, 1921-1945', *International Studies*, 28(3), 1991, p. 262. In the very same year, S.C. Bose established a more far-reaching relationship with Mussolini.

[173] *Hindu Outlook*, 12 Oct. 1938, p. 13.

[174] Ibid., 2 Nov. 1938, 'A great dictator – Signor Mussolini at work' (in ibid., 30 Nov. 1938.

Moreover, in late 1938, the *Völkischer Beobachter*, the mouthpiece of the German National Socialist Party, took an interest in Savarkar's activities.[175] The views expressed by RSS leaders about European fascist movements during this period resemble those of the Hindu Sabhaites in some respects but with the crucial difference that whereas the Hindu Mahasabha, as a political party, was interested in the role of the state the RSS was more concerned about the socio-political aspects of building the Hindu Rashtra.

In 1939, Golwalkar's book *We, or our nationhood defined* gave the RSS the charter it had previously lacked. Even more obviously than Savarkar's *Hindutva*, it reveals the strategy of stigmatisation and emulation of 'threatening Others' at work. On the one hand Golwalkar stigmatises the 'semi-barbaric life' of 'the chief nations of the world', which contrasts with the situation in India ('It seems as if we never were uncivilised', he writes[176]) and on the other he expresses an inferiority complex *vis-à-vis* western countries:

The European society, we maintain, is exceptionally defective and consequently in a constant state of unrest. And yet, Europeans, as nations, are free and strong and progressive. Inspite of their ugly social order, they are so, for the simple reason that they have cherished and do still foster correct national consciousness, while we in Hindusthan ignore this causa causans of our troubles and grope about in the dark..[177]

Golwalkar draws from this comparison the necessity of emulating the 'true' western conception of nationalism:

We believe that our notions today about the Nation concept are erroneous. They are not in conformity with those of the Western Political Scientists, we think we are imitating. It is but proper, therefore, at this stage, to understand what the Western Scholars state as the Universal Nation idea and correct ourselves.[178]

In other words, India's mainstream political culture, typified by Congress, wrongly interpreted the concept of nation in the framework of territorial nationalism. Golwalkar repeatedly indicts Congress for 'the amazing theory [...] that the nation is composed of all those who, for one reason or the other happen to live at the time in the country'.[179] He uses the so-called failure of Czechoslovakia as a multi-national state – after the annexation of the Sudetenland by Germany[180] – as an argument justifying

p. 7) and *Mahratta* (6 Nov. 1939, p. 10).

[175] *Völkischer Beobachter,* 30 Nov. 1938, in Savarkar papers, Reel no. 1, File no. 2.

[176] M.S. Golwalkar, *We, or our nationhood defined,* op. cit., p. 4.

[177] Ibid., p. 62.

[178] Ibid., p. 21.

[179] Ibid., p. 59.

[180] Golwalkar regarded the *Anschluss* and the annexation of the Sudetenland as 'logical', in

'the fears of many political scholars, regarding the wisdom of heaping together in one state, elements conflicting with the national life'.[181] Who are these political scientists to whom Golwalkar refers repeatedly? In fact Golwalkar draws most of his inspiration from German writers.

German sources of Golwalkar's ideology

Golwalkar quotes at length the definition of the nation proposed by 'Blunstley, the famous German writer', whose name, correctly spelt, is Johann.Kaspar Bluntschli:

It is a union of masses of men of different occupations and social states, in a hereditary society of common spirit, feeling and race bound together especially by a language and customs in a common civilization which gives them a sense of unity and distinction from all foreigners, quite apart from the bond of the state.[182]

Bluntschli – who is also referred to by Savarkar and M.S. Aney, another Hindu Sabhaite leader, the author of the preface to *We, or our nationhood defined* – was born in Zürich but studied in Germany where he spent most of his career as a professor of law.[183] In the book cited by Golwalkar, Bluntschli differentiates the German view of the nation from that of the English and the French in the following terms:

In English the word 'people', like the French 'peuple' implies the notion of a civilisation, which the Germans (like the old Romans in the word 'natio') express in Nation [...] Etymology is in favour of German usage, for the word natio (from nasci) points to birth and race.[184]

Since he opts for the German definition of the nation, Bluntschli openly criticises the notion of social contract because 'A mere arbitrary combination of men has never given rise to a People. Even the voluntary agreement and social contract of a number of persons cannot create one'.[185] In contrast he emphasises that 'The essence of a People lies in its civilisation [*Kultur*][...] It may be called an organism in so far as its character has received a visible expression in the physique of the race and in language and manners.'[186] Defining nations as 'organic beings' he concludes:

---

conformity with 'the true Nation concept' (ibid., p. 35).

[181] Ibid., p. 38.

[182] Cited in ibid., p. 19.

[183] Behaim-Bürkel, *Neue Deutsche biographie*, Berlin: Duncker and Humblot, 1955, pp. 337-8.

[184] J.K. Bluntschli, *The theory of the state*, Oxford: Clarendon Press, 1885, p. 82 (translation of *Lehre vom modernen Staat*, Stuttgart: I.G. Cotta, 1875-6).

[185] Ibid., p. 83.

[186] Ibid., p. 85.

We are justified, then, in speaking of a national spirit [*Volksgeist*] and a national will [*Volkswille*], which is something more than the mere sum of the spirit and will of the individuals composing the Nation.[187]

The other Western political scientists referred to by Golwalkar adopt a similar view of the nation. Burgess, who draws much of his inspiration from Bluntschli, considers, in the chapter quoted by Golwalkar, that 'A population of an ethnic unity, inhabiting a territory of a geographic unity is a nation'.[188] Referring once more to Bluntschli's *Lehre vom modernen Staat*, Burgess also emphasises that in a country composed of several nationalities 'The reigning nationality is in perfect right and pursues, from a scientific point of view, an unassailable policy when it insists, with unflinching determination, upon ethnical homogeneity here',[189] which means, among other things, the imposition of a common language. From R.G. Gettell, who often refers to Bluntschli and Burgess, Golwalkar borrows a similar definition[190] and even A.N. Holcombe, who criticises the element of racism in Burgess's definition on behalf of a more liberal view of nationalism, considers that the 'most fundamental characteristic [of the nation] is cultural unity'.[191]

Most of the books mentioned by Golwalkar are illustrative of the German ethnic definition of nationalism. He paid little attention to the English authors from whom the Congress leaders drew their idea of the nation in universalistic terms, such as the role of individual will and the social contract. Bluntschli and the other political scientists mentioned above led Golwalkar to look at the case of India in the light of five criteria for the concept of the nation, namely: geographical unity, race, religion, culture and language.

In spite of his original interest in the renunciation of the world, Golwalkar did not make religion a priority; he regarded it merely as a cultural manifestation which could be used to 'cement' national unity. (In this context the national religion of Russia was socialism, with Karl Marx

[187] Ibid., p. 87.

[188] John W. Burgess, *Political Science and Comparative Constitutional Law*, vol. 1, Boston: Ginn, 1890, p. 1.

[189] Ibid., vol. 2, p. 42.

[190] See Raymond Garfield Gettell, *Introduction to Political Science*, Boston: Ginn, 1922 (1st edn 1910), p. 9.

[191] Arthur N. Holocombe, *The foundation of the modern commonwealth*, New York: Harper, 1923, p. 134. For the passage quoted by Golwalkar, see ibid., p. 133. I have not been able to identify the book by Gumplowicz from which Golwalkar borrowed only a two-word long definition of the nation, 'a community of civilization'. Even though he was born in Poland, Gumplowicz spent his formative years in Austria and Germany (see the 'Introduction' by I.L. Horowitz to his *Outlines of Sociology*, New York: Paine-Whitman, 1963).

as its 'prophet'; it was irrelevant that this was 'a religion which does not believe in God'.[192]) He probably devalued the religious content of Hindu identity because the heterogeneity of Hinduism militated against the project for national unity. But the latter could be promoted by emphasising race. Thus the essential criterion remained race,[193] to which Savarkar had already given pride of place.[194]

A special kind of racism

In contrast with Savarkar, Golwalkar claims that 'Hindus came into this land from nowhere, but are indigenous children of the soil always, from times immemorial.'[195] This racial factor, in his eyes, 'is by far the important ingredient of a nation'.[196] Here Golwalkar claims inspiration from Hitler's ideology:

To keep up the purity of the Race and its culture, Germany shocked the world by her purging the country of the semitic Races – the Jews. Race pride at its highest has been manifested here. Germany has also shown how well nigh impossible it is for Races and cultures, having differences going to the root, to be assimilated into one united whole, a good lesson for us in Hindusthan to learn and profit by.[197]

Golwalkar applied this nationalist ethnic reasoning to the Muslim minority, which posed a threat not only because it enjoyed the backing of a whole series of Islamic states but also because it was a 'foreign body' lodged into Hindu society, which it thus undermined. He criticises the decision of a Muslim leader, Maulana Mohammad Ali, who had died abroad, to direct 'his remains to be taken not to the land which had fostered him and his forefathers before him, but to the foreign land of Mecca'.[198] He argues that Muslims 'take themselves to be the conquering invaders and grasp for power' and therefore Hindus are 'at war at once with the Moslems on the one hand and the British on the other'.[199] As Pandey has

---

[192] M.S. Golwalkar, *We, or our nationhood defined*, op.cit., p. 37.

[193] Golwalkar does not pay as much attention to territory as Savarkar, even though he points out Hindustan's 'definite geographical unity, deliminated naturally by the sublime Himalayas on the North and the limitless ocean on the other three sides' (ibid., p. 40).

[194] Moreover, Golwalkar mentions the book by V.D. Savarkar's brother, G.D. Savarkar, *Rashtra Mimamsa*, as one of his 'chief sources of inspiration and help' (ibid., p. 4).

[195] Ibid., p. 8.

[196] Ibid., p. 23.

[197] Ibid., p. 35.

[198] Ibid., p. 53.

[199] Ibid., p. 16. Golwalkar was later to describe Muslims, Christians and Communists as 'internal threats' (see the titles of three chapters of *Bunch of thoughts*, op. cit., pp. 233, 248 and 257).

noted, Golwalkar's definition of the nation was more restrictive than Savarkar's. Hindus appear in his writings 'as *the* nation in India'.[200]

However, the references to race are very vague and contradictory, as evident from the fact that Golwalkar applies this notion to Indian Muslims, who, in most cases, are only converts of the same blood. Race is often defined as an amalgam of predispositions which seem to lie not so much in the genes but are instead passed down by cultural tradition, so that its influence takes effect at the earliest age and hence makes a free choice in the matter of national identity impossible:

The aspiration of the individual, as also of the Race are conditioned by its mental frame. As is the mould into which the Racial mind is thrown – of course by its agelong traditions – so are its desires, its aspirations.[201]

More importantly, Golwalkar mentions only once 'the purity of the Race' in reference to Germany, and dealing with race in general terms he writes:

Even if there be people of a foreign origin, they must have been assimilated into the body of the mother race and inextricably fused into it.[202]

However, if this integration does not materialise, Golwalkar radically rejects the idea of a multi-ethnic nation, as suggested in the following paragraph:

The foreign races in Hindusthan must either adopt the Hindu culture and language, must learn to respect and hold in reverence Hindu religion, must entertain no ideas but those of glorification of the Hindu race and culture [...] or may stay in the country, wholly subordinated to the Hindu nation, claiming nothing, deserving no privileges, far less any preferential treatment – not even citizen's rights.[203]

These citations suggest that Golwalkar combined two sorts of references. On the one hand his concern with the integration of all the Indian communities into a common race does not echo the Nazis' obsession with the purity of the race but rather reflects the influence of the hierarchical principles of 'Indian traditional xenology'. Moreover, Golwalkar considered as *mlecchas* 'those who do not subscribe to the social laws dictated by the Hindu Religion and Culture'.[204] On the other hand, Golwalkar's concern with the promotion of a homogenous nation whose culture would be dominated by the Hindu Great Tradition harks back to his reading of Bluntschli and similar authors and to his admiration for their ethnic

[200] G. Pandey, 'Which of us are Hindus?', op. cit., p. 251.

[201] M.S. Golwalkar, *We, or our nationhood defined*, op. cit., p. 32.

[202] Ibid., p. 23.

[203] Ibid., p. 62.

[204] Cited in G. Pandey, 'Which of us are Hindus', op. cit., p. 258.

nationalism which, in Germany, prepared the ground for Nazism. Golwalkar considers cultural elements as inherent to the group, collectively
inherited from its forefathers. For instance he regards a national language –
such as Sanskrit, the 'mother language' of India – as 'an expression of the
Race spirit',[205] obviously an equivalent of the German *Völksgeist.*

One expression used by Pandey when dealing with Golwalkar's discourse – 'an upper-caste racism' –[206] identifies with precision the
specificity of this racism, which takes the form of socio-cultural domination rather than being based on biological claims and an obsession with
racial purity. Moreover, Golwalkar translated 'race' by '*jati* ', as Savarkar
did in *Hindutva.*[207] Like Savarkar, Golwalkar was in fact more interested
in cultural unity than racial homogeneity.

Religious minorities were required by Golwalkar to owe allegiance to
Hindu symbols of identity because these were the embodiment of the
Indian nation. RSS leaders used the word 'Hindu' less often than *rashtriya*
('national') or Bharatiya – this was the adjectival form of Bharat, the
name of the legendary first Aryan who unified the subcontinent and, by
extension, the term used to designate India in Sanskrit and Hindi texts.
These usages hark back to the conviction that Hindu culture contains
within it the essence of Indian identity. The concept implies assimilation
of religious minorities in a Bharatiya nation through removal of the
external signs by which their adherence to a particular community is
designated. Religious practice thus has to withdraw into the private
domain and the minorities have to pledge allegiance to Hindu religious
symbols, presented as national symbols. An example of this tenet of RSS
ideology is provided by the words of its joint General Secretary, K.S.
Sudarshan, speaking about the Muslims:

Islam has a strong imprint of Arabic culture as it was born there. But it did assume
different shades as it came in contact with European culture in Turkey,
Zoroastrians in Iran and Hindu culture in Indonesia. Islam did not prevent
Indonesian Muslims to proclaim Mahabharat and Ramayan as their cultural epics
and Ram and Krishna as their forefathers. What harm will come to the Muslim
way if they were to accept Ram and Krishna as their ancestors and Ghazni, Gauri
and Babar as foreign invaders?[208]

In *We, or our nationhood defined*, Golwalkar pays little attention to
the means of integrating the minorities because:

These questions arise in discussions about the 'state' with which we are not directly

---

[205] M.S. Golwalkar, *We, or our nationhood defined*, op. cit., p. 26.

[206] G. Pandey, 'Which of us are Hindus', op. cit., p. 26.

[207] M.S. Golwalkar, *We, or our nationhood defined*, op. cit., p. 52.

[208] Interview in *Indian Express*, 12 Feb. 1993.

concerned within the scope of the present work. We are out to understand the Nationhood of Hindusthan which done, all questions regarding the form of 'state' shall be worth entrusting to the 'Nation' as we find it to exist.[209]

This clarification suggests that Golwalkar's ideas regarding the state differed from fascist ideologies and even from German Nazism.

The primacy of social organism

Fascism, in the 1920s-1940s, implied a political voluntarism in which the state was both an object of conquest and a means to an end. Indeed a major characteristic of fascism lies in its aspiration to capture the state and transform it into a totalitarian apparatus. The word 'totalitarian' was first used regularly by Mussolini from 1925 onwards to describe his system, the 'totalitarian state'.[210] This was manifest even in Romania where, more evidently than in other fascist countries, the accent seemed to be on a social organicism in the 1920s-1940s.[211]

However, the situation was very different as far as the Nazis were concerned. While the Italian fascists did not see their movement as being above the state or even the nation and considered that 'their movement had come to an end with the seizure of power', the Nazis, as Hannah Arendt emphasises, 'kept aloof from this fascist form of dictatorship, in which the 'movement' merely serves to bring the party to power'.[212] Nazism, just like any other form of totalitarianism in Arendt's terminology, was 'above the state' for the sake of a direct identification with the people.'[213] The notion of '*totale Staat*' borrowed from the Italian experiment by Carl Schmitt did not survive – except under the garb of the '*volkische totale Staat*'[214] – largely because Hitler displayed a constant hostility to the state. According to Hitler this agency was artificial in comparison to the *Volk* and had to be subordinated to it. In *Mein Kampf* he argues repeatedly that the state is not an end in itself but that its only aim is the preservation of the race:

...the State represents not an end but a means. It is indeed the presumption for the formation of a higher human culture, but not its cause. On the contrary, the latter lies exclusively in the existence of a race capable of culture.[215]

209   M.S. Golwalkar, *We, or our nationhood defined*, op. cit., p. 50.
210   L. Schapiro, *Totalitarianism*, New York: Praeger, 1972, p. 13.
211   E. Weber, *Varieties of fascism*, New York: Van Nostrand, 1964, pp. 74-6.
212   H. Ardent, *The origins of totalitarianism*, New York: Harcourt, Brace and Co., 1958, p. 259.
213   Ibid., p. 265.
214   J.P. Faye, *Langages totalitaires*, Paris: Hermann, 1972, pp. 377-85.

In this context, *Rasse* and *Völk* are interchangeable words which occasionally refer to another concept, *Organismus*.[216] In fact, some Nazi ideologues wanted to re-establish the organic unity of the groups forming the *Völk* through a state based on the old corporations.[217] In organisational terms, the hostility of the Nazis towards the state found its expression in the clear separation of the NSDAP from the state apparatus.[218]

Golwalkar's ideology shares with Nazism a relative depreciation of state power but it proceeds essentially by taking society rather than race as the matrix of the Hindu nation. As is evident from the compilation of his undated writings and speeches published in 1966, he rejects the theory of a social contract which underpinned Western states because it implies an adherence on the individual's part to the body politic (and to society) and consequently the possibility of this adherence being withdrawn.[219] On the contrary, Hindu tradition, as Golwalkar interprets it, is characterised by an organicist 'harmony'.[220]

His analysis stems partly from his admiration for the system of *varnas*[221] although this reference occurs only fleetingly. The main theme in his work is that society must become an organic whole of a special kind: ultimately, this process will not require the existence of intermediate structures such as the *varnas*; individuals will find fulfilment by merging into a homogenous nation in which social differences will lose their meaning. From such reasoning the RSS derives its sense of vocation:

The ultimate vision of our work [...] is a perfectly organised state of society wherein each individual has been moulded into a model of ideal Hindu manhood and made into a living limb of the corporate personality of society.

Obviously, this is not a vision which can be realised within a few days or even a few years. It requires the untiring, silent endeavour of hundreds and thousands of dedicated missionaries.[222]

---

[215] Adolf Hitler, *Mein Kampf*, New York: Reynal & Hitchock, 1941, p. 592. Hitler also writes: 'The State in itself is for us only a form, while what is essential is its content, the nation, the people, it is clear that everything else must subordinate itself to its sovereign interests.' (ibid., p. 842).

[216] 'We as Aryans, are therefore able to imagine a State only to be the living organism of a nationality which not only safeguards the preservation of that nationality, but which, by a further training of its spiritual and ideal abilities, leads it to the highest freedom' (ibid., p. 595).

[217] G. Mosse, *The crisis of German ideology*, New York: Universal Library, 1964, p. 285.

[218] The Organisation Handbook of the NSDAP warned that 'The party must [...] take care that it does not become too much interwoven with the State administrative machinery. Otherwise it runs the risk of being devoured by the bureaucracy of the State...' (Cited in L. Schapiro, *Totalitarianism*, op. cit., p. 67).

[219] M.S. Golwalkar, *Bunch of thoughts*, op. cit., pp. 13 and 29.

[220] Ibid., p. 33.

[221] Ibid., p. 49.

The objective of the RSS is clearly the advent of a 'new man' and state power is of no help in this enterprise because it cannot 'mould the "inner man" after an ideal'.[223] Priority must therefore be given to work in society aimed at persuading its members to become aware that society constitutes a potential nation. The ideal social state is one where each 'individual has realised his oneness with others in society and is imbued with a spirit of sacrifice. [...] We, the individuals, appear on the surface like bubbles or drops for a moment then disappear. The "permanent", therefore, is the national life.'[224] The mission of the RSS was to fashion society, to 'sustain' it, 'improve' it, and finally merge[225] with it when the point had been reached where society and the organisation had become co-extensive. It was in this sense that *swayamsevaks* and hence *pracharaks* were presented as true 'missionaries'.[226] The millenarian plan sought to extend to the whole of society the Hindu nationalist concept of a man who denies his individual personality. Thus the RSS was totalitarian, first because it aspired to fill the whole space occupied by society, and second because it sought to endow individuals with the selflessness of the ideal *pracharak*. They could then become the units of an organic community by means of an indoctrination of which the discipline of the *shakhas* was the prototype:

[In a human body] Each cell feels its identity with the entire body and is ever ready to sacrifice itself for the sake of the health and growth of the body. In fact, it is the self-immolation of millions of such cells that releases the energy for every bodily activity.

The training that is imparted every day in the *shakha* in a strictly regulated fashion imparts that spirit of identification and well-concerted action. It gives the individual the necessary incentive to rub away his angularities, to behave in a spirit of oneness with the rest of his brethren in society and fall in line with the organised and disciplined way of life by adjusting himself to the varied outlooks of other minds. The persons assembling there learn to obey a single command. Discipline enters their blood.[227]

This must be the clearest formulation of the organicist concept of the RSS:[228] the basic social unit is not the *varna* but the individual, considered as a cell of the social body, which represses all free will according to the teachings of the *shakhas*. We might label this an organicism based on the

[222] Ibid., p. 88.
[223] Ibid., p. 98.
[224] Ibid., p. 60.
[225] Ibid., pp. 102, 520 and 545.
[226] Ibid., p. 539.
[227] M. S. Golwalkar, *Bunch of thoughts*, op. cit., p. 534.
[228] This formulation was still present in the ideology of the RSS leaders in the 1980s (H.V. Seshadri, 'RSS as life-force of society', *Organiser*, 16 Nov. 1980, p. 6).

sacrifice of the individual. These ideas bear comparison with those which were put forward by such nineteenth-century German nationalists as Fichte, who, as Thomas Hansen pointed out, considered that 'the will to loyalty and sacrifice of the individual ultimately determines the will to cohesion and organisation of the nationality.'[229] As in RSS writings, this line of reasoning leads to an emphasis upon the importance of education and character-building as the means of producing the new man, the man who readily accepts membership of the nation.

Golwalkar's ideology can be regarded as virtually totalitarian precisely because he concentrates so much on the relationship between the individual and the nation, a relationship in which a uniform system of socialisation prepares men and women to participate only in the one collective entity, the national community, without the aid of intermediate structures.[230] Golwalkar did not aspire to re-establish the ancient order of the *varnas* through the RSS, but to abolish caste so as to build a nation defined as 'an aggregate of individuals',[231] these individuals being of a special kind, since the RSS's mission was 'to build up in every walk of life men of pure and upright character, personal and national. In this sense the Sangh seeks to invade and "dominate" every sphere of national life.'[232] An important difference between this totalitarianism and fascism in its various forms or Nazism is that the Indian version chose to work patiently on society over a long period rather than seizing power and constraining society 'from above'.

The kind of metaphor used by Golwalkar in the above citations echoes his scientific education. Students of natural science were always strongly represented in the RSS, possibly because of the importance of organicism in its ideology. Hedgewar was a doctor, Golwalkar studied and taught zoology, Rajendra Singh, who became *sarsanghchalak* in 1994, graduated in physics; H.V. Seshadri, who was to become General Secretary of the organisation, in chemistry; and K.S. Sudarshan in engineering.

The organicist character of Golwalkar's ideology is reminiscent of certain aspects of Nazism. There are more obvious affinities between the two than between Hindu nationalism and Italian fascism since both share a strong emphasis on ethnic homogeneity. However, three differences remain. First, as emphasised in the previous section, the supreme concept in the RSS's doctrine is not race but society. In Golwalkar's works the promotion of an organic society is more important than the purity of the

---

[229] T.B. Hansen, 'Religion and ideology in the Hindu nationalist discourse', working paper, International Development Studies, Roskilde University (Denmark), 1992, p. 12.

[230] After independence, Golwalkar paid much more attention to intermediate structures when developing the affiliates of the RSS (see chap. 3).

[231] M.S. Golwalkar, *Bunch of thoughts*, op. cit., p. 7.

[232] Golwalkar, cited in *Organiser*, 30 Oct. 1964, p. 45.

race. Second, even though Nazism attributed more importance than did Italian fascism to the organic nation in comparison to the state, Hitler was nostalgic for the 'old Reich'[233] and valued the state as a means to promote the interests of the race. According to Hitler the 'mission' of the Nazi movement was 'the creation of a Germanic State'.[234] This explains his preoccupation with the need to capture power as a matter of urgency, as attested by the aborted coup of 1923. The RSS, by contrast, is not a putschist organisation and Golwalkar considered that Hitler's capture of the state was a mistake:

> Hitler's movement centred round politics. We try to build life without being wedded to politics. It is many times found that many are gathered for political purpose. But when that purpose fails, unity is lost. We do not want any temporary achievement but an abiding oneness. And so we have kept ourselves aloof from politics.[235]

Although such a claim of apolitism forms part of RSS propaganda, the movement is in fact eminently political. However it is true that it concentrates on long-term programmes rather than on the immediate capture of the state. In a way, this strategy made the RSS more dangerous and more difficult to eradicate through repression. Third, the movement lacked the obsession with the supreme leader which was characteristic of the European fascisms.

The organisation above men

RSS volunteers have been dedicated more to an organisation than to one man. In November 1929 the RSS adopted the principle of *ekchalak anuvartita* (following one leader) and Hedgewar was then appointed *sarsanghchalak* for life; even so, the organisation remained supreme and, interestingly, his death in 1940 did not affect it.

The routine activities of the RSS are specified and governed by a comprehensive framework of rules, whose strict application ensures that its intermediate and local units can function without day-to-day guidance from its central authorities. At each level of the organisation the supervision of the prescribed procedures is the responsibility of particular officers, such as the *mukhya shikshaks* and, most importantly, the *pracharaks*. The coping stone of this hierarchy is the *sarsanghchalak*. Charisma is not the basis of his authority. The incumbents of this office

---

[233] 'On the State form, the army and the body of officials rested the wonderful power and strength of the old Reich. These were primarily the causes of a quality which the present-day State lacks completely: the State authority!' (*Mein Kampf*, op. cit., p. 387).

[234] Ibid., p. 480.

[235] Cited in R. Kohli, *Political ideas of M.S. Golwalkar*, op. cit., p. 138.

are not seen as indispensable and when a new *sarsanghchalak* is appointed the basic framework of the organisation is unaffected. Hedgewar nominated Golwalkar as his successor in 1940 and Golwalkar nominated Deoras as his in 1973, but on neither occasion was it necessary for the new *sarsanghchalak* to win support from the members of the RSS by presenting himself and his ideas to them; their legitimacy was derived from the very procedure of nomination, much in the way that the succession of *gurus* at the head of a sect is endorsed. The cult of personality which undoubtedly exists within the RSS is focussed on the office rather than the incumbent, who is seen only as the guardian of a wider mission which is beyond the scope of any one individual.

The cohesion of the RSS derives more from its members' respect for a shared ideology than from loyalty to particular individuals who may hold high office in the organisation. This ideologically based cohesion coincides with a devaluation of individuality in the RSS; the 'new man' must sacrifice his personality to the cause. In 1991, the *pracharak* of Shivpuri pointed out: 'If there is a position of myself, then it is a wrong process. There must be position of Bhagwa Dwaj, Hindu Rashtra and Bharat Mata. [...] There is no man [in the RSS], but everything is based on men.'[236] The fact that the RSS organisation is above men and in particular that the movement does not rely on the authority of a supreme leader, differentiates it from fascist groups.

The difficulty of using the concept of 'fascism' in the case of the RSS has also been attributed to other aspects of the 'sectarian' dimension that we studied in the previous section. It was recently pointed out by authors not known for their Hindu nationalist sympathies that 'The RSS exaltation of the ascetic model (segregation of *shakhas*, celibacy of *sarsanghchalaks* and of most *pracharaks* and *pracharikas*) marks an important distinction between itself and other similar patterns for youth organisation. The fascists and the Nazi youth fronts had inculcated a hard macho attitude and an aggressive male sexuality.'[237]

To sum up: since a characteristic of the RSS's Hindu nationalism has been to down-play the role of the state we cannot classify it straightforwardly as a fascist movement.[238] As distinct from Nazism, the RSS's ideology treats society as an organism with a secular spirit, which is implanted not so much in the race as in a socio-cultural system and which will be regenerated over the course of time by patient work at the grassroots.[239] Finally, in contrast to both Italian fascism and Nazism the

---

[236] Interview on 26 Oct. 1991, Piparsod.

[237] T. Basu *et al.*, *Khaki shorts and saffron flags*, op. cit. p. 79.

[238] This observation had been already made by D.E. Smith (*India as a secular state*, Princeton University Press, 1963, p. 468).

RSS does not rely on the central figure of the leader. Nonetheless, the RSS can be classed as authoritarian in its emphasis on discipline, in its refusal to recognise the specific character of minorities and in its intention of reforming the Hindu mentality absolutely to prepare the advent of a new man, implying the need to extend the sway of the organisation over the whole of society.

In the last two sections, we have successively analysed two important dimensions of the RSS: its religious, 'sectarian' and Brahminical connotations and the anti-liberal characteristics of its Hindu nationalism. Both aspects must be kept in mind when we come to study the movement's development. The growth of the network of *shakhas* was logically a priority for its leaders and the uneven attraction the RSS exerted can hardly be understood if its dual character is forgotten.

Priority given to the expansion of the *shakha* network

The RSS represented the 'Hindu Rashtra in miniature' because of the very existence of its network of *shakhas*, one which constituted an 'imaginary community', to use Benedict Anderson's term. Just as (according to Anderson) the readers of daily newspapers in a given country form a nation by virtue of the fact that they engage in the same activity, within the same culture, at the same moment, and know that they are among thousands of millions similarly engaged,[240] so *swayamsevaks* carry out the same daily rituals and exercises in the *shakhas* in the knowledge that they are being reproduced simultaneously wherever the RSS has taken root. In addition, the discipline inculcated in this fashion produces a deliberate conditioning, as the writings of K.R. Malkani indicate:

Doing the same exercises, singing the same songs, listening to the same *baudhiks*, they came to think alike and feel alike. They had the same idiom, the same style

---

[239] Golwalkar's preference for a long-term socio-psychological reform in contrast with a fascist-style seizure of power was echoed among local RSS cadres, one of whom, interviewed in New Delhi in 1951, declared: 'Hitler, whom Guruji and we admired for his sense of discipline and his attempts to eliminate angularities for German culture, failed in his purpose because he did not elevate his program to the spiritual plane and he favored foolish aggression in Europe [...] We do not believe in dictatorship in the Western sense, but we also do not believe in the cultural anarchy and insipid, valueless secularism which now seem to dominate in the West. A disciplined society, deeply imbedded in our ancient culture, is our aim. Guruji promises to take us to this goal if only we have the patience and the will power to prepare for our day which will come.' (Cited in R.L. Park, ' "Angularities" and the secular state: An interview with India's RSS', *The Radical Humanist*, 5 Feb. 1961, p. 69).

[240] B. Anderson, *Imagined communities: reflections on the origin and spread of nationalism*, London: Verso, 1983, p. 39.

and the same smile. One *swayamsevak* would feel fully at home in the company of another *swayamsevak* even if he did not always understand his language.[241]

Development of the *shakha* network was a priority for the RSS in order to extend the 'imaginary' vanguard of the Hindu nation. The RSS's technique was to divide India into units which could be covered by the RSS network. This programme was the constant preoccupation of Hedgewar, as his last speech revealed:

Remember, we have to organise the entire Hindu society from Kanyakumari to the Himalayas. In fact our main area of operation is the vast Hindu world outside the Sangh. [...] Our object should be to show to the people the true path of national salvation. That true path is none other than ORGANIZATION [*sangathan*].[242]

Hedgewar concentrated on recruiting and training *pracharaks* who were to be responsible in turn for establishing as many *shakhas* as possible, first in Nagpur and then right across Maharashtra. The main task was thus to penetrate the entire social structure in order to forge a Hindu nation that would be physically, morally and socially sound. The *pracharaks* supplied the initial framework for this network. Later they were able to free themselves from operating on a purely local level. New stalwarts took on the functions of *mukhya shikshaks* (chief instructors trained in an Instructors' Training Camp) and secretaries of local branches, while the *pracharaks* supervised the operations at district, division and state level. These areas of activity did not necessarily correspond to previously established entities but rather to zones carefully mapped in relation to means of communication in order to shorten the journeys of itinerant *pracharaks*. From the late 1920s *pracharaks* set out in ever growing numbers to found *shakhas* all over Maharashtra. In 1928 there were eighteen, concentrated around Nagpur, in 1930 sixty and in 1933 about 125 (with 12,000 *swayamsevaks*).[243] In 1934 V.R. Oke, who had completed his Instructors' Training Camp and Officers' Training Camp in 1929-31, organised in Poona the first OTC outside Nagpur. In this zone, therefore, the RSS was now able to train its own cadres.

In the mid-1930s, it was really only in Maharashtra that the RSS had been firmly established by men such as Oke, Babasaheb Apte and S. Parmarth.[244] Elsewhere it had only a few outposts, such as that in the Benares Hindu University to which, in 1928, Hedgewar sent P.B. Dani, a *swayamsevak* from Nagpur district. Dani's assignment had the approval

---

[241] K.R. Malkani, *RSS story*, op. cit., p. 35.

[242] Cited in Deshpande and Ramaswamy, *Dr Hedgewar, the epoch-maker*, op. cit., p. 188.

[243] W. Andersen, 'The Rashtriya Swayamsevak Sangh – I', op. cit., p. 593 and W. Andersen and S. Damle, *The brotherhood in saffron*, op. cit., p. 38.

[244] Sitaram Parmarth was an early lieutenant of Hedgewar in Nagpur. He was also a Brahmin from the lower middle class (his father was a post office book-keeper).

of M.M. Malaviya, the University's founder and a leader of the Hindu Mahasabha.[245] Before Dani left for Varanasi, Hedgewar advised him to overcome timidity in order to mix with students, and to learn the language most used in Varanasi, Hindi, and even those of other regions from which students might come. It was important to make friends from all regions to allow the RSS thinking to spread there.[246]

During the second half of the 1930s, numerous *pracharaks* were sent from Nagpur to develop the *shakha* network. A common strategy was to get them enrolled like Dani in a university in order to recruit new followers among the student population. This method can be called 'Sangathanist' since its aim was to give concrete form to Hedgewar's ambition: an organisation (*sangathan*) of all Hindus through the multiplication of *shakhas*. Babasaheb Apte acted as an assistant to Hedgewar in the coordination of the *pracharak* network. He travelled continuously and provided a special kind of help to the *pracharaks* by identifying and meeting persons of importance (*ganmanya log*) in all the places he visited in order to win their patronage for the *shakhas*.[247]

The northward expansion and the pracharaks' modus operandi

The expansion was most vigorous in North India, especially in the Punjab where the separatism of certain leaders in the Muslim majority community was antagonising a growing number of Hindus. The RSS benefited from the support of eminent figures in the Hindu Mahasabha and the Arya Samaj such as Bhai Parmanand, whose son-in-law, Dharmavir, an English teacher, acted as a contact. In 1935, Babasaheb Apte had toured the province.[248] Three *pracharaks* – all Maharashtrian Brahmins – followed: A.B. Joshi was despatched to Sialkot; Moreshwar Moonje registered for a BA course at Dayananda Anglo-Vedic College in Rawalpindi in 1939, and while there, with the Principal's support, acted as a physical training instructor[249] before being transferred, first to Jhelum and then to Peshawar; Paturkar was sent to pursue his studies at the DAV College in Lahore.[250] Their *modus operandi* is illustrative of the way the RSS network was developed:

[245] *Organiser*, 14 June 1965, p. 8.

[246] C.P. Bhishikar, *Shri Bhaiyaji Dani*, op. cit., p. 13.

[247] P.G. Sahasrabuddhe, *Karmayogi Babasaheb Apte*, op. cit., p. 26.

[248] *Organiser*, 12 Aug. 1972, p. 7.

[249] Interview with Moreshwar Rao Moonje, 12 Dec. 1991, Bhopal.

[250] The first *shakha* in this town was established in the *akhara* that Bhai Parmanad had created in memory of Bhanda Vairagi, a *sadhu* who had fought alongside the Sikh armies during their struggle against the Muslims in the eighteenth century (interview with Bhai Mahavir, 4 Sept. 1992, New Delhi).

[The *pracharaks*] would meet the *swayamsevaks* in the day time in their respective schools and colleges.[...] Attempt was made to bring new students to these group meetings so that they could be introduced to the RSS and persuaded to become *swayamsevaks*. Similar meetings were held after the *shakha* was over on the ground or in the house or different *swayamsevaks*. These informal meetings followed by some refreshments played a very important role in spreading the *sangha* work and developing personal closeness which proved to be binding. There was not formal membership. But once a young man joined a *shakha* such close contact was maintained with him that he became an intimate part of the whole.[251]

DAV College was a judicious choice because, as Balraj Madhok wrote, 'the Arya Samajists were closest to Dr Hedgewar's way of thinking'.[252] Moreover, it was from among those students who were the most ardent disciples of the Arya Samaj that Paturkar recruited 'volunteers' called to a political role at the national level. One of them, Madhok, was from an Arya Samajist family in Jammu, from where he had come to study in Lahore. After attending some Communist meetings, he joined the RSS in 1938,[253] the same year as Bhai Mahavir, the son of Bhai Parmanand and a fellow-student at DAV College. In 1940, Madhavrao Muley, hitherto *pracharak* at Ratnagiri, was appointed to the newly-created post of provincial (*prant*) *pracharak* in Lahore to strengthen the organisation of the regional network of *shakhas*.[254]

The RSS headquarters at Nagpur despatched as *pracharaks* Vasant Rao Oke, to Delhi, in 1936; Murlidar Dattatraya ('Bhaurao') Deoras to Lucknow, in 1937;[255] and his brother Madhukar Dattatraya ('Balasaheb') Deoras to Bengal, in 1939.[256] In the United Provinces (UP), besides the BHU, the RSS concentrated on two other educational institutions. Bhaurao Deoras, though he was already a graduate, joined courses at Lucknow University 'to facilitate meeting young men'. In 1937 he recruited Madhusudan Waman Moghe, a Maharashtrian Brahmin from Indore, who was a student in the zoology department. Moghe became *pracharak* for Allahabad region in 1942 and gave special attention to the local University. Rajendra Singh, a Rajput from Bulandshahr who was studying for his M.Sc. in the physics department, was persuaded by Moghe to join the RSS in 1942 and in 1944 became *pracharak* in Pratapgarh district.[257] In western UP the Sanatan Dharma College of Kanpur was another focal point of the *pracharaks'*

[251] B. Madhok, *RSS and politics*, New Delhi: Hindu World Publications, 1986, p. 24.

[252] Ibid., p. 23.

[253] Ibid., p. 25.

[254] *Organiser*, Varshapratipada Special, 1979, p. 13.

[255] Concerning his use of the Sangathanist method at the BHU, see ibid., 24 May 1992, p. 2.

[256] Ibid., 25 Feb. 1968, p. 3 and June 1973, p. 5.

[257] R. Singh 'Bapurao Moghe – a brilliant and devoted personality', *Organiser*, 20 Feb. 1994, p. 8.

work. Babasaheb Apte went there in 1937. A *shakha* was then established and later that year Sunder Singh Bhandari, a student from Udaipur and Deendayal Upadhyaya, a student from Mathura district, who were both to become *pracharaks*, joined the RSS.[258]

By 1938 this expanding network consisted of around 40,000 *swayamsevaks*, 60,000 (divided between 500 *shakhas*) in 1939, and 76,000 in 1943, of which 35,000 were concentrated in the Central Provinces, 20,476 in Bombay Province and 14,000 in Punjab.[259] As far as the RSS cadres were concerned, some 1,400 *swayamsevaks* and would-be *pracharaks* were present at the Officers' Training Camp held at Nagpur in the spring of 1940. They came from the United Provinces, Bihar, Bengal, Madras Presidency, Bombay Presidency, the North-West Frontier Province, Sindh and Punjab, where there were already fifty *shakhas*.[260] In Sindh, the RSS was established in the late 1940s by Balraj Puri, a *pracharak* from Punjab.[261] In Madras Presidency, the first *shakha* was opened in Madras by S. Parmarth who remained *pracharak* there up to 1946.[262]

Explaining the RSS's relative attractiveness in the 1940s

At first glance it seems that the numerical strength of the RSS was artificially inflated since the majority of its participants were pre-adolescent. The latter were the main target of the organisation because they were more likely to absorb its message but they remained often barely aware of the movement's ideology. Even today, many *swayamsevaks* admit to having joined the RSS because their parents wanted them to take exercise; they were attracted by the games and the atmosphere of camaraderie, but did not have a clear idea of what the organisation represented.[263] Regular attendance at the *shakha* could, however, lead to genuine acculturation.[264]

---

[258] Interview with S.S. Bhandari, 24 Feb. 1994, New Delhi and D. Puchpa, *Sangh-ninva mein visarjit* (Hindi), op.cit. p.104.

[259] 'Notes on the Volunteer Movement in India' prepared by the Intelligence Bureau, 27 Jan. 1940; ibid., 23 Aug. 1940, in L/P & J/Coll. 17 – C81 IOLR, and W. Andersen, 'The Rashtriya Swayamsevak Sangh I', op. cit., p. 595.

[260] J.A. Curran, *Militant Hinduism in Indian politics*, op. cit., p. 14, and B.V. Deshpande and S.R. Ramaswamy, *Dr Hedgewar, the epoch-maker*, op. cit., pp. 165, 170 and 179.

[261] K.R. Malkani, *The Sindh story*, New Delhi: Allied Publishers, 1984, p. 85.

[262] Interview with K.Jana Krishnamurthi, 22 Feb. 1995, New Delhi and D. Puchpa, *Sangh-ninva mein visarjit* (Hindi), op. cit, p. 58, Three Maharashtrian *pracharaks* were sent to Kerala in 1942 (J. Chiriyankandath, 'Hindu nationalism and Indian regional political culture: a study of Kerala', paper prepared for the ECPR workshop on 'Political culture and religion in the Third World', Bordeaux, 27 Apr–2 May 1995, p. 15.

[263] This point is illustrated by this brief testimony of a senior *swayamsevak* in Delhi: 'In the first time I did not know about the RSS and about our Hindus, what is a Hindu and what we are, what we can do for Hindus. But after some time we know this Hinduism and

Andersen and Damle, on the strength of works by sociologists and psychologists specialising in India, emphasise how favourable for the enrolment into a movement of this kind are the critical years of youth

It is a time when, if G. Morris-Carstairs is right, Indian youth seek a person or a cause to which they can give their uncompromising support and obedience. The RSS appeals to this impulse by advocating the sacrifice of self for society, organizationally expressed through service in the RSS and by deference to RSS leaders.[265]

When we look for reasons to explain the RSS's appeal in the 1940s, the main object of this section, we often find the attachment to this 'model man' that is the *pracharak*. The experience of a former *swayamsevak* from Punjab illustrates this psychological process. R.L. Dhooria, who joined in 1942-3 at the age of about ten, has this significant memory of the head of his *shakha*, who was also a teacher in his school: .

The young man [...] became one of those few persons to whom I gave my heart unreservedly and uninhibitedly. He loved me immensely. [...] Not only I but most of the other boys were deeply attached to him.[...] Not a little of my devotion to the RSS was the result of my deep attachment to him.[266]

With maturity, attachment to this 'model man' tended to change into a respect based on the prestige associated with asceticism.[267] K.D. Jhari, a student from Ambala in the Punjab, was made a *pracharak* at the age of seventeen, after renouncing marriage on the instructions of his 'superiors' and because he was inspired by the example of Vasant Rao Oke, the RSS leader in the region, himself a celibate.

In 1944, when I first saw him I was immensely impressed by his personality. Till today my memory is engraven with the charm and fascination of his personality. At the time he appeared to me with the halo of a god irradiating his head.[268]

R.L. Dhooria remembers that 'going to the *shakhas* was in the nature of a passion grande, a specy of sacred routine to be observed and followed priestlike with a religious regularity.'[269] This testimony accords with that

---

what we can do for Hinduism.' (interview with the *mukhya shikshak* (chief instructor) of the *shakha* of Vikram mandal, 11 Oct. 1991, New Delhi).

[264] Interview with one of those in charge of the *shakha* of the Idgah (New Delhi), 11 Oct. 1991. See also the series of articles by S.R. Goel, 'How I became a Hindu', *Organiser*, 27 Sept., 4 Oct., 18 Oct. and 1 Nov. 1991.

[265] W. Andersen and S. Damle, *The brotherhood in saffron*, op. cit., p. 5.

[266] R.L. Dhooria, *I was a swayamsevak*, New Delhi: Sampradayikta Virodhi Committee, n.d., p. 15.

[267] This interpretation is implied in the study by Andersen and Damle, which defines the RSS as a living 'lay order' (p. 77).

[268] K.D. Jhari, 'Revealing details of pracharak's life', *Secular Democracy*, June 1970, p. 35.

[269] R.L. Dhooria, *I was a Swayamsevak*, op. cit., p. 18.

of Kewalram Ratanmal Malkani, who entered the RSS at Hyderabad (Sindh) in 1941:

Here were bright young men plying the *lathi*, playing nice Indian games and singing patriotic songs with a quiet discipline and a ready smile. The whole atmosphere was pure and elevating. [...] Being in the *Sangha* felt like having a purifying dip daily in the Ganga. My mental attitude was that of a devout novitiate with the prayer, *Sangham sharanam gachhami* [I surrender myself to the *Sangha*].[270]

Malkani also explains the attraction exerted by the RSS during these years on other comrades, not only for political reasons but also as an answer to their quest for a personal discipline formulated in terms of *samskars*:

I have often pondered over what drew lakhs of promising young men to the RSS in the forties and kept them glued to it thereafter. The appeal, I find, was total. The Congress with its taboos and totems like *ahimsa* and *charkha* was not considered a fit instrument for ushering in freedom. [...]

In addition the RSS alone could checkmate the continuing Congress ambivalence about Muslim communalism. [...]

Nor was the RSS appeal confined to public issues. The appeal was, if anything, even stronger to the individual – what he was, what he aspired to be. The atmosphere of purity and integrity was a standing invitation to self-improvement according to one's lights. And so some practised *asanas* [yoga exercises] to improve health. Others gave up meat. Some others foreswore smoking. Still others stopped seeing films.[271]

The prevalent brotherliness and egalitarianism in the RSS is admitted to have been a powerful motive for those joining the organisation:

While iron discipline prevailed, the atmosphere of sociability and camaraderie that prevailed there was truly remarkable.[...] The question of caste, for instance, was simply conspicuous by its absence. We all played together, sang together, ate together. [...] We were all Hindus and children of the Bharat Mata.[272]

The appeal of the RSS to young people appears to arise, in part, from the features of the movement as an ideological 'sect', such as solidarity among equals sharing the same doctrine and the atmosphere of religious ritual and self-discipline (defined in terms of *samskars*) guided by a *pracharak* whose role approximates to that of an ascetic. Here one can gauge the force of the strategy of emulation. The object of the RSS was to forge a Hindu nation on the Western model by concentrating on the

---

[270] K.R. Malkani, *The midnight knock*, New Delhi: Vikas, 1978, pp. 91-2.

[271] Ibid., pp. 92-3. K.R. Malkani was from a Congress background (his elder brother, Prof. N.R. Malkani, was one of Gandhi's lieutenants).

[272] R.L. Dhooria, *I was a swayamsevak*, op. cit., pp. 39-40.

individual. But it placed its mission within a familiar and prestigious indigenous framework, which contributed notably to its success.

The eye-witnesses we have quoted in fact explain their attachment to the RSS not so much by political motives – although all were from areas which were to become incorporated into Pakistan – as by personal ones. However, this was only one aspect of the RSS's attraction. The desire to protect the high castes, whose vulnerability had been exposed by the development of 'mass' politics stemming from the agitations of the Congress party, was a motivation which increased as Gandhi's methodology permeated the freedom movement. As indicated by Malkani, the RSS attracted opponents of Gandhian politics in Maharashtra and elsewhere in the 1940s, and most probably even before that date.

The movement's ideology was another potent binding factor, particularly at the moment of becoming an RSS cadre. It is striking to find impulses similar to those which prompted Hedgewar to form the RSS in the context of the Hindu-Muslim riots of the 1920s, in a letter from Deendayal Upadhyaya explaining to his family his choice of the 'career' of *pracharak*:

Muslim goondas [hoodlums] may, at a single stroke, besmirch the honour and reputation of the highest citizens. This is so because even though they stand high, the Samaj [society] to which they happen to belong is weak and degenerate, devoid of power and steeped in selfishness. [...] Do you believe the Samaj will stand by you in case of an emergency? No, it will not, and for the simple reason that it is disorganised. [...] Our sisters and daughters are carried away by the Muslims, they are victims of assaults by British soldiers in broad daylight and we, who are never tired of boasting of our honour and our exalted position in society are obliged to look on in utter helplessness.[273]

The sense of their community's collective inferiority that typified the Hindu nationalists underlies this statement. Interestingly, Upadhyaya feels especially concerned by the vulnerability of the Hindu upper-caste élite. His letter was written in 1942, when, for other reasons, events contributed to the rise of the RSS. Some of those who took part in Gandhi's 'Quit India' movement were deceived by its outcome because effective repression by the British prevented any tangible advance. Doubting the effectiveness of the methods of the Congress, they turned to the RSS,[274] sometimes after having been tempted by Communism.[275] Others made this choice even before the 'Quit India' movement because of the same distrust

---

[273] *Organiser,* 14 Apr. 1968, p. 9.

[274] This was the case with Rajendra Singh (R. Singh, 'Bapurao Moghe', *Organiser,* 20 Feb. 1994, p. 8) and with A.B. Vajpayee (ibid., 3 Jan. 1982, p. 8).

[275] This was the case with J.P. Mathur, a *pracharak* in the United Provinces from 1945 (interview, 18 Nov. 1989, New Delhi and S.S. Bhandari (ed.), *Jana Deep Souvenir,* Delhi: Rakesh Press, 1967, p. 11).

of the Congress. Lal Krishna Advani, a future Hindu nationalist leader who joined the RSS in Hyderabad (Sindh) in 1942, declares:

I joined at about the same time as the 'Quit India' movement. I joined a couple of months earlier but my motivation was the conviction that India would not attain independence by the methods the Congress was commanding. Much more was needed and the RSS approach used to be that unless we first build up, form a nucleus of people willing to sacrifice their life for the country India would not become independent.[276]

In the 1940s the development of the RSS was also fuelled by the desire of some Hindus to organise themselves in reaction to the growing mobilisation, sometimes in paramilitary form, of Muslim separatist movements. This response was strongest in areas where Hindus were in a minority. However it was not the only motivation, as the testimonies of the Punjabis Dhooria and Jhari make clear. In each adult *swayamsevak* a liking for paramilitary style, anti-Muslim attitudes, distrust of the Congress and admiration for a *prachrak-'guru'* who could offer a means of self-improvement, combined to hasten the growth of the RSS.

The RSS and the Hindu Mahasabha

Apart from its ability to attract support through its own methods, the RSS benefited from the support of local notables in developing its network. The *pracharaks* sent out on missions were recommended to such patrons by the headquarters in Nagpur, which was skilled in the management of its web of relations. In the RSS's strategic plan, these notables were to become referred to as *sanghchalak* (lit. directors). They functioned mostly as counsellors or even guides, and by sponsoring the activities of local *pracharaks* conferred on the movement a certain respectability:

In town after town the Sangha *pracharak* would arrive with a few letters of introduction to the local leaders, whether belonging to Congress, Hindu Mahasabha, Arya Samaj or whatever. He would put up in the local Bhavan of any of these organisations or in a temple or with any well-wisher.[277]

The first *sanghchalak* of the RSS was Hari Krishna (alias Appaji) Joshi, a Congress leader from Wardha, where Gandhi was to have his *ashram*. As early as 1926, Joshi became *sanghchalak* for the RSS unit of Wardha district, the first branch to be formed from Nagpur. He then left the Congress in 1931.[278] In fact, most of the public figures patronising the RSS belonged to the Hindu Mahasabha. In this organisation, in addition

[276] Interview with L.K. Advani, 11 Feb. 1994, New Delhi.

[277] K.R. Malkani, *The RSS story,* op. cit., p. 43.

[278] D. Puchpa, *Sangh-minva mein visarjit,* op. cit., pp. 75-6.

to M.M. Malaviya and B.S. Moonje, the RSS enjoyed during the 1930s the support of Padam Raj Jain. This Marwari from Calcutta had been impressed by the Nagpur *shakha* which he visited after the session of the Hindu Mahasabha in Poona in 1935. He told Hedgewar how much he appreciated his 'silent but highly important work'.[279] As General Secretary of the Hindu Mahasabha he helped Vasant Rao Oke establish the Delhi *shakha* by authorising him to set up his general headquarters – and the first *shakha* – in the central office of the Mahasabha.[280] From the 1940s onwards, the Delhi branch of the RSS benefited from the patronage of a leading industrialist, Hans Raj Gupta, an Arya Samajist who became *sanghchalak* for the Delhi region in 1947 (see below).[281] In the United Provinces, the British secret service believed that the RSS 'owe [d] its growth to Dr Moonje'[282] and his journeys in the region. The RSS also benefited considerably from the influence of local notables such as Narendra Jeet Singh. This patron, who became *sanghchalak* for the branch of Kanpur division in 1945 and then for the whole province in 1948, was a typical *sangchalak*: the son of a reputed lawyer who had been chairman of the Kanpur municipal board, he was himself a leading advocate (he presided over the local Bar Council for many years), and remained *Prant Sanghchalak* till his death in 1993.[283]

Having assisted the expansion of the RSS, the Hindu Mahasabha considered itself all the more entitled to ask for the support of its network of *swayamsevaks*. The Nagpur leadership, however, would not divert their organisation from its long-term vocation by becoming involved in political action. Here the RSS showed its divergence from the Hindu Mahasabha since it gave priority to the creation of a Hindu Rashtra as the necessary preliminary for a Hindu Raj (Hindu state), which could not be contemplated at this early stage. The lack of interest shown by the RSS in political activity aimed at winning power in the state reflected the belief that such action would only distract Hindus from the main object, i.e. the strengthening of the Hindu nation in socio-psychological and physical terms. At the end of the 1930s, Hedgewar apparently snubbed Jamanlal Bajaj, a Gandhian leader from Wardha, who, according to Appaji Joshi, had designs on the activist network of the RSS and had suggested to Hedgewar that his organisation affiliate to Congress.[284] The general stand

---

[279] Savarkar Papers, Reel no. 3, File no. 1. Letter of 27 July 1936, NMML.

[280] Ibid., Reel no. 4, File no. 1. Letter of Padam Raj Jain to Savarkar (29 Nov. 1936), and interview with V.R. Oke.

[281] Interview with Rajendra Gupta, 25 Feb. 1995, New Delhi.

[282] 'Note on the Volunteer Movement in India prepared by the Intelligence Bureau–28 Sept. 1940', op. cit.

[283] *Hindu Chetna*, 1 Dec. 1993, p. 10 (Hindi).

[284] A. Joshi, 'How Congress and Mahasabha tried to appropriate the RSS', *Organiser*, 15

of the RSS was that the anti-colonial struggle took second place to a Hindu nationalist social reform. When Hedgewar took part in the Civil Disobedience movement which Congress launched in 1930, he took care to emphasise that he was doing so strictly as an individual, and entrusted a friend with the task of running the RSS, demonstrating thereby his concern to keep the organisation aloof from the political arena. However his old connections with his two mentors, Moonje and Savarkar, made him amenable to doing business with the Hindu Mahasabha. The annual conference of the Mahasabha at Nagpur in 1938 benefited from the presence of RSS volunteers, who helped keep order. After he took over the organisation Golwalkar revoked all these concessions, obliging the Hindu Mahasabha in 1940 to develop its own paramilitary group, the *Ram Sena* (army of Ram).[285] A member of the Nagpur branch of the Hindu Mahasabha, who had enquired of the RSS leaders about this *volte face*, wrote in 1940:

They say that there is no difference between the Hindu Mahasabha and the Congress. [...] In Maharashtra Sangh flourished mainly due to the supports and efforts of Hindu Sabha workers. But when Sangh thought that it has become sufficiently powerful, it is now making attempts to destroy the Hindu Mahasabha.[286]

The same process occurred during the 1940s in North India where the RSS freed itself all the more easily from the subordinate position envisaged for it by the Hindu Mahasabha as new patrons presented themselves. Some of these were maharajahs anxious to find a counterweight to the Muslim paramilitary groups which were developing in their states, as in Alwar (Rajasthan), where the RSS was able to maintain training camps;[287] some – in the provinces claimed by Muslim separatists as part of the future Pakistan – were notables who feared for their lives and property. Thus R.L. Dhooria reported that in 1947 every rich person in Montgomery district in Punjab was a member of the RSS.[288] In the Punjab, financial support from these quarters was accompanied by an unprecedented growth in the organisation's membership as Partition approached: between January and June 1947 the number of *swayamsevaks* in the province rose from 46,000 to 59,200.[289]

Aug. 1970, p. 15.

[285] 'Hindu militia' (Ram Sena), M.G. Chitnavis Papers, File no. 91, NMML (mss. section).

[286] 'What should be the attitude of the Hindu Mahasabha towards the RSS?', anonymous note dated 7 Feb. 1940, M.G. Chitnavis Papers, File no. 19, NMML (mss. section).

[287] *Report of the commission of inquiry into the conspiracy to murder Mahatma Gandhi.* Part I, New Delhi: Government of India, 1966, pp. 242- 3.

[288] R.L. Dhooria, *I was a swayamsevak*, op. cit., p. 44.

[289] *Rashtriya Swayam Sevak Sangh in the Punjab*, Lahore, 1948, pp. 5-17.

A North Indian movement

At the national level, the membership of the RSS soared from 76,000 in 1943 (RSS sources had claimed that there were already 100,000 *swayam-sevaks* in 1940) to about 600,000 at the beginning of 1948.[290] The density of membership varied considerably from region to region, as indicated by the figures given by Curran for 1951, when the RSS had 600,000 members. The movement remained underdeveloped in the North-East (West Bengal, Assam and Orissa together accounted for only 16,000 *swayam-sevaks*) and in the South where there were only 31,000 members, about half of whom were concentrated in Karnataka. The RSS's Sanskritised culture was barely acceptable to many south Indians because it was regarded as antithetic to Dravidian identity.[291] The provinces of Madhya Bharat, Rajasthan and Vindhya Pradesh contained only 20,000 *swayam-sevaks* but the Congress was rather weak here too, mainly because the reigning princes usually succeeded in keeping political movements at bay. The provinces where the RSS was strongest were Bihar (50,000 *swayam-sevaks*), the Bombay area (60,000), Madhya Pradesh (125,000), Greater Punjab (Delhi and Himachal Pradesh included – 125,000) and Uttar Pradesh (200,000). A majority of these provinces formed part of the Hindi belt, which, even more than Maharashtra, was bound to provide the core area of support for the Hindu nationalists. Several features of this northern region made it an area receptive to the RSS: it was the centre of Hindi literary culture, it contained relatively high proportions of high caste Hindus, especially Brahmins (in Uttar Pradesh, for instance, in 1931 upper castes represented one-fifth of the population – including 9.2% of Brahmins) and some of its localities contained significant Muslim minorities.

In the late 1940s the fortunes of the RSS in the Hindi belt were undoubtedly linked to the circumstances of Partition. At that time the organisation tended to function as a militia, for both offensive and defensive purposes:[292] for example, *swayamsevaks* were involved in anti-Muslim riots in Delhi in September 1947.[293] Moreover the ability of the RSS to help Hindu refugees from the new West Pakistan added greatly to its prestige. In April 1947, a Hindu Sahayata Samiti (a body for assisting Hindus) was established, largely under the patronage of Hans Raj

---

[290] W. Andersen and S. Damle, *The brotherhood in saffron*, op. cit., p. 50, and J.A. Curran, *Militant Hinduism in Indian politics*, op. cit., pp. 14 and 43.

[291] Chiriyankandath points out that none of the festivals celebrated by the RSS were the prominent ones of Kerala. In this state the RSS's appeal was largely confined to Brahmins ('Hindu nationalism and regional political culture', op.cit., pp. 28-30).

[292] K.D. Jhari, 'Creating the urge to kill', *Secular Democracy*, July 1970, p. 367.

[293] I.H. Qurushi, 'A case-study of the social relations between the Muslim and the Hindus, 1935-1947', in C.H. Phillips and M.D. Wainright (eds), *The Partition of India*, London: Geo. Allen and Unwin, 1970, p. 367.

Gupta.[294] In 1947, when this city of 900,000 inhabitants was inundated
with some 470,000 refugees, the Hindu Sahayata Samiti – which was
associated with the RSS – distributed clothes and blankets in refugee
camps and enrolled children in their new schools.[295] The devotion and
discipline of the *swayamsevaks* turned out to be precious assets on which
to base the popularity of the movement. This decision to provide social
support, a 'welfarist tactic', in other words,[296] contributed to the evolution
of the RSS as a Hindu nationalist movement oriented towards psycho-so-
cial reform independent of any political patronage.

Throughout its formative stages the Hindu nationalist movement has
employed a threefold strategy of stigmatisation and emulation of
'threatening Others'. In the first phase, the dominating presence of these
Others, often exaggerated, aroused strong feelings of vulnerability. There
are other cases of majorities with a minority complex,[297] and probably all
ethnic nationalisms (the Herderian brand in Germany, for one) emerged
from excessive feelings of vulnerability,[298] but as far as Hinduism is
concerned, its extreme differentiation into castes and sects was (from the
Hindu nationalist perspective) an additional predisposition to such a
feeling. The second phase was characterised by efforts to reform Hindu
society through a selective imitation of those cultural traits from which
the Other was believed to have gained its strength and hence its superiority. This borrowing did not develop openly but rather under the pretext
of a reinterpretation of Hindu traditions. The cumulative process led
gradually to the construction of an ideology of Hindu nationalism.
    The origins of the movement lie in the socio-religious reform of the
nineteenth century when, in order to resist the European administrative
and missionary offensive, organisations like the Arya Samaj invented a

---

[294] *Organiser*, 21 Aug. 1947, p. 16, and July 1985, p.3.

[295] Ibid., 1 Jan. 1948, p. 7; 8 Jan. 1948, p. 9; and *Hitavada*, 9 Jan. 1948, p. 2.

[296] This formula – used to describe the provision of social assistance to those suffering from
material or moral deprivation when implemented by movements operating on the
borderline between social work and political or ideological action – owes its origin to
the reflections of a working group of scholars entitled 'Trajectoires du politique',
founded by Jean-Francois Bayard at CERI, Paris. No particular author has been credited
with its invention. In the following chapters I shall use the word 'tactic' to describe
practices which are part of strategies; here, for instance, I refer to the 'welfarist tactic'
as a part of the sangathanist strategy.

[297] A similar sentiment lies at the basis of Sinhalese nationalism, according to S.J. Tambiah
(*Sri Lanka: Ethnic fratricide and the dismantling of democracy*, London: I.B. Tauris,
1986, p. 92).

[298] Herder's sentiment towards Germany's fate in the context of French domination is well
analysed by R. Ergang in *Herder and the foundation of German nationalism*, New York:
Columbia University Press, 1931.

Vedic Golden Age. This ideological construction enabled them to regain self-esteem, defend their threatened identity and demonstrate how the values of the dominant power could be adopted with advantage. The system of the *varnas* was thus reinterpreted as a social model which could reinforce the cohesion of Hindu society (in contrast with the caste system), which conformed to Western standards of justice and individual merit and, at the same time, with the prestige of antiquity, legitimised the principle of social hierarchy. This analysis suggests how one might amend the theoretical framework provided by Geertz and Fallers: the ideology of the Vedic Golden Age was certainly created to vindicate 'patterns of belief and value' but these patterns were predominantly those of the élite Brahmins who served as the prime initiators of the socio-religious reform movements.

The strategic 'detour' by way of Vedic antiquity, of which so little was known that all fictions could be accepted as valid, was vitally important. It was this myth which first gave sustenance to Hindu ethnic consciousness and subsequently to Hindu nationalist ideology, when the strategy of stigmatisation and emulation was again set in motion by the Khilafat movement and the riots of the 1920s. In this context, Savarkar and then Golwalkar crystallised the identity of Hindutva while borrowing most of their political concepts from the West. They indeed internalised the western – mainly German – notion of ethnic nationalism as a means of strengthening Hindus against their 'enemies'. The Hindu Mahasabha aimed to retain a reinterpreted system of *varnas* as a model of the Hindu nation. This option, which contradicted certain modern aspects of Savarkar's ideology, was related to the presence within the movement of several conservative notables who did little to expand its base. The RSS chose a different way forward since in its case it was not the *varna* system but the Hindu sect that provided the framework. This approach proved more relevant to nation-building because the sect was the only Hindu institution that incorporated individualistic values, which form the basis of national cohesion in the western model.

Though it was an extreme form of ethnic nationalism, the ideology of the RSS as codified by Golwalkar differed from fascism and even Nazism in three respects. First, the organisation was not so closely associated with its leader. Second, the state, in contrast with fascism, was considered as a secondary agency. Third, race, in contrast with Nazism, was subordinated to the primacy of society. The RSS set itself to reform Hindu society by following a form of organicism based on the sacrifice of the individual. Its ambition was therefore to penetrate the whole of society through its network of *shakhas*. It took the form of a long-term project in which concerns of state power were not a priority.

The Hindu nationalist strategy of identity-building relies on both the emulation and stigmatisation of 'threatening Others'. This chapter has concentrated on the process of emulation, because it is difficult to identify and analyse, but the fact remains that the process of stigmatisation is its necessary concomitant. First, the origin of the strategy of emulation lies in a hostile reaction to the presence of the Other; second, stigmatisation is the logical outcome of the entire strategy since Hindu nationalist identity can better be strengthened and communicated to co-religionists through the demonisation of the Other, the diffusion of denigrating stereotypes and the exploitation of feelings of vulnerability.

The Hindu nationalist strategy of identity-building derives its paradoxical character from the fact that it simultaneously stigmatises and emulates the Other and eventually produces a Hindu nationalist identity which, as several authors have emphasised, has little to do with Hinduism. Dealing with the reaction of the Hindu nationalists to Christian influence, Romila Thapar writes that they 'attempted to defend, redefine and create "Hinduism" on the model of the Christian religion'.[299] They introduced into Hinduism many cultural traits which are foreign to it, such as proselytism. The overall aim of their ideological project seems incongruous to the extent that it was directed towards building an ethnic nation by reducing to uniformity a society distinguished by extreme differentiation. Hence the characterisation of Hindu nationalism by D. Gold and R. Thapar as 'organised' or 'syndicated' Hinduism.

Hindutva nationalism and Hinduism share common features which belong almost entirely to Brahminical culture. Its notion of ethnicity overlaps with 'Indian traditional xenology' – a Brahminical *Weltanschauung* – through what G. Pandey calls 'upper caste racism'. The emphasis on self-discipline through *samskars* is altogether consonant with the Brahminical ethic. Moreover, the potentially universal appeal of the *pracharak* – as an ascetic active in the world – was partly dissipated by the Brahminical ambience of the RSS .

The inability of the RSS and the Hindu Mahasabha to attract substantial support from the masses resulted from such fundamental contradictions. On the one hand they were intended to be the spearheads of a Hindu Rashtra evolved on the model of the western, egalitarian nation; on the other hand, in practice, they promoted the values of Brahminical culture. One way out was the possibility of developing a tactic of social welfare and an emphasis on Sanskritisation in order to attract and win over low

---

[299] R. Thapar, 'Syndicated moksha', op. cit., p. 18. A. Nandy develops the same interpretation: 'Hindutva is built on the tenets of a re-formed Hinduism of the nineteenth century. Reformed according to those who saw Hinduism as inferior to the semitic creeds, in turn seen as well-bounded, monolithic, well-organized, masculine, and capable of sustaining the ideology of an imperial state' ('Hinduism versus Hindutva', *The Times of India*, 18 Feb. 1991).

caste Hindus, a strategy employed by the RSS after 1947. Another could have been the mobilisation of Hindus around sensitive issues. The atrocities of Partition and the creation of a separate Muslim state on India's borders ought to have helped the Hindu nationalists to employ this strategy. However, the political conditions which emerged after Independence enabled India's secular leaders to hinder its implementation.

2

THE STRATEGY OF ETHNO-RELIGIOUS MOBILISATION AND THE POLITICS OF SECULARISM

'So far as I am concerned and the government I lead is concerned, I want to make it perfectly clear that communal forces will not be given the slightest quarter to sow seeds of dissensions among the people' (declaration by Nehru, 3 Oct. 1951, quoted in N.L. Gupta (ed.), *Nehru on communalism*, New Delhi: Sampradayikta Virodhi Committee, 1975, pp. 229-30).

For the Hindu nationalists an effective way of enlarging their audience after 1947 was by recourse to a strategy of ethno-religious mobilisation conceived in terms of an instrumentalist approach. Paul Brass defines the latter as 'a perspective that emphasizes the uses to which cultural symbols are put by élites seeking instrumental advantage for themselves or the group they claim to represent.'[1] Brass probably overstates the impact of the political organisations headed by these élites when he writes that: 'They shape group consciousness by manipulating symbols of group identity to achieve power for their group.'[2] The formation of Hindu nationalist identity is more easily understood as an ideological construct originating in the socio-religious reform movement of the nineteenth century. In this context the alternative approach suggested by Sudhir Kakar in his criticism of Brass's instrumentalism is highly relevant. According to Kakar, ethnic identity 'is evoked more, and differently, by shared cultural symbols and history – heavily mythological – which is shaped by the group's hopes and fears and distorted by its ambitions and ideals.'[3] This psychological analysis recalls the strategy of stigmatisation and emulation through which, we argue, Hindu nationalist ideology was formed in reaction to what were

[1] P. Brass, *Ethnicity and nationalism –Theory and comparison*, New Delhi: Sage, 1991, p. 102.

[2] P. Brass, *Language, religion and politics in North India*, Cambridge University Press, 1974, p. 45.

[3] S. Kakar, 'Reflections on religious identity', *Seminar*, no. 402 (Feb. 1993), p. 54. However, the characterisation of this approach as being 'primordialist' is difficult to accept since it implies a profound reinterpretation of the original identity.

perceived as 'threatening Others'. However, as Kakar himself suggests, both approaches are complementary. The instrumental use of symbols which have been reinterpreted and given significance by means of ideology flows logically from the process of constructing a nationalist identity. Mass mobilisation through the manipulation of symbols of identity reinterpreted to varying degrees is indeed the easiest means of communicating a new identity to those whom the ideologues are trying to represent.

One remaining problem concerns the 'mobilised masses'. Those authors employing such an instrumentalist approach generally consider them to be more or less passive, merely responding to stimuli sent from above, an attitude strongly criticised in recent years by the 'subaltern studies' school of historians. We shall return to this problem in chapter 12 where the success of the strategy of ethno-religious mobilisation in the late 1980s and early 1990s will be analysed. Till then, we shall concern ourselves only with the difficulties encountered by the Hindu nationalist movement in *implementing* an instrumentalist strategy.

The political situation in India after 15 August 1947 was *a priori* favourable to Hindu nationalism. Hindus formed an even larger proportion of the population in independent India than in British India, while the establishment of Pakistan had provided a more tangible focus for anti-Muslim feeling than the Muslim League of pre-independence politics. However, independent India did not prove conducive to Hindu nationalist propaganda since secularism emerged as one of the pillars of the state. That it did was due in large part to Jawaharlal Nehru, its main advocate. After Partition he found himself at odds, not only with the Hindu nationalists, but also with those Hindu traditionalists in his own party who accepted the primacy of Hindu values and were prepared to join with Hindu nationalists in campaigns of ethno-religious mobilisation. By the early 1950s, however, secularism had emerged as a legitimate norm of the Indian political system and organisations identified with Hindu nationalism were effectively marginalised; the Hindu Mahasabha could only obtain support in remote areas such as Madhya Bharat in central India.

The political context after 1947

The circumstances of Partition heightened the receptivity of the Hindu population to Hindu nationalist appeals in those areas which had received refugees – some 7 million in all – who had been dispossessed and witnessed appalling atrocities. Thus in Delhi on 7 December 1947, 50,000 people attended a meeting at which the Maharajah of Alwar, businessmen close to the Hindu Mahasabha, such as J.K. Birla and Gokul Chand Narang, and above all Golwalkar were present; Golwalkar praised his *swayamsevaks* for their work in the service of 'Hindutva' before criticis-

ing the government for the weakness it had shown in favouring Muslims.[4]
On 27 January 1948 a comparable number of Hindus in Delhi took part
in a meeting called by the Hindu Mahasabha leader Vishnu Ganashyam
Deshpande in condemnation of Gandhi, who he denounced as having been
responsible for the country's Partition.[5]

The moment seemed ripe to represent the Hindu nationalists as guardians of the interests of their community, which after all accounted for
84.98% of the Indian population in 1951 while Muslims now numbered
only one-tenth of the total. It was a strategy adopted by the Hindu
Mahasabha. As early as 9 August 1947 the party had exploited the
situation by proposing 'a programme for the Hindu nation' at a meeting
in Delhi presided over by V.D. Savarkar and largely organised by Narayan
Bhaskar Khare (chief minister of the princely state of Alwar).[6] However,
the wider political context was to prevent the Hindu Mahasabha from
carrying on with this strategy.

The political context was made up of two interacting elements. One
was the structure of the political arena, which was dominated by the
Congress, still benefiting from the prestige which it had acquired as a
movement of national liberation. The other was the public acceptance of
'normative rules' governing political competition. In F.G. Bailey's definition these rules 'express ultimate and publicly acceptable values':[7]

Normative rules do not prescribe a particular kind of action, but rather set broad
limits to possible action. [...]

They are used to judge particular actions ethically right or wrong; and within a
particular political structure they can be used to justify *publicly* a course of
conduct.[8]

A similar concept was developed by Pierre Bourdieu through the
notion of the 'legitimate problematic of politics',[9] which refers to what
the political class deems suitable for discussion in the political arena. In
the political context of post-independence India the dominant position of
the Congress and the nature of the norms supported by this party gradually
combined to marginalise the arguments of the Hindu nationalists.

---

[4]   *Report of the Commission of inquiry into the conspiracy to murder Mahatma Gandhi*,
op. cit., part II, p. 66.

[5]   Ibid., p. 57; and Hindu Mahasabha Papers NMML (section of the mss.), C-160.

[6]   N.B. Khare Papers, NAI, File no. 164.

[7]   F.G. Bailey, *Stratagems and spoils: A social anthropology of politics*, Oxford:
Blackwell, 1969, p. 4.

[8]   Ibid., p. 5.

[9]   P. Bourdieu, *La distinction. Critique sociale du jugement*, Paris: Minuit, 1979, p. 465
and 'La représentation politique – éléments pour une théorie du champ politique', *Actes
de la recherche en sciences sociales*, nos 36-7, Feb.-Mar. 1981, pp. 3-24.

From the 1930s onward, Hindu nationalism was declared by the leaders of Congress to be out of keeping with an Indian definition of nationality. This definition recognised as primary units of the nation either (in the case of Nehru) individuals in the abstract or (in the case of Gandhi) religious communities on a basis of equality. As a collection of individuals or of communities, the nation could not in any case be constructed as a hierarchy dominated by the Hindus – which was the ideal of the Hindu nationalists, who wanted to see the minorities assimilated into Hindu culture.[10] Furthermore, the Congress party promoted a definition of Indian nationality that was based on a composite notion of culture, as evident in the writings of Nehru, for whom the secular genius of India rested in its capacity to assimilate exogenous elements.

This led him to say that Indians were 'an odd mixture of many races',[11] a proposition the Hindu nationalists could certainly not accept. For someone like Nehru, the Hindu Mahasabha and the RSS embodied a Hindu *communalism*[12] which undermined Indian national unity. Clearly Nehru's nationalism embodied the territorial and universalist version of nationalism whereas Hindu nationalism was a variant of ethnic nationalism.

However, the Congress contained several variations of nationalism and that proposed by the party's Hindu traditionalists, who also considered that Hindu values and customs should be fostered, resembled Hindu nationalism in certain respects. This overlap seemed likely to work in favour of the Hindu nationalists in the context of post-Partition India.

Nehru's secularist struggle

Congressmen described by Bruce Graham as 'Hindu traditionalists'[13] were noted for their attachment to Hindu culture and hence became involved with associations to defend the cow and promote Hindi and Ayurvedic medicine. Hindu traditionalists differ from Hindu nationalists in that the former rarely have the ideological commitment of the latter, who are more xenophobic in outlook. While Hindu nationalism is built around opposition to the Other, whether Muslim or Christian, Hindu traditionalism is manifested simply by the promotion of culture, together

---

[10] This typology is presented in an elaborate manner in Pandey's *The construction of communalism in North India*, op. cit., p. 261.

[11] J. Nehru, *The discovery of India*, Delhi: Oxford University Press, 1989 (1946), p. 55.

[12] Before independence, Nehru used the term 'Hindu nationalism' (ibid. p. 273) even though he considered that it was not 'nationalism in the modern sense of the word' (J. Nehru, *Glimpses of world history*, Delhi: Oxford University Press, 1989 (1934-5) p. 720), but after 1947 Hindu communalism became the standard expression.

[13] B. Graham, 'The Congress and Hindu nationalism' in D.A. Low (ed.), *The Indian National Congress*, Delhi: Oxford University Press, 1988, p. 174.

with the interests of the community. In fact, initiators of the Hindu traditionalist current of thought, such as Madan Mohan Malaviya and Lajpat Rai supported the idea of the Indian nation but believed that the construction of such a nation necessitated the strengthening of the majority community.[14]

After Independence some of the traditionalists carried out projects which were highly regarded by the Hindu nationalists. One such example was the reconstruction of the temple of Somnath in Gujarat, which had been partly destroyed by the army of Mahmud of Ghazni in the eleventh century. Somnath was in the princely state of Junagadh whose Nawab announced the state's accession to Pakistan in 1947. Sardar Patel, who was both Vice premier and Home Minister, displayed his Hindu traditionalist credentials when he came to Junagadh on November 12, 1947 to direct the occupation of the state by the Indian army and, at the same time, announced that the temple would be rebuilt.[15] 'The restoration of the idols would be a point of honour and sentiment with the Hindu public,'[16] he added. The decision to proceed with this project was promoted by Kanaiyalal Maneklal Munshi, the Union Minister of Supply, who was from Gujarat and whose Hindu traditionalism had given him common ground with many of the Hindu nationalists.

Munshi had manifested his respect for traditional values when in 1938 he established the Bharatiya Vidya Bhavan (Institute for Indian Culture) in Bombay in order to promote 'the reintegration of the Indian culture in the light of modern knowledge and to suit our present day needs and the resuscitation of its fundamental value in their pristine vigour'.[17] This ideological inclination led him to eulogise the *varna*

---

[14] In 1909 Lajpat Rai justified the formation of the Punjab Hindu Sabha in this perspective: 'In my opinion it should be the business of a Hindu Congress or Conference to support and take so far as possible such steps which might conduct to their unity and strength as a religious nationality, as for instance, the language question, the question of character, the advisibility of having common text-books, the teaching of Sanskrit language and literature all over India, the taking of steps which might lead to the protection of Hindu orphans from the bands of proselytising agencies of other denominations [...] In the present struggle between Indian communities, I will be a Hindu first and an Indian afterwards, but outside India, or even in India against non-Indians I am and shall ever be an Indian first and a Hindu afterwards' (cited in G.V. Ketkar, 'The All India Hindu Mahasabha', op. cit., p. 277).

[15] *Hindustan Times*, 15 Nov. 1947, p. 6.

[16] Cited in P. van der Veer, 'Ayodhya and Somnath: eternal shrines, contested histories', *Social Research*, 59 (1), Spring 1992, p. 91. The ruins of the old temple were pulled down in October 1950 and in May 1951 Rajendra Prasad, the President of the Republic of India, performed the installation ceremony despite the opposition of Nehru (S. Gopal, *Jawaharlal Nehru – a biography*, vol. 2, London: Cape, 1979, p. 155).

[17] K.M. Munshi's preface to C. Rajagopalachari's translation of *Ramayana*, Bombay: Bharatiya Vidya Bhavan, 1957, p. 5. In the same book Munshi describes the *Ramayana*

system and manifest anti-Muslim attitudes.[18] He had resigned from the Congress in 1941 because he considered that the party had not shown sufficient determination in opposing the idea of creating a separate state of Pakistan. His subsequent campaign to uphold the principle of 'Akhand Hindustan' (undivided India) had won favour with the Hindu nationalists and in 1942 he had been invited to speak to the Working Committee of the Hindu Mahasabha.[19] Having rejoined the Congress in 1946, he was elected as one of its representatives on the Constituent Assembly where, as a member of the expert committee appointed to prepare the draft constitution, he proposed the idea of making Hindi the national language of India.[20]

Munshi was closely associated with the restoration of the temple of Somnath, which began in late 1947. The government decided to provide the funds for this purpose but on Gandhi's suggestion it agreed that the project should be financed by public subscription. The reconstruction project was supervised by an advisory committee under the chairmanship of Munshi,[21] who had visited the site of the Somnath temple in 1922 and had written a novel, *Jaya Somnath*, fifteen years later in praise of its historical importance.[22] In November 1947 Munshi was still celebrating the memory of those Hindus who had resisted Mahmud of Ghazni.[23]

During the autumn of 1947, while Patel was announcing the plans to restore the temple at Somnath, Nehru on several occasions appealed to Hindu refugees from the territories now inside Pakistan not to help themselves to the property left behind by Muslims fleeing in the other direction.[24] He also used the opportunity to propound the benefits of

---

and the *Mahabharata* as the 'collective unconscious of India' (ibid., p. 6) and Rajagopalachari writes that these 'classics really embody our national character in all its aspects' (ibid., p. 8).

[18] In July 1950 he gave a highly revealing lecture on the 'Social foundations of Indian culture': 'We, who are blinded by an admiration of the social apparatus of the West, fail to realise that *chaturvarnya* was a marvellous social synthesis on a countrywide scale when the rest of the world was weltering in a tribal state.' He added that India's 'modern Renaissance' could be traced to the end of the 17th century when Shivaji rose against 'alien rule' (K.M. Munshi, *Our greatest need and other addresses*, Bombay: Bharatiya Vidya Bhavan, 1953, pp. 43-57).

[19] V.B. Kulkarni, *K.M. Munshi*, New Delhi: Govt. of India, 1983, p. 89, p. 94 and p. 100.

[20] He had already expressed this view in 1945 as president of the Hindi Sahitya Sammelan (K.M. Munshi, *Our greatest need and other addresses*, op. cit., pp. 164-75). See also his speech at the Conference of the All-India Rashtra Bhasha Prachar Sammelan in December 1951 in which he criticised the constitutional provisions regarding Hindi (ibid. pp. 176-81).

[21] V.B. Kulkarni, *K.M. Munshi*, op. cit., p. 216.

[22] P. van der Veer, 'Ayodhya and Somnath', op. cit., pp. 89-90.

[23] *Hindustan Times*, 21 Nov. 1947, p. 5.

[24] Ibid., 28 Sept. 1947.

'Socialist Democracy'[25] rather than the 'Hindu state' urged by the Hindu Mahasabha, and to reassure the Muslim minority who had remained in India.[26] This last measure was met by inertia on the part of Sardar Patel and another Hindu traditionalist leader in Congress, Rajendra Prasad.[27] Nehru was spurred into action against the Hindu nationalists when he heard of a stratagem of the RSS in Delhi which consisted in sending *swayamsevaks* masquerading as Congress workers to convince the Muslims encamped at the Red Fort in Delhi that they should migrate to Pakistan 'for their protection'.[28] In addition, the government of Uttar Pradesh became concerned by the fact that members of the RSS were in possession of firearms, and were using them not only for defensive purposes. For this reason several of the movement's activists and cadres were arrested.[29] In a speech at Lucknow on 6 January 1948, Patel called upon the Hindu Mahasabha to amalgamate with Congress on the grounds that its members could not pretend to be 'the only custodians of Hinduism'. He held out the same invitation to members of the RSS:

> In the Congress, those who are in power feel that by the virtue of authority they will be able to crush the RSS. You cannot crush an organisation by using the *danda* [stick]. The *danda* is meant for thieves and dacoits. They are patriots who love their country. Only their trend of thought is diverted. They are to be won over by congressmen, by love.[30]

This attitude was partly explained by the assistance the RSS gave the administration; in September 1947 the commander of the Delhi military region asked Golwalkar for help in maintaining public order.[31] Patel's expression of qualified sympathy also reflected the long-standing disposition of a number of Hindu traditionalists within the Congress.

Gandhi was assassinated on 31 January 1948 by Nathuram Godse, a former *swayamsevak* who had joined the Hindu Mahasabha out of fascination with the personality of Savarkar and because he disapproved of

---

[25] Ibid., 7 Oct. 1947, and *The Hindu*, 1 Nov. 1947.

[26] *National Herald*, 20 Oct. 1947.

[27] S. Gopal, *Jawaharlal Nehru*, vol. 2, op. cit., pp. 15-17. Rajendra Prasad had been Chairman of the Reception Committee of the Hindu Mahasabha at the time of the Gaya session (1923) which marked the resurgence of the organisation. He attended other sessions in the 1920s (R.Prasad, *Autobiography*, New Delhi: National Book Trust, 1994 (1957), p. 182 and p. 232).

[28] Interview with M.C. Sharma, Oral History transcript (Hindi), op. cit., p. 157.

[29] *Hindustan Times*, 1 and 13 Jan., 1948.

[30] *Hindustan Standard*, 8 Jan. 1948, pp. 1 and 8. After this speech, Muslims complained to Gandhi about the attitude of Patel, who replied that he was 'a friend of the Muslims', but that their community had to change its mentality and 'forget the lesson which has been taught to them of the two- nation theory' (*Hindustan Times*, 17 Jan. 1948).

[31] W. Andersen and S. Damle, *The brotherhood in saffron*, op. cit., p. 49.

the RSS's inactivity on the political front. The plot had involved only a small group of Maharashtrian 'Savarkarites' who were exasperated by the attitude of Gandhi.[32] The latter had embarked on a fast to the death to force the new Indian government to pay 55 million rupees to Pakistan as compensation for losses incurred at Partition. The success of this moral pressure, to which the government succumbed on 18 January, was the immediate reason for which he was murdered. The event set off an enormous wave of popular revulsion. There were lynchings of prominent Hindu nationalists and, in Maharashtra, of Brahmins more or less at random because of their over-representation in the Hindu nationalist movement in the state.[33]

In the months following Gandhi's murder, Nehru showed his determination to deal firmly with the Hindu nationalists. This stemmed from his conviction that the Mahatma's killing was only the first stage in a 'fairly widespread' conspiracy[34] to seizè power, of which the prime mover was the RSS. Nehru suggested to Patel that he display more vigour in suppressing the movement.[35] Patel assured him that a wing of the Hindu Mahasabha had been responsible for the whole operation, and that the RSS as such was not implicated in the murder,[36] but Nehru was still expressing anxiety about the 'recrudescence of the RSS' in May 1948.[37]

That Nehru sensed there was a plot resulted from his reading of the Hindu nationalist phenomenon in terms of 'fascism'; it also explains the vigilance he had shown towards the RSS since he became Prime Minister. In December 1947 he wrote to the heads of the provincial governments:

We have a great deal of evidence to show that the RSS is an organisation which is in the nature of a private army and which is definitely proceeding on the strictest Nazi lines, even following the technique of organisation. [...] I have some knowledge of the way the Nazi movement developed in Germany. It attracted by its superficial trappings and strict discipline considerable numbers of lower middle class young men and women who are normally not too intelligent and for whom life appears to offer little to attract them.[38]

The strength of the RSS alarmed the authorities even more after Gandhi's

---

[32] Interview with Gopal Godse, brother of Nathuram Godse and a conspirator in the plot, 10 Nov. 1990, New Delhi.

[33] *Hitavada*, 4 Feb. 1948, p. 1; and D.P. Mishra, *Living an era*, vol. 2, Delhi: Vikas, 1978, pp. 57-8.

[34] J. Nehru, *Letters to Chief Ministers 1947-1964*, vol. 1 (G. Parthasarathi, ed.), Delhi: Oxford University Press, 1985, pp. 56-7 (letter of 5 Feb. 1948).

[35] V.D. Shankar (ed.), *Sardar Patel's select correspondence, 1945-1950*, Ahmedabad: Navajivan Publishing House, 1976, p. 282 (letter of 26 Feb. 1948).

[36] Ibid., p. 283 (letter of 27 Feb. 1948).

[37] Ibid., p. 268 (letter of 2 May 1948).

[38] J. Nehru, *Letters to Chief Ministers*, vol. 1, op. cit., pp. 33-4 (letter òf 7 Dec. 1947).

murder, when in the wave of repression carried out against it caches of arms and an unexpectedly large membership were revealed. Press reports pointed out that in Central Provinces and Berar, the movement's birthplace, there were 579 *shakhas*.[39] Furthermore, troops stationed in the region admitted to illicit links with the movement, which had always attracted soldiers into its ranks.

In the course of the repression, some 20,000 *swayamsevaks*[40] were arrested and the RSS was banned. The Hindu Mahasabha, however, was not subjected to this treatment. When Golwalkar was released in August 1948, on condition that he resided at Nagpur, he set about regaining his movement's legal right to exist. He wrote to Nehru, saying that the RSS, as a structure for guiding the young, was his best ally against Communism, which was then in full swing on the very borders of India.[41] Nehru replied that the government had proof that RSS activities were 'anti-national' by virtue of being communalist, and that the matter was the responsiblity of the Home Minister.

Golwalkar then asked Sardar Patel to lift the ban on the RSS and offered the movement's services in exchange. In his eyes, Congress, 'which is capable of doing good [to India] in the political field', and the RSS, 'which had achieved success in the cultural field by creating in the population a spirit of patriotism, fraternity and altruism which is unprecedented',[42] were destined to cooperate with each another. Patel had already proposed that RSS members should 'carry on their patriotic endeavour only by joining the Congress and not by keeping separate and by opposing'.[43] However the movement was loathe to lose its identity.[44] Patel then demanded, as an absolute pre-condition, that it adopt a written constitution. To the RSS this would have meant abandoning the one characteristic from which so much of its strength was derived – that of a network of activists capable of spreading more or less informally to the point where it could penetrate the whole of society. Acquiring a

---

[39] *Hitavada*, 11 Feb. 1948, p. 6.

[40] D.P. Mishra, who was then Home Minister in the Central Provinces and Berar, reveals that 16,421 arrests were made in five days, two-thirds of them in the Central Provinces and Berar (*Living an era*, vol. 2, op. cit., p. 61).

[41] *Justice on trial: A collection of the historic letters between Sri Guruji and the government (1948-1949)*, Mangalore: Prakashan Vibhag, 1969 (1958), p. 8 (letter of 24 Sept. 1948).

[42] Ibid., p. 33 (letter of 5 Nov. 1948).

[43] Ibid., p. 28 (letter of 11 Sept. 1948). Fifteen days later Patel expressed a somewhat different wish to Golwalkar:'... my only suggestion to you is that the Sangh should be brought to adopt fresh lines of technique and policy. That new techniques and policy can be only according to the rules of the Congress' (ibid., p. 29, letter from Patel to Golwalkar, 26 Sept. 1948).

[44] See Golwalkar's letter (ibid., pp. 80-2) and the press statement dated 3 Dec. 1948 by the Delhi Prant Organising Secretary (ibid., pp. 85-7).

constitution would mean constricting its ambitions and accepting an 'official vocation' in which it would be only a part of society instead of the whole.

Golwalkar responded to Sardar Patel's demands by launching a *satyagraha*̇ on 9 December 1948. This agitation made it plain that the movement was still a force to be reckoned with: more than 6,500 *swayamsevaks* were arrested in the Central Provinces and the total number of those detained reached 4,500 in the United Provinces by 17 December, while branches in Maharashtra, Bengal, Punjab and Gujarat participated fully.[45] In all 60,000 volunteers, of whom 50,000 were still in prison in July 1949, took part in the movement, the very scale of which prompted the government to resume negotiations with Golwalkar (who was now back in prison) and RSS leaders who were anxious to find a way out of the impasse.[46]

When the *satyagraha* was suspended at the end of January 1949, three RSS leaders – Eknath Ranade, P.B. Dani and Balasaheb Deoras – wrote a constitution for the organisation. This fell short of Sardar Patel's expectations in that it contained no mention of the holding of internal elections, the involvement of pre-adolescents in the movement (which henceforward would have to be authorised by their parents), the defining of the powers of the *sarsanghchalak* and allegiance to the Indian constitution as much as to the national flag or of the repudiation of violence.[47] Golwalkar tried to re-launch the agitation from his place of detention, but letters written with this objective, particularly to Deoras, were intercepted.[48] The text of the constitution was then amended, with the exceptions of the procedure for selecting the *sarsanghchalak* and the enrolment of pre-adolescents. Patel finally agreed to accept the constitution in June 1949 and the ban on the RSS was lifted on 11 July 1949.

Returning to Nagpur on 13 July, Golwalkar declared that he had not sacrificed any aspect of the RSS's identity;[49] in fact internal democracy within the movement, which had been written into the constitution, remained a dead letter. According to the relevant clause, local branches of the RSS were required to elect provincial assemblies whose members (including the *sanghchalaks* and *pracharaks* of the province) would nominate delegates to an Akhil Bharatiya Pratinidhi Sabha (ABPS – Delegate Assembly of All India). This body, which formed a *de facto* parliament of the RSS, elected the General Secretary, who was em-

---

[45]   Based on figures published on page 1 of *Hitavada* during December 1948.

[46]   W. Andersen and S. Damle, *The brotherhood in saffron*, op. cit., p. 53 and D.P. Mishra, *Living an era*, vol. 2, op. cit, p. 81.

[47]   See the letter from Patel's secretary to Golwalkar, 3 May 1949, in *Justice on trial*, op. cit., pp. 70-2.

[48]   D.P. Mishra, *Living an era*, vol. 2, op. cit., p. 77.

[49]   *Hitavada*, 14 July 1949, p. 1.

powered to nominate an executive committee of six to eleven members, the Kendriya Karyakari Mandal (KKM – Central Executive Committee). It was later renamed as the Akhil Bharatiya Karyakari Mandal (ABKM – All India Executive Committee) in 1972. In practice there would never be more candidates than posts to be filled, since the principle of a contested election was rejected as divisive. This concern with unity was also manifested in an absence of public debate among RSS members, and if discussion could take place behind closed doors, no public criticism or opposition was possible once a decision had been reached. It was admitted, in the constitution itself, that the backbone of the RSS, the *pracharaks*, should function independently of the system of elections but have a direct relationship with the General Secretary who, from his base in Nagpur, would nominate, tranfer or even suspend them in the first instance.[50]

The RSS's adoption in 1949 of a constitution which was not as restrictive as it might have been and the consecutive lifting of the ban were without doubt largely due to Sardar Patel's determination to achieve a result, not at any price (the negotiations lasted a whole year) but quickly enough. Even at the time of the *satyagraha* in December, he had repeated his invitation to *swayamsevaks* to join Congress. With the RSS barely legalised, he took advantage of Nehru's absence abroad to get a resolution passed by a Congress Working Committee (CWC) on 10 October 1949[51] authorising *swayamsevaks* to belong to the party. This vote and the preceding speeches – notably that by Purushottamdas Tandon, the Congress President in Uttar Pradesh – showed clearly that the Hindu traditionalist current of opinion enjoyed strong support.[52] Only six provincial committees of Congress demanded in November that the resolution should be reconsidered. In the event Nehru's campaign against the communalism of the RSS led to its speedy nullification.[53] However this was but the first episode in a trial of strength which would last throughout 1950. The champions of militant Hinduism returned to the offensive, in the purest expression of 'instrumentalist' logic, at the end of 1949.

The Hindu Mahasabha thus found itself in the front line of the battle. The party was not proscribed in 1948, thanks partly to the mediation of S.P. Mookerjee.[54] This scion of the Bengali *bhadralok* intelligentsia had joined the Hindu Mahasabha in 1937, and as its president in 1943-5 had

---

[50] The constitution of the RSS appears in an annex to K. Jayaprasad, *RSS and Hindu nationalism*, New Delhi: Deep and Deep, 1991, pp. 351-61.

[51] *Hitavada*, 11 Oct. 1949, p. 1.

[52] Ibid., 12 Oct. 1949, p. 1, and 1 Nov. 1949, p. 5.

[53] Ibid., 6 Nov. 1949, p. 3: 17 Nov. 1949, p. 1; and 18 Nov. 1949, p. 1.

[54] Letter from S.P. Mookerjee to Patel, 4 May 1948 in Durga Das (ed.), *Sardar Patel's correspondence, 1945-1950*, vol. 6, Ahmedabad: Navajivan, 1974, p. 63.

a more moderate programme to defend than had any of his predecessors in the 1930s and early 1940s. In August 1947 he became a member of the first government of independent India as a representative of militant Hindu opinion. At the same time he sought to liberalise his party,[55] especially after Gandhi's murder. At an extraordinary meeting of the Hindu Mahasabha on 6 February 1948, he recommended that it make a choice between two divergent paths: on the one hand, 'to break with its political activities and limit itself to social, cultural and religious problems', and, on the other, to 'abandon its communalist composition [...] and open its doors to every citizen, regardless of religion, who was ready to accept its economic and political programme'.[56] The Hindu Mahasabha Working Committee (HMWC) chose the first of these options on 15 February.[57] However the old guard, including Moonje, quickly protested against Mookerjee's 'alarmist advice'.[58] On 8 August the HMWC decided instead to renew its political activities, thus opting for the second alternative proposed by Mookerjee,[59] and on 6-7 November ratified it, without envisaging the admission of non-Hindus to the party. Consequently, on 23 November Mookerjee resigned from the party. Behaving increasingly like a small group or cell, the Hindu Mahasabha tried in 1949-50 to find the right conditions for renewal by means of an instrumentalist strategy of ethno-religious mobilisation. We shall first concentrate on the agitation launched in the town of Ayodhya, which is not only interesting in its own right but also foreshadows one of the most significant and ominous Hindu nationalist campaigns of the post-independence period.

The first attempt to exploit the issue of Ayodhya

To the Hindu Mahasabha, Ramjanmabhoomi (the birth site of Ram in Ayodhya, Uttar Pradesh) was undoubtedly a symbol which could be manipulated in such a way as to provoke a massive mobilisation of Hindus. A temple is said to have stood on this holy site and was supposedly demolished in 1528 at the order of Babur, the founder of the Mughal dynasty, in order to build there a mosque, the Babri Masjid. The conditional mode is necessary here, because there is no archaeological evidence

---

[55] B. Graham, 'Syama Prasad Mookerjee and the communalist alternative' in D.A. Low, *Soundings in modern South Asian history*, Berkeley: University of California Press, 1968, pp. 334-74.

[56] Quoted in B. Graham, *Hindu Nationalism and Indian politics*, Cambridge University Press, 1990, p. 13.

[57] *Hitavada*, 17 Feb. 1948, p.1.

[58] Hindu Mahasabha Papers, C-171 (letter from B.G. Khaparde to I. Prakash, April 1948).

[59] *Hitavada*, 10 Aug. 1948, p. 1.

to support the idea that a temple ever existed on the site,[60] or that this is the birthplace of Ram, or that present-day Ayodhya is the site of the capital city of the same name where Rama was born in the *Ramayana*.[61] It is entirely a question of belief.[62] In the late eighteenth century, it was commonly believed that Ram's birthplace was marked by a small platform close to the mosque; this was the object of worship by Hindu pilgrims.[63]

However, a conflict surrounding the site erupted in the 1850s. It seems that in 1853 Bairagis (Hindu ascetics) who claimed that the Babri Masjid was built on Ram's birthplace attacked the mosque.[64] In the mid-1850s a compromise was found whereby Hindus were to offer prayers at the *chabootra* (platform) outside the mosque. Hindu priests and devotees came to render homage to Ram on this site, which was regarded as his birthplace.[65] It was here in 1883 that a pandit demanded that a temple be built, the British authorities refusing to accede to the request because of the proximity of the Babri Masjid.[66]

This ploy was reactivated on the night of 22/23 December 1949, when someone[67] broke into the mosque and placed there idols of 'Ram Lalla [infant] and others'[68] – which the Hindu regarded as a 'miracle' and the

60   D. Mandal argues that the 'various structural remnants claimed to be the vestiges of 'pillar bases' are not contemporaneous,' which 'rules out the possibility of there having been one structure raised on a series of pillars' (*Ayodhya – Archaeology after demolition*, Hyderabad: Orient Longman, 1993, p. 39).

61   K.N. Pannikar, 'A historical overview' in S. Gopal (ed.), *Anatomy of a confrontation: The Babri Masjid – Ramjanmabhumi issue*, New Delhi: Viking, 1991, pp. 24ff.

62   Peter van der Veer, who did fieldwork in Ayodhya in the 1980s, emphasises how the pilgrims he met there had no interest in the 'true story' of Ayodhya while adhering fully to the legend (P. van der Veer, *Gods on earth: The management of religious experience and identity in a north pilgrimage center*, London: Athlone Press, 1988, p. 34.

63   This is based on the testimony of P. Tieffenthaler (a Jesuit missionary) in 1786 (G. Deleury, *Les Indes florissantes: Anthologie des voyageurs francais, 1750-1820*, Paris: Robert Laffont, 1991, p. 737).

64   S. Srivastava, 'How the British saw the issue' in S. Gopal (ed.), *Anatomy of a confrontation*, op. cit., pp. 38-57.

65   P. van der Veer, 'God must be liberated: A Hindu liberation movement in Ayodhya', *MAS*, 21 (2), 1987, p. 288.

66   S.K. Tripathi, One hundred years of litigation' in Asghar Ali Engineer (ed.), *Babri Masjid/Ramjanmabhoomi controversy*, New Delhi: Ajanta Publications, 1990, p. 17.

67   Anand Pathwardan recorded an interview with one of those who had been involved in the operation in his film 'In the name of God'. The interviewee mentions the name of K.K. Nair (see below) but the identity of the others who took part is not known. Recently, Ramachandra Paramahans, an influential religious figure in Ayodhya, claimed that he 'placed the *murthi* of Ramlala inside the structure in 1949' (*Frontline*, 9 Sept. 1994, p. 24).

68   This vague phrase is continuously used in the legal proceedings (see the suits cited in K. Prasad, *Report of the inquiry commission submitted to Citizens' Tribunal on Ayodhya* New Delhi: Secretariat, Citizens' Tribunal on Ayodhya, 1993, p. III).

Muslims as an act of sacrilege. There were several indications that the operation had been carefully planned in advance. Not long beforehand, Muslim tombs in the vicinity of the mosque had been desecrated, and the *Ramcharitmanas*, a very popular version of the *Ramayana*, had been recited uninterruptedly for nine days in front of the mosque. This recitation was organised by the Akhil Bharatiya Ramayana Mahasabha represented by Baba Raghava Das, Swami Karpatriji (see below) and the Hindu Mahasabha leader Digvijay Nath.[69] The local Congress secretary in Faizabad, who was opposed to the mobilisation, gave the following description of this operation:

Mass meetings were held. Loud-speakers fitted in tongas [horse-drawn carts] and cars kept on screaming day in and day out, calling upon the people to come for Darshan in the Mosque where yajna...was taking place, as the place of Ram's birth was being reclaimed. People began coming in thousands also from outside the town in cars sent by the organisers of the show. Inflammatory speeches were made and it was openly announced that the Babri Mosque had to be converted into a Sri Ram Temple. Mahatma Gandhi, Congress and congressmen were openly abused.[70]

On 23 December, the sub-inspector of police at Ayodhya estimated that 5-6,000 devotees who had been drawn to the town by news of the apparition of Ram were 'chanting bhajans [religious songs] and raising religious slogans'.[71] On the 26th, the District Magistrate, K.K. Nair, was ordered to remove the idols by the head of the United Provinces government, Govind Ballabh Pant,[72] after Nehru had asked·for a return to the *status quo ante*. Nair refused to carry out the order, ostensibly for fear of starting a riot, but probably also by virtue of his Hindu nationalist convictions. Together with his aide, Guru Datt Singh, he was removed from his post, but some time later Nair joined the Jana Sangh and in 1965 was elected MLA (Member of the Legislative Assembly) and in 1967 Member of Parliament for Bahraich on a Jana Sangh ticket.[73] His wife, Shakuntla Nair, seems to have been responsible for organising an *Akhand Kirtan* (uninterrupted recitation and chanting of songs) for which she recruited a *sadhu*, a ploy which made the removal of the idols from the mosque extremely difficult; hence they were ultimately left

---

[69] S. Srivastava, *The disputed mosque: A historical inquiry*, New Delhi: Vistaar Publications, 1991, p. 13.

[70] Quoted in A.G. Noorani, 'Legal aspects to the Issue' in S. Gopal (ed.), *Anatomy of a Confrontation*, op. cit., p. 68.

[71] Quoted in ibid., p. 71.

[72] Ibid., p. 72, and S. Gopal, 'Introduction' in ibid., p. 15.

[73] *Parliament of India: Fourth Lok Sabha who's who*, New Delhi: Lok Sabha Secretariat, 1967, p. 371.

there.[74] S. Nair was elected MP for Gonda in 1952 on a Hindu Mahasabha ticket, campaigning against the Hindu Code Bill (see below).[75]

It is highly likely that the idea of placing the images in the mosque originated with the Hindu nationalists.[76] Although this fact has not been definitively proved, the Arya Samaj and Hindu Mahasabha deliberately set out to exploit the issue in an instrumentalist manner. On 25 December, the Arya Samaj of Faizabad met to vote on a resolution demanding that

All religious institutions in India which had been damaged and converted into masjids should be restored to the Hindus for being used for the purposes for which they were originally meant.[77]

The case of the Hindu Mahasabha is even more instructive because the party clearly hoped to achieve political gain from the events at Ayodhya. It had been given a useful precedent shortly before, in 1948, at a by-election in the Faizabad constituency where the Congress had nominated a *sadhu* politician, Baba Raghava Das, as its candidate, and made every effort to have his socialist opponent, Acharya Narendra Deva, disqualified on the grounds of lack of religious fervour.[78]

This election had shown the Hindu Mahasabha the gains that could be achieved by using an instrumentalist strategy.[79] As soon as the 'discovery'

---

[74] D.R. Goyal, 'At peace with themselves' in A.A. Engineer (ed.), *Babri Masjid – Ramjanmabhoomi controversy*, op. cit., p. 127. No action was taken despite G.B. Pant's 'hope that a satisfactory solution may be found and the idols removed peacefully' (Letter from Pant to Nehru, 9 Feb. 1950 reproduced in *Sunday* (Delhi) 8 Nov. 1992).

[75] Hari Sharan Chhabra (ed.), *Opposition in the Parliament*, New Delhi: News Publishers, 1952, p. 63. S. Nair was again elected MP (for Kaiserganj) on the Jana Sangh ticket in 1967.

[76] It seems that K.K. Nair and Guru Datt Singh were members of the RSS and directly involved but without a precise plan in mind. (H. Gould, 'Religion and politics in a UP constituency' in D.E. Smith (ed.), *South Asian politics and religion*, Princeton University Press, 1966, p. 62).

[77] *The Leader*, 29 Dec. 1949, p. 6.

[78] Harold Gould described this campaign in the following terms: 'Pandit Pant went to Ayodhya and declared in his speeches that Narendra Deva didn't believe in the divinity of Lord Rama [...] as proved by the fact that he didn't wear the chhot, or tuft of hair at the back of head, displayed by all devout, genuine Hindus. Baba Raghava Das, for his part, moved among the faithful distributing tulsi leaves, another symbol of Hindu orthodoxy, to emphasise the spiritual difference between him and his Socialist-materialist adversary. Ayodhya voted overwhelmingly for the Baba over the Acharya and the elections went to Congress. The "Ayodhya strategy" had worked to perfection.' (H.A. Gould, *The Hindu caste system*, vol. 3, Delhi: Chanakya, 1990, pp. 76-7).

[79] At precisely the same moment the party's annual conference was being held in Calcutta, where it was decided to stage a political comeback. On 24 December 1949 its president N.B. Khare announced that the party's objective was the formation of a 'cultural state of Hindu Rashtra'. (*The Leader*, 25 Dec. 1949).

of the idols was made known, V.G. Deshpande, the party's General Secretary, visited Ayodhya twice. A circular was then issued calling on all activists in the Hindu Mahasabha to make 27 March 1950 the birthday festival of Ram (Ramnavami), 'Ram Janmabhoomi Day':

Attempts should be made to contact all the authorities of the temples in your town, particularly Shree Ram Temples. [...] All should be requested to conduct special prayer for retention of this shrine where Lord Ram was born, with the Hindus, and be asked to tell the congregation which assembles for celebrating the birth of Shree Ramchandra regarding the episode. The congregations in the temple also should be requested to pass similar resolutions.

It is hoped that this matter will be given urgent attention and every attempt will be made to see that the Day becomes a success.

Arrangements for the publicity also should be properly made and reports of the observance of the day should be sent to the Head-Officer here.[80]

In the wake of this agitation the party hoped to mobilise support around a theme which it knew to be particularly powerful in view of the veneration in which Ram was held throughout North India. This circular was followed by a personal note written by Deshpande, implying that the 'beautiful structure' of the temple was still standing, although the only remains attributable to it were 14 carved pillars in the fabric of the mosque, the origins of which are debated by archaeologists.[81]

Meanwhile these attempts to foment trouble in Ayodhya came to nothing in face of the determination of Nehru and Patel not to let the situation degenerate.[82] Several preventive arrests were made, including that of the secretary of the Hindu Sabha of Ayodhya, Gopal Singh Visharad.[83] The government's resolute response had prevented the Hindu

---

[80]   Hindu Mahasabha papers, C-187 (circular of 9 March 1950).

[81]   Certain historians are inclined to think that these pillars belonged not to a Vaishnavite but to a Shaivite temple (see the interview with Prof. Champakalakshmi in *Frontline*, 24 April, 1992, p. 100, and C.B. Asher, 'Architecture of Mughal India', *The New Cambridge History of India*, I-IV, Cambridge University Press, 1992, p. 30).

[82]   Letter from Patel to G.B. Pant, 9 Nov. 1950, in D. Das (ed.), *Sardar Patel's correspondence, 1945-1950*, vol. 9, op. cit., 1974, pp. 310-11.

[83]   In the suit G.S. Visharad filed on 16 January 1950 in the civil court of Faizabad, a declaration was sought that he be 'entitled to worship and visit without obstruction and disturbance Shri Bhagwan Ram Chandra and others' and that 'A perpetual injunction restraining the defendants from removing the idols' be issued. Understandably, the Hindu Mahasabha congratulated itself on this suit in a resolution at its December 1950 annual session (Hindu Mahasabha papers, C-186) since an interim injuction had been issued restraining anyone from removing the idols and from interfering with *puja*. Subsequently it was decided that the inner courtyard gates of the disputed structure be locked and that the keys remain with the Receiver of the property 'attached' in dispute, the chairman of Ayodhya Municipal Board, who had been appointed on 29 December 1949 by the Additional City Magistrate. However, a sentry opened the lock for the *bhog* (food offering to deities) and prayers. Pilgrims could now make their devotions only

nationalists from exploiting the affair for political ends.[84] The problem of the Hindus who had remained in the regions now forming Pakistan proved to be a more delicate issue in that it mobilised the Hindu traditionalists in Congress.

Hindu traditionalists and Hindu nationalists join together in defence of the Hindus of East Pakistan

In February 1950, East Bengal was the scene of anti-Hindu riots which recalled the horrors of Partition; between the 10th and the 20th of that month the death-toll in the violence was estimated at no less than 10,000.[85] The flow of refugees, which had been on a smaller scale in the East than in Punjab after Partition, recommenced and some 860,000 Hindus crossed the border in two months.[86] On 8 April Nehru concluded with his opposite number in Pakistan, Liaquat Ali Khan, the Delhi Pact whereby the two governments committed themselves to guarantee the security of their religious minorities and put a permanent end to migrations. This objective fell far short of being realised, however, since from 9 April to 25 July, nearly 1.3 million additional refugees entered West Bengal.[87]

The Hindu nationalists were not slow to exploit the situation. From March 1950 it preoccupied S.P. Mookerjee, himself a Bengali, who informed Nehru almost daily about Muslim persecution of Hindus in order that retaliatory measures might be taken.[88] The Delhi Pact, in his view, was nothing better than a sell-out. Mookerjee left the government on 12 April and launched a campaign for the defence of the refugees which culminated in July with an All India Refugee Conference. This drew some 15,000 visitors and 5,000 participants, including prominent Congressmen,[89] and slogans criticising Nehru were heard.[90] P. Tandon, who

---

through a lateral grille behind which a *pujari** was on duty. (K. Prasad, *Report of the inquiry commission*, op. cit., p. 111, and interview of Baba Lal Das – who became priest of the Ramjanmabhoomi temple in 1983 – in *Manushi*, no. 79, Nov.-Dec. 1993, p. 10).

[84] The *status quo ante*, however, was not restored as the Muslims demanded, and the interim injunction of the civil court legitimised, the worship of Ram in the mosque which was no longer accessible for *namaz*.

[85] *Times of India*, 9 Oct. 1950, p. 10.

[86] *Pioneer*, 22 May 1950, p. 1.

[87] *Statesman*, 2 Aug. 1950, p. 10.

[88] Mookerjee Papers NMML (mss. section), F. 159. In his correspondence with Patel, he did not exlude recourse to 'armed intervention' if an exchange of populations – which Patel came to favour – could not be organised (ibid., F. 162, letter of 26 March 1950).

[89] *Sunday News of India*, 30 July 1950, pp. 1 and 3.

[90] *Times of India*, 27 July 1950, p. 1.

presided over one of the seminars, spoke in the words of Mookerjee when he called on the government to levy a special tax to help the refugees.[91]

Tandon's invocation of certain Hindu nationalist tenets has a logical consistency with his earlier career; he was the man who, perhaps more than any other, personified the Hindu traditionalist current of opinion in Congress after 1947. He had begun his political career at Allahabad in the wake of M.M. Malaviya, through whom he entered the government of the princely state of Nabha in 1914. He had already held important positions in the Hindi Sahitya Sammelan (HSS – Conference of Hindi Literature), founded by Malaviya in 1910, which had as its objective the active promotion of Hindi. Gandhi had been a member of the HSS, and as such sought a definition of Hindi as a common language for both Hindus and Muslims, but he disagreed with the movement and resigned in 1945, leaving control in the hands of Tandon, who brought in traditionalists like Seth Govind Das.[92] Tandon was also involved with the Punjab National Bank (an Arya Samajist creation), of which he opened a branch in the United Provinces in 1925 before serving as the Bank's secretary from 1927-9.[93] From 1948 onwards Tandon presided over the United Provinces (later Uttar Pradesh) branch of Congress, in the name of an ideology which Nehru considered 'opposed to [the party's] basic principles'.[94] And indeed, from 1948 onwards, he spoke out increasingly against Indian Muslims preserving their own specific identity, as in June that year at Sultanpur:

The Musulmans must stop talking about a culture and a civilisation foreign to our country and genius. They should accept Indian culture. One culture and one language will pave the way for real unity. Urdu symbolises a foreign culture. Hindi alone can be the unifying factor for the diverse forces in the country.[95]

His endorsement of certain articles of belief expounded by Mookerjee exemplifies the fact that by 1950 the Hindu nationalist analysis had acquired a new legitimacy which enabled it to attract traditionalists in Congress.[96] Thus, as the result of what had taken place in East Bengal, the

---

[91] *Hitavada*, 30 July 1950, p. 1.

[92] J. Das Gupta, *Language conflict and national development*, Berkeley: University of California Press, 1970, pp. 112, 119, 122 and 219.

[93] *Statesman*, 3 Sept. 1950, p. 1; 16 Feb. 1955, p. viii; and 3 Sept. 1950, p. 1.

[94] S. Gopal, *Jawaharlal Nehru*, vol. 2, op. cit., p. 92.

[95] *National Herald*, 15 June 1948, p. 7. See also his speech at Kanpur (ibid., 2 June 1948, p. 3).

[96] Patel, who was very critical of Pakistan, was an inconsistent supporter of Nehru's moderate policies (S. Gopal, *Jawaharlal Nehru*, vol. 2, op. cit., pp. 86, 89 and 92), an attitude shared by Congress veterans and Hindu traditionalists such as C. Rajagopalachari (ibid., p. 94).

Hindu nationalists could now reasonably hope to exploit the situation arising from the trauma of Partition, having hitherto been prevented from doing so in the aftermath of Gandhi's murder.

In Parliament Mookerjee, by far the most effective orator on the opposition benches, harried Nehru on the refugee question[97] in his capacity as deputy for a constituency in Calcutta. Many Congressmen who had been brought round to Hindu nationalism by recent events ended up by agreeing with his views. The *Times of India* commented:

Congressmen belonging to this school of thought want to see the end of the policy of appeasement of Pakistan by Congress, which, they say, has continued even after partition of the country. They seem to support Dr Mookerjee and Mr Purushottamdas Tandon in their approach of these problems. They feel that it is not a question of supporting communalism or opposing secularism as the Prime Minister would like to interpret it, but one of showing grit and strength towards Pakistan who, they say, is determined to be anti-Hindu in her policies and aggressive towards India as a whole.[98]

Nehru, for his part, persevered in his attempt to resolve the question of the Hindu minorities in East Pakistan by negotiation:

That was the Gandhian approach to the communal problem. It meant an attempt not only to protect the minorities but to win them over and thus demonstrate the rightness of our policy.[99]

This evocation of the Gandhian heritage was not gratuitous. Nehru derived from it a charismatic legitimacy which would be useful to him in his confrontation with the Hindu traditionalists in Congress. The elections for the presidency of the party were thus a time of reckoning for Nehru in his fight against the Hindu traditionalists and led him to invoke Gandhi's name and to employ the latter's sometimes less than democratic methods.

Nehru and the Hindu traditionalists

The elections for the presidency of Congress were fought at the end of August 1950. As in October 1948, when Sardar Patel had given him his support,[100] Tandon stood on a Hindu traditionalist platform and did nothing to hide his differences with Nehru, whose fundamental views were represented instead by the other candidates, Shankarrao Deo and

---

[97]   E.g. see *Lok Sabha Debates* (1st series). Part II, vol. 14 (6-29 Aug. 1951), col. 355-66.

[98]   *Times of India*, 17 Aug. 1950, p. 6.

[99]   Letter from Nehru to Patel, 26 March 1950, in D. Das (ed.), *Sardar Patel's correspondence, 1945-1950*, vol. 10, op. cit., p. 12.

[100]   S.A. Kochanek, *The Congress party of India – The dynamics of one party democracy*, Princeton University Press, 1968, p. 21.

Kripalani (an aide of Gandhi who had already been president in 1946-7). Nehru, perturbed because Tandon had presided over the Delhi conference on aiding the Bengali refugees, tried to dissuade him from contesting these elections in a letter of 8 August 1950. He justified his advice by pointing out to Tandon that he had become 'to large numbers of people in India, some kind of a symbol of [the] communal and revivalist outlook'.[101] In a letter to Patel he added that because of this Tandon was 'widely supported by Hindu Mahasabha and RSS elements'.[102]

Sardar Patel backed Tandon throughout this controversy. For one thing, he did not believe him to be basically in disagreement with the ideals of Congress and his candidacy was, in his view, likely to rally Hindu nationalists and thus make them more moderate. According to Patel, this had been the effect of Tandon's participation in the refugee conference, where he had exercised 'a great restraining influence'.[103] In so far as Patel recognised positive qualities in the Hindu nationalists, he seems above all to have hoped or actually anticipated that their incorporation in Congress would soften their extremist tendencies and, once their ideology had become diluted, remove a current of militant opposition which could then be a source of strength for his own party or his faction within it.[104]

For the first time in its history, Congress had to choose between three candidates for a post which was usually uncontested. In the event the 3,000 delegates of the All India Congress Committee (AICC) gave Tandon a majority of 214 votes over Kripalani. At the session at Nasik in September, the new president put forward a programme tinged with Hindu militancy. Hindi, in his view, should take the place of English as India's official language in less than the fifteen-year period envisaged by the Constitution, notably to allow for an accommodation with the Dravidian states in the South.[105] While the Hindu Mahasabha was hesitant about setting Tandon apart from other Congressmen,[106] Mookerjee made no secret of his satisfaction,[107] and the RSS claimed with much self-congratulation that by choosing Tandon rather than Kripalani, the

---

[101] Cited in S. Gopal, *Jawaharlal Nehru*, vol. 2, op. cit., p. 93.

[102] Letter from Nehru to Patel, 27/28 Aug. 1950, in Durga Das (ed.), *Sardar Patel's correspondence, 1945-1950*, vol. 10, op. cit., p. 221.

[103] Letter from Patel to Nehru, 9 Aug. 1950, in ibid., p. 221.

[104] In 1949, this argument was developed in part by A.G. Kher, a minister of the United Provinces close to Patel (W. Andersen and S. Damle, *The brotherhood in saffron*, op. cit., p. 55).

[105] *Hitavada*, 21 Sept. 1950, p. 7, and *Times of India*, 21 Sept. 1950, p. 5.

[106] Hindu Mahasabha Papers, C-184 (Tej Bahadur Kaul, 'Tandon and Hindus').

[107] *Hitavada*, 4 Sept. 1950, p. 1.

Congressmen had shown 'their preference for Gandhism plus Patelism as compared to Gandhism plus Nehruism.'[108]

A *rapprochement* between Hindu nationalists and Hindu traditionalists seemed more likely now that the conditions in which Hindus were living in Pakistan were arousing public anger. But Nehru, who had at first refused even to take part in the Congress Working Committee, immediately denounced the penetration of Congress by communalist ideas. At the Nasik session, he threw all his weight against this development:

> If injustice is done to minorities in Pakistan, is it a valid reason to adopt a similar attitude here? If that is called democracy then I say, hell with such democracy. [...] True that people's passions had been aroused by events in Pakistan, but democratic principles could not be thrown to winds because of that. Congressmen should never compromise principles. [...] I am Prime Minister today because you have chosen me. If you want me as Prime Minister, you have to follow my lead unequivocally. If you do not want me to remain, you tell me so and I shall go. I will not hesitate, I will not argue. I will go out and fight independently for the ideals of Congress as I have done all these years.[109]

Nehru had inherited from Gandhi a moral ascendancy which stemmed as much from his privileged relationship with the Mahatma as from fidelity to his principles. Here he used this asset in the same way as Gandhi, who had not hesitated to violate a basic rule of democracy, that of numbers, by calling on his personal authority to bring erring majorities back to the right path.[110] It is precisely Gandhi's attitudes, according to F.G. Bailey, that perfectly illustrate the concept of 'normative rule';[111] Gandhi had effectively imposed a 'legitimate problematic of politics' based on an equal respect for all religions, and non-violence, and had thus disqualified 'communalists' and 'terrorists'.

By putting his continuance in office in the balance, Nehru give himself the means to ensure it. He regained the allegiance of many Congressmen at Nasik, and all the resolutions he proposed were passed. Tandon found himself thrown on to the defensive: he had to postpone the nomination of

---

[108] *Organiser*, 11 Sept. 1950, p. 3.

[109] *Statesman*, 23 Sept. 1950, p. 5.

[110] This attitude was seen, for example, in 1939 in the conflict between Gandhi and Subhas Chandra Bose, the new Congress president whose radicalism the Mahatma disapproved. Bose had no choice but to resign because a majority of Congressmen, among whom were some of his former sympathisers, could not bring themselves to dissociate themselves from Gandhi (L.A. Gordon, *Brothers against the Raj: a biography of Indian nationalists Sarat and Subhas Chandra Bose*, New York: Columbia University Press, 1990, pp. 376-92).

[111] 'In pre-Independence India Gandhi ruled that the roles of terrorist and communal (i.e. religious) agitator were unethical in the competition for nationhood' (F.G. Bailey, *Stratagems and spoils*, op. cit., p. 21).

the CWC, which had in the end shown itself to be 'composed largely of party bosses from the major states, many of whom opposed the social and economic policies of the Nehru government'. In the first rank of this 'old guard of the Congress, already in control at the state level',[112] were to be found Hindu traditionalists such as Seth Govind Das (Madhya Pradesh) and S.K. Patil (Bombay).[113] He also benefited from the support of regional 'bosses' like Dwarka Prasad Mishra (Madhya Pradesh), a close associate of Sardar Patel.

The death of Patel in December 1950 deprived Tandon of a vital ally. Consternation spread throughout the Hindu nationalist camp,[114] especially as Nehru continued waging a veritable war of attrition against Tandon. On 6 August 1951, Nehru resigned from the CWC in protest against its composition, Tandon having excluded from it Rafi Ahmad Kidwai, one of Nehru's close aides. But on 21 August Nehru obtained a vote of confidence from the Congress group in Parliament. Tandon then offered to resign in his favour to resolve the crisis. His resignation became effective on 8 September at a session of the AICC which was notable for a violently anti-communalist speech from Nehru – who was immediately elected as the new president of Congress and proceeded to appoint a CWC in his own image. Nehru had brought this off thanks to his ability to personify, and to impose, the secularist approach. Thus the *Times of India* during the summer of 1951 commented:

It is a strange phenomenon of present-day Congress politics that while the rank and file do not see eye to eye with the Prime Minister. [...] they idolize him and applaud his speeches even when he gets tough with them. [...] They went him at all costs because he alone comes nearest to the Father of the Nation [Gandhi] in his personal and political conduct, and has attained an international stature unique in the history of modern India.[115]

This description applied perfectly to a man like D.P. Mishra, who opposed Nehru to the extent of leaving Congress after the resignation of Tandon but who considered that 'as regards the premiership of free India we had always a vague idea that having been declared as his successor by the Mahatma, Nehru was bound to occupy that exalted office at the dawn of freedom'.[116] In electing Tandon, Mishra and those of like mind had not been challenging the supremacy of Nehru, whose legitimacy was of a higher order, but seeking to provide a balance: 'Democracy does not thrive without opposition and since there is no opposition party worth the name

[112] S.A. Kochanek, *The Congress party of India*, op. cit., pp. 21 and 29.
[113] For the complete list see *Congress bulletin*, Sept.-Oct. 1950 (no. 6.), p. 238.
[114] *Hitavada*, 16 Dec. 1950, p. 5.
[115] Cited in M. Weiner, *Party politics in India*, op. cit., pp. 77-8.
[116] D.P. Mishra, *Living an era*, vol. 2, op. cit., pp. 185-6.

in the country the Congress itself would have to be both the party in power and the opposition.'[117]

This capacity of the Congress to provide its own opposition in the field of secular policy was to constitute one of the constraints of the 'Congress system' to which Hindu nationalists would be subjected in states where 'bosses' such as Mishra preserved considerable influence until the 1960s (as we shall see in chapter 4). But at the beginning of the 1950s it was, of course, developments at the Centre which threw the plans of the proponents of Hindu politics into disarray. A convergence between the Hindu traditionalists and Hindu nationalists would have taken Congress in a different ideological direction. This possibility was given credence by the strategy of ethno-religious mobilisation of 1949-50 which was determined by a perceived Muslim or Pakistani threat. However, this strategy was checked by Nehru, who eventually succeeded in imposing a style of politics based on secularism.

Secularism as a legitimate norm of the Indian political system

Secularism does not mean in this context the separation of religion from the state but rather a benevolent neutrality towards all religions, which are treated equally. However, this universalist position exists alongside an effort to reduce the ascendancy of religion in society. The 1950 Constitution, strongly influenced by Nehru, did not recognise religious communities but only individuals, to whom it guaranteed in Article 25 'freedom of conscience and the right freely to profess, practice and propagate religion'.[118] This ideal concept of religion as a private matter implied a reduction in its sphere of influence through the impact of the state in its capacity as the agent of 'modernisation'. Nehru's principal achievement in this voluntarist perspective was undoubtedly the Hindu Code Bill.

The Hindu Code Bill was intended to provide a civil code in place of the body of Hindu personal law, which had been amended to only a limited extent by the British authorities. The bill was presented to the Constituent Assembly on 9 April 1948 but it caused a great deal of controversy and was subsequently broken down to three more specialised bills which came before the Lok Sabha in its 1952-7 term. The Hindu Marriage Bill outlawed polygamy and contained provisions dealing with inter-caste marriages and divorce procedures; the Hindu Adoption and Maintenance

---

[117] Ibid., p. 198.

[118] See the analysis of Article 25 of the Constitution in S. Mitra, 'The limit of accommodation: Nehru, religion and the State in India', *South Asia Research*, 9 (2), 1989, p. 113.

Bill had as its main thrust the adoption of girls, which till then had been little practised; the Hindu Succession Bill placed daughters on the same footing as widows and sons where the inheritance of family property was concerned.

These bills aroused strong opposition from the Hindu nationalists. In Parliament N.C. Chatterjee, the Hindu Mahasabha leader, and S.P. Mookerjee protested vehemently against what they took to be a threat to the stability and integrity of traditional forms of marriage and the family in Hindu society.[119] However, one of the most vehement critics of the government's proposals was Swami Karpatriji, a *sanyasi* who belonged to the Dandis, one of the orders founded by Shankara. He had won respect for his knowledge of Sanskrit texts, his asceticism (he had spent long periods in solitude in the Himalayas) and for his skill as an orator. It was a measure of his authority that he had been involved in the selection of some of the four major *Shankaracharyas*. In 1940 he had founded the Dharma Sangh (Association of Dharma), a cultural association for the defence of traditional Hinduism. In 1941 he founded a daily paper, *Sanmarg*. After 1948 he turned towards politics[120] and established the Ram Rajya Parishad (Council of the Kingdom of Ram) to serve as a political party. This body organised numerous demonstrations against the Hindu Code Bill; 15,000 people, including personalities such as the Princess of Dewas Senior (a former princely state in Central India), attended a week-long conference in Delhi at the beginning of 1949.[121]

The Hindu nationalists, for their part, were particularly exasperated that the civil law reform concerned only Hindus, whereas the Constitution enjoined (in article 44 of the Directive Principles) the State to give India a uniform Civil Code; hence Mookerjee's declaration that 'the government did not dare to touch the Muslim community'.[122] Nehru's secularism suffered here from a certain ambiguity or at least a lacuna, doubtless due to his concern to reassure the Muslims who had chosen to remain in India, Since he was prepared to condone the right of civil courts to apply Muslim personal law in cases affecting Muslims.[123] In his view, the majority

---

[119] R. Som, 'Jawaharlal Nehru and the Hindu code: A victory of symbol over substance?', *MAS*, 28(1) (1994), p. 174.

[120] B.D. Tripathi, *Sadhus of India*, op. cit., pp. 224-5, and Franco Fioccardi, 'Swami Karpatriji, il tradizionalismo del Vedanta nella cultura e nella società dell' India moderna', laurea thesis, Università degli Studi di Roma 'La Sapienza', Facoltà di Lettere (Studi Orientali), 1991 (see especially pp. 28 ff. on the Ram Rajya Parishad and pp. 198 ff. on Karpatriji's fight against the Hindu Code Bill).

[121] Hindu Mahasabha Papers, C-172 (letter from A. Lahiry to Bhopatkar, 10 March 1949).

[122] *Lok Sabha debates* (1st series) vol. XV, part II (17 Sept. 1951), cols 2705-223.

[123] His biographer explains that Nehru, 'in defiance of logic, refused to consider alterations in Muslim personal law on matters of monogamy and inheritance so as to place all Indian women on a par. There should be no impression of the Hindu majority forcing anything.

community had duties towards the minorities. As S. Gopal points out: 'He urged incessantly the importance of generous treatment of the minorities so that they would feel that they were Indians, and be completely at home.'[124] Such an attitude could be denounced as an anti-Hindu bias, while the RSS later described it as 'pseudo-secularism'. In the early 1950s, however, the campaigns undertaken in this direction succeeded in having the Hindu Code Bill amended and the parliamentary vote delayed but failed to mobilise widespread support or even win that of the traditionalists in Congress. Rajendra Prasad, who was elected President of the Republic in 1950, was distressed by a project whose 'new concepts and new ideas...are not only foreign to Hindu Law but may cause disruption in every family'.[125] He argued that the proposal for reform should first be included in the party's election manifesto and placed before the voters before any discussion in Parliament.[126]

Nehru had to make many concessions to the bill's critics, including Rajendra Prasad. Although the bills which were adopted by the new Parliament in the mid-1950s were thus less far-reaching in scope than Nehru had originally intended, they were a solid testimony to his ability to impose his views on others and to defy the Hindu traditionalists.[127] In this respect the composition of the new Parliament represented a political watershed in Indian politics.

Nehru's struggle with the Hindu traditionalists had been evident in his preparations for the first general elections of 1951-2, when he assumed that certain candidates would manipulate ethno-religious symbols and issues in an attempt to gain support. Congressmen were also likely to select candidates known for their militant Hindu tendencies especially at a time when these themes found a certain echo in the public mind because of the continuing tension between India and Pakistan. To obviate these risks, Nehru piloted into law a Representation of the People Act which specifically forbade the use of religious symbols or the invocation of the 'threat of divine displeasure' during an election campaign.[128] In Septem-

---

however justified, on the Muslim minority and changes would only be enacted when the Muslims wanted them' (S. Gopal, *Jawaharlal Nehru*, vol. 3, op. cit., p. 172).

[124] Ibid., vol. 2, p. 207.

[125] Quoted in D. Das (ed.), *Sardar Patel's correspondence, 1945-1950*, vol. 6, op. cit., p. 400.

[126] R. Som, 'Jawaharlal Nehru and the Hindu code', op. cit., p. 180.

[127] In his letter to Chief Ministers of 10 May 1956 he wrote that 'the passage of this legislation marks an epoch in India' (*Letters to Chief Ministers*, vol. 4, op. cit., p. 369).

[128] Quoted in E.W. Johnson, 'Comparative approaches to the study of the Hindu communal political parties in contemporary India: some limitations in the applicability of (1) systems analysis and (2) political modernization and development theory', unpubl. Ph. D. thesis, New York University, 1970, p. 81.

ber 1951 he addressed an outspoken circular to the Election Committee of the Congress:

The major struggle in India today, in the elections or elsewhere, is between the Congress, as representing a non-communal and secular State, and communal bodies which have an entirely different approach on this issue [...] Therefore, Congress candidates must be chosen with particular care so that they might represent the fully non-communal organisations should, therefore, be suspects from this point of view. This is important, as there has been a certain infiltration in the past of communal elements in the Congress.[129]

The overwhelming majority won by Congress in the 1951-2 general elections – seats out of 489 – was interpreted by Nehru as proof that his rejection of communalism was paying off politically and made the resort to Hindu slogans redundant.[130]

In November 1952 he authorised a circular which the AICC sent to party members requesting them not to associate themselves with an RSS campaign to protect the cow (see below). Nehru denounced the campaign as 'a political move without any attempt to do solid constructive work in this direction',[131] while in 1955 he opposed a bill with the same end in view tabled by Seth Govind Das.[132] In that year he proposed a Citizenship Act, which the militant Hindus opposed because of the universalist concept of the nation which it reflected.[133] Certain clauses had the effect of recognising the right to citizenship by registration on the part of an immigrant from Pakistan either of whose parents was born in undivided India, which was the usual case. Hindu traditionalist parliamentarians of the Congress party (such as Thakurdas Bhargava) and of the Hindu Mahasabha (such as N.C. Chatterjee) objected that this facility should be restricted to Hindu refugees, thus reflecting an ethnic concept of nationality. In an earlier debate on this subject in the Constituent Assembly, Nehru had rejected these views in the name of 'justice to the individual or the group',[134] and when the bill was put to the vote in 1955, the amendments proposed by the traditionalists were defeated.

---

[129]   N.L. Gupta (ed.), *Nehru on communalism*, op. cit., 223-4.

[130]   Ibid., p. 240.

[131]   *Hitavada*, 27 Nov. 1952, p. 5.

[132]   *Statesman* (Delhi), 3 Apr. 1955, p. 1. *The Citizenship Act, 1955 and Rules*, New Delhi: Government of India, 1988, p. 2.

[133]   The brother of G.C. Bhargava, the political heir of Lala Rajpat Rai in Punjab, Thakurdas Bhargava represented the same Hindu traditionalist school of thought within Congress as Seth Govind Das (S.P. Sen [ed.], *Dictionary of national biography*, vol. 1, Calcutta: Institute of Historical Studies, 1973, p. 175).

[134]   Quoted in A. Kashyap. *Communalism and constitution*, New Delhi: Lancer, 1988, p. 118. For the 1955 debate see pp. 127-8.

Thus, in the face of the Hindu traditionalist and nationalist champions of a closed ethnic concept of the nation, Nehru had succeeded by the mid-1950s in imposing a regime that subscribed to more secularist and universalist values, not only in terms of a 'legitimate problematic of politics' or of 'normative rules' but also on the grounds of legality reflected in the Constitution and the country's fundamental laws.

In consequence secularism became a legitimate norm of the Indian political system. The principles of secularism became norms because they were underpinned by the Fundamental Rights section of the Constitution of 1950, embodied in social legislation and defended by the courts. These norms were legitimised by the discourse of the Congress and the main opposition parties.

Nehru's policy of promoting secularism was accepted by the two main groups in the parliamentary opposition, namely the Socialists, who won 16.4 per cent of all votes cast in the 1952 general election and 10.4 per cent in 1957, and the CPI (Communist Party of India), which received 3.3 per cent of votes in 1952 and 8.9 per cent in 1957. The leaders of these parties and Nehru shared a determination to promote secularism, while the Socialist and Congress programmes overlapped at other points. Even before the Avadi resolution in January 1955, in which Congress declared itself in favour of a 'socialist model of society', Nehru had held discussions with the Socialist leaders (such as Jaya Prakash Narayan in 1953),[135] who considered it necessary to cooperate constructively with the ruling party with which it had some basic principles in common. Thus, during the 1950s a large segment of the political class had been won over to promoting secularism in a socialist perspective. This phenomenon gradually became a central part of the 'legitimate problematic of politics', or 'normative rules', and those political currents which challenged it automatically found themselves on the periphery of legitimate discourse. As P.C. Upadhyaya indicates:

In ideological terms, this secular consensus has been an important advance, particularly in the sphere of political language. It has become, to a considerable extent, an index of legitimacy in Indian politics. [...] On the other hand, communalism, like feudalism, has acquired a pejorative connotation, amounting almost to abuse.[136]

Thus the Hindu nationalists were largely isolated after 1950-1 and suffered from the way Nehru contested their legitimacy and repressed their propagandist activities.

---

[135] S. Gupta, 'Parties between the elections' in S.L. Poplai (ed.), *National politics and 1957 elections in India*, Delhi: Metropolitan Book Co., 1957, pp. 8ff.

[136] P.C. Upadhyaya, 'The politics of Indian secularism', *MAS*, 26 (4), 1992, p. 851.

The further marginalisation of the Hindu Mahasabha

The building of the secularist state by Nehru during the 1950s went in tandem with the Hindu Mahasabha's retreat into a few bastions. These developments were bound to occur together because the party was prevented from employing its instrumentalist strategy of ethno-religious mobilisation and became a victim of the vigilant anti-communalism of those in power. Between 1948 and 1952, repeated preventive arrests of its activists, especially V.G. Deshpande,[137] served to limit the impact of their propaganda. Subsequently, Nehru did not relax his vigilance, but his actions took different forms.

At the end of 1956, communal clashes followed the reprinting, with a foreword by K.M. Munshi, of Henry and Dana Lee Thomas's provocative book *Living Biographies of Religious Leaders of the World*, which aroused protests from Muslims because of its disrespectful portrayal of the Prophet. At Bareilly in Uttar Pradesh, a demonstration degenerated into a riot which cost six lives; and at Jabalpur, in Madhya Pradesh, Muslims, in an apparent act of retaliation, destroyed an image of Ganesh, provoking a riot which left five dead and forty-four wounded. Nehru reacted vigorously by ordering the imprisonment of those responsible for the provocation,[138] having the offending book withdrawn from sale, and announcing a new law which would prohibit the promotion of communalism through the printed word.[139] He was certain that the campaign and the violence accompanying it had been masterminded by the Hindu communalist parties 'to attract votes in the forthcoming [1957] elections'.[140]

In addition to the constraints which Nehru's anti-communalism imposed on any strategy of ethno-religious mobilisation, the Hindu Mahasabha was also the victim of its own refusal to open itself up in any way. Its reservations about accepting non-Hindu members had clearly contributed to the party's most able leader, Mookerjee, withdrawing his support. By taking refuge in extremist and conservative social attitudes it attenuated its base still further.

An extremist party

The Mahasabha's constitution, amended at a special session in Jaipur in 1951, assigned to the party the aim of 'establishing a Hindu

---

[137] *Hitavada*, 1 March 1950, p. 5; 19 March 1950, p. 7; 2 Apr. 1950, p 1; and *The Stateman*, 28 May 1952 in N.C. Chatterjee Papers NMML (mss. section), vol. IV.

[138] *Statesman*, 11 Sept. 1956, p. 1; and 23 Sept. 1956, p. 5, and J. Nehru, *Letters to Chief Ministers*, vol. 4, op. cit., p. 436.

[139] N.L. Gupta (ed.). *Nehru on communalism*, op. cit., p. 249.

[140] Ibid., p. 250.

state'.[141] 'Hindu cultural life [had to] receive official recognition'[142] – this involved state patronage for Hindu festivals and the teaching of Sanskrit in schools. Such proposals implied devolving more power to the state, an aim which had been a feature of the party's ideology before Independence.

The party did not spell out in plain language the constitutional provisions it envisaged for the Muslims for fear of provoking repressive measures against it. The most radical of these – enunciated by Mahant Digvijay Nath, the party's General Secretary, in 1950 – stated that 'if the Hindu Mahasabha attains power, it would deprive the Muslims of the right to vote for five to ten years, the time that it would take for them to convince the government that their interests and sentiments are pro-Indian.'[143] The president, N.B. Khare, declared that 'Muslims would be considered as second-class citizens': 'They should not be permitted any part in the political life of the country. That change should be made in the Constitution.'[144]

The most extreme of the Hindu Mahasabha's articles of faith concerned the annulment of Partition. The party called, in effect, and consistently, for the restoration of a united India – Akhand Bharat – if necessary by force. Here it confirmed the central place which the notion of territory occupies in its ideology.

Finally, the conservative socio-economic programme of the Hindu Mahasabha reflected its dependence on landowners and its organicist, Brahminical worldview. In 1949 N.B. Khare claimed that socialism was one of his party's planks.[145] However, as it turned out, this 'spiritual collectivism' was nothing other than a new version of the *varna* system.[146] This combination of extremist stands and conservative attitudes largely explain why the Hindu Mahasabha's only pockets of influence in the 1950s were located in ex-princely states, especially those of Central India.

---

[141] All India Hindu Mahasabha, *Constitution, aims and rules*, New Delhi, 1951, p. 1.

[142] All India Hindu Mahasabha, *Mahasabha and its ideals*, Calcutta: Bharat Publications, 1950, p. 25.

[143] *Statesman*, 13 June 1950, p. 7.

[144] Interview with N.B. Khare, Oral history transcript. NMML (accession no. 310), pp. 118-119.

[145] *Akhil Bharatiya Hindu Mahasabha, 28th session – Presidential address*, by N.B. Khare, Nagpur, 1949, p. 43.

[146] V.G. Deshpande, *Hindu socialism explained, being the presidential address delivered by him at the 45th annual session of the All India Hindu Mahasabha*, Delhi, 1960, p. 7 and *Hitavada*, 25 April 1961, p. 5.

The Hindu Mahasabha in Madhya Bharat

The socio-economic reforms announced by the Congress party on its accession to power naturally aroused anxieties among princes and land-owners. *Jagirdars, zamindars* and other *malguzars*, in organising their resistance, had already placed themselves within the confines of the Hindu Mahasabha, or resorted to it as a political mouthpiece. This phenomenon was especially evident in the state of Madhya Bharat, which came into being in May 1948 through the amalgamation of twenty-five former princely states. The most important of these had been ruled by princes of the Maratha dynasty, such as Gwalior – one of the largest Indian states, which accounted for 55 per cent of the land area of Madhya Bharat – Indore (21 per cent) and Dewas.[147] Abolition of the *jagirdari* and *zamindari* systems involved, respectively, 4,219 and 8,631 villages in Madhya Bharat.[148] The *jagirdars* were the quickest to organise themselves when their very considerable prerogatives began to be threatened, and particularly when authority over 5,146 *patwaris* (the instrument of the *jagirdars'* authority in the villages) was transferred to the government in 1948, along with their police powers.

Exasperated by the treatment inflicted on them by the Congressmen in power, some of these figures mobilised themselves behind the Hindu Mahasabha. The inspiration for this move was provided by Chandrojirao Angre.[149] He had been the second most powerful *jagirdar* in the state of Gwalior by virtue of his own landholdings,[150] and was the senior member of a clan which had always had a special relationship with the ruling dynasty of Gwalior, the Scindias. Having married a sister-in-law of Maharajah Jivaji Rao, he became his right-hand-man after Jivaji Rao's accession to the throne in 1936.[151] Thus from 1938 Angre was a powerful patron of the Hindu Mahasabha, and presided over its implantation in the state.[152] His son, Sambhajirao Angre, was the initiator of the local Hindu Sabha in Gwalior.[153]

[147] Other smaller principalities had been ruled by Rajputs (such as Ratlam, Narsingarh and Sitamau) or Muslims (Jaora).

[148] *Report on the general administration of Madhya Bharat, 1948-1949*, Gwalior: Government Central Press, 1952.

[149] Rajpramukh Papers, File no. 43, section 4 (1948-9), Bhopal State Archives (old secretariat).

[150] *Gwalior Today*, publicity department of the Government of Gwalior, 1938, pp. 31-2.

[151] V.R. Scindia with M. Malgonkar, *Princess: The autobiography of the Dowager Maharani of Gwalior*, New Delhi: Times Books International, 1985, p. 115.

[152] Savarkar, who went to Gwalior in 1938, seems to have been 'in good books with Sardar Angre' (Savarkar Papers, Reel no. 5, letter from D.B. Barve to Savarkar, 10 July 1940).

[153] Interviews with S. Angre, Shivpuri, 20 Nov. 1989 and with Laxmi Narayan Gupta, Bhopal, 22 Aug. 1992.

In 1951 C. Angre organised a conference of the All India Landowners and Jagirdars Association (of which he had been General Secretary since the 1930s), where it was decided to defend 'agricultural interests' at the elections.[154] But was the best policy to found a party with this specific purpose, or to unite with an existing body?[155] The question was settled by C. Angre in favour of the second option, which naturally militated in favour of an accord with the Hindu nationalist parties while cashing in on the influence of agricultural landholders to prevent these parties from being diverted from a right-leaning path. Angre made this clear in the *Hindu Outlook*, the newspaper of the Hindu Mahasabha, four months before the election:

We must shed this influence of foreign ideologies [which Congress's Marxist election manifesto betray] and base our aims and objects of the manifesto on our own Tradition, Culture, Religion and practicability. We must aim, not at a class conflict that would create chaos as this is not the time to do so but by ameliorating the interests of all the classes. [...] Confining myself to the class I belong to. [...] I can, with confidence assert that our class has a definite reckoning influence in the rural areas. They can only join hands with the Party whose aims and objects are more towards the sober Right than the frenzied Left.[156]

Angre was appointed 'zonal organiser' jointly with Digvijay Nath – *Mahant* of the Goraknath sect based at Gorakhpur (in Uttar Pradesh) – for Madhya Bharat, the state of Bhopal, Vindhya Pradesh and Rajasthan.[157] In this zone, by October 1951, he had already 'assembled about forty jagirdars and petty rulers to stand in the elections under the banner of the Hindu Mahasabha'.[158] The results of the 1951-2 elections revealed the influence which the Hindu Mahasabha had acquired in the region. The party returned eleven MLAs (Members of the Legislative Assembly, i.e. deputies in the assembly, or Vidhan Sabha, of Madhya Bharat) within the boundaries of the former state of Gwalior, and V.G. Deshpande achieved the remarkable feat of being elected to the Lok Sabha for two constituencies, Guna and Gwalior. He renounced the Gwalior seat in order to allow N.B. Khare, the party president who had been defeated at Nagpur, to win an easy

---

[154] *Hitavada*, 4 May 1951, p. 1.

[155] Hindu Mahasabha Papers, p. 128 (letter from C. Angre to V.G. Deshpande, 16 Apr. 1951).

[156] *Hindu Outlook*, 26 Aug. 1951, p. 5. In response to a questionnaire distributed in order to establish a 'Who's Who', C. Angre summed up his ideology as follows: 'One cannot strengthen the weak by weakening the strong, cannot help small men by crippling big men' (S.P. Singh Sud and A. Singh Sud (eds), *Indian elections and legislators*, Ludhiana: All India Publications, 1953, p. 171).

[157] *Hindu Outlook*, 7 Oct. 1951, p. 1.

[158] Hindu Mahasabha Papers, C-189 (letter from I. Prakash to Digvijay Nath, 4 Oct. 1951).

by-election. Furthermore, the Hindu Sabhaites defeated one minister and one state minister of the Madhya Bharat government and even the Chief Minister in a by-election at Mandsaur.[159]

The Hindu Mahasabha also owed its success to a group of Hindu nationalist activists from the urban middle class, in the vanguard of which stood S.D. Parchure, a medical doctor in Gwalior and an admirer of Savarkar (Parchure was suspected of having furnished Godse with the pistol that he used to kill Gandhi, but was finally acquitted).[160] The party's eleven MLAs included three barristers (Niranjan Verma, L.N. Gupta and P.L. Inamdar – Parchure's defending counsel), one medical doctor, one businessman and one optician (H.K. Vashya).[161] These Hindu Sabhaites had been elected almost *en masse* in Gwalior and the neighbouring districts – an area where they could not have succeeded without the assent of 'the palace'. Moreover some MLAs from the Hindu Mahasabha were themselves local notables (like Diwan Barjor Singh, an ex-*jagirdar* in Shivpuri), often related in some way to the Scindias.[162]

An illustration of the influence of militant and conservative Hindu groups in this area was the fact that the Ram Rajya Parishad won a seat in 1951 in the Vidhan Sabha of Madhya Bharat and came second in ten constituencies. Its greatest support was concentrated in the districts of Mandsaur, Shajapur and Dewas, where it was supported by the princess of the state of Dewas Senior – this being a reflection of the party's social standing throughout the region.

The support which the Hindu Mahasabha derived from the aristocracy of the former state of Gwalior deprived the Congress party at the same time of power in an important area of influence. As a result Nehru insisted that Vijaya Raje Scindia, the wife of Maharajah Jivaji Rao who had been Rajpramukh (Governor) of Madhya Bharat in 1948-51, should contest the

---

[159] S.R. Sharma, 'Madhya Bharat' in S.V. Kogekar and R.L. Park, *Reports on the Indian general elections, 1951-1952*, Bombay: Popular Books, 1956, pp. 195 and 203.

[160] *Report of commission of inquiry into conspiracy to murder Mahatma Gandhi*, part 1, op. cit., p. 265, and M. Malgonkar, *The men who killed Gandhi*, Delhi: Orient Paperbacks, 1981, p. 142.

[161] Interview with H.K. Vashya, 26 Nov. 1989, Gwalior. *Madhya Bharat Vidhan Sabha Sadasyon ka sankshipt parichay – 1952* Gwalior: Madhya Bharat Vidhan Sabha Sachivalay, [n.d.]; and P.L. Inamdar, *The story of the the Red Fort trial, 1948-49*, Bombay: Popular Prakashan, 1979, pp. 216-17.

[162] L.N. Gupta, an advocate who had been elected Director of Pichhore Cooperative Bank in 1940, admitted that he was helped by a couple of ex-*jagirdars* in his constituency (interview with L.N. Gupta). The Hindu Mahasabha was also well established in the (Muslim) former princely state of Bhopal, where it won an MLA seat and came second in seven of the other twenty-two constituencies; its leader obtained 36 per cent of the vote in the Lok Sabha election. (*Report on the first general elections in India, 1951-1952*, vol. II (statistical), New Delhi: Election Commission [n.d.]).

1957 elections on a Congress ticket.[163] Her entry on the electoral scene reduced the Hindu Mahasabha to seven assembly seats and only a single parliamentary one; V.G. Deshpande lost heavily against the Maharani. However, the Madhya Bharat region continued to be the stronghold of the Hindu Mahasabha, thanks to the support of the Angre clan. Sambhajirao Angre campaigned on behalf of Hindu Mahasabha candidates even though he officially worked for the Scindias.[164]

Outside this aristocratic pocket of influence in Central India, the Hindu Mahasabha suffered an overall electoral rout in the 1950s, which left it only three Lok Sabha seats in 1952 and two in 1957.

Although Partition appeared to have created favourable conditions for the expansion of Hindu nationalism, this ideology gradually lost its attraction in the 1950s. Such an outcome was largely due to Nehru's ability to limit the opportunities for Hindu nationalists to launch agitational campaigns aimed at manipulating sensitive issues, such as the status of the Ramjanmabhoomi or the situation of Hindus in East Pakistan. In both cases, he acted promptly to prevent groups from defying the law and taking matters into their own hands, while resisting pressure from Hindu traditionalists within Congress who sometimes advocated extreme measures. Furthermore, he succeeded in establishing the principles of secularism as legitimate norms of the Indian political system with the more or less explicit support of the opposition parties. Centres of resistance to the imposition of Nehru's views remained, however.

Our study of Indian politics after 1947 shows the extent to which the Hindu traditionalists within Congress constituted a brake on the development of secularism. While they remained within the Congress, they were inclined to see Hindu nationalists as opponents, but if organised as a separate group outside the Congress they might be persuaded to work with their former rivals.

A further portent for the future was the evident interest of Hindu nationalist organisations in using ethno-religious appeals to build up agitational movements. Yet their attempts to launch campaigns met with little response within a political regime in which the Congress was able to use its dominance to promote secularism. The Hindu Mahasabha was effectively prevented from using the strategy of ethno-religious mobilisation and it remained a political force only where it had the support of

---

[163] V.R. Scindia with M. Malgonkar, *Princess*, op. cit., pp. 172-3. Madhya Bharat had been absorbed into the post-1956 state of Madhya Pradesh by this stage.

[164] Interview with S. Angre, Shivpuri, 20 Nov. 1989.

conservative notables and princes, as in Madhya Bharat. The Jana Sangh, for its part, proved to be more robust and resilient.

The RSS-JS combination had no objection to the strategy of Hindu mobilisation. In late 1952, the RSS launched a petition with the aim of prohibiting cow slaughter. Hundreds of thousands of signatures were allegedly collected. These registers of names were loaded on bullock carts and presented to the Governor of Madhya Pradesh in Nagpur and to the representatives of the Union Government in New Delhi, where the procession of petitioners stretched for five kilometres .[165] This was clearly an attempt at ethno-religious mobilisation, although the priority for the RSS and the Jana Sangh in the 1950s lay in developing their network of activists rather than in mass mobilisation.

[165] *Hitavada*, 1, 3 and 9 Dec. 1952.

3

A SPECIFIC PARTY-BUILDING STRATEGY: THE JANA SANGH AND THE R.S.S. NETWORK

'Jana Sangh is a party with a difference... [It] is not a party but a movement. It springs from the craving of the nation to come into its own. It is the urge of the nation to assert and accomplish what it has been destined to.' (D. Upadhyaya in *Organiser*, Divali Special, 1964, p. 11)

Although they claimed to be apolitical, the RSS's leaders were driven to an interest in power by their advocacy of a Hindu Rashtra. Golwalkar may have thought that the government should accept an advisory and consultative role for the RSS on the model of the traditional relationship between temporal power and spiritual authority; he may also have regarded participation in party politics as the antithesis of the organisation's basic mission. But some *swayamsevaks* thought the RSS should be directly involved in party politics, and they therefore became associated with the Jana Sangh, a party initiated by S.P. Mookerjee.

The participation of some *swayamsevaks* in the work of the Jana Sangh and their subsequent takeover of the party was part of an elaborate division of labour within the total membership of the RSS. After Independence the RSS decided to build up a whole range of affiliated organisations within different sectors and institutions of Indian society as a means of infusing Hindu nationalist values into public life. To this end it formed a students' union and a trade union. The association of *swayamsevaks* with the Jana Sangh belonged to this context, and was therefore seen as an application in the sphere of party politics of the principle that the social and psychological reform of Hindu society was needed to provide the cultural basis for a Hindu Rashtra in every sector of national life.

With this in mind, RSS workers within the Jana Sangh felt that the new party should avoid the practice of winning elections by co-opting local notables. Their technique of party-building was essentially long term and relied on a network of disciplined and dedicated activists. This pattern is well illustrated by the *modus operandi* of those RSS organisers who were responsible for establishing the Jana Sangh in certain regions of Central India. The strategy which they employed was 'Sangathanist' in the sense that it relied on an integrated team of organisers (known as *sangathan mantris* – organising secretaries) and was designed to ensure that the party's support was a coherent constituency rather than an assemblage of individual followings belonging to particular notables.

The RSS and politics

Officially the RSS showed no interest in state power at the moment when India became independent. However the main objective of the RSS, the formation of the Hindu Rashtra, was eminently political and precluded the organisation from ignoring the sphere of the state after India won Independence. The only question, then, was what kind of rapport with politics the RSS was to establish. Certain of Golwalkar's statements after Independence virtually endowed the RSS with the role of a political counsellor by bringing the traditional connection between temporal power and spiritual authority into play:

The political rulers were never the standard-bearers of our society. They were never taken as the props of our national life. Saints and sages, who had risen above the mundane temptations of self and power and had dedicated themselves wholly for establishing a happy, virtuous and integrated state of society were its constant torch-bearers. They represented the *dharmasalta* [religious authority]. The king was only an ardent follower of that higher moral authority.[1]

Golwalkar was invoking from Hindu tradition the king's *guru* (*Raj guru*); and because of its promotion of a Sanskritised culture and respect for the values of renunciation, the chief of the RSS proposed for his organisation the traditional function of dharmic counsellor to the state power.[2] Expounding upon the mission of the RSS, Golwalkar wrote that:

We aspire to become the radiating centre of all the age- old cherished ideals of our society – just as the indescribable power which radiates through the sun. Then the political power which draws its life from that source of society, will have no other [goal] to reflect the same radiance.[3]

With this, one reaches the limit of Golwalkar's indifference to the state, since he visibly covets a role as counsellor to the prince. Thus, his apolitical orientation had already been amended by this opening up to the political domain, limited though it still was, when, at the end of the 1940s, it was actively questioned by the more 'activist' *swayamsevaks*.[4]

---

[1]   M.S. Golwalkar, *Bunch of thoughts*, op. cit., p. 93.

[2]   K.R. Malkani willingly attributes the function of *Raj guru* to the RSS and defines it as that of 'moral counsellor' (interview, 16 Nov. 1989, New Delhi).

[3]   . M.S. Golwalkar, *Bunch of thoughts*, op. cit., p. 103. See also his description of the articulation between the king and the *guru* (ibid., p. 100).

[4]   I borrow the term 'activist' from W. Andersen and S. Damle. In their typology of RSS

The birth of the Jana Sangh

The members of this 'activist' current were recruited from among the young *pracharaks* who had grown in maturity thanks to the experience of working relatively autonomously when the RSS hierarchy was affected by the ban and arrests of 1948-9; this had allowed them to take initiatives which had emancipated them from the control of Nagpur. Above all, the banning of the RSS had convinced them of the need to enter politics to defend their movement's right to exist, since no politician had stood up for their cause in Parliament or elsewhere. Shortly before becoming editor of the newspaper of the RSS, *Organiser*, Malkani wrote in it in December 1949:

Sangh must take part in politics not only to protect itself against the greedy designs of politicians but to stop the un-Bharatiya and anti-Bharatiya policies of the Government and to advance and expedite the cause of Bharatiya through state machinery side by side with official effort in the same direction. [...] Sangh must continue as it is, an 'ashram' for the national cultural education of the entire citizenry, but it must develop a political wing for the more effective and early achievement of its ideals.[5]

This endorsement of political action went against the RSS's traditional vocation of socio-psychological reform which its veterans (Golwalkar above all, but also P.B. Dani, E. Ranade and M. Muley) attributed to the movement. When the ban was lifted, Golwalkar looked to a compromise solution whereby the Congress would allow individual *swayamsevaks* to join the party.[6] But such a development in 1948-9 depended upon ratification of the position of Hindu traditionalists within the party, the expectation of which also determined S.P. Mookerjee's strategy.[7]

The death of Sardar Patel and Nehru's hardline attitude towards Tandon precipitated a rapprochement between the RSS 'activists' and Mookerjee, a move anticipated by the former – who were looking for a leader to form a new party – since 1949. Among their number were Vasant Rao Oke, the Delhi *pracharak*, and Balraj Madhok, who had gained political experience of a kind denied to most RSS members when, in November 1947, he had formed a politically-oriented Hindu movement in Jammu, the Praja Parishad (see below). Madhok had been expelled

---

members, the 'activists' are those 'who believed that the RSS should have a broader agenda' and the 'traditionalists' those 'who were wary of such moves outside the narrow character-building environment of the *shakha*' (W. Andersen and S. Damle, *The brotherhood in saffron*, op. cit., p. 108).

5   *Organiser*, 1 Dec. 1949, pp. 7-14.

6   W. Andersen and S. Damle, *The brotherhood in saffron*, op. cit., p. 124.

7   B. Graham, *Hindu nationalism*, op. cit., p. 26.

from the state of Jammu and Kashmir in 1948, and the fact that he settled in Delhi enabled him to meet Mookerjee regularly.[8]

The idea of a new party seems to have taken shape towards the end of 1949 when Mookerjee began to express open opposition to the 'pro-Pakistan' policy of Nehru in whose government he was still a minister. It was in any case necessary to obtain the approval – if not the outright support – of the controlling body of the RSS if the plan were to succeed. Mookerjee went to Nagpur several times between November 1949 and the spring of 1950,[9] and there met Golwalkar, who described the occasion some years later:

One of my old colleagues who had developed a liking for political work to a degree uncommon and undesirable for a Swayamsevak of the RSS, Sri Vasant Rao Oke, was in close contact with him for a long time and his association seems to have prompted Dr Mookerjee to seek my cooperation and help in the matter. [...] Naturally I had to warn him that the RSS could not be drawn into politics, that it could not play second fiddle to any political or other party since no organisation devoted to the wholesale regeneration of the real i.e. cultural life of the Nation could ever function successfully if it was tried to be used as a hand maid of political parties.[10]

Golwalkar, having made sure that Mookerjee was in full agreement with the ideals of the Hindu Rashtra, 'chose some of [his] colleagues, staunch and tried workers', to assist him. However the plan for a political party stalled, as much because it was hoped that the Congress would open its doors to Hindu nationalists as because of Golwalkar's reluctance to involve the RSS too closely in the affair. By the end of 1950, when Tandon was at loggerheads with Nehru, Mookerjee had gathered in Delhi a group consisting not only of *swayamsevaks* (V.R. Oke, B. Madhok, Bhai Mahavir), but also of Hindu traditionalist politicians such as M.C. Sharma (for his biography, see below, p. 122) and various Arya Samajists (Lala Yodh Raj, president of the Punjab National Bank,[11] his brother Balraj Bhalla, and Mahashe Krishnan, editor-in-chief of *Pratap*). This team, with the addition of Hans Raj Gupta and Dharmavir, met on 16 January 1951 to discuss the setting-up of a party in the Delhi region and in Punjab to prepare

---

[8]   Interview with B. Madhok, 10 Nov. 1990, New Delhi.

[9]   *Hitavada*, 6 Nov. 1949, p. 9. Mookerjee had already visited the previous *sarsanghchalak*, Hedgewar, asking him to help the Hindus of Bengal by developing the RSS there (K.R. Malkani, *RSS story*, op. cit., p. 31).

[10] *Organiser*, 25 June 1956, p. 5.

[11] The son of Hans Raj, one of the founders of DAV College in Lahore, Yodh Raj had become 'General Manager' of the bank in 1943 and then taken over control. After Partition, which had a highly detrimental effect on this well-established institution in West Punjab, he had engineered a rapid flotation of the stock (P. Tandon, *Banking century – a short history of banking in India and the pioneer: Punjab National Bank*, New Delhi: Penguin, 1989, ch. 16 and p. 338).

the constitution for a pan-Indian party.[12] The draft constitution of this All India People's Party (Bharatiya Jana Sangh)[13] was circulated to potential sympathisers.[14] It was accompanied by a 'note on the strength of the parties in opposition to the Congress' which contained the following passage:

The RSS has a strong volunteer organisation and a growing press under its management. It has a body of workers of startling merit. It is disinclined to contest the coming elections but its leader Guruji should be persuaded to lend the support of the organisation to the new party that may be formed to oppose the Congress in the coming elections.[15]

At Nagpur, the pressure from activists led some newspapers to suggest that the RSS might split into two factions: that of Golwalkar and the General Secretary, B.D. Dani, who had reservations about any political involvement,[16] and another, comprising the activists, who declared their readiness to put up candidates on an 'independent' ticket.[17]

Faced with the unresponsiveness of the RSS leaders, Mookerjee showed his determination by setting up a 'People's Party' in West Bengal on 23 April 1951. On 27 May, a meeting was held at Jullundur, at the instigation of Madhok,[18] to found a Jana Sangh which would represent Punjab and Delhi.

These developments undoubtedly spurred the leaders of the RSS into action, since the formation of a new Hindu nationalist party, attracting *swayamsevaks* but controlled by politicians, inevitably made them fear a loss of discipline in their ranks; the movement therefore had to enter the party on a massive scale in order to exert influence from the inside. This

---

[12] B. Madhok, *RSS and politics*, op. cit., p. 50, and B. Madhok, *Portrait of a martyr: Biography of Dr Shyam Prasad Mookerji*, Bombay: Jaico, 1969, p. 99. Mookerjee's attachment to the pan-Indian aspect of his project became unequivocal when he agitated for the amalgamation of the Bengali and Punjabi branches of the party (Mookerjee Papers, F-168. Letter from J.D. Mehta to Mookerjee, 27 June 1951).

[13] Ibid., 'Draft Constitution for Bharatiya Jan Sangh'. Although the word Hindu does not appear in the title of the party, the choice of 'Jana' to denote 'people' seems to be significant. According to Balraj Madhok, one of the party's founders, it was preferred to 'Lok' because of its ethnic connotations: 'We had discussed a lot whether our name should be Bharatiya Lok Sangh or Bharatiya Jana Sangh. We called it 'JAN' deliberately, because the word 'Jan' has a particular connotation. Only he can be called a 'Jan' of India, who looks upon Bharat his own Janani [mother, progenitrix] and who owns its past and owns its present' (B. Madhok, *What Jana Sangh stands for*, Ahmedabad: Ahmedabad Junior Chamber, 1966, p. 42).

[14] Such as the former mayor of Bombay with Hindu Sabhaite loyalties, Jamna Das Mehta (ibid., letter from J.D Mehta to Mookerjee, 27 June 1951).

[15] Mookerjee Papers, F-168, 'Draft Constitution for Bharatiya Jan Sangh'.

[16] W. Andersen and S. Damle, *The brotherhood in saffron*, op. cit., p. 127.

[17] *Hitavada*, 13 Feb. 1951, p. 6, and *The Hindu*, 8 Jan. 1951, p. 4.

[18] *Organiser*, 10 Sept. 1951, p. 14.

concern emerged during the summer, as the letters of Mookerjee and M.C. Sharma, awaiting a reply from Nagpur, make clear.[19] Once set in motion, the process gathered momentum. On 2 September, the Uttar Pradesh branch of the Jana Sangh was founded. Its president, Krishna Pal Singh, was a man of a similar type to Mookerjee or M.C. Sharma, representing the party's typical 'politician'. A member of the Provincial Assembly from 1926 to 1935, he belonged to the same tendency as M.M. Malaviya; at one time he was president of the state's Hindu Sabha, and later became prime minister of Datia state (Central India).[20] However, the secretary of the Jana Sangh in Uttar Pradesh was none other than D. Upadhyaya, who was well known as one of the leading *pracharaks* of the RSS. Nagpur thus assured itself of the means of controlling the Jana Sangh in the state. Most of the eleven regional branches which the Jana Sangh had acquired by the autumn of 1951 – Punjab, United Provinces, Bengal, Karnataka, Bihar, Rajasthan, PEPSU (Patiala and East Punjab State Union), Orissa, Madhya Bharat, Himachal Pradesh and Delhi – had such a dual leadership.[21]

On 21 October, the founding convention of the party in Delhi elected a 'working committee' which again showed the weight of the RSS: Mookerjee was its president, but Bhai Mahavir was named as General Secretary together with M.C. Sharma. Three of the ruling body of the party – Madhok, Upadhyaya and Sohni – were senior *swayamsevaks*.[22]

To sum up, the RSS had entered the political arena in response to political events and to pressure from 'activist' *swayamsevaks*, but with certain guarantees; in fact the movement gave itself the means to control the policy line of the Jana Sangh. When the 'politicians' among its founders sought to vary that line in any way or emancipate themselves from its control, the RSS would not hesitate to take power itself within the party.

First the part, then the whole

As Graham has shown, the ambitions of the Jana Sangh 'politicians' – of whom Mookerjee was the first – were incompatible with the outlook of the RSS, even of those belonging to the 'activist' tendency:

Mookerjee wanted to challenge Congress rule without delay, and he apparently believed that middle-class liberalism was compatible with Hindu traditionalism, if not with Hindu nationalism, but the young men of the RSS acted as though they

---

[19] Mookerjee Papers, F. 168. Letters of 7 and 26 June and 6 July 1951.

[20] *Organiser*, 10 Sept. 1951, p. 14.

[21] C. Baxter, *The Jana Sangh: a biography of an Indian political party*, Bombay: Oxford University Press, 1968, p. 73.

[22] Mookerjee Papers, F-170.

were a brotherhood for some future time, in which a new élite, imbued with Hindu values, would sweep aside that which had been formed under the British Raj.[23]

Once the People's Party of Bengal had been formed, Mookerjee's aim was to fashion his party into the key element of an opposition front capable of taking the place of Congress. He explained as much during the 1951 election campaign. However, the compromises which this aim implied were inconvenient for Nagpur.

The 1951-2 election, in anticipation of which Mookerjee had planned the setting-up of his party, immediately precipitated alliances and horse-trading with groups which were sometimes at odds with the party's ideology. For example, his election manifesto envisaged the abolition of the *jagirdari* and *zamindari* systems without compensation, in order to 'distribute the land to the tillers'.[24] But this did not prevent Mookerjee engaging in negotiations with organisations representing landed interests in one form or another. Electoral pacts were concluded with the Hindu Mahasabha in Bengal, the Praja Party (a party for the defence of land-owners) in Uttar Pradesh, and the Zamindar Mazdoor Party in Punjab.[25] Mookerjee would have been inclined to form electoral alliances with other parties but his efforts came to nothing.[26]

The Jana Sangh won only three seats in the Lok Sabha – two of them in Bengal, thanks to the influence of Mookerjee – and thirty-five in the Vidhan Sabhas (see election results, Appendixes D and E, pp. 554-5). But despite this reverse, Mookerjee contrived to become the main leader of the opposition in the new Lok Sabha by virtue of his eloquence and by gathering into a single parliamentary group, called the National Democratic Party, some forty members from the Jana Sangh, Dravida Kazhagam (a Tamil autonomist party in Tamil Nadu) and Ganatantra Parishad (a landowners' party in Orissa).[27] This group was the third largest after the Communists. For Mookerjee it was 'the beginning of the inter-communal, conservative, all-India party he had hoped to found'.[28] Fuelled as it was by Mookerjee's political ambition, this prospect was likely to displease the RSS since it implied a dilution of Hindu nationalist identity.

Mookerjee's leadership acted as a constraint on the Nagpur movement

[23] B. Graham, *Hindu nationalism*, op. cit., p. 55.

[24] 'Manifesto – 1951' in *Party documents*, vol. I, New Delhi: Bharatiya Jana Sangh, 1973, p. 51.

[25] C. Baxter, *The Jana Sangh*, op. cit., p. 90, and *Times of India*, 16 July 1951, p. 4.

[26] M.A. Jhangiani, *Jana Sangh and Swatantra – A profile of the rightist parties in India*, Bombay: Manaktalas, 1967, p. 141.

[27] *Organiser*, 5 May 1952, pp. 9-10, and 30 June 1952, p. 1; *Hitavada*, 27 June 1952; and Mookerjee Papers F. 259.

[28] C. Baxter, *The Jana Sangh*, op. cit., p. 109.

in other ways too. Despite Golwalkar's initial caution, the Jana Sangh leaders, both during and after the election campaign, expected the activists of the RSS to be at the service of their political cause. In August 1952, Mookerjee exhorted the *swayamsevaks* to abandon their 'isolationist policy'.[29] But the RSS's priority remained, now more than ever, the development of its Sangathanist (see above, Chapter 1, p. 66) network, which had been adversely affected by the ban of 1948-9,[30] rather than political activism, for which there had been such high demand during the election campaign. The resolutions passed by the Jana Sangh Working Committee after the election in February 1952 further reveal the determination of the RSS men within the party to steer it towards social issues. Resolution no. 8 declared:

The Working Committee feels that now that the General Elections are over, the workers of the Jana Sangh should take up more important work for organising a network of Jana Sangh bodies all over the country and carrying through them, constructive programmes for the cultural, social and economic regeneration of our society and for the building of a sound and stable political structure on the basis of democracy. The constructive programme shall be carried on particularly among those sections of society which need help either because they have been lacking in opportunities and resources, education, leadership, or organisation.[31]

There followed a detailed list of 'target' groups: workers, students, women, refugees, peasants and above all Scheduled Castes.

This position was re-stated in the form of a resolution entitled 'a massive constructive programme' at the first plenary session of the party, held at Kanpur in December 1952.[32] Represented at the top level of the party by D. Upadhyaya, who had succeeded Bhai Mahavir as General Secretary, it came to be imposed by force in the months following the premature disappearance of Mookerjee. The latter's death in 1953 during a campaign of protest against 'Kashmiri separatism' led to an intervention by the RSS in the internal affairs of the Jana Sangh, doubtless because of

---

[29] *Hitavada*, 6 Aug. 1952, p. 5. This appeal came shortly after a similar one from a socialist leader of Nagpur who was anxious to see the RSS ally itself to his party because of its ideas of equality. Unfortunately, he said, the RSS 'has now become a sect whose disciples seek to ensure a happy life for *gurus* [...]. Our Guruji always considers that the RSS has not achieved sufficient strength whatever practical work needs to be done' (ibid., 2 May 1952, p. 4).

[30] Only the hard core of *swayamsevaks* – numbering some 100,000 – were to remain faithful to the organisation throughout this period. In 1951, the RSS once more reached its 1947 level, i.e. 600,000 members (J. A. Curran, *Militant Hinduism*, op. cit., p. 43.)

[31] Mookerjee Papers, F. 174.

[32] 'Massive constructive programme' in Bharatiya Jana Sangh, *Party Documents*, vol. 5, New Delhi, 1973, pp. 87-8.

fears that the party would fall into the hands of another politician who would be less reliable than Mookerjee.

M.C. Sharma was the logical successor to Mookerjee as head of the party, but he had only a small support network concentrated in Delhi – its key figures were two RSS workers, Vasant Rao Oke and Kunwar Lal Gupta, a lawyer and merchant in the Old City linked to the Hindi Sahitya Sammelan.[33] Above all, Sharma was the very personification of a politician in the Mookerjee mould. The son of Din Dayal Sharma, one of the promoters of the Hindu Mahasabha in the 1920s who was close to M.M. Malaviya, M.C. Sharma had remained in the Congress without showing any great activism up to Independence; like a number of Hindu traditionalists, he became chief minister of a princely state. But at Partition he was particularly impressed by the help given to Hindu refugees by the RSS and by the movement's internal solidarity, which seemed well placed to promote Hindu interests.[34] He had acted as an intermediary with the authorities when the RSS was banned, and then appeared to play an active role in the setting-up of the Jana Sangh. These qualifications were still not significant enough to make the party cadres who had come from the RSS regard him as a legitimate president, and they were not slow to show their defiance in *Organiser*.[35] Sharma immediately had to compromise with the RSS over the composition of the Working Committee. Among its twenty-nine members were a number of RSS men: D. Upadhyaya, Bapusaheb Sohni, Bhai Mahavir, Nana Deshmukh, A.B. Vajpayee, B. Madhok, S.S. Bhandari, Bhairon Singh Shekhawat and Jagannath Rao Joshi.

Sharma attempted to reinforce his position when a meeting of the All India General Council (AIGC – the full authority of which the Working Committee was an offshoot) was held at Indore in August 1953, but this only served to provoke the hostility of the AIGC. He resigned in November, after having denounced the increasing interference of the RSS in party affairs.[36] The leaders of the Delhi branch (alone) followed suit. The Working Committee merely took note of these defections and made Sohni interim president until the session at Jodhpur (30 December 1954 – 1 January 1955) when Prem Nath Dogra, the RSS *sanghchalak* of Jammu and head of the Praja Parishad, was named president and the Delhi branch dissolved.[37] Dogra reappointed twenty-three of the twenty-nine retiring members of the Working

[33] *Fourth Lok Sabha who's who*, New Delhi: Lok Sabha Secretariat, 1967, p. 180.

[34] Oral History transcript. Interview with M.C. Sharma (Hindi), op. cit., pp. 154, 162 and 175.

[35] *Organiser*, 8 Feb. 1954, pp. 2-14.

[36] B. Graham, *Hindu nationalism*, op. cit., pp. 63-4.

[37] *Times of India*, 5 Jan. 1955, p. 3.

Committee, an indication of the extent to which the RSS had already penetrated the party apparatus.[38]

The main conclusion to be drawn from this episode is that, although the RSS leaders were willing to become involved in the work of setting up a political party because they were persuaded to agree with certain of their own 'activists' that party politics could not be ignored, they were not prepared to allow the Jana Sangh to be taken over by politicians who would ignore their organisation and make policy compromises in order to attract support rapidly. In order to prevent such an outcome, they virtually converted the Jana Sangh into a front organisation and thus kept it within the framework of the other groups affiliated to the RSS.

The RSS and its affiliates

Before 1947, the only organisation affiliated directly to the RSS was the Rashtrasevika Samiti, a women's organisation which had been founded on lines similar to the RSS in 1936. After Independence the RSS decided to form a set of affiliated organisations which became known collectively as the 'Sangh parivar' (the RSS family). The Jana Sangh had been formed separately by Mookerjee, and therefore lay partly outside the ambit of the RSS until *swayamsevaks* asserted their control in the mid-1950s. From that point onwards it was reshaped in the mould of the RSS and its role adapted to conform with the division of labour within the 'Sangh parivar'.

The Jana Sangh, replica and auxiliary of the RSS

From 1954 onwards, leaders of the Jana Sangh with an RSS background reshaped the political programme and organisation of the party in conformity with those of the mother organisation. The main architect of this transformation was D. Upadhyaya, who was to remain the party's General Secretary till 1967 with the full support of Golwalkar. In the eyes of his peers and of those in charge in Nagpur, he represented the 'ideal *swayamsevak*'.[39]

---

[38] In June 1956 former members of the Jana Sangh, including M.C. Sharma, who had now returned to Congress, held a meeting in Delhi at which the RSS's violation of democratic norms was subjected to much criticism, notably by V.R. Oke; the five hundred delegates then went on to set up the National Democratic Front. This disintegrated as early as February 1957, with most of its members rejoining Congress and Oke, its president, returning to the Jana Sangh, according to a press report, 'because he continued to regard the Sangh as a mother which had given him numerous political friends'. Indeed, leaving the RSS was, for a *swayamsevak*, tantamount to cutting oneself off completely from an ideological and social world in which the young volunteer had first achieved a socio-political identity.

[39] He was described thus on his death by Bhaurao Deoras (*Organiser*, 25 Feb. 1968 p. 3).

Upadhyaya abandoned his studies – after completing the first year of a MA in English literature – in order to dedicate himself entirely to the RSS, which he had first joined while in college at Kanpur in 1937. He worked for the organisation first as *pracharak* in Lakhimpur district, then as joint *prant pracharak* – he was the first non-Maharashtrian to hold this responsibility – between 1947 and 1951[40] and finally as an editor, launching a weekly publication, *Panchjanya*, which subsequently became a pan-Indian journal. Obliged to operate underground after Gandhi's assassination, he was one of the leading instigators of the *satyagraha* of 1949 in his province. He then went on to help frame the RSS's constitution and in effect founded the Jana Sangh in Uttar Pradesh.[41] Upadhyaya was considered the ideal *swayamsevak* not only because, with humility and discipline, he had consecrated his whole life to the cause, to the extent of refusing marriage, but also because, in the opinion of RSS veterans, 'his discourse reflected the pure thought current of the Sangh'.[42] It was therefore not surprising that he should have progressively taken on the task of endowing the Jana Sangh with a doctrine of its own, although one that seemed to be a variant of the ideology of the RSS.

The two principal texts in which he set out his political thought are *The two plans* (1958) and *Integral humanism* (1965); these were to provide the bases of the Jana Sangh's foundation of its 'Principles and Policies' in 1965. The salient point here was the diminution in importance of the state by comparison with society. This may have been in conformity with the ideology of the RSS, but was paradoxical in the case of a political party whose vocation was, in theory, the conquest of power.

For Upadhyaya the 'basic cause of the problems facing Bharat is the neglect of its national identity' shown by westernised and unprincipled politicians.[43] However his model of the nation was the Western one, and he recognised that 'nationalism is the oldest and strongest'[44] of the 'isms' invented in the West. By means of reference to the so-called 'historical' *varnas*, he tried in his turn to affirm the existence of a Hindu nation. His thought process thus remained within the framework that stigmatised and emulated the Other through a reinterpretation of tradition.

Following in the footsteps of Golwalkar, he rejected the theory of a social contract, explaining that 'society is "self-born"' as an "organic entity":[45]

---

[40] D. Puchpa, *Sangh-ninva mein visarjit* (Hindi), op. cit., p. 109.

[41] S. Raje (ed.), *Pandit Deendayal Upadhyaya – A profile*, New Delhi: Deendayal Research Institute, 1972.

[42] Babasaheb Apte, 'Panditji had a cool head and a warm heart'. *Organiser*, 10 March 1968, p. 5.

[43] D. Upadhyaya, *Integral humanism*, New Delhi: Bharatiya Jana Sangh, 1965, p. 5.

[44] Ibid., p. 8.

[45] Ibid., p. 32.

In our concept of four castes, they are thought of an analogous to the different limbs of Virat-Purusha. [...] These limbs are not only complementary to one another, but even further, there is individuality, unity. There is a complete identity of interest, identity of belonging. [...] If this idea is not kept alive, the castes instead of being complementary, can produce conflict. But then this is distortion. [...] This is indeed the present condition of our society.[46]

His reference to the schema of the four *varnas* should not be taken to mean that Upadhyaya favoured the restoration of this social system. Such a hierarchical organisation of society would have been regarded as illegitimate and hence rejected by RSS ideologues because they considered it to be divisive. When RSS writers refer to the *varna* system they are using it as a metaphor in the sense proposed by Schlanger, who shows that such metaphors can be used to promote a unitarian ideological project.[47] In this case, Upadhyaya is employing the framework of the *varna* system to make the point that the origins of contemporary Indian society reside in an ideal organic society, which was an integrated whole, harmonious and free of conflict, and which was therefore almost a nation. Moreover Upadhyaya often inverted the two terms; the accent on unity and submission to *dharma* (from which proceeded the genius – *chiti* – of the society of *varnas*) encouraged this assimilation of society and nation. The primacy accorded to society explains the ideal of decentralisation promoted by Upadhyaya, for whom the fulcrum of national life was to be found-in the local reality of the villages:

In our socio-political set-up, the king and the State were never considered supreme. [...] The mightiest of the kings did not ever disturb the Panchayats. Similarly there were associations on the basis of trade. These two were never disturbed by the State; on the contrary, their autonomy was recognised. [...] Thus the State was concerned only with some aspects of life of the Society.[48]

The ideology of the Jana Sangh, codified by Upadhyaya, followed the RSS in the value it accorded to the society-nation in comparison to the state. Certainly the reference to the *varnas* contrasted with the egalitarian mission of the RSS, but this difference was logical: it was this which separated the world of the sect from that of the actual society in which conflict had to be eliminated, a task that the RSS entrusted, in particular, to its affiliates.

The complementarity of the RSS and its affiliates

The RSS and the Jana Sangh were complementary in two respects. First,

---

[46] Ibid., p. 43.

[47] J.E. Schlanger, *Les métaphores du corps*, Paris: Vrin, 1971, p. 31.

[48] D. Upadyaya, *Integral humanism*, op. cit., p. 62.

the existence of the Jana Sangh enabled the RSS to be represented in party politics without being directly affected by the rules and working of this milieu. Secondly, and more importantly, the task of promoting a kind of social harmony relying on intermediate institutions, such as villages or corporations, could be undertaken by the Jana Sangh while the RSS concentrated on its long-term mission of preparing Indian society for its final transformation, when individuals would accept direct involvement and even fusion in the life of the nation. Two speeches made by Golwalkar between 1947 and 1952 can be usefully compared to illustrate this point.

The plan, conceived by Hedgewar, of an ideological brotherhood with a vocation to absorb the whole of Hindu society, was central in Golwalkar's speech to the ABPS at the end of 1947:

Continuously expanding amongst the Hindu society we hope to reach a stage where the Sangh and the entire Hindu Society will be completely identical. This is bound to happen in the course of time for there is no escape.[49]

These words have the millenarian emphasis inherent in the mission of the RSS. Five years later, in a speech that opened with a eulogy to the 'scientific' nature of the *varna* system, Golwalkar declared:

Today there is talk of a classless society. Such a society would be possible of achievement only if all persons in the society were seers who have realised the Soul and have transcended worldly bonds. As long, however, as social development does not reach this stage, a classless social structure is a danger. If a developed society realise that the existing differences are due to the scientific social structure and that they indicate the different limbs of the body social, the diversity would not be constructed as a blemish.[50]

In principle RSS leaders perceived the *shakhas* as the crucible of a nation of individuals 'liberated' from their original personality and social characteristics (such as their caste), who have 'transcended worldly bonds', in Golwalkar's words. As a preliminary stage towards this organicism based on the sacrifice of the individual, the RSS affiliates are expected to promote the 'restoration' of a certain holistic organicism referring metaphorically to a *varna* system located in an idealised past. The RSS was therefore prepared to coexist – for a lengthy period of transition – with a society based on corporate groups in the same way as sects might coexist with a caste system. Indeed, Golwalkar himself proposed a theory of social reform which presupposes that the state will rely on institutions mediating between itself and individuals. His project would combine territorial representation (election by constituencies, as already practised) with 'functional' representation consisting of each

[49] Cited in *Hitavada*, 31 Dec. 1947, p. 55.
[50] *Organiser*, 1 Dec. 1952, p. 7.

corporation nominating delegates at the request of both its local branches and the central organisation. This mechanism was described as merely giving concrete form to what was already practised in ancient India, where each of the *varnas* chose its representative for its village councils (*Gram panchayat*) and thence to the royal council.[51] Golwalkar did not hesitate to demand, if necessary, a revision of the Constitution to put this plan into action.

In its work of reforming society, the RSS relied not only on its own efforts but also on those of the Jana Sangh and of its other affiliated organisations, particularly its trade unions. While the RSS's *shakhas* formed a special world where egalitarian values could develop, the organisation's affiliates worked in the real world and were faced with organised groups in conflict – hence their mission of promoting a harmonious society based on an organicist scheme.

Unions were quickly developed by the RSS in order to resist Communist influence, which was heavily attacked because of its anti-national bias and the risk that the Communists' scheme of class struggle would provoke division in Hindu society.[52] In July 1948, Madhok – a teacher who argued that the infiltration of student organisations was a vital task – founded in Delhi, with approval from Nagpur, the Akhil Bharatiya Vidyarthi Parishad (ABVP). In conformity to RSS philosophy, the task of this organisation was to bring about collaboration between all those involved in university education, since 'the teachers and the taught are both wheels of the same car.'[53] It would be a rival to the All India Students' Federation, which was described as being dominated by 'Communist agitators'.

The front organisation of labour unions was developed above all by Datto Pant Thengadi, a Maharashtrian Brahmin and *swayamsevak* from Nagpur who began his service as a *pracharak* in Kerala and then served in Bengal and Assam from 1942 to 1948 before establishing the ABVP branch in Nagpur. After Independence, Golwalkar, who was extremely worried by the 'Communist threat', asked Thengadi to infiltrate 'red' labour unions in order to gain the experience that he would need in order to found his own workers' branch of the RSS. Thengadi directed his activities towards the INTUC (the labour union affiliated to Congress), whose Madhya Pradesh branch he revived in 1950, before finally setting up the RSS's own labour union.[54] Significantly, this new body, the Bharatiya Mazdoor

[51] M.S. Golwalkar, *Bunch of thoughts,* op. cit., pp. 37-8.

[52] The Hindu nationalists remained convinced throughout the 1950s that Congress was destined to disappear – the Communists being their long-term rivals (see, for example, *Organiser,* 6 June 1950, p. 5).

[53] Ibid., 6 Nov. 1948, p. 5.

[54] Interview with G. Prabhakar, General Secretary of the BMS, 5 Dec. 1990, Bhopal; *Who's who in Rajya Sabha – 1970,* New Delhi: Rajya Sabha Secretariat, 1971, p. 316, and

Sangh (BMS), was established in July 1955 with the approval of the preceding annual session of the Jana Sangh at Jodhpur.[55] The Jana Sangh functioned on this occasion more like a social movement than a political party since it released one of its own cadres, Thengadi, who was the Organising Secretary of the party in Madhya Pradesh, to take charge of the BMS, a task different from normal party work but conforming to Hindu nationalist plans. Thengadi, who declared Communism to be 'enemy number one' at the inaugural conference of the BMS in Bhopal on 23 July 1955, Tilak Jayanti Day,[56] entrusted his trade union with the task of rehabilitating Hindu social organicism. He wanted to substitute family for class in political discourse and proposed a corporatist scheme inspired by the 'functional' ordering of the representational system suggested by Golwalkar.[57]

The apparent division of the Jana Sangh's forces to assist other off-shoots of the RSS was perfectly in accord with the task assigned to the latter's affiliates: to work in society in order to 'restore' its supposedly lost harmony. This decision followed also from the conviction that the Jana Sangh should achieve political power only after society became deeply imbued with its ideals, as Upadhyaya himself pointed out:

As a matter of fact electoral success is only a means to achieve the realisation of our ideals. We do have to amass popular support, but only of those who can follow our ideals and become one with our organisation. We do not simply want popular support; it must be an idealistic popular support.[58]

Hence the party's truly political involvement was both progressive and selective. Electoral success could wait; first, the Jana Sangh had to acquire a network of propagandists of the Sangathanist type who would work upon society in such a way that, in the end, political power would fall into its lap like a ripe fruit. Although the Jana Sangh, like any other affiliate of the RSS, had been assigned a definite role to play within the division of labour of the 'Sangh parivar', this did not mean that it was expected to develop ideals and a structure different from the RSS. The Jana Sangh accepted that it was more important to concentrate on the

---

Hitavada, 3 March 1951, p. 4, and 30 Sept. 1951, p. 5.

[55] K. Saxena, 'The Hindu trade union movement in India –The Bharatiya Mazdoor Sangh', *Asian Survey*, 33 (7), July 1993, p. 687.

[56] *Organiser*, 1 Aug. 1955, p. 13. However, the BMS was legally constituted in Delhi on 13 August 1967 (M. Mehta, *Story of BMS*, New Delhi: Bharatiya Mazdoor Sangh, 1990, p. 4).

[57] Ibid., 24 Oct. 1955, p. 13. On this point, see my 'Note sur un syndicat nationaliste hindou. Le travail et les travailleurs dans l'idéologie et les stratégies du Bharatiya Mazdoor Sangh', *Purushartha*, no. 14, (1991), pp. 251-70.

[58] *Organiser*, 26 Jan. 1955, p. 13.

long-term process of building the *Hindu Rashtra* than on short-term methods of gaining control of government. Thus it also adopted organisational principles which conformed to those of the RSS.

Minimal public involvement: the party's organisational priority

Up till the end of the 1950s, only the pressing threats to national security called forth an active response from the Jana Sangh in the political domain.

The state of Jammu and Kashmir was the most characteristic example. In the party's view, Nehru had shown too conciliatory an attitude by conceding to Jammu and Kashmir, in Article 370 of the Constitution, a form of autonomy.[59] The Dogra community, the landlords of Jammu on which the Hindu ruling dynasty had been based, resented the changes which occurred in the state and supported the Praja Parishad (led, since 1950, by Prem Nath Dogra) that was active in opposing Article 370.[60] The Jana Sangh and the Praja Parishad – which served as its vanguard in Jammu and Kashmir – protested when Sheikh Abdullah, the leader of the regional party, the National Conference, and the head of the state government, announced the creation of a special flag for Jammu and Kashmir alone and the replacement of the Maharajah by an elected head of state. In January 1952 the Praja Parishad launched an agitation, which was put down with great severity.

In July 1952, by means of the Delhi Pact, Nehru obtained a compromise from Sheikh Abdullah, to which the Praja Parishad alone refused to give its consent because it confirmed the principle of regional autonomy. At a meeting in Kanpur, the Jana Sangh issued an ultimatum – demanding the complete integration of Jammu and Kashmir and rejecting the submission of the question to the United Nations – before organising a *satyagraha* in March 1963 with the aid of the Hindu Mahasabha and the Ram Rajya Parishad.[61] Mookerjee himself tried to enter Jammu and Kashmir in May, but was arrested by the Kashmiri police, and died in prison, apparently from pleurisy, on 23 June. This Kashmir Andolan (agitation) was suspended on 7 July. The fact that many *swayamsevaks*, from within the Jana Sangh and beyond it, participated in the agitation was because the

---

[59] B. Puri, *Kashmir – Towards insurgency*, New Delhi: Orient Longman, 1993, p. 27.

[60] This arrangement was even more disagreeable to the Praja Parishad in that it included, *inter alia*, the promotion of Urdu as the official language, an agrarian reform that was detrimental to the Dogras, and the demotion of the Hindu Maharajah, the young Karan Singh, to a purely honorific position (B. Graham, *Hindu nationalism*, op. cit., p. 36).

[61] Nehru then decided to order the arrest of the *satyagrahis* in Punjab and Delhi, forbad those in Uttar Pradesh from leaving their state, and toyed with imposing a ban on the Jana Sangh (S. Gopal, *Jawaharlal Nehru*, vol. 2, op. cit., p. 125).

problem was one that concerned national integrity and therefore justified a massive and unified response.[62]

The same analysis applied to the *satyagraha* in Goa. On the second anniversary of Mookerjee's death, in order to force the integration of this 'foreign enclave', which Nehru refused to obtain by armed intervention, Jagannath Rao Joshi led an agitation into Goa itself. An RSS man, Joshi was at that point the Jana Sangh's organiser in the South.[63] He was imprisoned with his followers by the Portuguese police. Then, on 15 August 1955, a Committee for the Liberation of Goa, in which the Jana Sangh was a leading participant, launched a new *satyagraha*, to which the Portuguese police responded by opening fire, killing thirty or so people. But in spite of the popularity of this patriotic action, the Goa *satyagraha* failed to mobilise opinion far beyond the Portuguese enclave.

Concern for national integrity led the Jana Sangh to embark on a second kind of movement, this time angled towards the unity of the country. In effect, from 1953 onwards, the government gave in to regionalist movements demanding a revision of state borders on linguistic lines. The Hindu nationalists, on the other hand, immediately demanded

> [...] the abolition of autonomous linguistic state with their emphasis on regionalism and their dangerous potential for secession. In their place we seek the reinforcing of democratic institutions at the village, district, divisional and zonal levels. [...] The divisional level *janapada* will be closer to the people than the present state governments.[64]

This emphasis on *janapadas*, defined as administrative divisions grouping together several districts, is explained by the advantages which this level of government could offer for national integration. As intermediary between state and district, it broke up linguistic zones and ensured that they did not become mini-nations. Further, if facilitated decentralisation at the local level, where the *panchayat* remained the principal unit in the Jana Sangh's schema (an issue which will be addressed in the next chapter).

Hostility towards linguistic states was naturally unpopular because of the growing tendency of local people to identify with their regional culture, and the Hindu Mahasabha did not hesitate to exploit these feelings before the election of 1957.[65] The Jana Sangh itself yielded briefly to this

[62] See the remarks of Golwalkar in *Hitavada*, 10 Apr. 1951, p. 3.

[63] *Who's who in Rajya Sabha – 1970*, op. cit., pp. 35-6.

[64] *Organiser*, 26 Jan. 1956, p. 5.

[65] For example N.C. Chatterjee in Bengal (*Hitavada*, 13 Nov. 1956, p. 2), N.B. Khare in Maharashtra (*My political memoirs or autobiography*, Nagpur: J.R. Joshi, 1959, pp. 409-18).

device in 1957 in Gujarat and Maharashtra.[66] The Jana Sangh's opposition to the division of Punjab, as demanded by the Akali Dal, into separate Hindi and Punjabi zones (the latter being the language of the Sikhs) cost it many votes. It urged that Punjab be amalgamated with Himachal Pradesh in order to re-establish Greater Punjab, the so-called cradle of Aryan civilisation in India.[67] In support of this configuration, it alleged that Punjabi, which the Sikhs claimed as being peculiar to the West of the province, was in fact spoken throughout its extent. However, this cause and its supporting arguments were highly unpopular with the Hindu population, who regarded Hindi as the sole language of the eastern part of the province where they were in the majority, and who at times aspired to hive off this region from the western half of Punjab and have Delhi as its capital.[68]

This concern to promote its ideology rather than seek short-term electoral advantage by exploiting regional identities was characteristic of the Jana Sangh's activists in the 1950s: fighting for parliamentary seats mattered less to them than building up a network of like-minded cadres able and willing to work its way through society from the grassroots in order to build a truly committed vote.

The Jana Sangh's Sangathanist party-building pattern

From top to bottom, the structure of the Jana Sangh rested upon 'activist' *swayamsevaks*. At the top level, two senior *pracharaks* were detailed to assist Upadhyaya in setting up the Jana Sangh network. Jagannath Rao Joshi, a graduate of Poona University, but originally from Karnataka where he had served the RSS as a *pracharak* for seven years,[69] dealt with the southern half of the country while Atal Bihari Vajpayee was put in charge of North India. Born in Gwalior in 1926, he joined the RSS in the early 1940s. He was one of the *swayamsevaks* whose commitment to Hindu nationalism derived from influences from the Arya Samaj (he was General Secretary of the Arya Kumar Sabha of Gwalior in 1944 and studied at DAV College in Kanpur, gaining an M.A. in political science) and whose activism had taken shape within the student movement (he was also President of the Gwalior Students' Federation in 1944). Vajpayee was sent as a *vistarak* to Uttar Pradesh in 1946 and quickly began working for Upadhyaya's newspaper – becoming editor of *Rashtra Dharma* in 1948-9 and later of *Panchjanya*. He then followed Upadhyaya into the

---

[66] C. Baxter, *The Jana Sangh*, op. cit., pp. 159-60.

[67] *Statesman* (Delhi), 28 May 1954, p. 7.

[68] On this question, see B. Graham, *Hindu nationalism*, op. cit., pp. 100-11.

[69] *Organiser*, 4 Aug. 1991, p. 7.

Jana Sangh, where Mookerjee made him his secretary.[70] In 1958 the team expanded when four veteran *pracharaks*, also deputed by Nagpur, were entrusted with organising the party.[71] Vajpayee was sent to the Delhi headquarters, where he assisted Upadhyaya; Madhok was given the north (Jammu and Kashmir, Punjab, Himachal Pradesh and Delhi) and J.R. Joshi the Dravidian South; the western area was entrusted to Sunder Singh Bhandari. Born in 1921 into a Jain family in Udaipur, he had begun a legal career in the High Court of the princely state of Mewar. A *swayamsevak* since 1937, he became a *pracharak* in charge of Jodhpur and Bikaner divisions in 1946 and then secretary of the Rajasthan branch of the Jana Sangh in 1951.[72] Nana Deshmukh, who had been sent as *pracharak* first to Rajasthan in 1938 and then to eastern Uttar Pradesh in 1940, was entrusted with the organisation of the Jana Sangh in Uttar Pradesh, Bihar, Assam, West Bengal and Orissa. He succeeded Upadhyaya as General Secretary of the Jana Sangh in UP in the 1950s.[73] These men were known as national secretaries, and all, with the exception of Madhok, were celibate *pracharaks*. Their task was to build up the Jana Sangh by applying the same organisational principles which had been used in the RSS. To this end, they had to coordinate the actions of the *sangathan mantris* (organising secretaries) who were entrusted with promoting the party in every state. These full time workers were usually RSS *pracharaks* who had been dispatched to the Jana Sangh in order to develop the party's structure. They were in charge of its organisation at the state level, in certain divisions and occasionally in districts that were regarded as priorities. We shall now consider the case of the Jana Sangh's organisation in Madhya Pradesh in order to identify the specific techniques which were employed in constructing its framework at both local and state levels.

The case of Madhya Pradesh

In Madhya Pradesh, which was to become one of the strongholds of the Hindu nationalists, the *sangathan mantri* who gradually took charge of

---

[70] Interview with A.B. Vajpayee, 23 Feb. 1994, New Delhi, *Who's who in Lok Sabha – 1957*, New Delhi: Lok Sabha Secretariat, 1958, p. 495 and S.S. Bhandari (ed.), *Jana Sangh souvenir*, Delhi: Rakesh Press, 1969, p. 52. He remained editor of *Vir Arjun* (Delhi) in 1952-3 (S. Vazirani (ed.), *Atal Bihari Vajpayee*, New Delhi: Popular Book Services, 1967, p. 15). Vajpayee was known for his gifts as a orator, but also for his poems, which were often memorised in the *shakhas* (*Organiser*, 3 Jan. 1988, p. 8).

[71] Ibid., 17 March 1958, p. 4.

[72] Interview with S.S. Bhandari, 24 Feb. 1994, New Delhi and *Who's who in Rajya Sabha–1970*, op. cit., p. 103.

[73] Interview with N. Deshmukh, 25 Feb. 1994, New Delhi and Parliament of India, *Sixth Lok Sabha's Who's who – 1977*, New Delhi: Lok Sabha Secretariat, 1977, p. 164.

the organisation of the Jana Sangh was Kushabhau Thakre. Born into a family of Maharashtrian origin in Dhar – a Maratha state – he had given up his medical studies in 1938 to devote himself to the RSS. He served the organisation first as a *pracharak* in Mandsaur, Ratlam and Ujjain districts during the 1940s before being attached to the Jana Sangh. He became the party's principal organiser for the south of Madhya Bharat (the region of Malwa) in 1951 before taking responsibility for the whole state in 1953.[74] In November 1956, Madhya Pradesh was created in the course of a rearrangement of boundaries within the federation along linguistic lines.

DISTRIBUTION OF CASTES, TRIBES AND RELIGIOUS
COMMUNITIES IN MADHYA PRADESH, 1931

Category	Madhya Pradesh	Vindhya Pradesh	Mahakoshal	Chhattisgarh	Madhya Pradesh
Upper castes	*18.5*	*20.6*	*11.7*	*3.2*	*12.9*
Brahmin	6.5	13.3	4.6	1.7	5.7
Rajput	9	4.5	5.6	0.9	5.3
Banya	2.2	2.1	1	0.5	1.4
Kayasth	0.7	0.7	0.5	0.1	0.5
Middle castes	*0.87*	*0.34*	*2.96*	*0.17*	*1.11*
Maratha	0.42		0.57	0.1	0.31
Kumbi	0.45	0.34	2.39	0.06	0.8
Backward castes	*37.3*	*42.25*	*39.29*	*50.13*	*40.67*
Ahir	2.6	6	4.8	8.4	5.3
Dhimar	1.14	2.92	2.64	0.8	1.65
Gujar	2.9	0.04	1.1	0.02	1.23
Kachhi	3.25	6	–	–	1.9
Kumhar	1.6	1.7	0.9	0.8	1.2
Kirar	2.1	0.09	–	–	–
Kurmi	1.6	4.7	2.6	2.9	2.6
Lodhi	2	2.7	4.4	0.9	2.25
Lohar	0.8	1.5	1.3	1	1.1
Mali	1	0.1	2.3	2.9	1.7
Nai	1.4	1.8	1.2	0.8	1.2
Teli	1.6	2.9	2.3	9.3	4.2
Others	15.28	11.8	15.75	22.3	16.34
Scheduled castes	16.7 (17.3)	14.7 (15)	11.9 (13.7)	12.5 (11.5)	14.05 (14.1)
Scheduled tribes	13 (14.7)	14.5 (20.2)	25 (27.1)	31.7 (33.1)	21.62 (22.97)
Muslims	7 (7.8)	2.7 (3)	4.4 (5.2)	1.1 (1.7)	3.85 (4.8)
Jains	1.2 (1.3)	0.4 (0.4)	0.8 (1.1)	0.1 (0.3)	0.7 (0.85)
Other religions	0.7	0.03	0.5	1.1	1 (1.09)
Other	4.73	4.48	3.45	–	4.1
Total	100	100	100	100	100

Sources: Census report 1931 for Gwalior State, Central India Agency and Central Provinces and Berar.
Note: The figures in parentheses are drawn from the 1981 census.

[74] Interviews with K. Thakre, 1 Nov. 1988, Delhi, and 23 Nov. 1989, Bhopal.

The new state included Madhya Bharat, the Bhopal region, the former Vindhya Pradesh, Mahakoshal and Chhattisgarh (the last two regions forming the Hindi-speaking parts in the former Madhya Pradesh; see map, pp. xxii-xxiii). Each of these regions had its own character, determined by geography and history. Madhya Bharat, Bhopal and Vindhya Pradesh were made up exclusively of old princely states grouped together after Independence. The Jana Sangh had enjoyed a moderate level of success there in the 1951-2 elections. In Madhya Bharat, it won four MLA seats and came second in nineteen of the seventy-six other constituencies and in Vindhya Pradesh it won two MLA seats and came second in nine of the thirty-nine remaining constituencies. Mahakoshal, by contrast, had been subjected by the British to direct rule as part of the Central Provinces and had long been an area where support for Congress was strong. Chhattisgarh, which included districts that had been directly administered by the British but also a large number of princely states, was a Congress stronghold too.

As shown in the table on p. 133, the distribution of castes and communities varied from region to region. Madhya Bharat and Vindhya Pradesh had the highest proportion of upper castes (about one-fifth of the population, a figure comparable to that in Uttar Pradesh) and the lowest of tribals whereas the opposite was the case in Mahakoshal and Chhattisgarh. As far as Madhya Pradesh as a whole was concerned, as many as 20.63% of the population (in 1961) were tribals while there was a relatively high proportion of Scheduled Castes (Untouchables): 13.14%. At only 5%, the number of Muslims was modest although their distribution throughout the state was uneven. In 1949 only the Bhopal region (a former Muslim princely state) and Madhya Bharat had a higher percentage of Muslims – 14 and 6% respectively. In Vindhya Pradesh it was only 3%.[75]

As far as socio-economic development was concerned, Madhya Pradesh remained strongly tied to agriculture, with 78% of the active population working on the land in 1951 – a figure which had dropped by only 9 percentage points in 1981.[76] This was in spite of certain regional disparities: there were more industrial towns with a population greater than 100,000 in Madhya Bharat (in the 1961 census these were, in descending order, Indore, Gwalior, Bhopal and Ujjain) than in Chhattisgarh (where Raipur and Durg-Bhilai were growing fast) or Mahakoshal, where Jabalpur was the principal town.[77] These variations were also

---

[75] *The Indian and Pakistan Year Book and Who's who*, vol. 35, Bombay: Times of India, 1949, p. 447.

[76] *Pocket compendium of Madhya Pradesh statistics-1958*, Gwalior: Government Regional Press, 1958, p. 17.

[77] *Pocket compendium of Madhya Pradesh statistics-1965*, Gwalior: Government Regional Press, 1965, p. 58.

reflected in the transport infrastructure, which was most developed in the west but much less so in the east and north. In 1956 there was only 4.3 km. of road per 100 sq. km. in the newly formed state of Madhya Pradesh. This had risen to 14.9 km. in 1982, but was still barely half the national average.[78]

At the moment when Madhya Pradesh was formed in 1956, Thakre's team was entrusted with the mission of establishing the Jana Sangh in a state which was not only the largest in India, with a land area equivalent to that of France, but also relatively inaccessible. It took its *modus operandi* from the Sangathanist methods of the RSS: namely developing and maintaining a network of activists capable of working locally in depth in order to inculcate Hindu nationalist ideals in the minds of the largest number of people. This technique of implantation can be termed 'Sangathanist' because of its emphasis on two kinds of organisation: first, development of the party apparatus was of prime importance, and, second, society was to be organised in the manner envisaged by the Hindu Sangathan movement of the 1920s. For a militant Hindu nationalist the two were indissolubly linked since the promotion of organisational structures involved the same qualities of discipline as social reform, the first being the instrument of the second. The organisation was the model of the Hindu Rashtra.

The 'Sangathanist' approach was deployed in two different ways in Madhya Pradesh. First, *sangathan mantris* were sent on prolonged tours of the state, recalling the first *pracharaks* despatched by Nagpur, and second, *swayamsevaks* attracted to political work were seconded to the Jana Sangh on the spot. The two methods occurred in varying proportions according to the demands of each region. In Madhya Bharat, the second was considerably more in evidence than the first, largely because the RSS was already firmly established, above all in Malwa.[79] Here the first *shakhas* had been set up in Indore and Dewas in 1929 by Hedgewar himself.[80] In 1936 a *shakha* was established in the now typical fashion in Ujjain – which was to become one of the main bases of the RSS in Madhya Pradesh. Digambar Rao Tijare, a Brahmin from Wardha district was deputed from Nagpur to Ujjain, one of the sacred towns of Hinduism. It had a Jyotirlingam (natural lingam of Shiva) and was a site for Khumba

---

[78] O.S. Shrivastava, *Techno-economic profile of Madhya Pradesh*, Bhopal: Vikas Publications, 1985, p. 147.

[79] Certainly, several *sangathan mantris* were despatched from one part of Madhya Bharat to another. Hari Moreshwar (alias Haribhau) Joshi, whose natural father was a Maharashtrian Brahmin, went to Susner (Shajapur district) and became its MLA in 1957 while he had led the ABVP at Ujjain (Ashfaq Ali, *Bhopal past and present*, Bhopal: Jai Bharat, 1987, p. 360).

[80] B. V. Deshpande and S.R. Ramaswamy, *Dr Hedgewar, the epoch-maker*, op. cit., p. 110.

Melas, which were organised every twelve years and drew large numbers of pilgrims. Although he was a matriculate, Tijare decided to work in one of the textile mills of the town while simultaneously developing RSS branches. Since he spoke only Marathi, he first approached the numerous Marathi-speaking students in Ujjain, which was part of Gwalior state, a Maratha state. He often came to the playground close to the Mahakal temple (which contains the Jyotirlingam) and talked to students of the Maharajah High School who practised football there and exhorted them to play Indian games such as *kabaddi*. Babasaheb Kasture, one of the young Maharashtrian Brahmins who was attracted to Tijare, said that he was fascinated by his physical strength and dedication. After some time, the physical training was coupled with baudhik sessions in the temple premises.

The Ujjain *shakha* developed quickly because of patronage from local notables of Maharashtrian origin. Bhaiya Saheb Asthewale, a Brahmin landlord, became the town's *sanghchalak* and persuaded Maharajah Jivaji Rao Scindia not to obstruct its functioning. In 1939, while the Maharajah of Indore prohibited the annual route march of the RSS at the festival of Dasahara, Gwalior state permitted it to take place in Ujjain.[81]

The network of *shakhas* expanded greatly in the 1940s under the direction of P.B. Dani, who officiated as prant pracharak for Madhya Bharat between 1940 and 1946 when he was nominated to his first term as General Secretary of the RSS.[82] From his headquarters in Indore, he coordinated the activities of pracharaks. Between 1939 and 1942 they went to Nagpur for their OTC and from 1942 onwards were trained on the spot. In that year the first OTC in Madhya Pradesh was held at Khandwa. It was attended, among others, by K. Thakre, Manohar Rao Moghe (a Maharashtrian Brahmin who was posted in Dhar and later Ujjain) and Moreshwar Rao Gadre, another Maharashtrian Brahmin based in Indore.[83] The fact that all of them were from Maharashtrian families – admittedly ones who had settled in central India over a long period – probably reflected the relative ease with which the pracharaks from Nagpur could communicate with them because of their common mother tongue and regional culture (which included pride in the achievements of Shivaji and the Peshwas).

By 1946, according to RSS sources, Dani had attained the objective set by Hedgewar of enrolling 3% of the urban and 1% of the rural population.[84] There was no doubt that this successful campaign had

[81]   Interview with Babasaheb Kasture, 21 Feb. 1994, New Delhi.
[82]   C.P. Bhirshikar, *Shri Bhaiyaji Dani*, op. cit., p. 24 and *Organizer*, 31 May 1965, p. 1.
[83]   Interview with M.R. Moghe, 26 Aug. 1992, Ujjain. M.R. Moghe was the elder brother of Madhusudan Waman (alias Bapurao) Moghe who was to become *baudhik pramukh* of the RSS
[84]   *Organiser*, 7 June 1965, p. 1.

benefited from the traditional hostility of the princes of the region to Congress. Being afraid that the latter would undermine their authority, they sought to prevent it from penetrating their respective states. This attitude, which had already found expression in Gwalior, was reproduced to a lesser extent in Dewas and Dhar. In Indore, the movement obtained most of its recruits among students drawn to the city from the surrounding area, often from a radius of several hundred kilometres.[85] For example, Gulab Chand Khandelwal, who came from a village in Sehore district close to Bhopal, joined the Indore branch of the RSS in 1939 when he was studying at Holkar College. His brother Pyarelal followed him to Indore in 1942, joined the RSS and became a *pracharak* in 1948.[86] As early as the late 1930s Indore had 30-35 *shakhas*, some of which had taken root in the textile mills. In order to attract workers, they met in the afternoon, before the evening shift began in the factories.[87] However, middle class members and students formed the largest categories within the RSS in Madhya Bharat by the late 1940s.

The legal proceedings against RSS members after the assassination of Gandhi and during the *satyagraha* in 1948-9 marked the first watershed at which it is possible to sketch a sociology of the movement. In Madhya Bharat most of the prosecuted leaders belonged to liberal professions or to the administration. The *satyagraha* got off to a vigorous start on 9 December 1948 in Indore. By 12 January 1949, 1,444 *swayamsevaks* had already been arrested. Police reports make it clear that among those detained were many 'lawyers, teachers and civil servants'.[88] The high proportion of public employees among the activists could not but cause anxiety to the government of Madhya Bharat.[89] However the most heavily involved group of those that participated in the movement were probably students. Of the 1,995 *swayamsevaks* who had been arrested by the end

---

[85] In 1947, its two colleges, Holkar College and Sanskrit College, accounted for more than 1,000 students and fourteen High Schools between them were responsible for the education of 2,552 boys. (R.W. Jones, 'Area, power and linkage in Indore: a political map of an Indian city', Ph. D. thesis, Columbia University, 1970, vol. 1, p. 62.)

[86] Interview with G.C. Khandelwal, 15 Oct. 1991, Bhopal.

[87] Interview with Ganesh Manohar Tare (who joined the RSS in 1939), 28 Aug. 1992, Indore.

[88] Madhya Bharat Cabinet papers, file no. 505/1948, Madhya Pradesh State Archives, Bhopal (Old Secretariat).

[89] In Madhya Pradesh, of the 571 'security prisoners' – the most dedicated activists of the 6,515 people arrested during the *satyagraha* – 355 were civil servants and ten were teachers (*Hitavada*, 30 March 1949, p. 3). The government sacked the civil servants who had been implicated (*Report on the general administration of Madhya Pradesh for the years 1946-1951*, Nagpur: Government Press, 1951, p. 6, and *Struggle*, 5 Nov. 1949 in Rajpramukh papers, S. no. 15, file no. 21, section 4, 1949 – Madhya Pradesh State Archives, Bhopal [Old Secretariat]).

of December 1948, 498 were from Ujjain district, 488 from Indore district and 209 from Shajapur district.[90]

The powerful presence of the RSS in Malwa explains the relatively early date by which the Jana Sangh was able to open its regional branch at Indore – on 2 September 1951 – at the same time as in Uttar Pradesh. K. Thakre admitted that in Madhya Bharat the Jana Sangh was built on the RSS network while in other areas of Madhya Pradesh it did not benefit from such a strong base.[91] The most revealing example of this phenomenon was the parliamentary constituency of Shajapur, from which the Jana Sangh has always succeeded in having outsiders returned, such as the Bombay-based pressman Baburao Patel (MP in 1967) and the all-India leader from South India, Jagannath Rao Joshi (MP in 1971). This stronghold persisted after the constituency was declared reserved for the Scheduled Castes in 1977: since then, Phool Chand Verma, a *swayamsevak* from Indore, has been elected four times. This safe seat, as P.C. Verma acknowledges, is primarily due to the density and activity of the RSS network.[92] As early as 1957, Haribhau Joshi had benefited from this network when he was returned as an MLA, an achievement he subsequently repeated on four occasions. The case of Shajapur, even though an untypical one, illustrates the way the Jana Sangh profited from the preparatory work of the RSS in order to establish safe seats in Madhya Bharat.

In 1956 the Jana Sangh had 203 local committees in Madhya Bharat representing 10,000 members – twenty at Ujjain, seventeen at Indore, fifteen at Gwalior and five at Bhopal.[93] The party's reliance on the technique of building up a Sangathanist network is exemplified by its work in three areas which became its first strongholds, namely the districts of Mandsaur, Ujjain and West Nimar.

Mandsaur.   Consisting of *tehsils* (an administrative area equivalent to a subdivision of a district) which had formerly been divided between the princely states of Gwalior and Indore, Mandsaur district manifested several signs of backwardness and isolation – as recently as 1981 barely

90   Madhya Bharat Cabinet papers, file no. 505/1948.

91   Interview with K. Thakre. When the formation of the new state of Madhya Pradesh was announced in 1956, he immediately contacted the *pracharaks* of this region to coordinate the activities of the RSS and the Jana Sangh (K. Thakre, 'Madhya Pradesh mein bhajpa sarkar – Bhagirthi prayason ka pratiphal', *Swadesh*, 1992, no. 19 [Hindi]).

92   Interview with P.C. Verma, 29 Aug. 1992, Indore. Virendra Singh Sisodia, who was elected as an MLA in Shajapur district in 1990, confirms this interpretation (interview, 21 Aug. 1992, Bhopal).

93   In contrast, Vindhya Pradesh had only 100 or so committees (*Organiser*, 13 Aug. 1956, p. 38).

one-third of the population was accessible by serviceable roads.[94] On the other hand, it derived wealth from the cultivation of cash crops such as betel-nut and opium, the principal merchandise of five out of twelve market towns in 1981.[95] Marketing these crops was to a large extent left in the hands of a sizeable Jain community who, in contrast to a nationwide proportion of 0.5%, averaged 2.25% in the district as a whole and about 10% in towns like Jawad and Mandsaur.[96] In this district the Jana Sangh encouraged its activists to build up a level of party-directed support which would enable it to contest elections without relying on notables and their followers. As a result, the party's local units were no longer dependent on those politicians whom Mookerjee had recruited in the early 1950s; these men were either pushed aside or absorbed into the Sangathanist structure.

In 1952, the only non-Bengali Jana Sangh MP, Umashankar Mulshankar Trivedi, was from this district. His was a profile typical of the 'politicians' who at that time were represented at the top of the party structure by Mookerjee (with whom he had studied law in England in the 1920s).[97] He had been an active Congressman – lending his services as defending counsel to participants in the 'Quit India' movement – until 1951, when he joined the Jana Sangh because of his opposition to Nehru's policy towards Pakistan.[98] He declared that he owed his electoral success to those very services which he had rendered as a barrister to disadvantaged sections of society.[99] His status as a notable, deriving from his presidency of the Bar Association of Neemuch (an important market town in Mandsaur district), also contributed to his success. Indeed, Trivedi typified the conservative politicians (for example, he opposed agrarian reform and defended *jagirdars* in court)[100] whom Mookerjee brought into the inner circles of the Jana Sangh.

The only Jana Sangh MLA elected in the district in 1952, Vimal Kumar Chauradia, also belonged to the class of urban notables. He was the son of a rich Jain merchant of Bhanpura, another *tehsil* administrative centre. His family, too, had been active in Congress and thus retained a certain

---

[94] *Census of India 1981 -- Series, II, Madhya Pradesh, District Census Handbook – Part XIII – A Village and Town Directory – Mandsaur District*, Bhopal, 1982, p. xxiii.

[95] Ibid., p. xxxii.

[96] *Census of India 1981 – Series II, Madhya Pradesh – Household population by religion or head of Household*, Bhopal, 1985, p. 53.

[97] C. Baxter, *The Jana Sangh*, op. cit., pp. 63 and 134.

[98] Trilochan Singh (ed.), *Indian parliament (1952-1957)*, New Delhi: Arunam and Sheel (n.d.), p. 286.

[99] H.T. Davey, Jr., 'The transformation of an ideological movement into an aggregative party: a case study of the Bharatiya Jana Sangh', unpubl. Ph. D. thesis, University of California, Los Angeles, 1969, p. 194.

[100] H.S. Chhabra (ed.), *Opposition in the parliament*, op. cit., p. 77.

popularity at the local level. He had joined the Praja Mandal in 1938, and his brother had been gaoled for nine months on account of the 'Quit India' movement. In January 1950, shortly after obtaining his law degree, he too decided to join the Jana Sangh on account of the policy of Congress towards Pakistan since Partition.[101]

The adherents of the Sangathanist method who dominated the Jana Sangh after 1954 saw this electoral strategy of co-opting notables as no more than a makeshift. In their eyes the party, as a priority, had to build up its network on the RSS model. Chauradia was finally converted to this tactic, and became *sanghchalak* while Trivedi was marginalised in the late 1960s (he had won a seat in the Lok Sabha for Mandsaur in 1962 on the Jana Sangh ticket).

For the Jana Sangh cadres, Mandsaur district was a propitious territory for experimentation with the Sangathanist method because of the dense network of *shakhas* that Thakre had helped to establish when he was a *pracharak* there in the 1940s.

The strength of the RSS in this area was largely a function of its high reputation not only among members of the upper castes but also among Jains, who evidently recognised in its puritanism and discipline virtues which they valued in their own community. The head of the RSS branch at Bhanpura, a Jain, considered the *samskars* of the RSS 'the most important thing', defining them as 'the effort to awaken a discipline of patriots [*anushasan deshbhakti*]'; this implied driving out all bad feelings (*bhedbhav*).[102]

In the 1950s, the Jana Sangh built upon the RSS network established in the 1940s by the *pracharaks* of Mandsaur district, with K. Thakre as one of their leaders. Those principally responsible for this method of

[101] Interview with V.K. Chauradia, 16 Oct. 1991, Bhanpura. Bhagvan Das Jain, the other Hindu nationalist MLA in the district, a Hindu Sabhaite returned at Mandsaur in a by-election, was also a notable from the Jain community. He owned a dispensary and had been mayor of Mandsaur (*Madhya Bharat Vidhan Sabha sadasyon ka parichay – 1952*, op. cit.).

[102] Interview with Harak Chand Harsoria, 16 Oct. 1991, Bhanpura. A Jain merchant who joined the RSS in 1944 related that Thakre sometimes went for three days without food, walking from one village to the next without a care for his bodily comfort: he could thus be compared to a *karma yogi*, totally dedicated to the work of the organisation (*sangathan*). This figure drew the Jain merchant into the RSS at the age of fourteen; the latter also participated in the *shakha* because he met there people who pursued 'good samskars' in fidelity to the high tradition (*sanskriti ke samskar*). (Interview with Jawaharlal Jain, 15 Oct. 1991, Mandsaur.) A Brahmin who at one time was a *mukhya shikshak* (chief instructor) joined the RSS in 1941 at the age of thirteen, and invoked similar motives to explain his action. Every day he visited Thakre for a sort of purification (*sanshodh*), because one's character and behaviour (*charitr*) were well formed there with good thoughts (*acche vichar*), echoing the Brahminical *samskars* (interview with Ratan Lal Mukhya, 15 Oct. 1991, Mandsaur).

organisation were *swayamsevaks* who were products of these *shakhas*: Virendra Kumar Sakhlecha and Sunderlal Patwa, both of whom were to head the state government many years later. Sakhlecha was from a modest Jain family in Jawad. His father, a cloth merchant, headed the local branch of the Arya Samaj.[103] Sakhlecha joined the RSS in 1945 at Jawad. After studying law at Holkar College (Indore) he established a legal practice at Mhow, the neighbouring town to Indore, in 1953, and then in 1956 transferred it to Jawad where he worked mostly for the Jana Sangh.[104] Patwa, who was also a Jain, entered the RSS at a very young age in 1940 and also served as a *pracharak* between 1945 and 1951.[105] His family were landowners and traders in the small town of Kukdeshwar (in the *tehsil* of Manasa).

The political base obtained by these men came primarily from their work in the field. Although deputed to the Jana Sangh, Sakhlecha and Patwa continued to develop the network of *shakhas*, even in the villages;[106] at the same time they launched agitations and pressurised the government to increase the purchase price of opium. These activities, together with the mobilisation of a network of rural *swayamsevaks*, explain their success in the 1957 elections when they became MLAs for, respectively, Jawad and Manasa.

In the case of Mandsaur we can see how teams of RSS activists succeeded in building up one of the Jana Sangh's first strongholds in the Madhya Bharat region. Their social background is interesting: although one of the most prominent, a teacher turned *pracharak*, was a Sondhya Rajput by caste,[107] most of the activists and potential election candidates were drawn from groups within the local merchant community, such as Jains (Sakhlecha, Patwa and Chauradia belonged to this community), Sindhis (such as Tillumal, who was the Jana Sangh candidate in the contest for Mandsaur town in the 1957 Assembly elections) and Khattris (including Chawla, a money-lender who had come from Lahore as a refugee and had become the President of the city unit of the party).[108]

Ujjain.   Ujjain had been the first centre of RSS activity in the Malwa

[103]   This organisation had been very active 'in all the urban areas' of Mandsaur district for a long time (R. Verma, *Madhya Pradesh District Gazetteers – Mandsaur*, Bhopal: District Gazetteers Department, 1993, pp. 46 and 65).

[104]   Interviews with V.K. Sakhlecha, 12 Oct. 1991 and 16 Feb. 1994, Bhopal.

[105]   Interview with S. Patwa, 17 Feb. 1994, Bhopal and *Madhya Pradesh Vidhan Sabha sadayson ka sankship parichay – 1977*, Bhopal: Madhya Pradesh Vidhan Sabha sachivalay, 1977, p. 114.

[106]   Interview with Thakur Kishore Singh Sisodia (see below), 15 Oct. 1991, Mandsaur.

[107]   This *jati* is not accepted by the Rajputs as Kshatriyas in Mandsaur district (R. Verma, *Madhya Pradesh District Gazetteers – Mandsaur*, op. cit., p. 59).

[108]   Interview with K. Chawla, 4 Feb. 1994, Mandsaur.

region and it was here that Jana Sangh activists first succeeded in using the Sangathanist organisational technique to establish party-directed support in a working class area. According to M.R. Moghe, who had been sent to Ujjain as a *pracharak* in 1942, within the next eight years the town had 60 *shakhas*, half of them situated in the rural periphery.[109] As elsewhere, the Hindu nationalist movement was more firmly established among the upper-caste middle class, a tendency accentuated after the opening of Vikram University since students were the chosen target of the RSS.[110] Of the prominent figures in the local Jana Sangh in its formative years, one finds a preponderance of Brahmins, such as K.P. Bhargava (an advocate and town *sanghchalak* who contested the general elections in 1957)[111] and Vishwanath Vyas, again an RSS man[112] and the scion of one of the main priestly families of the Mahakal temple.

However, the Sangathanist method was developed as early as the 1950s, either in the form of trade unionism or as part of a welfarist tactic to sow the seeds of the Jana Sangh in unfamiliar surroundings, given the classic social basis of the RSS. Ujjain being a traditional centre of the textile industry, in which 42,224 workers were employed in 1961,[113] the RSS had established *shakhas* in the mill area as early as the 1930s through D. Tijare. Relying on this RSS network, the Jana Sangh made inroads among the workers thanks to *swayamsevaks* who also worked in the mills and had gained recognition for their union activism in the BMS. One of their number, Hukum Chand Kacchwai, a member of the Scheduled Castes, had taken part in emergency relief work during a famine in the neighbouring Jhabua district and helped refugees after Partition.[114] He became an MP in 1962. The then chief organiser of the Jana Sangh in Ujjain, Babulal Jain, admits that his party succeeded in making inroads among the Scheduled Castes because of Untouchables attracted to the RSS (like Kacchwai). This presence never diminished; Ujjain returned a Hindu nationalist MP at every election from 1962 to 1991, except in 1984. The social and political profile of S. Jatiya, who became the town's MP

---

[109] Interview with M.R. Moghe.

[110] Ashfaq Ali, *Bhopal past and present*, op. cit., p. 382 and interview with Babulal Jain, a *swayamsevak* who built up a pharmaceutical business and had joined the RSS in 1945. He worked for the ABVP in the 1950s before assuming organisational reponsibilities in the Jana Sangh from 1962 onward (21 Aug. 1992, Bhopal).

[111] Interview with Rajesh Upadhyaya (another Brahmin lawyer who had joined the RSS in 1945 and then risen through all the stages of the local Jana Sangh hierarchy till he became president of the BJP in Ujjain), 26 Aug. 1992, Ujjain.

[112] Interview with V. Vyas, 25 Aug. 1992, Ujjain. Vyas belongs to the All India Brahman Association.

[113] R. Verma and S.D. Guru, *Madhya Pradesh District Gazetteers – Ujjain*, Bhopal: District Gazetteers Department, 1982, pp. 128-31.

[114] *Who's who in Lok Sabha – 1967*, New Delhi: Lok Sabha Secretariat, 1967, p. 219.

for the first time in 1980, was similar to Kacchwai's. Originally from Jawad (Mandsaur district), where he joined the RSS as a boy before becoming a *vistarak* and studying sociology at Indore, Jatiya first served the BMS in 1966 as an employee of the Madhya Pradesh Electricity Board, where he worked in order to pay for his studies. Then he became a *sangathan mantri* for the Jana Sangh in Shajapur and Bhopal districts in 1972-5, and finally was elected MLA for Agar in 1977. He took the oath in the Vidhan Sabha in Sanskrit – one of the reasons for his entering the RSS was a certain yearning for Sanskritisation, a phenomenon discussed in Chapter 1. But this did not deflect him at all from his efforts on behalf of workers from the low castes.[115] In 1989 he was re-elected to the Lok Sabha with more than 58% of the vote. His popularity as a workers' leader had been given a fillip shortly before the elections, in the logic of the welfarist tactic, when he made an intervention in favour of workers who had been victims of an escape of gas at the Vinod mill. His reputation extended beyond his own community; thus the brother of the *qazi* (Muslim judge) of Ujjain declared: 'May be we will vote for Jatiya who has an impeccable record as a leader of workers and the down trodden. He has faced police lathis for the labourers.'[116]

At the Vidhan Sabha elections in 1990, another workers' leader, Babulal Mehere, a Brahmin, won the seat of Ujjain South, a constituency with a high concentration of industry. Mehere had been an early where he recruit of the RSS and was the founder of the BMS in Ujjain, where he acquired a specially high reputation among workers in the town by developing a workers' cooperative bank. This pioneer institution, which Mehere founded in 1955, attracted the savings of textile workers against a small rate of interest, and offered loans, also at lower rates of interest than other banks in either the public or private sectors. This scheme, added to his defence of the workers through the BMS and his newspaper, *Avantika*, must partly explain his election as MLA even though he had never won an elected post except at the municipal level.[117] He also benefited from a very well entrenched activist network; in the area of Ujjain, there were numerous RSS *shakhas* in the working-class quarters as also in the surrounding villages.

By contrast, labour in Indore, the principal industrial town in Madhya Pradesh, for a long while continued to be dominated by INTUC (which

---

[115] Interview with Jatiya, 4 Dec. 1990, Ujjain.

[116] *Indian Express*, 22 Nov. 1989, p. 4.

[117] Interview with Babulal Mehere, 4 Dec. 1990, Ujjain.

had provided Congress with some of its leaders) and by the Communists.[118] The BMS failed to take root here.[119]

West Nimar.   Sangathanist techniques were also applied through a tactic of social work in the tribal areas of West Nimar. At Khargone, the Jana Sangh's first chief organiser was Balchandra Badgare, a lawyer and Maharashtrian Brahmin who had already founded a local RSS branch in 1939. He worked in his district party with Ram Chandra Bade, another Maharashtrian Brahmin lawyer, from Sendhwa, who had left Congress after Partition and joined the Jana Sangh, under whose colours he was elected an MLA in 1952.[120] These two men tried to implant the party among the tribal peoples in West Nimar and Jhabua districts, who suffered from chronic unemployment. In Jhabua a socialist leader took up their defence, which gave his party a strong foothold there.[121] But in West Nimar Bade acted as the spokesman of the tribals and led a delegation to Indore to air their grievances in August 1953. In 1960 the state government, in an attempt to counter deforestation, tried to move the tribals who cultivated land in that district. The Communists then launched an agitation, but Bagdare countered it by sending Jana Sangh militants into the tribal areas 'to befriend adivasis, to know their problems'.[122]

Parallel to this, Bade campaigned on behalf of the tribals' right to clear the forest to provide cultivable land and sell timber. In June 1962 the government sent in the police to destroy the harvest of the villages concerned. Bagdare went to Bhopal and submitted a memorandum to the Minister of Forests who suspended the expulsion of the tribal cultivators. Then a delegation of tribals joined Bade and other local Jana Sangh leaders in a demonstration at Bhopal. Finally the Madhya Pradesh government set up a commission of inquiry, whose report dissuaded the authorities from pursuing their policy.[123] In 1962, the Jana Sangh won a parliamentary seat and six of eight MLA seats in West Nimar, of which four were reserved for tribals.

The Sangathanist technique of implantation, which was in full swing in Malwa, was hardly producing any results in the north of Madhya

[118] W. Wilcox, 'Trade unions, the middle class and a communist MP: The Indore parliamentary election of 1962' in M. Weiner and R. Kothari (eds), *Indian voting behaviour: Studies of the 1962 general elections*, Calcutta: K.L. Mukhopadhyay, 1965, pp. 69-84.

[119] R.W. Jones, 'Area, power and linkage in Indore', op. cit., vol. 2, p. 418.

[120] *Fifth Lok Sabha's who's who*, New Delhi: Lok Sabha Secretariat, 1971, p. 29.

[121] *Statesman* (Delhi), 23 Aug. 1953, p. 4.

[122] Interview with Bagdare, 12 Nov. 1990, Bhopal.

[123] *Hindustan Times*, 11 and 17 July 1962, p. 5; *Times of India*, 16 July 1962, and *Organiser*, 9 Apr. 1962, p. 4.

Bharat, around Gwalior. Here the Jana Sangh was being built up primarily by Narayanrao Krishnarao Shejwalkar, again a Maharashtrian Brahmin, who was the son of the local *sanghchalak* and followed his example by becoming a lawyer.[124] He had achieved a certain degree of popularity working with the Hindu Sahayata Samiti to help Sindhi refugees during Partition.[125] But in the Gwalior region the rise of the Jana Sangh was blocked by the strength of the Hindu Mahasabha and the revivification of Congress after Maharani Scindia's affiliation to it. Gwalior differed from Malwa in this respect because in the latter region the princely family and the *jagirdars* of Indore state had disappeared from the political scene in the 1950s.[126] They did not help the Hindu nationalist movement, but neither did they hamper its development.

Outside Madhya Bharat, the Sangathanist party-building pattern was hardly to be found except in Vindhya Pradesh, where the Jana Sangh was again represented by RSS men with a Maharashtrian Brahmin background (like M.S. Newalkar, a local lawyer from Chhatarpur),[127] belonging to the Jain community (like Hukumchand Jain in Satna)[128] or from the Hindu Banya group (like Ram Hit Gupta, a businessman and local lawyer who was responsible for physical training in the regional branch of the RSS and was the Jana Sangh's most dependable candidate for the Vidhan Sabha, to which he was elected for five terms from 1957 onwards at Amarpatan).[129] In Satna district one of the party's main figures was Sukhendra Singh, an RSS man elected as MLA in 1962 who was also a lawyer but from a Rajput background.[130]

In Mahakoshal and Chhattisgarh, where the RSS existed only in urban

[124] Interview with N.K. Shejwalkar, 27 Nov. 1989, Gwalior.

[125] Their situation was even more critical at Gwalior where half of the Muslims who had abandoned 1,268 dwellings in 1947-8 returned from Pakistan or elsewhere; the refugees installed there found themselves threatened with expulsion due to laws enacted only recently. The Hindu Sahayata Samiti was able to perform its charitable mission to the full in this instance (*Hitavada*, 26 Mar. 1949, p. 14; 9 Dec. 1949, p. 3; 17 Dec. 1949, p. 2; 19 Feb. 1950, p. 1, and 3 Sept. 1951, p. 5; *Report of the general administration of Madhya Bharat, 1948- 1949*, op. cit., p. 60).

[126] R.W. Jones, 'Area, power and linkage', vol. 1, op. cit., p. 74.

[127] Ashfaq Ali, *Bhopal past and present*, op. cit., p. 367.

[128] Mookerjee Papers, F. 173.

[129] *Madhya Pradesh Vidhan Sabha sadasyon ka Sankship parichay – 1957*, Bhopal: Madhya Pradesh Vidhan Sabha sachivalay, 1961 and interview with R.H. Gupta, 20 Aug. 1992, Bhopal. Beyond local RSS support, Gupta attributes his electoral successes to the reputation of his family, one which he managed to perpetuate; his grandfather and his father had been known for their philanthropy and he too involved himself in social welfare. He therefore combined an activist profile with features typical of the local notable.

[130] *Parliament of India Ninth Lok Sabha who's who*, New Delhi: Lok Sabha Secretariat, 1992, p. 468.

'islands' like Jabalpur, Bilaspur or Raipur, the party failed to win a single seat throughout the 1950s. In these regions, which had in large part been directly administered by the British, the supremacy of Congress was unchallenged; it had been able to develop more freely than in the princely states and had thus become synonymous with the independence movement. The socialists of the PSP were also well established in these areas where in 1957 they won two-thirds of the twelve seats in the Vidhan Sabha, making them the principal opposition party.

In Mahakoshal the RSS had been developed since 1938 by Eknath Ranade, who had been despatched from Nagpur as *prant pracharak*; he was P.B. Dani's successor as General Secretary of the movement between 1956 and 1962. Among the *swayamsevaks* who 'joined because of his efforts'[131] in 1938-41 were the four founders of the local Jana Sangh, among whom two were Banyas working as lawyers, including Baburao Paranjpe, a Maharashtrian Brahmin.

Given Chhattisgarh's proximity to Nagpur, *shakhas* had been installed there since the 1930s, but in 1941, when Moreshwar Rao Moonje was transferred there as *pracharak* they numbered only thirty or so, concentrated in the towns.[132] One of the young *swayamsevaks* he had trained in Raipur, Y.R. Meghawale, who was from a landlord Maharashtrian Brahmin family, became a *pracharak* and worked for the Jana Sangh from its foundation, but all through the 1950s the party lacked the resources to put forward a significant number of candidates and had only 'three or four active members throughout Chhattisgarh'.[133]

The weakness of the Jana Sangh in Chhattisgarh and Mahakoshal prompted the party's leaders to send to those regions *sangathan mantris* already trained in the techniques required for 'long-distance missions' by virtue of their past experience as *pracharaks*. Moreshwar Rao Gadre, a *swayamsevak* trained by B.D. Dani in the 1940s,[134] was thus transferred in 1957 from Indore to Raipur, and Narayan Prasad Gupta, a *pracharak* at Bhopal since 1947, was detailed in 1962 to build up the party in Mahakoshal, starting with Jabalpur and Sagar.[135]

Thakre's typically Sangathanist aim of achieving a presence in the forty-five districts of Madhya Pradesh was realised by the end of the 1950s. He then worked to implant the Jana Sangh in each of the *tehsils* corresponding to Vidhan Sabha constituencies and embodying the party's strategic framework of *mandal samitis* (local committees), its local

---

[131] Interview with Baburao Paranjpe, 3 Nov. 1991, Jabalpur.
[132] Interview with M. Moonje.
[133] Interview with Meghawale, 12 Oct. 1991, Bhopal.
[134] M. Gadre, 'At the feet of Bhaiyaji', *Organiser*, 7 June 1965, p. 4.
[135] Interview with N.P. Gupta, 17 Nov. 1990, Bhopal.

decision-making units. This aim was fulfilled on the eve of the 1962 elections.[136] However, reaching the villagers from the *tehsil* headquarters was not easy since there were then 14,000 *gram panchayats* (village councils), with 15 to 80 *panchayats* per *tehsil*. Thakre therefore evolved the notion of *shakti kendras* (centres of power).[137] Each unit dealt with five or six *panchayats* and was to become the basic building-block of the Jana Sangh network.

This survey of party-building practices in Madhya Pradesh suggests two principal conclusions about the social background of the cadres in this state and the status of the prominent figures among them, the *sangathan mantris*. All the party cadres about whom relevant biographical information is available belonged to the upper castes and of these a majority were Brahmins and Banyas (either Hindus or Jains).[138] Members of the Maharashtrian high castes were particularly numerous, whether Brahmins or – like Thakre – CKPs (Chandraseni Kayasth Prabhus – Kayasths who came originally from Maharashtra). This over-representation was probably due to their common language and cultural references with the RSS *pracharaks* sent from Nagpur. Thus the RSS's expansion northwards can be said to have coincided with that of the Maharashtrian community in areas to which the latter had migrated from the eighteenth century onwards. This community was more receptive to the *pracharaks*' propaganda and provided the RSS with a nucleus in Madhya Bharat. However, in the long run, the over-representation of upper caste Maharashtrians turned out to be a handicap.

First, it was difficult to expand from such a narrow social base because it failed to provide the Hindu nationalist movement with enough contacts in a large number of communities, including the Rajputs. Second, the Marathi-speaking population, if it numbered one-fourth of the population of the city of Indore in 1931, accounted for only 2.24% of the population of Madhya Pradesh in 1951 (compared to 76.77% in the case of Hindi-speakers). Third, the over-representation of Maharashtrian Brahmins among the Jana Sangh cadres exposed it to Congress propaganda. In Indore, for instance, R.W. Jones noticed that:

To Hindi-speakers Congress politicians emphasize that Maharashtrian Brahmans are alien to the region and usurpers of Hindi-speakers' political opportunities, to the common people that Maharashtrian Brahmans [being associated with the organisations responsible for the assassination of Gandhi] are anti-Gandhian (and therefore against the common people), to Muslims that Maharashtrian Brahmans

[136] Interview with Thakre, and *Organiser*, 1 Dec. 1958, p. 13.

[137] K. Thakre, 'Madhya Pradesh mein, bhajpa sarkar bhaghirthi prayason ka pratiphal', op. cit.

[138] Aggarwal, Gupta and Khandelwal are Banya names.

are communalist, and to lower castes that Maharashtrian Brahmans view them-
selvs as socially superior and politically exclusive.[139]   ?

The fact that the Hindu nationalist cadres were mainly recruited among
the Maharashtrian upper castes and the merchant community partly
reflected and explained the uneven implantation of the Jana Sangh in
Madhya Pradesh. Logically enough, the party was stronger in the former
Madhya Bharat and Vindhya Pradesh regions where the upper castes
accounted for about one-fifth of the population. But even in these areas
the Jana Sangh was bound to suffer from its narrow base. Thus the
Sangathanist party-building techniques implemented in Madhya Pradesh
were hindered by an élitist bias.

The *sangathan mantri* – and this is our second conclusion – was the
central figure in the Jana Sangh's party-building pattern, cither through
conversion 'on the spot' or through 'long-distance missions'. Thakre, who
in this context was no more than *primus inter pares*, attributed a great part
of the credit for the Jana Sangh's expansion to M. Gadre, N.P. Gupta and
P. Khandelwal, who succeeded Gadre in charge of Madhya Bharat after
spending ten years as *pracharak* in Indore district. Most of the *sangathan
mantris* were experienced *pracharaks* who brought to the Jana Sangh the
values and *modus operandi* of the RSS.

These men were supposed to dedicate themselves solely to organisation and not to electoral politics; the party's candidates were recruited
rather from activists of a different type, who were attracted by public
action and the prospect of power. The explanation for this dual structure
is to be found primarily in the necessity of preserving the key cadres from
the compromises inherent in day-to-day politics.[140] Staying out of the
mainstream of political life, *sangathan mantris* were required by their
vocation to embody the values of the RSS and be models for *swayamsevaks* exposed to political temptations. Furthermore, they often still lived
celibate lives of spartan simplicity, a discipline which reinforced their
moral authority, on the model of relations between a *pracharak* and
young *swayamsevaks*. They were sometimes directors of conscience,

---

[139] R.W. Jones, 'Area, power and linkage in Indore', vol. 1, op. cit., p. 87. In Indore, the
Maharashtrian upper castes were particularly over-represented within the RSS and the
Jana Sangh. In the municipal councils, from 1950-65, the Maharashtrian Brahmins and
CKP accounted for two-thirds or three-fourths of the Hindu nationalist representation
(ibid., vol. 2, p. 258).

[140] This mistrust of politics among certain members of the RSS was revealed in an interview
with a *swayamsevak* of mature years in Bhopal: 'Those swayamsevaks who are in
politics, they say politics is such a bad or dirty game that we are liable to get spoiled in
that. "You have thrown us in the mud and it is your duty to draw us from that mud." It
is our duty to tell them that they are getting spoiled' (interview with P.P. Bapat, Bhopal,
25 Nov. 1989).

recalling certain aspects of the status of a *guru*, as the following description of K. Thakre by one of the BJP's leaders in Bhopal makes clear:

Kushabhau Thakre is our great man. He organised the whole party last forty, thirty years. He knows each and every worker form tehsil to city. [...] He is the Bhishma Pithamaha[141] of our party. he is very simple. He lives in a small place, just like a small *takht* [throne]...unmarried...and donated his whole life to the nation, to RSS. [...] If he thinks that I am not good and I am not working in the interest of party or nation, he will first guide me. Slowly, slowly he will say do this, do this, for our party. When someone will not go according to lines of party then he will say alright thank you.[142]

Here we see the prestige and respect conveyed in the Hindu world by asceticism – and, by implication, the figure of the ascetic in politics personified by the *pracharak*. The ideal *sangathan mantri* is therefore expected to attract followers mainly because of the ethic he represents through his discipline, his actions and his words.

This appeal – which is where our two conclusions intersect – relies in good measure on high caste values and more especially on a Brahminical culture. Consequently, it could not but be restricted, at least in the short term, except where it was supplemented by a tactic of social welfare as in Ujjain or in West Nimar. Undoubtedly, the case of the Jana Sangh in Madhya Pradesh suggests an original party-building pattern although its efficiency was limited in the short term. We must now return to the national level to take a more complete view and compare it to other methods of party building.

A counter-model of party-building

The organisational structure of the Jana Sangh obviously resembles that of the RSS. First, the *sangathan mantris* are the functional equivalent of *pracharaks*: just as the latter worked under the direct authority of Nagpur, the true hierarchy at the heart of the Jana Sangh linked the *sangathan mantris* to the General Secretary (Upadhyaya) via the national secretaries in charge of the four zones and the state organisers. Second, the party presidents at the state as well as the national level play the same role as the *sanghchalaks*.[143] After 1954 the party president was in effect a figurehead who (like the *sanghchalaks*) was selected to enhance the respectability of the Hindu nationalists.[144]

---

[141] The abdicating king in the Mahabharata who tried to reconcile the Pandavas' and the Kauravas' ambitions to succeed him.

[142] Interview conducted on 22 Nov. 1989, Bhopal.

[143] In Madhya Pradesh the Jana Sangh presidents were not 'encouraged to play an active administrative role' (interview with K. Thakre, 23 Nov. 1989).

[144] Prem Nath Dogra (party president, 1954-6), a District Officer in Jammu under British

The existence of an inner and an outer circle, separating those who were able to capitalise on links with the RSS from the rest, took institutional form in the early 1960s. As amended in 1963, the Jana Sangh's constitution distinguished between the party's ordinary and its active members. The latter were effectively defined as those who had been active in one of the party's executive or plenary bodies or in one of the affiliated organisations, which would have included the RSS. Whereas ordinary members could participate in elections to the executives of their local units, only active members could serve on bodies above that level.[145] This two-tier membership structure practically ensured that the RSS, whose workers would have been concentrated in the category of active members, retained a strong presence within the district and state levels of the Jana Sangh's organisation.

Just as in the RSS, the party's internal elections tended in any case to be a formality. According to the constitution of the Jana Sangh the president, at the national level as well as in the states, embodied supreme authority, above all because it was he who nominated the Working Committee. In fact, true control was exercised by the General Secretary and the national secretaries, who also dominated the Working Committee.[146] The election to the presidency took place every two years, with the party's state units electing an All India General Council (AIGC) which in turn nominated the president, but at each level the process was supervised by the *sangathan mantris*. The controlling authorities at state level were appointed in the same way.

Even if there was debate, the actual voting was generally unanimous in conformity with the RSS code of discipline: once a majority choice had emerged, all were commanded to rally to it. Here the *sangathan mantris* naturally relied on their moral authority, in particular when it came to preventing factionalism among the inevitable losers when appointments to posts of responsibility were being made and candidates nominated in the party before elections. Their proven disinterestedness – they refused all public appointments – contributed greatly to their power of persuasion. Given their devotion to the 'cause' of Hindu nationalism, their appeal for

---

rule, had been chosen as *sanghchalak* of that region in 1942 (*Organiser*, 29 Nov. 1954, pp. 3-14); Dev Prasad Ghosh (1956-60), an advocate of the Calcutta High Court and a prominent academic, was first a luminary of the Congress Nationalist Party of Malaviya and then of the Hindu Mahasabha, before joining the Jana Sangh in 1951 (ibid., 30 Apr. 1956, p. 8); Pitamber Das (1960-1) was a veteran Congressman who became *sanghchalak* at Mawana (UP) in 1943 and was later chosen as the Jana Sangh's president in Uttar Pradesh (*Uttar Pradesh Vidhan Parishad ke sadasyon ka jivan parichay*, Lucknow: Uttar Pradesh Vidhan Parishad sachivalay, 1965, p. 48 [Hindi]).

[145] B. Graham, *Hindu nationalism*, op. cit., p. 78.

[146] H.T. Davey, 'The transformation of an ideological movement into an aggregative party', op. cit., p. 164.

unity in the name of the movement's ideological objectives was generally both credible and effective.

The Jana Sangh thus benefited from the dual party structure described above. On the one hand, Jana Sanghis involved in public action contested elections and assumed charge of the presidentship at the local, state and national levels. On the other hand, *sangathan mantris* were not supposed to face the electorate or assume power in official, government bodies. They formed the organisational backbone of the party and drew their discipline and like-mindedness from their shared training in the RSS. Most of them were former *pracharaks* and cohesiveness was their norm. The *sangathan mantris* derived prestige and a particular authority from their position in the party structure. This enabled them to defuse factional fights between party leaders from other sectors (MLAs, MPs or other office-bearers) who might compete for a post. However, the division between the two categories must not be exaggerated; after 1954 the Jana Sangh also owed its cohesion to the fact that most of its cadres and leaders were members of the RSS, imbued with the ideology and discipline of this organisation.

The form of the Jana Sangh reflected a conception of party structure which was relatively original in the Indian context. Many Indian parties took shape as the result of co-option and 'aggregation'. Local or regional leaders regarded as having influence because of their wealth, the size of their landholdings or their prestige within a caste association were given political responsibility or put up as candidates at elections. This led to the creation of a pyramid of influence. A political notable would attract 'associates' prepared to guarantee their support according to a clientelistic logic; multiplied many times, this would give the party in question a base of considerable size, like a vast coalition. The Hindu Mahasabha worked on the same principle, but the notables within it represented only a narrow periphery of society and thus could not assure it of any substantial political weight. Congress came close to the classic form of this type, and functioned as a great interlocking mass of personal fiefs, also called 'vote banks'. Myron Weiner emphasised the fact that 'Congress is primarily concerned with recruiting members and winning support. It does not mobilize; it aggregates': 'In its effort to win, Congress adapts itself to the local power structures. It recruits from among those who have local power and influence.'[147]

The Jana Sangh adheres to a different logic, close to the method used by the RSS, one we have described as 'Sangathanist': it gives precedence to building a solid network of activists, capable at one and the same time

---

[147] M. Weiner, *Party building in a new nation: the Indian National Congress*, Chicago University Press, 1967, p. 15.

of implanting the party at the local level through social work and of propagating Hindu nationalist ideology, albeit at the cost, if necessary, of unpopularity. This was discernible in Punjab and Rajasthan as well as Madhya Pradesh.

In 1952 the party in Punjab nominated, out of forty-three candidates for election to the Vidhan Sabha, thirty 'little-known RSS workers and alumni rather than co-opting local notables'.[148] The result was all the more disastrous because the party refused to campaign on regionalist themes that were of growing concern to the voting public. In 1957, the Jana Sangh in Punjab succumbed to this demagogic temptation. Since it recognised that two languages were spoken in the region, it campaigned for the promotion of Hindi, with the result that it won nine MLA seats and its ranks were swollen by defenders of Hindi, including many Arya Samajists. However this increase in its manpower by 'aggregation' made it vulnerable to dissension; in particular, Congress was able to negotiate some concessions with the Arya Samaj leaders. The RSS then immediately applied itself to re-establishing its authority in the Jana Sangh, which cut it off from its fringe supporters. Partly as a consequence, it lost support at the polls in 1962.

The Jana Sangh also ignored the possibility of mobilising support from influential sections of society in Rajasthan, where it did not hesitate to alienate Rajput landlords. As the 1951-2 elections approached, associations of landowners were looking for a political mouthpiece to reinforce their opposition to Congress, which had just announced the abolition of the *zamindari* and *jagirdari* systems. They first opted for the Jana Sangh;[149] then the Kshatriya Mahasabha (which was dominated by Rajput landowners) sponsored the formation of a Samyukta Dal (Party of Unity) in association with the Ram Rajya Parishad and Hindu Mahasabha. The Jana Sangh refused to join the Samyukta Dal so as to remain faithful to its position on agrarian reform, S.S. Bhandari fearing 'feudalism coming in by the back door of democracy'.[150] Finally the Rajputs concentrated their support on the Ram Rajya Parishad and helped the party to gain a clear success in the state.[151] However, the majority of the 8 MLAs returned on a Jana Sangh ticket were Rajput landlords and they abandoned the party when it appeared that it was not likely to amend its stand on the question of land reform.[152] The refusal by the Jana Sangh to seek growth by binding

---

[148] G.A. Heeger, 'Discipline versus mobilizaiton: Party building and the Punjab Jana Sangh', *Asian Survey*, 12, 10 (Oct. 1972), p. 868.

[149] Mookerjee Papers, F. 168 (letter from Vijay Singh to Mookerjee, 27 June 1951).

[150] Ibid., F. 173 (letter from Bhandari to Mookerjee, 23 Nov. 1951).

[151] B. Graham, *Hindu nationalism*, op. cit., pp. 179-81.

[152] Interview with S.S. Bhandari.

itself to particular social groups was on a par with its hostility to any alliance likely to be prejudicial to its discipline or dilute its identity.

After the elections of 1951-2, S.P. Mookerjee, who was always anxious to form a large opposition party, had sought a *rapprochement* between the Jana Sangh and the Hindu Mahasabha, since the rivalry between them had injured the electoral performance of both. This cause was taken up on Mookerjee's death by N.C. Chatterjee, president of the Hindu Mahasabha.[153] But in December 1953, doubtless under pressure from the RSS, M.C. Sharma, who till then had favoured the project, described the Hindu Mahasabha as a 'communalist creation' which 'welcome[d] princes and zamindars and defend[ed] vested interests'.[154] This was the end of the first attempt at amalgamation. However Chatterjee, together with V.G. Deshpande, persevered. In January 1955 they had an abortive meeting with Golwalkar,[155] and in February 1956 they negotiated with Upadhyaya but without being able to agree on a name for the intended new party. The Jana Sangh was unwilling to change its name.[156] Many Hindu Sabhaites then joined the Jana Sangh, including Hardayal Devgun, who was one of the mainstays of the Hindu Sabha in Delhi and secretary of the Hindu Mahasabha till 1958.[157] He was followed by V.G. Deshpande. The Jana Sangh had at last attained its objectives, because since the outset the party had conceived of an alliance with the Hindu Mahasabha solely in terms of the latter rallying to its own programme or even being completely absorbed by it.[158]

The Sangathanist strategy adopted by the Jana Sangh meant that its practical policy in the 1950s boiled down essentially to the creation of a militant network dedicated, like the RSS, patiently to imposing its vision of the world over a long period by working at the grassroots. Up to the early 1960s the Jana Sangh's leaders considered that they had to resist any drift into propaganda or alliances that would be counter to the party's ideology.[159] In 1962, Upadhyaya justified this attitude by arguing that united fronts of the opposition were bound to 'degenerate into a struggle for power by opportunist elements coming together in the interest of expediency.'[160] He wanted to build the Jana Sangh into an alternative party

[153] *Amrita Bazar Patrika*, 11 July 1952, in N.C. Chatterjee Papers, vol. VIII.

[154] *Statesman*, 7 Dec. 1952 in ibid.

[155] *Hindu Outlook*, 31 Jan. 1955, p. 1.

[156] Ibid., 28 Feb. 1956, p. 1.

[157] *Who's who in Lok Sabha – 1967*, op. cit., p. 132.

[158] M. Weiner, *Party politics in India*, Princeton University Press, 1957, pp. 208-9.

[159] See the resolution of the party general executive in July 1956 in M.A. Jhangiani, *Jana Sangh and Swatantra*, op. cit., p. 143.

[160] D. Upadhyaya, 'Jana Sangh', *Seminar*, no. 29, Jan. 1962, p. 20.

to the Congress and looked upon elections as an 'opportunity to educate the people on political issues and to challenge the right of the Congress to be in power'.[161] The Jana Sangh rejected alliances with particular groups or their political representatives because in future it would convert sectional (i.e. regional or casteist/corporatist) interests to the irenicism or organicism of its Hindu nationalism, and thus win over its competitiors – as it had already done with the Hindu Sabhaites. Here one finds oneself in the presence of an alternative model of party-building, as G. Heeger has already suggested:

Parties can be more than aggregates put together to form a winning coalition. As might be surmised from the term 'party' itself, they can reflect a claim by the party that it – a party – address itself correctly to and for the nation as a whole.[162]

Heeger added that 'for the Jana Sangh leadership, their party is to be a microcosm of an ideal India' and that the distinction these leaders made 'between the "party-building" and mobilising support has exacted a price' in electoral terms. In the eyes of those who controlled the party after 1954, electoral results were certainly less important than local implantation and propaganda, and indeed between 1954 and 1959 the number of members and local committees increased, respectively, from 143,000 and 2,000 to 215,370 and 2,551[163] while the number of candidates nominated by the party in the Vidhan Sabha elections fell between 1952 and 1957 from 727 to 582.

In the 1950s *swayamsevaks* became involved in the political arena through the Jana Sangh, a party modelled on the image of the RSS The Jana Sangh aspired to develop through a Sangathanist network of activists that would make it co-extensive with society. Conceived as a front organisation of the RSS, like the ABVP or the BMS, it plunged into social work with the intention of establishing, or re-establishing, an organicist type of society – one purged of tension. The traversing of social and political space by means of a network largely borrowed from the RSS and the implementation of social welfare activism were to be the two complementary wings of the Sangathanist strategy. This strategy of penetration of the body of society, according to those who conceived it, would, in the long term, naturally bring the Jana Sangh to power because the Hindu nation would eventually recognise it as its appointed political representative.

The involvement of the RSS in the political arena introduced an

---

[161] Ibid.

[162] G.A. Heeger, 'Discipline versus mobilization', op. cit., pp. 864-5.

[163] For more details, see B. Graham, *Hindu nationalism*, op. cit., pp. 78-9.

important innovation into Hindu nationalist politics. For the first time the network of *swayamsevaks* made themselves available – partly at least – for political action. This was made clear in Madhya Pradesh during the 1951-2 elections, just as in Uttar Pradesh where 100,000 activists took part in the election campaign.[164] Ten years later, in the 1962 elections, the Jana Sangh in UP announced its deployment of 100,000 activists: according to press reports they canvassed bank employees in Kanpur, worked their way through the suburbs of Lucknow, infiltrated villages in Gorakhpur district, and organised half of the election meetings held in Varanasi.[165]

However, it remained to be seen whether the strategy of building up the Jana Sangh by the use of Sangathanist techniques would result in electoral success. By the late 1950s the party's workers were still concentrating on the tasks of spreading and strengthening its organisational framework; they engaged in propaganda and agitational campaigns only where an issue seemed to them of special importance. It was therefore possible for the Jana Sangh's leaders to claim that the poor election results of their party were only to be expected, but the fact remained that a weak electoral performance was bound to arouse concern.

Each of the three chapters of Part I has dealt with one strategy of the Hindu nationalist movement. At the level of ideology, we have analysed the formation of Hindu nationalism in terms of a strategy of stigmatising and emulating the Other. However, the Hindu traditionalism of certain members of Congress presented an alternative position which suggested to men like Mookerjee the need for a strategy of *rapprochement* in relation to the Congress up till 1951.

As far as the mobilisation of support was concerned, this attitude corresponded to an effort at integration which, with Mookerjee, took the form of a search for allies at the price of a certain dilution of Hindu nationalist ideology. The other strategy to mobilise support which Hindu nationalists employed was the manipulation of symbols and exploitation of issues such as Ramjanmabhoomi and refugees from East Pakistan. This approach was hampered by the political context, the political class being largely attached to a politics of secularism to the point of supporting the sometimes repressive measures introduced by Nehru.

At the level of party-building strategy, the Jana Sangh was based essentially on its Sangathanist network, which devoted its main efforts

---

[164] S.V. Kogekar and R.L. Park, 'Uttar Pradesh' in S.V. Kogekar and R.l. Park (eds), *Reports on the Indian General Elections, 1951-1952*, Bombay: Popular Book Depot, 1956, p. 159.

[165] *Organiser*, 21 Aug. 1961, p. 16; *Statesman* (Delhi), 4 Jan. 1962, p. 7, and 7 Jan. 1962, p. 7; *National Herald*, 10 Jan. 1962, p. 3 and 1 Feb. 1962, p. 4; *Indian Express*, 30 March 1962.

during the 1950s to consolidating itself. The alternative method, on which the Hindu Mahasabha relied and which Mookerjee explored in the early 1950s, could have consisted of an 'aggregation' of local notables and politicians, but this would have made the Jana Sangh vulnerable to a dilution of its identity and undermined the internal discipline on which it had set such store.

It is apparent from these strategies that a moderate combination would involve cooperation with Hindu traditionalists and a pragmatic effort at integration in mainstream political activity – notably by means of alliances and increased reliance on local notables – while a more militant, even aggressive, combination would consist, for the Jana Sangh, of placing its Sangathanist network at the service of an instrumentalist strategy designed to use Hindu nationalist themes for the purpose of mobilisation. From 1954 onwards, this was the preferred combination. However the three strands of which it consisted did not come together till the late 1980s, due essentially to the weaknesses of the Sangathanist approach and the constraints imposed by the political context.

By choosing the Sangathanist method, the Jana Sangh was distancing itself from the rivalries between notables which had always undermined the organisation of the Hindu Mahasabha. But in doing so it denied itself the advantage of either their influence or their popularity. It relied mainly on the appeal of its cadres and their Hindu nationalist ideology which, in the 1950s, proved less attractive to voters than the Congress's promises of socio-economic development. This partly explains the party's modest results in elections: in 1952 it won three seats in the Lok Sabhas and thirty-five in the Vidhan Sabhas and in 1957, respectively, four and forty-six, an unremarkable development. At the end of the 1950s, the Jana Sangh faced a dilemma: should it pursue the Sangathanist logic of a slow penetration of the whole of Indian society, in the style of the RSS, if this entailed repeated electoral defeats? The Sangathanist method seemed ill-suited to the demands of a political party, as Bhaurao Deoras later implicitly admitted:

In politics, as pandit Deendayal [Upadhyaya] used to say, the measuring rod of success is the number of seats that you win; but for Sangh, it is the quality of the *swayamsevaks* we develop and the social influence that we wield which matters.[166]

From the 1960s the party oscillated between a strategy of integration with legitimate politics and one of militant ethno-religious mobilisation. The first option involved acquiescence in secularist norms, the elaboration of an economic programme likely to challenge the government's policies, the maximisation of the patriotic content of its ideology and a growing

[166] *Organiser.* 11 Nov. 1984. p. 18.

reliance on notables. Such a course would allow the Jana Sangh to normalise its position within the political system but not without diluting its identity, which the Sangathanist network, close to the RSS, would find intolerable. For the latter the second strategy, based on the manipulation of symbols of Hindu identity, ought to have been its preferred electoral strategy. However, it demanded two significant changes to the variables of our model: first, the activists' network had to expand and be supplemented by religious figures in order to amplify its mobilisatory capacity; and second, but more importantly, the instrumentalist strategy could not function effectively unless the constraints placed on it by the political context, particularly through the defence of secularism as a legitimate norm, were relaxed.

Part II. OSCILLATION AND HYBRIDISATION IN THE 1960s

4

TOWARDS STRATEGIES OF MODERATION?

By the late 1950s the Jana Sangh had developed in North India a relatively strong party apparatus and began to try to project itself as an alternative to the Congress. However its leaders ultimately did not envisage a strategy which appealed primarily to Hindu ethno-religious feelings. This choice can be explained by several factors, most of them related to the prevalent political context and especially to a certain duality of the Congress. On the one hand, at the local level, many Congressmen proved to be Hindu traditionalists whose policies and discourses deprived the Jana Sangh of some of its political arguments, at least in the Hindi belt. On the other hand, the central government displayed a vigilant anti-communalism and a strong commitment to issues devoid of ethnic connotations. In fact, during the 1950s Nehru imposed a politics of secularism and gave priority to socio-economic development. The latter contributed greatly to his popularity. Overwhelmingly, the economic themes in the programme of Congress, and of the other major political groupings (Socialists and Communists), tended to raise economic development, besides secularism, to the status of a legitimate norm of Indian politics.

This, added to its poor results in the 1957 elections, spurred the Jana Sangh to redirect its strategy towards a better understanding of socio-economic problems than its theme of Hindu nationalism. The party exploited the vulnerability of the government on two themes that were not associated with militant Hindu nationalism and were in accordance with Gandhian ideals: the fight against increasing state intervention in the economy and the defence of national integrity. Its principal target consisted of the middle classes, notably peasants owning their own land and businessmen already attracted by the Jana Sangh's promotion of economic decentralisation.

Besides adjusting to the constraints of the political context, the Jana

Sangh leadership probably realised in the late 1950s and early 1960s that it could not rely merely on its Sangathanist network for contesting elections. On the one hand, the party evolved a *rapprochement* with the non-communist opposition, certain components of which were interested in alliances provided the Jana Sangh toned done its Hindu nationalist identity. On the other hand, this development was accompanied, in so far as the Jana Sangh's party-building strategy was concerned, by a greater readiness to co-opt notables and politicians who did not belong to the RSS or to its affiliates but whose local influence could attract votes. This was the first hybridisation of the Sangathanist model.

Adjusting to the political context

The electoral strength of Congress barely diminished until 1967. In 1962 the party held on to 361 of the 488 seats in the Lok Sabha and 44.1% of the votes. Furthermore, it was in power in every state (except Kerala, for a while). It was able to maintain this supremacy largely through its ability to remain a party of consensus, and this was due to its capacity for adaptation in response to its internal divisions; as Rajni Kothari explains, its fringe factions exerted a pressure which generally brought the party into step with organised public opinion:

There is plurality within the dominant party which makes it more representative, provides flexibility, and sustains internal competition. At the same time, it is prepared to absorb groups and movements from outside the party and thus prevent other parties from gaining in strength.[1]

As far as the Jana Sangh was concerned, the exploitation of issues with militant Hindu connotations was made all the more difficult because of the presence in Congress of a Hindu traditionalist current of opinion.

The dual constraints of the 'Congress system'

Nehru may have considerably reduced the influence of Hindu traditionalists at the Centre in the name of secularist values, but their leaders fell back on the states, especially in North India. Hence the Jana Sangh found itself caught in a vice between the vigilant secularism of the Centre and local Congressmen encroaching on the themes it regarded as its own. This reduction in its room for manoeuvre was especially well illustrated in the debates about the place of Hindi and the protection of the cow.

---

[1]   R. Kothari, 'The Congress system in India', *Asian Survey*, 4 (12), Dec. 1964, pp. 1164-5.

The Hindu traditionalists and state politics.   In 1950, the Constituent Assembly, responding to demands from the non-Hindi-speaking populations, gave English an extended lease as India's official language for an interim period of fifteen years, after which it would be succeeded by Hindi – which it was hoped would then have spread sufficiently to make this practical. This compromise, whose accommodating character betrayed the influence of Nehru, was sharply denounced by the Jana Sangh. Mookerjee pleaded for Hindi to be accorded the status of a national language without delay.[2] The report of the Official Language Commission of 1957, half-way through the designated interim period, also exasperated the Jana Sangh on account of its laxity; the party demanded solid advances such as the systematic use of Hindi in communications between the Centre and the states.[3] In fact, Nehru was determined to tread a path of conciliation with the southern states, which dreaded the expiry of the interim period in 1965. Thus, in 1963 he obtained the passage of an Official Language Act which kept for English the status of 'associate additional official language', to the great displeasure of the Jana Sangh, which denounced it as a 'colonialist language bill'.[4] In 1967, Congress reiterated its guarantee that English would remain an associated language, under an Official Languages (Amendment) Act.

Meanwhile, in two of the states where the Jana Sangh was most active– Uttar Pradesh and Madhya Pradesh – it found itself confronted by traditionalist Congressmen who were already won over to the promotion of Hindi. In Uttar Pradesh, at the end of 1947, G.B. Pant, who headed the state government, had pronounced Hindi to be the language of the courts and of the administration generally.[5] In 1951 Hindi was declared the official language, without any guarantee in favour of Urdu-speakers. The Anjuman-e-Taraqqi-e-Urdu, as authorised by Article 347 of the Constitution, petitioned the President of the Republic for official recognition of Urdu as a language used by a 'substantial proportion of the population'. More than 4 million signatures were collected for the petition in 1954, and in reply Azad, the Minister of Education, recommended that Urdu classes

2   See his speech of 13 Dec. 1949 at the Constituent Assembly in *Dr Syama Prasad Mookerjee*, New Delhi: Lok Sabha Secretariat, 1990, pp. 45-52.

3   Resolutions of 8 May 1954 and 24 Nov. 1957, *Party documents*, vol. 5, New Delhi: Bharatiya Jana Sangh, 1973, pp. 21 and 28.

4   Resolution of 6 April 1963, ibid., p. 30.

5   B. Graham, *Hindu nationalism*, op. cit., pp. 113ff. Although not a Hindu traditionalist, Pant had affinities with Patel's attitude towards Muslims. While Nehru thought that it was the Hindus' responsibility to help the religious minorities to feel at home in India after Partition, Pant declared in 1948 that Muslims 'should try to win over the good will of the majority'. He added that 'if they persisted in their old ways the establishment of a purely Hindu raj was inevitable' (cited in L.Brennan, 'The state and communal violence in UP, 1947-1992', *South Asia*, 17, 1994, p. 23).

be set up. The Jana Sangh immediately protested at this pressure, and expressed the hope that 'the government of Uttar Pradesh will keep control of these anti-national tendencies arising under cover of Urdu, and will act as firmly as before'.[6] This hope was not disappointed by Dr Sampurnanand, who headed the state government from 1954 to 1960.

Originally from Varanasi, Sarvasri Sampurnanand was a veteran of the school of Malaviya and Tandon, whom he had met in the 1920s. Having been exasperated by the Khilafat movement, he was also one of those who brought about the renewal of the Hindu Mahasabha in 1922[7] before being seduced by socialism. However he remained attached to Hindu traditionalist ideas. He studied Sanskrit in order to read the Vedas in the original, after which he proudly insisted that India had been the original home of the Aryans and their starting point for their migrations to the east and to the west.[8] Between 1954 and 1958 he curbed the implementation of instructions received from the Union government about Urdu. The Centre reiterated them in 1958 on the basis of a constitutional amendment guaranteeing to every linguistic minority the possibility of instruction in its own language. Then the state government made a concession in favour of Urdu in six districts in the north-west of the state where more than one-fifth of the population were Muslims, but no fundamental change in its linguistic policy was made. The report of the Language Committee set up by the state in 1961, just when the census showed that more than 10% of the population in Uttar Pradesh spoke Urdu, did not suggest any measures that would challenge Hindi's monopoly in the high schools and in written examinations. Graham concludes:

The decision in favour of a Hindi-only policy meant that the Congress government in Uttar Pradesh was reasonably protected against any attack from the Jana Sangh, which had therefore to concentrate its fire upon the Anjuman-i-Taraqqi-i-Urdu and other groups campaigning on behalf of Urdu-speakers.[9]

In the same way, Hindu traditionalists within Congress in Uttar Pradesh prevented the Jana Sangh from making protection of the cow a political issue. In 1955, the state government announced before a jubilant Vidhan Sabha the outlawing of cow slaughter, as it was authorised to do under the Constitution. Nehru, while admitting the legislative freedom of

---

[6] *Organiser*, 26 April 1954, p. 8.

[7] Sampurnanand, *Memories and reflections*, Bombay: Asia Publishing House, 1962, p. 28, and J. Lütt, 'Die regionalen Wurzeln der Hindu Mahasabha' in H. Kulke and D. Rothermund (eds), *Regionale Tradition in Südasien*, Wiesbaden: Franz Steiner, 1985, p. 224.

[8] Dr Sampurnanand, *Introduction to Vedic studies*, Belgaum: Academy of Comparative Philosophy and Religion, 1969, p. 6.

[9] B. Graham, *Hindu nationalism*, op. cit., p. 117.

the states in this matter, described the decision as a 'wrong step'.[10] This comment did not induce Sampurnanand to amend the new law. A comparable measure was passed at the same time by the Congress governments of Bihar, Rajasthan and Madhya Pradesh.

In fact the partial eviction of the Jana Sangh from its chosen territory was even more decisive in Madhya Pradesh. In this state, and especially in Mahakoshal, its traditional heartland, Congress had been dominated since the 1920s by men whose prestige was partly due to their talents as writers in Hindi. Seth Govind Das, the son of a rich Marwari from Jabalpur, president of the Mahakoshal branch of Congress in 1928-34 and 1946-57, and elected to Parliament uninterruptedly up till 1971, wrote about 100 plays; and Dwarka Prasad Mishra, a minister in the governments of Ravi Shankar Shukla in 1937-9 and after Independence, was an equally prolific Hindi author; he also founded or collaborated in numerous Hindi newspapers in Jabalpur.[11] R.S. Shukla, who became Chief Minister of Madhya Pradesh for ten years after Independence, did not share this interest in Hindi literature but favoured the promotion of Sanskrit. He had been introduced to Congress around 1915 by Moonje[12] and like many Hindu traditionalists had been an active member of M.M. Malaviya's Independent Congress Party in the 1920s.[13]

After Independence, these Congressmen asserted their presence in associations defending the cause of Hindi. Since 1947, from the platform of the Central Provinces and Berar Hindi Sahitya Sammelan (Conference of Hindi Literature), over which he had presided since 1920, Seth Govind Das had been calling on the government to make Hindi the official language and on the 'Muslims to adopt the general language of the people on their own and also to imbibe the general civilisation of the country'.[14] He repeated this proposition in 1948 as president of the All India Hindi Sahitya Sammelan, over which he once again presided from 1963 to 1971. D.P. Mishra, whom he invited to speak from this platform in 1949, expressed the same ideas. He chaired the congress of the movement in

---

[10] Cited in D.E. Smith, *India as a secular state*, op. cit., p. 487.

[11] P.B. Mayer, 'Development and demise: The Congress as the Raj' in J. Masselos (ed.), *Struggling and ruling: The Indian National Congress, 1885-1985*, London: Oriental University Press, 1985, p. 184. In the early 1930s, Seth Govind Das and D.P. Mishra launched *Lokmat*. The former provided the funds while the latter was editor of what was the first Hindi newspaper in Central India (interview with D.P. Mishra, Oral History Transcripts, Accession n° 510, NMML, p. 94-Hindi).

[12] D.E.U. Baker, *Changing political leadership in an Indian province: The Central Provinces and Berar, 1919-1939*, Delhi: Oxford University Press, 1979, p. 36.

[13] S.C. Sharma, *Pt. Ravi Shankar Shukla: Life and times*, New Delhi: Bhartiya Bhasha Peeth, 1991, pp. 52-4.

[14] *Hitavada*, 20 Dec. 1947, p. 3.

1956 to defend the same points of view, along with Sampurnanand and R.S. Shukla.[15]

The Congressmen of Madhya Pradesh were important protagonists of the traditionalist tendency at the national level. In 1949 Seth Govind Das, together with Raghuvira – a Sanskrit scholar (see p. 179) –, was one of the principal backers in the Constituent Assembly of the amendment by Thakurdas Bhargava which led to the prohibition of cow slaughter being included among the Directive Principles of State Policy.[16] Moreover in 1949 Seth Govind Das headed the All India Cow Protection League.[17]

The traditionalist hostility of the Madhya Pradesh Congressmen towards Nehru and their support for Tandon – who nominated Seth Govind Das to the Congress Working Committee in October 1950 – came into the open in September 1951 in the decisive vote of the AICC: only the Mahakoshal branch of Congress, dominated by R.S. Shukla, Seth Govind Das and D.P. Mishra, declared itself against Nehru's replacement of Tandon.[18] Mishra resigned from the party the following day and discreetly joined the newly-founded Jana Sangh.[19] His closeness to the Hindu nationalist movement had already become apparent at the time of the ban on the RSS in 1948-9 , when he had been Home Minister of the Central Provinces and Berar. True to 'Patelist' logic, he had then invited the RSS to join Congress because 'the Sangh, if conducted on the right lines may be able to doing a lot of good'.[20] In the Vidhan Sabha of Madhya Pradesh, where he announced his resignation from the Shukla government, Mishra resorted to militant Hindu language against Nehru, notably over East Bengal:

Both our national honour and our plighted word to the Hindu minority demand that we issue an ultimatum to Pakistan that if she does not ensure conditions of security and self-respect for her Hindu population, we would ourselves invade Pakistan and occupy the territory necessary to rehabilitate the entire Hindu minority. [...]

And this secularism, sir, is a chapter by itself. Although both the central and

[15] Ibid., 10 Dec. 1948, p. 6; 28 Feb. 1949, p. 4; 1 Jan. 1956, p. 1, and 12 Jan. 1957, p. 1.

[16] Ibid., 25 Nov. 1949, p. 3.

[17] B. Hooja, *A life dedicated: Biography of Govind Das*, Delhi University Press, 1956, p. 124. Seth Govind Das frequently took a Hindu traditionalist position during debates in the Constituent Assembly. See, for example, his intervention on 5 November 1948 when he took exception to the decision that the text of the Constitution would be written in English, objected to the choice of Jana Mana Gana rather than Vande Mataram as the national anthem, and protested at the use of any other than "the ancient name, 'Bharat' " to designate the newly independent country (*Constituent Assembly Debates*, New Delhi: Lok Sabha Secretariat, 1989, pp. 222-3).

[18] *Hitavada*, 9 Sept. 1951, p. 1.

[19] Mookerjee Papers, F-173, letter of Mookerjee to Bhai Mahavir, 30 Nov. 1951.

[20] *Hitavada*, 11 Dec. 1948.

state governments have successfully ensured full civic rights and equality of opportunity of the minorities, our Prime Minister never misses an opportunity to showing in effect as if he is the sole protector and guardian angel of the Muslims, and that but for him they would be nowhere.[21]

D.P. Mishra did not remain in the Jana Sangh, where his main ambition was to gain national prominence, but instead founded the Bharatiya Lok Congress before joining the PSP and, finally, returning to Congress. He became Chief Minister of Madhya Pradesh in 1963. The Madhya Pradesh branch of Congress numbered many other leaders who could in no way be suspected of communalism, such as Kailash Nath Katju and Bhagwati Rai Mandloi (the Chief Ministers in between the incumbencies of R.S. Shukla, who died in 1957, and D.P. Mishra). However the presence of Hindu traditionalists in the Congress fold served to deprive the Jana Sangh of many of its strongest arguments on which its appeal was based, such as the promotion of Hindi, the protection of the cow and the fight against Christian missions.

In Madhya Bharat, Hindi had been recognised as the language of public administration in 1948;[22] in Madhya Pradesh it was declared the official language, along with Marathi, in October 1950,[23] while cow slaughter was at first restricted in 1951[24] and later prohibited altogether in the mid-1950s. The regional challenge presented by missionary proselytism, especially in the tribal areas, was largely shielded from Hindu nationalist propaganda by the attitude of the Congress. In 1954 the Jana Sangh launched an 'Anti-Foreign Missionary Week' protest movement,[25] but the agitation was suspended when the government set up its own commission of inquiry, the Niyogi Committee, whose report took a view close to that of the Hindu nationalists. It proposed in effect the legal prohibition of conversions which were not completely voluntary.[26] But Congress refrained from enacting such a law, which would have been difficult to formulate and indeed to apply without contravening the principles of religious liberty enshrined in the Constitution. The Hindu nationalists proposed two new laws, in 1958 and 1961, which were rejected,[27] but they were unable to exploit the issue further because of the vigilant control Congress was already exercising over missionaries. D.P.

---

[21]   D.P. Mishra, *Living an era*, vol. 2, op. cit., pp. 238-9.

[22]   Madhya Bharat Cabinet Papers, File 505/48.

[23]   *Hitavada*, 6 Oct. 1950, p. 1.

[24]   Ibid., 25 Sept. 1951, p. 1.

[25]   *Statesman*, 19 Nov. 1954, p. 11.

[26]   *Report of the Christian missionary activities enquiry committee*, vol. 1, Indore: Government Regional Press, 1957, p. 170. For more details, see ch. 5.

[27]   *Hitavada*, 13 April 1961, p. 6.

Mishra was thus reminded by his own Minister of Justice, when the proposed Hindu nationalist law received its final reading, that the Centre delegated to the state the task of taking measures against missionaries.[28] This call to order was undoubtedly the result of factional competition. Indeed, the Hindu nationalists found themselves all the more firmly excluded from their chosen field of action because certain Congress factions, vying with those that held power, were exploiting similar themes in order to embarrass the Chief Minister. This explains, for example, why Seth Govind Das demanded that D.P. Mishra – who was one of his rivals – devote more energy to the substitution of English by Hindi in the administration.[29]

The Hindu nationalists seemed to be held in a vice-like grip by the 'Congress system'. On the one hand, in the states we have been considering – Uttar Pradesh and Madhya Pradesh – Congress traditionalists appropriated some of their arguments; on the other, Nehru was denouncing them at the Centre in the name of the secular state.[30]

Nehru and the politics of secularism. Nehru's reaction to communal riots in the early 1960s illustrates perfectly the determined secularism prevailing at the Centre, but also some of its limitations. The reappearence of rioting in the 1960s has been largely attributed to the emergence in the Muslim community, which had lost many of its political and business élite in 1947, of a class of successful small entrepreneurs. Hindu industrialists and businessmen, faced with this new competition, were all the more willing to resort to violence in order to preserve their position.[31] The riot at Jabalpur in Feburary 1961 seemed to be the result of such local socio-economic rivalries and thus to correspond with this pattern. The facts of the case were apparently as follows.[32] On 3 February, employees of the second-largest producer of *bidis* (small cigarettes) in the region, a Muslim, broke into the house of a Hindu merchant and raped his daughter, who then committed suicide. Several hundred fellow-students of the dead

---

[28] Ibid., 2 Oct. 1963, p. 1.

[29] Ibid., 24 Nov. 1963, p. 3.

[30] The secularism displayed by the Congress government was not totally unbiased. Some expressions of communalism by the minorities were tolerated, especially when the party might benefit from them. In 1959 the Congress made an alliance with the Muslim League in Kerala in order to form a new government after dislodging the Communists from power. This bias was consistent with the idea, implicit since Partition, that the Hindus, because they formed a majority, had more obligations than the minorities.

[31] C. Jaffrelot, 'Les émeutes entre hindous et musulmans – essai de hiérarchisation des facteurs culturels économiques et politiques', *Cultures et Conflits*, 5 (spring 1992), pp. 25-55.

[32] This reconstruction is taken from reports in *Hindustan Times*, 5, 8, 9, 10, 11 and 13 Feb. 1961.

girl, with support from the ABVP, organised a demonstration. This degenerated into a riot, which the army brought under control without any serious harm, on the 5th. But on the 7th, after the army had been withdrawn, Hindus attacked the town's Muslim quarters. The violence and looting continued till late into the night, leaving forty-two dead – of whom only two were Hindus.[33] According to the left-wing newspaper *New Age*, this second phase of the riot was attributable to alarmist rumours put out by *Yugadharma*, an RSS paper, that the forces of law and order had been attacked by the Muslims.[34] The premeditated character of the violence could be deduced from the fact that Hindu houses situated within the Muslim quarters had been marked beforehand so that they would be spared.

Nehru, convinced that the riot had been carefully organised,[35] came to Bhopal to tell the local Congressmen how much he had been disturbed by the violence, all the more so because those he was addressing had remained 'sitting inside their house like purdah ladies during the riots'.[36] He ordered the head of the state government to resort at will to the Preventive Detention Act in order to prevent the communalists from doing harm.[37] Before his visit, he appointed a special committee of Congress to look into the possibilities of prohibiting the communalist parties from contesting elections,[38] an idea that naturally alarmed the leaders of the Jana Sangh. Vajpayee and other Jana Sangh MPs pressed Lal Bahadur Shastri, the Home Minister, for a definition of a communalist party[39] – which seemed to be lacking. The report of the Congress special committee pronounced in favour of a ban, but at the same time two obstacles came to light: the imminence of elections and the hostility to the proposal of two Muslim members of the Committee.[40] Furthermore, some Muslim MPs announced simultaneously the holding of a Muslim Convention.[41] Those who Nehru considered as potential beneficiaries of his plan – namely the Muslims – did not seem prepared to make a major effort to eradicate political communalism.[42]

---

[33] P.C. Joshi, 'Jabalpur – the lessons', *New Age*, 12 March 1961, p. 4.

[34] L.N. Malhotra and M.K. Bajpai, 'Ghastly communal carnage in Jabalpur', ibid., 26 Feb. 1961.

[35] S. Gopal, *Jawaharlal Nehru*, vol. 3, op. cit., p. 173.

[36] Cited in *Hitavada*, 25 April 1961, p. 1.

[37] S. Gopal, *Jawaharlal Nehru*, vol. 3, op. cit, p. 173.

[38] *Hitavada*, 4 April 1961, p. 1.

[39] *Lok Sabha Debates*, vol. IV, New Delhi: Lok Sabha Secretariat, 1961 (debate of 4 May 1961).

[40] *Hitavada*, 21 April 1961, p. 1.

[41] Ibid., 15 May 1961, p. 1.

[42] It should be noted that at that time 'there were some signs of a revival of the Muslim

Finally the Congress special committee recommended an interim measure, the imposition of collective punishments for rioters,[43] while the central government opted for the creation of a National Integration Council (NIC) whose task was to accelerate the emotional integration of India.

Nehru's determination was fortified by the riot which broke out in October 1961 at Aligarh Muslim University (AMU). Since its foundation in 1911, AMU had educated members of the Muslim intelligentsia. It was perceived by militant Hindus as a hotbed of Muslim militancy which needed to be treated with the utmost vigilance. At the end of September 1961, a student union election resulted in numerous non-Muslim candidates appearing on the slate, including one who belonged to the ABVP. None of these was elected, and Muslims held victory processions on the night the results were announced in which effigies of the defeated candidates were paraded. This provoked counter-demonstrations by Hindus. Jana Sangh activists organised student meetings and, notwithstanding the dispersal by the police of a procession of 7-8,000 people, their demonstration degenerated into a riot in which fourteen people, mostly Muslims, were killed. The violence spread to Moradabad district and Meerut where there were seventeen deaths resulting from students spreading news of the other disturbances, and propaganda by the Hindu nationalist parties. The Jana Sangh and the Hindu Mahasabha organised protest meetings where rumours that an ABVP candidate had been intimidated into withdrawing his candidacy and that a number of Hindus had been stabbed, were circulated. Charan Singh, the state's Home Minister, denounced such 'political' activities and responded by charging 1,189 individuals.[44] Nehru's government persisted in its repressive vein even to the extent of arresting Jana Sangh militants involved in the riots as much as two months after they took place.[45]

Struggling against Hindu propaganda in the name of democracy proved difficult.[46] Golwalkar had been sentenced to a fine of 500 rupees or six months' imprisonment for a speech encouraging communal hatred in 1959, but was acquitted on appeal on 15 November 1961

League', as D.E. Smith points out, 'partly as a result of the new respectability which it acquired through participation with the Congress and other groups in the anti- communist United Front in Kerala, and probably more because of Muslim frustrations, fears and grievances' (*India as a secular state*, op. cit., p. 420).

[43] *Hitavada*, 25 May 1961, p. 1.

[44] This paragraph derives from a report by Charan Singh reproduced *in extenso* in the *National Herald*, 15 Nov. 1961.

[45] *Times of India*, 21 Dec. 1961, p. 8.

[46] It also seemed impossible to impose the idea that the status of a civil servant was incompatible with membership of the RSS, the *swayamsevaks* winning numerous law suits around this theme (*Organiser*, 27 April 1975).

because of the difficulty of proving what the effect of his speeches had been.[47] The same phenomenon was seen after the Jabalpur riot, with those charged being acquitted.[48] Nonetheless, the firmness of the Nehru government did force the Hindu nationalists to act with a certain prudence, the bleak years of the ban remaining a potent memory within the RSS. In 1965, Balasaheb Deoras and E. Ranade admitted that 'direct participation in communal riots would result in a ban.'[49] On the eve of the 1962 elections, the government announced its intention to amend the Representation of the People Act of 1951 in order to enact 'a new electoral offence, the promotion of disaffection among the people on the grounds of religion, race, caste, or language during elections.'[50]

This constraint enforced by the political system explains why the Jana Sangh was prevented from *openly* resorting to Hindu slogans, as was seen in the 1962 election campaign in Uttar Pradesh:

[In] Lucknow, the Jana Sangh is shy of parading itself as a Hindu party, although it is seriously taken as such by its followers and itself behaves as such in its publicity and propaganda; the house to house propaganda is different from platform speeches.[51]

The party confined its use of militant Hindu arguments to its door-to-door propaganda – a method which the density of its network of militants made possible – while in its public discourse, and the agitation which it engendered, it concentrated on themes seen as 'legitimate' in the eyes of the régime, namely those concerning the economy or the welfare of the nation as a whole. This shift in emphasis was due not only to the difficulties met by the Jana Sangh in launching an ethno-religious mobilisation but also because of the need to be showing concern for socio-economic issues at a time when the Congress presented development as the national priority and drew most of its popularity from this measure, even at the village level.[52] The Jana Sangh leadership decided to oppose the

[47]   Ibid., 16 Nov. 1961, p. 7.

[48]   *Hitavada*, 12 Nov. 1961, p. 5, and 4 Feb. 1962, p. 5.

[49]   Interviews cited in H.T. Davey, 'The transformation of an ideological movement into an aggregative party', op. cit., p. 93.

[50]   Quoted in E.W. Johnson, 'Comparative approaches to the study of the Hindu communal political parties in contemporary India', op. cit., p. 83.

[51]   *National Herald*, 8 Jan. 1962, p. 1. Harold Gould's observations of the 1962 campaign in Faizabad confirm this disjunction between public and private discourses: 'Privately, the Jana Sangh spokesmen were intimating to all who should listen that all Muslims would be sent to Pakistan following a Jana Sangh victory at the polls. The élite castes in the villages were told that their lost prerogatives would be restored to them' (H.A. Gould, 'Religion and politics in a U.P. constituency', op. cit., p. 67).

[52]   In a village in Central India, Nehru was lauded in women's songs as the 'builder of canals' who had thus given good land to all (J.L. Chambard, 'La chanson de Nehru: de

state-controlled economy in reaction to Nehru's socialist reforms, and to allude to Gandhi's economic ideas in doing so. It thus began to project itself as the spokesman of the middle classes, a goal which was very different from that of the 'Hindu nation'.

The Jana Sangh's opposition to public ownership of the economy

In the late 1950s the Jana Sangh launched a campaign against the growing role of the state in the Indian economy, objecting, in particular, to Nehru's plan for joint co-operative farming. This decision implicitly recognised that the normative constraints produced by the government's insistence on secularism had made it difficult to demonstrate about communal issues. Thus the Jana Sangh manifested a growing interest in preserving a measure of economic decentralisation and in representing the concerns of sectors of the Indian middle class.

The desire for decentralisation. From its early years the Jana Sangh had favoured increasing the degree of political and economic decentralisation in India. Although its ideas about the inherent unity of Indian society led it to propose a unitary rather than a federal state, it was also attracted to the idea of some powers being retained at the level of the small locality. The formula proposed by the Jana Sangh since its first election manifestos of the 1950s and codified in the 'Principles and policies' largely inspired by Upadhyaya,[53] bore the name '*janapada*'. These administrative entities, which were given a name that referred to the territorial unity of the ancient kingdoms, would number around 100; they would be much smaller than the states of the Indian federation, thus favouring a traditional type of self-government which would be applied, above all, at the village level. In its election manifesto of 1954, the Jana Sangh committed itself to making the *panchayats* 'the foundation of administration', granting them an increase in financial resources and re-establishing the rule – which it claimed to be traditional – that their members should be elected unanimously.[54]

The desire to decentralise was ideological; it clearly derived from the prestige which attached to the *panchayat* concept, re-interpreted for more than a century in a traditionalist vein. The first British administrators

---

Ram à Nehru, ce que pensent de leurs rois les femmes d'un village indien', paper given at the seminar 'Nehru: l'homme et le visionnaire', UNESCO, Paris, 27-9 Sept. 1989, p. 6).

[53] 'Manifesto – 1951', Bharatiya Jana Sangh in *Party documents*, vol. 1, op. cit., p. 56; 'Manifesto – 1954' in ibid., p. 68, and 'Principles and policies' in ibid., p. 18.

[54] 'Manifesto – 1954', op. cit., p. 62.

considered Indian villages to be little democratic republics, which ignored caste by virtue of their 'primitive communism' and were indifferent to (because independent of) outside events, in particular the rivalries between kingdoms. But this is an idealised vision, because villages traditionally gave up at least one-sixth of their agricultural produce to the kingdoms, and, far from being unitary, sheltered different sub-castes related to *jatis* which transcended the limits of the villages.[55] All the same, this 'romantic utopia' had been propagated by the nationalist movement, which saw in it a flattering image of the Indian past. Gandhi was nurtured on this myth to such an extent that he envisaged the development of independent India on a basis consisting essentially of villages.[56] In the 1950s his principal disciple, Vinoba Bhave, expounded this theme through the *sarvodaya* movement.

Politically, however, it was not the successors designated by Gandhi to be at the head of Congress – such as Nehru, who had opted instead for rapid modernisation – but socialists like Jaya Prakash Narayan[57] and, in a more organicist form, the Jana Sangh, who developed these Gandhian themes. This is clear from the statements of Upadhyaya, for whom 'the villages have been self-contained units of Bharatiya life [...]. They were self-sufficient and self governing; the village panchayat has descended from Vedic times.'[58] This ideological sanctification of the village entity ran parallel to a sanctification of the family as the basic element of Indian life. In his programme for the Jana Sangh, originated in October 1951, Malkani entrusted to the party a mission to 'reorganise society in a way to restore the family unit of cooperative effort and social security'.[59] Here the family is seen as the ideal productive unit, just like the village, the economic vocation of which was emphasised in the opening paragraph of the Jana Sangh's election manifesto of 1951:

The village has been the centre of Bharatiya life in all times. The ideal of 'Sarvodaya' cannot be achieved until and unless the village is restored to its original position as the basic economic unit.[60]

---

[55] L. Dumont, 'La communauté de village, de Munro à Maine' in *La civilisation indienne et nous*, Paris: A. Colin, 1975, p. 121.

[56] M. Gandhi, 'Village republic', *Harijan*, 18 July 1946, and Pyarelal, *Mahatma Gandhi – the last phase*, vol. 2, Ahmedabad: Navajivan, 1956, p. 548.

[57] The latter retired from active politics in 1954 to work for the Bhoodan movement of V. Bhave (appealing for gifts of land for the benefit of poor peasants). Socialist thinking remained no less imbued with Gandhian ideals (M. Weiner, *Party politics in India*, Princeton University Press, 1957, pp. 28 and 34).

[58] *Organiser*, 26 Jan. 1956, p. 10.

[59] Malkani papers, NMML (section of mss.), F.2. 'Speeches and writings'.

[60] 'Manifesto – 1951', op. cit., p. 50.

This profession of faith was in complete contradiction to the policy of Nehru, whom Upadhyaya never ceased to denounce:

By taking up programmes of heavy industries the [Planning] Commission intended to bring about a structural change in our society. Their aim is to build an industrial in place of an agricultural society. But we cannot build a pyramid from the top downwards.[61]

Basing his argument on statistics, he challenged the lack of investment in agriculture[62] and above all in 'decentralised small scale industry', which, in his view should have been the chief agent of industrialisation.[63] From 1951, the Jana Sangh declared in favour of a division of tasks between the state (which would run heavy industry) and the private sector. The production of consumer goods would be reserved to the latter, but the state would be required to prevent economic conglomeration so that family enterprises might flourish.[64] This socio-economic programme led Deepak Lal to say that the economic ideas underlying the Jana Sangh, and subsequently the BJP, were 'close to those espoused by Gandhi, with the major difference being that, unlike him, they do not want completely to reject the modern world'.[65]

The contrast between the Jana Sangh's programme and Nehru's economic policy was made plain in the resolution passed by delegates to the Nagpur session of Congress in January 1959. Land redistribution would be speeded up and areas of land exceeding the authorised limits would be given to landless peasants to be run as cooperatives.[66] These cooperatives, which were intended to become the basic units of rural life, would at first be concerned only with services, such as credit and the supply of seed. Common ownership of land and collective labour would operate only on a voluntary basis and private property rights would be retained. Even so, this was nothing less than a new peasant structure, created by the initiative of the state.

Such a challenge to the 'village order' immediately became a major element in the political debate. Undoubtedly the element of Gandhian doctrine associated with this order remained a point of reference for many

---

[61] D. Upadhyaya, *The two plans – promises, performances, prospects,* Lucknow: Rasthradharma Prakashan, 1958, p. 258.

[62] Ibid., pp. 241-2.

[63] Ibid., p. 268.

[64] 'Manifesto – 1951', op. cit., p. 52. See also 'Manifesto – 1954', op. cit., p. 64.

[65] D. Lal, 'The economic impact of Hindu revivalism' in M.E. Marty and R. Scott Appleby (eds), *Fundamentalisms and the state,* University of Chicago Press, 1993, p. 418.

[66] F. Frankel, *India's political economy, 1947-1977,* Princeton University Press, 1978, pp. 162-3.

Indians.[67] In putting the resolution to the vote in Nagpur, Nehru appeared to be undermining the mythical village unit and thus drew the ire of landowners. Meanwhile the small peasants who were supposed to be the beneficiaries of his project had not yet proved that they were sufficiently politically aware to be relied upon. This disequilibrium was all the more harmful to Nehru given that even smallholders, who traditionally have a special attachment to their land, were mistrustful of his reform.

This combination of factors explains the 'enormous wave of criticism which followed [the Nagpur resolution]'.[68] It was in this context that the Swatantra Party (Liberal Party) was set up, gathering in both Congress veterans such as Rajagopalachari, Gandhi's one-time lieutenant in Madras, and others with a vested interest in free enterprise. The Jana Sangh was also quick to exploit the unease in the countryside. Besides ideological motives, its anti-government campaigns were launched because the party wished to attract those sectors of the middle class which were likely to be affected by the Nagpur resolution and which it regarded as its strongest potential support base.

The Jana Sangh as spokesman for 'the middle world'.   In March 1959 the Jana Sangh Working Committee passed a bellicose resolution, containing the following pointed comments:

The Congress (Nagpur) Resolution makes a futile and misleading reference to the retention of property rights in land in the name of members of the cooperative farms. But, such entry of property rights in the books of the farm is farce, since the owners are prevented from operating on their lands as masters with the full rights of disposal and management on their own responsibility and in accordance with their own plan of life.

In actual effect, cooperative farms are not radically different from the next state of collectives after the Russian and Chinese patterns (before the Communes). [...] The Kisans [peasants] everywhere should be apprised of the fate that is awaiting them so that any irretrievable social catastrophe might be avoided.[69]

On 8 July 1959, the All India General Council called on activists to mobilise for three weeks of agitation that coming October.[70] In Uttar Pradesh, Nana Deshmukh campaigned actively against cooperative farming. He had written a pamphlet criticising the scheme as early as 1956 when Nehru had sent a delegation to study the Chinese

---

[67] Francine Frankel has shown clearly how Gandhi's cooperative project was itself based on a certain irenicism or social organicism which had made it possible for numerous landowners to rally to Congress (ibid., p. 11).

[68] Ibid., p. 163.

[69] *Party documents*, vol, 2, New Delhi: Bharatiya Jana Sangh, 1973, p. 65.

[70] Ibid., pp. 68-9.

system.[71] In 1959 Deshmukh announced that 5,000 activists would be enrolled by each district-level branch of the party in order to explain in the state's 50,000 or so villages[72] the 'inherent dangers of cooperatives'.[73] This campaign had much to do with the party's membership in UP increasing from 43,107 in 1958 to about 80,000 at the end of 1960.[74]

The same phenomenon occurred in Madhya Pradesh, where the government had, in addition, first passed a Land Ceiling Act (1959) limiting a single family's holding to 28 acres,[75] thereby posing a direct threat to 268,456 proprietors who, in 1954-5, on average owned 30 or more acres.[76]

Without doubt this measure hastened the mobilisation of the middle and wealthier peasantry against the planned cooperatives, which the Jana Sangh denounced vigorously. K. Thakre recalled this agitation, which affected some 5,000 villages, as one of the principal factors in his party's 'take off'.[77] S. Patwa, who took part in the agitation as he travelled from village to village, regarded it as one of the foundations of the Jana Sangh's success in the 1962 elections.[78] Of more immediate significance was the transformation of the movement through its growth in manpower. Thakre explained the increase from twenty-nine *mandal samitis* in 1959 to forty-nine in January 1961 – embracing 500 local committees and a membership of 23,000 – by the fact that the agitation against cooperatives 'gave the Jana Sangh workers an opportunity of establishing contacts with the peasants'.[79] S.S. Bhandari, then in charge of the Rajasthan unit of the Jana Sangh, considers that its movement against cooperative farming in the state 'was the party's first attempt to enter the rural areas'.[80]

Across the nation, the Jana Sangh organised meetings to oppose cooperatives in 55,000 villages.[81] This agitation succeeded not only because of the support it received from agriculturalists who would have suffered from cooperative farming but also because smaller peasants who had an intense

[71] Interview with N. Deshmukh, 25 Feb. 1994.

[72] *Hindustan Times*, 31 Aug. 1959, p. 5.

[73] Ibid., 23 Sept. 1959, p. 10.

[74] *Organiser*, 16 March 1959, p. 17 and *Statesman*, 4 Jan. 1961, p. 9.

[75] This limit was fixed at 56 acres in the case of land which could produce only a single harvest, and 84 acres in the case of dry farming.

[76] Farmers with less than 30 acres numbered more than 4.6 million (*Pocket compendium of Madhya Pradesh statistics – 1964*, op. cit., pp. 144-5).

[77] Interview with K. Thakre, 1 Nov. 1988, New Delhi.

[78] Interview with S. Patwa, 18 Nov. 1988, Bhopal.

[79] *Organiser*, 2 Jan. 1961, p. 7.

[80] Interview with S.S. Bhandari, 24 Feb. 1994, New Delhi.

[81] H.T. Davey, 'The transformation of an ideological movement into an aggregative party', op. cit., p. 351.

attachment to their land felt threatened by the proposed reform. [82] This level of activism contributed to a surge in the number of local committees, from 2,551 in 1959 to 4,313 in 1960;[83] however this figure was also a reflection of the rise in the party's popularity among the urban middle class, especially businessmen.

In 1958 merchants were forced to accept the establishment of state control over the trade in grain; it was hoped that centralised regional distribution of produce would reduce inflationary shortages. The Jana Sangh immediately condemned the decision, arguing that it would lead to the nationalisation of small business[84] and the disappearance of 30,000 wholesalers and 3 million retailers.[85] By quoting such figures, it sought to awaken the anxieties of traders, a number of whom were already predisposed in its favour because of its promotion of economic decentralisation and opposition to sales taxes in the 1950s.[86]

In Madhya Pradesh, a state which produced a grain surplus, merchants who had hitherto achieved highly profitable speculative sales to Maharashtra found themselves penalised when these 'food zones' were introduced in April 1959. However the expected damage did not materialise due to the lack of enthusiasm on the part of the state government to enforce these commercial restrictions,[87] an attitude which converged with one that was observable nationally. Between 1959 and 1963, the Minister of Agriculture, S.K. Patil, deliberately relaxed controls so that grain merchants could again benefit from selling into areas of deficit where prices had been forced up.[88] The Jana Sangh occasionally took up the defence of the grain merchants when the authorities decided to buy cereals in order to hold up prices when they would otherwise have fallen in the wake of a good harvest, such as in Madhya Pradesh in 1958-9. But, the party risked alienating the rural middle class through practices of this kind.

Fortunately for the Jana Sangh's leaders, at the beginning of the 1960s the party was in a position to exploit the financial crisis which led the

[82] N. Deshmukh admitted as much (interview).

[83] *Organiser*, 1 Feb. 1960, p. 9, and 2 Jan. 1961, p. 9. For a state by state break-down of these figures, see S.S. Bhandari (ed.), *Jana Deep Souvenir*, New Delhi: Rakesh Press, 1967, p. 93.

[84] *Hindustan Times*, 8 March 1959, pp. 1-2.

[85] Resolution passed at the party's annual session, 28 Dec. 1958 (*Party Documents*, vol. 2, op. cit., p. 61). In the mid-1960s, India had about 100,000 small businesses (B. Graham, *Hindu nationalism*, op. cit., p. 163).

[86] Ibid., p. 168.

[87] W. Wilcox, 'Madhya Pradesh' in M. Weiner (ed.), *State politics in India*, Princeton University Press, 1968, p. 159.

[88] S.K. Patil, *My years with Congress*, op. cit., p. 97.

government to penalise the middle classes *as a whole* by introducing a Compulsory Deposit Scheme (CDS) to which payers of agricultural, income and sales taxes, salaried workers and urban landlords would all be subject. The party organised agitations against a plan which, according to Upadhyaya, would penalise simultaneously the 'rural sector and the salaried middle class'.[89] The Madhya Pradesh branch of the Jana Sangh, for instance, was thus provided with an opportunity to bridge the gulf between urban and rural society and so present itself as a mouthpiece for the entire middle class.

In Madhya Pradesh, tax increases brought in after the 1962 election had already sparked off demonstrations by the Jana Sangh in thirty-five districts including Bhopal, where the party sent successive waves of *satyagrahis* in July and August, 680 of whom were arrested.[90] The Communists meanwhile rivalled the Jana Sangh in militancy on the same theme. In one demonstration in July, all the opposition parties joined together and 771 arrests were made – 411 Communists, 183 Jana Sanghis and 177 members of the PSP.[91]

The following year the government introduced a Sales Tax (Amendment) Bill, the effect of which would be to raise certain sales taxes from 7 to 10% on prices and impose a tax of 1% on the price of grain. This amplified protests from the Jana Sangh, ever-ready to defend the interests of traders, and partly as a result of this agitation the grain tax was withdrawn.[92]

The Rationalisation of Land Revenue Bill, which would have increased agricultural taxes on the most prosperous third of the peasantry from 20 to 50%,[93] led the party to launch a much bigger campaign when the state governor resolved to promulgate the Act. Thakre propagated the idea that a farmer would now pay an additional 125% to the state, if one included the CDS.[94] In Vindhya Pradesh, which hitherto the Jana Sangh had barely penetrated, Congress was surprised at the campaign's success.[95] When Upadhyaya visited Hoshangabad in support of the campaign, he lamented that 'the weight of the increased taxation and of forced economies fell mainly on the middle classes'.[96] Public opinion, dominated as it was by the middle class, proved receptive to these protests.

[89] *Organiser,* 24 June 1963.
[90] Ibid., 4 June 1962, p. 5; 16 July 1962, p. 4; 30 July 1962, p. 13; 6 Aug. 1962, p. 11; and 20 Aug. 1962, p. 12.
[91] *Hindustan Times,* 11 July 1962, p. 5; 19 July 1962, p. 5; 21 July 1962, p. 6; 31 July 1962, p. 12.
[92] *Madhya Pradesh Chronicle,* 1 Apr. 1963, p. 1.
[93] *Hindustan Times,* 31 July 1962, p. 4, and 1 Aug. 1962, p. 12.
[94] *Madhya Pradesh Chronicle,* 27 June 1963, p. 1.
[95] Ibid., 30 June 1963, p. 3.
[96] Ibid., 24 July 1963, p. 3.

In September 1963, Nehru amended the Compulsory Deposit Scheme so that only payers of income tax would have to comply with it, while in Madhya Pradesh the government, of which D.P. Mishra had been in charge for only five days, finally abandoned the Rationalisation of Land Revenue Bill on 3 October,[97] after also having faced pressure from certain Congressmen.[98]

At the beginning of the 1960s the Jana Sangh had established its presence on the political scene as an adept in agitation, thanks to its activist taskforce. Its protests were aimed above all at the policies of Nehru that favoured increasing intervention by the state in the economy, ideas which had little legitimacy in the eyes of certain sections of the population and were contrary to the ideology of the RSS. This campaign had quickly taken on a purely political dimension in so far as it gave the Jana Sangh an unexpected opportunity to portray itself as the defender of the independent middle classes and thereby supplant its political rivals by mobilising its network of activists.

In Madhya Pradesh such organisational strength attracted to the Jana Sangh the then leaders of the Hindu Sabha: V.P. Tiwari, MLA for Guna and president of the Hindu Sabha group in the Vidhan Sabha; Niranjan Verma, MLA for Vidisha; and Udho Das Mehta, leader of the Hindu Sabha in Bhopal since the 1940s. They joined the Jana Sangh together with their followers in the wake of the agitation of 1962-3.[99]

The Jana Sangh's electoral fortunes in 1962 enabled it to become the second largest party in the Vidhan Sabha in Uttar Pradesh and in Madhya Pradesh, where it won forty-one seats. In the latter state the PSP won only thirty-three seats and the Socialist Party fourteen. This electoral expansion derived in part from the party's skill in exploiting the Congress's shift towards a Socialist programme. This was unacceptable to a large section of the middle classes, and it was the ambition of many of the Jana Sangh's leaders to build their party in exactly such a way as to represent these voters.[100] Moreover, the upper limit of 30 acres which it had recommended in its agrarian project of 1957 was dropped from its election manifesto of 1962.[101] The Jana Sangh also reiterated its opposition to cooperatives as the best means of wooing this class of intermediate landholders whom its

[97]   Ibid., 4 Oct. 1963, p. 1.

[98]   W. Wilcox, 'Madhya Pradesh', op. cit., p. 158.

[99]   *Madhya Pradesh Chronicle*, 25 Oct. 1963, p. 6.

[100]   T.H. Davey, 'The transformation of an ideological movement into an aggregative party', op. cit., p. 364.

[101]   Upadhyaya was to offer an unconvincing justification for this development, in particular by stating that the imposition of land ceilings would make some farms unviable because of their small size ('Your vote (8) – Agriculture continues to be neglected by government', *Organiser*, 29 Jan. 1962, p. 4).

campaigns had targeted. In the same context B. Madhok opposed the lowering of the land-ceiling in demagogic tones:

Why should any man invest in agriculture if he knows that he will have to hold 25 acres of land only? [...] Why should you want Indian villagers to remain in perpetual poverty? Why should not rural people also be given an opportunity to grow up along with their fellow urban countrymen? Therefore the ceiling on land should be, the number of acres of land which any individual can look after himself.[102]

With the merchant middle classes in its sights, the Jana Sangh relaunched its campaign against the government's restrictions on trade following the reintroduction in 1964 of zones from which grain could not be exported. The Jana Sangh fought for the cancellation of the system and the forced purchases which formed part of it.[103] Parallel with this, it continually demanded that increased credit be given to small enterprises, as part of the five-year national plans.[104] Thus the party appeared during the 1960s very much as the potential representative of what Bruce Graham called the 'middle world' – of the middle classes threatened 'from above' by the intervention of the state in the economy and the development of capitalism, and 'from below' by the increasing political awareness and mobilisation of the backward classes.[105] In 1966, the most heavily represented sector within the Jana Sangh General Council was that of business, with 129 delegates, against eighty-three from the liberal professions and seventy-six farmers.[106]

At the same time, the Jana Sangh had the smallest number of Scheduled Caste deputies.[107] Of the few that there were, many had not been attracted to the party itself but came from the small group of RSS-trained Scheduled Caste members. Furthermore, they often owed their election to non-Scheduled Caste voters who were always in a majority in their constituencies.[108] At this time the Congress, which had initiated reforms such as the admission of Untouchables to temples, was thought of as the official

[102] B. Madhok, *What Jana Sangh stands for*, op. cit., pp. 26-7.

[103] 'Manifesto – 1967' in *Party documents*, vol. 1, op. cit., p. 160.

[104] B. Graham, *Hindu nationalism*, op. cit., p. 165.

[105] Ibid., p. 158.

[106] M.M. Sankhdher, 'General elections in Delhi' in S.P. Varma and I. Narain (eds), *Fourth general election in India*, Bombay: Orient Longmam, 1968, p. 168.

[107] W.H. Morris-Jones and B. Das Gupta, 'India's political area: interim reports on ecological electoral investigation', *Asian Survey*, 9 (6), June 1969, p. 412.

[108] N.P. Gupta acknowledged this fact about Madhya Pradesh, and especially about the three reserved assembly seats that the Jana Sangh won in the 1962 elections in the districts of Chhatarpur, Panna and Satna. One of these MLAs was an RSS member. (Interview with N.P. Gupta and *Madhya Pradesh sadasyon ka sankshipt parichay*, 1962, op. cit., p. 6).

guardian of the Scheduled Castes and accordingly received massive electoral support from them.

In Madhya Pradesh the 'middle world' overlapped considerably with the 8.16 million people (out of a total population of 26 millions) described in the 1951 census as 'self-supporting', the remainder gaining their livelihood from work for their employers. These 'independents', two-thirds of whom belonged to the rural sector, certainly included many very small peasants but their mentality was none the less similar to that of bigger proprietors hostile to any reform, simply because they too owned assets. Yet the heart of this 'middle world' resided in the one million 'independent workers' and owners of small businesses and industries.[109]

In the 1960s the Jana Sangh found the Congress withdrawing from many aspects of its socialist programme. After the vote of the Nagpur resolution Nehru had faced opposition from within his own party, which had cadres who were all the more hostile to the system of cooperatives because they themselves possessed land or enjoyed the support of landowners. Hampered by a lack of volunteers needed to establish the cooperatives planned for the next three years, Congress staggered the projects and then buried the dossier *de facto* with the Third Plan,[110] announcing in addition that henceforth joining cooperatives would be entirely voluntary.[111] This reversal of policy enabled Nehru to disentangle himself from a controversy which might have strengthened the legitimacy of the Jana Sangh. But India's military reverses had the effect of restoring some advantage to the Jana Sangh and especially of making it an acceptable partner for other parties of the non-communist opposition, given its patriotic pedigree.

From dogmatism to pragmatism?

The only other non-communal cause around which the Jana Sangh had always been strongly mobilised, apart from decentralisation, was that of territorial integrity, an issue that grew in importance in the 1950s. In 1959, the Jana Sangh Working Committee reacted to the Chinese incursions along the Indo-Tibetan frontier by demanding from the government 'that national security be accorded total priority' and that the territories that had

---

[109] *Pocket compendium of Madhya Pradesh statistics – 1958*, op. cit., pp. 19 and 22.

[110] F. Frankel, *India's political economy*, op. cit., pp. 195ff.

[111] In a series of three articles the *Organiser* objected that such a formula, based on free choice, was bound to fail and that therefore the peasants would finally be compelled to surrender their independence on the collectivist model (23 July 1962, pp. 5-14; 30 July 1962, pp. 6-12; 6 Aug. 1962, pp. 7-10).

been occupied should be liberated.[112] In protest against the invitation to Chou En-lai to visit Delhi, the Jana Sangh organised an 'Act with Firmness Week' in April 1960.[113] And when the advance signs of the impending Chinese invasion appeared in May 1962 with the capture of two Indian frontier posts, the AIGC called for massive reprisals and the breaking-off of diplomatic relations.[114] In September, after the first attacks, the party presented a list of recommendations, which grew as the invasion progressed.[115] It could pride itself on having always given warning of Chinese intentions to a Prime Minister who, because of his idealism, had greatly neglected this menace and the military security of the country.[116] The Jana Sangh continued this didactic role during the long months of negotiations when Chinese soldiers remained stationed on Indian territory.

In assuming the role of defender of the national interest – with a legitimacy acquired through ten years of agitation for territorial integrity – the Jana Sangh attracted several Congressmen who had been disillusioned by Nehru's apparent weakness. Among the most prominent of these was Dr Raghuvira, an eminent parliamentarian who had been a professor of Sanskrit before being nominated to the Constituent Assembly.[117] At the annual session of the Jana Sangh in 1962, when he was elected party president, he criticised the aimlessness of Nehru's defence policy.[118] His early death in 1963 deprived the party of a recruit of substance, who none the less demonstrated the party's new attractiveness.

By revealing the country's vulnerability, the war of 1962 had been a 'traumatic event' for the whole Indian population – so much so that it redefined the 'legitimate problematic of politics'.[119] The war had heightened the prestige of the Hindu nationalists within the political system, their new respectability being reflected – and increased – by the invitation to the RSS to take part in the Republic Day parade; 3,000 *swayamsevaks* in uniform marched in the ceremony along Rashtrapati

---

[112] Resolution of 20 Sept. 1959 in *Party documents*, vol. 3, New Delhi: Bharatiya Jana Sangh, 1973, pp. 66-8.

[113] Resolution of 20 March 1960, ibid, pp. 78-9.

[114] Resolution of 24 May 1962 in ibid., p. 86.

[115] Resolutions of 29 Sept. 1962 and 30 Dec. 1962, ibid., pp. 88-9 and 89-93.

[116] S. Gopal, *Jawaharlal Nehru – A biography*, vol. 3, op. cit., pp. 212 and 224.

[117] *Statesman*, 15 May 1963, p. 12.

[118] *National Herald*, 31 Dec. 1962, p. 5.

[119] On the connection between the two notions, see J.F. Bayart, *The state in Africa:the politics of the belly*, London: Longman, 1993, p. 247. S. Gopal opens the penultimate chapter of his biography of Nehru with the sentence: 'No one who lived in India through the winter months of 1962 can forget the deep humiliation felt by all Indians, irrespective of party' (*Jawaharlal Nehru*, vol. 3, op. cit., p. 232).

Road in New Delhi.[120] Yet this more open attitude at the Centre did not imply any slackening of secularist vigilance or of the determination of those in authority to marginalise the Hindu nationalists. Rather, the development of the non-communist opposition marked an erosion of the politics of anti-communalism in so far as, in the aftermath of the elections and the war of 1962, several mainstream parties proved receptive to the Jana Sangh's efforts at integration.

The origins of integration with the legitimate opposition

The Jana Sangh began to reconsider its hostility to electoral alliances after the 1962 elections, the results of which were a blow to Upadhyaya despite his party's progress in Uttar Pradesh and Madhya Pradesh.[121] While the party aspired to present itself as an alternative to Congress and, accordingly, reaffirmed its refusal to enter into electoral alliances while putting up a record number of candidates (196 to the Lok Sabha and 1,140 to the Vidhan Sabhas), it still made little progress, from 5.97% in 1957 to only 6.44% of the votes cast for the elections to the lower chamber in 1962, where it could count only fourteen MPs (it increased its number of MLAs to 116). This slow progress was connected partly to the presence of numerous opposition candidates whose positions were often close to that of the Jana Sangh. The latter had to fight the Ram Rajya Parishad in twenty-six Lok Sabha and ninety-eight Vidhan Sabha constituencies, the Hindu Mahasabha in, respectively, twenty-five and 105, and the Swatantra Party in sixty-four and 397.[122] These other opposition contestants deprived the Jana Sangh of many seats it might otherwise have won, due to the simple majority voting system.

Thus the 1962 election results prompted the Jana Sangh's leaders to seek alliances. In accordance with its new strategy of integration, it did not turn to the Hindu parties but to those of the 'legitimate opposition', namely the ones whose programme was free of communalism and which addressed socio-economic problems. This desire for greater integration within the opposition would not have been reciprocated if the major parties had remained faithful to the strictly secularist approach that had prevailed in the 1950s. But, whether from necessity or for ideological reasons, two groups were amenable to collaboration with the Jana Sangh: the Socialist and Swatantra parties.

The first, which came into being in 1955, at the instigation of Ram

---

[120] This figure is from an RSS source (*RSS spearheading national renaissance – 60th anniversary year 1985*, Bangalore: RSS (Prakashan Vibhag), 1985, p. 29).

[121] See his post-electoral report in *Organiser*, 28 May 1962, pp. 2-4, 14 and 16.

[122] Figures obtained from C. Baxter, *The Jana Sangh*, op. cit., pp. 238-40.

Manohar Lohia, when a faction broke away from the PSP on account of what was seen as its accommodating attitude towards Congress, analysed the election results of 1962 in much the same way as had the leaders of the Jana Sangh. Lohia had been anxious, even before the elections, to unite all opposition forces against Congress,[123] and the latter's success at the polls encouraged him to press ahead with a unified strategy in opposition to the dominant party.[124] This determination was further hardened by the 1962 war. Although 'for years the Party ranks had been taught to fight the communalists',[125] they now found themselves caught up in a rapprochement with the Jana Sangh. In April 1964, following anti-Hindu riots in East Pakistan set off by the disappearance of a precious relic – a hair of the Prophet – from the Hazratbal mosque in Srinagar, Lohia and Upadhyaya published a joint communiqué. They appealed for calm, and later declared in favour of a confederation reuniting India and Pakistan.[126] This declaration reflected certain nationalist tendencies on Lohia's part, which also found expression in his vigorous defence of Hindi as the national language.[127] His plan for a unified opposition corresponded with a conception of political activity largely stripped of ideology, as one of his then lieutenants, Madhu Limaye, explains:

For Lohia the 'main distinction' among parties related neither to their Leftism or Rightism nor their adherence to Democracy or Totalitarianism. It was between those in the Government and those who were 'out of it'. A state of permanent opposition or the prospect of being kept out of power produced frustration or a sense of despair. Lohia wanted the opposition parties to overcome this by joining hands in the achievement of the urgent goal of throwing the Congress out of power.[128]

The other alliance which the Jana Sangh forged during the 1960s was much more concerned with ideological affinities. Its partner was the Swatantra Party, whose leaders included advocates of Western-style free enterprise, such as Piloo Mody or M.R. Masani, and conservatives of two kinds. Of the latter, there was on the one hand C. Rajagopalachari, a veteran of the Independence movement who had removed himself from Congress and personified traditionalism of the Gandhian type. His return to politics was the direct consequence of his opposition to Westernisation

---

[123] The Jana Sangh also supported his candidature against Nehru in the constituency of Phulpur (*Pioneer*, 24 Jan. 1962, p. 5).

[124] M. Limaye, *Birth of non-congressism*, Delhi: B.R. Publishing Co., 1988, p. 84.

[125] Ibid.

[126] Ibid., p. 97, and *Organiser*, 20 April 1964, p. 2.

[127] E.g. see his article 'Hindi – here and now', ibid., Republic Day Special, 1965, p. 19 (reproduced in *Seminar*, no. 68, 1965, pp. 27-31).

[128] M. Limaye, *Birth of non-congressism*, op. cit., p. 102.

and state control of the economy by those in power – contrary to the Gandhian model of decentralisation based on more or less autarkic village units.[129] On the other hand, K.M. Munshi represented Hindu traditionalism.[130] The Swatantra Party also recruited veteran Hindu Sabhaites like N.C. Chatterjee[131] together with more 'legitimate' figures such as Sardar Patel's son Dahyabhai or his former aide V.P. Menon. All the same, the Swatantra Party appeared to be fully 'legitimate' in so far as its identity lay essentially in its economic programme. Like Lohia's party, the Swatantra Party aimed at federating opposition forces so as to checkmate the Congress: according to Erdman, 'broadly speaking, the governing principle of Swatantra's efforts was "my enemy's enemy is my friend" '[132] Thus the party tended to incorporate regional parties (the Ganatantra Parishad in Orissa) and caste associations (the Gujarat Kshatriya Mahasabha). This technique was implemented at the expense of creating a network such as the Jana Sangh possessed and the Swatantra Party regarded with envy.[133] This was an additional motive for rapprochement, albeit one hampered by the reservations felt by elements within the Swatantra Party – such as the Ganatantra Parishad and the Gujarat Kshatriya Mahasabha – over the Jana Sangh's 'communalism'.[134] Thus the secularist approach once again come into play. In 1962, only the Rajasthani branches of the two parties concluded an electoral pact of any substance. Meanwhile, certain obstacles to collaboration being pursued further were removed in the climate created by the Sino-Indian conflict.

The first important step in the integration of the Jana Sangh in the legitimate opposition was accomplished when, in the aftermath of the war, in May 1963, the Socialist party, the Swatantra Party and the Jana Sangh decided to put up only a single candidate in all four Lok Sabha by-elections. Upadhyaya was unsuccessful, but J.B. Kripalani (a respected veteran Gandhian and ex-Socialist who stood as an independent), Lohia and Masani were returned. In the latter two instances, at Farrukhabad and Rajkot, the opposition candidates appreciated the efficacy of Hindu nationalist activists in the campaign.[135]

---

[129] H.L. Erdman, *The Swatantra Party and Indian conservatism*, Cambridge University Press, 1967, p. 95.

[30] Ibid., p. 99. See also his article 'Wanted: an active Hindu religion', *Organiser*, Diwali special issue, 1963.

[131] H.L. Erdman, *The Swatantra Party and Indian conservatism*, op. cit., p. 133.

[132] Ibid., p. 212.

[133] Ibid., pp. 161 and 165.

[134] Ibid., p. 218.

[135] R. Roy, 'Congress defeat in Farrukhabad' in Centre for the Study of Developing Societies, *Party system and election studies*, Bombay: Allied Publishers, 1967, p. 213, and R. Maru, 'Fall of a traditional Congress stronghold', ibid., p. 232.

This success was followed up by Kripalani appealing for unity among the opposition. The PSP then immediately announced its refusal to collaborate with reactionary forces such as the Swatantra Party and the Jana Sangh – a move which the latter, significantly, regretted.[136] Negotiations were held with the Socialist party[137] and then especially with the Swatantra Party. At the beginning of 1964, Vajpayee announced that the three parties were ready to form a common parliamentary group, at the same moment as Madhok declared his support for the fusion of the Jana Sangh and the Swatantra Party, a plan which apparently took shape in Punjab before running into difficulties.[138] First, the Jana Sangh leaders, including Upadhyaya, regarded themselves as closer to the 'socio-democrats' than to the Swatantra Party;[139] and second, the latter had greater sympathy than the Hindu nationalists with Kashmir's claims to autonomy in the spring of 1964.[140] So although the rapprochement proceeded no further, the principle of electoral collaboration among the opposition parties had been established. This already marked the Jana Sangh's new integration into the realm of 'legitimate politics'.

Parallel to this achievement, the leadership of the Jana Sangh initiated another pragmatic move destined to improve the party's electoral showing, namely the recruitment of notables. As with the negotiation of alliances, this reorientation remained partial. The party did not shift towards an aggregative pattern of party-building pure and simple but instead chose an intermediate strategy which retained the principal features of the original Sangathanist technique.

The 'cluster technique', a party-building pattern borrowing from both Sangathanism and the aggregative method

The rise of the Jana Sangh at the polls in 1962 seemed to have little to do with 'Sangathanism'. Along with its tendency to exploit discontent with Nehru's economic policy among certain sections of the middle and upper classes, the Jana Sangh resorted – to a certain extent – to the method of expansion by social aggregation; defending these classes went hand in hand with an effort to co-opt notables. The latter term refers, in this case at least, to a generic category. Max Weber defines notables as persons

---

[136] Resolution of Central Working Committee, 13 June 1969, *Party documents*, vol. 4, New Delhi: Bharatiya Jana Sangh, 1973, p. 162.

[137] *Statesman*, 17 July 1963, p. 7, and 11 Aug. 1963, p. 9.

[138] *Pioneer*, 14 Jan. 1964, p. 4; *Statesman*, 23 Jan. 1964, p. 7, and 8 Feb. 1964, p. 1; *Hindustan Times*, 31 Jan. 1964, p. 6, and *Patriot*, 9 Feb. 1964, p. 4.

[139] *Organiser*, 15 Nov. 1962, pp. 21-2.

[140] B. Graham, *Hindu nationalism*, op. cit., p. 213.

'(1) whose economic position permits them to hold continuous policy-making and administrative positions in an organisation without (more than nominal) remuneration; (2) who enjoy social prestige of whatever derivation in such a manner that they are likely to hold office in virtue of the members' confidence, which at first is given and then traditionally accorded.'[141]

According to the second aspect of this definition, 'notable' designates personalities of local influence, in a rural or an urban context. Among the criteria of notability, the possession of capital and/or land or industrial and/or financial activities are prominent because they imply a direct power over tenants, employees or debtors. But the notable can also exert a more subjective influence because of the social prestige of his status. This criterion overlaps the former but indicates also that certain professionals (lawyers, doctors, journalists) who are publicly known and respected must be included as notables. At the local level, notability is often revealed by and associated with membership of social, economic and political associations. By contrast with the activist's profile, it did not imply any strong ideological commitment. The category of local notables must also be differentiated on the one hand from politicians whose strength usually lies in their party affiliation and, on the other, in the Indian context, from the princes whose influence has a long pedigree and covers a large geographic area.

The Sangathanist method was an electoral handicap since, unlike the notables who were so numerous in Congress, the Jana Sangh's cadres with a RSS background could not draw on a 'vote bank'. They owed almost their entire influence to their capacity for effective propaganda and to the prestige deriving from their conduct. Since these characteristics were ones that could not be established overnight, and thus threatened to slow the party's advance, its leaders seemed to have resolved, with the 1962 elections in view, to co-opt notables. This decision resulted also from the characteristics of the notables mentioned in the first part of Weber's definition. He emphasises that notables are 'able to live for politics without living from politics'[142] because of their private resources. In the late 1950s and early 1960s the Jana Sangh was interested in both aspects given its lack of both activists and money. From 1956 the General Secretary of the RSS, E. Ranade, had made it known that his movement could not allow new *pracharaks* to be deputed to the Jana Sangh.[143] The financial resources of the Jana Sangh were also insufficient to support the ambitions of its party leaders. In Madhya Pradesh, in 1964-5, Thakre

---

[141] M. Weber, *Economy and Society*, New York: Bedminster Press, 1988 p. 290.

[142] Ibid.

[143] W. Andersen and S. Damle, *The brotherhood in saffron*, op. cit., p. 113.

decided to solicit funds from among party members, but only 850 Jana Sanghis responded, donating 100 rupees each.[144] Thus by co-opting notables the Jana Sangh hoped to tap a new source of funds to pay for its election campaign.

However, the recruitment of an increasing number of notables by the Jana Sangh in the 1960s was only a relative change of direction. For one thing, notables already had a place in the Sangathanist scheme of things, even if they were content for this to consist largely of patronising Hindu nationalist activities as RSS *sanghchalaks* or presidents of local branches of the Jana Sangh, whereas now they seemed instead to be in the first rank of possible candidates in elections. For another, this 'notabilisation' remained under control, as the situation in Madhya Pradesh showed.

Here one can often use membership of the institutions of the Panchayati Raj and cooperatives as a criterion of notability. In most cases these bodies had not lived up to the ideal of political and social democracy that Nehru had hoped for. In fact, local notables were quick to occupy the new positions of power represented by the *gram panchayats* (councils elected by several villages, which themselves appointed a leader, called a *sarpanch*), the *janapada panchayat, parishad* or *sabha* (an analagous system operating at *tehsil* level, intermediate between the villages and the district), the Mandi Samitis (committees for marketing agricultural produce)[145] and the credit cooperatives,[146] control of which 'became an important new source of economic patronage and political influence for the propertied castes'.[147]

In Madhya Pradesh, doubtless in a more clear-cut fashion than in other regions, traditional authorities continued to dominate village politics, notably through the new local institutions of the *Panchayati Raj*. This state of affairs was especially pronounced in Madhya Bharat and Vindhya Pradesh where it was probably due to the numerical strength of the upper castes compared to the intermediate castes (in Madhya Bharat, the Rajputs were three times more numerous than the biggest intermediate caste, the Gujars – see Table, p. 133). The continuing survival of the princely states till the late 1940s also delayed politicisation of the population by

---

[144] K. Thakre, 'Madhya Pradesh mein, bhajpa sarkar bhaghirthi prayason ka pratiphal', op. cit.

[145] For the influence of these institutions on the peasants in a district of Malwa (Dewas), see A. Mayer, 'The dominant caste in a region of central India', *South West Journal of Anthropology*, 14, 4 (1958), p. 423.

[146] On the proportion of notables among those holding responsible positions in the cooperatives (they were often elected to the bodies of the *Panchayati Raj* as well) at the end of the 1950s, see D. Thorner, *Agricultural cooperatives in India – a field report*, London: Asia Publishing House, 1964, pp. 3-4 and 8-11.

[147] F. Frankel, *India's political economy*, op. cit., pp. 190 and 193.

screening them from exposure to ideas which had been in common currency in British India for decades.

Adrian Mayer revealed the extent to which, in the region of Dewas, the traditional village headmen, often of Rajput origin, were quick to dominate the new seats of power introduced by the *Panchayati Raj* and became what he called 'rural leaders'.[148] Jean-Luc Chambard's study of the village of Piparsod (in Shivpuri district), begun in 1957, reported a similar situation: here the dominant personalities on the political scene were recruited from among moneylenders, 'the network of borrowers and that of political clients [...] merging to form a clientele, in the widest sense, of several "patrons" (*malik*)'.[149] Since the 1950s factions headed by the village's biggest moneylenders have been dominating the *gram panchayat*.

The sociological profile of its victorious candidates in the Vidhan Sabha election of 1962 bears witness to the fact that the Jana Sangh in Madhya Pradesh tended to take over these sources of local power and co-opt their office-holders, a strategy which may have been favoured because many notables had either turned away from the Congress Party or found that opposition parties other than the Jana Sangh lacked sufficient activists to make electoral success possible. Congress was alienating many local leaders because the lack of discipline in the party encouraged group rivalries and because it was interested in relying on leaders who had sufficient local power to win elections; the Congress thus established what was in effect a competition between aspiring politicians, many of whom were inevitably disappointed and therefore turned to other parties which had their own constituencies and team of workers. The Jana Sangh was especially well placed to attract such notables.[150]

---

[148] A. Mayer, 'Some political implications of community development in India', *Archives Européennes de sociologie*, IV (1963), pp. 86-106 and *Caste and kinship in Central India – A village and its region*, London: Routledge and Kegan Paul, 1960, pp. 112-18.

[149] J.L. Chambard, *Atlas d'un village indien*, Paris: EHESS, 1980, p. 32.

[150] One of Angela Burger's case studies in her book on the opposition parties in Uttar Pradesh illustrates this process. In Pratapgarh, a district in southern Oudh, where the Jana Sangh had been established in 1951 by a *pracharak* who was a local lawyer, the party failed to make inroads into the countryside, where former *taluqdars* of the Rajput caste were still dominant. In 1958 one of their number, Thakur Pratap Singh, embittered at finding his ascent within Congress blocked, switched to the Jana Sangh, which was only too happy to elect him to the Rajya Sabha and persuaded him to stand for election to the Lok Sabha in 1962. The party's campaign was directed mainly against the agricultural cooperatives, which were denounced as a means of confiscating land. However Raja Pratap Singh did not need such propaganda to rally support to the Jana Sangh, as he had access to his own network of 'taluqdars and their families, employees (including children of former employees) and ex-zamindars with their subsidiary "shopkeeper network", primarily of businessmen and moneylenders and their clients.' The system that emerged linked the Jana Sangh network to a much larger circle of notables who made it possible for the party to penetrate the countryside. In 1962 the Raja was elected to the Lok Sabha

The electoral map of the poll (see appendix J, p. 560) reveals the permanence of the party's areas of strength and of weakness – with two exceptions, Betul and Raipur. The Jana Sangh installed itself at Maha-koshal in Betul district thanks to the labours of N.P. Gupta, who on the one hand devoted himself to obtaining property rights for tribals who were clearing land illegally,[151] and on the other was making use of notables. In the town of Betul, for example, he had won over G.H. Khandelwal, a well-known lawyer and former Congress member who had turned against the government; he stood as the Jana Sangh candidate in 1962.[152]

This recourse to influential substitutes also took place in Chhattisgarh. In the south of Raipur the party won three seats of which one, Dhamtari, went to a relatively unknown candidate, Kridutt, whose only political asset was his membership of the RSS. Sivaha was won by a tribal leader – the village *sarpanch* and member of the development committee of the *tehsil* – and Kurud by Y.R. Meghawale, a RSS man who at the time was director of the cooperative bank of Raipur.

Here one is aware of the nuances in the recruitment of notables by the Jana Sangh in Madhya Pradesh, compared with aggregation. Through this method of party-building, a 'cluster' effect was achieved, represented on the map by dark spheres (see Appendix J, p. 562). Jana Sangh swayamsevaks co-opted local notables to add new constituencies to their nucleus of influence obtained in the 1950s while ensuring that they remained in command of the local party. In each 'cluster' the 'hard core', made of activists, is more or less permanent while the periphery, composed of notables, is subject to renewal in the case of those reluctant to comply with party discipline or who had lost their local influence. It should be noted that in this party-building pattern, some swayamsevaks – such as Y.R. Meghawale – themselves underwent a process of 'notabilisation'.

In Malwa, the Jana Sangh enlarged its base more decisively than

California Press, 1969, pp. 185-7). The Jana Sangh in Uttar Pradesh was already profiting in 1957 from the influence of Raja Datta Singh at Lakhimpur; the same had been true of Yadavendra Datt Dubey, the Maharajah of Jaunpur since 1956, but this was a special case since the prince had belonged since 1942 to the RSS, of which he had become *sanghchalak* for Varansi division (*National Herald*, 19 Apr. 1957, p. 3, and *Who's who in U.P. Legislative Assembly*, Lucknow: U.P. Legislative Assembly Secretariat, 1959, p. 287).

151   In July 1962 he also organised a demonstration of 2,000 tribals in Betul against tax increases (*Organiser*, 18 July 1962, p.4).

152   Interview with N.P. Gupta and *Madhya Pradesh Vidhan Sabha sadasyon ka sankshipt parichay* – 1962, Bhopal: Madhya Pradesh Vidhan Sabha Sachivalay, 1964 – unless otherwise stated, the source of information in this section.

anywhere else by means of this 'cluster' technique. Among the successful candidates at Mandsaur were to be found the hard core of the party's organisers: Sakhlecha (who became leader of the opposition in the Vidhan Sabha), Patwa (who became Chief Whip of the Jana Sangh group in the assembly) and Onkar Lal. All of them were *swayamsevaks* whose network was based on that of traders, their own milieu. However a new circle of Rajput notables made its appearance in 1962. The MLA for Sitamau, Thakur Mohan Singh, was a former *zamindar* of the princely state of Gwalior who had become both a *sarpanch* and president of a Mandi Samiti. In 1964 he was replaced in a by-election by Thakur Kishore Singh Sisodia (the son of a *jagirdar* of Gwalior state) who had been *sarpanch* of three different *panchayats* since the early 1950s and, from 1962, president of the Mandi Samiti at Mandsaur. Both men had belonged since the early 1950s to the Ram Rajya Parishad, which had won 14.2% of the votes cast in Madhya Bharat in 1952, and joined the Jana Sangh in 1962, having been wooed by Sakhlecha, Patwa and Chauradia,[153] a decision which exemplified the method of expansion 'in clusters'.

In 1967 the Jana Sangh won seven of the eight Vidhan Sabha seats in Mandsaur district, largely because its reliance on notables as electoral candidates had become institutionalised. Sakhlecha, who was re-elected for Jawad, had now become a politician of stature in the region. Patwa, for his part, lost in the elections but was in the process of becoming a local notable, having been elected president of the cooperative bank of Mandsaur district in 1967 following a decision taken by the party.[154] He remained in this position up to 1973. Parallel with their notabilisation, these *swayamsevaks* continued to receive support from Rajput notables like Mohan Singh (MLA for Mandsaur) and Kishore Singh Sisodia, whose son Rajendra Singh Sisodia succeeded him as *sarpanch* of his village, Nimbod, in 1964 and as MLA for Sitamau in 1967.[155] This 'cluster' was further crowned by the victory in Mandsaur's Lok Sabha constituency of a Marwari based in Calcutta who was a well known chartered accountant.[156] Sakhlecha, a relative of his, preferred him to his predecessor, U.M. Trivedi.[157] This development is highly revealing of the way the 'cluster technique' functioned. Even though Trivedi was a national leader of the Jana Sangh over the long term, he still belonged to the periphery of Mandsaur's 'cluster' because he did not have an RSS background. The hard-core of

---

[153] Interview with Thakur Kishore Singh Sisodia.

[154] Patwa also worked in the local marketing cooperative societies (interview with S. Patwa, 17 Feb. 1994, Bhopal).

[155] *Madhya Pradesh Vidhan Sabha sadasyon ka sankshipt parichay – 1967*, Bhopal: Vidhan Sabha Sachivalay, 1970, pp. 56, 122.

[156] *Who's who in Lok Sabha – 1967*, op. cit., p. 249.

[157] Interview with Thakur Kishore Singh Sisodia.

Mandsaur's 'cluster', as elsewhere, comprised RSS cadres who decided, among other things, the party's nominees at the time of elections.

Another instance of successful cooperation between a Jana Sangh activist and a rural notable took place in Dewas district. Here Kailash Joshi, a *swayamsevak* who was called on to become Chief Minister in 1977, built up his own 'cluster' with the help of landed proprietors in the area. Joshi had joined the RSS in 1943 while a student in Indore.[158] In the 1950s he pursued a strategy of 'notabilisation' by being elected as head of the municipality of Hatpiplia with the help of Thakur Sajan Singh, one of the sons of the *jagirdar* of Bagli (formerly a part of Gwalior state) who was already the municipality's vice-president. In 1957 the Thakur contested the election to the Vidhan Sabha on the Jana Sangh ticket, but he was not elected and in 1962 declined a further offer to stand – to the benefit of Joshi, who won at Bagli with his patron's help and has retained the seat since then.[159] The collaboration between Joshi and the Thakur lasted till the 1967 elections.[160] The structure of this 'cluster', where *swayamsevaks* cooperated with rural leaders, corroborates Adrian Mayer's comment that in the early 1960s the Jana Sangh had a stronger presence in the countryside than in Dewas town – unlike Congress.[161]

Thus the Jana Sangh in Madhya Pradesh seemed set to resolve the conflict which had arisen at the end of the 1950s between the aim of a long-term Sangathanist approach and the need to put up influential candidates at elections: the mingling of networks of notables and *swayam-sevaks* offered a third alternative. Although it was increasing, the number of notables among the Jana Sangh's candidates in Madhya Pradesh remained limited. This was certainly due to the party's attachment to the Sangathanist model, which had merely become hybridised through the 'cluster technique'. The party had in fact sought a compromise which would allow it to improve its electoral position while remaining faithful to a method inherited from the RSS: on the one hand, it continued to be

---

[158] Interview with K. Joshi, 15 Nov. 1988, Bhopal.

[159] Interview with K. Joshi, 24 Nov. 1989, Bhopal.

[160] Subsequently the Thakur shifted to the Congress and disputed elections against Joshi in 1980 and 1985.

[161] A. Mayer, 'System and network: An approach to the study of political process in Dewas' in T.N. Madan (ed.), *Indian anthropology – essays in honour of D.N. Majumdar*, Bombay: Asia Publishing House, 1962, pp. 272-3. One can demonstrate a similar pattern in an urban setting in Shajapur district. A 'hard core' of *swayamsevaks* was represented by the ex-*pracharak* H. Joshi (elected MLA at Susner) and M.L. Bhandari (Agar) a Banya, who provided a link between the party and the merchant community and illustrated the process of 'notabilisation' of *swayamsevaks* since he was a member of the municipal council of Agar. The dimension of 'urban notability' was well represented in this cluster by R.C. Dube, the editor of a local newspaper and president of the municipal council of Shajapur, whose MLA he became in 1962.

run in each district by *swayamsevaks* who were simply ordered to build up their 'cluster' by co-opting notables, and, on the other hand, it encouraged a form of 'notabilisation' of activists which would on occasion allow it do to without notables altogether. In all, of thirty-two MLAs whose life-histories are known, twelve bore the usual characteristics of notables, while twenty were activists trained by the RSS, of whom seven had been engaged in a notabilisation process (see Appendix F, pp. 556-7).

It may be that the Jana Sangh also used this 'cluster technique' in other states. In Uttar Pradesh, of the 49 Jana Sangh MLAs returned in the 1962 elections, 49% were former *zamindars or taluqdars* and 45% belonged to the RSS; although these two categories would have overlapped, they indicate the extent to which the party was relying on large landholders to win seats as well as working for the return of RSS men.[162] In Rajasthan more than one-third of the 15 MLAs returned in 1962 were Rajput landowners.[163] The political circumstances in these states differ, and more research needs to be done before we can tell whether the 'cluster technique' was used in particular regions, and with what success, before taking the comparison further.

In the first half of the 1960s, the Jana Sangh leadership developed a moderate strategy which combined three basic elements. First, it amended the Sangathanist model by intensifying its reliance on notables, who often had only a certain sympathy with Hindu nationalist doctrine, in order to strengthen its electoral foundations. Second, this development, which was carefully controlled, went hand in hand with an effort to break out of its isolation – in the wake of the traumatic events of 1962 – by making alliances with other parties in the area of legitimate politics. This integration strategy depended largely on the attitude of these groups; while the political class tended during the 1950s to recognise secularism as a normative value and hence reject communalist parties like the Jana Sangh, the latter began to benefit in 1962-3 from a waning of this conviction among certain opposition parties, above all because of a desire to supplant the Congress. The collaboration of 1963 began to erode the secular approach as a legitimate norm of Indian politics which hitherto

---

162 R.C. Meyer, 'The political élite in an underdeveloped society: the case of Uttar Pradesh in India', University of Pennsylvania, unpubl. Ph.D. dissertation, 1969, pp. 158, 162 and 228.

163 H.T. Davey, 'The transformation of an ideological movement into an aggregative party', op. cit., pp. 202-4. The one-third roughly corresponds to 29 and 7% of the Jana Sangh MLAs who have functions in the cooperatives and the *Panchayati Raj*' (R. Sisson and L. Shrader, *Legislative recruitment and political integration: Patterns of political linkage in an Indian state*, Berkeley: University of California Press, 1972, pp. 39-40).

had doomed the Jana Sangh to isolation. Third, the Jana Sangh displayed a shift of emphasis from militant Hindu themes in favour of more legitimate articles of faith, such as patriotism and opposition to state intervention in the economy, an issue already present in its programme but used more intensively to attract support from the 'middle ground of politics'.

The strategy of moderation – contrasting with the preferred strategy of the RSS combining Hindu nationalism, Sangathanism and ethno-religious mobilisation – had been adopted because the Jana Sangh could hardly exploit a Hindu feeling of vulnerability (the minorities being in a non-militant phase) and because of the constraints imposed by the political context. On the one hand, the structure of regional politics prevented the Jana Sangh from fully exploiting symbolic issues like the promotion of Hindi because the 'Congress system' already dealt with them. On the other hand, the Centre was vigorous in its fight against Hindu communalism. Furthermore, Nehru had established socio-economic development as a major priority and nobody could ignore it, not even the Jana Sangh. The latter developed an alternative programme which was hostile to state intervention in order to profit from the relative unpopularity of government schemes such as collective farming. This was a significant development because in campaigning on socio-economic issues, the party was diverted from ethno-religious themes.

This situation was to change somewhat in the mid-1960s. In 1964 Nehru died, and the following year India fought its second war against Pakistan. By contrast with what happened in 1962, the Indian Army's victorious offensive at the beginning of September precluded the Jana Sangh from strengthening its image as a 'patriotic party'.[164] Its Working Committee could only applaud 'the magnificent response given by the nation – the Government, the defence forces and the people – to the challenge posed by Pakistan's aggression.' It admitted that 'never before in these 18 years of independence, have the Government policies and actions been so completely in accord with the people's will as they have been during these past few weeks.'[165]

---

[164] On 30 June 1965 Nehru's successor, Lal Bahadur Shastri, accepted the compromise worked out through Britain's good offices to obtain a cease-fire. The text recognised Pakistan's claims in the frontier zone of Kutch (in the west of Gujarat) and Sindh. The Jana Sangh challenged the validity of the agreement, with Upadhyaya even declaring: 'A government which cannot defend the border had no right to exist' (*Organiser*, 8 Aug. 1965, p. 1). On 15 August his party organised a demonstration outside Parliament which drew 100,000 people from all over India, each regional branch being requested to send 1,000 participants (*Statesman*, 22 July 1965, p. 1; 27 July 1965, p. 3; 29 July 1965, p. 3 and 8 Aug. 1965, p. 7). The party was on the way to being able to exploit the situation when the Indian army launched its offensive.

[165] Resolution of 27 Sept. 1965, *Party documents*, vol. 3, op. cit., pp. 128-9. *Swayamsevaks*

However, the 1965 war, by revealing to public opinion the permanence of a Pakistani menace, reinforced the legitimacy of the Jana Sangh, which not only cast itself as the defender of the national interest but also defined this in purely Hindu terms.[166] In a speech before 1,000 *swayamsevaks* in Delhi, Golwalkar mentioned the 'suspicious conduct'[167] of certain Muslims during the conflict. This intensification by the RSS of Hindu nationalist propaganda could only hinder the strategy of integration pursued by the Jana Sangh.

Even before the 1965 war the hold of the RSS-trained local cadres on the party appeared to be a major internal constraint on the execution of a moderate strategy. In July 1964 the breaking-off of negotiations with the Swatantra Party on amalgamation had been explained by the Jana Sangh as being due not only to their disagreements over the Kashmir question but also by virtue of the fact that, since its own strength was based on an activist network, 'alliance discussion should be on their own terms'.[168] The local party cadres, meanwhile, most of them *swayamsevaks*, remained attached to the Sangathanist model, which gave priority to internal growth rather than alliances involving a dilution of Hindu nationalist discipline and doctrine.

This doctrine was to guide most of the Jana Sangh's electoral strategy at the local level, as was shown by its participation in the mobilisation of 1966-7 against cow slaughter, in which the initiative belonged more to the RSS and its new offshoot, the Vishwa Hindu Parishad.

---

enrolled in the army and ensured the efficient running of administrative services, such as keeping the traffic moving in Delhi. They had been summoned to carry out such tasks by Golwalkar, in answer to requests for support from the government. Furthermore, the leader of the RSS had been invited by Shastri to a conference bringing together all currents of Indian politics (*Organiser*, 12 Sept. 1965 and 19 Sept. 1965, p. 13).

[166] The President of India, Radhakrishnan, in a radio broadcast 'congratulated the Muslims in India on their unshaken loyalty' (S. Gopal, *Radhakrishnan – A biography*, Delhi: Oxford University Press, 1989, p. 341) but the war awoke memories of Partition and the suspicions of some Hindus about the Muslims (see the case of Gujarat as analysed in J. Reddy, *Inquiry into the communal disturbances at Ahmedabad and other places in Gujarat on and after 18th September 1969*, Gandhinagar: Government Central Press, 1971, pp. 47 and 212, and Imtiaz Ahmed, 'Pakistan and the Indian Muslims', *Quest*, Jan.-Feb., 1975, p. 40). The RSS busied itself with exploiting such feelings during the war, even going to the length of denouncing the presence of infiltrators within Muslim organisations (*Organiser*, 15 Aug. 1965, p. 8) and the refusal of Muslims to become assimilated. An anonymous contributor wrote in the *Organiser*: 'They cannot, in the name of "religion" sympathise with invaders and run down liberators [...] why can't Muslims stop thinking as Muslims and start talking as Indians?' (ibid., p. 6).

[167] Ibid., 21 Nov. 1965. See also his speech at Udaipur (ibid., 12 Dec. 1965, p. 2).

[168] *Statesman*, 10 July 1964, p. 7.

5

THE MIXED STRATEGY:
HINDU MOBILISATION AND
ELECTORAL ALLIANCES

Although the Jana Sangh increased its support from the late 1950s to the mid-1960s partly as a result of socio-economic protest movements, it never relinquished its Hindu identity. The latter was not strongly emphasised, largely because it was difficult to capitalise on Hindu nationalist themes within the limits prescribed by the anti-communalist policy of Jawaharlal Nehru. Promotion of Hinduism was taken up instead from 1964 onwards by the Vishwa Hindu Parishad (VHP – World Hindu Council), a creation of the RSS, which was less susceptible than the Jana Sangh to the constraints of the government's secularist approach because it kept itself outside the sphere of politics.

In fact the VHP became the advocate of a programme of socio-cultural reform which was consistent with the strategy of stigmatisation and emulation. It had been founded by RSS leaders mainly to meet the challenge posed by proselytising religions in India and had taken over some of the organisational features of such religions in order to resist their influence more effectively.

Although the VHP's original mission was to defend Hinduism, its network of contacts within the Hindu religious institutions gave it the capacity to engage in ethno-religious mobilising campaigns, such as that developed in late 1966 to bring an end to cow slaughter. The conditions for such a campaign were propitious. Nehru's death in May 1964 had left the Hindu traditionalists with more latitude to express their views and Mrs Gandhi, who became Prime Minister in January 1966 following the death of Lal Bahadur Shastri, appeared to lack the experience to counter the threat from this new source of opposition. However, the Jana Sangh's commitment to the campaign was qualified; its was a 'mixed strategy', designed to foster ethno-religious mobilisation while permitting a pragmatic approach to building up support by appeals to non-ideological interests. It was successful in recruiting notables and princes to contest the 1967 elections and concluded a number of electoral alliances with other non-Congress groups.

193

The Vishwa Hindu Parishad: the strategy of stigmatisation/
emulation and the religious network

Pracharaks and 'modern gurus'

While the VHP was launched by the RSS, from its inception onwards the
VHP obtained the crucial support of *gurus* who shared many ideological
affinities with Hindu nationalism.

The first man to head the VHP was Shivram Shankar Apte, a
Maharashtrian Brahmin from Baroda who had joined the RSS in Bombay
in 1939 when he was studying for his LL B. As a lawyer in Bombay he
had been close to K.M. Munshi, who was then practising law. He also
worked as a journalist at United Press of India, acquiring skills which
served the RSS several years later. His meeting with Golwalkar led him
to embrace the career of a *pracharak* and he was first sent to Tamil Nadu.
After the 1949 ban on the RSS he was given the task of developing a Hindi
news agency.[1] In 1961, Apte published in *Kesari* – the Marathi newspaper
founded by Tilak – a series of three articles about the need to bring
together representatives of all the currents of Hinduism in order to
stengthen its coherence.[2] In 1963, an article by Swami Chinmayananda
suggested that a 'world Hindu conference' should be convened in order
to achieve this goal. From then onwards, the collaboration between
Chinmayananda and Apte symbolised the association of *pracharaks* and
'modern *gurus* ' which is the cornerstone of the VHP.

A Brahmin from Kerala, Swami Chinmayananda had obtained a MA
in English literature in the early 1940s before becoming a journalist in
Delhi.[3] While he was reporting on the *sadhus* of Rishikesh, he became a
disciple of Swami Shivananda, the founder of the Divine Life Society, in
1949.[4] Two years later he initiated a series of conferences in English on
the Vedanta, called *jnana yajna* (sacrifice or worship of knowledge),
whose aim was to bring back to the fold of Hinduism the Westernised

---

[1]   N.B. Lele, 'Shri Shiv Shankar Apte' in *Shraddhanjali Smarika*, New Delhi: Vishwa
      Hindu Parishad, [n.d.], pp. 26-28 (Hindi).

[2]   *Hindu Vishva*, Sept.-Oct. 1980, p. 18.

[3]   His writings revealed his anti-Gandhian views. In May 1947, for instance, he wrote in
      Blitz: 'By the over-emphasis laid on non-violence we have come to witness the pathetic
      situation of today, when thousands, in cowardly fear take to precipitate flight, leaving
      their innocent children to be butchered and their unarmed helpless women to be
      dishonoured or converted or killed.' (article reproduced in *Organiser*, Swami
      Chinmayananda special, 28 Aug. 1994, p. 4).

[4]   N. Patchen, *The journey of a master: Swami Chinmayananda*, Berkeley, CA: Asian
      Humanities Press, 1989, p. 56.

middle class, 'the modern educated illiterates'.[5] The first of his speeches, in Poona, was entitled 'let us be Hindu':

My proposal is that the wise thing would be for us to try and bring about a renaissance of Hinduism so that under its greatness – proved through many centuries – we may come to grow into the very heights of culture and civilisation that was ours in the historical path.[6]

The *jnana yajna* attracted more and more followers in the 1950s and the patronage of personalities such as Rajendra Prasad, the Indian President, who inaugurated one of Chinmayananda's conferences in 1956. His success, like that of most of those van der Veer describes as 'modern *gurus*', is probably attributable to the relevance of his message for the middle class. As with other 'modern *gurus*', the emphasis was on 'individual growth', 'social concern' and religion as 'a code of conduct for every man to make life a success'.[7] And because Swami Chinmayananda's speeches dealt with the Vedanta, they were appropriate also to Westernised Hindus who tended to reject popular, ritualistic Hinduism but were still attached to their culture.

Parallel to his *jnana yajnas*, in the 1950s Swami Chinmayananda patronised a Chinmaya Mission whose main activity was the training in Hinduism of children and teachers. In 1963, this mission collected 10,000 Rs for the Vivekananda Rock Memorial that the RSS was building in Kanyakumari (Tamil Nadu). In the same year Swami Chinmayananda established his *ashram* in Bombay, the Sandipany Academy, to provide training for Hindu preachers:

A new type of swami is emerging in this country who will serve as missionatries to their own people. At this crucial time in our history, we do not need those who live in a cave and meditate.[8]

Soon afterwards, in 1965, Swami Chinmayananda followed abroad a businessman who was looking for 'ammunition to export yoga to America'.[9]

Swami Chinmayananda is representative of many 'modern *gurus*' who were active in the VHP and shared a common set of characteristics: their spiritual practice is based on discourses[10] in English and hence both

---

5   Interview with Swami Chinmayananda, 10 June 1993, Puteaux (France).

6   Cited in N. Patchen, *The journey of a master*, op. cit., p. 155.

7   P. van der Veer,' Hindu nationalism and the discourse of modernity: the Vishva Hindu Parishad' in M. Marty and R. Scott Appleby (eds), *Accounting for fundamentalisms*, University of Chicago Press, 1993.

8   Cited in N. Patchen, *The journey of a master*, op. cit., p. 215.

9   Cited in ibid., p. 229.

10 Swami Chinmayananda considered his tongue as his 'one square inch assets' (cited in ibid., p. 220).

language and message were adapted to the urban middle class; they often shared the same background as that of the latter; the *guru-shishya* relation is accorded less importance than that of mass contact (for example, Swami Chinmayananda does not initiate disciples individually but gives 'the mantra from the platform'[11]); the 'modern *gurus*' do not emphasise their sectarian affiliation but rather their 'Hindu' allegiance; they have often founded their own *ashram*; and, lastly, they attend conferences all over the world.

S.S. Apte was very interested in Swami Chinmayananda's 1963 article, and the notion of a 'world Hindu conference' took shape partly through the collaboration of these two men. For nine months, Apte toured India in order to contact personalities likely to participate in it, and in 1964, 150 people were invited to the inaugural conference of the VHP at the Sandipany Academy.

The VHP, a consistory for Hinduism ?

The foundation of the VHP fulfilled the criteria of the strategy of stig-matisation and emulation since it resulted from a reactivation of the majoritarian inferiority complex, namely the feeling that Christian proselytisation posed a threat to Hinduism and that close attention had to be given to imitating its techniques in order the better to resist it. The arousal of this sense of vulnerability, even in certain official circles, had been in evidence since the 1950s, as the publication of the Niyogi Report in 1957 suggests.[12] In a summary of the Niyogi Report intended for

---

[11]   Interview with Swami Chinmayananda.

[12]   Following an intensification of Christian missionary activity in the tribal zones of Madhya Pradesh (in Surguja district, more than 4,000 conversions took place in 1952, compared to only forty the previous year—*Report of the Christian missionary activities enquiry committee*, vol. 1, op. cit., p. 21), the government of R.S. Shukla set up a commission of enquiry under B.S. Niyogi (a former chairman of the Civil Service Commission), which discovered that the number of foreign missionaries active in India increased from 4,377 in 1951 to 4,877 in 1955, of whom 480 – more than half of them Americans – were in Madhya Pradesh; and between 1950 and 1954 the missions had received grants totalling 2.9 billion rupees from abroad, two-thirds being from the United States. This money was used to build schools, orphanages and hospitals where conversions were sometimes obtained fraudulently (ibid., p.100 and pp. 99-135). The report stated, among its conclusions:

> Evangelisation in India appears to be part of the uniform world policy to revive Christendom for re-establishing Western supremacy and is not prompted by spiritual motives. The objective is apparently to create Christian minority pockets with a view to disrupt the solidarity of the non-Christian societies, and the mass conversions of a considerable section of Adivasis [tribal peoples] with this ulterior motive is fraught with danger to the security of the State (ibid., p. 137).

propagandistic purposes, a Hindu association defined the enemy as 'an extremely centralised organisation which exists throughout the whole world, with its power concentrated in the Pope'.[13]

In August 1964 the Pope announced that the International Eucharistic Congress would be held in November in Bombay. Immediately, the *Organiser* protested against this 'invasion'.[14]

Catholicism is not merely a religion. It is a tremendous organisation allied with some foreign powers. [...] The large scale conversion of tribal people in the industrial heartland of India [South Bihar] poses a serious danger to future national security. Because the Catholic position is that in the case of conflict between their country and the Church, their first loyalty will always be to the Pope![15]

This partly mythical image (especially since most missionaries in India were Protestant) of an enemy whose strength came from its organisational solidity and transnational character, stimulated the Hindu nationalists to endow their religion with a multinational ecclesiastical body.[16] This sheds light on the task assigned to the VHP at its inception on 29 August 1964 in Bombay. Its General Secretary, S.S. Apte, explained the movement's foundation as follows:

The declared object of Christianity is to turn the whole world into Christendom – as that of Islam is to make it 'Pak'. Besides these two dogmatic and proselytising religions, there has arisen a third religion, communism. [...] The world has been divided into Christian, Islamic and Communist, and all these three consider the Hindu society as a very fine rich food on which to feast and fatten themselves. It is therefore necessary in this age of competition and conflict to think of, and organise, the Hindu world to save itself from the evil eyes of all the three.[17]

The principal example cited by Apte in support of his argument was the autonomist movement of the Naga tribes in the North-East, who were largely Christianised[18] and to whom a separate Nagaland had been granted

---

The demand for a separate state by the partly Christianised tribes of Jharkhand in South Bihar was analysed, in this perspective, as being the result of missionary activity (ibid p. 50.), thus supporting the thesis of the Hindu nationalists that conversion was a process of 'denationalisation'. The strength of the aggressor was above all attributed to its capacity to mount coordinated action internationally.

[13]   *Report of the Christian Missionaries Activities Enquiry Committee – Madhya Pradesh – Abridged Version*. Delhi: All India Arya (Hindu) Dharma Sewa Sangha (n.d.), p. 12.

[14]   *Organiser*, 31 Aug. 1964, p. 1.

[15]   Ibid.

[16]   The very name of the organisation – World Hindu Council – reflects their international ambitions. The VHP leaders relied mainly on the Hindu diaspora in their effort to establish the organisation abroad.

[17]   *Organiser*, Diwali Special, 1964, p. 15.

[18]   Four-fifths of the people included in the census for Nagaland declared themselves to be Christians, a sign of how wide-ranging the conversions had been.

in 1963. The RSS attributed this fact to their 'denationalisation' by the missions. The selection of this example confirmed that Christianity was regarded as the chief aggressor. It also explains the structure of the VHP, which was in fact a scheme for federating the sects of Hinduism on a Christian model.

Present at the founding congress were not only politicians like K.M. Munshi and V.G. Deshpande but also representatives of different sects like Tara Singh and Gyani Bhupendra Singh, president of the SGPC, for Sikhism was, in the eyes of Hindu nationalism, merely a branch of Hinduism. Simultaneously the VHP was given an 'Advising Council which included the *Shankaracharyas*, the spiritual leaders and the *gurus* of all the *Sampradaya* and *Pantha* [sects]'.[19] A decision was also taken to organise a major international conference at Allahabad, in 1966, on the occasion of the Kumbh Mela[20] in order to develop among the sects 'a sense of oneness and unity underlying the apparent diversities'.[21]

Up till then, representatives of Hindu sects had been more closely associated with Hindu nationalist movements other than those belonging to the 'Sangh Parivar'. Thus the Hindu Mahasabha had enrolled into its ranks the Shankaracharya of Karweer Pith and the Mahant Digvijay Nath of Gorakhpur. In the 1950s Hindu religious figures tended on the whole to respond to the solicitations of a new party led by one of their own number, Swami Karpatriji, namely the Ram Rajya Parishad.[22] The Shankaracharya of Puri, Niranjan Tirth, who was appointed in 1964, had been secretary of the Ram Rajya Parishad and editor of its journal, *Sanmarg,* in Varanasi.[23]

Gathering the various *Shankaracharyas* within the VHP was made no easier because of their traditional rivalries. Thus the first International Hindu Conference, which was held at Allahabad (or Prayag, the Sanskrit name used by Hindu nationalists), on 22-24 January 1966, suffered from the defection of the *Shankaracharyas* of Badrinath and Sringeri. Among the 25,000 delegates were to be found at least as many founders of their own *ashrams* or heads of modern associations as spiritual masters who had been initiated and invested according to the rules of sects which

---

[19]   *Organiser*, Diwali Special., 1964, p. 15.

[20]   The religious gathering held every twelve years at the confluence of the Ganges and Jamuna rivers, attendances at which often surpass several million people.

[21]   *Organiser*, Diwali Special, 1964, p. 15. In 1969 S. S. Apte repeated his desire to promote 'the integration and indivisible unification of all the folds and layers, castes, communities and Sampradayas [sects] to make this multipetal society a living organism' (ibid., 21 June 1969).

[22]   *Hitavada*, 9 Nov. 1956, p. 3, and 25 Nov. 1956, p. 3.

[23]   *Organiser*, 20 July 1964, p. 7.

carried on an ancient tradition. Among the former we can single out three prominent personalities.

The first was Prabhu Datt Brahmachari. He had taken part in the Independence movement, to which he had been drawn by Gandhi, along with Hindu traditionalists like M. M. Malaviya, P. Tandon and Sampurnanand, who brought him in to become editor of *Aj*, a Hindi newspaper in Varanasi, in the 1920s. He renounced the world soon afterwards and founded his *ashram* at Jhusi, near Allahabad, where he helped to organise the Kumbh Mela.[24] In 1948, the RSS leader in Allahabad, Rajendra Singh, got to know him. Soon after, Prabhu Datt Brahmachari tried unsuccessfully to meet Rajendra Prasad in order to petition for the ban on the RSS to be lifted. He also became close to Golwalkar in the early 1950s[25] and in the 1951-2 elections Rajendra Singh and Golwalkar persuaded him to stand against Nehru on the cow protection platform and in opposition to the Hindu Code Bill. Prabhu Datt Brahmachari was typical of the 'modern *gurus*' who founded their own *ashrams* and were politically active.

The second was Sant Tukdoji (1901-68), who personified the Hindu traditionalist line in the VHP (also represented by K.M. Munshi) in his capacity as president – at the time of its creation and again in the mid-1960s – of the Bharat Sadhu Samaj (Society of Indian Sadhus). This institution had been founded under the auspices of the Congress government with two aims in view: 'to act as the Unifying force for re-organising all religious sects and Orders for utilising in the maximum the spiritual and moral potentialities for all-round development of the country'.[26] A *sant* from Maharashtra, Tukdoji had taken part in the Sarvodaya movement. In 1949, President Rajendra Prasad honoured him as a Rashtriya Sant and during the 1962 and 1965 wars he had gone to the front to support Indian soldiers. He propagated his ideas not in America but in Japan and Malaysia.[27] He explained his decision to join the VHP by

---

[24]　Ibid., 26 Oct. 1990, p. 9.

[25]　Rajendra Singh, 'Do shabd', preface to Shri Prabhadatt Brahmachari, *Hamare shri Golwalkarji ki punya smritiyan*, Jhusi (Prayag): Sankirtan bhawan (n.d.), pp. 2-4 (Hindi).

[26]　'Note from Secretary, Bharat Sadhu Samaj' in *Report on the Hindu religious endowment commission 1960- 1962*, New Delhi: Ministry of Law, n. d., p. 510. This institution, in the spirit of Nehru, who presided over it in the year it was founded (*Statesman* [Delhi], 27 March 1957), was established with the aim of encouraging *sadhus* to participate in economic development through *shramdan* (voluntary labour) (*Hitavada*, 15 April 1956, p. 4). The content of the project piloted by G. Nanda (the Union Planning and Labour Minister who was Chairman of the Central advisory Committee) was heavily influenced by Gandhian notions such as *bhoodan*, the prohibition of alcohol consumption, and protection of the cow (ibid., 2 March 1956; 1 May 1956, p. 5; 24 Sept. 1956, p. 7; and 25 Sept. 1956, p. 6).

[27]　'Sant Tukdo ji Maharaj' in *Shraddhanjali Smarika*, op. cit., p. 46 (Hindi).

reference to the need to protect Hinduism against Christianity and Islam as well as to counteract the anti-Hindu bias of the government.[28]

Brahmachari Dattamurti Maharaj (1901-66) was a disciple of Bhaskar Masurkar Maharaj, a *sadhu* who had been very active in the *Shuddhi* movement in Goa (he claimed to have reconverted 10,000 Christians). After completing his studies in engineering Dattamurti joined Masurkar's *ashram* in 1924 and developed the *Shuddhi* movement in Maharashtra, Gujarat and Karnataka. In 1955 he assumed the leadership of the *ashram* and eleven years later took part in the foundation of the VHP.[29]

Among representatives of historic religious currents, especially notable was the participation – destined to become institutionalised – of Swami Vishvesh Tirth of Pejawar Math (from Udipi in Karnataka), the spiritual head of the Vaishnavite sect of Madhva.[30] Born in 1931, he had been initiated into the Madhva Sampradaya when he was seven years old and after several years of study had been appointed head of the Sri Krishna *math* of Udipi in 1951. He had then acquired a reputation as a patron of Hindu culture through the Madhva Mahamandal (Great Madhva Circle), which actively promoted a classical Indian, i.e. Sanskrit-based, education.[31]

The under-representation of spiritual masters heading prestigious sects suggests that the VHP, like the Hindu Mahasabha in its time, above all attracted *swamis* in search of a platform and greater legitimacy. This indicated a source of weakness, though not necessarily an insurmountable handicap, since the authority of a Hindu spiritual master may derive from sources other than being the official head of a recognised sect. Knowledge of texts, ascetic discipline and oratorical gifts can mitigate the lack of an official position and enable those so endowed to proclaim themselves as religious spokesmen.

Although it was far from representative of all currents of Hinduism, the Allahabad meeting of 1966 set itself up as a sort of parliament[32] and consistory of Hinduism. A sub-committee was nominated to 'draw up a code of conduct suitable for the promotion and strengthening of the Hindu *samskars*'.[33] This Videvat Parishad (learned assembly) was convened to simplify the purification rites, bestow on the five principal festivals in the Hindu calendar an 'official' status, and above all draw up this

[28] *Organiser*, 26 Dec. 1965.
[29] 'Bramachari Dattamurti "Maharaj" ', *Shraddhanjali Smarika*, op. cit., p. 40 (Hindi).
[30] *Organiser*, 30 Jan. 1966, p. 1 and 3 May 1981, p. 4.
[31] *Hindu Vishva*, May 1981, p. 39.
[32] S.S. Apte considered furthermore that its members were 'representatives' of Hindus dispersed throughout the world and living under different regimes (*Organiser*, Republic Day Special Number, 1966, p. 9).
[33] Ibid., 30 Jan. 1966, p. 2.

famous code of conduct. Significantly, these procedures were justified in the *Organiser* by reference to Christianity and Islam.

Christians and Muslims are generally found observing, strictly and scrupulously, some religious rules of conduct. Besides, every Christian and Muslim has some outward symbols significant of his religion. The Parishad happily arrived at a 'code of conduct' which would be agreeable to all the sects and creeds. They decided that Pratashnan [bathing in the morning] and Ishwarsmaran [remembering God] should be the minimum rules of conduct.[34]

Besides these efforts to bring about greater uniformity of beliefs and practices in Hinduism, the VHP also strove to make itself the central authority in an entire religious network, one that would be based not only in monasteries but also in temples. Priests were thus called upon, at the Allahabad assembly, to make temples places of 'dissemination of ... *dharma* and *sanskriti*'.[35]

Reviewing this development, the *Organiser* wrote that it was the first time that such an assembly had taken place since that convened by the Emperor Harsha in the seventh century, which had brought together at Prayag representatives of the different religious currents in India in order to foster mutual harmony and understanding. In fact this decision reflected the Buddhist influences to which Harsha had been exposed.[36] But for the *Organiser* the important thing was to find 'national' terms of reference to legitimise the meeting, whose character had little that was Hindu about it. The invocation of this illustrious past was in fact aimed at presenting a cultural transfer – the principle of an ecclesiastical structure – as a simple restoration within the logic of a strategy of emulation.

With the Vishwa Hindu Parishad the RSS – whose leader, Golwalkar, was present both at the foundation of the organisation and at the Allahabad meeting – had opened up a new front, one that conforms to our interpretation of Hindu nationalism in terms of a strategy of stigmatisation and emulation. Its ideology is constructed by means of a very precise rationale that is defined by three principal characteristics: first, being subjected to a real or imagined external threat, Hindu militants stigmatised it and developed strong feelings of vulnerability and hostility towards the 'threatening Other'; second, they undertook to reform their community, borrowing cultural features from the aggressor to which they attributed the latter's strength; and third, such reform is experienced or presented as a return to the past, from which they could extract pride to legitimise this imitation of the Other. This process of imitation, whereby the VHP used the adversary's own weapons against it, was well illustrated by the

[34] Ibid., 11 June 1967, p. 14.
[35] Ibid., 30 Jan. 1966, p. 15.
[36] D. Devahuti, *Harsha: a political study*, Oxford: Clarendon Press, 1970, pp. 96 and 157.

despatch of 'counter-missionaries' to the tribal zones of the North-East affected by Christian proselytism.[37] The Hindu nationalist identity which developed from this logic still seemed to show little fidelity to Hinduism in so far as it meant borrowing features from the Other which were foreign to it, such as a centralised church-like structure or proselytism. Swami Chinmayananda admitted as much explicitly:

I know that religious organisation is against the very principle of Hinduism, but we have to move with the time. We seem to have entered today all over the world, in every walk of life, in every field of endeavour into an age of organisation. You cannot send a rocket up without an organisation. If disorganised, there is no strength, no vitality. Therefore, in the spiritual field, even though the individuals proceed forward and develop, if religion wants to serve the society, it also has to get organised.[38]

As well as pursuing its own mission in the socio-cultural field, the VHP expanded the edifice of Hindu nationalism. In symbiosis with the hard core cadres formed in the RSS – represented here by S.S. Apte – two new networks were established. One was linked to important per-sonalities deriving their power either from landholdings or personal wealth who were attracted to the organisation because of its role in defending Hinduism in accordance with their traditional vocation as patrons of Hindu institutions;[39] thus the Maharajah of Mysore served as president of the VHP before being succeeded by the Maharana of Udaipur in 1968.[40] Capitalist families like the Dalmias also supported the move-ment in the same way as J.K. Birla helped the Hindu Mahasabha. The other principal linkage of the RSS (via the VHP) was naturally to a religious network of growing importance consisting of *sadhus* and the leaders of sects.

The VHP appeared to be the effective agent of a Hindu instrumentalist strategy precisely because its religious network was a means by which a Hindu nationalist mobilisation could be achieved. In 1966 the VHP was one of the protagonists in the campaign against cow slaughter, which the Jana Sangh tried to exploit politically in the run up to the February 1967 elections.

[37] W. Andersen and S. Damle, *The brotherhood in saffron*, op. cit., pp. 133-4.

[38] Swami Chinmayanandji, 'Why you should work for Vishwa Hindu Parishad' in *Shraddhanjali Smarika*, op. cit., p. 69.

[39] Concerning the rajahs' patronage of temples, see, for the case of Puri, H. Kulke, 'Royal temple policy and the structure of medieval Hindu Kingdoms' in A. Eshmann et al. (eds), *The cult of Jagannath and the regional tradition in Orissa*, Delhi: Manohar, 1978, p. 133.

[40] *Organiser*, 12 April 1968, p. 6.

Ethno-religious mobilisation under a double constraint

In 1966, the shift towards the strategy of Hindu mobilisation seemed to have been made possible by a new political context. The power of the Centre appeared weakened after the death of Shastri on 11 January 1966. Indira Gandhi, who succeeded Shastri as Prime Minister, was at once inexperienced and cautious *vis-a-vis* the control exercised by the Congress 'bosses'. Of these Gulzarilal Nanda (interim Prime Minister in 1964 and 1966 and Indira Gandhi's Home Minister) and S.K. Patil (Minister of Railways) were known for their Hindu traditionalist views. The latter had been close to Sardar Patel during his rise to power as leader of the Congress in Bombay and had been vigorous in his support of Tandon in 1950. Faithful to Sardar Patel's plan to enrol the RSS in Congress, he had also proposed that the party should 'nominate' certain *swayamsevaks* as candidates before the elections of 1951-2.[41] He even agreed in 1965 to inaugurate a local branch of the VHP, and in 1967 to take part in a ceremony to mark the despatch of ABVP activists to the North-East. [42]

For Nanda,[43] Hindu traditionalism was above all expressed through his campaign for recognition of the Ayurvedic medical system – the practitioners of which the government refused to consider as being equal to those of 'modern' medicine –[44] and the setting up of the Bharat Sadhu Samaj under his personal patronage in February 1956 while he was Minister of Planning and Labour. His close relations with high profile religious figures was illustrated in 1964 when he met with Swami Karpatriji in order to invite him to join in the battle against corruption.[45] Moreover his contacts with Hindu nationalists became more and more frequent, as his interviews with the *Organiser* in 1964-6 reveal.[46] In 1964,

---

[41] W. Andersen and S. Damle, *The brotherhood in saffron*, op. cit., p. 152. For a while in 1966 S.K. Patil seemed, like G. Nanda, to be a potential rival to Indira Gandhi (*Statesman Weekly*, 4 June 1966, p. 3.).

[42] *Organiser*, 1 Aug. 1965, p. 15, and 16 July 1967, p. 10.

[43] For a biographical sketch of G. Nanda see B.S. Gujrati, *Prime Ministers of India*, Delhi: Metropolitan Book Co., 1967, pp. 51-2.

[44] P. Brass, 'The politics of Ayurvedic education: A case study of revivalism and modernization in India' in S.H. and L.I. Rudolph (eds), *Education and politics in India – Studies in organization, society and policy*, Delhi: Oxford University Press, 1972, pp. 361-2. In 1962, Nanda appointed as President of the Ayurvedic Congress Pandit Shiv Sharma, whom the Scindias and the Jana Sangh managed to get elected to the Lok Sabha in 1967 as MP for Vidisha.

[45] *Organiser*, 10 July 1964, p. 16. In the editorial of the following issue, the *Organiser* commented: 'He [Nanda] evidently thinks association with *sadhus* can be a political asset in a religious country. And we think he is right too.'

[46] One of these concluded with this recommendation to the editor: 'Please do not hesitate to contact me for any information clarification. We must all cooperate in the national cause' (ibid., 31 Aug. 1964 p. 2).

he launched a project for a Sadachar Samiti (Society of Good Moral Conduct) in order to gather together representatives of religious associations and the worthier citizens; he thought that 'the *Organiser* would be the first to welcome [it] heartily'.[47] In June 1965 he invited Golwalkar to a meeting at which he informed him of the growing tensions with Pakistan and asked for his help in maintaining law and order.[48] The *Organiser* also congratulated itself on the fact that Nanda had defended in the Rajya Sabha the idea that the RSS was a cultural movement and not a political one – in the face of opposition from the parliamentary left, which tried to scotch this myth by making the status of a civil servant incompatible with membership of the RSS, as it was with membership of any political party.[49]

The cow protection movement

Indira Gandhi's inexperience and the Hindu traditionalism of certain Congress bosses help to explain why the Jana Sangh felt able to take up the issue of cow protection to build up the Hindu vote in 1966-7. The cow, as a symbol of Hindu identity, had been manipulated by interested parties on several occasions. Originally its sacred character in Hinduism had been comparable to that of the Brahmin.[50] This status, which has numerous explanations,[51] is recognised by all currents of Hinduism, thus endowing it with great potential for mobilisation. The Arya Samaj exploited the issue at the end of the nineteenth century to aid its penetration of the countryside.[52] Since then, appeals for protection of the cow have been, by implication, directed against the Muslims (who sometimes, though rarely, slaughter them for ritual purposes), thus heightening communal tension.[53] This was treated as a legitimate theme by a major body of opinion in Congress; Gandhi expressed his veneration for the cow on several occasions, but made it clear that the issue should not be used in any way against the Muslims.[54]

[47]   Ibid., p. 1.

[48]   Ibid., 21 June 1965, p. 1.

[49]   Ibid., 27 Nov. 1964.

[50]   In the code of Manu (the principal *Dharmashastra*), a man who kills a cow has to undergo very severe purification and expiation.

[51]   On this debate see S.M. Batra, 'The sacredness of the cow in India', *Social Compass*, 33 (2-3), 1986, pp. 163- 75.

[52]   S. Freitag, 'Sacred symbol as mobilizing ideology: the north Indian search for a "Hindu community" ', *Comparative study of society and history*, 22 (4), Oct. 1980, p. 614.

[53]   P. Brass, 'Elite groups, symbol manipulation and ethnic identity among the Muslims of South Asia' in D. Taylor and M. Yapp (eds), *Political identity in South Asia*, London: Curzon Press, 1979, p. 44.

[54]   G. Chakravartty, *Gandhi – A challenge to communalism*, New Delhi: Eastern Book Centre, 1967, pp. 202-3.

In 1949-50, there were prolonged debates in the Constituent Assembly between secularists, such as Nehru, and Hindu nationalists and Congress traditionalists, which resulted in an ambiguous compromise over cow slaughter. Its prohibition was recommended by Article 48 of the Constitution, i.e. at the level of the 'Directive Principles' to guide the states of the Union. Nehru had insisted on the fact that legislation against cow slaughter had to be a matter of relevance solely to the states. But apart from the refusal of certain states like Kerala to restrict the practice, a judgement of the Supreme Court in 1958 limited the scope of laws passed against cow slaughter in the other states to draught animals.[55]

There had already been protests against these restrictions from the RSS (in 1952 and 1954, in association with Prabhu Datt Brahmachari),[56] as well as narrowly targeted political attempts to exploit them. In 1962 the Chief Minister of Madhya Pradesh, Kailash Nath Katju, and Nehru were denounced by Hindu nationalists as non-believers; in Katju's constituency, Jaora, in Ratlam district, the Jana Sangh employed slogans such as 'A vote for the Jana Sangh is a vote for the protection of the cow' and circulated a pamphlet, the cover of which showed Nehru killing a cow with a sword.[57] Political propaganda of this sort contributed to the success of Laxmi Narayan Pandey, a medical practitioner and member of the RSS, who defeated Katju, and was symptomatic of a political manipulation of symbols that attained a new dimension during the 1960s.

The Bharat Gosevak Samaj (BGS, or Society to Serve the Cow) – whose patrons in Delhi, its base, were Hans Raj Gupta, Vasant Rao Oke and the businessman, Jai Dayal Dalmia – organised a conference in August 1964 to demand that the government should take upon itself the task of banning cow slaughter.[58] Officially the initiative for this came from the BGS, but the fact that Golwalkar opened the conference, that Prabhu Datt Brahmachari was there to give the event his blessing, and that D. Upadhyaya delivered an address, made it clear that there was a close connection with the 'Sangh parivar'. Furthermore, the date of the conference coincided with the launching of the VHP.[59]

The question of the prohibition of cow slaughter was put decisively to the test in August 1966 by Jana Sangh MPs, including. Swami Rameshwaranand, an Arya Samajist from Haryana.[60] The response of

55   D. E. Smith, *India as a secular state*, op. cit., p. 487.

56   *Organiser*, 17 March 1968, p. 12.

57   *Hindustan Times*, 3 March 1962, p. 5, and *Times of India*, 6 March 1962, p. 6.

58   On the politics of the BGS, see Prabhudatt Brahmachari, *Hamare shri Golwalkar*, op. cit., p. 27.

59   B. Graham, *Hindu nationalism*, op. cit., pp. 148-9, and *Organiser*, 31 Aug. 1964, p. 8.

60   *Madhya Pradesh Chronicle*, 5 Aug. 1966, p. 3; 14 Aug. 1966, p. 2 and 25 Aug. 1966, p. 2. At the same moment, a demonstration by *sadhus* took place outside Parliament House

the Minister of Agriculture was to exhort the governments of the states, where the prohibition was only partial, to intervene, an approach that found favour with many Congress traditionalists. On 5 September a delegation led by Seth Govind Das sent a memorandum on the subject to G. Nanda, the Home Minister, who was reputed to support it. Meanwhile in Parliament Swami Rameshwaranand had exclaimed 'Glory to our mother the cow!', despite calls to order from the Speaker, as the result of which he was suspended for ten days.[61]

On 25 September 1966, a Sarvadaliya Goraksha Maha-Abhiyan Samiti (SGMS, Committee for the Great All-Party Campaign for Protection of the Cow) was founded, headed by Prabhu Datt Brahmachari. He announced that a huge *satyagraha*, consisting of 100,000 participants, would be held on 7 November followed by a mass hunger-strike if a decision was not reached immediately. The steering group of the SGMS contained members of the VHP and the RSS, including Golwalkar, but also Congressmen (such as Seth Govind Das) and representatives of the Bharat Sadhu Samaj, the Arya Samaj (Ram Gopal Shalwale), the Hindu Mahasabha (Digvijay Nath) and above all the Ram Rajya Parishad (Swami Karpatriji and the Shankaracharya of Puri).[62]

The Union Territory of Delhi was alone in amending its laws in favour of greater protection for the cow.[63] On 7 November a very large demonstration went ahead in Delhi. Estimates of the number of participants in the whole of North India varied between 125,000 and 700,000.[64] The Delhi march ended with a meeting in front of the Lok Sabha. On the platform close to Parliament House, along with the organisers of the SGMS (including Golwalkar) and Congressmen such as Seth Govind Das, were the leaders of the Jana Sangh, whose Working Committee had given the movement its support.[65] Vajpayee was joined by Swami Rameshwaranand who, flouting his ten-day suspension, had provoked such disorder in the Lok Sabha that he was barred for the rest of the current session, and had come to harangue the crowd instead. His appeals for an assault on the Lok Sabha caused some *sadhus* to attempt (without success) to break the police cordon and commit acts of vandalism against public buildings.[66] These

(*Statesman Weekly*, 6 Aug. 1966, p. 3).

[61]   *Madhya Pradesh Chronicle*, 6 Sept. 1966, p. 5.

[62]   C. Baxter, *The Jana Sangh*, op. cit., p. 260.

[63]   *Madhya Pradesh Chronicle*, 18 Oct. 1966, p. 4. This was what Nanda would have liked to achieve in all the states by means of a negotiated settlement within the framework of the Constitution.

[64]   *Hindustan Times*, 8 Nov. 1966, and *Patriot*, 11 Nov. 1966.

[65]   Resolution of 2 Nov. 1966 in *Party documents*, vol. 2, op. cit., pp. 78-9.

[66]   *The Hindu*, 8 Nov. 1966, and review by Y.B. Chavan in *Rajya Sabha Debates*, vol. 58, 17 Nov. 1966, col. 1774.

acts of violence and the disorder which followed left eight dead, including one policeman.

The Jana Sangh tried to evade responsibility for the debacle, and Vajpayee and U.M. Trivedi tried to calm the most ardent demonstrators who, by launching an assault on the Lok Sabha, had not only discredited the party with regard to the secular norm of the régime but also challenged the authority of Parliament. This was especially damaging just at a time when the Jana Sangh was pursuing its rapprochement with the legitimate opposition (see below). The party could not hide the fact that the person who had sought official permission for the demonstration was none other than Kedar Nath Sahni, the General Secretary of its Delhi branch.[67] Above all, even if two-thirds of those arrested were *sadhus*, including followers of Karpatriji,[68] processions took place in the days that followed consisting of political activists who tried to exploit public resentment against the government's rough treatment of the *sadhus*. Madhok (the president of the Jana Sangh), Hans Raj Gupta and Hardayal Devgun were among the 1,400 people arrested at the moment when Golwalkar, far from looking for a compromise, was calling the SGMS to pursue its action 'firmly and pacifically'.[69]

A few days after the demonstration, according to the SGMS's plan, the Shankaracharya of Puri and Prabhu Datt Brahmachari began their fast; they were quickly arrested, which, as anticipated, aroused public ire. The RSS expressed its satisfaction at seeing the Shankaracharya continue his fast after being released,[70] and members of the Jana Sangh orchestrated fasts in solidarity and as acts of protest which spread throughout the country.[71] This was a tactical decoupling. On the one hand, the Jana Sangh's national leaders busied themselves defending a liberal image. In parliament Vajpayee denied that Swami Rameshwaranand was representative of the Jana Sangh's policy, and Trivedi accused the government of having encouraged the violence by its inadequate security measures. He even went on to support the demand of the Swatantra Party for a commission of inquiry.[72] These efforts resulted from the desire to pursue a strategy of integration. On the other hand, instrumentalist practices prevailed at the local level. In addition to the cow the Hindu nationalists

---

[67] Ibid., 10 Nov. 1966, col. 817 (intervention by J. Hathi, Home State Secretary).

[68] *Times of India*, 9 Nov. 1966.

[69] *Indian Express*, 10 Nov. 1966, and *Madhya Pradesh Chronicle*, 9 Nov. 1966, p. 5.

[70] *Times of India*, 29 Nov. 1966.

[71] *Free Press Journal*, 21 Nov. 1966.

[72] *Rajya Sabha Debates*, vol. 58, 17 Nov. 1966, col. 1774, and *Lok Sabha Debates*, vol. 60, 7 Nov. 1966, col. 1674.

also sought to exploit another universal symbol of Hinduism, the *sadhu*. The police's ruthless handling of these allegedly non-violent individuals led to the very public resignation of some MLAs from Uttar Pradesh.[73]

The firm secularism of the Centre

Indira Gandhi remained firm throughout the agitation. After the violence on November 7, she dismissed G. Nanda, whom she had only included reluctantly in her government.[74] On the surface, at least, this was because the forces of order had been outflanked by the rioters, but other motives might have influenced her decision. Nanda's lack of rigour could be attributed to his sympathy for *sadhus* (notably those of the Bharat Sadhu Samaj) and even for their cause in an agitation which he might have hoped to exploit in order to discredit the Prime Minister.[75] Nanda, who spoke out in favour of the banning of cow slaughter by the Centre after his dismissal,[76] was in a way the victim of Indira Gandhi's concern to respect secularist principles and, it would seem, to marginalise a potential rival.

The Prime Minister then trained her guns on the RSS, perhaps as much because it seemed to be coordinating the movement as on account of its past record, which made it more vulnerable than the SGMS and similar associations. She emphasised that the RSS could be classed as a political party to emphasise the incompatibility between attachment to it and membership of the civil service.[77] The RSS did not yield to this pressure. The next day its executive, upholding the cause of the SGMS, called on the government 'to amend the constitution in such a way as to produce central legislation on this matter' and called ' upon the people to continue to cooperate whole heartedly with the peaceful and non-violent movement of the Samiti for securing this legitimate and noble demand.'[78]

Tension increased following the death of one of the *sadhus* fasting in Delhi.[79] Indira Gandhi set up an Emergency Committee within the government, and firm action was much in evidence. The suspension of the fasts was the pre-condition for any negotiation, since the government would

[73] *Hindustan Times*, 6 Dec. 1966.

[74] P. Jayakar, *Indira Gandhi: a biography*, New Delhi: Viking, 1988, p. 184. Some commentators alleged that the violence on 7 November – on the basis of which Nanda was dismissed – had been engineered by *agents provocateurs* in order to discredit the Home Minister.

[75] *Statesman Weekly*, 12 Nov. 1966, pp. 1 and 4.

[76] *Statesman* (Delhi), 5 Jan. 1967, p. 6.

[77] *The Hindu*, 27 Nov. 1966.

[78] Ibid., 28 Nov. 1966.

[79] *The Times*, 1 Dec. 1966.

decide nothing under pressure.[80] This did not prevent the new Home
Minister, Y.B. Chavan, from negotiating with the SGMS, but without
success. The movement refused to entertain the idea of a temporary ban
(with a decision being reached after negotiation), which would have
applied only to calves, just as it rejected the setting up of a committee of
experts. The government nonetheless proceeded with the idea of establishing such a committee, and invited representatives of the states and the
SGMS to join it.[81] On 28 December Madhok, who had just come out of
prison, declared that the publication of a presidential ordinance was 'a
pre-condition for breaking the fasts'.[82]

The refusal of any compromise was partly due to the benefit the Hindu
nationalists hoped to derive from dramatising the situation as part of its
election campaign. The Jana Sangh was willing to capitalise on the
emotion generated by the agitation, while Golwalkar – habitually more
withdrawn from political activity – considered it legitimate to call for a
vote against Congress on the issue.[83]

The cow protection movement in Madhya Pradesh

The development of the Jana Sangh's election campaign at the local level
(in our test-case of Madhya Pradesh) was especially revealing in this
regard. One of the party's principal themes during the summer had been
food shortages and the rise in prices,[84] but in the autumn it returned more
strongly to the theme of defence of the cow. In September 601 activists
of the Madhya Pradesh branch of the party, led by its president N.K.
Shejwalkar, tried to invade the Vidhan Sabha, shouting slogans against
price rises and in favour of cow protection.[85] To promote the latter theme,
the branch benefited from the help of Satyamitranand Giri, the
Shankaracharya of Bhanpura Pith in Mandsaur district. This small
religious centre was considered in its own locality as having been created
by Shankara himself, since his birthplace was nearby (hence the title of
Shankaracharya accorded to Satyamitranand Giri). As the person responsible for the SGMS in Madhya Pradesh, he stirred up the agitation in the

[80] *Hindustan Times*, 26 Dec. 1966.
[81] *Statesman* (Delhi), 5 Jan. 1967, and *Times of India*, 6 Jan. 1967.
[82] *Statesman Weekly*, 31 Dec. 1966. Two days later, Golwalkar invited the government to
      do the same in order to save the lives of the two hunger-strikers (*Organiser*, 1 Jan. 1967).
[83] *Hitavada*, 18 Jan. 1967, and M.S. Golwalkar, 'The cow and elections', *Organiser*, 26
      Jan. 1967, p. 7.
[84] *Madhya Pradesh Chronicle*, 10 July 1966, p. 3; 25 July 1966, p. 3; 17 Aug. 1966, p. 6;
      27 Aug. 1966, p. 3; 29 Aug. 1966, p. 3; 30 Aug. 1966, p. 3.
[85] *Statesman Weekly*, 17 Sept. 1966, p. 8.

state in advance of the demonstration of 7 November,[86] after which the mobilisation grew apace. On 9 November, responding to the repression in Delhi, Goraksha Sammelans (conferences in defence of the cow) were organised in Jaora, Sironj, Basoda and Vidisha. Orders for a *hartal* – or general strike – were accompanied at Bhopal and Khandwa by sympathy fasts and at Indore by a procession of 5,000 people led by Gangaram Tiwari (a local Congress leader) and Ram Narain Shastri (the RSS *prant sanghchalak* for Madhya Bharat).[87] This was an isolated case of association but it revealed that certain Congressmen, whether Hindu traditionalists or not, wished to avoid at all costs being perceived as 'enemies of the cow'. Elsewhere in Madhya Pradesh one of the main centres of the agitation was Raipur.[88] The cow protection question was the *leitmotiv* of Upadhyaya's speeches during his tour of the state. In Bhopal he said:

Such high dignitaries and religious leaders of the top were never detained even when India was under foreign rule. Even Aurangzeb dare not touch the Shankaracharyas. Evidently the Government has lost all sense of proportion. Its policy appears not only to continue the slaughter of cows but to humiliate the Hindus by desecrating everything that they hold in veneration. Before their arrests both these leaders [the Shankaracharya of Puri and Prabha Datt Brahmachari] had advised the people to maintain peace and continue the agitation till the end. The government has thrown a challenge. The people should accept it.[89]

The *Statesman* commented that the Shankaracharya's 'death might swing more votes away from the Congress than may be suggested by the present status of public feeling on cow slaughter.'[90] However, the inflexible attitude of the SGMS served to thwart the Jana Sangh's strategy of Hindu mobilisation.

The unreliability of religious leaders

The attitude of the *sadhus* compromised the Jana Sangh's strategy of integration and from the outset revealed signs of the political motivation of religious personalities outside the RSS–VHP combination.
Eventually the Jana Sangh offered its good offices as a mediator

---

[86] *Madhya Pradesh Chronicle*, 19 Oct. 1966, p. 3, and 22 Jan. 1967, p. 6.

[87] Ibid., 8 Nov. 1966, p. 3; 9 Nov. 1966, p. 3, and 11 Nov. 1966, p. 3. At Ratlam the Shankaracharya of Dwarka appealed to voters to support candidates who demanded a ban on cow slaughter (*Hindustan Times*, 18 Dec. 1967, p. 3). His counterpart in Sringeri had reservations about the methods previously employed to attain this aim (*Organiser*, 21 May 1967, p. 1).

[88] *Madhya Pradesh Chronicle*, 9 Nov. 1966, p. 2, and 21 Nov. 1966, p. 6.

[89] Ibid., 23 Nov. 1966, p. 1.

[90] *Statesman* (Delhi), 8 Jan. 1967.

between the government and the hunger-strikers. Upadhyaya called on the Shankaracharya of Puri to suspend his fast, even if the government's concessions did not go far enough,[91] in all likelihood because he was disturbed by the strategy being adopted by religious and political leaders like Swami Karpatriji. On 7 January Karpatriji, who was against the suspension of the fasts, visited the Shankaracharya of Puri (his old lieutenant in the Ram Rajya Parishad)[92] in his capacity as temporary substitute for Prabhu Datt Brahmachari as head of the SGMS. He then announced the creation of a single issue political party, the National Front, which would campaign against cow slaughter and field 150 candidates in the Lok Sabha elections and 2,000 in the Vidhan Sabha polls.[93] Upadhyaya repeated his demand to the Shankaracharya of Puri the day after the announcement.[94] His concern was to avoid the exploitation by another party of this increasingly tense situation.

Prabhu Datt Brahmachari and the Shankaracharya of Puri finally suspended their fasts at the end of January having gained nothing from the government except its proposal for a committee of experts somewhat different from that initially envisaged. The committee was empowered to propose a reform of the Constitution if protection of the cow required it,[95] and Golwalkar and the Shankaracharya of Puri were to be the chief representatives of the SGMS on it.[96] The indifference with which this constructive step was greeted suggested that the issue was only important in the context of the election campaign. In the event, Golwalkar declared that he was unable to attend the committee meetings over a period of three months.[97] The SGMS representatives, led since February 1967 by the Shankaracharya of Puri,[98] resigned when the government appeared reluctant to implement any major reform. Without the support of the RSS, however, their agitation had only a marginal impact.[99]

[91] *Hindustan Times*, 1 and 7 Jan. 1967.

[92] At the same time the son-in-law of the Shankaracharya of Puri sent him a telegram 'alleging that some political elements in the Goraksha Samiti have taken a rigid stand so that the Jagadguru may die and that they sweep the polls in the elections using the Shankaracharya's name' (*Statesman*, 7 Jan. 1967, p. 1). Soon afterwards his secretary accused a group of 'political agents surrounding him day and night' of preventing the Shankaracharya from accepting a compromise proposal by the authorities (ibid., 25 Jan. 1967, p. 1).

[93] *Times of India*, 8 Jan. 1967, and *Hindustan Times*, 17 Jan. 1967.

[94] *Statesman* (Delhi), 9 Jan. 1967.

[95] Ibid., 1 Feb. 1967, p. 1, and *Organiser*, 5 Feb. 1967, for the text of the agreement.

[96] *Times of India*, 30 June 1967.

[97] *Hindustan Times*, 21 April 1968, p. 1.

[98] Ibid., 26 Feb. 1967, p. 4, and 6 July 1968, p. 12.

[99] *Times of India*, 11 Feb. 1967, p. 3, and *Hindustan Times*, 19 Oct. 1968, p. 11.

In 1966-7 the strategy of ethno-religious mobilisation of the RSS and its affiliates was subjected to two series of constraints which hampered its effectiveness: the first were external and concerned the political context, and the second were internal and concerned its religious network. The Jana Sangh had probably dared to undertake its campaign because the Centre seemed less inclined than in Nehru's time to repress Hindu activism. The government may have appeared weak because Indira Gandhi had yet to establish her authority, particularly with the Congress party bosses. Another explanation might be that certain Congress leaders (such as S.K. Patil and especially Nanda) may have seemed better disposed to a cause which their Hindu traditionalism inclined them towards. Both calculations proved mistaken. The Centre, under the firm control of a Prime Minister who had emancipated herself from the party bosses, dealt steadfastly with the Hindu nationalists, as was shown by her replacement of Nanda.

This strategy was not without repercussions at the state level. In Madhya Pradesh Satyamitranand Giri was accused of having infringed the secularist rules of the Constitution while campaigning on behalf of Jana Sangh candidates in his district of Mandsaur. As a result, the accused MLAs were suspended and by-elections were held in the constituencies of Garoth and Neemuch, where the Jana Sangh lost the seats it had won in 1967. Thus the party and the Shankaracharya were dissuaded from pursuing their political collaboration and from using slogans such as 'Vote Jana Sangh to protect the cow'.[100]

This robust response by the Centre was one reason why the Jana Sangh finally decided to abandon its experiment; another was the character of its religious allies. The latter showed themselves to be less than wholly reliable since Karpatriji had not ruled out the possibility of deriving electoral profit from the affair. The weakness of the religious network, a key element in the strategy of Hindu mobilisation, must have led the RSS to regret the slow growth of the new Vishwa Hindu Parishad. If it had been better structured, the RSS and its affiliates would have had a dependable means of implementing its strategy of ethno-religious agitation. Failing this, it had been compelled to turn to organisations like the SGMS, in which the RSS was certainly represented but was not strong enough to exercise any real control.

The Jana Sangh thus had to strike a balance in the cow protection movement because its campaign came under the double constraint of the political context and the weakness of the 'religious network'. Under such circumstances its capacity for mobilisation proved to be very variable.

---

[100] Interviews with Kishore Singh Sisodia, B. Bagdare and V.K. Sakhlecha, whose election was also suspended until the Supreme Court, before which he appealed, declared it valid.

Haryana, where 5,000 demonstrators had been mobilised, seemed very receptive, and Congress leaders in the state identified the agitation as the chief reason for their electoral reverses. But for their counterparts in the Punjab it was only the third most important reason.[101] In Rajasthan the region of Jodhpur and in Maharashtra that of Vidarbha appeared the most highly mobilised.[102] In Madhya Pradesh, Madhya Bharat had been receptive but in Mahakoshal the Jana Sangh had concentrated on economic problems which, in Jabalpur especially, had been seen as the outstanding ones even if the trading community had given strong support to the calls for a *hartal*.[103] In Uttar Pradesh the high concentration of Muslims in certain localities had made the question more acute than elsewhere, not so much in Kanpur, Meerut or Varanasi as in towns like Muzaffarnagar. In Bihar, the agitation was taken up enthusiastically in Bhagalpur, where the Marwaris lent considerable support,[104] but it was on a limited scale elsewhere. These variations were seen again in the 1967 election results. The Jana Sangh improved its position appreciably, but without gaining power except in Delhi.

This breakthrough was also made possible by the increased emphasis given to its strategy of co-opting notables and concluding electoral alliances. Indeed the 1967 elections are especially interesting because of the Jana Sangh's effort to combine an instrumentalist approach through its association – locally at least – with the cow protection movement and the pursuit of a pragmatic strategy.

Electoral progress and increased reliance on notables and princes

In 1967 the Jana Sangh achieved a new record both for votes cast (9.35% for the Lok Sabha and 8.77% for the Vidhan Sabhas) and seats won (respectively thirty-five out of 520 and 268 out of 3,487). This progress seemed to be linked as much to its campaign for cow protection as to its ever-increasing recruitment not only of notables but also of princes. This process was still largely driven by the disenchantment of many Congressmen with their party,[105] a phenomenon which was particularly in evidence in Madhya Pradesh.

---

[101] M. Brecher, *Political leadership in India*, New York: Praeger, 1969, p. 179. The representatives of the Indian élite questioned by Brecher agreed that the cow protection movement was only of secondary importance in explaining Congress losses at an all-India level (ibid., p. 25).

[102] *Statesman* (Delhi), 8 Jan. 1967, p. 9.

[103] Ibid., 1 Jan. 1967, p. 7, and *Indian Express*, 26 Dec. 1966, p. 2.

[104] *Statesman* (Delhi), 8 Jan. 1967.

[105] A columnist even argued that 'a great many of the men catapulted into legislative office on the Jana Sangh ticket are fair weather friends without any deep commitment to the

The Jana Sangh branches at Indore, Ujjain and Dewas remained faithful to the Sangathanist model, a development that can be explained by the strength of the RSS in this zone. In 1963 Ram Narain Shastri declared that 4,000 *swayamsevaks* were involved in Ujjain *shakhas*;[106] and in 1970, he revealed that 6,000 people regularly attended *shakhas*, which were concentrated around Indore and Ujjain.[107] Although at Indore the Jana Sangh did not always succeed in overcoming the dual challenge from Congress and the Left (the latter being firmly established in working-class areas), in Ujjain district it was winning a growing number of seats and H.C. Kachhwai was re-elected to the Lok Sabha. On the eastern border of Malwa, in the district of Bhopal, this Sangathanist formula was being applied to open up new territory.[108]

In Bhopal itself, Babulal Gaur, a *swayamsevak* leader of the BMS trade union at the Bhopal Textile Mill, where he worked from 1947 till 1966, was preparing the ground for the Jana Sangh among the workers and accordingly founded several *shakhas*; but his former mentor in the AITUC, Shaker Ali Khan of the CPI, still exerted a hold, and this, combined with his support among Muslim voters, deprived the Hindu nationalists of victory at the elections.[109] On the other hand, Laxmi Narayan Sharma was elected for the first of many occasions at Berasia, the constituency just to the north of Bhopal town where he worked with another long-term *swayamsevak*, Gauri Shankar Kaushal. Like Sharma, Kaushal was a teacher in Bhopal who worked among the peasants, putting as much effort into improving their social and economic conditions (a hospital was opened at Berasia thanks to their efforts) as to promoting Hindu nationalist themes such as Hindi and cow protection.[110]

---

party. One estimate suggests that a good 50% were men in search of tickets whom the party conveniently adopted – rather than chose on its own (*Statesman Weekly*, 30 Dec. 1967, p. 2).'

[106] *Madhya Pradesh Chronicle*, 5 Nov. 1963, p. 6.

[107] *Hindustan Times*, 6 Aug. 1970.

[108] The capital of a former Muslim princely state, Bhopal had not been a place of early implantation for the RSS. Babasaheb Kasture, the *pracharak* in charge of Bhopal between 1945 and 1957 met many difficulties in establishing *shakhas* given the state's administration had prohibited the RSS (interview with B. Kasture, 21 Feb 1994, New Delhi). In the early 1950s, the district had only 10 *shakhas* (interview at Bhopal, 31 Aug. 1992, with U.C. Israni, secretary of the Madhya Bharat unit of the RSS, who was one of the 12,000 Sindhis who settled in Bhopal). However the Jana Sangh benefited from an influx into the area of refugees from Pakistan, many of whom (and Sindhis in particular) considered that Congress was responsible for Partition and approved of the Hindu nationalist ideology regarding the Muslims. In 1961, there were 23,870 Sindhi speakers in Bhopal (P. N. Srivastav and S.D. Guru, *Madhya Pradesh District Gazetteers – Bhopal and Sehore*, Bhopal: Directorate of Gazetteers, 1989, p. 99).

[109] Interview with Babulal Gaur, 21 Nov. 1989, Bhopal.

[110] Interviews with L.N. Sharma, 23 Nov. 1989, and G.S. Kaushal, 24 Nov. 1989, Bhopal.

That the party's strength in the region relied essentially on the network of RSS activists is borne out by the fact that in 1967 Jagannath Rao Joshi was elected to the Lok Sabha for Bhopal, a constituency where he was virtually unknown except among the *swayamsevaks* who served his cause devotedly throughout the election campaign.

In other parts of Malwa – such as Mandsaur district – and to the east of Madhya Bharat, the Jana Sangh continued to develop its implantation according to the 'cluster technique'. Simultaneously, and of greater significance, in 1967 the Jana Sangh embarked on a rapprochement with the local princely families.

In Madhya Pradesh the former princes represented a considerable political force. It was a state which, apart from Mahakoshal and portions of Chhattisgarh, consisted above all of former princely states: there were some 35 in Vindhya Pradesh, 25 in Madhya Bharat, and a dozen – often with tribal populations – in Chhattisgarh.[111] It was estimated that 170 out of 296 Vidhan Sabha and 20 out of 37 Lok Sabha constituencies were to be found in the former territory of those states.[112]

Up till 1967, when the princely families became involved in politics, they usually opted for Congress, sometimes out of concern to be close to official power and sometimes because they had not dared to ignore the solicitations to which they were subjected. In Madhya Bharat, Congress had benefited from the candidatures of Bhanu Prakash Singh (Maharajah of Narsingarh)[113] and Vijaya Raje Scindia after 1957. In Vindhya Pradesh it had always been supported by the one-time Rajpramukh, the Maharajah of Rewa, a state equal in size to all the others in that region. In Chhattisgarh it had fielded as candidates, from 1952 onwards, the Maharajahs of Sarangarh (in Raigarh district) and Surguja, as well as obtaining support from the Rani of Khairagarh (Padmavati Devi), the Maharajah of Kanker and, from 1961, the former reigning family of Sakti in Bilaspur district.[114] This assiduous use of princes who commanded banks of votes on account of their past and present influence was typical of the 'aggregative' strategy of the Congress.

In 1967 this coalition broke up. Of the 36 princes who stood in the

[111] V.P. Menon, *The integration of the Indian States*, Hyderabad: Orient Longman, 1985 (1956), pp. 211 and 223.

[112] *New Age*, 10 Jan. 1971, p. 4.

[113] C. Hurtig, *Les maharajahs et la politique dans l'Inde contemporaine*, Paris: Presses de la FNSP, 1988, p. 191.

[114] *Hitavada*, 5 Jan. 1952, and 10 Nov. 1956, p. 3; *Madhya Pradesh Chronicle*, 1 May 1963, p. 3, and 19 Jan. 1962, p. 6. This was partly due to the long-established relations between the Shuklas and princely families: like many other Hindu traditionalists, the young Ravi Shankar Shukla had served – as a tutor – the states of Khairagarh, Kawardha and Bastar (S.C. Sharma, *Pt Ravi Shankar Shukla*, op. cit., pp. 7-8).

election 17 did so under the Congress banner, which was also supported by the Maharajah of Rewa.[115] But many defected. This malaise resulted from the concern of D.P. Mishra, head of the Congress-ruled state government, to assert his authority over the former princes who wished to obtain special treatment in exchange for the influence they were placing at the party's disposal. They insisted especially on having sight of files that concerned their former territories. This independent spirit was shown particularly by the Maharajah of Bastar who had accepted the Congress ticket in 1957 only to resign his seat as an MLA when the government refused to return to him property it had sequestered allegedly because of his generosity to his subjects. He soon became an enemy of the Congress government, which held him in prison for a time and then stripped him of his titles, which were transferred to his brother. On 26 March 1966 he was assassinated in his palace. The opposition pointed the finger of guilt at the state government, and anxiety spread in princely circles,[116] where an attempt to organise themselves now took place: a Kshatriya Mahasabha was formed in Rewa and a Rajput Parishad in Bhopal.[117]

At the same time, D.P. Mishra tried to show that, in the region of Gwalior, he had control of Congress nominations by refusing to confirm candidates proposed by Vijaya Raje Scindia, who had assumed the title of Rajmata after the Maharajah's death in 1961. In 1966 he refused to accept her candidature for her own seat in Gwalior, and suggested that she contest that of Mandsaur instead.[118] Soon afterwards she left Congress, which was now being deserted by a growing number of princes.

The Ram Rajya Parishad had till then been the main opposition party to receive support from princes, such as Dewas Senior, Jashpur (in Surguja district, where the party obtained half of its 10 MLAs in 1962) and Kawardha (Rajnandgaon district).[119] In 1966-7 the desire of numerous princes to depose D.P. Mishra led them to form an alliance with the Jana Sangh, the best organised of the opposition parties, which welcomed them without too many quibbles over agreement on ideology. In Chhattisgarh the princes who had been disturbed by the 'Bastar affair', like the heir-apparent of Raigarh and the Maharajah of Jashpur, took the initiative in joining the Jana Sangh.[120] From this time onwards the Jashpur family

---

[115] B.R. Purohit, 'General elections in Madhya Pradesh' in S.P. Varma and I. Narain (eds), *Fourth general elections in India*, op. cit., p. 304.

[116] On the 'Bastar affair' see C. Hurtig, *Les maharajahs et la politique*, op. cit., pp. 195-8.

[117] *Hindustan Times*, 20 Aug. 1966, p. 3 and 11 Oct. 1966, p. 1.

[118] Interview with S. Angre, 2 Dec. 1989, Delhi, and *Madhya Pradesh Chronicle*, 7 Oct. 1966, p. 3; 18 Nov. 1966, p. 1, and 22 Nov. 1966, p. 3.

[119] The Jana Sangh had not sought to develop close relationships with princes other than with Bhanu Prakash Singh, an independent candidate whom it supported at Rajgarh in 1962 (*Hitavada*, 3 Jan. 1962, p. 6).

was to support the Hindu nationalists. The Maharajah himself was elected to the Rajya Sabha in 1968 on the Jana Sangh ticket in gratitude for his championing of the party, and in 1967 the party returned three MLAs in Surguja district and two in Raigarh district, an achievement also due to the work of the RSS which had just been established in the tribal area.[121]

However the chief benefit that accrued to the Jana Sangh arose from the electoral pact it made with the Scindias: 25 of the 55 Vidhan Sabha constituencies within the borders of the old state of Gwalior, where the Scindias' influence counted most, were reserved for the Jana Sangh – which, in return, did not put up candidates against those of the Rajmata in the remaining constituencies.[122] For the party this was the chance to win seats in a region where the Scindias' influence had always kept its room for manoeuvre within narrow limits. Thus in 1967 a new zone of support for Hindu nationalism appeared on the electoral map in Gwalior.

The three MLAs elected in the town and its environs were *swayam-sevaks*. Naresh Johri and Shitla Sahai had begun their careers as student leaders in the early 1950s at Victoria College in Gwalior; Johri was later sent as a *pracharak* to organise the RSS and then the Jana Sangh in Morar district, for which he became the MLA in 1967.[123] Sahai continued with student politics, and was twice chairman of the student union at Victoria College, before obtaining his LL B at Agra in 1956. He then moved on to trade unionism, and in 1954 supported a strike in the Jivaji Rao Cotton Mills at Gwalior which opened the way for the BMS to establish itself in the factory.[124] Following in his wake, Jagdish Prasad Gupta, the son of a factory foreman at J.C. Mills who had been initiated into Hindu nationalism by Johri and Sahai while preparing his LL B, developed the BMS in this industrial area of Gwalior[125] and in 1967 overturned the majority previously enjoyed there by the CPI, with support from the Scindias. Sahai did the same at Lashkar, a district of Gwalior where he had maintained his popularity as a notabilised *swayamsevak* by arranging for Hindi schools, libraries and later on a cancer clinic to be opened.[126]

The Jana Sangh also won numerous seats in the vicinity of Gwalior. In the district of Shivpuri the party was developed by RSS cadres. The first *shakha* had been inaugurated in 1940 and the local Jana Sangh branch was

[120] *Madhya Pradesh Chronicle*, 25 Oct. 1966, p. 3; 27 Oct. 1966, p. 3 and 30 Oct. 1966, p. 3.

[121] Kasture established the first *shakhas* there in the early 1960s (interview with B. Kasture).

[122] *Madhya Pradesh Chronicle*, 27 Nov. 1966.

[123] Interview with N. Johri, 19 Nov. 1989, Shivpuri.

[124] Interview with S. Sahai, 28 Nov. 1989, Gwalior.

[125] Interview with J.P. Gupta, 25 Nov. 1989, Gwalior.

[126] This strategy of notabilisation had been begun in Gwalior by N.K. Shejwalkar, who was elected mayor of the town in 1961 and a member of the Rajya Sabha in 1968. Interview with N.K. Shejwalkar.

organised in the early 1950s by Babulal Sharma, a lawyer and member of the Arya Samaj who had joined the RSS in 1946 during a stay in Delhi where he passed his LL B.[127] From 1957, the candidate for the Vidhan Sabha seat at Shivpuri was Sushil Bahadur Asthana, another *swayam-sevak*, who had joined the RSS in 1942 and remained in the organisation when he became a civil servant.[128] In 1955 he had been elected to the town council, and in 1967 became a MLA thanks to support from the Scindias.[129] Further south, in another district of Gwalior state renamed Vidisha, the seat in the principal town was gained by the Jana Sangh. The victorious MLA, Raghavji Lakhamsi Savala, a Jain lawyer and well known tax consultant, had joined the RSS in 1946.[130] He emphasised the fact that the Jana Sangh had set out from the start to establish its network in the villages – and succeeded in so doing – but recognised that in 1957 the party did not have the means to fight elections, and that in 1962 both the Hindu Mahasabha – supported by Sambhajirao Angre – and Congress – represented by Rajmata Scindia – had left the Jana Sangh with no chance of victory. In 1967 the party owed its success to the support it received from the Rajmata.

A new zone of influence thus emerged which at first glance seemed to conform to the Sangathanist model, since it was largely based on the grassroots activity of RSS cadres. The dependence of this stronghold on local notables and princes was more marked here than anywhere else. All these successes were in fact made possible by the efforts of the Rajmata and her adviser Sambhajirao Angre. First, she gave direct assistance to the Jana Sangh candidates by campaigning on a Jana Sangh ticket in the Karera constituency – without, however, identifying herself with this party, as is apparent from the fact that she was simultaneously standing for election to the Lok Sabha on a Swatantra Party ticket. Second, many notables loyal to the princely house of Gwalior (mostly Rajput land-owners and former *zamindars* or *jagirdars* of the Scindias) had fol-lowed the Rajmata into opposition and were now associating themselves with the Jana Sangh. At the time of its formation Madhya Bharat contained 1,300 *jagirdars*, who were mostly dependent on the state of Gwalior, and nearly 122,000 *zamindars*.[131] A *jagirdar* like Thakur Kishore Singh Sisodia described this category as 'subordinates' of the

---

[127] Interview with Babulal Sharma, 27 Nov. 1988, Shivpuri.

[128] Interview with S.B. Asthana, 26 Nov. 1988, Shivpuri.

[129] Since Shivpuri had been their summer capital before Independence, the Scindias were especially influential there.

[130] Interview with R.L. Savala, 12 Oct. 1991, Bhopal and Parliament of India, *Ninth Lok Sabha Who's who*, op.cit., p. 347.

[131] *The Indian and Pakistan Year Book and Who's Who*, Bombay: *Times of India*, 1951, pp. 482-3.

princely family.[132] This helps explain why there were large numbers of rural notables, most of whom had links with the Scindias, who became MLAs in Gwalior region in 1967 (see appendix F, p. 556).

The terms of the agreement between the Jana Sangh and the Scindias were such that the latter could remain 'masters in their own house'. Numerous constituencies were partly disbarred to the Jana Sangh because the Gwalior princely house was supporting candidates there without troubling to obtain the party's agreement. These were sometimes 'allies of the family' without any special affinity to the Hindu nationalists, like the Rajmata's personal secretary, Y.S. Kushwaha, an influental Thakur, who was elected to the Lok Sabha for the Bhind constituency.[133] To some extent, the Jana Sangh went along with the logic of autonomous 'vote-banks' growing by 'aggregation', which was something quite different from expansion by the 'cluster technique'. The *swayamsevaks* acting as political entrepreneurs no longer coopted just a few local notables but depended on a whole chain of them headed by the 'super-notables' of Gwalior Palace – the Rajmata Scindia and S. Angre – who presided over the choice of a number of unremarkable candidates.

The influence of 'the palace' came from various sources. Most of the former princes retained a clientele, inherited from the British period, of ex-*jagirdars* or other 'vassals' of their states. In the case of the Scindias, this clientelistic relationship was tied to an economic patrimony – landed but also industrial – employing thousands and bringing in a vast income.[134] And one cannot overlook the clientele created by numerous gifts to institutions, especially in education (Jivaji Rao founded Vikram University at Ujjain in 1956 with an endowment of 5 million rupees).[135] This phenomenon was a reflection of the attention which the Scindias had traditionally paid to the development of their state, especially since Maharajah Madhav Rao (1877-1925), who established the family's reputation by building irrigation canals and introducing industrialisation on a considerable scale. Beyond clientelism, popular veneration for the person of the prince remains a potent force in Gwalior, and in this respect the return from Oxford of the Rajmata's son, Madhav Rao, in November 1966 only heightened the influence of the Scindias. He made a tour through the former state which attracted many politicians – including

---

[132] Interview with Kishore Singh Sisodia.

[133] *Who's who in Lok Sabha* – 1967, op. cit., p. 543. Kushwaha had been one of the Ministers of Jivaji Rao Scindia's government before 1948. He had been a member of the Congress from 1936 to 1966 and an MLA from 1948 to 1952 and from 1957 to 1962.

[134] Among the Scindias' assets were the Scindia Steam Navigation Company Ltd (based in Bombay, where the Scindias had many properties) and the Scindia Potteries (based in Delhi where they owned a huge estate).

[135] *Hitavada*, 16 Oct. 1956, p. 1.

some Congressmen – seeking his patronage, which was regarded as being more useful than that of his mother.[136]

Within the borders of the former state of Gwalior, only 1 of the 55 seats escaped the alliance of the Jana Sangh and the Scindias in 1967, which resulted in 78 MLAs standing on the Jana Sangh ticket, seven on the Swatantra ticket, and 25 as independents supported by the Scindias. Yet even this electoral surge did not succeed in ousting Congress, led by D.P. Mishra, which held 176 seats out of 296.

A comparable phenomenon was seen on the western frontier of Madhya Bharat, in Rajasthan, an administrative entity born after Independence out of the fusion of the Rajput princely states. In 1962, some *swayamsevaks* seconded to the Jana Sangh had gained a foothold in urban pockets, for example at Jaipur. In 1967, as in the region of Gwalior, this implantation spread thanks to the support given by two former royal families, those of Jhalawar and Kota, whose territories bordered the western part of Madhya Pradesh. The two Maharajahs, dissatisfied with the Congress government's allocation of ministerial portfolios, chose the strongest opposition party in their region in order to get elected – one to the Lok Sabha, the other to the Vidhan Sabha – and procure the election of eight Jana Sangh MLAs around Kota.[137] The party was supported by an increasing number of landowners. Of the Jana Sangh MLAs interviewed by S.L. Puri, 22% were Rajputs; in other words double the share of Brahmins and 5% more than the overall proportion of Rajputs in the Vidhan Sabha.[138] Nonetheless, the party was unable to increase the number of these strongholds due to competition from the Swatantra Party, which was preferred by many of the princes (such as the Maharani of Jaipur, Gayatri Devi and the Maharana of Udaipur) and carried off 48 seats as against the Jana Sangh's 22. Notwithstanding their alliance, the two parties could not prevent Congress from forming a new government with the help of independents.

As well as resorting to 'vote banks' made up of notables and princes, in 1967 the Jana Sangh decided to form electoral alliances and participate in coalition governments.

[136] *Madhya Pradesh Chronicle*, 22 Nov. 1966, p. 1; 1 Dec. 1966, p. 3, and 16 Dec. 1966, p. 3.

[137] K. Bhargava, 'Rajasthan politics and princely rulers: An analysis of electoral processes', *Indian Journal of Political Science*, 33 (4), Oct.-Dec. 1972, p. 424.

[138] S.L. Puri, *Legislative elite in an Indian state*, New Delhi: Abhinav, 1978, pp. 35-6. The Jana Sangh MLAs achieved the strongest representation in the *Panchayati Raj* institutions and cooperatives (ibid., p. 64).

Electoral alliances and coalition governments

The Jana Sangh's strategy of Hindu mobilisation in the 1966-7 election campaign on the theme of cow protection was, *a priori*, incompatible with the quest for alliances with the legitimate opposition. Yet the Jana Sangh high command remained committed to developing links which would enable it to become integrated in mainstream politics and maximise its gains at the polls. Parallel with this, the strategy of certain socialists and the Swatantra Party continued to be dominated by the objective of achieving an anti-Congress front. The Samyukta Socialist Party (SSP) of Lohia – which came about in June 1964 from the amalgamation of the Socialist Party and the PSP, whose principal tendencies split off once again in February 1965 – continually expressed its wish to reach an electoral agreement throughout 1966.[139] The Jana Sangh's participation in the overtly 'communal' cow protection movement appeared not to be an obstacle in this search for agreement. In Madhya Pradesh, the Jana Sangh, the SSP and the Jana Congress (a Congress splinter group) avoided putting up rival candidates in 17 Lok Sabha and 117 Vidhan Sabha constituencies.[140] Competition from the socialists (PSP and/or SSP) deprived the Jana Sangh of victory in only fourteen cases.[141]

However, this rapprochement was less marked than that of the Jana Sangh and the Swatantra Party, the co-signatories of an electoral pact in the spring of 1966.[142] Here were to be seen genuine ideological affinities. The inclusion of a demand for the prohibition of cow slaughter in the election manifesto of the Swatantra Party was only turned down after long debate, and many of the party's 'individual candidates were side by side with the Jana Sangh in exploiting the cow-slaughter issue'.[143] The electoral accord between the Swatantra Party and the Jana Sangh resulted in the former putting up rival candidates in only 403 of the 1,607 constituencies contested by the Jana Sangh. The two parties were rivals for a small number of seats in Rajasthan (where the accord was enforced most forcibly), Gujarat, Madhya Pradesh, Orissa, Assam, Haryana, Punjab, Maharashtra, Andhra Pradesh and West Bengal. The accord proved less

---

[139] M. Limaye, *Birth of non-congressism*, op. cit., p. 105, and *Statesman Weekly*, 1 Jan. 1966, p. 3, and 26 Nov. 1966, p. 8.

[140] T.H. Davey, 'The transformation of an ideological movement into an aggregative party', op. cit., p. 226.

[141] These were cases where the Jana Sangh could have taken the lead if there had been a united opposition to Congress and it had thus had access to the votes cast for Socialist candidates (calculations based on *Madhya Pradesh Vidhan Sabha general elections – 1957-1980 Results – statistical data*, Parts I and II, Bhopal: Chief Electoral Office, 1980).

[142] *Statesman Weekly*, 28 May 1966, p. 3.

[143] H.L. Erdman, *The Swatantra Party*, op. cit., p. 264.

conclusive in Uttar Pradesh, where the Jana Sangh contested 193 of the 207 Vidhan Sabha seats where Swatantra candidates were standing, and in Bihar.[144] Thus the agreement played a far from negligible part in the Jana Sangh's electoral advance.

Soon after the election the party entered coalition governments which included the principal opposition groups. In a number of northern states the Jana Sangh had achieved such a substantial parliamentary presence that its MLAs were an indispensable element in the functioning of a non-Congress government. Parties like the SSP and Swatantra were prepared, in order to realise this objective, to admit the Jana Sangh, and most significant of all the Jana Sangh was ready to mask whole sections of its ideology for the sake of sharing power.

Such pragmatism may be explained by a number of motives. Upadhyaya resigned himself to coalitions because the demand for political change expressed by the electorate had to be honoured and a new means found to 'eradicate the political untouchability' from which the Jana Sangh suffered.[145] But he saw coalitions as only a temporary expedient. Vajpayee, for his part, was a forceful advocate of coalitions, and proposed a resolution in their favour at the AIGC in April 1967. He justified his decision by the need to rescue the people, who had been subjected for decades to Congress rule.[146] However, when challenged to explain the participation of his party in coalitions that lacked any ideological coherence, he replied that the Jana Sangh's reason for being in politics was to gain power.[147] Such a pragmatic, power-oriented approach was the most important motive affecting the party leadership's decision to enter coalition governments.

Even though the Jana Sangh had repeated its refusal in principle to be associated with the Communist parties before the 1967 elections, its winning candidates in Bihar were invited by party headquarters in New Delhi to join a coalition government which included the CPI. This option had been accepted with the explicit admission that such governments could not share any ideological orientation, but would simply have to govern their states to the best of their ability.[148] In fact, the Jana Sangh abstained from upholding Hindu nationalist arguments in its ministries, and even assumed a low profile when its partners pronounced in favour

---

[144] C. Baxter, *The Jana Sangh*, op. cit., pp. 286-7.

[145] *Organiser*, 31 Dec. 1967, p. 7.

[146] Ibid., 30 April 1967, p. 4

[147] H.T. Davey, 'The transformation of an ideological movement into an aggregative party', op. cit., pp. 210-11.

[148] See the resolution passed by the 23 Jana Sangh ministers who met in Bhopal under the auspices of the party leadership several months into the first coalition government in order to take stock of the experiment (*Organiser*, 5 Nov. 1967, p. 1).

of projects which went against its principles. The issues which determined the life and death of these coalition governments were not ideological ones, as the case of Madhya Pradesh demonstrates.

In that state, so as to be able to fight more effectively against the Congress Party under D.P. Mishra, Rajmata Scindia formed a parliamentary group (Jana Kranti Dal – Party of the People's Revolution) with 'her own' MLAs in the Vidhan Sabha, among whom were members of the Swatantra Party. She soon recruited SSP and then Jana Sangh MLAs'into a new Samyukta Vidhayak Dal (SVD – united parliamentary group in the Vidhan Sabha). In July 1967 it was able to form a coalition government when the Rajmata contrived to bring 35 Congress MLAs over to the opposition in the train of Govind Narain Singh, the leader of a faction who was disgruntled at being refused a ministerial portfolio by D.P. Mishra.[149] G.N. Singh was made head of the government at the request of the Rajmatas who remained active behind the scenes. The Congress dissidents were over-represented in ministerial posts in recognition of the decisive importance of their votes.[150] Having inherited an interest in character-building from the RSS, the Jana Sangh wanted to have the Ministry of Education but had to settle for the Home Ministry;[151] this went finally to Sakhlecha, who was also appointed Deputy Chief Minister. One of his first measures was to lift the ban on certain civil servants belonging to the RSS.[152] He was also anxious about 'altering the composition of the police bureaucracies at the highest levels, transferring opponents out and bringing sympathizers into strategic spots.'[153] Noronha – the state Chief Secretary between 1963 and 1968 – who had shown some sympathy for the RSS while posted in Berar, mentions in his autobiography that the SVD government suspended a superintendent of police because he had arrested some Jana Sangh workers during a communal riot and that 'great care was taken to see that no key post in any department went to a Muslim'.[154]

However, G.N. Singh tried to take sole responsibility for deciding on transfers and promotions in order to benefit his clientele.[155] This was

---

[149] *Patriot*, 18 July 1967.

[150] Ibid., 23 July 1967.

[151] According to the Chief Secretary, R.P. Noronha, G.N. Singh reasoned that the Jana Sangh 'could build up a permanent following through the primary schools whereas the police would follow them only so long as they were in power' (*A tale told by an idiot*, New Delhi: Vikas, 1976, p. 150).

[152] *Times of India*, 11 Aug. 1967.

[153] R. W. Jones, 'Area, power and linkage', vol. 2, op. cit., p. 533.

[154] R.P. Noronha, *A tale told by an idiot*, op. cit., pp. 18-19 and pp. 148-9.

[155] *Times of India*, 28 April 1968, *Hitavada*, 27 April 1968, *Statesman* (Delhi), 27 April 1968, and *Organiser*, 5 May 1968, p. 1.

probably one of the reasons why, in June 1968, the Jana Sangh forced him to declare a programme of action and dismiss from the government Congress dissidents who were notoriously corrupt.[156] Singh yielded to the demand of the Rajmata and the Jana Sangh to expel nineteen ministers from his government, but then brought back most of them in January 1969 when he found that he had sacrificed some of the most effective channels of his personal influence.[157] In March he returned with twenty of his supporters to Congress, which was thus able once again to command a majority.[158]

One of the few ideologically slanted measures which the Jana Sangh enacted was one seeking to outlaw conversions to Christianity which had not passed a strict test guaranteeing that they had been entirely voluntary. This measure was called the 'Dharma Swatantra – religious freedom – Act'. In addition, the party campaigned for the suspension of government aid to educational institutions run by missionaries in the tribal zones, where Christian proselytisation was most rife.[159] The only MLAs on the left to protest against these intended measures were from the PSP, which had first given its support to the SVD government without participating in it, and which withdrew that support in November 1967 as a protest against the appointment of Sakhlecha to the Home Ministry, where he was said to be giving protection to the RSS. The PSP was demanding that the latter be proscribed.[160]

This experience was repeated in other states.[161] In Bihar the 26 Jana Sangh MLAs had been instructed to join up with 68 from the SSP, 18 from the PSP, 28 Communists, 3 from Swatantra and about 20 independents in a pro-government majority – again known as Samyukta Vidhayak Dal – clearly dominated by the Left. The Communists aspired to make Urdu the second official language of the state, an issue that was bound to stir up a lively debate within the coalition. The Jana Sangh opposed it – successfully – but did not consider the matter one over which it might withdraw from the coalition. Eventually the latter collapsed in January 1968 after the defection of MLAs from the Scheduled Castes and Scheduled Tribes (three of whom belonged to the Jana Sangh) who after founding a Shoshit Dal (Party of the Exploited) joined Congress to form a new majority. This in turn disintegrated and was replaced in March 1968 by a new govern-

---

[156] Ibid., 15 June 1968, and C. Hurtig, *Les maharajahs et la politique*, op. cit., p. 211.

[157] *Statesman Weekly*, 4 Jan. 1969, p. 1.

[158] Ibid., 15 March 1969, p. 1. The SVD had tried unsuccessfully to install the Maharajah of Sarangarh in his place.

[159] Ibid., 21 Dec. 1968, p. 8.

[160] Ibid., 14 Oct. 1967, p. 8, and 18 Nov. 1967, p. 8.

[161] For a detailed study see Bruce Graham, 'The Jana Sangh and Party Alliances: 1967-1970', *South Asian Review*, 4 (1), Oct. 1970, pp. 9-26.

ment again containing two Jana Sangh ministers. The heterogeneity of this administration was such that it could not survive beyond June. The Centre declared President's rule until such time as elections could be held. The episode had shown the risks that participation in coalition government at state level could pose for the Jana Sangh's discipline and credibility.

In Uttar Pradesh, the Jana Sangh, with its 98 seats, was now the second-ranking party in the state after Congress. It was able to share power thanks to the secession of Charan Singh's group from Congress, which till then owed its small majority to the support of independents. The group formed a majoritarian Samyukta Vidhayak Dal with the Jana Sangh, the SSP and the CPI.[162] As in Bihar, this ill-assorted coalition divided over the question of Urdu. The Communists wanted to establish it as the state's second official language against the advice of the Jana Sanghis, who threatened to leave the government.[163] But they did not dare to put its warnings into action[164] and even mediated between Charan Singh and the SSP and the CPI when those parties withdrew their ministers from the government after having failed to achieve their main objective, the abolition of land revenue.[165] Obviously the Jana Sangh was anxious to see the SVD government continue, probably in order to use its new accession to power to its own advantage.

What proved to be an important apple of discord between the Jana Sangh on the one hand and the SSP and CPI on the other, was the partisan policy of some of their Jana Sangh colleagues. The Deputy Chief Minister and Minister of Education, Ram Prakash Gupta, a former *pracharak* and deputy mayor of Lucknow, was accused of promoting the Saraswati Shishu Mandir schools,[166] while Ganga Bhakt Singh, the Minister of Cooperation, was denounced for recruiting Hindu nationalist sympathisers to administrative posts in his gift.[167] Charan Singh took the initiative of removing the most important portfolios from the Jana Sangh,

---

[162] According to the correspondent of *Organiser* in Lucknow, Nana Deshmukh, the national secretary of the Jana Sangh in charge of Uttar Pradesh, contributed to persuading Charan Singh to quit Congress (*Organiser*, 3 Sept. 1967, p. 4).

[163] Ibid., p. 14.

[164] Ram Prakash Gupta even declared: 'There will never be any crisis in the SVD ministry over the issue of Urdu' (ibid., 20 Aug. 1967, p. 5). The main success of the Jana Sangh regarding the language issue consisted in making English an optional subject in high school examinations.

[165] M.S. Verma, *Coalition government – U.P.'s first experiment*, Lucknow: Department of Public Administration, 1971, p. 62.

[166] The 'temple of the pupils of Sarasvati' (goddess of learning) was a network of private schools launched by the RSS to purvey a highly ideological education.

[167] B. Kapoor, *The dragon unmasked – Role of the Jana Sangh in SVD government in UP*, New Delhi: Sampradayikta Virodhi Committee, n.d., p. 9.

but by doing so he created a demand within the latter's ranks for a change of Chief Minister. His resignation was followed by the proclamation of President's rule in February 1968.[168] The Congress, notably through the *National Herald*, was quick to point out that 'the Jan Sangh, specially the RSS part of it which is represented in the government has been making a many-pronged attack to spread its influence in as many spheres of life as possible'.[169] This kind of discourse made a certain impact which revealed the limitations of the Hindu nationalists' legitimacy and acceptability in the framework of coalition politics.

An analogous scenario unfolded in Haryana where the Jana Sangh chose to support the government without participating in it, and in Punjab where it was associated, in government, not only with Communists but with Akalis, against whom it had struggled until 1966 to prevent the state being partitioned between a Hindi-speaking Haryana and a Punjabi-speaking Punjab. In these two states, the government fell not because of ideological conflicts but as the result of opportunistic defections by some of the Jana Sangh's partners.

Except in Delhi, where it obtained an absolute majority,[170] the party had intensified its strategy of integration after the elections of 1967 at the price of important concessions. There is little doubt that its flexibility was not gratuitous but motivated by a willingness to share power in order to promote the interests of the Hindu nationalist movement. This tendency was made explicit in issues such as the transfer of police officers in Madhya Pradesh or the official support provided to the Saraswati Shishu Mandirs in Uttar Pradesh. However, this opportunism challenged some pillars of Hindu nationalism such as the promotion of Hindi and uncompromising opposition to the Communists. The Jana Sangh's tendency to dilute its principles manifested itself, at the plenary session in December 1967, in the form of questioning the priority it had hitherto accorded to Hindi. The Jana Sangh had already conceded in its 1967 election manifesto that the public service entry examinations could be taken in the regional languages; now it deliberately failed to set a deadline for making Hindi the national language and furthermore emphasised that its adoption had to be voluntary.[171] This development was again due to pragmatic con-

[168] For a detailed analysis see P. Brass, 'Coalition politics in North India', *American Political Science Review*, 62 (4), Dec. 1968, p. 1186.

[169] Cited in M.S. Verma, *Coalition government*, op. cit., p. 54.

[170] The Union territory was untypical in that, as G. Puri has demonstrated, the party habitually won a large proportion of the votes of refugees from Pakistan (*Bharatiya Jana Sangh, Organisation and Ideology – Delhi: a case study*, New Delhi: Sterling, 1980., pp. 163-7).

[171] *Organiser*, 14 Jan. 1968, p. 6.

siderations since it was expected to help the Jana Sangh to penetrate the Dravidian South where the party had never won a seat.

From the late 1950s to the late 1960s the Jana Sangh oscillated between two different approaches. It opted first for a form of notabilisation and a programme of socio-economic and patriotic agitation which was intended to challenge the policies of Nehru's government and facilitate the party's integration in the political system and, more especially, the mainstream opposition. Then in 1966-7 it became associated with a cow protection campaign which placed in jeopardy its standing as a party acting within the Constitution. Immediately afterwards, it showed itself ready to tone down the more obvious features of its Hindu nationalism and to question the original Sangathanist party-building pattern while relying more heavily on notables and princes and concluding opportunistic alliances. These oscillations are largely explicable in the light of our model of three strategies and their variables.

The move towards a strategy of ethno-religious mobilisation and later one of pragmatic integration in the legitimate opposition was linked to the evolution of two parameters, the religious network and the political context. The formation of a religious network associated with the VHP was likely to reinforce the capacity for mobilisation of the Hindu nationalists due to the activism and prestige of different kinds of *sadhus*. But this network appeared too weak and indisciplined reliably to execute a strategy of mobilisation. Second, and more importantly, much of the Jana Sangh's strategy was directly conditioned by the political context. Nehru's emphasis on socio-economic reforms, his vigilant secularism and the Hindu traditionalism of certain Congress factions in North India combined to persuade the Jana Sangh of the need to tone down its strategy of militant Hinduism compared with a socio-economic approach based on decentralisation. The accession to power of an inexperienced Prime Minister, Indira Gandhi, and the increased influence of traditionalist Congress bosses apparently convinced the Hindu nationalists – wrongly, as it turned out – that it was now possible to implement a strategy of ethno-religious mobilisation. Parallel to this, certain opposition parties witnessed an erosion of their anti-communal traditions. This development stemmed not only from the emergence of the Swatantra Party, which inherited certain features of Hindu traditionalism, but also from the growing determination – expressed notably by Lohia – to forge an alternative to Congress independent, within certain limits, of ideological affinities.[172] This determination was not hindered by the Jana Sangh's

---

[172] The PSP was more critical of the Jana Sangh as it took the influence of the RSS into account (*Statesman Weekly*, 8 Feb. 1969, p. 6).

resorting to a strategy of Hindu mobilisation during the 1966-7 election campaign, which allowed it to initiate a 'mixed strategy' combining the advantages of instrumentalism (in terms of popular mobilisation) with those of alliances (in terms of sharing out constituencies). This paradoxical conjunction undoubtedly contributed to the party's electoral gains in 1967. One must note that the same mechanisms were operating, though on a larger scale, when the Bharatiya Janata Party (BJP), the heir of the Jana Sangh, began its expansion in 1989.

The Jana Sangh's pragmatic integration strategy after the 1967 elections, when the party joined a whole series of heterogenous coalitions, can also be explained by reference to our model. The political context, especially Indira Gandhi's anti-communalist stance and the weakness of the religious network, doubtless convinced party leaders that they could not deploy a strategy of Hindu mobilisation in any sustained fashion. It is also likely that the mixed reception among the electorate to the cow protection movement persuaded them to abandon this line of attack. Simultaneously, the mainstream opposition parties seemed prepared to cooperate with the Jana Sangh, which in response proceeded to tone down the Hindu nationalist themes in its public statements. This development strengthened the position of those in the Jana Sangh's national leadership who were willing to make the party's ideology more acceptable to moderate opinion and thus improve its chances of taking power, even if this meant participating in coalition governments.

H. T. Davey and C. Baxter deduced from this development that the Jana Sangh would soon cast off its Hindu nationalist ideology; here they saw the effect first of electoral competition, which forced it to 'aggregate' notables and princes and to take a stand on the socio-economic issues which concerned the population as a whole,[173] and second of the impact of 'socialisation' within the parliamentary system on the party's national leaders. In effect the Jana Sangh members of the Lok Sabha were more concerned with socio-economic and foreign policy questions than with the themes of Hindu nationalism.[174] This analysis was especially apposite in the case of Vajpayee and Madhok. The former was the Jana Sangh parliamentary leader in the Lok Sabha, while the latter was elected president of the Jana Sangh in 1966 in order to provide the party with a dynamic figurehead.

With the benefit of hindsight not available to Davey and Baxter we can show that this approach had only limited value because of the residual role which it offered to the Sangathanist network and the extra-parliamentary

---

[173] C. Baxter, *The Jana Sangh*, op. cit., pp. 315-16.

[174] H.T. Davey, 'The transformation of an ideological movement into an aggregative party', op. cit., p. 360. See also pp. 3, 16 and 209.

Hindu nationalist forces, above all the RSS. Up till now, we have considered the way the Jana Sangh's leaders evolved the party strategy under certain external constraints. The strategy of ethno-religious mobilisation, for instance, was described as conditioned by the political context and the reliability of the 'religious network'. However, the Jana Sangh also appeared to be subject to internal constraints in the shaping of its party strategy. In fact, the oscillations of the 1960s between strategies of militancy and moderation partly reflected the tension between the efforts of all-India leaders to become integrated into mainstream politics and the staunch Hindu nationalism at the grassroots. While Vajpayee and Trivedi were apologetic about the violent events of 7 November 1966 in Delhi, the agitation on behalf of cow protection gained momentum in the countryside.

By the end of the 1960s strategies of moderation were being criticised by local cadres of the Jana Sangh and by the RSS because of the dilution of Hindu nationalist identity they implied. Thus the RSS-trained activist network was a variable which constrained the Jana Sangh's leaders within the parameters of our model: if its action hitherto had only been measured by its impact on the strategy of Sangathanist party-building, one must also see in it an internal brake on the moderate strategy pursued by party leaders. The latter were therefore persuaded, in the 1970s, critically to examine the possibility of pursuing a policy that would remain pragmatically oriented towards the quest for power and at the same time be compatible with the doctrine of its grassroots members as well as the RSS.

Part III. THE CONTRADICTIONS OF THE 1970s

6

LOCAL CADRES AND POPULISM

At the end of the 1960s the Jana Sangh could no longer avoid a debate on the dilution of its ideology because of its participation in various coalition governments in the states after the fourth general election. The debate took place at two levels. First, it was contested between the pragmatists, namely the all-India leaders who wanted to give the party an opportunity to exercise power, and local cadres close to the RSS line who rejected strategies which would effectively have questioned the Hindu nationalist programme of the Jana Sangh. Second, it was fought out between those leaders, including Balraj Madhok, who were seeking integration with the Hindu traditionalist sector of Indian politics and others, such as Atal Bihari Vajpayee, who favoured the use of populist appeals and were concerned with the protection of the party's separate identity. It was the latter group which finally prevailed.

Their victory revealed that the Sangathanist network and the RSS had retained its hold over the party. Indeed Vajpayee's line was more in tune with the the aspirations of the party's local activists than Madhok's views. Madhok was expelled from the Jana Sangh in 1973 without much difficulty; nor did many of his followers leave the party. This episode and the change of strategy in the late 1960s and early 1970s suggest that the real division within the Jana Sangh was not vertical, of the factional type, but horizontal. It pitted against each other the all-India leaders and the local cadres who were deeply imbued with the RSS's ethic. In other words, the Sangathanist network played a greater role than rivalries at the top in shaping the Jana Sangh's strategy.

The strategy which the party adopted in the early 1970s entailed a new social and economic radicalism and an appeal to the patriotic sentiments engendered by the war of 1971 between India and Pakistan. However, in pursuing this course of action, Vajpayee and his colleagues found themselves at odds with the conservatives among the ranks of the party's notables and with the parties which were allied to the Jana Sangh. In any case, it was difficult to use populism as a means of building support when the Congress (R) under Mrs Gandhi was also exploiting the same appeal with considerable success.

The main division within the Jana Sangh is not vertical but horizontal

The influence of the Sangathanist network in shaping party strategy

At the meeting of the All India General Council in April 1967, which had the task of pronouncing on the question of the Jana Sangh's being associated with coalitions, numerous delegates (including N. Johri for Madhya Pradesh) spoke out against cooperation with the Communists, which such coalitions entailed. They reminded their audience that the Jana Sangh's vocation was to replace Congress, not merely inflict reverses on it at the price of ideological compromises.[1] They concluded by adopting an amendment recognising the party's right to oppose those decisions of coalition governments which went against its policy and interests.[2] This was in keeping with the position of the RSS, to which the Jana Sangh's local cadres had generally remained close. In April 1967, the general council of the RSS had given its approval to coalitions in the hope

[...] that the present coming together of several parties will help understanding one another at close quarters, wipe out political 'untouchability' and animosity and bring about amity and harmony among the various political groups as envisaged by the Sangh.[3]

This formulation was symptomatic of the persistent desire of the movement to make Hindu nationalism a philosophy for society as a whole rather than one associated with a single party within a system of alliances.

It is important not to neglect these responses to the way the Jana Sangh was evolving. The RSS certainly did not exercise tight control over the Jana Sangh; in general it gave its affiliated organisations considerable autonomy and was willing to take account of their advice concerning areas of policy in which they were expert. However, the RSS insisted on its right to oversee and orient the general activities of the 'Sangh parivar', and held

---

[1] *Organiser*, 30 April 1967, p. 4.

[2] Ibid., p. 15.

[3] Resolution of the ABPS in *RSS resolves*, op. cit., pp. 56-7.

annual meetings with representatives of its affiliates to discuss the co-ordination of their work. The Jana Sangh was represented at these meetings by Upadhyaya and subsequently by Deshmukh and then Bhandari. Second, and more importantly, the party's most specific attribute was its dependence on the network of activists which derived from the RSS and remained close to it. While those involved in electoral and ministerial politics might be amenable to compromises and could be convinced of the utility of forging alliances because of their interest in state power, the activists of the Sangathanist network revealed their unwavering attachment to doctrinal purity and the RSS. This strong bond was easy enough to apprehend at the local level, where the organisers of RSS affiliates (the BMS, the Jana Sangh etc.) traditionally consulted *pracharaks*, simply because they represented the heart of the Hindu nationalist combination and their constant journeying gave them an overall view of the local context, allowing them not only to give advice but also to coordinate the activities of the different organisations.[4] While the leaders of all ideological parties are constrained by the reluctance of their local cadres to compromise on 'doctrine', even to a small degree, this phenomenon assumes a particular importance in the relationship of the Jana Sangh leaders with the RSS and their Sangathanist network. In fact, the coalition governments disintegrated in 1968-9 partly because of the attitude of the Jana Sangh's local cadres. On one level they were prepared to make concessions about issues – such as the status of Urdu – which the national leadership was reconsidering; while on another they did not want to go too far in compromising the party's identity and were eager not to betray their social basis or hinder the promotion of interests close to the Hindu nationalist fold – e.g. transfers of civil servants or education policy. This ambivalent attitude undoubtedly aroused the suspicions of partners of the Jana Sangh. Among the Jana Sanghis working at the state level, the Sangathanist cadres were naturally the least flexible. While the Jana Sanghi 'politicians' (MLAs and ministers) were willing to make concessions 'to maintain the delicate unity of the coalition' in Uttar Pradesh, the organising wing, 'called on the party's district units to oppose a [grain procurement] scheme' (which the legislative wing supported) because it contradicted the ideology of the Jana Sangh and the interests of its social base.[5]

In 1969 the Jana Sangh decided that it would no longer associate itself

---

[4] I was, in particular, able to observe the importance of this set-up in Shivpuri district. Here, the heads of various offshoots of the RSS gathered every month to meet the *pracharak* in the RSS office.

[5] M.H. Johnson, 'The relation between land settlement and party politics in Uttar Pradesh, India, 1950-63, with special reference to the formation of the Bharatiya Kranti Dal', unpubl. Ph.D. thesis, University of Sussex, 1975, pp. 198-9.

with non-Congress coalitions given its unrewarding experiences of earlier experiments. It blamed its participation in the SVD government in Uttar Pradesh for the electoral reverse which it suffered there in the mid-term elections of 1969, when it won only 49 seats compared with 98 in 1967 and therefore lost its position as the principal non-Congress party to the Bharatiya Kranti Dal (BKD), which captured 98 seats in the 1969 poll.

The reservations of the party's local cadres towards the strategy of moderation were an important factor in the search for a new strategy by the Jana Sangh's leaders, one of whom, Madhok, openly criticised the participation of Jana Sanghis in coalition governments in the late 1960s. However, his campaign failed to make an impact because his alternative proposals also implied a dilution of the party's identity. By contrast, Vajpayee's populist line was more in tune with the expectations of the grassroots and the RSS.

The choice between traditionalist integration and Sangathanist populism

Madhok, who was president of the Jana Sangh in 1966-7, made a deter-mined stand against participation in any government that included Com-munists.[6] But this was only so that he could propose a different type of alliance. He had long been in favour of an accord with the Swatantra Party, with·which he sought to form a common parliamentary group in March 1967.[7] A Swatantra faction, headed by N.G. Ranga, had welcomed this attempt to forge an understanding.[8]

Madhok aspired to make the Jana Sangh the focal point of a loose grouping of conservative forces in opposition to the alliance which was taking shape between Indira Gandhi's Congress Party and the Com-munists. A step in the direction of British-style bi-partisanship seemed to have been taken in the autumn of 1969 with the formation of the Congress (O) – the 'O' standing for Organisation – by Congress leaders who were out of sympathy with Mrs Gandhi. In their forefront was Morarji Desai, who had always been opposed to the Nehru line in the name of a Hindu traditionalism manifested with Gandhian overtones. As Francine Frankel has written:

Desai's scorn for socialist ideology was ultimately an expression of essentially religious convictions that moral and spiritual development rather than material

---

[6] Letter from Madhok to S.S. Bhandari, 22 Nov. 1972, cited in M.R. Varshney, *Jana Sangh, RSS and Balraj Madhok*, Aligarh: Varshney College (n.d.), p. 106.

[7] *Hindustan Times*, 2 Feb. 1968.

[8] Ranga even presided over a gathering of the RSS at Nagpur (*Statesman Weekly*, 12 Oct. 1968, p. 2).

progress were the true yardsticks of human civilization. A man of ability as well as integrity, his challenge to Nehru's approach came less from a well-articulated liberal philosophy than a life style of personal austerities, religious devotion, and 'social' work that evoked memories of Gandhi and gained for him a substantial personal following inside the Congress party.[9]

Madhok saw the split in Congress as being one between 'Patelists' and 'Nehruists'.[10] Therefore he called on the leaders of the former group (chiefly M. Desai and S.K. Patil) to promote a conservative party which would project itself as the defender of Hindu interests.[11] For Madhok, this plan went hand-in-hand with a militant Hinduism: at a conference in Patna in December 1969 he set forth his arguments for the necessary 'Indianisation' (in effect 'Hinduisation') of Muslims and Christians.[12] He suggested that the Jana Sangh should renounce the Sangathanist model and its specific identity to submerge itself in the tide of 'Hindu traditionalism' – as Mookerjee had envisaged at the time when Sardar Patel and Tandon represented a similar outlook in the top ranks of the Congress. The way forward indicated here prefigures what in fact happened in the later 1970s.

However, this conservative option was immediately criticised, especially by Vajpayee, who believed in the need to take greater account of social problems. In September 1968 he had supported the strikes for higher pay by employees in the central administration and demanded that the Lok Sabha should establish a minimum salary, to the considerable annoyance of Madhok,[13] while in 1969 he had criticised Madhok's opposition to the nationalisation of the banks, which ran the risk of making the Jana Sangh appear as the defender of 'business' – whereas, according to Vajpayee, it had to become the champion of the 'common man'[14] with populist overtones.

Populism is a problematic notion in India as elsewhere. It is, as pointed out by Ionescu and Gellner, an 'elusive and protean' concept.[15] In this chapter the term is synonymous with demagogy but is also used in the sense proposed by Edward Shils:

[9]   F. Frankel, *India's political economy, 1947-1977*, op. cit., p. 227.

[10]   *Statesman* (Delhi), 9 Nov. 1969.

[11]   *Times of India*, 17 and 28 Sept. 1969. Desai excluded any amalgamation but revealed that he wished to conclude an electoral alliance with the Jana Sangh and the Swatantra Party in January 1970 (*Statesman Weekly*, 10 Jan. 1970, p. 2).

[12]   These arguments figure in his book *Indianisation? What, why and how*, New Delhi: S. Chand, 1970.

[13]   *Hindustan Times*, 26 Sept. 1968.

[14]   *Statesman* (Delhi), 3 Sept. 1969.

[15]   In 'Introduction' to G. Ionescu and E. Gellner (eds), *Populism – its meanings and national characteristics*, London: Weidenfeld and Nicolson, 1969, p. 1.

Populism proclaims that the will of the people as such is supreme over every other standard, over the standards of traditional institutions, over the autonomy of institutions and over the will of other strata. Populism identifies the will of the people with justice and morality.

It exists wherever there is an ideology of popular resentment against the order imposed on society by a long-established, differentiated ruling class, which is believed to have a monopoly of power, property, breeding and culture.[16]

Hindu nationalism had latent affinities with populism. In fact it could be considered as a potentially populist doctrine to the extent that it placed a high value on the general will of Hindu community, and implied that existing institutions, including those of the state, were not expressions of that will and therefore lacked legitimacy. But it was difficult for the RSS and the Jana Sangh to make these ideas explicit because they also represented the social and political interests of upper and intermediate castes, and thus the principle of hierarchy. Gradually, however, these organisations added populist overtones to their election campaigns. Upadhyaya, who had frustrated Madhok's efforts to ally the Jana Sangh with the Swatantra Party in 1964, had been taking the party in a populist direction before his death in February 1968. In his presidential address to the party in 1967, Upadhyaya had put forward an argument in which he combined his social preoccupations with a certain activism:

Those who are keen to preserve the *status quo* in the economic and social spheres, are unnerved by popular movements. They are wont to create an atmosphere of despair. We are sorry we cannot cooperate with them. For many of these public agitations are natural and necessary.[17]

According to Andersen and Damle, the orientation sought by Vajpayee not only had affinities 'with the world view of the RSS' but was also probably more in tune 'with the class background of most *swayam-sevaks*'.[18] Within the RSS this strategic change of direction was supported by Balasaheb Deoras, an 'activist' who had succeeded E. Ranade as General Secretary in 1965 and was committed to a more egalitarian social order than Golwalkar, who was ailing in the early 1970s.[19]

At the same time the RSS had tightened its hold over the Jana Sangh. In 1967 Upadhyaya had taken over the presidency of the Jana Sangh from Madhok.[20] The Jana Sangh's decision to strengthen the party by

---

[16] E. Shils, *The torment of secrecy*, Melbourne: Heinemann, 1956, pp. 98 and 100-101.

[17] *Organiser*, 21 Dec. 1967, p. 7.

[18] W. Andersen and S. Damle, *The brotherhood in saffron*, op. cit., p. 182.

[19] When he became *sarsanghchalak* in 1973, Deoras made it clear that he did not consider the *varna* system worthy of emulation.

[20] S.S. Bhandari had been promoted to General Secretary, while J. Joshi and N. Deshmukh, as well as Vajpayee, remained in their posts as national secretaries.

reinforcing discipline of the Sangathanist variety was also widely evident – in the context of the SVD experiments – in its treatment of its MLAs, who 'were required to report to the local party organisation and to take their instructions from it'.[21] Parallel to this, Upadhyaya announced that the party's network of paid full-time activists charged with the task of spreading its message was being enlarged;[22] henceforward, only *swayam-sevaks* would be accepted.

The intensification of RSS control over the Jana Sangh was at the expense of the alliance plans of Madhok. His preferred option had in fact been automatically set aside, since any formula jeopardising the identity of the party to which the Sangathanist network was closely attached had been ruled out.

The primacy of the organisation over individuals

In June 1972, Madhok publicly denounced – in the name of a more liberal programme – the leftward drift of the party, which he blamed for its electoral reverses in 1971 and 1972 (see below).[23] He took up this argument again in February 1973 in a note which he presented before the party's executive committee at the start of the meeting at Kanpur, where he also took a stand against the control which the RSS exerted over the Jana Sangh and called for the party's internal workings to be made more democratic by the abolition of the *sangathan mantris*.[24] Advani, Vajpayee's successor as president of the Jana Sangh in 1973, described Madhok's attitude as characteristic indiscipline, and he was expelled from the party for a period of three years – which, in the event, proved permanent.[25]

Madhok was told that the reason he had been expelled was because of the dissenting views he had expressed publicly over the years (for example, over nationalisation of the banks). Here Advani referred to the party's unwritten rules whereby discussion of matters over which a majority decision had already been taken was inadmissible. Furthermore, Advani accused Madhok of having an 'inflated ego',[26] which had caused him to push himself forward as an individual: the Jana Sangh had inherited from the RSS a concern to subordinate personalities to its organisation.[27]

21   W. Andersen and S. Damle, *The brotherhood in saffron*, op. cit., p. 180.
22   *Statesman* (Delhi), 30 July 1967.
23   *Times of India*, 7 June 1972.
24   Note reproduced in M.R. Varshney, *Jana Sangh – RSS and Balraj Madhok*, op. cit., pp. 112-24.
25   *Motherland*, 14 March 1973, pp. 1 and 7.
26   *Organiser*, 17 March 1973, p. 13.
27   At first, Madhok considered himself to be the victim of this principle more than of

It seems that Madhok had never been completely accepted by the high command of the 'Sangh parivar'. Even today, senior *swayamsevaks* of the BJP will point out that he never completed his OTC course and that he achieved prominence because of his familiarity with the state of Jammu and Kashmir, which was an early and important focus of attention for Hindu nationalists in the post-independence period. In addition, he had been one of the first *swayamsevaks* to explore the idea of forming a new party and to discuss the idea with Mookerjee, even before the RSS leaders accepted it. By contrast, Advani was a product of the RSS. A *swayamsewak* since 1942, in 1947 he became *pracharak* of the Karachi branch where he developed numerous *shakhas* while simultaneously working as a teacher. After Partition, he served as a *pracharak* in the Alwar, Bharatpur, Kota, Bundi and Jhalawar districts of Rajasthan until 1952 when he was appointed secretary of the state Jana Sangh in order to assist S.S. Bhandari, the General Secretary. In 1957 Upadhyaya asked him to come to Delhi to look after parliamentary work when the session was on and in 1958 he became secretary and later vice-president of the Delhi unit of the Jana Sangh; after the 1967 elections he was leader of the city's metropolitan council. Parallel to this, from 1960 onwards he assisted another Sindhi, K.R. Malkani, in editing *Organiser*.[28] That he was imbued with the doctrines of Hindu nationalism was clearly evident in his articles. Even though he had become a member of the Jana Sangh's national executive in 1966 he had remained withdrawn from the national political scene till he became party president, at the suggestion of Vajpayee, in 1973. At that time the *Organiser* compared him to Upadhyaya[29] probably because he shunned publicity and was the incarnation of RSS ideology.

Madhok attracted no more than a handful of activists from the Jana Sangh, which was very surprising given that he nad been one of the party's co-founders. His failure in dividing the party reflects the primacy of the organisation over individuals; as we tried to show in Chapter 3, Jana Sanghis did not owe allegiance to personalities but rather respected the authority of *sangathan mantris* as the embodiment of the organisation. This arrangement explains the party's tight discipline and why it was largely free from factionalism, a phenomenon that rests primarily on allegiance towards personalities and clientelistic linkages.

The predominant type of leadership was rather that of a tightly bound elite sharing a common doctrine and sense of discipline learnt from the RSS. Debates were confined to private meetings and public differences

---

ideological disagreement (interview). It was precisely to avoid personality cults that the presidentcy of the party, which became a more important post after 1966, was rotated.

[28] Interview with L.K. Advani, *Who's who in Rajya Sabha – 1970*, op. cit., p. 4 and G. Vazirani, *Lal Advani: The man and his mission*, New Delhi: Arnold, 1991, pp. 11-17.

[29] 'Second Deendayal at helm of BJS', *Organiser*, 17 Feb. 1973, p. 1.

between party chiefs were very rare. In fact personalities did not count for much in comparison to the organisation. Moreover the replacement in 1973 of Vajpayee by Advani was not the product of any kind of competition and nor did it imply any shift of emphasis in the political programme. The primacy of the organisation over personalities also explains the influence of the local cadres – the backbone of the party – in shaping the party's programme. Therefore, one can state with confidence that the main division within the Jana Sangh was not vertical but horizontal. In the early 1970s, this division explains the preference for populism and Sangathanism in comparison to Madhok's alternative. At that time the populist line was also a better option than a militant Hindu conservatism of the type advocated by Madhok because the central government, reacting to increased inter-communal rioting, was actively reaffirming its secularist principles.

The central government's fight against communalism

Between 1954 and 1966 the average number of communal riots per annum was 70.2. This figure rose to 209 in 1967, 346 in 1968, 519 in 1969 and 521 in 1970 (see Appendix B, p. 552). Hindu nationalists were alleged to have been involved in the three major communal riots of the 1967-70 period – at Ranchi, Ahmedabad and Bhiwandi.[30]

The central government reacted to this renewal of violence by adopting a tougher attitude towards the Hindu nationalists, especially since a Home Ministry report revealed that the RSS had become the largest association of volunteers in the country.[31] In 1968, the National Integration Council was reconstituted and the Ministry submitted to it a plan to prohibit 'communalist activities',[32] though this was never followed up. The Congressmen close to Indira Gandhi, such as Jagjivan Ram, meanwhile adopted the same anti-communalist stance as the Communists, with whom they had had frequent contact in the Sampradayikta Virodhi Committee (SVC – committee for the struggle against communalism).[33]

---

[30] See *Report of the commission of inquiry on communal disturbances – Ranchi-Hatia (August 22-29, 1967)*, 1968, pp. 10 ff.; *Report – Inquiry into the communal disturbances at Ahmedabad*, op. cit., p. 67; and D.P. Madan, *Report of the Commission of Inquiry into the communal disturbances at Bhiwandi, Jalgaon and Mahad in May 1970*, vol. 1, pp. 163 ff.

[31] This report noted 73,000 *swayamsevaks* in Maharashtra, 31,500 in Rajasthan, 29,000 in Madhya Pradesh, 20,000 in West Bengal, 18,800 in Bihar, 18,000 in Karnataka, 17,000 in Uttar Pradesh, 14,500 in Delhi ,13,700 in Andhra Pradesh, 9,000 in Kerala and Punjab, 8,600 in Gujarat and 6,000 in Haryana (*Statesman Weekly*, 6 Sept. 1969, p. 3).

[32] Ibid., 15 June 1968.

[33] Ibid., 30 May 1970, p. 7.

In the summer of 1970, the SVC launched a petition for the banning of the RSS.[34] Indira Gandhi herself denounced the fascism of the Jana Sangh, whose appeal for the Indianisation of the minorities she compared to that of Hitler's persecution of the Jews.[35] She asked Y.B. Chavan, the Home Minister, who had accused the Jana Sangh of involvement in the riots at Ahmedabad,[36] to sound out the state governments on the possibility of banning the RSS. A majority of states believed that such a measure would risk triggering off a mobilisation of the RSS and its sympathisers, as had happened in 1949. The Congress leadership in the states, however, argued that prompt action was called for.[37] Indira Gandhi finally ordered a stricter implementation of the existing laws: thus in Delhi there was enacted a two-month ban on the 'practice of physical exercises, in uniform or without it, with or without *lathis* or any other weapon, or objects resembling one, by a group of five or more persons in a public place';[38] furthermore, it was announced that police files on 'functionaries and active members of the RSS would be reexamined and appropriate measures taken'.[39]

The RSS attempted to resist this vigilant secularism by instructing Hans Raj Gupta to organise a petition for submission to the President of India; 400,000 signatures were collected protesting against the ban on the Delhi *shakhas*. In 1972 a Criminal Law (Amendment) Bill was introduced which gave the government new means of combating communalist and regionalist paramilitary organisations. Aware that the implementation of this bill could weaken the position of the RSS, the Jana Sangh opposed it in parliament, but the measure was passed into law.[40]

Partly as a result of these events, the Jana Sangh opted for a low profile, eschewing any Hindu militancy. In adopting the Vajpayee formula – distancing the party from Hindu communal themes – it once again showed how its actions were influenced by the context of the political arena. When Upadhyaya was mysteriously assassinated in February 1968, Vajpayee succeeded him as President of the Jana Sangh. His re-election during the

[34] *National Herald*, 20 July 1970.
[35] Ibid., 15 Jan. 1970; see also *Statesman Weekly*, 16 May 1970, p. 1, and *Hindustan Times*, 25 Nov. 1970.
[36] *Statesman Weekly*, 11 Oct. 1969, p. 7.
[37] *Times of India*, 23 June 1970.
[38] Ibid., 26 June 1970.
[39] *National Herald*, 11 July 1970. The list of Indira Gandhi's recommendations to the heads of the state governments included the imposition of fines, a closer watch on communalist meetings, sanctions against civil servants who proved ineffective in the fight against communalism, and the development of a network of informers (*Statesman Weekly*, 6 June 1970, p. 10). Significantly, the executive committee of Congress (O) took no part in this campaign (ibid., 27 June 1970, p. 2).
[40] *Statesman Weekly*, 10 June 1972, p. 6.

period 1969-72 allowed him to set in train his populist strategy. Claiming that it represented the people, the Jana Sangh, with its eye increasingly on future electoral success, began to promise social reforms that were often unrealistic.

The patriotic and populist roles of the Jana Sangh: the problem of outdoing the Congress

The populist theme was developed by Vajpayee in a similar fashion to the strategies of moderation and pragmatism tried out earlier by the Jana Sangh. 'People are interested not by ideologies,' he said, 'but by fundamental bread-and-butter needs.'[41] At its meeting in Patna in December 1969, from which Madhok walked out as a mark of his disapproval, the party voted for a four-page resolution proposing a 'real new deal'.[42] Its most 'revolutionary' clauses related to the strict implementation of maximum acreages in agriculture, the distribution of surplus land to the low castes and Adivasis, security of tenure for *bataidars* (tenant farmers working on large estates), lowering the cost of credit to cultivators and of the price of water and electricity and a massive programme of low-cost construction.[43] The party's election manifesto in 1971 took up all these proposals and many more under the title 'A National War on Poverty':

> The Jana Sangh declares a National War on poverty. It is committed to the objective of total victory in this war. We are out to break once and for all the vicious circle of low incomes, low demand, low savings, low investments, low employment and low production. We shall generate the healthy trend of more employment, higher incomes, greater demand, larger savings and greater investment, leading to higher production at lower costs.[44]

This populism sought to exploit the constant deterioration in the economic situation of the poorest in society at a time when India was suffering from bad monsoons. The effects of the Green Revolution had been gathering pace since 1966, but socially this meant that landowners with the capacity to invest were getting richer while the rest became

---

[41] *Hindu*, 21 July 1970.

[42] *Link*, 4 Jan. 1970, p. 17.

[43] Resolution XVI of 28 Dec. 1968 in *Party Documents*, vol. 2, op. cit., pp. 176-9. In 1970, Vajpayee launched a nationwide petition demanding the inclusion of the right to work among the Fundamental Rights, the redistribution of land to landless peasants and the granting to small peasants' of interest-free loans for five years. 50,000 activists are believed to have signed the charter. (*Statesman Weekly*, 20 June 1970, p. 7, and 12 Sept. 1970, p. 14).

[44] 'Manifesto – 1971' in *Party documents*, vol. 1, op. cit., p. 175.

relatively poorer.[45] In such a context the populist option was bound to pay political dividends. However, the Jana Sangh was far from being the only party to follow this path. In this struggle for the votes of the poor, the Congress, with its socialist allegiance, had an advantage on which Indira Gandhi was determined to capitalise.

She used populist themes to strengthen her position as head of government. After its reverses in the 1967 elections, Congress made a special point of showing its fidelity to the socialist principles of Nehru by producing a 10-point programme envisaging, *inter alia*, nationalising the banks and insurance companies, limiting the incomes and property holdings of the urban population and abolishing the privileges and 'purses' accorded to the princes. This programme met with the disapproval of party bosses like S.K. Patil and Morarji Desai. From the spring of 1969, when it became clear that these leaders would do all in their power to unseat her, Indira Gandhi chose to rely increasingly on the radicals by presenting this tactical formulation as a fixed ideology against the conservatism of her opponents. On 16 July she took the finance portfolio away from Desai, who promptly resigned from the government, and on the 19th she arranged for a presidential ordinance which nationalised fourteen important banks. She then called for a free vote in the impending election of the President of India, a move which led to the final division of the Congress into two parts, Congress (R) – for Ruling or Requisitionist – and Congress (O) – for Organisation. Unlike the undivided Congress, Mrs Gandhi's Congress (R) was not a 'system', in the sense that it no longer spanned almost the whole ideological spectrum. Rather it had come to embody a socialism which it increasingly claimed to be the sole legitimate option.[46]

Indira Gandhi presented this reconstitution of the ruling party – whose new chief, Jagjivan Ram, was a Scheduled Caste politician – as the precondition for genuine social reform, which the Congress notables had previously obstructed. In effect, she nationalised the insurance companies and announced the abolition of the privileges and purses of the princes, by means of a constitutional amendment which the Rajya Sabha rejected on 5 September 1971, and then by a presidential decree on 7 September which the Supreme Court declared unconstitutional. Such institutional blocking by conservatives of potentially popular initiatives led Mrs Gandhi to call elections in which she expected to regain a majority in the Lok Sabha. The announcement was made in December 1970, and she immediately concluded an alliance with the CPI while redoubling her determination to appear, independently of any party, personally committed to the fight against poverty. This she put across in the course of an

[45] F. Frankel, *India's political economy, 1947-1977*, op. cit., pp. 335-9.

[46] Ibid., p. 427.

extensive national campaign under the slogan '*Garibi hatao!*' (let us eradicate poverty).

This populism, in the more or less novel form of an appeal to the masses, was the deciding factor in the success of the Congress (R), which exceeded all expectations and gave the party 352 out of the 518 seats in the Lok Sabha. The Jana Sangh now had 22 seats on the basis of 7.4% of the votes cast, as against 35 on the basis of 9.4% in the previous house; its own populism had been no match for that of Mrs Gandhi. But the party chose to persevere with the same strategy for the Vidhan Sabha elections due to be held in 1972.

The Jana Sangh approved of the nationalisation of insurance companies,[47] and at its AIGC conference, held at Ghaziabad, Uttar Pradesh, in November 1971, resolutions were passed demanding a ceiling on urban property and the 'honest implementation of all land-reforms'.[48]

The Jana Sangh was merely adopting a position associated very closely with that of Congress (R). After its victory in 1971, the government undertook to alter the constitutional guarantees concerning property law so that it could carry out its populist commitments. This procedure permitted the abolition of the privileges and purses of the princes, for which Indira Gandhi had campaigned in the 1972 election. In that campaign she had also promised a new ceiling on agricultural property: '10 to 18 acres of perennially irrigated land or irrigated land capable of growing two crops or the equivalent amount for other categories of food'. This was a measure directed specifically for the benefit of the Scheduled Castes.[49]

Indira Gandhi's government outstripped the Jana Sangh in a much more spectacular fashion with its military successes against Pakistan. In March 1971 the Pakistan army had tried to put down seccessionists in East Bengal led by the Awami League, which organised its own guerrilla fighters and appointed a provisional government. For the Jana Sangh this was an unexpected opportunity to weaken the hereditary enemy, and it called on Indira Gandhi to recognise the provisional government and put to the vote a resolution in the Lok Sabha expressing India's solidarity with the new régime.[50] The prudence of the Prime Minister – which some regarded as a 'wait and see' policy – allowed the Jana Sangh to exploit the nationalist sentiment which was beginning to affect certain sectors of opinion.[51] On

---

[47]   *Motherland.* 14 May 1971, p. 1, and 3 July 1971, p. 1. In the name of the 'common man' Vajpayee launched a major campaign against the budget of 1971-2, which included an increase in indirect taxes on consumption to finance the government's social projects (ibid., 29 May 1971, p. 1; 1 June 1971, p. 2, and 7 June 1971, p. 1).

[48]   Resolution of the AIGC of 27 Nov. 1971 in *Party Documents*, vol. 2, op. cit., p. 199.

[49]   F. Frankel, *India's political economy, 1947-1977.*, op. cit., p. 476.

[50]   *Motherland*, 29 March 1971, p. 1, and 30 March 1971, p. 1.

[51]   Ibid., 25 May 1971, p. 1.

12 August the party organised a *satyagraha* that the *Organiser* claimed comprised 13,000 participants and half a million sympathisers.[52]

At this point the government retook the initiative, to some extent, by signing the Indo-Soviet Treaty, a measure which the Jana Sangh had no choice but to approve given the risks of isolation on the part of the Americans. Indira Gandhi, who wanted above all to gain time in order to prepare the army, declared war on 24 November in response to a Pakistani attack. The Jana Sangh immediately gave its support to the government: its own activists and those of the RSS offered their services, as in 1965, to maintain law and order in Delhi and were apparently the first blood-donors to come forward.[53]

Once the war was won, Hans Raj Gupta sent the Minister of War, Jagjivan Ram, a sword and a copy of *Bhagavad Gita*, suggesting – not without condescension – that the government had acquitted itself well in its patriotic duty, an obligation of which the Hindu nationalists claimed to be the exemplars.[54] However, those in power had no need for the Hindu nationalists' blessing; they had gained total victory, Pakistan having surrendered unconditionally on 16 December after only two weeks of fighting. All the Jana Sangh could do was to offer its congratulations.[55]

The war of 1971 marked a revealing stage in the government's evolution towards a form of nationalism which had hitherto been the preserve of the Jana Sangh. As Ashis Nandy observed, the reign of Indira Gandhi meant that two of 'the main elements of the country's political identity' became 'aggressive affirmation of Indianness' and 'tough-minded pursuit of national interest which rejects nothing as ethically taboo'.[56]

This transformation of the position of the Congress (R) left the Jana Sangh at a disadvantage. In the 1972 state elections, Congress cashed in on the Indian army's military successes to help it recapture power in all the northern states. The Jana Sangh's losses in this region (see Appendix E, p. 555.) were partly due to the impossibility of competing with Congress on the issue of patriotism – just as it had been over populism.

The Jana Sangh's impotence when it found itself competing with Congress on populist terrain also arose, in 1972 as in 1971, from its inability to make the party-building strategy consistent with its electoral plans and the wishes of local cadres: two distinct tendencies collided with each other when the party chose to preach a radical social policy at the

[52] *Organiser*, 21 Aug. 1971, p. 1.

[53] *Motherland*, 7 Dec. 1971, and 10 Jan. 1972, p. 3.

[54] Ibid., 20 Dec. 1971, p. 1.

[55] *Organiser*, 11 Dec. 1971, p. 2. Thus Golwalkar and Deroas sent congratulatory telegrams to Indira Gandhi (*ibid.*, 25 Dec. 1971, p. 15).

[56] A. Nandy, *At the edge of psychology*, Delhi: Oxford University Press, 1980, p. 113.

same time as it turned increasingly to notables and princes (whom, naturally, Congress had alienated) in order to expand. This contradiction was all the more damaging to the party when Indira Gandhi herself sought to move with the 'political awakening' of the masses while by-passing Congress notables.

The sociological limits of populism: the Jana Sangh's inability to widen its base

The few electoral surveys relating to the elections of the 1960s situate the main supporters of the Jana Sangh in the higher castes and the professional, white-collar, merchant and other middle-class groups.

Research carried out in 1967 by the Centre for the Study of Developing Societies revealed an over-representation among Jana Sangh voters of 'white collar' occupations (13.8% as against 7.6% in the population as a whole), but also – though to a lesser extent – of the liberal professions (2.9% as against 2.5%) and merchants (8% as against 7.3%).[57] From this it emerged that 35% of its voters lived in towns, compared with less than 22% in the case of Congress. Its sympathisers were also concentrated largely in the middle-income categories. Similarly, peasant landholders who supported the Jana Sangh owned medium-sized properties while those of the Swatantra Party tended to be larger. The Jana Sangh thus remained firmly anchored in the 'middle world', mostly among the higher castes.

Surprisingly, perhaps, 18.1% of its supporters were from the Scheduled Castes and Scheduled Tribes. This proportion, which was only slightly below the percentage of those categories in Indian society as a whole (22%, of whom 14.5% were Scheduled Castes), represented quite an advance. The research of Morris-Jones and Das Gupta shows a positive connection between the presence of a high proportion of Scheduled Castes and Scheduled Tribes and the return of a Jana Sangh candidate in a growing number of districts between 1957 and 1967; yet in 1962 the Jana Sangh was the party with the smallest number of successful candidates who were members of the Scheduled Castes or Tribes.[58]

This tendency for the party's social base to widen was compromised in the early 1970s by an increasing reliance on notables and princes. This became a handicap just at the time when techniques for mobilising the electorate were undergoing a profound change.

---

[57]　D.L. Sheth, 'Profiles of party support in 1967', *EPW*, 6 (3-5), Jan. 1971, p. 314.

[58]　W.H. Morris-Jones and B. Das Gupta, 'India's political area: interim report an ecological electoral investigation', *Asian Survey*, 9 (6), June 1969, p. 412.

The appeal to the masses and the decline of 'vote banks'

Until the very end of the 1960s, all parties cultivated the active support of those notables who had a personal power base, as a means of entrenching the party in a given area. However, in 1969 Charan Singh's BKD in-augurated a new strategy in the mid-term elections for the Uttar Pradesh state assembly. This consisted of directly targeting peasants from middle and 'backward castes':[59] Jats, Yadavs, Gujars, Lodhis, Kurmis etc. In this state the Jana Sangh suffered heavy losses – its share of the votes cast had declined, from 21.67% in 1967 to 17.93% in 1969 – partly because of its increasing dependence on notables – mostly ex-*zamindars* – [60] whom Charan Singh had by-passed through his direct appeal to the lower caste peasants.[61] This anticipated the strategy Indira Gandhi was to adopt throughout India.

By means of tours, during which she presented her populist programme directly to the masses, the Prime Minister also sought effectively to 'short-circuit' the notables who had generally remained loyal to Congress (O) and were the traditional backbone of the party.[62] Her strategy was based on the assumption that the rural population was beginning to respond to direct mass appeals and that the probable shift to mass politics would undermine the political power of the notables, especially in those states which had been provinces of British India and where the authority of the former royal families and their *jagirdars* or *zamindars* had practi-cally disappeared.

The effect of such propaganda on the Scheduled Castes seems to have been particularly noteworthy, as was shown by the upswing in the Congress's vote in those constituencies reserved for them (the increase was 23% as opposed to 15% overall).[63]

Such a shift towards a direct appeal to the masses, thereby reducing

[59] F. Frankel, *India's political economy, 1947-1977.*, op. cit., p. 386.

[60] Thakurs represented 21.57% of its MLAs in 1969 and 22.95% in 1974 (Z. Hasan, 'Power and mobilization: patterns of resilience and change in Uttar Pradesh politics' in F. Frankel and M.S.A. Rao (eds), *Dominance and state power in modern India*, Delhi: Oxford University Press, 1989, p. 189).

[61] V.B. Singh, 'Jan Sangh in Uttar Pradesh: Fluctuating fortunes and uncertain future', *EPW*, 6 (3-5), Jan. 1971, p. 314. Nana Deshmukh recognised this state of things when explaining the defeat of the Jana Sangh (*Organiser*, 22 Feb. 1969, p. 2).

[62] S. Kaviraj, 'Indira Gandhi and Indian politics', *EPW*, 21 (38-9), 20 Sept. 1986, p. 1699.

[63] W.H. Morris-Jones, 'India elects for change and stability', *Asian Survey*, 9 (8), Aug. 1971, p. 735. This was confirmed by a poll of 641 opinion-formers in Gujarat held in 1971-2. Of 178 Harijan leaders questioned, 102 had voted for Indira Gandhi in 1971 out of a clear perception that this served their interests (G. Shah, 'Voting behaviour of Adivasi and Harijan leaders: a study of the 1971 elections', *Indian Journal of Political Science*, 33 (4), Oct.-Dec. 1972, pp. 439-40).

the importance of vote-banks, was at odds with the Jana Sangh's practice in two ways. First, the party was involved in 1971 in a conservative Grand Alliance, including the SSP, the Swatantra Party and the Congress (O), which resulted in electoral pacts affecting 300 out of the 520 Lok Sabha constituencies;[64] and second, it persevered with a party-building strategy which depended increasingly on princes. In 1971 and 1972, as the case of Madhya Pradesh suggests, the Jana Sangh suffered on account of these methods, which were preventing it from widening its base there.

The cost of relying on princes

From 1970 onwards, the Jana Sangh was adversely affected by the inconsistency of its policy towards the princes. On the one hand it was slowly coming round to the idea of making a direct appeal to the princes to give up their purses voluntarily; on the other, the party was welcoming, and indeed canvassing, a growing number of the princes who were looking for allies among those who opposed the plans of Indira Gandhi. In August 1967 some sixty princes, mostly from North India, had met in Delhi to form a movement in defence of the privy purses which they had been guaranteed under Article 291 of the Constitution. When it became clear that Mrs Gandhi was intent on abolishing this and their other privileges, the princes gave active support to the opposition, most obviously by backing the Grand Alliance in the campaign for the mid-term Lok Sabha elections of March 1971.[65]

In Rajasthan, the Jana Sangh kept the support of the Maharajah of Kota, who was re-elected to the Lok Sabha, and gained that of the Maharana of Udaipur, who strongly opposed Indira Gandhi's policy towards the princes.[66] The Jana Sangh thus won Kota's two seats and two of the four which made up Udaipur division, where the Maharana, who was not himself a candidate, backed minor *rajahs* like Hemendra Singh Banera (Bhilwara constituency), the president of the Mewar Kshatriya Mahasabha, or 'magnates' like the Marwari, B. Jhunjhunwala, who was elected for Chittorgarh.[67] In Rajasthan the Swatantra Party was already well established and benefited from the support of numerous princes, including the Maharani of Jaipur and the Maharajah of Bikaner, but the Jana Sangh

---

[64] W. Andersen and S. Damle, *The brotherhood in saffron*, op. cit., p. 182. In Uttar Pradesh in January 1970, the Jana Sangh supported an ephemeral government formed by the leader of Congress (O), C.B. Gupta, in association with the Swatantra Party and the Socialists (*Statesman Weekly*, 31 Jan. 1970, p. 8). An alliance of the same type also took shape in Bihar (ibid., 7 Feb. 1970, p. 8).

[65] See C. Hurtig, *Les maharajahs et la politique*, op. cit., p. 87-127.

[66] *Organiser*, 5 Sept. 1970.

[67] *Who's who in Lok Sabha – 1971*, op. cit., pp. 44 and 251.

faced no such competition in Madhya Pradesh. There the Scindias remained the Jana Sangh's principal supporters among the princes. The experience of the SVD had finally sealed the ties between the party and the house of Gwalior. In 1968, disillusioned by the opportunism of the other members of the coalition, the Rajmata teamed up with the Jana Sanghis; her association with the Hindu nationalist movement took on a more ideological colouring, in keeping with the orientation of her adviser, S. Angre. In May 1968, together with S.S. Apte and the Shankaracharya of Bhanpura, she presided over the joint committee of the VHP units of Madhya Pradesh, Rajasthan and Gujarat, and declared on that occasion:

Under the pretext of sham secularism, many of our misguided compatriots hesitate to call themselves Hindus. The greatest need of the time is to make our people understand the true meaning of Hindutva and to carry its glorious light to every corner of the world.[68]

From 1970 onwards she campaigned on behalf of the Jana Sangh throughout Madhya Pradesh, outside her traditional domain.[69] In February 1970 her son Madhav Rao formally joined the Jana Sangh in a ceremony at which he announced that other princes, including the heir to the Maharajah of Chhatarpur, in Vindhya Pradesh, had done likewise.[70] The chief explanation for this phenomenon was the existence of a veritable princely network centred on the Scindias of Gwalior.

As the pre-eminent state in the region, Gwalior had traditionally assumed the leadership of the surrounding principalities. The Scindias were able to play on personal links to rally princely houses which were in any case being driven into the arms of the opposition by Indira Gandhi's policies. Many friendships had been formed in the 'Colleges' reserved for princes under the British raj; for example, S. Angre, H. Singh Banera and the Maharajahs of Narsingarh, Khairagarh, Kota and Panna had all been educated at Mayo College, in Ajmer (Rajasthan).[71]

In 1969 the princes began deserting the SVD to rejoin the party in power, but the following year the Scindias did not have to work particularly hard to rally the former Maharajahs, embittered as they were by Congress's policy, to the state's principal opposition party. In October 1970 there was a gathering of Vindhya Pradesh princes in support of the Grand Alliance, led by the Maharajah of Rewa, who had hitherto been on the side of Congress. It was held at Panna, the capital of a former princely state, and its Maharajah, Narendra Singh, who had been deputy Rajpramukh of Vindhya Pradesh and a Congress MLA since 1952, turned

---

[68] *Organiser*, 3 May 1968, p. 6.
[69] Ibid., 25 Apr. 1970.
[70] Ibid., 28 Feb. 1970.
[71] Interview with S. Angre, 2 Dec. 1989, New Delhi, and *Patriot*, 13 March 1970.

out to be an ally of particular worth to the Hindu nationalists.[72] Some princes joined the Jana Sangh without the Scindias' intervention, for example Bhanu Prakash Singh of Narsingarh, who resigned in August from the central government after Indira Gandhi denied his right to vote against the proposed law abolishing the princely privileges and purses. With the approach of elections, he joined the Jana Sangh.[73]

In 1971 half a dozen princes stood as Jana Sangh candidates for the Lok Sabha: Rajmata Scindia at Bhind, her son at Guna, Bhanu Prakash Singh at Bhopal, Narendra Singh at Satna, and the Rajmata of Saraipali (the mother-in-law of the Maharajah of Sarangarh) at Mahasamund. The party also campaigned on behalf of princes standing for election on the Congress (O) ticket, such as Rani Padmavati of Khairagarh, or as independents like the Maharajah of Rewa.[74] Finally, the Jana Sangh received support from princes who could not, or would not, stand as candidates themselves, for example, the princely family of Kawardha and the Begum of Bhopal. The latter made an election tour on behalf of Bhanu Prakash Singh with the Maharana of Udaipur, who was especially incensed by the abolition of the purses.[75] This massive rallying of princes to the Jana Sangh naturally drew in ex-*zamindars* and ex-*jagirdars* who still owed them obligations or aspired to enter this circle.[76]

The impression that the Jana Sangh had become a party of 'haves' was further strengthened by the fact that the Scindias were supporting the candidature of big businessmen, such as Ramnath Goenka, a press magnate, at Vidisha. The party's central leadership tolerated these practices all the more willingly because its national leaders themselves also profited from the princely connection; Jagannath Rao Joshi stood for the Rajgarh constituency and Vajpayee for Gwalior itself, where the Scindias' influence guaranteed an easy victory. There was thus a clear divorce between the Jana Sangh's populist rhetoric and the rallying of princes.

The Jana Sangh's position was further weakened by Congress's '*Garibi Hatao*' campaign. Indeed a new political consciousness seemed to be emerging in the Scheduled Castes and Scheduled Tribes. For example, the Kachi and Jatav castes promised their support to Congress

---

[72] One of the most prominent Hindu nationalist leaders in Madhya Pradesh, R.H. Gupta, acknowledges that Narendra Singh's influence proved very useful to the Jana Sangh in Panna district and in two constituencies of the districts of Chhatarpur and Satna (interview with R.H. Gupta).

[73] C. Hurtig, *Les maharajahs et la politique*, op. cit., p. 110, and *Motherland*, 5 Feb. 1971, p. 4.

[74] *Statesman Weekly*, 23 Jan. 1971, p. 6.

[75] *Motherland*, 11 Feb. 1971, p. 7; 16 Feb. 1971, p. 7, and 17 Feb. 1971, p. 7.

[76] This was observed at Bhopal (ibid.); Durg (ibid., 11 Feb. 1971, p. 4); and Raipur (ibid. 5 Feb. 1971).

in meetings at Morena,[77] and certain Scheduled Caste leaders, as at Mandsaur, deserted the Jana Sangh for Congress.[78]

The election of 1971 marked the limit of the Jana Sangh's expansion in Madhya Pradesh, with 11 seats won compared to 10 in 1967, and revealed its reliance on Madhya Bharat, the source of 10 of its winning candidates. Above all, the party appeared, from this point on, to be dependent on the princely network which, directly or otherwise, had given it most of its victories: the Scindias at Bhind and Guna, B. Patel and Goenka at Shajapur and Vidisha, Narendra Singh at Satna (the only new conquest, and a princely one at that, in the east of Madhya Bharat) and Vajpayee, who perhaps would not have won at Gwalior without the Scindias and certainly could not have beaten them. In contrast to this princely support in the north of Madhya Bharat, Hindu nationalists were well implanted in the south (Malwa) – L.N. Pandey at Mandsaur, R.C. Bade at Khargone and P.C. Verma at Ujjain.

These developments gave the impression that while the Jana Sangh's identification with the princely network had enabled it to impose itself in areas where princely influence remained strong, this same factor had hindered it from widening it social base where the princes had lost their foothold and the populism of Congress had attracted a significant number of votes. In fact, certain princes were defeated (Bhanu Prakash Singh at Bhopal and the Rajmata of Saraipali at Mahasamund), and in Chhattisgarh, as in Mahakoshal, the Jana Sangh lost several of the bridgeheads which it had built in those constituencies reserved for Scheduled Castes, like Sagar.

In 1972 the Jana Sangh perservered with this paradoxical strategy. In July 1971, Madhav Rao Scindia had been nominated to the Jana Sangh's Central Working Committee.[79] He allegedly obtained a promise from the Maharajah of Rewa to support Jana Sangh candidates.[80] But the party was soon to discover that the backing of the princes had its disadvantages, for once their privileges and purses had been abolished, their interest in backing the opposition evaporated and they returned to where power lay. Thus the Maharajah of Rewa finally opted for Congress, eight of whose candidates he supported in Vindhya Pradesh during the Assembly elections;[81] in Rajasthan the Maharana of Udaipur decided to end his support for the Jana Sangh against Gayatri Devi, who was determined to develop the Swatantra Party; and, above all, the Maharajah of Kota went back to

[77] *Link*, 7 March 1971, p. 20.

[78] *National Herald*, 18 Feb. 1971, and *Hindustan Times*, 31 Jan. 1971.

[79] *Motherland*, 6 July 1971, p. 1.

[80] Ibid., 5 Dec. 1971, p. 21.

[81] Ibid., 20 Feb. 1972.

Congress in exchange for a promise of favourable treatment, which helped the government party to win the 16 seats within that zone in the Assembly elections of 1972.[82]

The Jana Sangh leadership was now able to calculate the risks inherent in its reliance on princes. In Madhya Pradesh this belated realisation prompted an energetic return to the Sangathanist technique of social work at the grassroots, notably with a campaign against the nationalisation of forest production, which penalised Adivasis especially. Thakre himself led a demonstration in Delhi against the measure,[83] and the agitation was to have an effect on the electoral map of Madhya Pradesh in 1972: it was throughout the constituencies reserved for tribals that the party implanted itself in the very heart of Mahakoshal, which it had already penetrated by the same tactical means at Betul, namely by work at the grassroots. It managed to make a strong showing in Mandla district, where it won two of the five seats reserved for tribals.[84] In Chhattisgarh, the Jana Sangh established a presence based on the support of the Maharajah of Jashpur in Raigarh district and the success of the agitation led by Larang Sai, the re-elected MLA for Samri (Surguja). In Raigarh and Surguja districts the Jana Sangh retained five of the 11 seats reserved for tribals.[85]

These rare victories were mainly the result of strenuous local activism, and where such work had not been done the 'appeal to the masses' of Indira Gandhi's Congress proved invincible. At Bhopal, during one of her election tours, she denounced the 'archaic princely order'[86] on which the Jana Sangh, incapable of promoting the cause of the poor, had to depend. Such rhetoric proved very effective.

In Madhya Bharat Congress won 50 seats, compared with 22 in 1967. The Jana Sangh's candidates were all beaten in Mandsaur district;[87] in Dewas and Shajapur districts only Kailash Joshi – who became leader of the opposition in the Vidhan Sabha – and Haribhau Joshi succeeded in getting elected. In all, the Jana Sangh won only 8 seats in the Malwa and Bhopal area (compared to 12 in 1967). By contrast, the Scindias' influence in the Gwalior area helped it to win 21 seats, 5 going to *swayamsevaks* and the others to notables in the Scindia network such as a former landlord, Mahendra Singh, of

[82] K. Bhargava, ' Rajasthan politics and princely rulers', op. cit., pp. 428-9.

[83] *Motherland*, 23 Feb. 1972, p. 7.

[84] Ibid., 13 June 1972, p. 1, and Ashfaq Ali, *Bhopal past and present*, op. cit., p. 365.

[85] The rest of its gains in Chhattisgarh, other than those it had merely confirmed at Bilaspur and Raipur, were accomplished mainly in Tribal constituencies, as in Bastar district where the party received the support of Adivasi leaders like Baliram Kashyap, who had been elected MLA for Jagdalpur.

[86] *Statesman Weekly*, 11 March 1972, p. 5.

[87] Sakhlecha then obtained a Rajya Sabha seat.

Kalukheda[88] in Ashok Nagar, a constituency in Guna district (see Appendix F, p. 556). However, even in the region of Gwalior the Rajmata's personal network was not enough to guarantee systematic electoral success. In 11 of the 31 constituencies, victory went to Congress in alliance with the Communists. In each case candidates from backward castes or the working class were elected: in Sabalgarh, Joura, Attair, Bhind, Dabra and Seondha Thakurs, or candidates sponsored by the princes, like Yashwant Singh Kushwaha, were defeated by such rivals. In the working-class constituency of Gwalior, Jagdish Prasad Gupta, who had backing from the Scindias, lost to a Communist, a scenario repeated in identical fashion in the other industrial centres of Madhya Bharat such as Indore and Bhopal. This tendency was emphasised in the by-election at Gird in June 1972. It had been brought about by the resignation of the Rajmata Scindia who faced with the choice of sitting in either of the two houses, preferred the Lok Sabha; her Jana Sangh candidate was defeated by a Communist who had worked for thirty-five years among the peasants, whose support proved decisive.[89] The victory of the people's candidate over that of the 'palace' was the abiding image of this contest. Nor must one forget that it happened after the passing of a law establishing a ceiling of 10 acres on landholdings owned by individuals and 15 acres on those owned by families of five individuals, a measure which Congress had promised before the elections and was supported by the CPI.[90]

Thus, in 1972, the Jana Sangh found itself dependent on princes whose patronage it had sought to accelerate its growth not only in Madhya Bharat (with the Scindias) but also in Vindhya Pradesh, where the party relied increasingly on the Maharajah of Panna and lesser *rajahs* like Yadavendra Singh at Bijawar to maintain its presence.[91] However, this princely support did not compensate for the growing attraction of the Congress (R), especially among the poor. Scheduled Caste leaders in Vindhya Pradesh and Sagar, for example, seemed to have deserted the Jana Sangh.

The Jana Sangh in Madhya Pradesh found its total number of seats reduced to 48 despite an infinitesimal increase – from 28.28 to 28.72% – in its share of the votes cast. This reverse was repeated in all the states and territories of the Union where polls took place in 1972, including Delhi, where the Jana Sangh barely succeeded in enlarging its base.[92] Soon after

[88] Mahendra Singh was the Scindias' secretary for parliamentary affairs (*Madhya Pradesh Vidha Sabha sadasyon ka sankshipt parichay – 1972*, Bhopal: Madhya Pradesh Vidhan Sabha sachivalay, 1972, p. 121).

[89] *Link*, 18 June 1972, p. 28.

[90] *Statesman Weekly*, 22 April 1972, p. 7.

[91] *Motherland*, 23 Feb. 1972, p. 7.

[92] One study revealed that the Jana Sangh vote was largely the result of a massive turnout at one polling station of well-educated voters and businessmen (R. Chandidas, 'Elections

the municipal election, S.P. Sumnaskar, who had been returned to Alipur, a key rural constituency reserved for Scheduled Castes, left the party with three other low caste municipal councillors after denouncing the 'alliance of the Punjabis and the Banyas'.[93] The Jana Sangh's greatest loss – of a large part of the Punjabi electorate, which transferred its vote to Congress – was probably due to the Bangladesh war. The refugees who had previously voted for the Jana Sangh were now finding in Indira Gandhi a Prime Minister prepared to deal firmly with Pakistan.[94]

The electoral strategy emphasising populist and nationalist themes which the Jana Sangh adopted at the beginning of the 1970s was largely a compromise between the demands of the local cadres – who were worried by the dilution of the party's identity since the late 1960s – and the aspirations of the leadership to join mainstream politics. It was also a response to the need to project the Hindu nationalist movement as being one that respected the Constitution. The vigilant secularism displayed by the government strengthened the conviction among the Jana Sangh's leaders that resorting to techniques of ethno-religious mobilisation was not only largely ineffective in terms of electoral mobilisation but also completely impractical. By contrast, populist and nationalist arguments were quite legitimate, and capable of attracting numerous voters. The parameters (or constraints) of the political context and local party network largely conditioned the Jana Sangh's electoral strategy.

In 1971–2, three internal contradictions brought about the failure of this strategy. The Jana Sangh was laying claim to the same populist and nationalist themes which Indira Gandhi had already begun to build up into a dominant political culture, one that almost amounted to a new norm of Indian politics. In thus copying its own approach from that of the party in power, the Jana Sangh effectively prevented itself from capitalising on its own distinctiveness and competed against a ruling party which was much more adept than it could be at using populist appeals. This contradiction first emerged at the 1969 meeting in Patna, at which Vajpayee, with no little embarrassment, tried to explain that 'no one can have any quarrel with socialism's concern for the underdog or its insistence on social justice and equity', while criticising the socialism of Indira Gandhi for its statism.[95] Such a nuance was difficult to put across to party activists in the election campaign and, more importantly, was unlikely to prove

---

to Delhi Municipal Metropolitan Council', *EPW*, 28 June 1975, p. 970).

[93] Cited in G. Puri, *Bharatiya Jana Sangh*, op. cit., p. 57.

[94] *The Hindu*, 18 March 1972.

[95] Ibid., 3 Jan. 1970, p. 10.

convincing to the poor in question; thus the Jana Sangh had condemned itself to act as a populist understudy to the Congress without the means of competing with it. All this made it seem as if the party had tried to integrate itself with the political régime in too radical a fashion by adjusting its programme to that of the dominant party.[96]

Nor had the Jana Sangh trimmed its party-building strategy in accordance with this electoral strategy in so far as it continued to look for support among a growing number of princes and notables, although the vote banks the latter were capable of delivering had in many cases been reduced by Indira Gandhi's tactics. This contradiction was all the more plain since the Jana Sangh had allied itself with another conservative force, the Congress (O), which had dominated the opposition since 1969.[97]

The electoral and implantation strategies of the Jana Sangh were not only virtually contradictory; they were also contrary to the ideology and interests of the Sangathanist network, which was the effective base of the party and had denounced electoralism and populist over-bidding. At a meeting of the AIGC in November 1971, one delegate rejected the way the party had gone in for 'a sort of competition with the Congress in radicalism', while another criticised populism as an 'electoral expedient', and a third suggested that 'if the idea was to outdo the other parties, the Jana Sangh has only to raise the slogan of total nationalisation .[98] Yet the party cadres were worried by the conservatism of the notables whom the party leaders had gathered around them, and by the Grand Alliance.[99] Although he tried to justify this policy, Vajpayee admitted that the 'defeat in the elections had deeply disappointed party workers' and that they were 'asking themselves whether the party would have been in a better position if it had not entered into an alliance.'[100] The Grand Alliance was rejected after the 1971 elections when the AIGC delegates decided in July that the party would fight the 1972 elections on its own.[101]

---

[96] At the AIGC meeting in Bhagalpur that marked a first move towards activism, Vajpayee declared: 'We go from here to fight, fight and fight. [...] We are going neither right or left. We are certainly going forward, *adjusting ourselves to the time and the demands of the time'* (emphasis added, ibid., 13 May 1972, p. 6).

[97] The contradiction became very apparent at the AIGC meeting in July 1970 which radicalised the social programme of the Jana Sangh while pronouncing in favour of the Grand Alliance formula of the Congress (O) (*Statesman Weekly*, 25 July 1970, p. 6).

[98] *Motherland*, 28 Nov. 1971, p. 2.

[99] *New Age*, 31 Jan. 1971, p. 5.

[100] Interview in J.P. Mathur (ed.), *Jana-Deep souvenir*, Delhi: Rakesh Press, 1971, p. 2.

[101] In Madhya Pradesh, the Jana Sangh found itself competing against opposition parties – Swatantra Party, Congress (O) and the Socialists – in 130 constituencies. This did not affect its tally of seats in 110 cases, where the party had no chance of winning, but deprived it of victory in some 20, if we admit that the percentage of votes polled by the other parties would have gone to it if electoral pacts had been in place.

The defeat that occurred while this consultation was taking place was attributed by the delegates to the conservative image which the party still retained, a manifestation not of populism but of the inherent and long-standing tendency of the Sangathanist network to look at problems at the grassroots level with a view to promoting a RSS style of social reform. The 190 interviews conducted by Andersen between 1968 and 1971 confirmed this social profile. For example, a reduction in income differentials was almost unanimously considered to be a priority, so as 'harmoniously' to strengthen the nation irrespective of considerations of social class.[102]

The local cadres thus once again instigated a reshaping of political strategy by the Jana Sangh's leadership, in a move which was in tune with the RSS's wishes.[103] Its electoral reverses made the Jana Sangh leadership more sensitive to recommendations from its grassroots. It even brought about a certain rejection of the parliamentary system: the simple majority voting system had deprived the party of the representation to which it considered itself entitled on the basis of its shares of the vote and postponed its possible accession to power to the very distant future. After the 1972 election, the Jana Sangh concentrated on demanding electoral reform.

Thus, discouraged in its efforts at integration within the institutional system and anxious to find itself in step once again with its network of cadres and the RSS, the leaders of the Jana Sangh set about redefining its populist tactic in favour of activism. At a future date this would enable it to return to the strategy of integration, albeit within the 'JP movement', an alliance that would be directed against the institutional system and based on an activist ideology in accord with RSS principles.

---

[102] W. Andersen and S. Damle, *The brotherhood in saffron*, op. cit., p. 195. Furthermore, 72% of the Jana Sanghis interviewed considered strikes to be legitimate.

[103] In 1973, Golwalkar turned his efforts towards the ABVP and the BMS, both of which participated in a strike, together with other labour unions and the Communists, against the state-owned insurance companies.

7

THE HINDU NATIONALISTS IN THE 'J.P. MOVEMENT'

'Bihar movement and RSS's work are fundamentally the same. [...] Both are aimed at complete change in the entire society through a process of evolution of thoughts and actions of the people for the betterment of the whole nation' (speech by 'JP' to *swayamsevaks* at a training camp in Calicut in May 1975).[1]

In 1972 the government's inability to carry out its promises and confront the economic crisis led to a rapid fall in its popularity.[2] In such a social and political context, the time was propitious for a reorientation of the Jana Sangh's populist tactic along activist lines. Activism had already been adopted by a growing number of opposition movements ready to provide an outlet for the effervescence in society or indeed to stimulate it further. The Jana Sangh's desire to gain admission to mainstream politics without betraying the identity it had inherited from the RSS began to take solid form from 1974, when its particular populist-activist strategy converged with that of the Gandhian movement of Jaya Prakash Narayan (known as 'JP') who shared with the Hindu nationalists their concern for political decentralisation and reshaping society.

The integration of the Jana Sangh in the legitimate opposition was accelerated when the government's attempt to curb the 'JP movement' culminated in the imposition of a state of emergency. Many opposition leaders were imprisoned under the emergency, and the Jana Sanghis among them found themselves coming to terms with some of their former rivals.

The activist turn: the Jana Sangh leadership, its local cadres and the RSS back in step

In 1973 Madhok's departure gave supporters of the populist option and

[1] *National Herald*, 18 May 1975; and *Organiser*, 24 May 1975.

[2] Agrarian reform remained very incomplete and the rhythm of price increases continued to accelerate (30% in 1973-4 compared to 13% in 1972-3 (F. Frankel, *India's political economy, 1947-1977*, op. cit., pp. 493-5 and 506-15).

its intensification through activism greater room for manoeuvre. This was reflected in the principal resolution passed at the Kanpur meeting in February 1973:

The BJS today resolved to organise mass unrest and to lead the struggle on the economic and social fronts for all aggrieved sections of the society.[3]

This move towards agitational methods was expressed in numerous *satyagrahas* – for example, against the rise in prices and on behalf of the Scheduled Castes.[4] Agitation over socio-economic issues became the party's permanent mode of operation. In Madhya Pradesh, 2,500 Jana Sanghis broke into the precinct of the Vidhan Sabha to protest against the tax increases which were expected to feature in the budget then being discussed in the assembly;[5] in Rajasthan, demonstrations against unemployment and inflation had to be put down by the police in Jaipur and Jodhpur;[6] in Maharashtra, 10,000 Jana Sanghis blocked buses in protest at a rise in fares;[7] and in Delhi a similar number demonstrated against a fare increase on the railways.[8]

These are only a few examples of the mobilisation of the Jana Sangh, which became adept at organising street protests in 1972-3. The importance of its agitation was based on the strength of its network of activists who favoured this kind of approach. The policy was probably launched in conjunction with the RSS or even on the initiative of its leadership, given the personality of the new *sarsanghchalak*.

Golwalkar died in 1973 but had already – according to RSS tradition if not its constitution – designated as his successor Balasaheb Deoras.[9] The profile of this *swayamsevak*, a disciple of Hedgewar, was classic: a Maharashtrian Brahmin, he had obtained his LL B at the University of Nagpur and became RSS secretary in the town before being sent to Bengal as a *pracharak*. He later returned to the headquarters of the movement from where he directed the publication of *Tarun Bharat* (a Marathi daily founded by N.B. Khare before Independence and subsequently acquired by the RSS) and *Yugadharma* (a Hindi-daily belonging to a publishing house of the RSS).[10] In 1965 he succeeded P.B. Dani as General Secretary of the RSS and played his part promoting activism in the movement. Then,

---

[3]   Organiser, 17 Feb. 1973, p. 4.
[4]   *Motherland*, 14, 17, 19 Aug. 1972.
[5]   Ibid., 5 Aug. 1972, p. 1.
[6]   Ibid., 14 and 16 Nov. 1972, pp. 4 and 8.
[7]   *Organiser*, 14 Oct. 1972, p. 10.
[8]   *Motherland*, 9 March 1973, p. 3.
[9]   Ibid., 10 June 1973.
[10] Ibid., 26 March 1971, p. 5; and *Organiser*, 23 June 1973.

as Golwalkar's health declined, he began to take on an increasingly prominent role. Since 1948-9, Deoras had been the archetypal RSS activist, in contrast to Muley, the other possible successor, who became General Secretary on Golwalkar's death.

His personal experience had already found expression in Deoras's interest in politics.[11] In 1965 he had even set a precedent by addressing the annual conference of the Jana Sangh.[12] However, the activism of the new *sarsanghchalak* was already tinged with populism, a tendency that grew out of his wish to speed up RSS penetration of the whole body of society by combining the Sangathanist method with propaganda of a kind that could rally whole sections of public opinion *en bloc*. Hitherto Hedgewar and Golwalkar had promoted the view that the long-term priority for the RSS was essentially to work in close touch with society while shunning publicity; this now had to be amended.[13] The change of emphasis was behind the following resolution on social movements, passed by the ABPS in March 1974 – the first since the arrival of Deoras at the head of the RSS:

It cannot be denied that the masses have risen in revolt for having been hard put to meet their primary necessities of life – a situation arising out of rampant corruption and wrong and unrealistic policies pursued by the Central and State Governments under the garb of progressiveness. [....]

The RSS believes that the present atmosphere of all-round corruption and selfishness can be cleansed only by the generation of a pure stream of patriotism. Having directed all its energies to that end, the Sangh hereby extends its cooperation to every such effort from any direction.

The ABPS is confident that the Swayamsevaks of Sangh will not be unduly ruffled by any such baseless charges or threats of ban. They will continue to fortify the faith of the people in RSS through their conduct and close contacts with them. [....] For the people are with the Sangh and the Sangh stands by them.[14]

It was in this context that the RSS and the Jana Sangh came to participate in the 'JP movement'. Their mutual involvement relaunched the strategy of integration, allowing Hindu nationalists to be associated with a well-known leader and a popular movement, and at the same time bringing the Jana Sangh and the RSS closer together in activist-populist work. Furthermore, this participation was not solely opportunistic: the coalescence of veteran Gandhians like 'JP and *swayamsevaks* was in keeping with the reformist aspect of their respective ideologies.

---

11   W. Andersen and S. Damle, *The brotherhood in saffron*, op. cit., p. 114.
12   Ibid., p. 209.
13   Ibid., p. 115.
14   *RSS resolves*, op. cit., pp. 76-8.

The political convergence of social reformers

Strictly speaking, the 'JP movement' marked the culmination of a phase of socio-political agitation that was first manifested in Gujarat. This state was suffering the effects of a sharp economic crisis and a particularly corrupt leadership with the result that, in January 1974, there occurred a popular uprising, in which the main protagonists were students. The RSS's student wing, the ABVP played an active role and tried to link the students' agitation with the campaign organised by the Jana Sangh against price rises.[15] The agitation spread to Bihar in the form of a 'JP movement' that quickly gained momentum.

In Bihar, too, students spearheaded the agitation, but the ABVP found itself more obviously in the front line than it had been in Gujarat. In December 1973, the executive committee of the Bihar ABVP, meeting in Dhanbad, had decided to launch a Gujarat-style agitation along with the Socialists' Youth Wing.[16] This led to the formation of a Chhatra Sangharsh Samiti (Student Committee for Struggle) in Patna on 17 February 1974, its plan of action being concerned with the living conditions of students as much as with the development of 'Bharatiya education.' The Samiti included in its membership representatives not only of the ABVP but also of the Socialist fold and the Congress (O). Nevertheless, according to G. Ostergaard, 'the CSS had its origin in the successful move, inspired by the ABVP [...] to challenge the influence of the Students' Federation of India, a body associated with the CPI.'[17] The Communists in Bihar tried to establish a rival committee, the Chhatra Yuva Sangharsh Morcha (Battle Front of Student Youth), but the Chhatra Sangharsh Samiti had the benefit of the ABVP's infrastructure, which had made great strides in the state since 1972 when it had won over the CPI's All India Students' Federation on many campuses. Full-time organisers had been appointed, like Ram Bahadur Rai and Lal Muni Choubey, who were both expelled from the Benares Hindu University in 1972 because of their activism, especially the campaign against the central government-sponsored plan to give BHU a more secular name.[18]

The RSS network was deeply involved in this particular student movement. K.N. Govindacharya, who before becoming an RSS

---

[15] G. Shah, *Protest movements in two Indian states – A study of the Gujarat and Bihar movements*, Delhi: Ajanta, 1977, pp. 32ff.

[16] P.C. Sahasrabuddhe and M.C. Vajpayee, *The people versus the Emergency: a saga of struggle*, New Delhi: Suruchi Prakashan, 1991, p. 67.

[17] G. Ostergaard, *Non-violent revolution in India*, New Delhi: Gandhi Peace Foundation, 1985, pp. 92-3. This interpretation is corroborated by G. Shah, *Protest movements*, op. cit., p. 87.

[18] I am grateful to Anand Kumar, a student leader from the BHU and then convenor of the 'JP movement' in Jawaharlal Nehru University, for this information.

pracharak in 1965 had gained a   M. Sc. in mathematics at BHU, was the *pracharak* of Patna.[19] He had personally overseen the development of the ABVP (by the beginning of 1974 it had a presence in every district of the state) and was one of the instigators of the Chhatra Sangharsh Samiti.[20]

On 18 March 1974 the last-named organisation staged a *gherao* in front of the Vidhan Sabha in Patna in order to bring about its dissolution and the resignation of a government widely believed to be corrupt. The agitation mobilised a crowd of about 10,000 and was put down with the utmost severity: twenty-two people were killed and a curfew was imposed. The next day, Govindacharya – and later a delegation of the Chhatra Sangharsh Samiti, including members of Congress (O), the Socialist Party (which had come into being in 1971 after the fusion of the SSP and the PSP) and the ABVP – went to request the support of 'JP',[21] one of the most prominent Bihari personalities of the time.

'JP' had been a Socialist from the start – in 1934 he was one of the founders of the Congress Socialist Party and then, in 1944, of the Socialist Party itself. He was also a veteran of the Independence movement, having led a guerrilla action in 1942 as part of the 'Quit India' movement. In 1954 he renounced political action to join Vinoba Bhave in the Sarvodaya movement in his native Bihar. This movement, represented principally by the Sarva Seva Sangh (Association for the Service of All), had failed to redistribute more than a marginal amount of land.[22] 'JP' had come to believe that the Gandhians had finally been marginalised by the 'Nehru dynasty', which had been won over to the industrialising option and an ever-greater centralisation of power.[23] From the end of the 1960s, this state of affairs fuelled criticism of the apolitical stance of Vinoba Bhave as part of a whole current of opinion within the Sarva Seva Sangh, for which 'JP' had to some extent been a spokesman.[24] If in March 1974, at the age of seventy-two, he agreed to return on to the political scene, it was because

---

[19] For biographical details, see S. Gupta, 'The face the BJP needs to present', *The Independent*, 9 Feb. 1994, p. 6 and *Times of India*, 1 May 1991.

[20] Interview with Govindacharya, 19 Nov. 1990, New Delhi.

[21] Article by 'JP' in *Everyman's* (30 March 1974) in J. Narayan, *Towards total revolution*, vol. 4, Bombay: Popular Prakashan, 1978, p. 50.

[22] For a critical assessment, see Mohan Ram, 'The Sarvodaya farce', *EPW*, 3 May 1975, p. 720.

[23] See the article by 'JP' in *Everyman's* (19 Jan. 1975) in J. Narayan, *Towards total revolution*, vol. 4, op. cit., p. 119. He later stated: 'Nehru made the sad mistake of assuming that a new India could be created merely through the power and resources of the State' (interview with Brahmanand, 27 June 1976, in ibid., p. 180).

[24] G. Ostergaard, *Non-violent revolution*, op. cit., ch. 2. 'JP' himself decided to rein in the Sarvodaya movement. See his article in *Everyman's* (13 July 1974) in J. Narayan, *Towards total revolution*, vol. 4, op. cit., p. 78.

he had seen in the student movements in Gujarat and Bihar a chance to rehabilitate certain Gandhian priorities.

At first 'JP' was reluctant to agree to ally himself with the Chhatra Sangharsh Samiti, because of the propensity of students to resort to violence. The Tarun Shanti Sena (Youth Peace Force), the Sarvodaya movement's youth organisation, was represented on the CSS. It had worked hard to ensure that the 18 March demonstration went off peacefully but its efforts had largely failed. However, on 23 March the CSS organised a 'Bihar Bandh' (a suspension of all activity in the state) in protest against the curfew. It received strong support and passed off peacefully. 'JP' associated himself with the demand for the lifting of the curfew and announced that he would defy it on 29 March if it had not been lifted by that date. It was in fact lifted on the 28th, but many students and Sarvodaya movement activists were arrested. Around that time 'JP' agreed to 'direct and guide' the student movement. On 8 April he led a silent march at Patna which was an impressive display of non-violent protest.[25]

'JP' wanted to create a non-partisan, value-based opposition to the government but he could not help but accept the support of the Socialists and the Hindu nationalists. The latter tended to dominate the governing body of the Chhatra Sangharsh Samiti (CSS): one-third of its 24 members belonged to the ABVP, 4 were Socialists, 2 were from the Tarun Shanti Sena and 2 from the Congress (O). The headquarters of the Bihar CSS was located in the TSS's building in Patna but at the local level, 'where there were no offices, the residence of a prominent political leader, usually of the Jana Sangh, was used as a meeting place by the CSS leaders.'[26] G. Shah goes on to say that:

The ABVP dominated the CSS at many places, and at some places RSS workers were either office-bearers of the CSS or guided the members of the CSS. RSS members worked as volunteers in processions and at JP meetings. [...] ABVP maintained its office as centre of activities, and made attempts to recruit boys from the movement.[27]

'JP' would later acknowledge the preponderance of politically affiliated activists in his movement. But he justified it by saying that, first, he had not started the movement; second, that 'it is just not possible to keep political parties from coming into an open mass movement'; and third, that it could be regarded as a positive development because, in this case, the parties had 'undergo[ne] a sea-change in the process'.[28] As far

---

[25] G. Ostegaard, *Non-violent revolution*, op. cit., pp. 75-6.

[26] G. Shah, *Protest movements*, op. cit., p. 97.

[27] Ibid., p. 131.

[28] J. Narayan, *Prison diary*, Bombay: Popular Prakashan, 1977, pp. 56-8.

as the Hindu nationalists were concerned, he was probably willing to let them develop their ideology of social reform, which had some similarities to his own. Indeed, while the collaboration between 'JP' and the RSS and its affiliates in the Bihar movement was primarily due to the Hindu nationalists' search for a leader capable of integrating them in legitimate politics, such a rapprochement would not have been possible without some previous affinities, on the basis of which 'JP' could hope to change the Hindu nationalists' programme.

The RSS and the leaders of the Sarvodaya movement in Bihar and eastern Uttar Pradesh had already been in contact with each other for a long time.[29] This was probably accounted for by the RSS's decision to support the Sarvodaya movement in Uttar Pradesh,[30] which 'JP' later joined. Nana Deshmukh – a key Hindu nationalist figure in Uttar Pradesh – had taken part in the *bhoodan* programme of the Sarvodaya movement in 1953.[31] According to Deshmukh, their differences of outlook at that time were quite obvious, but they found more in common during the 1962 war with China when they

[...]addressed together common meetings to arouse the people against the aggression and to cooperate with the government. After 1962 we were not working together but discussed often about rural development. I used to go to his projects. He also used to see my things.[32]

In 1967, 'JP' and the RSS collaborated in relief work for drought victims in Bihar.[33] On 5 June 1973, 'JP' presided at a mourning ceremony in memory of Golwalkar, and in January 1974 Govindacharya allegedly took part in a meeting of the Tarun Shanti Sena in his capacity as a member of the RSS.[34] One of the reasons for the rapprochement between 'JP' and

---

29 In May 1952, 'JP' had already shown himself well-disposed towards the RSS, which he dissociated from the communalist parties: 'With such parties who are given to politics by religion we can have no truck and our policy of uncompromising opposition to them must be pursued vigorously. But towards the frustrated youth of the Rashtriya Swayamsevak Sangh we may well have a sympathetic attitude. The young boys and girls who belong to the RSS are all drawn from the lower middle classes. They are a disciplined lot. If in this hour of their frustration and disillusionment the Socialist Party can hold forth an effective alternative to them it may be possible to win over the best of them.' (J. Narayan, *Towards total revolution*, vol. 2, Bombay: Popular Prakashan, 1978, p. 166)

30 *Hitavada*, 31 May 1952, p. 4. Golwalkar had already invited some *swayamsevaks* to take part in V. Bhave's movement in 1949 (W. Andersen and S. Damle, *The brotherhood in saffron*, op. cit., p. 111).

31 Deshmukh and 'JP' had come into contact in 1946 in Gorakhpur, then the headquarters of the North Eastern Railways; 'JP' had visited the town as chairman of a railway trade union and Deshmukh had been the RSS *pracharak* there since 1940.

32 Interview with N. Deshmukh, 25 Feb. 1994, New Delhi.

33 'JP' had inaugurated an RSS relief centre (*Organiser*, 26 Feb. 1967, p. 5).

34 Interview with Govindacharya.

the Hindu nationalists in 1974 was because they regarded social reform as a priority in comparison with work within the political arena. 'JP' assumed that policies to promote social welfare were justified on purely humanitarian grounds whereas the Hindu nationalists saw such policies as serving the ultimate aim of endowing Hindu society with a new ideology; but despite this important difference of outlook they were agreed on the immediate desirability of particular social welfare projects. This principle reflected the primacy of society vis-a-vis the state expressed through a constant emphasis on decentralisation.[35]

The catchphrase which 'JP' popularised some time after taking charge of the agitation was 'total revolution'. This refers to a complete reform of society inspired by Gandhi's ideals:[36] the abolition of Untouchability and cast and, above all, an institutional transformation to make possible the primacy of society over the state, through the rehabiliation of politics at the local level:

What you see happening in Bihar is a struggle between 'chhatra shakti' [student power] and 'jan shakti' [people's power] on the one hand and 'rajya shakti' [state power] on the other. And the struggle is not for the capture of power, in other words, for replacing the Congress government with the opposition, but for purification of government and politics, including those of the opposition and for fashioning instruments and conditions for taming and controlling power, irrespective of which party or parties happen to be in power for the time being. Secondly it is for removal of corruption from other fields of social life, such as business [black-marketeering, hoarding, etc.] industry, education, and lastly but most important of all, it is for basic social, economic, political, cultural and educational changes. [....] In this revolutionary process governments and political parties will certainly play a role but the main moving force will be the direct action of the youths and the people.[37]

35   Advani wrote on this theme in 1970: 'Our plea for a unitary set-up has [...] been widely misunderstood, and sometimes even misrepresented, as being the advocacy of a stronger centre. This is *not* correct. We are fully alive to the fact that in essence our Constitution is already unitary, that it has armed the Centre with powers unimaginable in any proper federation, and that any abridgement of the authority presently vested in the provincial units would seriously impair the functioning of responsible government in these units. Therefore, far from suggesting any curtailment of the powers of the states we feel that there is need of enlargement of these powers, particularly in financial matters' (*Organiser*, 15 Aug. 1970, p.9). See also the Jana Sangh's election manifesto of 1971 ('Manifesto – 1971' in *Party documents*, vol. 1, op. cit., p. 177).

36   For example he designated the week beginning 24 April as 'People's awakening week': 'This movement to be successful must lead to a moral revolution in the State. [...] An interesting feature of the week will be that sons and daughters of corrupt persons including ministers, officers, businessmen and big farmer hoarders will observe a 12-hour fast in their homes to impress upon their elders that they must end corrupt and anti-social practices.' (Article by 'JP' in Everyman's, 27 April 1974, in J. Narayan, *Towards total revolution*, vol. 4, op. cit., p. 62.)

Such words were likely to interest the RSS, whose method, if not its spirit, was compatible with the scheme of action set out by 'JP'. His desire to strengthen civil society through local initiatives was expressed in the importance he accorded to agricultural development based on a peasantry of smallholders, his emphasis on family enterprises and the priority of decentralisation itself.[38] This programme explicitly followed the Gandhian logic of the village-republic, which already lay at the heart of the Sarvodaya movement and to which he wanted to give concrete form.[39] To this end he advocated the establishment of Janata Sarkars, 'governments of the people', which would exist at the *panchayat* level in Bihar as 'parallel centres' of power – decentralised in the truest sense.[40]

The affinities between 'JP' and the RSS led Richard Fox to analyse the presence of Hindu nationalists in the Bihar movement as not so much 'opportunistic' as the fruit of 'a real conjunction [...] in terms of certain common cultural convictions and political practice.'[41] Deoras was also anxious to acknowledge the existence of a very gratifying kinship between Gandhi and the RSS, which nonetheless expressed only one dimension of the Mahatma's ideals, and at a subordinate level. The *sarsanghchalak*, who was acquiring an increasingly high public profile, declared in December 1974 that 'Sri Jayaprakash [was] fulfilling the mission of noble leaders like Mahatma Gandhi, Acharya Vinoba Bhave, and Guruji Golwalkar because, following in their image, He is like sannyasis of old who remained aloof and yet did not hesitate to lead the people when the rulers went astray.'[42]

The figure of Gandhi was invoked here for tactical reasons, certainly, on account of his fame, but also because he represented a political tradition that was presented as genuinely indigenous: in this tutelary figure the RSS and 'JP' found a symbolic resource to oppose modernism

---

[38] For more details, cf. ibid., p. 113.

[39] Article by 'JP' in *Everyman's* (22 Dec. 1974) in ibid., p. 116. 'JP' called for the formation of non-partisan Jana Sangharsh Samitis (People's Struggle Committees) which, acting at the local level, would unanimously elect representatives to the Vidhan Sabhas to act as guardians of democracy (article by 'JP' in *Everyman's*, 25 May 1974, in ibid., p. 69).

[40] *Hindustan Times*, 13 and 24 Jan. 1975; *Indian Nation*, 11 Feb. 1975; interview with 'JP' in *Economic Times* (10 May 1975) in J. Narayan, *Towards total revolution*, vol. 4, op. cit, p. 155; and article by 'JP' in *The Sunday Standard* (11 May 1975) in ibid., p. 170. 'JP' also declared himself in favour of a system of local administration consisting of three levels: at the bottom, a 'community' consisting of 100 families; above it, the neighbourhood; and, at the top, the local 'municipality'. This three-tier arrangement should also operate at the level of economic production units ('Total revolution – some clarifications' in ibid., p. 195).

[41] R.G. Fox, 'Gandhian socialism and Hindu nationalism: cultural domination in the world system', *Journal of Commonwealth and Comparative Politics*, 25, 3 (Nov. 1987), p. 238.

[42] *Organiser*, 7 Dec. 1974, p. 1.

imported from abroad. 'JP' also argued that the revival of interest in Gandhi's ideas was

[...] largely due to the disenchantment that has spread over the past years with so-called socialist planning and policy-making and programming. As this disenchantment deepens, more and more of our intellectuals who had their hands [*sic*] in the clouds of America and Russia until now, will become conscious of their own skies under which they live.[43]

The area of ideological overlapping between the RSS and 'JP' came to be articulated around the theme of Indian-style decentralisation, involving cottage industries and the *panchayat* system – directed against the modernisation which had been promoted first by Nehru and then by his daughter.

However, these affinities did not conceal the numerous points of divergence in the realm of ideas as well as over a strategy for converting these ideals into action.[44] The Hindu nationalist activists disapproved of the socialist references with which the speeches of 'JP' abounded and which amounted at times to criticising the 'conservative' parties, including the Jana Sangh.[45] In order to force the MLAs to resign, the ABVP activists participating in the Chhatra Sangharsh Samiti willingly gave a boost to coercive methods (such as the *gherao*) which, in the eyes of 'JP', betrayed the ideal of non-violence.[46] And finally 'JP' did not subscribe to the more political aspects of the students' claims, notably their demand for the resignation of the state government; in fact he even tried to dissuade the student leaders – the most prominent of whom were Hindu nationalists – from explicit political affiliations.[47] It was this original divergence of opinion that was to prove the most serious.[48]

These tensions meanwhile tended to become reabsorbed in action. The

---

[43]   Interview with 'JP' (*Hindustan Times*, 26 Aug. 1974) in J. Narayan, *Towards total revolution*, vol. 4, op. cit., p. 94. In another interview he declared: 'I think Bihar and all other states suffered from Mr Nehru's giganticism. Build the largest dam, build the largest this, largest that. [...] Bihar is one state where there are several heavy industries. But I think Bihar needs much more widely spread small-scale industries' (interview with *The Economic Times*, 10 May 1975, in ibid., p. 153).

[44]   According to Advani: 'The bond between "JP" and the Jana Sangh was not ideology, it was idealism. Ideologically we might not agree. But the mutual respect that we had come to develop for each other was because "JP" accepted that the Jana Sangh was in politics for the seeking of certain ideals, it was not a power-oriented party as the others were, (interview with L.K. Advani).

[45]   Interview with K.N. Govindacharya and article by 'JP' in *Everyman's*, 3 Aug. 1974, in J. Narayan, *Towards total revolution*, vol. 4, op. cit., p. 96-7.

[46]   Article by 'JP' in *Everyman's* (27 April 1974) in ibid., p. 60.

[47]   In April 1974, 'JP' called in participants in the movement to adopt a 'non-partisan spirit' (article by 'JP' in *Everyman's* 27 April 1974, in ibid., p. 59).

[48]   Interview with K.N. Govindacharya.

two sides had a shared interest in emphasising their points of agreement rather than their differences – the Hindu nationalists in order to profit from the patronage of an eminent leader and 'JP' to benefit from the network offered by the Hindu nationalists (according to Govindacharya, they had 12,000-15,000 activists in Bihar). Thus 'JP' came gradually to admit the political – even partisan – nature of his movement.

On 16 April 1974, following a disproportionate use of force to suppress a demonstration at Gaya, 'JP' demanded the setting up of an official commission of enquiry. When the government of Bihar refused his request, he decided to bring about its resignation. Together with the Chhatra Sangharsh Samiti, he set up a 'Paralyse the Government Association'. Students organised demonstrations throughout the state in the course of which several hundred activists were gaoled. Linked into the disciplined network of *shakhas*, ABVP activists managed to extend the agitation to some rural districts.[49] The movement entered its next phase in June 1974 with a march on Patna, of which the students of the Chhatra Sangharsh Samiti, now renamed Chhatra Yuva [Youth] Sangharsh Samiti, were again the principal organisers. 'JP' seemed anxious to contain the influence of the Hindu nationalists in the movement and asked the ABVP 'not to politicise' it.[50]

'JP''s aspiration to be a non-political social reformer and his prejudice against the Hindu nationalists nonetheless became blurred that summer. First, his capacity for mobilisation lost its cutting edge in the face of determined opposition.[51] From August onwards the forces of law and order were unleashed on Bihar: many people died and thousands were arrested. Second, 'JP' began to see his secure Gandhian base eroded. In July 1974, a large minority of the delegates to the half-yearly meeting of the Sarva Seva Sangh criticised the 'JP movement' as being purely political. Vinoba Bhave himself objected to the demand for the dissolution of the Bihar Vidhan Sabha. Nevertheless a compromise was reached whereby 'JP''s 'experiment' would be tried for a few months

---

[49] *Motherland*, 14 and 20 April 1974, pp. 1 and 7, and 11 and 13 May 1974, pp. 1 and 7. The ABVP had taken care not to merge itself totally with the Chhatra Sangharsh Samiti the better to profit from the mobilisation which had resulted from the movement's activities. At each level – from the *tehsil* to the district – the ABVP installed a structure parallel to the Samiti to give itself a denser network once the agitation ended (interview with K.N. Govindacharya).

[50] *Motherland*, 27 July 1974.

[51] Starting in June, he launched waves of *satyagrahis* against the Vidhan Sabha, a campaign to withhold taxes, a *gherao* against Congress MLAs, a 'Three Day Bihar Bandh [general strike]', a number of fasts and a boycott by students of the new university term. But the movement ran out of steam as repression was intensified (*Indian Express*, 8 June 1974; *Times of India*, 2 July 1974; *Motherland*, 2 and 5 Aug. 1974; *Statesman* (Delhi), 13 Oct. 1974; *The Hindu*, 4 Oct. 1974; *National Herald*, 9 Oct. 1974).

longer.[52] By December, opposition to the Bihar movement within the Sarva Seva Sangh had intensified. Vinoba Bhave decided at this juncture to observe a vow of silence for one year, but his disapproval of the 'JP movement' was unambiguous.[53]

Faced with the weakening of the movement and the defection of part of his Gandhian base, 'JP' accepted the unofficial support of some political parties, in the forefront of which was the Jana Sangh, while the ABVP was already providing him with substantial backing.

A windfall and a dilemma: associating without losing one's identity

The 'JP movement' was a veritable godsend for the Jana Sangh's leaders in that it allowed them to get back in step with the Sangathanist network and integrate with the legitimate political opposition through an activist campaign outside the institutional system, which the party had increasingly distrusted since the 1971-2 elections.

Editorials in the Hindu nationalist press approved of the 'Total Revolution', emphasising that, far from following the path of violent Marxist-style revolution, 'the country needed a moral revolution, a spiritual revolution'.[54] In April 1974 the Jana Sangh officially embraced 'Total Revolution'.[55] When the first camp for training party cadres 'in agitation work' was held[56] at Hyderabad in September 1974, Vajpayee and Advani justified the Jana Sangh's support for the 'JP movement' by citing the 'total crisis' which was affecting the country culturally as well as politically and economically.[57] This rallying to the 'Total Revolution' implied an explicit challenge to republican legality, as the language used by Vajpayee bears witness: 'It is becoming increasingly difficult to dislodge the Congress by the ballot-box since elections proved to be an unequal battle, since the Congress has money power.'[58]

Such arguments had been heard within the Jana Sangh ever since the setback of 1972 that had provoked the demand for a new electoral law. In 1974, Vajpayee pursued the same theme in words that revealed how the value he placed on parliament had been eroded: 'The fight inside the

[52] G. Ostergaard, *Non-violent revolution*, op. cit , p. 108.

[53] Ibid., p. 146.

[54] *Motherland*, 10 Feb. 1975. See also ibid., 5 May 1974, p. 5, and 1 April 1975, p. 5.

[55] *The Hindu*, 18 April 1974.

[56] *Motherland*, 1 Sept. 1974.

[57] *Organiser*, 21 Sept. 1974. The *Organiser*, too, congratulated the Jana Sangh for penetrating to 'the very roots of the matter' (ibid.).

[58] *The Hindu*, 16 Sept. 1974.

legislature has to be supplemented by the fight *inter alia*, for bringing about the necessary electoral reform.'[59]

The Jana Sangh's position supported that of *Panchjanya*, a Hindi-medium RSS newspaper whose editor-in-chief wrote in the *Organiser*:

Masses have to be prepared for the active intervention and purification of the democratic process. It is not at all necessary that such an intervention should be violent but it has to be aggressive. [...] the forces of status quo have blocked all meaningful progress to democratic change. They have mobilised all the resources of the state to keep themselves in power – even against the popular wish and without using that power of improving the economic conditions of the masses.[60]

'JP' tended to legitimise language of this type when he attacked a legally elected government and condemned the 'loopholes and defects' of the electoral law which vitiated the democratic process.[61] In addition to this convergence of views, the Jana Sangh supported the agitation in Bihar because it was the work of a popular movement inspired by a prominent leader who did not feel perturbed in the company of Hindu nationalists.

In May 1974, 18 Jana Sangh MLAs in Bihar resigned in the full glare of publicity at the instigation of 'JP',[62] and a month later those who had not done so were expelled.[63] Even if the Socialists involved themselves in the battle alongside 'JP', the resignation of socialist MLAs in response to his call to all opposition MLAs to resign, proved a more laborious and ill-disciplined affair.[64] From May onwards 'JP' was assisted by Nana Deshmukh, the Jana Sangh's organiser in Uttar Pradesh and Bihar for the previous twenty years. Deshmukh's first real act after joining 'JP' was at Ahmedabad, where he organised the preparations for a visit to mark the linking of the student protest movements of Gujarat and Bihar.[65] From the autumn he concentrated his efforts in Bihar.

The 'Bihar Bandh', launched by 'JP' on 3, 4 and 5 October, owed its success partly to the work of Deshmukh and his activists who toured the state, including wide swathes of the countryside.[66] A month later, another

[59] *Organiser*, 17 July 1974.

[60] Ibid., p. 28; and see also Vashishtha, 'Parliament, a soap opera', *Motherland*, 14 Sept. 1974, p. 8.

[61] Article by 'JP' in *Everyman's* (25 May 1974) in J. Narayan, *Towards total revolution*, vol. 4, op. cit., p. 67.

[62] Article by 'JP' in *Everyman's* (18 May 1974) in *ibid.*, p. 64.

[63] *Statesman Weekly*, 11 May 1974, p. 4, and 8 June 1974, p. 1. In August 1974, after Congress (O) had belatedly rallied to the 'JP' movement, only 5 of its 23 MLAs resigned (ibid., 31 Aug. 1974, p. 6).

[64] M. Limaye, *Birth of non-congressism*, op. cit., pp. 465-6.

[65] *Motherland*, 9 April 1974, and N. Deshmukh, *RSS victim of slander*, New Delhi: Vision Books, 1979, p. 65.

[66] Ibid., pp. 66-7; and *Organiser*, 26 Oct. 1974, p. 13. Vajpayee then arranged a *dharna*

dharna, aimed at forcing the government's resignation, which 'JP' announced after the 'Bihar Bandh', drew thousands of participants thanks
partly to propaganda work by Deshmukh, who was twice expelled from
Bihar.[67] A procession held at Patna in November illustrated *par excellence*
the Gandhian nature of the movement when the demonstrators faced the
police without making the slightest aggressive reaction. On this occasion
Deshmukh acted as 'aide-de-camp' to 'JP' and was himself injured.

But the repression continued on a particularly heavy scale, and its
effect was to hinder the movement, which again began to wither. In
November 1974, 'JP' gave up the attempt to dislodge the Bihar state
government in favour of an agitation on a nationwide scale against Indira
Gandhi. He now directed his activities explicitly towards winning over
the political parties, all of which were keen to exploit the new leader's
capacity for mobilisation. The Jana Sangh was still anxious to integrate
itself into the legitimate opposition but the new political strategy of 'JP'
forced it to consider the risks of diluting its identity in a movement
incorporating other parties.

In 1971, as noted above, the party had rejected tactical alliances partly
under pressure from its Sangathanist network.[68] At the beginning of 1974,
the party gave its approval to the amalgamation, under the auspices of
Charan Singh, of the BKD, a fraction of the Socialist party, the Swatantra
Party and four other small groups within a single Bharatiya Lok Dal
(BLD), but refused to participate in it.[69] Eight months later, the Jana Sangh
resolved in favour of a form of unity within the opposition. There could
not have been a better opportunity for it to become integrated with
legitimate politics, given the position of strength of the Hindu nationalists
after six months of agitation with 'JP', and the fact that the latter's
ideology had been proved to be compatible with several of their major

---

(sit-in) in an effort to obtain authorisation to visit certain prisoners, victims of the
repression in Bihar, and was himself detained for 48 hours (ibid., 5 Sept. 1974, p. 1).

[67] *Statesman* (Delhi), 1 and 9 Nov. 1974.

[68] It then followed a line of action which J.P. Mathur, one of its national secretaries, spelled
out in 1973: 'The usual terminology "need to replace Congress" is sheer euphemism for
desire to share power with utter disregard to ideological convictions. Bluntly putting,
merger of parties without achieving a well-defined common ideological base and with
no long-term mental preparedness to struggle would be bare opportunistic approach to
power' (*Organiser*, 20 Oct. 1973, p. 33).

[69] *Motherland*, 16 April 1974, p. 5, and 28 April 1974, p. 1. The Jana Sangh even abstained
from making electoral alliances with the other opposition parties when elections to the
Vidhan Sabha in Uttar Pradesh became due in 1974 (*Statesman Weekly*, 26 Jan. 1974,
p. 3). A leader-writer for the *Organiser* rejected this idea of amalgamation in words
that were revealing and prophetic: 'A party has to be an integrated and integral whole if
it is to function meaningfully and become a credible alternative. [...] Only people
working and suffering together can develop the tradition and camaraderie necessary for
the successful working of the party' (*Organiser*, 14 Dec. 1974).

principles. Although the party remained wary of diluting its identity, and continued to reject the idea of joining a much larger grouping, it could envisage an improvement in its status on the political chess-board without being exposed to this danger, given that it remained one of the principal supporters of 'JP'.

At the end of November 1974, consultations which 'JP' was holding in Delhi with the political parties resulted in the formation of a National Coordination Committee consisting of twenty leaders representing the Jana Sangh, Congress (O), the BLD, the Socialist party and the Akali Dal. The involvement of the Jana Sangh seemed especially justifiable since 'JP' had agreed to take part in its annual meeting, which was held in Delhi in March 1975, just before a demonstration organised by the National Coordination Committee was due to take place (on 6 March). The marchers were to proceed to the Lok Sabha to hand over a 'Charter of Demands' which called for elections to be held in Bihar and Gujarat and formalised the spirit of the 'Total Revolution' with a list of demands (for reforms leading to greater social justice, respect for civil liberties, electoral reform, anti-corruption measures, etc.).

The scheduling of the meeting of the Jana Sangh at the same time as this demonstration led the party's organisers to try to make it a significant event in order to boost their representation in the procession: between 22,000 and 35,000 delegates were directed to the Ambedkar stadium, which was reserved for the occasion.[70] That the Jana Sangh was trying to portray itself as a motivating force of the 'JP movement' was evident from the meeting. An enormous painting of 'the people marching towards Parliament' served as a backdrop to the platform; this attempt to integrate itself into the popular opposition movement was partly vindicated by the speech of 'JP'. He used the occasion to launch a process which would lead him to participate in the meetings of every opposition party; but he made it clear that, in his view, the Jana Sangh was the best organised among them. He proffered his thanks for its support in Bihar before uttering the following, in reference to attacks by Congress: 'If you are a fascist, then I too am a fascist.'[71] The rest of the speech consisted of an appeal to the parties to cooperate ever more closely within his agitational movement, with the ultimate aim of giving India a bi-partisan system.[72]

This invitation to the political parties to merge had not been taken up by Advani in his presidential address, which endorsed the line adopted at the party's Central Working Committee in Jammu in November 1974:

[70] *Motherland*, 2 Mar. 1975, and *Hindustan Times*, 4 Mar. 1975.
[71] He added that he had incurred a debt towards the Jana Sangh and Deshmukh in particular for his help in Bihar (*Organiser*, 15 Mar. 1975).
[72] *Statesman* (Delhi), *Hindustan Times* and *Motherland*, 6 Mar. 1975.

[...] on the one hand continuance of the policy of relentlessly strengthening the organisational base and on the other optimum utilisation of the strength so accumulated to bringing about Total Revolution in conjunction with other similarly minded forces. [...] Thus working together the movement can form a joint block in Parliament and a concerted election strategy based upon a common minimum programme, common Janata candidates, a common symbol, are the measures which we think can lead to an institutional alternative to the Congress.[73]

The limits this placed on the unity which 'JP' desired could be explained partly by the pressure exerted by numerous delegates, who provoked a two and a half hour debate on the second day of the meeting during which they warned the leadership that the party risked losing its identity and protested against the strategy of ensuring that the opposition would put forward only one candidate in each constituency.[74] The expression of such reservations concerning the unitary approach reflected the strength of the RSS's ideological objectives – of a monopolistic nature – within the Sangathanist network and led Advani to speak forcefully at the Delhi meeting; but his own position was not radically different. It became the Jana Sangh's official objective at the working committee meeting held on 12 June at Mount Abu.[75]

The Jana Sangh thus tried to cope with a dilemma that was inherent in its very nature and which it had already confronted after the 1967 elections. As a front for the RSS, it had a vocation to represent the Hindu nation. This was an exclusive and long-term mission that could be realised only through the RSS and its activist network, which was more sound doctrinally than party headquarters. On the other hand, as a political party the Jana Sangh was obliged to make compromises to elude the vigilant secularism of the Centre and integrate itself in legitimate politics to gain power, even if this meant making alliances. In 1975 it found in the 'JP movement' a framework which was ideologically compatible with both the secularist norm of the régime and RSS doctrine, notably because of its decentralising emphasis. The 'JP movement', furthermore, responded to the concern of the Jana Sangh leadership to integrate with mainline politics, but *against* the institutional system. Above all, at the organisational level, the party was in a position to preserve its separate identity, on which the Sangathanist network showed that it set great store. It could thus capitalise on its association with the 'JP movement'. Moreover the *Organiser* strongly urged the Jana Sangh to collaborate with the opposition political parties.[76]

[73]   Ibid., 4 Mar. 1975, pp. 1-4.

[74]   *Statesman* (Delhi), 6 Mar. 1975.

[75]   *Hindustan Times*, 4 May 1975, and L.K. Advani, *The people betrayed*, Delhi: Vision Books, 1979, p. 67.

[76]   *Hindustan Times*, 17 May 1975.

Of these the BLD and the Congress (O) showed some reluctance when Vajpayee proposed the formation of a single parliamentary group, the BLD because Charan Singh refused to consider any option other than a full merger and Congress (O) because of its reservations about sacrificing its identity.[77] But in December 1974 a by-election at Bhopal gave the Jana Sangh, the Socialist party and Congress (O), which was very weak in that region, the chance to put up Babulal Gaur as the first of its candidates with the label 'Janata' (of the people); he won the seat, polling 13,000 votes more than the Congress candidate.[78]

A few weeks later, at a by-election (this time for the Lok Sabha) in another Madhya Pradesh constituency, Jabalpur, all the opposition parties, including the BLD, supported a Janata candidate from the Socialist camp, Sharad Yadav. The latter polled 87,000 more votes than the nephew of Seth Govind Das, who had held the seat since 1952 and whose death had caused the election.[79] Thus the Jana Sangh's formula of a close electoral pact was shown to be a highly effective means of making political capital out of the wave of opposition to Congress aroused by the 'JP movement''s appeal to public opinion. The other parties now joined in, and Congress (O) even adopted the idea of a 'federal party'.[80]

Thus in the spring of 1975 the Jana Sangh, without having had to renounce its identity, was able to appear as a linchpin of the opposition alongside 'JP', whose movement was gaining in popularity. The procession on 6 March brought about half a million people on to the streets of Delhi; 'JP' followed up this success with a nationwide tour, in the course of which he was seen by millions of people all over India. He now represented a serious threat to Indira Gandhi. Mobilisation of the opposition was intensified when Morarji Desai undertook a fast on 7 April with the object of having elections called in Gujarat, his home state. On 13 April, Indira Gandhi decided to hold elections there scheduled for 13 June. With the launching of the election campaign, a Janata Front (Front of the People) was immediately formed, thus providing an ideal platform for the Jana Sangh, since its four constituent parties – Congress (O), the BLD, the Socialist party and the Jana Sangh – agreed to put forward, under a single symbol, candidates whom the respective party members had already chosen unanimously. The Jana Sangh could thus survey the great electoral progress it had made, from 3 to 18 MLAs, a by no means minor contribution to Congress's reversal in the state.

---

[77] Ibid., 11 Jan. 1975, p. 3.
[78] Interview with Babulal Gaur, 22 Nov. 1989, Bhopal.
[79] Interviews with Chandra Mohan and Baburao Paranjpe (then mayor of Jabalpur), 3 Nov. 1991, Jabalpur; and *Statesman Weekly*, 25 Jan. 1975, p. 3.
[80] Ibid., 19 April 1975, p. 4.

To the defeat in Gujarat was added a more serious reverse for Indira Gandhi in mid-June: namely the invalidation by the Allahabad High Court of her own election to the Lok Sabha in 1971, which had allegedly been obtained by illegal means. Her appeal to the Supreme Court was rejected on 24 June.

On 25 June the parties forming the Committee of National Coordination set up the Lok Sangharsh Samiti (LSS – Committee for the People's Struggle), a new and better-structured coordinating body. Morarji Desai was its president, Deshmukh its general secretary while Thengadi and Advani were members. 'JP' announced that a vast *satyagraha* would take place to force the resignation of Indira Gandhi; however it was Deshmukh who presented the 'detail of the opposition's plans for agitation' that would consist mainly of daily *satyagrahas* by groups of demonstrators.[81]

This programme received support from all the opposition parties, especially Socialists like George Fernandes, a trade unionist well versed in agitational techniques; however, its activist aspects were more suited to the Jana Sangh which, together with the RSS, had at its disposal a reservoir of disciplined activists and a logistical superiority to the other opposition parties (by early 1975 the RSS had established 10,000 *shakhas*).[82] At the same time as it participated in the 'JP movement' the better to integrate itself with the opposition and propagate its own ideology, the Jana Sangh did its utmost to retain its identity, to appear as the motive force behind the agitation and even to ensure that the activist techniques for which it was the best prepared would be employed.

The proclamation of the state of emergency would allow the Hindu nationalists to strengthen their showing within the opposition, precisely because of the strength of their network of activists, who were more capable than many others of standing the test of clandestine action and organising the *satyagrahas* announced for June 1975.

The Emergency: crucible of integration

From Mrs Gandhi's point of view, the proclamation of the state of emergency was not only a response to the judgement of the High Court of Allahabad; it was also a move against the increasingly effective agitational campaign of the opposition parties. On the night of 25/26 June 1975, she ordered the arrest of the principal opposition leaders and on 4 July pronounced a legal ban on the RSS and the Jamaat-e-Islami,[83]

[81] *National Herald*, 26 June 1975, p. 2.
[82] *Indian Express*, 1 Feb. 1975.
[83] On the Jamaat-e-Islami, see Violette Graff, 'La Jamaat-e-Islami' in O. Carré and P. Dumont (eds), *Radicalismes islamiques*, Paris: L'Harmattan, 1986.

doubtless to maintain a balance by subjecting different communalist organisations to similar measures. The RSS was her particular target, as her speech on 27 June clearly shows:

Forces seeking to strangle Indian Democracy were similar to those which backed the rise of Nazism in Germany before World War II. It was in order to combat these forces that the government had been obliged to act swiftly and decisively. It is a mistake to equate Nazism with the use of police and army. The method often adopted was to create discord and confusion by infiltrating small groups into various facets of national life. This was indeed the method which the RSS had adopted in India.[84]

As early as August 1975, the CPI published a brochure supporting the government's idea that '29 June 1975 was to be the day of action planned by these forces [the rightist combine that united under the umbrella of 'JP'] in which the RSS and other similar stormtroopers were to become the spearhead of action' and that the 'conspiracy to capture power was drawn up in meticulous detail.'[85] In her speech at the plenary session of the Congress at Chandigarh in December 1975, Indira Gandhi declared that 'If the Jana Sangh comes to power, it will not need emergency. It will chop off heads. Heads were chopped off in Bangladesh and Chile. Persons there were not just detained. They were murdered.'[86] During the Emergency, as part of her battle against communalism, Indira Gandhi had secularism written into the Constitution, in which it had not previously featured up to that point.

The RSS's reaction to the ban was a twofold strategy. At first Deoras – who was imprisoned on 30 June and replaced by Muley – sought to adopt a conciliatory attitude. On 25 August he wrote to Indira Gandhi, congratulating her on the level-headedness of her last speech on 15 August but requesting that she rescind the ban on the RSS. In another letter, on 10 November, Deoras even proposed putting the RSS at the service of the development work being undertaken by the government.[87] These letters,

---

[84] *Times of India*, 28 June 1975.

[85] S. Mukherjee, *Fascism and the politics of power*, New Delhi: Communist Party Publication, August 1975, pp. 34-5. The author draws his inspiration from a document published by the government of India, *Why Emergency?*

[86] Cited in A. Moin Zaidi (ed.), *The Annual Register of Indian Political Parties* [hereafter *ARIPP*] – *1974-6*, New Delhi: S. Chand, 1976, pp. 418-19.

[87] Letter reproduced in P. Brahm Dutt, *Five headed monster – A factual narrative of the genesis of Janata Party*, New Delhi: Surge Publications, 1978, pp. 138-48. Deoras had made a similar offer in February-March 1975, when the possibility of a ban had seemed likely, thus forcing him to cease his displays of bravado (at the end of January, he had given the numerical strength of the RSS as a reason to dissuade the Congress deputies from persisting in their demand for a ban on the movement) (*Indian Express*, 1 and 17 Feb. 1975).

the existence of which was not made public till October 1977, revealed the concessions which the RSS was prepared to make to save itself from being banned, for it had been fearful, ever since 1948-9, of seeing the movement hindered from functioning properly or being dismantled altogether. The preservation of the organisation remained a top priority.

As more and more *swayamsevaks* were arrested, confirming that the RSS was one of the government's principal targets, the movement opted for resistance, but without relinquishing its efforts to get the ban lifted, notably through the mediation of V. Bhave, to whom Deoras wrote (without success). The movement went underground to organise itself for a long-drawn-out campaign. Of 1,356 *pracharaks*, only 186 had been arrested and most of the others continued their activities secretly. By the beginning of July, the national leaders who had gone underground had reconstituted the movement's network while seeking new local cadres to replace those in custody.[88] During July a meeting of the principal *pracharaks* who were still at liberty was held in Bombay. The programme agreed upon considered the restoration of democracy and the lifting of the ban on the RSS as two indivisible objectives.[89] The fact that the RSS fought against the Emergency above all to regain its legal status reflected the organisation's ambiguous attitude towards democracy, as suggested by Thengadi's subsequent analysis:

It is accepted on all hands that the present democratic process in India is not a growth of the soil and it is neither adequate nor favourable nor capable from the point of view of conditions in and requirements of the country. But its protection can save the country from dictatorship. It can afford scope for the thinking and action necessary for a new system that accords with the tradition, nature and circumstances of the country. In a dictatorship this is not possible. So opposing the dictatorship of the Emergency became a natural duty of the Sangh.[90]

Thus the RSS decided to work actively against the Emergency, an option which further increased the weight of the Hindu nationalists within the opposition.

The RSS, of course, was not the only movement to engage in active resistance to the Emergency. Socialists, capitalising on their experience as leaders of labour unions (such as the Fernandes brothers), became renowned for their clandestine activity. But here the RSS had two advantages. First, it had at its disposal a dense network of volunteers hardened in the techniques of more or less secret action who were well disciplined and had a feeling of solidarity with each other. This network,

---

[88] K.N. Sahni, 'My underground experience', *Organiser*, 7 Nov. 1977, p. 9, and P.G. Sahasrabuddhe and M. C. Vajpayee, *The people versus emergency*, op. cit., pp. 30, 303.

[89] See a letter sent by Muley to the *swayamsevaks*, cited in ibid., p. 119.

[90] See preface in ibid., p. 29.

after being restructured at the Bombay meeting in July, would not be broken – despite the arrest of key figures like Yadavrao Joshi, the Jana Sangh's organiser in the Sough, whose work was immediately carried on by H.V. Seshadri, the *prant pracharak* for Karnataka.[91] And second, the RSS was strongly represented in the clandestine LSS, thus increasing its ability to take action and bolstering its own legitimacy. After almost all the LSS leaders and been arrested, Deshmudh – who was subsequently detained in August – played a role in that body which was all the more important given that of the most active members of his team – Ravindra Verma (Congress O), Surendra Mohan (Socialist Party), Radhakrishna (secretary to 'JP'), Madan Lal Khurana, S.S. Bhandari, D. Thengadi and Subramaniam   Swamy – the majority (the four last-named) were *swayam- sevaks.*[92]

On 14 November 1975, the LSS started a ten-week *satyagraha* to give concrete form to the announcement made by 'JP' on 25 June. The movement received vital support from *swayamsevaks* who, organised in small cells, courted arrest by distributing tracts and shouting slogans against the regime; of the 80,000 *satyagrahis* (15,000 in Karnataka,[93] three-quarters were claimed by the RSS.[94] Even if this share is exaggerated, the high proportion of *swayamsevaks* in Indian prisons was real enough, as the accompanying table shows – the apparently modest level of the statistics is explained by the fact that many members of banned organisations or political parties were arrested as 'criminals' or 'anti-social elements.'

The RSS claimed that of a total of 105,000 detainees (25,000 in the first weeks of the Emergency and 80,000 as the result of the *satyagrahas*), seventy had died in custody; they also said that the police were searching for more than 50,000 activists.[95] The fact that *swayamsevaks* were helping the families of political prisoners increased their prestige among the population as a whole.[96] This strengthening of the RSS at once benefited and complicated the political unity of the opposition. On the one hand,

91   L.K. Advani, *A prisoner's scrapbook*, New Delhi: Arnold-Heinemann, 1978, p. 12.
92   N. Deshmukh, RSS: Victim of slander, op. cit., p. 110.
93   Accoring to J. Shettigar, a lecturer in economics at the University of Mangalore and the then *vidyarthi pramukh* of this town, the large number of *satyagrahis* in Karnataka was due mainly to the mobilisation of the youth of Mangalore, an historical stronghold of the RSS in the state (interview with J. Shettigar, 11 Feb. 1994, New Delhi). 9,000 in Kerala, 8,000 each in Bihar and Uttar Pradesh, 5,000 in Delhi).
94   *Organiser*, 4 June 1977, p. 11.
95   L.K. Advani, *A prisoner's scrap-book*, op. cit., p. 170, and Organizer, 28 May 1977, p. 5.
96   G. Puri, Bharatiya Jana Sangh, op. cit., pp. 238-9.

ANALYSIS OF INDIVIDUALS IMPRISONED DURING THE EMERGENCY

States[1]	Members of banned organisations	Of which...			Members of political parties	JS	CPI (M)	SP	Of which...		
		RSS	CPI (ML)	JEI					C (O)	BLD	DMK
Andhra Pradesh	512		350		210	130					
Assam	143	74	28	4	203	20	86	33			
Bihar[2]	269	128			530	247					
Gujarat	135				404						
Haryana[2]	24				172						
Himachal Pradesh	8	8		20	17	6					
Karnataka	165	129	7		156	124	1	8	15	1	
Kerala	476	115	360		221		139				
Madhya Pradesh[2]	1,593	1,578			1,807						
Maharashtra	1,717				780	503		207			
Meghalaya	14	13			2						
Nagaland[2]	0				9						
Orissa	112	57			141					55	
Punjab	16		13		33	14		6			
Rajasthan	154	127			213	113					
Tamil Nadu	139	47	72		570						419
Tripura	9				18		12				
Uttar Pradesh	637	475			785	178	145			148	
West Bengal	186	31	65		41						
Chandigarh	6	4			15	14					
Delhi[2]	146				180						
Goa	9	8			9	9					

[1] The states or Union territories not included here did not provide data which the Commission could utilise.

[2] Apportionment not disclosed.

Key: CPI (ML): Communist Party of India (Marxist-Leninist); JEI: Jamaat-e-Islami; CPI (M): Communist Party of India (Marxist); DMK: Dravida Munetra Kazagham; C (O): Congress (O); BLD: Bharatiya Lok Dal; SP: Socialist Party; JS: Jana Sangh.

Source: Shah Commission of Inquiry – Third and final report, 6 Aug. 1978. Government of India Press, 1978. The figures for Delhi are on p. 32 of the second report.

the lukewarm attitude of the Hindu nationalist movement towards the unity of the opposition decreased because it felt it was in a strong position; while, on the other hand, the increasing hold of the RSS over the opposition movements was beginning to arouse mixed feelings among other political forces.

Unity 'from above'

The principal opposition party leaders were arrested in the first hours of the Emergency: Vajpayee, Advani, Madhu Dandavate (Socialist) and Shyam Nandan Mishra (Congress O) were detained together on 26 June in Bangalore, where they had gone to take part in a parliamentary commission. In Delhi, Malkani and Bhai Mahavir were arrested with many other leaders, most of whom were in the city for the combined meeting of their parties; among these were Morarji Desai, 'JP', Charan Singh, Jaipal Singh (CPI – M) and Raj Narain (BLD).

The political parties themselves had not been banned, but the detention of their leaders had much the same effect. The presidency of the Jana Sangh devolved on Om Prakash Tyagi, an active Arya Samajist and former MP from Uttar Pradesh.[98] Gathering together the chief opposition leaders in prison fostered mutual understanding between them. The prison where the largest number of top leaders were incarcerated was Rohtak (Haryana), where Sikander Bakht and Ashok Mehta (both Congress O); Chandra Shekhar (a Congress dissident); Samar Guha (Socialist); Biju Patnaik, Piloo Mody and Raj Narain (BLD); Jaipal Singh (CPI-M); and Bhai Mahavir (Jana Sangh) were held for a long time, with the occasional company of Charan Singh, Devi Lal and a number of Jana Sangh leaders: Advani, Bhairon Singh Shekhawat, J.R. Joshi and Malkani.[99] Tihar jail in Delhi, where Malkani was also held, had a comparable group which included Nana Deshmukh, Hans Raj Gupta, J.R. Joshi, S.S. Bhandari; Charan Singh and Sardar Badal (BLD); Surendra Mohan (Socialist party); and all the leaders of the Jamaat-e-Islami.

This shared experience of prison promoted unity and the integration of the Hindu nationalists in the 'legitimate opposition', which could no longer avoid recognition of their part in the struggle against the Emergency. But for the accomplishment of complete unity it was necessary for the parties which were most chary of amalgamation – first and foremost, the Jana Sangh – to overcome their reluctance to become fully integrated in a new organisation.

Charan Singh relaunched the idea of an amalgamation of the four main

[98]   *Motherland*, 3 April 1975, p. 3 and *Fourth Lok Sabha Who's who*, op. cit., p. 628.

[99]   K.R. Malkani, *The Midnight knock*, New Delhi: Vikas, 1978, p. 45.

opposition parties in 1976[100] and obtained the agreement of those gaoled
with him – among whom was Deshmukh – in Tihar prison.[101] The following month, 'JP', who had been freed because of his poor health, brought
together the interim presidents and other officials of the four parties for
the same purpose. However only the BLD, whose leader Charan Singh
was freed in March 1976, made the necessary deliberations which resulted
in the proposal, at the end of May, of a formula involving the dissolution
of the various parties and their coming together in a new grouping.
Congress (O) remained loath to the idea of losing its identity – as did the
Jana Sangh, whose working committee invoked, in mid-May, the fact that
thirty of its members, including the party president, were in prison to
explain the postponement of any decision. This attitude largely reflected
the views of the Jana Sangh's regional branches. As ever, local cadres
viewed any dilution of their party's identity with deep reservations.
Furthermore, the sense that they were representatives of a different
political culture led those among them who were in prison to adopt an
attitude different from that of their leaders: Brahm Dutt suggests that in
Lucknow and Varanasi they did not mix with prisoners from other parties,
whom they saw as 'Vibhishana',[102] namely opportunists ready to exploit
the mobilisation by *swayamsevaks* on the ground in order to gain power.
In Madhya Pradesh, the Hindu nationalists did not believe that there had
been a genuine rapprochement between the state's political leaders in
prison. Shejwalkar argued that the whole process had occurred outside,
around 'JP', and while he was imprisoned in Bhopal the opposition leaders
had done nothing more than coexist.[103] Potnis, the Jana Sangh's president
in Gwalior district at the time, expressed the same opinion about the prison
in Gwalior, where the exchanges between opposition leaders had only
really begun after the constitution of the Janata Party had been distributed
among the activists who were still held in prison in the spring of 1977.[104]
According to S. Patwa, who was held in Indore jail with socialist leaders
such as Raghu Thakur and Sharad Yadav:

---

[100] The first negotiations between the opposition leaders appear to have taken place at
Rohtak prison where Ashok Mehta, S.N. Mishra, Sikander Bakht, Biju Patnaik, Piloo
Mody, Samar Guha, Madhu Dandavate, Bhai Mahavir and L.K. Advani were
incarcerated. They had three 'sessions', but the only subject of discussion was
'inter-party relations'(L.K. Advani, *A prisoner's scrap-book*, op. cit., p. 46).

[101] N. Deshmukh, *RSS: Victim of slander*, op. cit., p. 91.

[102] The younger brother of Ravana, in the *Ramayana*, who seeks to make him respect a
moral code and then betrays it to join Ram, from whose victory he profits to accede to
the throne of Lanka (Brahm Dutt, *Five-headed monster*, op. cit., pp. 22, 25).

[103] Interview with Shejwalkar.

[104] Interview with Potnis, 28 Nov. 1989, Gwalior. The situation was very similar in Dhar
jail, where K. Joshi was detained (interview with Vikram Verma, 17 Feb. 1994, Bhopal).

We did not think about the Janata Party then. It came a few months before the lifting of the Emergency. Negotiations were going on outside. We did not come very much closer [to the Socialists in jail with them].[105]

Such reactions on the part of the Jana Sanghis were also prompted by the demands of some of those supporting amalgamation. During the first discussions at Tihar, in February 1976, Surendra Mohan had insisted that the RSS and the volunteer organisations of the Congress (O) – the Congress Seva Dal – and of the Socialist Party – the Rashtra Seva Dal – should be fused into one volunteer organisation. Hindu nationalist leaders such as Deshmukh had objected that 'the distinct identity of the RSS could never be compromised.'[106] Then, after negotiations between the four parties resumed, in July 1976, Charan Singh emphasised that the new party should refuse admission to Jana Sanghis who were members of the RSS, as they would find themselves in a position of dual adherence[107] on account of their deep allegiance to the Hindu nationalist movement. Such proposals betrayed the disquiet of those who made them. The strength of the RSS, which had been revealed in the struggle against the Emergency, perturbed the most ardent partisans of a single party; if it (the RSS) was unwilling to merge in a unitary structure, it would be necessary to remain completely separate from it. Apparently such considerations convinced the Jana Sangh cadres that they were right to play a waiting game. At the meeting on 8 July, O.P. Tyagi drew attention to the resolution passed by the working committee in April that no decision should be taken until the Jana Sangh leaders were released.[108]

Meanwhile, on 13 May 1976, Advani had written to Tyagi, with an eye to the working committee meeting in mid-May, stating that all the Jana Sanghis whom he had been able to consult in prison were, like him, firmly on the side of amalgamation.[109] Eighteen years later, Advani chose to

---

[105] Interview with S. Patwa, 17 Feb. 1994, Bhopal.

[106] Personal communication from Surendra Mohan, 13 July, 1993.

[107] Brahm Dutt, *Five-headed monster*, op. cit., p. 55.

[108] At the same time, he distributed copies of a letter written by Muley saying that the RSS was actively considering adopting two amendments to its constitution: first, that followers of different faiths would be free to join it, and second that its office-bearers and full-time workers would not hold office in political parties or contest elections (personal communication from S. Mohan).

[109] 'With the declaration of emergency in June 1975 a new chapter has commenced. Democracy has come under eclipse. Those who believe in democracy have had to undergo many kinds of suffering and have had to make sacrifices. As a result of this the cordiality, closeness and mutual trust generated during this last one year among parties and persons committed to democracy could not have been ordinarily created even in one decade. The emergence of a strong and unified opposition party with democracy as its main plank should be regarded as a natural culmination of this chain of events' (L.K. Advani, *A prisoner's scrap-book*, op. cit., p. 300). In February 1976 Advani, with Madhu

emphasise the peculiar situation of those who were in jail: 'The reason why we joined [what was to become the Janata Party] was that when we were in jail during emergency, it seemed as a situation where, unless we all combine, this may become a permanent thing.'[110] Malkani, who had not favoured an amalgamation in 1975, reached a similar conclusion during his time in prison.[111] Here one can plainly see the difference in approach between those on the outside and the prisoners, which coincided by and large with the gulf between the secondary and local leaders on one side and the national leadership on the other. For national leaders, like Advani or Vajpayee, the amalgamation was accepted as a precondition for the return to democracy, and this reorientation went hand in hand with an amendment on the ideological plane.[112]

It seemed that these men were prepared to dilute their political identity in a new political culture. 'JP' appeared to be the guarantor of this synthesis, which would have to serve as the ideological line for the party that was to be created. Advani repeatedly emphasised the need for this party to be sponsored by 'JP'.[113] According to the logic of their integration strategy, the Jana Sangh's leaders would no doubt have preferred not to pursue the road to amalgamation to the end, but circumstances seemed to thrust it upon them.

In 1977, the Jana Sangh considered abandoning its separate existence because of the particular combination of circumstances created by the Emergency, but also because of the specific conditions of its integration with other forces in the wake of the 'JP movement', which possessed characteristics with which the Jana Sangh had some features in common. These ideological affinities, slender though they were, partly explain why the party's leaders accepted amalgamation, having previously refused even to consider it with partners like the Swatantra Party or the successive parties of Charan Singh.

All that occurred in 1977 made it seem as if the leaders of the Jana Sangh had resolved to conceal the more aggressive features of their Hindu

---

Dandavate, had written a letter to Ashok Mehta with the intention of supporting Mehta's efforts to convert Congress (O) to the idea of amalgamation.

[110] Interview with L.K. Advani, 11 Feb. 1994, New Delhi.

[111] K.R. Malkani, *The midnight knock*, op. cit., p. 48.

[112] This is clear from a note sent by Advani from prison to the underground activists: 'In the *baudhik* [ideological training of the *swayamsevaks*] food [...], a commitment to democratic values ought to be consciously built up. In the pre-emergency days our emphasis has been almost exclusively and rightly so, on nationalism. Now it has to be a twofold emphasis – on nationalism and democracy.' (L.K. Advani, *A prisoner's scrap-book*, op. cit., pp. 304-5).

[113] Ibid., pp. 307 and 314.

nationalism – for example, its attitude towards the minorities. Instead they emphasised less important parts of their doctrine, namely decentralisation at the village level and the primacy of civil society in comparison to the state. These were central tenets of the Bihar movement that 'JP' had expressed in a Gandhian perspective. Thus 'JP' seemed to have achieved one of his aims in 1974-5, namely, to provoke a change in the politically minded partners participating in his movement.[114]

This shift of emphasis in the ideology of the Hindu nationalists underwent a further change when the leaders of the Jana Sangh found in Morarji Desai a Gandhian of Hindu traditionalist allegiance capable of integrating them into a new ideological synthesis. However the latter would not be acceptable to all Hindu nationalists, and especially to local cadres to whom 'JP''s analysis proved largely inapplicable.

---

[114] In 1976, just after his release from jail, he wrote to friends: '[...] the RSS also has undergone a change and is still changing. Whatever the past of this organisation, today it is not exactly the same. It is alleged that the RSS and Jana Sangh are communal. But today its workers include the name of Mahatma Gandhi among those worth being remembered at the time of their morning prayer. Therefore, by including these organisations in the movement for total revolution I have made an attempt to de-communalise them and now they are not communal.' (*JP's jail life – A collection of personal letters*, New Delhi: Arnold-Heinemann, 1977, p. 31).

8

THE IMPOSSIBLE ASSIMILATION

On 16 January 1977, Indira Gandhi announced that elections would be held in March. In the following week, the BLD, Congress (O), the Socialist Party and the Jana Sangh regrouped in a Janata Party of which the National Executive Committee included six representatives of each constituent party, with Morarji Desai as chairman. The influence of the Janata Party was reinforced when it was joined by Jagjivan Ram, who had just resigned as Union Minister for Agriculture and Irrigation, taking with him his new Congress for Democracy (CFD), which immediately made an electoral pact with the Janata Party. In the election, this alliance won 295 out of the 542 seats in the Lok Sabha. The assignment of seats by party revealed a sharp increase in the fortunes of the former Jana Sangh, whose candidates obtained 93 seats, equal to 31% of the Janata Party's entire representation, compared to the BLD with 19%, the Socialists with 17%, Congress (O) with 15%, CFD with 10% and the Congress dissidents, led by Chandra Shekhar with 2%.[1] Yet despite this result, the ex-Jana Sanghis accepted their under-representation in the government headed by Morarji Desai and were given only three ministerial posts: A.B. Vajpayee (External Affairs), L.K. Advani (Information and Broadcasting) and Brij Lal Verma, a former socialist from Madhya Pradesh who had joined the Jana Sangh in 1973 (Industries).

The leaders of the former Jana Sangh probably consented to this sacrifice as a mark of goodwill, to allay the suspicions of some of their partners, because they regarded the Janata Party as the means by which they could join the mainstream of Indian politics. They attached importance to the fact that the Prime Minister, Morarji Desai, had a Hindu traditionalist outlook. They may also have calculated that, under Desai's auspices, a section of the Janata Party might develop a political culture similar to that which Sardar Patel and his colleagues had represented in the Congress Party after Independence .

However at the state level the former Jana Sangh activists did not approve so readily of relinquishing elements of their political identity for

---

[1] L.I. Rudolph and S.H. Rudolph, *In pursuit of Lakshmi – The political economy of the Indian state*, Hyderabad: Orient Longman, 1987, pp. 167-8.

the sake of assimilation.[2] The contradiction between the political strategy of the former Jana Sangh's leaders and the priorities of the party activists, whose influence had been strengthened by the Emergency, helps explain the instability of the Janata Party, but it was simultaneously weakened by the activities of Charan Singh and his lieutenants who, partly because of a genuine concern to preserve secularism and partly to gain political advantage, were trying to make an issue of the 'communalism' of the former Jana Sanghis.

Towards a political culture of synthesis?

It seem that the Jana Sanghis considered their amalgamation within the Janata Party to be a momentous act to which they were permanently committed. This was borne out by the solemn character of the meeting of 1 May 1977 when 5,000 delegates voted in favour of it without a dissenting voice. The Jana Sangh consciously renounced its separate identity, as Malkani wrote two years later, so as to represent a mere 'sub-culture' 'in a new Janata political culture'.[3] But for the Hindu nationalists it was less a renunciation than a major shift of emphasis in their own ideology. In effect, 'Janata political culture' was in keeping with a Gandhian and Hindu traditionalist outlook which overlapped with that of the former Jana Sangh.

The constitution of the Janata Party committed it to promote 'decentralisation of economic and political power'.[4] Its election manifesto was more specific in proposing smaller administrative units, a reactivation of the *panchayats* and a division of labour more favourable to cottage industry.[5] All these measures had already featured in the programme of the Jana Sangh, and in the election campaign Advani was one of the main advocates of this central aspect of his new party's manifesto.[6] Once the Janata Party was in power, these options were expressed by means of a reorientation of the five-year plan for 1978-83 in the direction of small-scale industry and agriculture, and by the allocation of new financial

---

[2]   After the Vidhan Sabha elections in June 1977, in a 'tacit bargain' struck between the former BLD and the former Jana Sangh, the followers of Charan Singh were given control of four state governments (Uttar Pradesh, Bihar, Haryana and Orissa) while the Hindu nationalists were assigned Himachal Pradesh, Delhi, Rajasthan and Madhya Pradesh.

[3]   *Times of India*, 3 May 1979.

[4]   *Constitution of Janata Party*, New Delhi: Janata Party, 29 April 1977, p. 1.

[5]   'The Janata Party election manifesto' in J.A. Naik, *The great Janata revolution*, New Delhi: S. Chand, 1977, pp. 144-7.

[6]   K. N. Kumar, 'The ideology of the Janata Party', *India Journal of Political Science*, 39 (4), p. 591.

resources to the states of the federation to implement this policy. At the same time, the government set up commissions of experts to investigate how to galvanise the process of decentralisation at the *panchayat* level.[7]

This logic, which had already been seen at work in the 'JP movement', was apparent in the more constructive and less contentious behaviour of the former Jana Sangh at the time when the Janata Party came to power. Deshmukh (one of the three General Secretaries of the Janata Party), after refusing the post of Industry Minister, threw himself into a rural development project set up in Gonda (Uttar Pradesh) by the Deendayal Research Institute.[8] This focused on encouraging the peasants of this under-privileged district to sink wells and helped them obtain loans for small rural industries.[9] Deshmukh justified his interest in the project and his retreat from politics in the following terms:

In the tradition of India, the social transformation should be totally free from politics. I left politics to create the feeling amongst the people that they can develop themselves, that for their development they should not depend upon the government.[10]

The convergence of Deshmukh with the Gandhians was made 'official' by the presence of 'JP' at the inaugural meeting of the Gonda project.[11] A similar convergence of principles took place at the top, where the Jana Sangh's ministers manifested liberal attitudes while Morarji Desai demonstrated that he was willing to consider policies favouring Hindu interests.

L.K. Advani suppressed – belatedly – the blacklist of public figures forbidden to take part in radio or television broadcasts[12] and introduced a law to strengthen the independence of the media. This modest measure

[7]   J. Das Gupta, 'The Janata phase: reorganisation and redirection in Indian politics', *Asian Survey*, 29, 4 (April 1979), pp. 398-9.

[8]   Based in Delhi and named after Deendayal Upadhyaya, the DRI had been founded in 1972 as the research institute of the 'Sangh parivar' (it publishes a journal – *Manthan* – and its library contains archives relating to the RSS. Under the aegis of Deshmukh it became involved in development projects.

[9]   *Gonda Gramodaya Project – Evaluation*, New Delhi: Deendayal Research Institute, 1982, and *A pilgrimage to nation-building*, New Delhi: Deendayal Research Institute, n.d.

[10] Interview with N. Deshmukh, 25 Feb. 1994, New Delhi. See also his article 'A motivated campaign' (*Indian Express*, 3 April 1979).

[11] A similar undertaking was launched in an area of Andhra Pradesh devastated by a cyclone where the RSS had already won respect by carrving out rescue operations: a new model village was built there by the Deendayal Research Institute. The projects were not without ulterior motives since they made it possible for new Saraswati Shishu Mandirs – networks of schools launched by the RSS – to be established and were themselves seen in the context of a welfarist tactic.

[12] *Times of India*, 5 and 6 June 1979.

proposed entrusting the control of national radio and television to an agency whose director would be appointed by the Union President, and which would be obliged to follow government directives.[13] Though a small step, such a decision was likely to improve the image of the ex-Jana Sangh. At the same time, Vajpayee, at the Ministry of Foreign Affairs, gave clear signs of impartiality by making determined efforts to normalise his country's relations with the two enemies of the Hindu nationalists, Communist China and Pakistan. Negotiations with China began in October 1978,[14] but were suspended when China attacked Vietnam. As regards Pakistan, Vajpayee went to Islamabad in February 1978 with the hope 'of being the harbinger of a new era of understanding and friendship between [... the two] countries.'[15] He made a number of industrial and commercial agreements[16] and proposed the signing of a non-aggression pact[17] and the simplification of visa formalities for families which had been divided at Partition. This offer, although finally rejected by Islamabad, made Vajpayee more acceptable to Indian Muslims.

The Emergency had already brought the Hindu nationalists and the Muslims closer together, since members of the Jamaat-e-Islami and the RSS had been imprisoned together. This had led to the 'miracle'[18] of a dialogue; but, more significantly, the Muslims had been subjected to the same persecutions as the rest of the population during the Emergency. In Delhi they suffered especially from plans to improve urban sanitation, which consisted of 'cleansing' certain shantytowns and derelict buildings; thus in mid-April 1976, resentment against two measures – demolition works in the Muslim quarter of Turkman Gate in Old Delhi and a campaign of forced sterilisation – led to a riot that was bloodily suppressed.[19] These

[13] Ibid., 22 and 29 May 1979.

[14] On September 30, 1977, Vajpayee had declared at the Council of Foreign Relations in New York that with China, India was willing 'to normalise and develop relations on the basis of the principles of co-existence and good neighbourliness' (A.B. Vajpayee, *Dynamics of an open society*, n.p., 1977, p. 32).

[15] Speech made at a dinner hosted in the honour of Vajpayee by Agha Shahi, Adviser on Foreign Affairs, Government of Pakistan, at Islamabad on February 6, 1978 (cited in A.B. Vajpayee, ed., *New dimensions of India's foreign policy*, New Delhi: Vision Books, 1979, p. 191). Agha Shahi came to Delhi in April 1978 and Vajpayee saw in this visit one more sign of the 'wind of understanding' which could 'bring into being a wholesome climate of truth and cooperation' (ibid., p. 195).

[16] J. Das Gupta, 'The Janata phase', op. cit., p. 396.

[17] *Statesman Weekly*, 9 April 1977, p. 13.

[18] Badr-ud-din Tyabji, 'Minorities and Janata – lessons of the miracle in jail', *Times of India*, 12 May 1977.

[19] *Shah Commission of Inquiry – Interim Report II, 26 April 1978*, New Delhi: Government of India Press, pp. 96-8, and J. Dayal and A. Bose, *Delhi under Emergency*, Delhi: Ess Publications, 1977, ch. 2.

events persuaded Imam Bukhari, of the Jama Masjid, the Great Mosque of Old Delhi, to join the Janata Party, and in part explains why he spoke out in favour of lifting the ban on the RSS, his ally in the fight against Indira Gandhi.[20] This new harmony culminated in a visit to Delhi by Deoras, when there were scenes of fraternisation between activists of the Jamaat-e-Islami and the RSS.[21]

In order to keep in step with the official government line, the ex-Jana Sanghis tended to stress the Gandhian elements in their political culture so as to mitigate the anti-Muslim bias inherent in Hindu nationalism. Yet certain elements seemed to pull in the opposite direction by virtue of a Hindu traditionalism which sometimes claimed kinship with Gandhianism and of which Morarji Desai was the personification.[22] Comparing Desai and 'JP', Advani considers that 'In the case of Morarji Desai there was a greater identity with us, even in thinking [than with 'JP']'.[23] Three episodes during the life of Desai's administration illustrate this process.[24]

The campaign against cow slaughter was traditionally associated with the Hindu nationalist movement. However, during the Emergency Vinoba Bhave threatened that he would undertake a 'fast unto death' to force the authorities to ban the practice,[25] and he did so again in 1979. The government then immediately introduced a bill to amend the Constitution with a view to placing the right to make laws regarding the protection of the cow into the 'Concurrent List' so that parliament would have power

---

[20] ,*Indian Express*, 2 March 1975; A. Gupta, *Revolution through ballot*, Delhi: Ankur, 1977, p. 96; and *Times of India*, 10 April 1977.

[21] *Hindustan Times*, 10 April 1977. In March 1978, Imam Bukhari even gave a speech in a *shakha* in Punjab after saluting the saffron flag (*Organiser*, 19 March 1978, p. 16). The change in the attitude of the Hindu nationalists was reflected in their position concerning the status of Aligarh Muslim University. The reform which this institution had undergone in 1965 and 1972 greatly reduced its autonomy, but in the election campaign some leading ex-Jana Sanghis promised to restore its privileges. A bill to this effect was prepared but there was no time for it to become law (V. Graff, 'Aligarh's long quest for "Minority" status', *EPW*, 11 Aug. 1990, p. 1173).

[22] He campaigned from the start for the extension of Hindi to the states of South India (*Statesman Weekly*, 24 Sept. 1977, p. 6) at the moment when Vajpayee made it a point of honour to speak in Hindi at the UN (ibid., 8 Oct. 1977, p. 13).

[23] Interview with L.K. Advani, 11 Feb. 1994, New Delhi. According to Advani, the ideological rapprochement between Desai and the Jana Sanghis started in the late 1960s (*Organiser*, 23 April 1995). Bruce Graham deduced from Desai's writings that he saw Indian culture 'as an expression of Hindu values' (B.D. Graham, 'The Prime Minister and the Hindu right' in J. Manor, ed., *Nehru to the Nineties*, London: Hurst, 1994, p. 199).

[24] On the following paragraphs see P.N. Bazaz, *The shadow of Ram Rajya over India*, New Delhi: Spark, 1980.

[25] At that time, 'JP' had approved of this move, alleging that prohibition of cow slaughter was not a communal issue (*JP's jail life*, op. cit., p.48).

to legislate in this field.[26] During the debate in the Lok Sabha some ex-Jana Sanghis defended the plan against secularist MPs, who included a member of the Janata Party, the socialist Madhu Limaye. The amendment won a majority of votes, but the government did not have time to complete the necessary parliamentary procedures for it to become law. Meanwhile another point of ideological agreement between the Hindu nationalists and Morarji Desai had been reached.

For some time Desai had supported the 'Freedom of Religion Bill' which was introduced on 22 December 1978 by O.P. Tyagi. The Bill sought to prohibit 'conversion from one religion to another by the use of force or inducement or by fraudulent means'.[27] This proposal, which was backed by the RSS,[28] was intended to offer tribals the 'protection of the state'[29] against the missionaries. Morarji Desai later withdrew his support for the measure[30] because of an agitation by Christians and the Minorities Commission,[31] in which they were well represented, and the Janata Party was therefore forced to drop the bill. Christian leaders cited in particular the violence to which comparable legislation had given rise in Arunachal Pradesh. In this Union territory, the government had allowed a vote on a 'Freedom of Religion Bill' specifying that no place of worship could be built without the plans being submitted for administrative authorisation. The law, which was adopted in 1978, was at first concerned with Christian churches, some of which had already been destroyed. This at least was the argument used by opposition deputies in the Lok Sabha to criticise Tyagi's bill, which the Home Minister. H.M. Patel, strongly defended on several occasions.[32]

Morarji Desai revealed the intensity of his Hindu traditionalist outlook in the 'Textbook Controversy'. In May 1977, he received an anonymous memorandum demanding the withdrawal from public circulation of four history books, of which three were intended for use in teaching. The books in question were *Medieval India,* by Romila Thapar, *Modern India,* by Bipan Chandra, *Freedom Struggle,* by A. Tripathi, Barun De and Bipan Chandra, and *Communalism and the Writing of Indian History*, by Romila Thapar, Harbans Mukhia and Bipan Chandra. The memorandum

---

[26] *Times of India,* 19 May 1979.

[27] For the complete text of this bill see *Organiser,* 15 April 1979, pp. 1-15

[28] See the ABPS resolutions in ibid., 8 April 1979, p. 14.

[29] *Times of India,* 29 May 1979.

[30] *Indian Express,* 15 May 1979.

[31] The Minorities Commission had been established by the government in January 1978 for the regulation of religious and linguistic minority affairs. For details, see T.P. Wright Jnr., 'The failure of the Minorities Commission of India, 1977- 81', *Indian Journal of Politics,* vol. 20 (Jan.-June), no. 182 (1986), pp. 1-2.

[32] *Lok Sabha debates,* 27 March 1979, vol. 24, cols 245ff.

criticised the works above all for not condemning forcefully enough
certain Muslim invaders in the Medieval period and because they emphasised the responsibility of leaders like Tilak and Aurobindo for antagonism between Hindus and Muslims. The RSS campaigned separately
for the withdrawal of these textbooks.[33] At the end of May, V. Shankar, a
former secretary to Sardar Patel who was in charge of Morarji Desai's
secretariat, indicated to the Minister of Education that the Prime Minister
was willing to see these works withdrawn from circulation. This confidential note was leaked to the authors of the books, who protested by invoking
secularist values. Nonetheless the government passed an act in July 1978
withdrawing another school textbook, *Ancient India*, by R.S. Sharma, an
archaeologist who was the target of critical articles in *Organiser*[34] and had
already been relieved of his post as head of the Indian Council of
Historical Research. Since this body was seen by the new government as
accommodating a number of Communist intellectuals who propounded
an erroneous view of history, it gave its support instead to an alternative
institution, the Bharatiya Vidya Bhavan, which had published a *History
and Culture of the Indian People* under the direction of R.C. Majumdar,
the veteran of Indian nationalist historiography whose pro-Hindu bias was
allegedly becoming more pronounced.[35]

As the Rudolphs have written, 'Desai's Hindu cultural revivalism,
noblesse oblige high caste attitudes and economic conservatism provided
the political and ideological conditions for an evolving *rapport* between
him and like-minded members of the Jana Sangh faction.'[36] For the latter,
this *rapport* reflected their efforts to become integrated in a 'Janata
culture' inspired by Hindu traditionalism. In a sense the wing headed by
Desai was the functional equivalent of the Congress traditionalists –
Congress (O) had been to some extent their institutional expression –
whose suitability as allies of the Hindu nationalists had already been
evident, notably in the early 1950s when Tandon had become president
of the Congress with the support of Patel. These developments suggested
that Mookerjee's alternative integration strategy of entry into a Congress
controlled by Hindu traditionalists was actually coming to pass. Given

[33] *National Herald*, 31 June 1977, A.R.G. Tiwari, 'A true history of India is yet to be
      written' (*Organiser*, 23 July 1978, pp. 8-9) ; see also the editorial entitled 'Wanted, a
      proper history of India', ibid., 19 March 1978, p. 3.

[34] S.P. Gupta, '48 archaeological objections to Sharma's history of Ancient India' (ibid.,
      15 Jan. 1978, pp. 8- 9).

[35] See the debate between R.C. Majumdar and Romila Thapar in *Indian Express*, 29 and
      30 Aug. 1977; also the articles by Majumdar in *Organiser*, which Malkani did his best
      to tone down! (*Organiser*, 12 Dec. 1977).

[36] L.I. and S.H. Rudolph, 'Cultural policy, the textbook controversy and Indian identity'
      in A.J. Wilson and D. Dalton (eds), *The States of South Asia*, London: Hurst, 1982, p.
      139.

this ideological convergence the integration strategy was gradually being accompanied by a genuine effort to become assimilated within a 'Janata' current of opinion. Had this happened, the latter would have become dominated by Hindu traditionalist values and retained from Gandhianism the emphasis on decentralisation and the theme of cow protection reinterpreted in a militant perspective.

The *Organiser* published a number of special editions, on the cover of which were cartoons of Morarji Desai in the attitude of Gandhi turning his spinning-wheel, and of the Mahatma himself. The newspaper approved of the evolution of Desai's policy towards a political culture of synthesis.[37] P. Parameswaran, the director of the Deendayal Research Institute, called for a greater ideological cohesion based on the teachings of Gandhi, Lohia and Upadhyaya.[38] Deoras strongly affirmed the attachment of the RSS to Gandhi, whose 'emphasis [...] on quiet constructive work' it shared; the only remaining difference, in his view, was the policy to be followed towards the Muslims.[39]

The RSS accepted the amendment to its ideology and practice[40] brought about by the ex-Jana Sanghis partly because the new political constellation made possible its involvement – in an unofficial role which it had long hankered after – as ally and adviser to those in power. This function had already been prefigured by Golwalkar in the 1960s, and since then it had been spread throughout the organisation, as is shown in remarks made by 'grassroots' *swayamsevaks*.[41] In 1977, the RSS appeared more and more willing to serve as a collective *Raj guru*. Advani indirectly referred to this matter in interesting terms:

---

[37] Political economy, giving special attention to small enterprises and the countryside, as Charan Singh demanded of him, was particularly valued (J. Dubashi, 'The Janata revolution', *Organiser*, 26 Jan. 1978, p. 5. See also 2 April 1978, p. 3, and 17 Dec. 1978, p. 15, and Malkani's panegyric on Desai, 'Morarji Desai: the man with clear head and clean hands', ibid., 7 Nov. 1977, p. 7).

[38] 'Janata must chose between ideological cohesion or drift and disintegrate', *Organiser*, 7 Nov. 1977, p. 6. The DRI published a book on this theme: P. Parameswaran (ed.), *Gandhi, Lohia and Deendayal*, New Delhi: DRI, 1978.

[39] *Organiser*, 7 Jan. 1979, p. 1.

[40] See the interview with Rajendra Singh in ibid., 5 Feb. 1978, p. 5. However, Deoras was critical of Vajpayee's visit to China.

[41] One member of the RSS in Bhopal established an implicit connection between the world-renouncing quality of RSS cadres and their potential status as *Raj gurus*: 'Our old tradition is of a raja and a *guru*. A king rules but he has control from the *guru* who used to stay in the jungle, who never had any selfishness. [...] This person never wanted anything. So the RSS is playing a part but they don't expect anything. [...] Previously there used to be a king and a *guru*. And today it is transformed into a group of people who are selfless, and who control the situation, who look if everything is alright for the prosperity of the nation' (interview with P.P. Bapat, 25 Nov. 1989, Bhopal).

The *sadhus* and the *sannyasis* or, I would say, even the RSS have a moral and ethical influence on us. After all, there are thousands of *pracharaks* who are our peers, our equals in all respects, who never aspired for any office. Therefore we respect them.[42]

During the elections of March 1977, although many of its members were still in prison, the RSS placed its activist network at the service of Janata Party candidates[43] and then offered the government its help in tasks aimed at 'raising the national and social consciousness of our people'.[44] The Janata government had agreed to associate the RSS with an adult literacy programme, to which the ABPS devoted a solemn resolution.[45] In the same spirit the President of the Republic, Neelam Sanjiva Reddy, and Jagjivan Ram had attended the opening ceremony of the Saraswati Shishu Mandirs, at which 15,000 children were present.[46] Parallel to this Deoras held meetings with members of the government – not least with Morarji Desai himself, especially when the unity of the Janata Party was breaking up – or individuals close to the seat of power like Charan Singh and 'JP'. Deoras asked Charan Singh to cease his dissidence, and to 'JP' he announced, in October 1977, a plan of action to strengthen harmony between India's different communities.[47]

This attempt at exerting moral authority, coupled with work in society, tended to turn the RSS into a 'supra party' and 'extra-constitutional authority'[48] that was incompatible with the logic of democracy, simply because its centre of power was not subject to the verdict of the polls. The movement's new role reinforced the apprehension of secularist sections of opinion towards it, not least because the creation of a denser network of *shakhas* remained one of Deoras's priorities.[49]

Thus it was that a reshaped political scene appeared to be in the making, as much in terms of alliances – where the combination that was established by the ex-Jana Sanghis and Morarji Desai's former Congress (O) gradually emerged as the linchpin of the Janata coalition[50] – as in terms

---

[42] Interview with L.K. Advani, 11 Feb. 1994, New Delhi.

[43] *Organiser*, 4 June 1977, p. 5.

[44] Ibid., 28 May 1977, p. 1.

[45] *RSS resolves*, op. cit., pp. 86-7.

[46] *Statesman Weekly*, 9 Dec. 1978, p. 8, and *Organiser*, 19 Nov. 1978, p. 1.

[47] *Hindustan Times*, 31 Oct. 1977, and *Statesman Weekly*, 29 July 1978, p. 4.

[48] On this point see D.R. Goyal, *Rashtriya Swayamsevak Sangh*, New Delhi: Radha Krishna Prakashan, 1978, p. 196.

[49] *Organiser*, 16 April 1978, pp. 1-2.

[50] Apart from ideological affinities, this rapprochement was helped, from the spring of 1978, by the tensions in the northern states resulting from growing differences about the question of reservations for the Backward Classes between the ex-BLD and the ex-Jana Sanghis; these developments pushed the latter towards the ex-Congress (O) (see below).

of the values or legitimate norms invoked by this grouping, which harked back to Gandhism, albeit in a new form reinterpreted towards Hindu traditionalism and even Hindu militancy. The RSS could be sure of having a role in this arrangement. The ex-Jana Sanghis, who were its chief beneficiaries, would do all in their power to perpetuate this situation, especially from the moment when the first factional struggles appeared within the government.

The ex-Jana Sanghis and the question of unity

The rivalry between Morarji Desai and Charan Singh was set in motion after the March 1977 elections when it became necessary to decide who should be Prime Minister.[51] 'JP' and Acharya Kripalani (another Gandhian veteran), who were invited to settle the matter, decided in favour of Morarji Desai; but Charan Singh, who was appointed Home Minister, could not accept his defeat. He had also failed to obtain the presidency of the Janata Party on behalf of a leader of the former BLD since it was ultimately given to Chandra Shekhar. In May 1978 Charan Singh denounced the economic policy of the government, arguing that it discriminated against the rural areas. On 28 June 1978 he described its members as a 'collection of impotent men' for their pusillanimity towards Indira Gandhi whom he wanted to see stand trial for her actions during the Emergency. The following day Desai forced him and Raj Narain, the Minister of Health, who was his ally in the struggle against the Prime Minister, to resign. The two men also resigned their seats on the National Executive Committee of the Janata Party.

However a troop of mediators immediately stepped in, among them Vajpayee, Advani, George Fernandes and Biju Patnaik, who had found Desai's resignation demand excessive.[52] At a committee meeting of the Janata Party's National Executive on 10 July, Vajpayee repeated, along with Nana Deshmukh, how necessary it was to maintain party unity in a spirit of 'forgiveness'. Hence the Executive passed a resolution expressing its 'desire' that Charan Singh and Raj Narain should not resign from it, which they accepted, although they were not brought back into the government.[53] During July and August 1978, the mediators continued their efforts to reintroduce Charan Singh into the government, and Vaj-

[51] Jagjivan Ram was also standing as a candidate and had Jana Sanghi support, partly because the Hindu nationalists hoped in this way to improve their image in the eyes of the Scheduled Castes (A.B. Vajpayee, 'All responsible for Janata crisis', *Indian Express*, 2 Aug. 1979).

[52] L.K. Advani, *The people betrayed*, op. cit., p. 68; N. Deshmukh, *RSS: victim of slander*, op. cit., p. 58.

[53] *Link*, 16 July 1978, p. 9

payee declared: 'Actually we are the peacemakers of the party, whenever it faces collapse.'[54]

Vajpayee and the other mediators obtained a postponement of the organisational (party) elections in the Janata Party (to replace the *ad hoc* committee formed in 1977) by arguing that such an election, conducted in his absence, 'would be humiliating to Charan Singh'.[55] These conciliatory moves were not to bear fruit till January 1979 when the danger that Indira Gandhi might return to the political scene appeared more real given her success in a by-election at Chikmagalur (Karnataka) in November 1978. On 24 January 1979, Charan Singh rejoined the Desai government as Minister of Finance and Deputy Prime Minister – a title he would share from now on with Jagjivan Ram. Advani and Vajpayee, along with George Fernandes, Madhu Dandavate and Chandra Shekhar, had done much to engineer his return.[56]

This conciliatory strategy, seeking to build the former Jana Sangh into the key component of a movement inspired by Hindu traditionalism, was above all suited to the all India leaders of the Janata Party but it was not evident in the states, as was shown by the situation in Madhya Pradesh. There, the 'culture of the *shakha*' appeared to be largely incompatible with 'Janata culture'.

'Shakha culture' or 'Janata culture'?: the Janata Party in the Hindi belt

The reluctance of local Jana Sangh activists to accept any dilution of their party's identity has already been analysed in previous chapters as a major constraint on the leadership's conduct. In 1977, many of these cadres, who often had an RSS background, were elected as MPs or MLAs, partly because of their role in the Emergency and the repression to which they had been subjected,[57] and partly because of the unpopularity of Congress, largely on account of its programme of forced sterilisations. This scenario gave the Hindu nationalist leaders the opportunity to dispense with notables in order to compete with Indira Gandhi's party, whose candidates suffered from a severe handicap, regardless of who their opponents were. These factors contributed to the electoral success of Hindu

---

[54] Ibid., 6 Aug. 1976, p. 14.

[55] *Organiser*, 30 July 1978, p. 2.

[56] L.I. and S.H. Rudolph, *In pursuit of Lakshmi*, op. cit., p. 175, and L. K. Advani, *The people betrayed*, op. cit., p. 69.

[57] It also seemed that during the Emergency fewer Jana Sanghis than members of Congress (O) were willing to renounce their party in order to join the party in power (*Statesman Weekly*, 14 Feb. 1976, p. 9, 20 March 1976, p. 13 and 10 April 1976, p. 9).

nationalist activists in the Lok Sabha election of March 1977.[58] The same phenomenon was to be seen in the Vidhan Sabha elections of June, especially in Madhya Pradesh (where 1,803 out of the 1,807 political prisoners arrested in 1975-7 under MISA, the Maintenance of Internal Security Act, were reportedly Jana Sanghis).[59]

The era when the party solicited candidates from among notables and princes seemed to be over in Madhya Pradesh as elsewhere. Moreover in 1977 more princes sided with the Congress – for which one finds part of the explanation in the political fortunes of the Scindia family of Gwalior. The imprisonment of Vijaya Raje Scindia during the Emergency had harmed her health, and this, combined with her conviction that the democratic process had been permanently warped, led her to announce her retirement from politics. Her son had resigned from the Jana Sangh, and stood successfully in March 1977 as an independent before joining the Congress.[60] Only one other Congress candidate was elected in the entire state. The only prince to be put up by the Janata Party and elected was the Maharajah of Panna, Narendra Singh. He was a former member of the Jana Sangh and had been in prison throughout the Emergency. Rajmata Scindia meanwhile decided to support the Janata Party before the Vidhan Sabha elections of June 1977.[61]

To have opposed the Emergency and forfeited one's liberty in the process was one of the principal criteria for selection as a Janata Party candidate in these elections. Within the Hindu nationalist camp this worked in favour of *swayamsevaks*, whether or not they were active members of the Jana Sangh. In Shivpuri, for example, Babu Lal Sharma, who had given up his responsibilities in the Jana Sangh – because, in his words, he disliked politics – and then became *sanghchalak* of the local RSS, found himself continually proposed for adoption by the Janata Party because his 22 months in detention had singled him out as a valuable candidate.[62] By contrast, the local Jana Sangh MLA since 1962 had put his personal security before opposition to the new régime, and this was enough to disqualify him. Babu Lal Sharma declined the offer of a candidacy but

---

[58] Only a dozen deputies had been elected on the basis of local power or princely status. By contrast, some thirty deputies were pure products of the RSS who had often held the post of *pracharak* and for whom it was their primary electoral function, as in the case of Murli Manohar Joshi (*Sixth Lok Sabha Who's Who*, New Delhi: Lok Sabha Secretariat, 1977, p. 252).

[59] *The Hindu*, 23 Jan. 1977, and *Hindustan Times*, 18 Feb. 1977.

[60] V.R. Scindia with M. Malgonkar, *Princess*, op. cit., pp. 252 and 259. Close allies like Yashvant Singh Kushwaha followed Madhav Rao Scindia into Congress (*Statesman Weekly*, 26 Feb. 1977, p. 4).

[61] Ibid., 4 June 1977, p. 9. This was also the case with Bhanu Prakash Singh, Maharajah of Narsingarh (ibid., 11 June 1977, p. 15).

[62] Interview with Babulal Sharma, 27 Nov. 1989, Shivpuri.

another local activist, Mahavir Prasad Jain, accepted. A RSS member since 1945, he had been arrested in November 1975 for making a public speech against the Emergency in the context of a *satyagraha*.[63] He was elected even though he had never contested an election before.

This profile of an 'apolitical' activist trained by the RSS applied to a large proportion of the victorious candidates in the 1977 elections. Of the 93 ex-Jana Sangh MLAs for whom pertinent biographical information is available, 71 had been in prison for between 17 and 21 months during the Emergency, 6 had turned to underground work, and 49 of these – a majority – had been well-known members of the RSS. This progression in the number of Hindu activists was paralleled by an increase in representatives of the liberal or intellectual professions (22 lawyers, 7 teachers, 9 doctors of medicine); farmers (23) and merchants (12) made up smaller percentages. It should be emphasised that notables (*sarpanchs*, directors of cooperatives) who were not members of the Jana Sangh, at least before gaining those positions, numbered only 18 out of 93. But this downward trend was accompanied by an increase in the number (11) of *swayam-sevaks* who had been 'notabilised' as municipal councillors and *sarpanchs*.[64]

These developments suggest that the gains in legitimacy won by the Hindu nationalists and the RSS, combined with the unpopularity of the government, relieved them of the need to seek out notables as candidates and thus allowed for a reaffirmation of the Sangathanist model. Senior *sangathan mantris*, like N.P. Gupta and N. Johri, also stood in the elections so as to form the backbone of the legislative group, which was certainly going to be needed.[65]

This move contained the seeds of a contradiction since it brought to the fore cadres who were particularly attached to the specifics of their own ideological tendency, just when the national leadership was aiming at integration within a broader group. The reservations felt at the grassroots level towards the constraints imposed by amalgamation in the Janata Party found expression at the elections in June through the rebel candidacies of numerous ex-Jana Sanghis who were not prepared to leave the field free for their new Socialist or BLD allies. Such was the case with Baburao Paranjpe at Jabalpur.[66] After the elections, this reluctance to 'play the unity game' persisted, especially among the ex-Jana Sanghis, because they

[63]   Interview with Mahavir Prasad Jain, 29 Nov. 1990, Shivpuri. In Gwalior region, another (successful) candidate for the Vidhan Sabha, standing for the first and last time, was Indrapurkar, a lawyer in Gwalior gaoled there during the Emergency (interview with Indrapurkar, 28 Nov. 1989).

[64]   *Madhya Pradesh Vidhan Sabha Sadasya Parichay – 1977*, Bhopal: Madhya Pradesh Vidhan Sabha Sachivalay, 1977 (Hindi).

[65]   Interview with N.P. Gupta.

[66]   Interview with Baburao Paranjpe.

constituted the strongest contingent in the Janata Party parliamentary group, with 128 out of 231 seats (in an assembly of 320 members).[67] Thus they occupied more than half of the seats of the Janata Party majority, while the balance consisted mainly of Socialists (about 80)[68] with a small group of ex-BLD members.

The policy enacted during the two and a half years of Janata Party rule in Madhya Pradesh varied according to who was in charge of the government. However one constant feature did emerge: a concern to perpetuate the Jana Sangh's mode of operation without really allowing space to partners with other party affiliations.

One important decision taken with the views of the Socialists in mind was the choice of K. Joshi as head of the government. The Socialists had opposed the nomination of Sakhlecha, who was the choice of Thakre but who they thought personified Hindu nationalist rigidity.[69] However, the reasoning of the ex-Jana Sanghis was based not in terms of the Janata Party but of a coalition whose component parts would be granted ministerial portfolios in proportion to their weight in the government majority; thus the ex-Jana Sanghis received 20, the Socialists 8, the ex-BLD 2, and the ex-Congress (O) and ex-CFD 1 each. Far from acquiescing in under-representation, as they had done at the Centre, the ex-Jana Sanghis sought a proportionality which, in qualitative terms, meant that they took control of all the important ministries: Home (K. Joshi), Commerce and Industry (Sakhlecha), Finance (Ram Hit Gupta), Agriculture (Y. Meghawale), Health (S. Sahai), Labour (L.N. Sharma) and Education (Haribhau Joshi). One consequence of this development was that certain Socialists decided that they would support the government without participating in it and thus launched a mission to save Madhya Pradesh from the 'forces of the right'.[70] Far from trying to win over this Socialist group, K. Joshi preferred to persuade a fraction of its members to share power by offering

---

[67] Some newspapers gave a rather different figure: the ex-Jana Sanghis were supposed to have had 147 seats in 1979 according to the *Statesman* (Delhi), 26 Oct. 1979, but the *'Who's who in the Vidhan Sabha'* does not substantiate this estimate.

[68] While Madhu Limaye was in prison in Madhya Pradesh during the Emergency he developed good relations with Thakre. After the Janata Party was formed he obtained the presidency of the State Election Committee, which selected candidates, for a Socialist, Y.P. Shastri. This helped the Socialists to obtain a large number of nominations, but they did not know how to turn this advantage to good use 'because of their internal differences or may be lethargy' (interview with M. Limaye, 21 Oct. 1991, New Delhi).

[69] Joshi was selected through a combination of local factors in Madhya Pradesh, but also as a result of his acts of resistance during the Emergency, with which nothing in Sakhlecha's record could compare. Sakhlecha was freed 'on parole' after several months in prison, whereas Joshi was beaten while he was in jail (P.G. Sahasrabuddhe and M.C. Vajpayee, *The people versus Emergency*, op. cit., p. 411).

[70] *Times of India*, 13 Aug. 1977.

them three portfolios,[71] which they accepted. The national leadership of the Janata Party finally called on the ex-Jana Sanghis to relinquish one of their ministries.[72] Thereafter the Madhya Pradesh state government's policy was clearly Jana Sanghi in its inspiration and implementation.

The government's strategy was to resort to ordinances rather than laws, which enabled it to avoid a compromise when its partners disapproved of its policy. Thus in October 1977 K. Joshi promulgated an ordinance authorising imprisonment for three months without trial, a measure introduced to break a strike by employees of the Madhya Pradesh Electricity Board. Immediately certain Socialists denounced what they described as a 'mini-MISA'.[73] This authoritarian tendency became even more marked in January 1978 when Sakhlecha succeeded Joshi as head of the government, Joshi having succumbed to health problems.

Though he was confirmed in office with the votes of a majority of the Socialists, Sakhlecha's appointment went against the wishes of this group[74] and 25 Janata Party MLAs voted for another candidate.[75] He gave every indication of being austere, disciplined, well organised and industrious – characteristics of *shakha* culture. He changed the composition of the government he had inherited from Joshi without altering the proportions of the different currents of opinion and adopted a policy combining decentralisation with concern for discipline. He organised municipal elections in the state's 15,000 *panchayatas*, the first to be held for a decade,[76] for which panchs and sarpanchs were to be directly elected. The government also enlarged their functions; every village *pannchayat* was given a secretariat (*sachivalay*) which included all the village's functionaries, who could thus be seen collectively by the villagers at least one day a week.[77] Moreover, the local administration was empowered to act on plans submitted to it by the *panchayat*; previously they had to be referred to state level. Apart from these decentralising initiatives, which constituted the area of overlap between Hindu nationalist ideology and 'Janata culture', little was achieved,[78] and the authoritarian aspect of '*shakha culture*' predominated in the exercise of power.

In February 1978, the police were given a free hand to deal with a

71   *National Herald*, 9 July 1977.
72   *Organiser*, 18 July 1977, p. 13.
73   *Link*, 16 Oct. 1977.
74   Ibid., 17 July 1977, p. 18, and interview with Raghu Thakur 31.10.95, N.D.
75   S. Rajput, *Role of the Chief Minister in state administration*, New Delhi: Radha Publications, 1994, p. 36.
76   *Times of India*, 21 June 1978 and 18 Jan. 1979.
77   Interview with V.K. Sakhlecha.
78   U.T. Joshi, 'Janata: One-year rule. Expectations mostly belied in M.P.', *Times of India*, 8 June 1978

demonstration by students demanding better conditions; on 5 April a long strike by miners was put down with bloodshed at Neemuch; and in October the government issued an ordinance, in response to a strike by state functionaries for better pay, providing for a fine of 500 rupees or six months' imprisonment for any employee guilty of disturbing public services.[79] Under pressure from the Socialists, this plan ultimately was to affect only those public services, such as hospitals, where the right to strike was already regulated – which did not prevent 30 ex-Socialist Party and BLD MLAs from voting against it. In addition, the government encouraged the regular use of Hindi in the local courts of justice,[80] while Christians complained of being presented with questionnaires by the administration which demanded to know the circumstances of their conversion and the age at which this had taken place (the conversion of minors would have led to prosecution under the Dharma Swatantra Act (1968)[81] – see p. 224).

These measures naturally evoked protests from the Socialists, but the ex-Jana Sanghis considered their partners more as an embarrassment, impeding their imposition of a new '*shakha* culture', than as one of the elements of a new 'Janata culture'. The way one of the then ministers describes the Socialists of that time, some ten years later, is revealing on this point:

They were few people, one thing. And secondly, since more members were out of the stock of the Jana Sangh, so we were smoothly working in the government and delivering the goods to the people of Madhya Pradesh. [...] Socialists, they are in habit of deciding, or criticizing people who are in front of them. [...] So that was actually not a matter for consideration.[82]

Babulal Jain, who became Minister of Education at the end of the Janata experiment in Bhopal, was even more explicit:

Jana Sanghis never wanted to join these people, the Socialists. We wanted to keep our separate identity. [... the Socialists] belonged to a culture that is the Congress culture. [...] Just to save democracy we had to forget our identity and join such fellows in whom we had no confidence.[83]

Vajpayee, anxious to change such attitudes, asked Sakhlecha to treat the Socialists tactfully when there was a ministerial re-shuffle in October 1978.[84] Sakhlecha's only concession was to give Mineral Resources to a

---

[79] *Link*, 26 Feb. 1978, p. 14; *Patriot*, 11 April 1978; *Link*, 17 Sept. 1978, p. 21 and 8 Oct. 1978.

[80] *Statesman Weekly*, 27 Aug. 1977, p. 6.

[81] *Link*, 4 June 1978.

[82] Interview with S. Sahai.

[83] Interview with B. Jain.

[84] *Patriot*, 20 Oct. 1978.

Socialist minister previously in charge of Rehabilitation and the Waqf. In spite of Socialist protests, Sakhlecha amassed for himself eleven portfolios, accounting for 50-60% of the budget, before handing back Electricity to K. Joshi. The Socialists were dealt with in a similar fashion within the Janata Party in the state.

The presidency of the Janata Party was given to Thakre, whose organisational talents were universally acknowledged. He was backed up by five General Secretaries in an *ad hoc* committee representing all the former parties which made up the Janata Party. With the help of one of these General Secretaries in particular, Pyarelal Khandelwal, he sought to turn the Janata Party into another Jana Sangh. The party had been founded on 23 January 1977 by the Jana Sangh, the Socialist Party, the Congress (O) and the BLD at the residence of Babulal Gaur, the first 'Janata' candidate to be elected from Bhopal. It was not a 'neutral' venue, because the headquarters of the party were subsequently established in the Jana Sangh's former premises at Mookerjee Chowk in the city.[85]

In February 1978, the Socialists accused Thakre of having dismissed from their posts the officers (not former members of the Jana Sangh) in charge of fifteen Janata Party local branches, who in each case had been nominated with the agreement of local activists rather than being elected, since inner-party elections were continually being postponed (see below).[86] Some weeks later, Raghu Thakur, the Socialist General Secretary of the Janata Party in the state, announced the formation of eighteen parallel district branches of the party. Thakre immediately suspended him for 'anti-party activities', with the approval of Morarji Desai.[87] Chandra Shekhar then worked out a compromise by dissolving the parallel committees in exchange for the lifting of the sanctions imposed by K. Thakre. However, shortly afterwards the parallel committees were reformed and placed under the 'umbrella' of a 'non-Jana Sangh Front' of which Raghu Thakur was the guiding spirit.[88] Thakur then organised a conference of minorities, with Raj Narain's participation, to protest against the government's Hindu bias, and he denounced unremittingly the infiltration of the administration by members of the RSS.[89] At the beginning of 1979, this Socialist fraction chose not to support K. Thakre when for the first time he contested a Lok Sabha seat (Khandwa) in a by-election

---

85 *National Herald*, 7 July 1977. The partners of the ex-Jana Sanghis later had it transferred to the 'MLAs' Rest House' (an area of deputies' lodgings), but since Thakre continued to live at Mookerjee Chowk, the party's activity remained centred there (*Hindustan Times*, 7 Jan. 1978).

86 *Sunday Standard*, 26 Feb. 1978.

87 *Times of India*, 2 and 7 May 1978.

88 Ibid., 8 May 1978 and 18 June 1978.

89 *Link*, 7 May 1978 and 10 Dec. 1978.

– successfully, as it turned out.[90] Finally, in July 1979, while the Janata Party was breaking up at the Centre, three Socialist members of the government resigned and about 32 MLAs were expelled.[91]

The instability of the Janata Party in Madhya Pradesh was at first sight due to the obstructive strategy followed by the Socialists. Such an attitude largely reflected their fear of being overwhelmed by the ex-Jana Sanghis – a fear which the latter's actions could not fail to inspire. Rather than seek compromise, the ex-Jana Sanghis abused their position of strength, a pattern of behaviour witnessed at both the governmental level and inside the Janata Party, where the Socialists were unwilling to contest organisational elections for fear of being submerged by the local ex-Jana Sangh network.

The way in which power was exercised in Madhya Pradesh neatly illustrates the difference between the Hindu nationalists at the regional and national levels during 1977-9. If the Jana Sangh leaders, in pursuit of their strategy of assimilation, were ready to dilute their ideology and work for the unity of the Janata Party at the national level, the Hindu nationalist leaders in the states remained true to the Sangathanist model and, as long as they were in a position of strength, sought exclusive power rather than power-sharing.

The situation was a little different in the other states and Union territories where the post of head of government had fallen to a leader who had formerly belonged to the Jana Sangh. In Rajasthan, B.S. Shekhawat was more accommodating than Sakhlecha and tried to turn words into action, as was shown by his *antyodaya* plan designed to assist the poorest families; in Delhi, K.N. Sahni, the Chairman of the Metropolitan Council, displayed a degree of goodwill towards the Muslims of Turkman Gate who had lost their homes; and in Himachal Pradesh, the policies of Shanta Kumar were closer to those of Sakhlecha.

Relations between the different components of the Janata Party were also difficult in Uttar Pradesh, Haryana and Bihar. In these states the growing divergence between the ex-BLD and the Socialists on one side and the ex-Jana Sangh on the other was the result of the decision taken by the Uttar Pradesh and Bihar Janata governments, both led by Chief Ministers who had belonged to the BLD, to reserve a proportion of posts in the state's bureaucracy and educational institutions for members of the Other Backward Classes.

In Bihar, a member of the former BLD, Karpoori Thakur, was elected as leader of the Janata Legislature Party (JLP) on 21 June 1977 by 144 votes against 84 cast for his Congress (O) rival, Satyendra Sinha. The

90 *Organiser*, 18 Feb. 1979, p. 16.
91 *Statesman Weekly*, 4 April 1979, p. 7.

ex-Jana Sanghis in the JLP had evidently voted for Karpoori Thakur, allegedly under pressure from their senior leaders.[92] Having taken office as Chief Minister, Karpoori Thakur chose a ministry which, for the first time in the state, contained more backward caste (38% of the total) than forward caste ministers (29%).[93] He subsequently decided to propose the implementation of the recommendations contained in the report of the state's Backward Class Commission (1976), especially those concerning the need to reserve places in the government services for members of the Other Backward Classes (OBC). The high caste members of his cabinet (who were mainly former Jana Sanghis) took the line that a new Commission should be appointed to study whether certain castes had moved ahead over the years and if the caste criterion should be abandoned in favour of one based on economic resources. The Backward Classes Commission had proposed that 26% of appointments to the civil service should be reserved for members of the OBCs, but in an effort to find an acceptable compromise Karpoori Thakur proposed that this proportion should be reduced to 25% and then, after a wave of protest, to 20%. However, the proposals sparked off violent demonstrations from high caste students who were reported to have received informal encouragement from the Janata Party's upper caste leaders, and especially from those who were former Jana Sanghis.[94] These leaders 'stepped up their efforts to destabilize the state government'[95] and in April 1979 Thakur lost a vote of confidence in the JLP after a number of Scheduled Caste MLAs (who were followers of Jagjivan Ram) had joined forces with the former Jana Sanghis against him.

Though the reservation issue was not as important in Uttar Pradesh as in Bihar, a similar controversy occurred there. The Chief Minister, Ram Naresh Yadav, was also a former member of the BLD. The government agreed to implement the recommendations contained in the report of the UP Backward Classes Commission, which had been submitted in 1977, and especially that places should be reserved in the state administration for members of the OBCs. The decision to grant a 15% reservation was debated in the UP Assembly in May 1978,[96] during which

---

[92] Sinha complained about the part which Nana Deshmukh played as central observer (*Statesman* (Delhi) 22 June 1977 pp. 1 and 7 and *National Herald*, 24 June 1977, p. 1); according to him, high-ranking Hindu nationalist leaders had to 'force' the ex-Jana Sangh MLAs to vote for Kapoor (interview with S.N. Sinha, cited in F. Frankel, 'Caste, land and dominance' in F. Frankel and M.S.A. Rao, eds, *Dominance and state power in modern India*, op. cit., p. 108).

[93] H. Blair, 'Rising kulaks and backward classes in Bihar', *EPW*, 12 Jan. 1980, p. 69.

[94] F. Frankel, 'Caste land and dominance in Bihar', op. cit., p. 109.

[95] Ibid., p. 111.

[96] *National Herald*, 12 May 1978, p. 4 and 8 June 1978, p. 1.

ex-Jana Sanghis 'expressed the disapproval of the upper castes towards the challenge to their power'.[97]

Besides the attitude of the ex-Jana Sanghis in state politics, the obdurate and indeed unrestrained attitude of some local Hindu nationalist leaders was revealed when fresh riots between Hindus and Muslims flared up in 1978-9. Violence at Aligarh claimed two dead in October 1978 and in November twenty-six, nineteen of whom were Muslim. In its report of enquiry the Minorities Commission alleged that Krishna Kumar Navman, former head of the local Jana Sangh and at that time of the Janata Party 'seem [ed] to have played a prominent role', along with close associates, in this riot.[98] In November, 16 of the 29 Janata Party members in Aligarh demanded his resignation, but in vain.[99] In April 1979, for the second time, a riot broke out at Jamshedpur, in which 108 people were killed, 79 of them Muslims.[100] The report of the resulting commission of inquiry pinned the blame on D.N. Pandey, the local MLA, a former Jana Sanghi elected on the Janata Party ticket.[101]

The number of riots per annum had fallen from 520 in 1969-70 to 248 in 1974; in 1976 there were 169, in 1977 188, and then the figures rose sharply again to 230 in 1978 and 304 in 1979. The intensity as well as the frequency of these later riots was exceptional: in 1978 three times more people died than was the case in 1977 (see Appendix B, p. 552).

In 1979 two tendencies attributable to local ex-Jana Sanghi activists combined to awaken the anxieties of their partners in the Janata Party: first, the limits of united action, which made them doubt the sincerity of these allies, and second, the renewal of inter-communal violence. These two phenomena, manipulated for political ends from the time of Charan Singh's return to government, were factors in the break-up of the Janata Party despite the efforts of the ex-Jana Sanghis at the Centre.

Return to 'political untouchability'

The apprehensions of the 'legitimate opposition' about being associated

---

[97] Z. Hasan, 'Patterns of resilience and change in Uttar Pradesh', op. cit., p. 187.

[98] *First annual report of the Minorities Commission*, New Delhi: Government of India Press, 1973, p. 73. See also E.A. Mann, *Boundaries and identity*, op. cit., pp. 175ff.

[99] V. Graff, 'Religious identities and Indian politics: A case study: Aligarh (1971-1981)', paper presented at the 10th European Conference on Modern South Asian Studies, Venice, 25 Sept. 1988, pp. 69-71.

[100] For more details, see C. Jaffrelot, 'Processions hindoues, stratégies politiques et émeutes entre hindous et musulmans' in D. Vidal, G. Tarabout and E. Meyer (eds.), *Violences et non-violences en Inde,Purushartha*, no. 16 (1993), pp. 261-87.

[101] *Report of the three-member commission of inquiry headed by Shri Jitendra Narain, former judge of Patna High Court*, New Delhi, 1981, p. 40.

with Hindu nationalists had first surfaced during the negotiations in prison, notably among the BLD and Socialists. They arose as much from scruples over having a communalist movement as an ally as from the fear of being smothered by it. Moreover the RSS, which had flourished in the Emergency and was always concerned to spread its network, could boast of an increase in manpower. The number of *shakhas* grew to over 10,000 in April 1977, rising to 11,500 a year later and 13,000 in 1979.[102] This expansion – which would have brought the number of *swayamsevaks* to one million after an alleged increase of 25% in 1978-9 – was also geographical, since the RSS had strengthened its base during the Emergency in Kerala and Karnataka. But the expansion also involved affiliates of the RSS. The BMS had seen the number of its adherents grow from 1.2 to 1.8 million between 1977 and 1980, while the ABVP's manpower increased from 170,000 to 250,000 between 1977 and 1982.[103]

The impression of strength generated by the RSS aroused fears of an internal threat among the former parties of the 'legitimate opposition', since the organisation was credited with the ability to control the former Jana Sanghis in the Janata Party. However, the allies of this group were also able to see advantages in having the RSS at the service of the Janata Party.

These two lines of thought undoubtedly merged in May 1977, when the president of the Janata Party, Chandra Shekhar, requested the RSS to join the former Jana Sangh in the process of amalgamation. In this he was supported by the Socialists and former BLD leaders like Madhu Limaye and J.A. Naik, who also proposed amalgamation with the Janata Party's social work and youth associations; the Seva-Dal, the youth movement of the Congress (O) and the Socialist Rashtra Seva Dal had already fused into one Janata Yuva. At the mid-August meeting of the Janata Party National Executive Committee, Limaye presented a note stating that the outline negotiations towards this end that he had held in May with Balasaheb Deoras and Muley had proved encouraging: the leadership of the RSS were pondering the proposal.[104] But the reaction of the RSS to these discussions, published at the same time in the form of an interview with Muley, was unambiguous:

The *swayamsevaks* of the Sangh are not volunteers who will spread durries [rugs] and fix the mikes for some leaders to come and make speeches. It should be clearly understood that we are nobody's boy scouts. The RSS is a great

---

[102] *Organiser*, 12 March 1978, p. 15; *Hindustan Times*, 19 April 1977; *Indian Express*, 15 May 1978; and *Balasaheb Deoras with Delhi newsmen in the press club of India March 12 1979*, New Delhi: Suruchi Sahitya Publications, pp. 7 and 32.

[103] W. Andersen and S. Damle, *The brotherhood in saffron*, op. cit., p. 215.

[104] Interview with M. Limaye.

socio-cultural organisation. It is devoted to the inculcation of national character, eradication of untouchability, casteism, communalism, provincialism and lin-guism.[105]

Being in charge of the youth wing of the Janata Party and of its workers' branch, Limaye then tried to amalgamate the youth organisations and also the labour unions that had traditionally been linked to the components of the new party. Thengadi, on behalf of the BMS, flatly rejected the plan by virtue of his refusal, in principle, to contemplate any relationship between labour unions and political parties.[106] As for the youth organisa-tion, parallel to the Janata Yuva, a Janata Yuva Morcha with close links to the former Jana Sanghis was formed at this time. It contained some Congress (O) members but no Socialists.[107]

'JP', still convinced that the RSS had a mission of social reform to accomplish, also believed that the new political constellation implied a change in the movement's way of operating. This would have involved the RSS either in becoming integrated with the Janata Party or, if it wished to preserve its independence, opening its doors to non-Hindus and so becoming representative of the nation in its totality. At a training camp in Patna on 3 November 1977, 'JP' invited the RSS to open itself to 'followers of other religions, especially of those religions which were not born in Bharat such as Islam and Christianity, but are Bharatiya in the same way as the Hindus are'.[108]

The RSS leaders showed little enthusiasm for his appeal.[109] Soon afterwards 'JP' retired from politics; he died in 1979. Their reaction confirmed that the RSS remained permeated by one major constituent element of Hindu nationalism: opposition to the Muslims as a cultural community. It contented itself with organising forums for mutual under-standing between communities,[110] and Muley wrote a somewhat cool letter to 'JP' saying that the RSS was doing all in its power where minorities were

---

[105] *Organiser*, 29 Aug. 1977, p. 1.

[106] See Thengadi's letter to Limaye of 5 Sept. 1977 (ibid., 19 Sept. 1977, pp. 9-14), and M. Limaye, *Politics after freedom*, Delhi: Atman Ram, 1991, p. 261.

[107] *Statesman Weekly*, 7 Jan. 1978, p. 15 and interview with Venkaiha Naidu (the former vice president of the Janata Yuva Morcha), 23 Feb. 1995, New Delhi.

[108] *JP's call to RSS*, Bangalore: Jagarana Prakashana, 1979, p. 1. Later in the speech, he added: 'You are people committed and devoted to ideals and also disciplined and imbued with many qualities. It is my expectation from you and, as an elder, it is my prayer, that God may bless you with strength enough to give a new shape to Bharat so that you are able to create a new Bharat in which human beings behave as brothers to each other and where there is no distinction of high and low, rich and poor' (ibid., pp. 5-6).

[109] At a personal meeting in June 1977, Deoras had already told 'JP' that such a change would take time (*Organiser*, 20 June 1977, p. 15).

[110] See the ABPS resolution of March 1978 (ibid., 12 March 1978).

concerned.[111] Balasaheb Deoras and Hans Raj Gupta then declared in November 1977 that Muslims would have to accept the principles and rituals of the RSS if they were to be admitted.[112] In line with this development, the RSS invited Muslims to its local branches during the Raksha Bandhan celebrations,[113] and praised those Muslims who already belonged to *shakhas*.[114] The acceptable Muslim remained one who had renounced his culture, at least where public life was concerned.

Certain Janata Party leaders – like Satyendra Narain Sinha, a member of the National Executive Committee – demanded that the ex-Jana Sanghis should dissociate themselves from the RSS,[115] citing article 5 of the Janata Party's interim constitution: that membership of the party was incompatible with that of any other political or communalist organisation. But the hostility of the Hindu nationalists towards any debate on this subject prevented discussion of the matter at the National Executive Committee meeting on 21 December 1977, at a time when the implementation of the government's programme claimed priority. Desai settled the question out of hand by declaring the RSS a cultural organisation.[116] This controversy, first raised in 1976 by Charan Singh, did not resurface within the Janata Party until 1979, when it served his purposes.

In 1978, the RSS once again became the target of the Congress and the Communists. Congress had warned the country against the infiltration of the Janata Party by the Hindu nationalists at a meeting of the AICC in March 1977, and did so again at its working committee meeting in August.[117] From July 1977 onwards the CPI published leaflets denouncing the fascism of the Hindu nationalists.[118] In January 1978, the Sampradayikta Virodhi Committee, which had close connections with the Left and Congress secularists, organised a seminar on the theme of the 'Character of the RSS'. The only leading figure in the Janata Party to take part was Raghu Thakur, who denounced the RSS's fascist tendencies.[119] The opposition then organised a demonstration in Delhi to protest against the involvement of the RSS in the adult literacy scheme,[120] from which it

---

[111] Ibid., 3 Oct, 1977, p. 3.

[112] *Hindustan Times*, 26 Nov. 1977, and *Indian Nation*, 1 Nov. 1977.

[113] *Organiser*, 12 Sept. 1977, p. 16.

[114] Ibid., 1 March 1978, p. 16.

[115] *Patriot*, 19 Aug. 1977.

[116] *Organiser*, 12 Sept. 1977, p. 13.

[117] *Times of India*, 8 March 1977, and G. Jain, 'The future of the RSS', *Times of India*, 31 Aug. 1977.

[118] See, for instance, K.L. Mahendra, *Defeat the RSS fascist designs*, New Delhi: Communist Party Publications, July 1977.

[119] *Hindustan Times*, 28 Jan. 1978.

[120] *Times of India*, 13 June 1978.

was excluded soon afterwards.[121] The Congress (I) ('I' for Indira Gandhi), formed in January 1978, did its utmost to exploit in the most visible manner possible the very fragile claim of the Hindu nationalists to public recognition of their respectability as political actors – always in the name of the secularist heritage of the 'fathers of the nation' and of the Constitution. This pressure was kept in check for a long time during 1978 by the good conduct of the ex-Jana Sanghis as mediators and conciliatory guardians of the Janata government's unity. But things changed at the end of 1978, when the alleged involvement of Hindu nationalist cadres in the riots at Aligarh and Jamshedpur gave added impetus to the arguments of the Congressite opposition. In the Lok Sabha debate on the Aligarh riot on 4 December, Vasant Sathe, of Congress(I), highlighted the responsibility of the 'fanatical' and 'paramilitary' RSS, and denounced the way in which Desai had recognised its status as a 'cultural organisation'. He called on all non-communalist parties 'to evolve a national consensus' to isolate this 'cancer in the body politic'.[122] Govinda Nair, of the CPI, was even more explicit, demanding that M. Limaye and Raj Narain should distance themselves from the Janata Party in the name of a 'democratic and secular society'.[123] The next day Indira Gandhi herself, mounting the podium in the Lok Sabha in order to undermine the unity of the Janata Party, returned to the same theme:

The other constituents of the Janata Party should try to wake up to the realities of the situation and the dangers to our country. [...] I am not saying that Jana Sangh should be removed from Government but there must be an effort to at least convert them that their attitude will not be tolerated. If you use the RSS, for instance, for adult education, then this kind of attitude is spread, it is not curbed and contained. [...] Whether it is culture, politics or education, the main thing is that this kind of attitude must be curbed by the Government.[124]

This appeal to secularist vigilance, combined with a hint of repression, was in the Nehruvian tradition but had a strong tactical dimension in that it suggested a political re-alignment. Desai immediately decided to 'calm passions',[125] but he could not escape from either renewed criticism by virtue of his association with the RSS, or denunciation of the Freedom of Religion Bill.[126] Both sincere and opportunistic secularists inside the

---

[121] *Patriot*, 26 Sept. 1978.

[122] *Lok Sabha debates*, 4 Dec. 1978, vol. XX, cols 271-8.

[123] Ibid., col. 33. At the same time, the CPI published a brochure about the activities of the RSS, notably its implication in the Aligarh riot (P.V. Parakal, *RSS double-talk exposed*, New Delhi: Communist Party Publication, 1979).

[124] *Lok Sabha debates*, 5 Dec. 1978, vol. XX, col. 281.

[125] Ibid., col. 289.

[126] Ibid., cols 295 and 350.

Janata Party combined their efforts to raise again the question of Hindu 'communalism' in political debate.

In November 1978 Raj Narain (who was still an associate of Charan Singh's dissident faction) was the first prominent politician to visit the devastated scene of the rioting in Aligarh and to accuse the Hindu nationalists of complicity in it. He also demanded that any ex-Jana Sangh ministers – at the Centre and in the states – who took part in RSS meetings should be dismissed.[127] Chandra Shekhar and Morarji Desai, who were probably anxious not to lose the support of the former Jana Sangh in their battle with the Charan Singh faction, rejected all notion of the RSS's involvement in the riots.[128] This led M. Limaye, after a visit to Aligarh, to denounce the Desai government for its complacency over the Hindu communalists. He did so in an open letter to Morarji Desai in which he took up many of the arguments used by the opposition:

The recent outbreak of communal riots in Aligarh and the role of the local RSS had not only completely alienated the sympathy of the Muslim minority, it has created doubts in the minds of many secular-minded Indians about the ability of the Janata Government to preserve the great traditions established by the national government under the leadership of Mahatma Gandhi. [...]

The fact that you gave a certificate to the RSS as a cultural organisation was interpreted by them as a licence for their aggressive activities. They have been using the position of their sympathisers in the administration not only to collect funds but to spread their tentacles in the remotest parts of the country. [...]

As Prime Minister it was your responsibility to control members of your government and also to influence the Chief Ministers to do the same in the matter of ministers attending RSS functions.[129]

A political realignment was now underway between secularists and opportunists of the former Socialist Party and the ex-BLD on the one hand, and members of the ex-Congress (O) and ex-Jana Sangh on the other. This realignment also reflected differences in terms of social bases and obligations, as the reservations controversy testified.

---

[127] *Amrita Bazar Patrika*, 13 Nov. 1978, and *Times of India*, 20 Nov. 1978.

[128] Chandra Shekhar modified his statement after a visit to Aligarh and called on the national leaders of the former Jana Sangh to exert stronger control over their local militants. However an inquiry by members of the Janata Party whitewashed the RSS in contrast to that published shortly before by Congress (I), which demanded the banning of the movement.

[129] Extracts on pp. 1, 3, and 6 of the open letter of 24 Nov. 1978, distributed by the AMU Students' Union. I am grateful to Violette Graff for providing this document. Desai replied in July 1979 that 'he had yet to come across any positive evidence of the involvement of the RSS as a body in these incidents [the recent communal riots]. Some individual members of the RSS may have figured but they may have figured as citizens involved in these incidents' (cited in B.D. Graham, 'The Prime Minister and the Hindu Right', op.cit., p. 201).

The second phase of the confrontation took place in Uttar Pradesh where, on 19 November 1978, Deoras organised a meeting at Lucknow to launch a counter-offensive. The ex-Jana Sangh ministers attended, some of whom, like the 500 *swayamsevaks* present, wearing uniform.[130] On the same day (24 January 1979) Charan Singh rejoined the government, he gave his fullest support to the expulsion by Ram Naresh Yadav, the head of the Uttar Pradesh government who was also his protégé, of two ex-Jana Sangh ministers who were continuing to participate regularly in *shakhas*. The ex-Jana Sanghis in the state joined with those in the CFD to overturn the government, but Charan Singh got another of his followers (Barnasi Das) elected as Chief Minister thanks to the support of CFD leaders whom he had won over while denouncing – with Raj Narain as his 'mouthpiece' – the fascism of the ex-Jana Sanghis.[131] This argument, when taken in tandem with the exposure of the ex-Jana Sanghis' upper-caste attitudes, began to hit home, placing the latter on the defensive. In February 1979 the Uttar Pradesh government prohibited the use of public places for *shakhas*.[132] Charan Singh's faction moved over very visibly to the theme of secularist legitimacy which the opposition had kept alive.

The strategy of the Charan Singh/Raj Narain faction was to weaken Morarji Desai by attacking his ex-Jana Sanghi allies. At the beginning of March, Raj Narain called for the dismissal of Vajpayee and Advani in a letter to the Prime Minister.[133] This campaign was echoed to some extent among members of the ex-Socialist Party where M. Limaye, who focussed his attack on the hold of the Hindu nationalists over the media, was its main proponent.[134] He made himself the mouthpiece of the secularist viewpoint by denouncing 'dual membership':

RSS believes in the theory of Hindu Rashtra, Hindu Sangathan. They never changed. [...] A Jana Sangh man are expected to have allegiance to the RSS, in that capacity he is a votary of the Hindu Rashtra. He signs our pledge and he becomes a votary of territorial nationalism. Can the same man perform two parts?[135]

In early April, the meeting of the Janata Party's National Executive Committee contented itself with entrusting to a sub-committee the task of examining relations between ex-Jana Sangh ministers and the RSS.[136] At this same meeting, the ex-Jana Sanghis repeated their demand for elections in the party to replace the *ad hoc* committee set up in the spring of

[130] *Times of India*, 20 Nov. 1978.
[131] Ibid., 4 April 1979.
[132] Ibid., 11 Feb. 1979.
[133] *Link*, 18 March 1979, p. 8.
[134] *Times of India*, 3 March 1978.
[135] Interview with M. Limaye.
[136] *Times of India*, 5 April 1979.

1977. Their persistence had begun to take effect by June 1978, but the elections were postponed till October and then put off indefinitely because of the apprehensions of the other partners in the Janata Party, particularly the ex-BLD, who were all too well aware of the Hindu nationalists' powerful network in northern India.[137] Such anxiety led the ex-BLD to boycott certain consultations that took place. Some Socialists, like M. Dandavate, also favoured – in April 1979 – the reconstitution of an *ad hoc* committee by consensus.[138] The ex-Jana Sangh's insistence on internal elections reinforced the mistrust of some of its partners, a feeling that was fully exploited after the riot at Jamshedpur, which created a propitious moment for Charan Singh to go on to the offensive. In a letter to Chandra Shekhar he demanded the expulsion of the Hindu nationalists from the Janata Party. In his opinion their presence was liable to lose the party support among the Muslims. There was also a danger that the Hindu nationalists would infiltrate the party, since they had a predisposition, resulting from their RSS background, to resort to anti-democratic practices. Charan Singh also announced a campaign on this theme, which Raj Narain intended to launch in Bihar.[139]

On 12 June, Raj Narain was expelled from the National Executive Committee of the Janata Party on the grounds of indiscipline. He then quit the party altogether, citing principally his hostility to the Freedom of Religion Bill, which had stirred up sharp controversy at that time. He founded a Janata Party (S) – 'S' for 'Secular' – which was soon able to count 47 MPs, mainly from the ex-BLD. Defections to this group finally deprived Morarji Desai of his majority and on 15 July he resigned as Prime Minister before the house could vote a motion of no-confidence in his administration. The resulting crisis was brought to an end on 28 July, when Charan Singh took office at the head of a minority government which had the open support of Janata (S) and the Congress Party led by Y.B. Chavan and the indirect backing of Mrs Gandhi's Congress (I). Charan Singh had thus made a bogey of the RSS to further his bid for power and had incidentally revealed how isolated the Hindu nationalists had become within the party system. The secularist approach had once again proved that it embodied a legitimacy that could be invoked to frighten certain

---

[137] Baru Sen Gupta, *Last days of the Morarji Raj*, Calcutta: Ananda, 1979, p. 19, and P.R. Goyal, *Rashtriya Swayamsevak Sangh*, op. cit., p. 193.

[138] *Times of India*, 5 April 1979.

[139] Ibid., 29 April 1979. In this state the ex-Jana Sanghis who had brought about the fall of the government of Karpoori Thakur could not prevent the defeat in May of their candidate Ram Sunder Das, partly because of the campaigns of Raj Narain and K. Thakur in which they warned against the danger of associating with Hindu communalists (ibid., 6 May 1979).

sections of the political class away from the Hindu nationalists, and thus be manipulated for reasons of self-interest.

Faced with this 'anti-communal' offensive, the RSS on the whole stood its ground despite certain superficial compromises. At the same time, the leaders of the former Jana Sangh largely agreed to the concessions required of them to remain in the Janata Party.

Deoras responded with determination to the attacks against his movement. On 4 March 1979 he hit back at those who ascribed political aims to the RSS. The occasion was the annual ceremony at the RSS's Delhi branch. This was a particularly grand affair since the 25,000 *swayamsevaks* who gathered together on the Ram Lila Ground were also joined by some 100 deputies and many ministers.[140] This tough stance was not to the taste of a man of compromise like Vajpayee, who was reluctant to be seen at an RSS celebration and therefore refused to be seated in the front row on this occasion.[141]

A conciliatory line tended to prevail in turn among the ex-Jana Sanghis. Thus, apparently at the suggestion of Bhandari, it was accepted that ministers should not be obliged to attend *shakhas*.[142] This symbolic gesture showed that even if membership of the RSS was non-negotiable for ex-Jana Sanghis, certain concessions were possible if they enabled them to keep their places at the heart of Janata. Their desire to be assimilated was also reaffirmed by Vajpayee in May 1979:

We have left the politics of Jana Sangh for ever. We should forget these things now and get participated in the only nationalist stream of the Janata Party based upon the four principles of nationalism, democracy, religious equality and social equality.[143]

To save the Janata government, the ex-Jana Sanghis did not hesitate to dissociate themselves from their former allies, the ex-Congress (O).[144] Although Morarji Desai had resigned as Prime Minister on 15 July, he at first refused to give up the leadership of the Janata Parliamentary Party. The former Jana Sanghis were among those who were pressing him to relinquish his party post in favour of Jagjivan Ram, who was thought to have a better chance of appealing to the Socialists as candidate for the post of Prime Minister, but it was not until 27 July that Desai stood down. By that stage Charan Singh had obtained sufficient support, including a

---

[140] *Times of India*, 5 March 1979.

[141] *India Today*, 16 March 1979, p. 27.

[142] *Link*, 18 March 1979, p. 8.

[143] *Times of India*, 13 May 1979.

[144] Both groups had made a particular point of collaborating – successfully – a few weeks earlier in the elections for the posts of leader and deputy leader of their parliamentary group against the ex-BLD group (*Statesman Weekly*, 19 May 1979, p. 7).

promise of backing from Congress (I), to justify the President in commissioning him to form a'government. However, Congress (I) withdrew its offer of support a few weeks later and on 20 August Charan Singh resigned from office. On the following day the President dissolved the Lok Sabha and called for fresh elections.

In the following months the ex-Jana Sanghis persisted in remaining in the Janata Party, even though this meant accepting ever larger concessions. In response to an explicit request by Chandra Shekhar, the new General Secretary of the RSS, Rajendra Singh (who had succeeded Muley in 1978) announced in July 1979 that the RSS was ready to consider, at the next meeting of the ABPS, an amendment to its constitution forbidding MPs and MLAs from engaging in politics while involved in *shakhas*.[145] But only a week after Rajendra Singh's announcement, the Janata Party enacted a rule change whereby it would no longer admit those who believed in a theocratic state.[146] Then Vajpayee proposed new concessions: organs of the RSS should not take part in political debate and nor should its members belong to youth organisations affiliated to a party or a labour union.[147] The important consideration, in retrospect, is that all this goodwill was in vain. After the election of January 1980 which brought Indira Gandhi back to power and reduced the Janata Party to a 9% share of the vote and 31 seats, Jagjivan Ram, its principal leader, reactivated the debate on 'dual membership' within the Janata Party. He wrote to Chandra Shekhar on February 26 that, in his view, 'no member of the Janata Party shall have any association with the RSS'[148] and resigned the following day in the name of this anti-communal crusade and the secularist values it embodied.

His defection can be explained in the same way as earlier ones. Jagjivan Ram was probably prepared to collaborate with the Hindu nationalists if they agreed to put their network of activists at his service, but since the RSS refused to take part in the election campaign – doubtless to show its disagreement with the 'politicians' – [149] he preferred to leave the party in order not to be subjected to the domination of the Hindu nationalists and to regain some prestige on the terrain of secularism. On March 18, the Janata Party's Parliamentary Board passed a resolution saying that 'no legislator or office-bearer of the Janata Party shall participate in the day-to-day activities of the RSS'.[150] The inclusion of this regulation in the

---

[145] A.M. Zaidi, *ARIPP-1980*, op. cit., p. 731.
[146] *The Hindu*, 20 July 1979.
[147] A.B. Vajpayee, 'All responsible for Janata crisis', op. cit.
[148] A.M. Zaidi, *ARIPP-1980*, op. cit., p. 733.
[149] *Times of India*, 29 Sept. 1979, 22 Oct. 1979 and 13 Feb. 1980.
[150] A.M. Zaidi, *ARIPP-1980*, op. cit., p. 732.

constitution of the RSS had already been proposed by Rajendra Singh to Chandra Shekhar in July 1979, and the ex-Jana Sanghis were content to wait for the meeting of the ABPS planned for 22-23 March to ratify it in the form of an amendment. However, Rajendra Singh's formula was not put to the vote at the RSS meeting. This failure to arrive at a decision could be explained, according to Andersen and Damle, by the change in the political context. Indira Gandhi's return to power would make the RSS a target for government action if it contributed to the unity of Janata, the principal rival of Congress (I), by passing a resolution – as formulated in July 1979 – to all intents and purposes dictated by tactical considerations.[151] The ex-Jana Sanghis took refuge in a 'wait and see' attitude, hoping this time for an act of mediation by Morarji Desai, who in fact proposed a compromise at a meeting of the Janata Party National Executive Committee on 3 and 4 April 1980. But this formula was rejected, which led to the ex-Jana Sanghis deciding to leave the party.[152]

They had tried to defer an outcome which seemed unavoidable, at the price of great symbolic concessions, because this schism would mean a return to 'political untouchability', as Advani himself commented.[153] This metaphor suffers from an obvious bias, for what was at stake was the illegitimate tie which the ex-Jana Sanghis still retained with the RSS. But it reveals the resentment of one of the national leaders who at that time was a keen proponent of assimilation.

The strategy of integration put into effect by the Hindu nationalists in the 1970s went through several variations, all of which failed as a result of internal contradictions between electoral and party-building strategies and/or the interplay of the activist network and the structure of the political arena.

The Jana Sangh's attempt in the early 1970s to compete with the Congress Party on the basis of a more effective programme in which populism took the lead over Hindu militancy, was immediately blocked by Indira Gandhi's superiority in this respect and counteracted by a strategy of party-building that involved an increasing dependence on notables and princes. The prestige that the Hindu nationalists later acquired during the 'JP movement' and the Emergency gave them cause to hope for their cooptation by their opposition partners in a 'Janata culture'; the latter – at least in the version epitomised by Morarji Desai – embodied

---

[151] W. Andersen and S. Damle, *The brotherhood in saffron*, op. cit., p. 226.

[152] A.M. Zaidi, *ARIPP-1980*, op.cit., p. 734 and L.K. Advani, 'Good Friday for the BJP!', *Organiser*, 26 April 1981, p. 2.

[153] L.K. Advani, *The people betrayed*, op. cit., pp. 72-5.

concerns such as decentralisation, deriving from Gandhi, and a certain Hindu traditionalism, with which RSS ideals had affinities. From a strategy of integration within the 'legitimate opposition' they moved on to what was essentially one of assimilation in which ideology was also at stake – such as Mookerjee had in mind when Tandon became president of Congress before founding the Jana Sangh, which in effect disappeared in 1977. This strategy failed to bear fruit, for two principal reasons.

First, the former Jana Sangh's local cadres continued to transmit a political culture which proved incompatible with the spirit of the Janata Party. This activist network was all the more feared because, had organisational elections been held, they might have allowed the Hindu nationalists to take control of local branches of the Janata party in much of North India, the regions in which the ex-BLD had its strongholds.

Second, throughout Janata's period in government, both Congress and the CPI continued to base a part of their propaganda on the denunciation of Hindu communalists, and in so doing appealed to secularism as a norm of the political system, something which nobody could contravene without betraying the 'Founding Fathers' of modern India. For some while this appeal was attenuated by the opprobrium which attached to its main advocate, Indira Gandhi; but its usefulness in political debate made it an instrument with which Janata Party politicians of a more secularist allegiance could turn the presence of RSS members in the 'party-coalition' into a decisive issue. Their secularism was probably sincere but in the case of Charan Singh the invocation of this 'normative rule' was at least partly tactical. In fact the way he behaved in 1978-9 is illustrative of a remark by F.G. Bailey:

It would be naive to assume that every leader or every member of a political community has thoroughly internalized its normative rules. Most leaders certainly manipulate normative rules in a pragmatic and cynical fashion to achieve prizes. Indeed, the prizes themselves may be pragmatic as when a position of honour carries with it substantial material perquisites.[154]

In the space of a few months, Charan Singh's campaign helped to erode the recognition gained by the Hindu nationalists.

Here one sees how the action of the legitimate opposition towards the Hindu nationalists was contradictory, given that its underlying considerations would always be those of power. In the 1960s its component elements became associated with the Jana Sangh primarily out of anti-Congress pragmatism. But ten years later, when this integration seemed to imply a certain dilution of Hindu nationalist ideology among the leaders of the former Jana Sangh, other Janata Party leaders dissociated themselves from them because they did not represent the same social grouping –

[154] F.G. Bailey, *Stratagems and spoils*, op. cit., p. 22.

Charan Singh's faction being more representative of the peasantry – and because anti-communalism was now a useful tactic. Thus certain sections of the former legitimate opposition successively helped to strengthen the Hindu nationalist current by enhancing its legitimacy and forming electoral alliances with it, and then partly hindered its normalisation and pushed back the more radical elements into Hindu militancy. The Janata episode thus confirms the role of the political context as an important factor contributing to the rise, marginalisation and transformation of the Hindu nationalist current.

Indeed the integration of the ex-Jana Sangh leaders in the Janata Party introduced a new distance between them and the RSS, as was seen at the end of 1977 when the latter formed joint action groups (Samanvaya Samitis) in which all its affiliates, with the exception of the ex-Jana Sanghis, took part[155] – probably as much for fear of revealing their illegitimate connections as because they were already involved in new ideological commitments.

In 1980 the Bharatiya Janata Party was presented by its ex-Jana Sangh promoters as the inheritor of the Janata Party, while the RSS was meanwhile reverting to the sources of its Hindu nationalism. Indeed, concluding from the Janata experience that 'the politicians can only divide',[156] Deoras turned his energies back towards Sangathanism by calling on the activist network to explain – and to establish – the organisation·in as many places as possible.[157] And, as we shall see in Chapter 10, he considered building the 'Hindu' vote as the best means of putting pressure on the political class. The failure of the Hindu nationalists' attempts at integration in the 1970s certainly appeared to be a factor in the progressive return of the RSS and its affiliates to Hindu militancy during the 1980s. Since this failure was partly the result of 'secularism' being used in the framework of a struggle for power, the 'political context' variable was once again shown to have had lasting consequences.

---

[155] W. Andersen and S. Damle, *The brotherhood in saffron,* op. cit., p. 142.

[156] *Organiser,* 14 Oct. 1979, p. 12.

[157] In Maharashtra, 2,500 activists covered 3,500 villages in the course of the campaign (ibid., 18 Nov. 1979, p. 4), and in Karnataka 6,500 villages were visited (ibid., 25 Nov. 1979, p. 9).

Part IV. THE CONVERGENCE OF HINDU NATIONALIST STRATEGIES IN THE 1980s

9

THE CONTRADICTIONS OF THE B.J.P AND THE EROSION OF SECULARISM

Advani: '...in India, a party based on ideology can at the most come to power in a small area. It cannot win the confidence of the entire country – neither the Communist Party nor the Jana Sangh in its original form.'
Panchjanya: 'But by ignoring the ideological appeal will you be able to keep together the cadres on the basis of these ideals?'
Advani: 'Effort is being made to make them understand. That is why I want the debate to go on.'
Panchjanya: 'However, despite its ideological anchorage, the Jana Sangh's appeal was steadily increasing.'
Advani: 'The appeal increased to the extent the ideology got diluted. Wherever the ideology was strong, its appeal diminished.'
(Interview published in the 1980 Diwali issue *Panchjanya*, a RSS weekly newspaper, and quoted in *Frontline*, 13 Oct. 1990, p. 29)

'The vibrations of Indira Gandhi's recent posturings in Assam, Punjab and Jammu (including Kashmir) have sparked speculation about the possibility that the Congress (I) is to be fashioned into a tribute of Hindu assertion. [...] She is obsessed with the business of retaining power at all costs, and whatever the consequences to the nation.'
(Romesh Thapar, 'Communalising our politics', *EPW*, 2 July 1983, p. 1163)

[About the 1984 parliamentary elections]. 'It was a conscious Hindu vote, consciously and deliberately solicited by the Congress Party as a Hindu Party. And this is what steered the party to a grand victory, decimated the "revisionist" BJP and reincarnated Cong (I) as BJP.'
(*Organiser*, 6 Jan. 1985, p. 1)

The three extracts quoted above suggest the beginning of a political and ideological 'reversal of roles'[1] that would have weighty consequences. And indeed the first half of the 1980s saw an important transformation in the parameters of our study. The ex-Jana Sanghis created a Bharatiya Janata Party (BJP) – Party of the Indian People – through which they aspired to inherit the mantle of the Janata Party. This approach entailed placing more emphasis on appeals to socio-economic interests rather than on the characteristic themes of Hindu nationalism, more reliance on politicians capable of appealing to group and sectional interests instead of ideologues, and a certain willingness to form electoral alliances with mainstream opposition parties. One could argue that this tactic of opening up was the result of a new variant of the strategy of integration; but it was more thorough-going than that which had been pursued in the early 1970s and, in consequence, aroused considerable resistance from local organisers and the RSS hierarchy, especially once it became clear that it would not result in electoral gains.

However, just at the stage when the BJP appeared to be moderating its use of Hindu nationalism, the will of the authorities to uphold secularism began to weaken. Instead of claiming consistently that religious appeals should not be used in the political arena the Congress leaders showed an increased interest in accommodating certain communal organisations in order to gain political advantage.

The BJP: heir to the Janata Party?

On 5 April 1980 the ex-Jana Sanghis inaugurated a new party, the Bharatiya *Janata* Party, which saw itself as the Janata Party's heir. Vajpayee – the BJP president – explained that the ex-Jana Sanghis could claim this special relationship because of the exemplary way they had conducted themselves while a part of Janata, where their attachment to the values of the 'JP movement' took pride of place.[2] This new move by the Hindu nationalists was aimed primarily at widening its base.

For Vajpayee it was imperative above all to avoid any comparison with the Jana Sangh, which had been condemned to an existence on the very fringes of mainstream politics.[3] In this spirit the BJP welcomed Janata Party leaders who had no previous association with Hindu nationalism, like Ram Jethmalani, a well-known Bombay lawyer who had become an

---

[1] R.E. Frykenberg, 'Hindu fundamentalism and the structural stability of India' in M. E. Marty and R. Scott Appleby (eds), *Fundamentalisms and the State*, University of Chicago Press, 199?., p. 244.

[2] *Hindustan Times*, 7 April 1980.

[3] *Times of India*, 6 April 1980.

MP for the first time in 1977; Shanti Bhushan, once Morarji Desai's Minister of Justice; and Sikander Bakht, also a former Janata minister and one-time leader of Congress (O).[4] Jethmalani and Bakht were appointed vice-presidents of the BJP – along with Vijaya Raje Scindia, Advani and Murli Manohar Joshi – and given the task, together with S.S. Bhandari, of writing the party's constitution.[5] This opening-up of the BJP was confirmed at the party's first plenary meeting in Bombay in December 1980, when a former Supreme Court judge, K.S. Hegde,[6] who had served as Chairman of the Lok Sangharsh Samiti for Karnataka during the 'JP movement' and as Speaker of the Lok Sabha in 1977-9, was appointed vice-president of the party in place of Advani, who now became one of its four general secretaries.

As well as co-opting some of its leading political figures, the BJP also claimed a part of Janata's programme. At a constituent conference in April 1980, its leaders announced that their electoral manifesto for the Vidhan Sabha elections, scheduled by Indira Gandhi for the coming June, would be none other than that of the Janata Party of 1977. This decision was confirmed at the meeting in Bombay when Vajpayee proposed as the party's creed 'Gandhian socialism' and 'positive secularism'. He went to great lengths to present the former as a cooperative third path that was particularly close to the Jana Sanghi tradition because of its decentralising and social reformist implications.[7] As for the latter, Vajpayee emphasised that it was different from Congress secularism, which he claimed was biased in favour of minorities in order to create 'vote banks'.

This attempt to appropriate the Gandhian message of the Janata found expression in the party's constitution, where the word 'Hindu' did not make a single appearance. The only discernible reference to the old Jana Sangh creed was to Upadhyaya's 'integral humanism', which was used as the heading under which the party's 'Five Commitments' were set out.[8] This, it was explained, was insofar as 'decentralised economy, integral humanism and Gandhian socialism are all manifestations of one and the same continuing theme'.[9]

---

[4] This was a sign of the ideological dilution affecting the Hindu nationalists. In 1952, Bakht's marriage to a younger Hindu woman was greeted with strong protests of an anti-Muslim character from the RSS camp (*Organiser*, 19 Feb. 1952, p. 1).

[5] *Times of India*, 7 April 1980.

[6] In 1973, K.S. Hegde had been one of the three judges of the Supreme Court entitled to become Chief Justice. He was bypassed by Indira Gandhi because he had pronounced against the government and subsequently resigned.

[7] A.B. Vajpayee, *India at the crossroads*, New Delhi: BJP Publication, 1981, pp.3-5.

[8] *BJP Constitution and Rules*, New Delhi: BJP Publication, 1981, p. 1. Apart from 'Gandhian socialism', and 'positive secularism', these were 'nationalism' and 'national integration', 'democracy' and 'value-based politics' (*Our five commitments*, New Delhi: BJP Publication, 1981, pp. 3-5).

In addition, the BJP wanted to distance itself from the former Jana Sangh through its actions rather than its defining principles. In July 1980, Jethmalani, with the active support of S. Bakht, introduced a Bill in the Lok Sabha that would once again legalise religious conversion. His justification for this initiative was the need to dispel anxieties engendered by O.P. Tyagi's Freedom of Religion Bill and to give credibility to the secularist image that the BJP wanted to promote.[10] In the same spirit, the party suspended Dina Nath Pandey's BJP membership (he had been re-elected as MLA for Jamshedpur on the BJP ticket) after he was implicated in the report of the commission of inquiry into the Jamshedpur riot.[11] In its efforts to distance itself from the Jana Sangh, the BJP moved towards a recognition of the composite character of the Indian nation. The party's Lok Sabha election manifesto of 1984 contained the following: 'Unity in diversity has been the hallmark of Indian culture, which is a unique, multi-hued synthesis of the cultural contributions made over the centuries by different peoples and religions.'[12]

Simultaneously, socio-economic issues were highlighted in a manner which recalled the populism of the Jana Sangh in the 1970s.[13] Campaigns were launched on themes such as inflation and corruption in October 1981.[14] After the electoral setbacks of 1983, which are discussed below, the party turned its attention to a more constructive programme of action. Vajpayee proposed to the National Council (the equivalent of the Jana Sangh's AIGC) that it should exploit the gaps in the Integrated Rural Development Programme (IRDP) launched by Indira Gandhi's government and do so in the framework of a welfare policy that had always been one of the Hindu nationalists' strong points. Peasants were to be helped in their dealings with the administration (to seek loans from local agencies, for instance) and, above all, corruption would be denounced at the local level. As Vajpayee explained,

It is hardly necessary to spell out the impact the BJP will make on the hearts and minds of the rural people if the BJP goes to the villages and declares that now that we are here, we would like to see which corrupt official tries to exploit these helpless people or harass them if they do not pay the demanded bribe. Any party, which takes up such a programme and honestly implements it, will surely win the

[9] *Economic Policy Statement*, New Delhi: BJP Publication, 1986, pp. 2-3.

[10] *Patriot*, 31 July 1980, and *Nagpur Times*, 3 Aug. 1980.

[11] *Tribune*, 16 Sept. 1981. Soon afterwards Pandey was exonerated of any charge, a decision greeted with a burst of publicity in the *Organiser* (28 Oct. 1981, p. 16).

[12] Cited in K. Choudhary, 'BJP's changing view of Hindu-Muslim relations', *EPW*, 17 Aug. 1991, p. 1901.

[13] *Resolution on the economic situation*, Cochin: BJP National Council, 25 April 1981, pp. 5-6.

[14] *Indian Express*, 11 and 13 Oct. 1981.

goodwill and trust of the rural masses and they will surely identify themselves with it.[15]

After the setbacks they had suffered through participating in the Janata Party, the founders of the BJP decided that they would never amalgamate with another party. In the long term, this choice involved making the BJP an alternative to Congress but it did not exclude the possibility of forging alliances, which, in fact, was an aspect of the party's effort to present a more open image.[16] This tactic, spurred forward by Vajpayee, took shape especially in the run-up to the general elections of 1984, during which he called on 'all the nationalist democratic forces in the country to heed the call of the hour [and] to accept our hand of friendships extended for the pursuit of a united national effort.'[17]

Charan Singh, who was as keen as ever to knit together an opposition which he could lead, responded positively to this appeal to form a National Democratic Alliance (NDA) devoid of any particular ideological slant.[18] Meanwhile, on the eve of the 1984 elections, he decided to dissolve his BLD in order to form a new party oriented more towards the peasants' interests – thus justifying the annullment of his agreement with the BJP. The latter investigated the possibility of collaborating with the Janata Party, but this could go no further than *ad hoc* electoral pacts. Now bereft of allies, it was all the more vulnerable in the face of the wave of sympathy which followed the assassination of Indira Gandhi by her Sikh bodyguards on 31 October 1984. In December 1984 Indira's son Rajiv Gandhi won a parliamentary majority greater than any obtained by Congress hitherto (415 in a house of 542); the BJP, though coming second in terms of votes (7.4%), gained only two seats. Then, in March 1985, when Vidhan Sabha elections were organised in the eleven states where the previous election had taken place in April 1980, overall the BJP suffered a reverse, its total number of seats falling from 198 to 169.

In the mid-1980s the party seemed to have reached an impasse. The tactic of openness, intended to make it the heir to Janata and thus an alternative to Congress by virtue of a socio-economic 'people-oriented' programme, had not enabled it to enlarge its base, and its policy of making alliances had misfired. In addition such openness had risked demobilising

---

[15] *Presidential address by Sri A.B. Vajpayee*, BJP 4th National Council Session, New Delhi, 15-17 April 1983. See details of the resolution in *Organiser*, 22 May 1983, p. 16.

[16] Interview with K.L. Sharma, 23 Nov. 1989, New Delhi. On this line of conduct see the resolutions passed by the National Executive in early 1982 (*Organiser*, 28 Feb. 1982, p. 8).

[17] *Presidential address by Sri A.B. Vajpayee*, op. cit., p. 9.

[18] See text of the agreement in *Organiser*, 21 Aug. 1983, p. 5.

the local cadres and alienating the RSS's hierarchy without attracting many new recruits.

Risks of divorce from the grassroots and the RSS

The ex-Jana Sanghis had withdrawn from the Janata Party partly in response to the demands of local cadres and activists, of whose discontent Advani and Bhandari had become well aware in the course of a national tour in February 1980.[19] But the BJP did not reflect either their ideology or their style of political action. At the party's first plenary session in Bombay, numerous delegates made no secret of their reservations. Vijaya Raje Scindia was one who spoke for this group: she circulated a note challenging the validity of 'Gandhian socialism' as one of the party's articles of faith, because in her eyes the concept of 'integral humanism' incorporated elements of social harmony (such as the extended family and the veneration of the old) that the word 'socialism', with its notion of class conflicts and its materialist connotations, lacked. And, above all, 'Gandhian socialism' represented a contradiction in terms, since 'socialism' related it to the state, whereas the message of Gandhi was one that concerned decentralisation and rural self-sufficiency.[20]

In Bombay, Rajmata Scindia's interpretation was well received by many delegates. The BJP's secretary in Madhya Pradesh, Kailash Sarang, spontaneously and outspokenly expressed the hostility of the activists in his state to the concept of 'Gandhian socialism'.[21] (And, as at the last plenary meeting of the Jana Sangh, in 1975, the delegates from Madhya Pradesh were the most numerous of all, after those of the state where the meeting was held.[22]) Altogether, 257 amendments to the resolution on 'Gandhian socialism' were tabled, but the leadership made no concessions of any substance. Only five delegates out of more than 50,000 defied party discipline and voted against it.[23]

As well as its diluted ideology, local and regional cadres were perturbed by the BJP's institutional framework, which seemed to have

---

[19] W. Andersen and S. Damle, *The brotherhood in saffron*, op. cit., p. 224.

[20] Interview with V.R. Scindia, 1 Sept. 1987, New Delhi and *Hindustan Times*, 27 Dec. 1980.

[21] *Nagpur Times*, 30 Dec. 1980, and *National Herald*, 28 Jan. 1980. A senior leader from Madhya Pradesh said of Vajpayee: 'He created confusion in the minds of the old workers by adopting Gandhian Socialism' (interview with Shejwalkar).

[22] In Bombay, the largest number of delegates (7,900) was from Madhya Pradesh, and the second largest (4,750) from Rajasthan out of a total of 54,632 (*Organiser*, 11 Jan. 1981, p. 2). In 1975, there were 5,214 from Madhya Pradesh (compared to 5,026 from Uttar Pradesh), out of about 40,000 (ibid., 8 March 1975, p. 16).

[23] *Hindustan Times*, 31 Dec. 1980.

incorporated many features of the Janata Party's organisation. The post of *sangathan mantri* disappeared; henceforward power was to be concentrated, below national level, in the party presidents of the different states. However, these presidents were often former *sangathan mantris*,[24] and the BJP continued to rely largely on the Sangathanist network, as the case of Madhya Pradesh makes clear.

Notabilised *swayamsevaks* and ideological notables and princes

In Madhya Pradesh, the persistence of the network of activists trained by the RSS and serving as a basis for the BJP was apparent from the lists of candidates in the elections of 1980 and 1985.

The Lok Sabha elections in January 1980 were remarkable, here as elsewhere, for demonstrating a general decline in the Hindu nationalists' fortunes; its only pockets of resistance were in Gwalior and most of all in Malwa, where the Janata Party in the state won three of its four seats. The defeat prompted Sakhlecha to resign in favour of Patwa but the state came under President's Rule following the dissolution of the Vidhan Sabha on 17 February. Elections for a new Vidhan Sabha were scheduled for 28 and 31 May; by this stage the state unit of the BJP, headed by Kushabhau Thakre, was in place. The BJP obtained 30.34% of the votes and won 60 seats in a house of 320. Of the 60 seats captured by the BJP, 41 were in Madhya Bharat but only 11 in the Gwalior area, where Madav Rao Scindia's attachment to Congress (I) had strengthened that party's position. Most of the successful BJP candidates were experienced Hindu nationalist activists. Almost 60% of those whose backgrounds were published[25] – 36 out of 51 – had entered politics by way of the RSS (20) or one of its branches (BMS, 1, ABVP, 4), or had been elected on the Jana Sangh ticket between 1962 and 1972 (11). The over-representation of such activists and veterans coincided with the heightened importance of Madhya Bharat – out of the 20 *swayamsevaks*, 19 were from that region, as were all the BMS and ABVP members.

About a dozen MLAs were elected on the strength of being local notables: managers of cooperatives (4), directors of *mandi samitis* (3) or elected members of local *gram panchayats* (2), *janapad panchayats* (1) and municipal councils (2). Often they obtained a post within the party and then became indoctrinated with its ideology. Himmat Kothari, for instance, the son of an important Jain moneybroker from Ratlam (a town where, in 1981, 8.5% of the population were Jains), thus entered the

24 Ibid. 8 Apr. 1980.

25 See *Madhya Pradesh Vidhan Sabha Sadasya parichay – 1980*, Bhopal: Madhya Pradesh Vidhan Sabha Sachivalay, 1980 (Hindi).

municipal council and then the Jana Sangh in 1972; in 1977 he began working for the BMS at the same time as he became a Janata Party MLA. He retained his seat for the BJP in the 1980, 1985 and 1990 elections, whereas in the past Jana Sangh candidates with a RSS background had never been able to capture it. Kothari regarded himself as completely in harmony with the Hindu nationalist line in spite of never having belonged to the RSS.[26] Such ideologisation of local notables was a natural dimension of party-building in 'clusters'. Over time, the public figures who were cultivated for the sake of their local influence became permeated by the doctrinal elements of the 'hard core' cadres who had passed through the RSS. Interestingly, half of the notables elected in 1980 had belonged to the Jana Sangh in the 1960s or early 1970s.

The Sangathanist approach was also converging with the ideologisation of notables since *swayamsevaks* who entered electoral politics tended in ever larger numbers to follow the path of 'notabilisation'. In 1980, 15 of the 20 MLAs with RSS backgrounds had obtained positions on local elected bodies or were in charge of cooperatives (9), or had combined these with some experience in government, which strengthened their influence over the local communities (5). Such 'notabilisation', which developed to the greatest extent in Malwa, helped the party by reducing its dependence on notables alone so it could remain as faithful as possible to genuine Sangathanist methods.

In all, the BJP seemed to have rallied only a modest number of new personalities capable of enlarging its following (only 8 MLAs, half of whom had entered politics via the 'JP movement', and the Janata Party satisfied this criterion). The fact that it held its own in Madhya Bharat was thus largely because of the old Sangathanist network, which was now being 'notabilised' and strengthened by notables who had become ideological over time. This development was reinforced by the elections of 1984-5. In the 1984 parliamentary election, the 'Congressite tide', helped by the adherence of a half-dozen *jagirdars* and maharajahs in the circle of Madhav Rao Scindia (who beat Vajpayee at Gwalior), left the BJP without a single seat in the state. In the Vidhan Sabha elections of March 1985, the party's share of the vote did not make any notable progress – 32.4%, as against 30.34% in 1980 – and though it won almost as many seats (58) as in 1980 (60), their distribution had changed: Madhya Bharat was no longer a party stronghold, since the BJP won only 22 seats there although its vote remained largely unchanged. The other regions of the state – Mahakoshal, Vindhya Pradesh and Chhattisgarh – provided the party with between 8 and 15 seats each.

In Chhattisgarh this breakthrough stemmed from a particularly effec-

---

[26] Interview with Himmat Kothari, 15 Oct. 1991, Bhopal.

tive network of activists, notables and princes centred on those associated with the Vanavasi Kalyan Ashram (VKA – Centre for Tribals' Welfare). The VKA had been founded in 1952 by Ramakant Keshav Deshpande, a Brahmin lawyer from Amraoti (now in Maharashtra), with the support of the state government and the RSS. Based in Jashpur (214 km. from Raigarh), it established schools in Raigarh and Surguja districts, an area with a large tribal population, with the aim of countering the appeal to the tribals of Christian mission schools.[27] The latter had been active among the Oraon tribes since the late nineteenth century. R.K. Deshpande worked from 1948 till 1957 in an official capacity with the Tribal Welfare Department, which feared that such missionary work would encourage separatism among the tribes.[28] He won the support of the Maharajah of Jashpur who, together with Golwalkar, in 1963 inaugurated permanent premises for the VKA[29] before the Maharajah joined the Jana Sangh. His son Dilip Singh Judeo proved a far more active official patron; in 1992 he declared himself to be a member of the RSS and a missionary.[30] Indeed, from 1984 onwards he made journeys into the hinterland in order to 'reconvert' Christianised tribals to Hinduism.[31] He drew most of his influence from his status as the scion of a royal house and an industrialist, which helped him to become president of the Municipal Council of Jashpur from 1975-85. In 1987 he was appointed vice-president of the BJP in the state and his political activity intensified.

The VKA, which had been closed down during the Emergency, benefited from the presence of former members of the Jana Sangh in the state governments in 1977-9 in its efforts to obtain funds.[32] It now grew rapidly, so much so that in 1977 it acquired national status (expressed in its new name, Bharatiya Vanavasi Kalyan Ashram), incorporating the tribal section of the VHP. From 1978 to 1983 the number of its full-time activists rose from 44 to 264 (56 of whom were tribals).[33] In Jashpur

---

[27] *Organiser*, 14 Jan. 1990.

[28] I. Sen, 'Women and proselytisation: A case study of Christian missionary and Hindu revivalist attitudes towards women in Raigarh district of Madhya Pradesh', paper presented at the World Sociological Congress, Madrid, July 1990, p. 7.

[29] *Organiser*, 5 June 1983, p. 5.

[30] *Parliament of India Ninth Lok Sabha Who's who*, New Delhi: Lok Sabha Secretariat, 1992, p. 176.

[31] For more details, see C. Jaffrelot, 'Les (re)conversions à l'hindouisme (1885-1990)', op. cit., p. 91.

[32] R.K. Deshpande also admitted that in 1968 the SVD had voted to extend credits to the VKA, which Congress rescinded after its return to power (*Organiser*, 12 Dec. 1977, p. 15). The VKA undoubtedly benefited from the patronage of Larang Sai who was Minister of State in the government of Morarji Desai, whose interest in this institution took him to Jashpur in 1977 (ibid., p. 1).

[33] In 1993, of the 315 full time workers, 50 were women and over one hundred were

district it established a hospital, a hostel, schools and set up centres for apprenticeship in manual trades in 40 villages. A sister-organisation even made its appearance – the Vanavasi Vikas Samiti (Committee for the Development of Tribal Zones) – which also established centres of this type at Bhanpuri (Bastar district), Mandla and Raipur. The Hindu nationalists also made 'a strong attempt to organize village women into *bhajan mandalis* [groups for religious singing] where lectures on spiritual and religious topics [were] regularly arranged and where a simultaneous programme of construction of village-level Hanuman temples [... was] going on.'[34]

In Chhattisgarh, between 1980 and 1985, the number of constituencies reserved for tribals which elected BJP candidates rose from 4 to 8. This success, in Raigarh district at least, was facilitated by the support of the Jashpur princely house, in addition to the efforts of the activists. In general, the establishment of the BJP in Chhattisgarh owed much to the support of local notables in 1985. This could have been taken as a sign of weakness, however some of the latter were deeply influenced by Hindu nationalism and thus very unlikely to desert the BJP. Lakhi Ram Aggarwal provides a good illustration of such a figure. A local magnate in Kharsia who owned several businesses in Raipur and Bilaspur, notably those dealing in *tendu* leaves, used in the making of *bidis*, in 1988 he financed the by-election campaign of Dilip Singh Judeo, who stood in Kharsia against Arjun Singh, head of the Madhya Pradesh state Congress government. Then, in 1990, he replaced Patwa as BJP president in the state. But this notable, whose family had financed the VKA from the outset, had joined the RSS in 1946 in reaction to the riots preceding Partition, and subscribed fully to the 'Hindu Sangathan' ideology which he also promoted as a Jana Sangh candidate in the 1960s.[35]

Thus the BJP in Madhya Pradesh still relied on a network of *swayam-sevaks* involved in local politics who were becoming 'notabilised', especially in Madhya Bharat. Where the party's eastward expansion was concerned, it depended more on local notables who in this particular case were now less likely to dilute the party's identity. From this point of view, the methods of the party's implantation in Chhattisgarh began to replicate the techniques it had used in the 1960s in Madhya Bharat: the primary network of *swayamsevaks* worked in a Sangathanist perspective (il-

---

Adivasis. From 1984 onwards this team was directed by Bhaskarrao, a veteran *pracharak* who had worked for about 40 years in Kerala (*Tribals: treasure trove of India*, Bharatiya Vanavasi Kalyan Ashram, 1993).

[34] I. Sen, 'Women and proselytisation', op. cit., p. 9. Hanuman was presented as a tribal divinity close to Ram whose army he commanded in the *Ramayana*.

[35] L.R. Aggarwal was also imprisoned during the Emergency (interview with L.R. Aggarwal, 17 Nov. 1990, Bhopal).

lustrated by the VKA) and served as the base for an expansion in 'clusters', involving the integration of notables and princes. This opening up was subject to control, for two main reasons: first, the 'core' of the clusters continued to be dominated by *swayamsevaks*; and second, some notables and even some princes proved to be deeply committed to Hindu nationalist ideology. In certain cases, they embodied the qualities of the most dedicated cadres of the RSS – who of course appreciated this attitude to the full. For example, the *pracharak* of Shivpuri district did not hide his admiration for Rajmata Scindia.[36] The same arrangement occurred in Vindhya Pradesh, where veterans trained in the RSS (R.H. Gupta, Sukhendra Singh) collaborated with notables and a prince (the Maharajah of Panna) who had been won over to Hindu nationalist principles.[37] In Chhattisgarh, Dilip Singh Judeo, who belonged to the RSS, in the 1980s began to play a role similar to that of Vijaya Raje Scindia and Narendra Singh in their respective areas.

This pattern of party-building was specific insofar as it combined the 'Sangathanist' and 'aggregative' techniques, with the former remaining the more important of the two. Such a point of equilibrium was reached at the moment when the BJP opted for a tactic of openness, challenging the Sangathanist model – which was apparent when the post of *sangathan mantri* was abolished. As could be seen in places other than Madhya Pradesh, the persistence of a predominantly Sangathanist party-building pattern only hindered the new strategy of the party leadership.

The strategy of openness failed to engender a massive rallying of leaders from other political parties. Dr Dharamveer, the head of a clinic who was Congress president in Gwalior district, joined the BJP in 1985.[38] He represented exactly the kind of recruit most sought after by the BJP leadership, namely prominent figures unconnected with the Hindu nationalist movement (Dharamveer was well acquainted with the RSS but had done nothing more than 'value' its work) who were more active than typical notables (he owned a local newspaper). In short, such recruits were 'publicists' of a political character, as personified by Ram Jethmalani and Shanti Bhushan on the national scene, but they remained few in number, especially in the case of regional counterparts of Sikander Bakht.

Only a small number of Muslim politicians joined the party in Madhya

---

[36] '[...] she is royal lady, in spite of that she is wandering in rural area [...] she goes in villages of the interior where I cannot go. Because sacrifice is there'.

[37] In the Vindhya Pradesh BJP the princes were represented by more than one individual, since Lokendra Singh, the son of Narendra Singh, began to stand in elections from 1977 onwards and Nagendra Singh, heir to the princely house of Nagod, a relation of Sukhendra Singh, was elected as MLA for Nagod in 1977 and 1980 (interview with Lokendra Singh, 30 Oct. 1991, Panna).

[38] Interview with Dr Dharamveer, 27 Nov. 1989, Gwalior.

Pradesh: Hamid Qureshi, a former minister under Sakhlecha, did so in 1980, as did Hasnat Siddiqui in 1984. Siddiqui was a journalist who had campaigned against the Emergency, and when the Congress (of which he had been a member since his youth) refused to sponsor him in 1980, he turned to the BJP. He was elected MLA for Bhopal South on the BJP ticket in 1985. But both men soon deserted the party, Hamid Qureshi on the eve of the 1984 election, and Hasnat Siddiqui in 1986 – in favour of the Congress – because he disapproved of the BJP's demand for a uniform civil code in the wake of the Shah Bano controversy (see below).[39]

These defections undoubtedly owed as much to the opportunism of the Muslim leaders concerned – to which the BJP's new strategy exposed itself – as to the party's practices, which in fact had changed little. As for the Muslims, a man like Sikander Bakht was integrated into the innermost circles of BJP leaders because he subscribed to the fundamental tenets of the Hindu nationalists: in his view, 'in a secular state [...] there cannot be any room for religious minority'[40] whereas it was acceptable to recognise the heroes of the Hindu epics as national symbols because Hinduism epitomises the values of tolerance.[41]

In Madhya Pradesh, where the BJP had maintained its position in 1980 mainly because of its network of RSS-trained activists, there appeared to be less need to reform its practices in a way calculated to attract large numbers of active members from outside the '*shakha* culture'. Thakre – who had been ill at ease in his role as BJP president in the state and had surrendered the post to Kailash Joshi at the end of 1980[42] to return to his function as an organiser – also pursued the policy of recruiting politicians which he had perfected while with the Jana Sangh. But just as the notables who were co-opted remained in every district under the control of *swayamsevaks*, politicians were only admitted on condition that they submitted to the party's rules, especially those regarding discipline. Thus it was more a case of their coming to the party than of the party knocking on doors, as Thakre made clear:

As we grew, they came. Because we have people from the Socialist party, from Congress, from the Hindu Mahasabha. We are swallowing. [...] And we are giving them due respect and due responsibility and all that. Once they come.[43]

---

[39] Interview with H. Siddiqui, 31 Aug. 1992, Bhopal.

[40] Interview in *India Week*, 29 June 1990, p. 6.

[41] Interview with S. Bakht, 3 Sept. 1987, New Delhi, and *Newstrack* (current affairs programme available on video cassette), Nov. 1990.

[42] That this action did not reduce Thakre's authority was made clear by the way his national status increased: he had already been appointed as the Jana Sangh's *sangathan mantri* for Madhya Pradesh and Orissa in 1967 (*Organiser*. 30 April 1987, p. 15), and in 1980 he also became national secretary of the BJP.

[43] Interview with K. Thakre, 23 Nov. 1989, Bhopal.

In the 1960s, this power of attraction was seen to be effective in relation to the Hindu Sabhaites. In the 1970s some Congressmen and Socialists were drawn to the party. One such was Brij Lal Verma, an MLA for Baloda Bazar who left the Congress to become a.member of the SVD government in 1967-9 and joined the Jana Sangh in 1972, becoming its state president in 1974. He was also one of the party's ministers in the Desai government.[44] Arif Beg, a Muslim from Indore who was first associated with the Socialist Party, joined the Jana Sangh in 1973 to become *sangathan mantri* of the party for the division of Bhopal. He was nominated to stand for Bhopal's Lok Sabha seat in 1977 and 1980.[45] In the 1980s the BJP was again successful in attracting recruits such as Shiv Prasad Chanpuria – a former Socialist minister in Sakhlecha's government who had turned to the BJP in 1980 – and Dharamveer, who became one of its MLAs for Gwalior. But this step-by-step expansion, even though it included such high-profile conversions to the cause, still fell short of the speedy increase in numbers that the national leadership had hoped to achieve.

The model of party-building which reached maturity according to a mainly Sangathanist logic in the 1980s contradicted the tactic of openness initiated by the national leadership. The 'activist network' once again exerted a restraining influence on the more pragmatic strategy envisaged by the party leadership. And it was strengthened further by the fact that the RSS became increasingly critical of the BJP.

The RSS's reservations regarding the BJP

The experience of the Janata Party confirmed the RSS's conviction that it needed to become larger to have real political influence. In 1979 Deoras appealed to the VHP to build, as we shall see below, a 'Hindu vote bank' while at the same time calling on *swayamsevaks* to make 1980 the year of the *shakha*. In 1981 their number rose to 17,000 (2,500 in Kerala, 1,500 in Karnataka, 1,200 in Andhra Pradesh and, in 1982, 400 in Tamil Nadu; clearly the South was a priority target).[46] In 1981, there were 22 training camps (Officers' Training Camps) through which 11,180 actual or future RSS cadres passed.[47] The RSS did not envisage that this activist force would be placed at the service of a political party. The ideological dilution

---

[44] *Sixth Lok Sabha who's who*, op. cit., p. 720. A similar trajectory was followed by Dharampal Singh Gupta, who was the Chief Whip of the Congress Legislature Party when he joined the SVD in 1967 and then the Jana Sangh.

[45] Ibid., p. 63.

[46] *Organiser*, 5 April 1981, p. 3, and 14 Feb. 1982, p. 4.

[47] Ibid., 12 July 1981, p. 5.

manifested by the BJP and its electoral reverses seemed to have substantially added to the RSS's doubts over whether it was capable of promoting the Hindu nationalist cause. In April 1983, the *Organiser* published an article, signed by the pseudonymous 'Sindu', containing barely concealed criticism of the BJP and an evident nostalgia for the Jana Sangh as shaped by Upadhyaya:

Basically it has to become something more than a party; it has to become a movement – to be able to fire the imagination of the country and offer a significantly superior alternative to the ruling party. [...] BJS was popularly known as some kind of a 'Hindu Party'. The BJP has a tendency to play down its Hindu character. Nobody need quarrel with its efforts to attract non-Hindus. But many may also view it as a certain weakening of character.[48]

Some sections of the RSS did not attempt to conceal their disapproval of the BJP's efforts to attract Muslims. Thus Ram Jethmalani was criticised for trying to participate in the Id prayers, as was a BJP official in Bombay for offering *namaz* in a mosque.[49] The *Organiser* was also very sceptical of the strategy of forming alliances which was being pursued by the BJP, and even more so of its plan to form a coalition government.[50] The weekly was even more critical after the 1984 electoral defeat of the BJP, which it attributed to its 'revisionist' attitude which was all the more counter-productive as the Congress(I) had been successful because he had acted 'as a Hindu party'.[51] An increasing number of articles suggested that the BJP should carry on its struggle alone, exploiting Hindu feelings:[52]

The political ideology is or at least should be the main justification of its existence. BJP should, therefore, shed the politics of alignment and focus on its ideology and political strategy to promote correctional and creative politics. [...] The Hindu vote is going to be politically important in the coming decade. The political parties feel shy about the usage of the word 'Hindu'. But BJP should have no shyness complex and to organise its idea of Hindu renaissance.[53]

In 1987, the General Secretary of the RSS, H.V. Seshadri, who till then had been in charge of organisation in the South,[54] let it be known that his

---

[48] Sindhu, 'BJP: A strategy for victory', ibid., 10 April 1983, p. 5.

[49] Ibid., 8 Aug. 1982.

[50] See the interview with Advani (ibid., 10 April 1983, p. 5).

[51] Ibid., 6 Jan. 1986, p. 1.

[52] See another interview with Advani, who was apparently given the task of convincing the RSS of the beneficial character of the BJP's strategy (ibid., Republic Day Special, 1985, p. 25).

[53] B.K. Kelkar, 'BJP and the crisis of political alignment', *Organiser*, 10 April 1988, p. 7.

[54] Seshadri had first worked as a *pracharak* in Karnataka from 1946 onwards. In 1987, Rajendra Singh left the post of General Secretary and became Joint General Secretary apparently because of health problems.

movement would not give the BJP its support unconditionally: 'RSS workers' support to the BJP also depends on the latter's attitude for the party has to show it to workers that they believe in Hindu consolidation and high moral values.'[55] By contrast, the Congress(I), which the RSS was probably keen not to antagonise in order to avoid repressive measures at a later date,[56] appeared to the RSS to be well placed in certain areas to safeguard Hindu interests – more so, at least, than the BJP. In Kerala the bipartisan political contest had been fixed since the 1950s at a point where the only alternative to the Communists was the Congress (I). From the late 1970s onwards the Communists had shown increasing hostility to the RSS, especially after the latter's growth during the Emergency (from 900 to 1,500 *shakhas* and from 20,000 to 35,000 members).[57] This expansion was one of the root-causes of the repeated clashes between the Communists and *swayamsevaks* – 164 violent incidents were recorded between January 1978 and March 1979.[58] The *swayamsevaks* were urged to put their new-found strength at the service of the Congress (I), rather than of a BJP incapable of winning power, in order to obstruct the CPI and CPI (M) in the Vidhan Sabha elections of January 1980, and also in those of 1982 in which the BJP itself participated. A sympathiser of the local RSS wrote: 'Up to the 1982 elections in the State, normally the pro-RSS votes went to the Congress camp, against the worst enemy, the communists.'[59] This pattern was repeated, after a fashion, in the Delhi and Jammu and Kashmir elections.

The election of 1983 in Delhi crystallised all the contradictions of the BJP's tactic of openness. While only just beaten on votes, it retained a mere 19 seats out of 56 on the Metropolitan Council and 37 out of 100 on the Municipal Corporation. The party had tried to increase the number of its rural and Muslim candidates, but the gains obtained by these efforts were marginal. The BJP won only two rural constituencies of the Metropolitan Council and Municipal Corporation, and of its Muslim candidates two were elected to the former body and three out of five to

[55] *Organiser*, 5 April 1987, p. 13.

[56] Such measures were again on the agenda after the riot at Moradabad in 1980, when the reactivated National Integration Council – which had already been reconstituted without much effect in 1968 and 1973 – embraced a plan of action which sought in particular to 'exclude from official forums and bodies persons who had attracted adverse notice in communal situations.' (*Patriot*, 13 Nov. 1980).

[57] K. Jayaprasad, 'The impact of Hindu nationalism on Kerala society and politics – a case study of the RSS', unpubl. Ph.D. thesis, Trivandrum University (Dept. of Politics), 1989, pp. 207-41.

[58] Ibid., p. 170.

[59] K. Jayaprasad, *RSS and Hindu nationalism: Inroads in a leftist stronghold*, New Delhi: Deep and Deep, 1991, p. 298. Remarks from Seshadri have supported this analysis (*Organiser*, 4 July 1982, p. 6).

the latter.[60] This 'opening-up' antagonised the activists and cadres of the local RSS, most of whom were Punjabi in origin, and they tended to withdraw their support from the party or transfer it to the Congress (I), as happened in the Karol Bagh constituency,[61] mainly to record their approval of Indira Gandhi's firm policies against Sikh separatists.[62]

Such a development affected both the BJP's traditional electorate and RSS activists in the election in Jammu, where not one of the party's candidates was elected – 17 of whom, out of 25, lost their deposits. Once again, this setback was explained largely by the attraction of the Congress (I) in Hindu nationalist circles. Indira Gandhi's campaign had in fact been directed against the National Conference of Farooq Abdullah whose government was accused of victimising the Hindus in Jammu. Malkani's reading of this campaign is particularly instructive:

Here was a new and interesting situation. As the Hindus of Jammu saw it, the BJP could at best sit in the Opposition and articulate grievances. But the Congress (I) could come to power and redress complaints. [...] No wonder many Jammu Hindus decided to vote for the Congress (I). BJP candidates may have been defeated but the BJP platform has won. Ideas are more important than seats.[63]

This interpretation applies to some extent also to the parliamentary elections of December 1984. On the eve of the poll, Deshmukh declared that Rajiv Gandhi deserved 'cooperation and sympathy' because on the one hand the BJP 'should not lose its credibility by joining hands with discredited people and parties', as in the National Democratic Alliance, and on the other because 'political parties should also take up constructive works to help the people'.[64] After Rajiv Gandhi's success, an official of the RSS confided: 'most of its [the BJP's] active workers who were RSS people generally preferred the Congress (I) in the elections.'[65]

The following is Andersen and Damle's explanation of these developments:

The pervasive view that a solid victory for Rajiv Gandhi was necessary to keep in check the forces of disintegration has a compelling appeal for many RSS members, as it must have had for a large part of the BJP's traditional constituency.[66]

---

[60] Lists of results provided by the 'Electoral Officer' of Delhi (Kashmir Gate), and an interview with M. Arya, 8 Dec. 1990, New Delhi.

[61] *Hindustan Times*, 12 Feb. 1983.

[62] *Times of India*, 16 Feb. 1983.

[63] K.R. Malkani, 'Updating "Hind Swaraj"', *Statesman* (Delhi), 4 July 1983, in *BJP Today*, Bombay: BJP office [n.d] p. 15.

[64] *Organiser*, 17 Feb. 1985, p. 1.

[65] Quoted in B. Graham, 'The challenge of Hindu nationalism: The Bharatiya Janata Party in contemporary politics', *Hull Papers in Politics*, no. 40 (Oct. 1987), p. 15.

[66] W. Andersen and S. Damle, *The brotherhood in saffron*, op. cit., p. 234.

At first sight, one finds the 'exclusion effect' observed in 1971-2: just as the Jana Sangh had been unable to outbid Indira Gandhi in nationalistic fervour at the time of the war over Bangladesh, so the BJP was beaten by Congress (I) on its own chosen ground. But, with eleven or twelve years between them, the two situations were not directly comparable. If the Indian nationalism of Congress, however bellicose, had the interests of the state behind it, its new drift towards Hindu nationalism presented a challenge to secularism.

All in all, the BJP's choice of a pragmatic strategy of openness was doubly counter-productive. The party's ambition to be a new embodiment of the Janata Party collided with the Hindu nationalist culture of its grassroots and of the RSS, on which it continued to be heavily dependent: the moderate strategy of the controlling group was thwarted once again by the – mainly Sangathanist – implantation that was still being pursued at the local level. The Congress (I), for its part, was undergoing a change that tended to weaken the constraints that the secularist norm had hitherto imposed on the Hindu nationalist movement.

The erosion of secularism as a political norm

In the early 1980s two factors combined to allow the tenets of Hindu nationalism to attain a certain legitimacy. First, the Congress (I) was trying to exploit communalism, thus contributing to a devaluation of the secularist norm; and second, this development was hastened by a revival of proselytisation and separatism on the part of certain minorities.

The Congress (I) was responsible for the erosion of secularism on several counts. As far as symbols were concerned, the new religiosity of Indira Gandhi prompted her to visit a growing number of holy sites: in the first six weeks after her return to power she visited a dozen temples situated all over India.[67] In 1983 she attended the inauguration of Satyamitranand Giri's Bharat Mata Mandir (see below) and took part in the ceremonies marking the centenary of the Arya Samaj.[68] More importantly, on returning to power she set about thwarting the opposition governments in the states by all possible means – including the questioning of some secular principles – in the name of stability at the Centre and national unity.

In Jammu and Kashmir, Congress (I) had already sought to weaken Farooq Abdullah's National Conference by resorting to specifically

---

[67] I. Malhotra, *Indira Gandhi: A personal and political biography*, London: Hodder and Stoughton, 1989, p. 231. This new religiosity was largely precipitated by the untimely death of her son Sanjay in 1980 (P. Jayakar, *Indira Gandhi*, op.cit., part 8).

[68] *Organiser*, 1 Feb. 1984, p. 16.

Hindu themes in the elections of June 1983, as mentioned above. It stepped up this strategy in November with a campaign against the discrimination manifested by Srinagar towards the (Hindu) south of the state, and against the 'anti-national role' played by Abdullah.[69] The second accusation referred particularly – according to a Congress (I) commission of inquiry – to a statement by Abdullah that he aimed to 'place Kashmir on the international map' and would seek 'Gulf money for the development of the State'.[70]

In Assam successive waves of immigration, mostly from Bangladesh, but also from West Bengal, had finally evoked defensive reactions on the part of the indigenous Assamese.[71] From 1979 the main demand of their representative organisations, the All Assam Students' Union (AASU) and the Assam Gasom (People's) Student Party (AGSP), was that 'foreigners' should be eliminated from the electoral roll. 'Foreigners', in fear of being deported, supported the Congress (I), which therefore did not wish to lose this source of votes. Since no measures had been taken against 'foreigners' voting before the 1983 elections, the indigenous Assamese called for a boycott and organised themselves to persuade 'foreigners' to desist from voting, by force if necessary. The government decided to go ahead and sent in the armed forces, but they failed to prevent the massacre of 3,000 Bengali immigrants during the elections. Congress (I) won a solid majority with 91 seats out of 109, despite a derisory turn-out.

In Punjab the rise to prominence of the Sikh militant, Sant Bhindranwale, appeared to have been promoted by Delhi in the hope of weakening the Akali Dal, Congress (I)'s principal political rival in the state. It seems that this Sikh holy man, whose activities were at first aimed at the lax orthodoxy of the Nirankari sect of Sikhism, had been urged to enter politics by Indira Gandhi's younger son Sanjay.[72] Bhindranwale had been arrested in 1981 for the assassination of the editor-in-chief of *Hind Samachar*, a newspaper which was highly critical of Sikh nationalism, but was released two months later and shortly afterwards took refuge in the

---

[69] B. Puri, 'Congress (I)'s shortsighted game', *EPW*, 3 Dec. 1983, p. 2501.

[70] B. Puri, 'Who is playing with national interest', ibid., 11 Feb. 1984, p. 236. These arguments were probably advanced, at least in part, to legitimise the alliance of the Congress (I) with the faction of Farooq Abdullah's brother-in-law, thanks to which the party formed a new majority in the State Assembly in July 1984.

[71] What follows is indebted to M. Weiner, *Sons of the soil*, Delhi: Oxford University Press, 1978, ch. 3; M. Weiner and M.P. Katzenstein, *India's preferential politics*, University of Chicago Press, 1981, ch. 6; S. Barnah,'Immigration, ethnic conflict and political turmoil: Assam 1979-1985', *Asian Survey*, 26, 11 (Nov. 1986).

[72] K. Nayar and Kushwant Singh, *Tragedy of Punjab*, New Delhi: Vision Books, 1984, p. 31, and M. Tully and S. Jacob, *Amritsar: Mrs Gandhi's last battle*, London: Jonathan Cape, 1985, pp. 57-61.

Golden Temple at Amritsar. No proof of his involvement in the killing was ever produced, but he had publicly praised the killers.[73]

The policy of Congress (I) in Jammu and Kashmir, Assam and Punjab took on a 'communalist' character with the intention of enfeebling its rivals in those states. This tactic implied a combination of contradictory elements for it appealed alternatively to Hindu, Muslim or anti-Sikh feelings. However its general effect was the establishment of communal idioms in political discourse at the expense of secular themes. Moreover the outcome of the new Congress (I) alignment was pro-Hindu. With the emergence of centrifugal tensions among non-Hindus in Kashmir and Punjab, the government tended to confuse the safeguarding of national integrity with the mobilisation of the majority community. As explained by James Manor, this 'astonishing development of the early 1980s, the adoption by Indira Gandhi of themes that have traditionally belonged to the Hindu chauvinist right' was part of a far more ambitious strategy.

First, Indira Gandhi saw 'the move toward the communalist right as an exercise similar to her move towards the Marxist left in and after 1969. It was a means of undermining the parties that stood to the right of the Congress (I) – mainly the BJP, but also to a degree the Lok Dal, which had elements within it susceptible to Hindu chauvinist appeals.' Second, 'the move to the right was also probably based on a cautious belief by Mrs Gandhi that only she (and her son) stood between India and serious communal strife. So, still more curiously, she apparently believed that, by catalyzing communalist sentiments, by becoming the main mouthpiece for Hindu communalism, she was protecting India from the dangers of it.'[74]

The decline of secularism was also manifested in the treatment of intercommunal violence. The riots of the years 1980-7 were exceptional as much for their extent and frequency as for the attitude shown by the authorities towards the minority victims of the violence. Such an erosion of one of the pillars of the secularist rule of law can be explained in part by political calculation. The anti-Sikh riots that followed the assassination of Indira Gandhi on 31 October 1984 were a case in point. The whole of North India was affected, but the epicentre was undoubtedly Delhi where about 2,000 adult males were killed.[75] In the capital the police failed to intervene and the slaughter developed in some localities at the instigation of local Congressmen.[76] Now that Sikh terrorists had struck a blow at a

---

[73] R.A. Kapur, *Sikh separatism*, Delhi: Vikas, 1987, p. 226; B. Puri, 'Understanding Punjab', *EPW*, 21 July 1984, pp. 1127-8.

[74] J. Manor, 'Parties and the party system' in A. Kohli (ed.), *India's democracy – An analysis of changing state-society relations*, Princeton University Press, 1990, p. 82.

[75] 'Who are the guilty? Causes and impact of the Delhi riots', *EPW*, 24 Nov. 1984, p. 1979.

[76] The army was not called in till 3 November, after which the violence ceased.

mainstay of the security of the state, in the person of the Prime Minister, Hindus, who constituted the heart of that state, had to 'teach a lesson' to Sikhs in general. When peaceful demonstrators passed through the city chanting *'Hindu-Sikh Bhai-Bhai!'* (Hindus and Sikhs are brothers), the looters and killers, in a frenzied state, replied *'Indira Gandhi zindabad!'* (long live Indira Gandhi) and *'Hindu-Hindu Bhai-Bhai!'* [77] Rajiv Gandhi subsequently organised his campaign around the theme of national integration with a pro-Hindu bias in the run-up to the election of December 1984, with great success. [78]

The principal Hindu-Muslim riots of 1980-7 were further inflamed, if not actually triggered off, by the police, who showed an anti-Muslim bias – in every case accompanied by killings – in the riots at Moradabad (1980), Biharsharif (1981), Meerut (1982 and 1987), and Delhi (1987). [79] These explosions of violence are explained partly by the attitude of police in the states, especially the PAC (Provincial Armed Constabulary) in Uttar Pradesh. But this tendency seems also to have been encouraged by the accommodating attitude of the state, thus marking a radical departure from the practices introduced by Nehru. Commissions of enquiry submitted reports which remained unpublished, or were not laid before the legislative assemblies, [80] and punishments were by no means proportionate to the crimes committed. In 1983, for instance, Indira Gandhi refused to recognise that the PAC had been at fault in the Moradabad and Meerut riots; [81] only the officer in command of the PAC at Meerut was suspended. [82] Another notorious indication of the erosion of secularism was seen in certain aspects of the relationship between the central government and the Muslim community.

In 1980, the Congress government introduced a bill seeking to revise the constitution of Aligarh University. This was less generous than the one prepared by the Janata Party, but its object was to initiate a phase of negotiations. The reservations expressed by certain Muslims in fact led

---

[77] 'Who are the guilty?', op. cit., p. 1980.

[78] M. Weiner, 'India's minority: Who are they? What do they want?' in J.R. Roach (ed.), *India 2000: the next fifteen decades*, Riverdale: South Asia Books, 1986, p. 119, and J. Manor, 'Parties and the party system', op. cit., p. 81.

[79] S. Saberwal and M. Hasan, 'Communal riot in Moradabad, 1980: Economy, policy and administration regression', *Occasional papers on history and society*, NMML (Delhi), no. 19; A.A. Engineer, 'Biharsharif carnage: a field report', *EPW*, 16 May 1981, p. 889, and A.A. Engineer (ed.), *Delhi-Meerut Riots*, New Delhi: Ajanta, 1988.

[80] K. Balagopal, 'Meerut 1987: Reflections on an inquiry', *EPW*, 17 April 1988, p. 770, and 'Communal violence: The Biharsharif report', ibid., 18 Feb. 1984.

[81] A. Banerjee, 'Comparative curfew: changing dimensions of communal politics in India' in V. Das (ed.), *Mirrors of violence: Communities, riots and survivors in South Asia*, New Delhi: Oxford University Press, 1990, p. 46.

[82] A.G. Noorani, 'Amnesty reports on Meerut killings', *EPW*, 12 Dec. 1987, p. 2140.

the central government to propose, within a very short time, a second and then a third draft bill, which was finally voted into law in 1981: it reaffirmed the university's Muslim identity and accorded it considerable autonomy.[83]

The 'Shah Bano affair' was even more revealing of the government's propensity to allow politics to become increasingly 'communalised'. Shah Bano had been the spouse, since 1932, of a lawyer from Indore who married for the second time in 1975 and separated from her according to Muslim customary law in 1978. Invoking Section 125 of the Code of Criminal Procedure,[84] she sued him and as a result established her right to alimony. When, in 1980, she demanded a review of her allowance, her former husband appealed to the Supreme Court, pleading that according to Shariat law he was not obliged to continue payments to her after the *iddat* (a period of three months after the divorce).[85] The Supreme Court dismissed the appeal on 23 April 1985, pointing out that Section 125 of the Code of Criminal Procedure applied to people of all faiths, and that the Quran itself required that a divorced wife should be paid an allowance. At the same time as they passed down this decision, the judges expressed regret that no effort had been made by the administration to draw up a uniform civil code, as Article 44 of the Directive Principles section of the Constitution required it to do.[86] The Supreme Court's decision angered some Muslim parliamentarians (such as Syed Shahabuddin of the Janata Party) and organisations like the Muslim League, the Jamaat-e-Islami and the Muslim Personal Law Board, which in 1973 had tried to have Muslims exempted from Section 125 during a revision of the Code of Criminal Procedure. These organisations also denounced the Supreme Court for presuming to interpret the Quran. These shifting currents of opinion coalesced in an All India Muslim Personal Law Board (AIMPLB), which

[83] A.G. Noorani, 'Indira Gandhi and Indian Muslims', ibid., 3 Nov. 1990, pp. 2419-20 and V. Graff, 'Aligarh's long quest for minority status, AMU (Amendment) Act, 1981', ibid., 11 Aug. 1990.

[84] The clause says that 'If any person having sufficient means neglects or refuses to maintain his wife, unable to maintain herself [...] a Magistrate of the first class may, upon proof of such neglect or refusal, order such person to make a monthly allowance for the maintenance of his wife ...' (*The code of criminal procedure*, Madras: Swamy Publishers, 1974, pp. 54-5).

[85] It must be recalled here that, in contrast with the Hindus, whose customary law was reformed by the Hindu Code Bill in the 1950s, the Parsis, Christians and Muslims have kept theirs. As far as the latter are concerned, the Shariat Act (1937) and the Dissolution of Muslim Marriages Act (1939) are still applied. A. R. Momin, 'Conflict of law and religion in contemporary India', *Social Compass*, 33 (2-3), 1986, p. 226.

[86] 'In the Supreme Court of India Criminal Appellate Jurisdiction – Criminal Appeal no. 103 of 1981' in A. A. Engineer (ed.), *The Shah Bano controversy*, Hyderabad: Orient Longman, 1987, pp. 23-34.

organised a 'Shariat protection week' in October 1985. At the numerous meetings that resulted, slogans such as 'Muslim personal law is in danger' and 'Shariat is our religious right, we will die to protect it', were propagated. The main tendencies of Indian Islam were represented in the demonstrations.[87]

Asghar Ali Engineer, a liberal Muslim reformer, considers that 'this agitation [was] the biggest ever launched by Muslims [since Independence]'.[88] He mentions a rally of 400,000 people in Bihar and one of 300,000 in Bombay.[89] In his view this mobilisation could be explained from three points of view: first, Muslims felt insecure because of the VHP's campaign following the Meenakshipuram conversions (see below) and the Supreme Court judgement was then 'perceived by them as yet another attempt to destroy the autonomy of their religion'; second, for the Muslim leaders who articulated the protest movements this judgement was 'a blessing in disguise in as much as it [had] united all Muslims of different sects and opinions to oppose it,'[90] a phenomenon likely to enhance their influence as representatives of a mobilised community; and third, because among such leaders the *ulema* predominated, just as they had led their community since the migration of most of the Muslim élite to Pakistan after 1947.[91] Thus, the 'Shah Bano affair' presented an image of the Muslim community likely to activate a Hindu sense of vulnerability.[92]

In July 1985 the AIMPLB had sent a memorandum to Rajiv Gandhi calling for Section 125 of the Code of Criminal Procedure and Article 44 of the Constitution to be amended so as to exempt Muslims. The Prime Minister had hitherto remained unmoved, but his determination seemed to weaken after the demonstrations of October 1985 and, in his anxiety not to alienate these Muslim leaders, he gave an assurance that no plans were afoot to challenge the customary law of minorities. On 21 December, Rajiv Gandhi made a definitive switch in policy when he promised a delegation of the AIMPLB that Section 125 of the Code of Criminal Procedure would be amended. Then on 27 February the government introduced a Muslim Women (Protection of Rights on Divorce) Bill

[87] Z. Hasan, 'Minority identity, Muslim women bill campaign and the political process', *EPW*, 7 Jan. 1989, p. 46.

[88] A. A. Engineer, 'Introduction' in A. A. Engineer (ed.), *The Shah Bano Controversy*, op. cit., p. 1.

[89] Ibid., p. 12.

[90] A. A. Engineer, 'Forces behind the agitation' in ibid., p. 36.

[91] Ibid., p. 40.

[92] All the more so given that some editorials in activist newspapers sounded provocative: see, for example, 'Long live Balasahev Deoras' (*Sangam Urdu Daily*, 26 Dec. 1985) in ibid., p. 204.

whereby a Muslim man would not be obliged to pay alimony to his divorced wife beyond the term of *iddat*. After that period, the divorced wife had to be supported by her family and if she had no relatives to care for her the magistrate could compel the *waqf* to provide for her needs – a clause which would have little effect in view of the financial condition of these bodies.[93] Some progressive Muslims protested – Arif Mohammed Khan, for instance, left Rajiv Gandhi's government – but they remained a minority.

In the first half of the 1980s a certain reversal of roles took place, with the BJP persisting in its strategy of moderation at the price of distancing itself somewhat from the RSS, while Congress opted to exploit religious identities. These divergent developments changed the parameters which had guided the strategy of the Hindu nationalists since Independence. Till the 1980s, the Congress central government had maintained socio-economic development (from Nehru's socialist path to Indira Gandhi's populism) and secularism as two pillars of what we have called the legitimate norms of Indian politics. During the 1980s, the Congress (I) withdrew from both commitments. Even though the theme of social development remained part of the official rhetoric, it was not pushed to the forefront, economic liberalisation becoming an emerging priority. At the same time, the Congress (I) manipulated communal themes at the highest level as part of its political strategy. Previously such a phenomenon had been observed only in local politics, especially when the Hindu traditionalists were in power in North India. Inevitably, this strategy led to an increasing legitimisation of communal idioms in political discourse.

Both tendencies – the marginalisation of social development in the Congress programme and the erosion of secularism – were interrelated: the party shifted from populist promises, which the Indian electorate treated with less and less respect, to communal categories to attract support. Their effects were also cumulative. As indicated by Rajni Kothari, 'the failure of the development paradigm of the Indian state in this respect led to a completely different agenda' in which communalism has become prominent.[94]

The communalisation of politics tended therefore to remove the restraints which the government's promotion of secularism – combined with threats of repression – had hitherto imposed on the Hindu nationalists' instrumentalist strategy. This strategy had retained numerous supporters in the BJP – at the grassroots if not at the top – and among the

[93] 'The Muslim Women (Protection of Rights on Divorce) Bill, 1986', in ibid., pp. 85-8.
[94] R. Kothari, 'Class and Communalism in India', *EPW*, 3 Dec. 1988, p. 2590.

ranks of the RSS. The return to the strategy of ethno-religious mobilisation was precipitated by the renewed Hindu sentiment of vulnerability *vis-à-vis* 'threatening Others'. This in turn set in motion a new strategy of stigmatisation and emulation and accordingly led a new set of prominent religious figures to rally to militant Hinduism.

10

THE HINDU SENSE OF VULNERABILITY
AND THE R.S.S.'s POLITICAL OFFENSIVE

> 'India is the only country where the majority community is still afraid of the
> minorities. This sense of insecurity sometimes breeds extreme reaction.' (Uma
> Bharti, *Sunday*, 11 April 1993, p. 9)

In 1985 the president of the AIMPLB compared the mobilisation of
Muslims in the 'Shah Bano affair' to the Khilafat movement.[1] From the
early 1980s, this agitation, added to the conversion of Untouchables to
Islam and the development of Sikh separatism, began to engender in
certain areas of Hinduism a sense of vulnerability comparable to that
which had been provoked by the Muslim mobilisation of the 1920s.

The reaction of the Hindu activists also seemed to be analogous to that
expressed in the Hindu Sangathan movement in that it took the form of a
new strategy of stigmatisation and emulation: Hindu nationalism was
re-forming itself in opposition to the 'Other', borrowing its methods. At
the heart of this process was the VHP, which not only attracted an
increased number of religious figures but also tried to persuade them to
accept an integrated ecclesiastical structure, as if to match the organisational features of the religions to which it was opposed.

The RSS showed renewed interest in the process of identity-con-
struction and went beyond it to adopt a strategy of ethno-religious
mobilisation which was intended to boost the electoral success of Hindu
nationalism. As we shall see, its elaborate extension of the processional
technique to a nationwide pattern of demonstrations focussing on symbols
such as the Ganges and Ayodhya revealed a greater willingness to
intervene directly in party politics.

The inferiority complex of the majority revisited

Muslim mobilisation over the 'Shah Bano affair' was seen by militant
Hindus as part of the same pattern as an earlier renewal of Islamic
militancy. In their view, Indian Muslims were participants in the interna-

[1] Z. Hasan, 'Minority identity', op. cit., p. 44.

338

tional Islamic revivalism which had found expression in the Iranian revolution;[2] the presence on India's frontiers, among the Afghan refugees in Pakistan, of Islamist movements financed mainly by Saudi Arabia was merely adding further cause for concern. The idea that Indian Muslims were potentially the final link in this pan-Islamic front gained momentum on account of the increasing number of them who were finding employment in the Middle East and Persian Gulf at the end of the 1970s. From 223,000 in 1975 the number of official Indian expatriate workers in the Gulf had reached 333,000 in 1979 while they were about 266,000 in other countries of the Middle East.[3] Although it is not easy to determine the religious affilation of these migrants, most authors who have addressed the problem agree that Muslims represented a higher proportion than the percentage of Muslims in the population of India might suggest.[4] D.K. Vajpayi, after making inquiries among 125 Muslims returned from the Gulf, detected major changes, both in their psychology and in their socio-economic status:

Being away from home and family, religion brought them closer. Their leisure time was spent in discussing their 'commanlity' – Islamic heritage. When they returned to India they not only brought money, watches and expensive transistor radios (boom-box ghetto-blasters), they also came back with a new awareness and assertive spirit of *din e-ilahi* (the religion of light). The new money gave them confidence, new mosques, and new madrasas for religious education for children which were deemed necessary to thank Allah (God) for their prosperity. It also generated increased social, religious and political consciousness, and naturally brought them in a direct collision course with other communities.[5]

2   Hansen points out that, in the wake of the Iranian Revolution, 'The emergence of small groups of bearded, traditionally dressed and highly active Muslim Youths in Bombay propagating an Islamic revival among Indian Muslims, served to re-activate the myths of Muslim fanaticism among broad sections of Hindus ('Democratisation, Mass-politics and Hindu identity: The communalisation of Bombay', paper prepared for the workshop 'Political Culture and Religion in the Third World', ECPR Joint Sessions Workshops, Bordeaux, 27 April-2 May 1995). The outbreak of war between Iraq and Iran was blamed on the expansionism of the latter by the *Organiser*, where one could read that 'Iran's target is not just Iraq but the entire Muslim world...' (*Organiser*, 23 May 1982, p. 6).

3   M.Weiner, 'International Migration and Development: Indians in the Persian Gulf', *Population and Development Review*, 8 (1), March 1982, pp. 2 and 31. In 1994, there were about 2.1 million persons of Indian origin in the Middle East and Persian Gulf (Lok Sabha debate cited in *Muslim India*, no. 142, Oct. 1994, p. 437).

4   T.P. Wright, Jr, 'Indian Muslims and the Middle East', *Journal of South Asian and Middle Eastern Countries*, 6 (1), 1982, and D.K. Vajpayi, 'The politics of paradise: Religion, identity and politics in Indian', paper presented at a conference entitled 'Religion, Identity and Politics', Centre for Indian Studies, University of Hull, 24-6 Oct. 1991, p. 24.

5   Ibid., pp. 24-5. See also 'Elections, Congress (I) and minorities', *EPW*, 15 Dec. 1984, p. 2098.

Myron Weiner has been more cautious in drawing conclusions regarding the situation in Kerala, which in 1979 had 300,000 of its residents living abroad:

Some observers have noted that the improvement in the financial and social status of returning Muslims in Kerala has contributed to the growth of Islamic schools, mosques, and other Muslims institutions in the state. !6 Howmuchofthepolitical awareness, militancy, and, in some localities, fundamentalism on the part of the Muslims is a result of return migration is unclear. !7

However, militant Hindus' sense of insecurity was heightened in the wake of a series of conversions to Islam in South India in early 1981. On 19 February, some 1,000 members of the Scheduled Castes in the village of Meenakshipuram (in the district of Tirunelveli in Tamil Nadu) converted to Islam. The conversion was made under the auspices of Muslim League leaders, one of whom laid the foundation-stone of the village mosque on 4 March. !8 Duringthefollowingmonthsthousandsofmembers of the Scheduled Castes were converted to Islam in South India. Research carried out by Abdul Malik Mujahid showed that those who were converted were mainly concerned to escape from a hierarchy of castes which confined them to the lowest stratum in society. The first converts were relatively well educated and economically secure people who were no longer prepared to tolerate the social ostracism to which they were subjected as Untouchables. What most attracted them about Muslim society was that, in their view, it was egalitarian and free of caste distinctions. !10

6   Oh this point see P. Kurien, 'Non-economic bases of economic behaviour: the consumption, investment and exchange patterns of three emigrant communities in Kerala, India', *Development and change*, vol. 5 (1994), pp. 767-9.

7   M. Weiner, 'International Migration', op. cit., pp. 32- 3 and p. 5. Weiner also points to the problems which Hindus face when they wish to take part in public worship or religious rituals in the Gulf states. While there is a 100-year-old temple in Bahrain, 'elsewhere Hindus must observe their festivals in less conspicuous locations, or in private. The Indian community recognizes that the conspicuous display of religion – in the form of temples, religious or marriage processions – can be provocative in Islamic states.' Such problems – and their political exploitation in India – may have contributed to the feeling that Muslims and Hindus find co-existence difficult, not only in Muslim countries but also in India itself (ibid. p. 6).

8   G. Mathew, 'Politicisation of religion – Conversion to Islam in Tamil Nadu', *EPW*, 19 June 1982, p. 1031; Office of the Director for SC/ST, Government of India, Madras, 'A report on the mass conversion of harijans of Meenakshipuram, Terkasi Taluk, Tiruneveli District into Islam', *Sunday*, 9 Nov. 1982, pp. 16-25; *Times of India*, 22 Nov. 1982.

9   It is not possible to give a precise assessment of the number of converts. According to Abdul Malik Mujahid it ranged from 2,000 to 22,000. (*Conversion to Islam – Untouchables' strategy for protest in India*, Chambersburg, PA: Anima Books, 1988, p. 9). To these conversions were added threats to abandon Hinduism if the condition of the Scheduled Castes was not ameliorated.

10   Ibid., pp. 51, 69 and 89. See also M.A. Kalam, 'Why the Harijan convert to Islam views reservations with reservation', *South Asia Research*, 4 (2), Nov. 1984, p. 157.

Many observers attributed the conversions to the external funds available to Muslim proselytising organisations. Leading articles in newspapers, not known for their support of Hindu nationalism, suggested that the converts had been paid sums of money,[11] which allegedly had come from Arab countries;[12] hence the claims of a conspiracy, illustrated by a front-page article in the *Times of India*, entitled 'International Islamic conspiracy for mass conversion of Harijans':

Plans to convert poor Harijans to Islam and setting up of a host of organisations of journalists, youths trade-unions and kisan sabhas [peasant associations] with the help of 'friendly' Arab countries and Islamic organisations in London and Europe have come to light. The Union Home Ministry is perturbed at these developments and is investigating reports on the activities of extreme Muslim organisations such as Jamaat-e-Islami.[13]

At the same time, a secret note prepared for the Minister of Home Affairs emphasised that:

Financial aid from Gulf countries to Muslim institutions, mosques and groups has [...] been coming in, in many cases not through proper channels.

There is enough indication that the zeal which the Jamaat- e-Islami-Hind and other revivalist groups are working in this area to accelerate the conversion of Harijans, is at least partly attributable to the resources these parties have acquired from the Muslim countries and the pan-islamic organisations over the last two or three years.[14]

The note, like the article in the *Times of India*, referred to an article published in the *Arab Times* of Kuwait about a report from the Islamic Cultural Centre in London announcing the conversion of betweeen 80 and 120 million Hindus thanks to funds from Arab countries and to the effort of the Jamaat-e-Islami to develop its trade union activities. Such reports greatly exaggerated the strength and organising capacity of the Jamaat-e-Islami. It was very weak in Tamil Nadu[15] and its national membership had risen only slightly, from 2,157 in 1974 to 2,792 in 1981.[16] This organisa-

---

[11] *Statesman* (Delhi), 20 July 1981.

[12] *Hindustan Times*, 18 July 1981.

[13] *Times of India*, 21 March 1981. A few months later press reports indicated that, except in Kashmir, intelligence agencies had not come up with positive evidence to link the speculation about the flow of petro-dollars with the construction and renovation of mosques (*Indian Express*, 12 Oct. 1981).

[14] 'Note prepared for the meeting of the consultative committee in the Ministry of Home Affairs to be held on the 14th September, 1981' reproduced in *Muslim India*, 1 (2), Feb. 1983, pp. 89-91. The note was leaked to the press in 1982 (see *The Statesman* [Delhi], 16 Nov. 1982, p. 1)

[15] A.M. Mujahid, *Conversion to Islam*, op. cit., p. 71.

[16] V. Graff, 'The Jama'at-e-Islami Hind', op. cit., p. 95.

tion was in fact the embodiment of political Islam, the implantation of which had always been harder than that of socio-religious reform movements like Tabligh-e-Jamaat, which was making great advances and had become established in a network covering the Arab countries and beyond.[17] The reality of a threat was nevertheless of less significance than the Hindus' subjective perception of one.

In such a context the conversions in Meenakshipuram had a profound effect, as was evidenced by the rumour that the president of Jamaat-e-Islami, at a meeting in Hyderabad, had called on Muslims to double their demographic strength.[18] The *Indian Express* published statistics indicating that Hindus would become a minority in the Indian population by the year 2281 or even 2231.[19] Opinion polls revealed that 57% of those interviewed wanted the government to stop conversions (78% in the cities of northern India).[20] These preoccupations took on an exacerbated form inside the Hindu nationalist camp, where former obsessions were revived. Thus H.V. Seshadri wrote:

Untouchability, besides engendering forces of internal disruption, has opened the doors to the onslaught of foreign forces. The *Arab Times* report as also the Action Committee resolution of the Islamic meeting at Hyderabad on February 19, 1981, proclaimed in unambiguous terms their plan in this regard. It is to convert 10 crores of Harijans to Islam and see that the Muslim percentage becomes sufficiently high to enable them to carve out, in the first instance, independent, Islamic States in Bharat [India], and finally to Islamise the entire Bharat. The pan-Islamic zealots in Bharat have always been dreaming of this vision.[21]

From now on, the underlying theme of all public discussions among militant Hindus was 'Hindu society under siege'. This was also the title

---

[17] M. Gaborieau, 'The transformation of Tablighi Jama'at into a transnational movement, 1944-1965', London SSRC Workshop on Tablighi Jama'at, London, 7-8 June 1990. For an analysis of the limitations on fundamentalists posed by the characteristics of South Asian Islam, see I. Ahmed, 'India – Surprising isolation', *World Focus*, 5 May 1980, pp. 23-6.

[18] The government itself was worried by these tendencies. In a report, the Union Home Minister suggested that the states should legislate to prevent fraudulent conversion. He was worried also by the revival of activity among Muslim organisations such as the Jamaat-e-Islami, the Muslim League and Tabligh-e-Jamaat, and by the inflow of finance from the Gulf states (*Statesman* (Delhi), 16 Jan. 1982).

[19] These figures reflected an old Hindu nationalist psychosis reawakened after each census. See S.K. Misra, 'Will Muslims outnumber Hindus?', *Motherland*, 26 June 1973. The 1971 census revealed a minor diminution of the proportion of Hindus from 83.4% in 1961 to 82.7% while the Muslims slightly increased from 10.7% to 11.2%.

[20] All these figures are cited in A.M. Muhajid, *Conversion to Islam*, op. cit., pp. 92 and 96.

[21] *Organiser*, 16 May 1982, p. 6. From July 1981, the paper's editorials were written in this vein (see, for instance, ibid., 5 July 1981, p. 3). See also J.R. Gupta, *Role of foreign money in conversion of Hindus*, Delhi: VHP, n.d.

given to a series of six articles published by a regular contributor to the *Organiser*, Sita Ram Goel, in which he analysed the three sources of danger with international ramifications: Christianity, 'Macaulayism' (the Westernisation of the Indian upper classes stemming from the educational reforms of T.B. , later Lord, Macaulay in the 1830s), and Islam (regarded as the most dangerous of the three because of its financial backing). Goel's conclusion was that 'the death of Hindu society is no longer an eventuality impossible to envisage'.[22]

The distinguishing feature of the 1980s undoubtedly lay in the way this feeling of vulnerability was discussed and communicated to other Hindus through the appearance of other 'threats' such as Sikh separatism, the influx of Bangladeshi immigrants into Assam, the visit of Pope John Paul II and the government's 'pro-Muslim bias' in the 'Shah Bano controversy' and the 'Rushdie affair'.

From the autumn of 1983, Bhindranwale's guerrillas set about transforming the Punjab into a *de facto* Sikh state by provoking a general exodus through the random murder of Hindus.[23] In 1983 there were 75 such Hindu victims, mostly passengers on buses; the number killed in 1984 was nearly five times higher (359) because, from March onwards, mobile murder squads began to attack villages.[24] After an agreement reached between the government and the Akali Dal, 1985 saw a lull, but in 1986 the slaughter was renewed: 520 civilians were killed in that year, 910 in 1987 and 1,949 in 1988. This fresh outbreak of terrorism caused thousands of families to flee to the towns – not only of the Punjab but also of Haryana, Himachal Pradesh and Delhi. The exodus made other populations feel insecure, an effect reinforced by the extended radius of the terrorists' activity from 1985. In May that year there were bomb explosions in Haryana, Rajasthan, Uttar Pradesh, and above all in Delhi where they claimed more than 80 victims. Moreover, striking at Delhi caused alarm to be magnified by means of the national press.

In the case of Assam, there was anxiety among militant Hindus from 1979 onwards owing to the so-called 'calculated infiltration' of Bangladeshi Muslims, a claim they reinforced by pointing to the expulsion of Hindu refugees from Bangladesh itself.[25] Above all the Hindu nationalists feared the risks of regional separatism which, they argued, reducing the number of Hindus in Assam could not fail to create.[26]

[22] *Organiser*, Independence Day Special, 1981, p. 7. See also the articles of 23 Aug. 1981, pp. 8-9; 30 Aug. 1981, p. 6; 6 Sept. 1981, p. 8; 20 Sept. 1981, p. 8 and B. Suseelan, *India under siege*, New Delhi: VHP, 1988.

[23] R.A. Kapur, *Sikh separatism*, New Delhi: Vikas, 1987, p. 227.

[24] Ibid., p. 229, and *India Week*, 16 June 1989, p. 14.

[25] *Organiser*, 21 Nov. 1979, p. 16.

[26] On this matter see the resolutions of the ABPS (ibid., 3 April 1983, p. 8).

The Pope's visit at the beginning of 1986 aroused similar, though less pronounced, fears. Catholic missionaries were said to be threatening a Balkanisation of India[27] in so far as all Catholics were obliged to render the Pope unconditional allegiance – a transnational tie which this visit was designed to reactivate.[28] The Pope's journey had a considerable rallying effect on Catholic communities.

The early 1980s was thus marked by the emergence or re-affirmation of threats – real or perceived as such – from the minority communities. From 1985 these anxieties were intensified among some Hindus who felt the Centre had revealed a pro-Muslim bias in the 'Shah Bano affair' and was discriminating against them. In the RSS, as in the AIMPLB, some leaders saw the mobilisation of Muslims as a new version of the Khilafat, which had given rise, according to Seshadri, 'to a horrible "Jihad" against the Hindus of Kerala'.[29] The ABPS reacted vehemently to the passing of the Muslim Women (Protection of Right on Divorce) Bill with a resolution attributing this concession to the government's electoral calculations,[30] and Deoras repeated the demand for a uniform civil code, without which, in his opinion, India would remain at the mercy of Muslim separatism.[31] On 8 May 1986, Advani attacked the bill in the Rajya Sabha; claiming that it was directed against the interests of Muslim women, he was able to present the BJP as a party whose advocacy of a common civil code was based on a modern and progressive outlook.[32] Thus the banning of *The Satanic Verses* by the government of Rajiv Gandhi in October 1988 was similarly interpreted as a concession motivated by electoral self-interest.

In differing degrees and in different forms, the supposed threats that presented themselves in 1981-6 contributed to the sense of vulnerability among Hindus, which the RSS and its affiliates wished to amplify. One of its leader-writers, implicitly recognising the element of irrationality in this state of mind, posed the following questions:

'Why are the Hindus feeling threatened in their own country? What is the exact nature of their fears? Are they real or imaginary? What can we do about them?'[33]

---

27 Ibid., 2 Feb. 1986, p. 1.

28 This argument was developed by H.V. Seshadri in a series of four articles (see above, all ibid., 2 Feb. 1986, p. 1).

29 Ibid., 19 Jan. 1986, p. 9.

30 Ibid., 30 March 1986, p. 6. See also the very aggressive editorial of 18 May 1986, p. 3.

31 Ibid., 22 Feb. 1986, p. 13. Interestingly, the BJP leaders were more moderate in their reaction; they mainly stressed the validity of the verdict of the Supreme Court (*Resolutions, BJP National Executive Meeting*, 3-5 January, 1986 (Chandigarh), pp. 3-5).

32 *Manthan*, 7 (2), p. 57.

33 M.V. Kamath, 'On being a Hindu', *Organiser*, 7 Sept. 1986, p. 2. The irrational aspect of this anti-Muslim phobia has been confirmed by the findings of Sudhir Kakar, a

In this context the RSS adopted a twofold strategy that combined old and new elements. On the one hand, as in the 1920s, the feeling of being vulnerable to alien communities prompted an attempt to reform Hinduism according to the logic of the strategy of stigmatisation and emulation. On the other hand, an effort at instrumentalist mobilisation was undertaken in a more political perspective with the aim of forming the Hindu community into a vote bank. The political climate in the first half of the 1980s would speed up the return of the RSS to the militant Hinduism which had emerged at the end of the Janata regime.

The VHP and building the Hindu nation against the Other

In Punjab, many *shakhas* were attacked by Sikh terrorists, causing the deaths of dozens of *swayamsevaks*,[34] and the Hindu community retaliated by lynching suspected militants. Yet the RSS and the BJP hardly exploited the resulting atmosphere of hatred in the 1980s. Not only were they content to limit themselves to orchestrating protests, like the general strike in the summer of 1989,[35] but they also ensured that such events were peaceful. This restraint had an ideological rationale.[36] In the Hindu nationalist view Sikhism, far from being the enemy, was the martial face of Hinduism, as a BJP resolution recalled:

The Sikh Panth was born to protect Hinduism and venerable Gurus sacrificed themselves and their dear children to protect Hindu honour. The Sikh contribution to the strength and prosperity of India is magnificient, and the nation is truly grateful.[37]

---

psychoanalyst: '[...] in a large number of cases, the *bhuta* or evil spirit possessing Hindu men and women who went for help to village exorcists or to well-known healing temples and shrines, turned out to be a Muslim. [...] In that Muslim *bhutas* were universally considered to be the strongest, the vilest, the most malignant and the most stubborn of evil spirits, the Muslim seemed to symbolise the alien and the demonic in the unconscious part of the Hindu psyche.' (S. Kakar, 'The communal devil', *India Today*, 31 Oct. 1986, p. 44. This article is a synthesis of some of the ideas the author put forward in an earlier work: S. Kakar, *Shamans, mystics and doctors: a psychological inquiry into India and its healing traditions*, New York: Alfred A. Knopf, 1982, pp. 63 and 87). Such psychological tendencies were probably in existence long before the 1980s, but they could not but be intensified by the developments we have just reviewed.

34 *Organiser*, 9 July 1989.

35 *Hindustan Times*, 26 June 1989, p. 1.

36 A good example is to be found in Seshadri's explanations after the attack on the Ludhiana *shakha* (*Organiser*, 20 April 1986, pp. 8-9.).

37 *Action unavoidable, situation avoidable – Hindu-Sikh unity at all cost*, New Delhi: BJP Publication, 1984, p. 3. As well as this conviction there was the attachment to Punjab as the cradle of Vedic civilisation (*Resolutions, BJP National Executive Meeting*, April 6 and 7, 1988, Agra, p. 12).

While the Hindu nationalist organisations did not generally represent Sikhs as being a menace to the Hindu community they had few reservations about depicting the Muslims as a threatening force. As on previous occasions when there had been tension between Hindus and Muslims, they both stigmatised the Muslim Other and sought to discover and imitate the sources of its strength. In order to describe the 'Muslims in unfavourable terms, Hindu nationalists simply used the traditional themes of Hindu xenophobia and played upon the feeling of vulnerability which the 'Sangh parivar' had fostered in the past. Addressing the plenary session of the BJP as the party's incoming president, Advani stated that in the 'Shah Bano affair' some Muslim leaders had acted as 'obscurantists' and 'fanatics' in their disregard of the right of their community's wives.[38]

Thus the paradox that stigmatisation was accompanied by emulation – the most interesting feature of Hindu nationalist strategy – appears yet again. When we turn to the evolution of the VHP from the late 1970s to the mid-1980s, we find that both processes occurred simultaneously.

The VHP as the spearhead of the RSS's new political strategy

The Vishwa Hindu Parishad became the spearhead of Hindu militancy at the beginning of the 1980s. Its primary vocation was to counter the conversions that were weakening Hinduism but the RSS pushed it to the forefront in the framework of a new electoral strategy which had taken shape as early as 1979.

At the end of January 1979, the second International Hindu Conference was held in Allahabad under the auspices of the VHP. This was just at a time when relations between the RSS and the Janata were deteriorating rapidly, and the conference ushered in a long-term strategic reorientation of the movement by Deoras, as his own speech bore eloquent witness:

The Government thinks that the Hindus have no right to ask for even basic rights while other religious communities shout loud and get special treatment from this very Government. [...] Politicians only think of the next election and personal gains for themselves. Hindus must now awaken themselves to such an extent that even from the elections point of view the politicians will have to respect the Hindu sentiments and change their policies accordingly. [...] If others put up demands, they were accepted, but even genuine demands by Hindus are ignored. This is because Muslims and other minorities usually vote *en bloc* while Hindus are divided. Once Hindus get united, the government would start caring for them also.

[38] *Presidential address by L.K. Advani – President, BJP*, Plenary session, May 9, 1986 (New Delhi), pp. 4-5. This sort of discourse probably made a positive impact on the modern middle class, whose affinities with Hindu nationalism will be studied in chapter 12.

[...] Therefore the need of the moment is to awaken our Hindu consciousness as Hindus.[39]

This speech made an implicit reference to the pressures being exerted by the minorities, in particular against O.P. Tyagi's Freedom of Religion Bill, to which the conference devoted a resolution of support. But, apart from this, a change of strategy was perceptible. Originally the RSS had not regarded the conquest of state power as a priority. For Hedgewar, and later Golwalkar, the most important goal of the organisation was enunciated in terms of a socio-psychological reform of which the *shakhas* were the main instrument. Deoras, who had already let the RSS get directly involved in political agitation through its association with the 'JP movement', now considered electoral politics to be of crucial importance for the Hindu nationalist activists, even when they did not belong to any party. The so-called lack of concern for the Hindus shown by the Janata politicians, with whom the ex-Jana Sanghis had unhesitatingly compromised themselves, had persuaded him of the need to build a 'Hindu vote', for which, it appeared, the VHP would have to be primarily responsible.

The laborious relaunching of the VHP (1979-81). Despite setbacks,[40] the movement remained pledged to the promotion of Hindu unity on a religious basis. Thus the 1979 conference could claim to have been a true cross-section of Hinduism (following the example of the first conference, held in 1966), but with greater credibility given the number (estimated at 100,000) and truly representative nature of the delegates. All the different strands of the 'Hindu nation' were represented, Buddhism included, since the Dalai Lama opened the conference.

The logic of these efforts at unity implied perseverance with a strategy of stigmatisation of the 'threatening Other' and of emulation of those cultural traits deemed to be the source of his strength and effectiveness. Hinduism was said to be facing a threat from the proselytising religions, which lacked its 'tolerance' and imperilled its majority status. The situation demanded the eradication of untouchability – an important incentive to conversion – and the unification of Hinduism in a coherent whole. These two remedies were again proposed in reaction to the cultural characteristics of the 'aggressors'. The organisational unity of Islam and

---

[39] *Hindu Vishva – Special number, Second World Hindu Conference*, March-April 1979, p. 13.

[40] In 1977, the VHP, which had 65 full-time activists, admitted that it 'had still not been able to make much headway in propagating standardised religious rituals (*vidhi*) among Hindus' (*Organiser*, 4 July 1977, p. 6).

Christianity had to be imitated in order to be successfuly resisted, a point made by Swami Chinmayananda:

Christianity and Islam were well organised. Hindus, on the other hand, were still speaking with different voices and thus had no voice in their own country. Let us convert Hindus to Hinduism, and then everything would be all-right.[41]

Accordingly the VHP once again proposed a 'minimum code of conduct for the daily life of every Hindu', the object of which was to unify religious practices and references. Article 1 called for all Hindus to venerate the sun every morning and evening; Article 2 for the regular use of the symbol 'Om' (as a pendant and on visiting cards, for example); while Article 3 was even more explicit:

Bhagavad Gita is the sacred book of the Hindus irrespective of various *sampradayas* [sects] which contains the essence of Hindu Philosophy and way of life. Every Hindu must keep a copy of the Gita in his house.[42]

This move to endow Hinduism with a sacred Book converged with a desire to provide it with a Church on the model of the Semitic religions, though without denying 'the Tradition'. The 1972 conference, like that of 1966, was thus compared with the meeting summoned at Kannauj by Harsha in order to fashion a Hindu consistory, but in spite of the large number of delegates who attended, the comparison was exaggerated because the figures of real authority were either not present (like the most eminent *Shankaracharyas*) or non-participants in the VHP (like the *Shankaracharya* of Badrinath). The principal religious figures who endorsed this claim were recognised as heads not of sects but merely of their own ashrams: as in 1966, they were Swami Chinmayananda, Prabhu Datta Brahmachari, Vishvesh Tirth and Satyamitranand Giri, whose background was very revealing. In 1963 he had resigned his post as *Shankaracharya* of Bhanpura *pith* 'because it restricted his activities, particularly his travel abroad'.[43] Soon afterwards he began to work on behalf of the VHP, which tends to corroborate our interpretation that the organisation proves especially attractive to religious leaders on whom it bestowed an alternative source of legitimacy. In 1983 Satyamitranand had built at Hardwar a Bharat Mata Mandir (Mother India Temple) with a mission to educate (each of the seven floors of the building brought together figures representing one aspect of the Hindu nation).[44] Thus, in

---

[41]   *Hindu Vishva*, March-April 1979, p. 40.

[42]   Ibid., p. 89.

[43]   L. McKean, 'Towards a Politics of Spirituality: Hindu religious organizations and Indian nationalism', unpubl. Ph. D. thesis, Department of Anthropology, University of Sydney, 1992, p. 117. .

[44]   Jaydee 'Bharat Mata Mandir', *Dharm Marg*, 1, 4 (Jan. 1984, pp. 39-41).

1979, the attraction of the VHP, though expanding, remained confined – in so far as active involvement was concerned – to a limited number of 'modern *gurus*'.

To a large extent the new VHP, relaunched in 1979, became a reality in the early 1980s in response to the sense of Hindu vulnerability aroused by the Meenakshipuram conversions. On 12 July 1981 the ABKM of the RSS voted for a resolution which – while demanding a law against conversions that were deemed not to have been completely voluntary – recognised the need for social reform. It called:

upon the entire Hindu Society to bury deep the internal caste dissensions and the pernicious practice of untouchability and stand up as one single homogenous family, so that the neglected and down-trodden sections will be assured of a place of equality, security and honour in the Hindu fold.[45]

This text recalled themes developed by the Hindu nationalists in the Hindu Sangathan movement, out of which the RSS had come into being. With this resolution the RSS affirmed its social mission, but the VHP was asked to help it in the task, in addition to intensifying its reconversion activities. On 14 July 1981 it held a Hindu Solidarity Conference under the auspices of Swami Vishveth Tirth, at which numerous *swamis* from Madurai, Tanjore and Madras were present. They saw themselves as an embryonic ecclesiastical authority, declaring at the conference:

We, the religious heads assembled today at Meenakshipuram solemnly declare that our Vedas and Shastras have not mentioned untouchability in any form, anywhere but have propounded only complete brotherhood. [...] We therefore ardently appeal to all our Hindu brethren to individually and collectively throw out these evils lock, stock and barrel and strive to ensure equality and fraternity among all sections of our Hindu people.[46]

A second Hindu Solidarity Conference was held less than a fortnight later, on 27 July, at Ramanathapuram, with the blessing of the *Shankaracharyas* of Kanchi and Sringeri. These conferences were the points of departure for a whole series of gatherings throughout India – the South having priority as the scene of the Meenakshipuram conversions. During 1981 Swami Vishvesh Tirth coordinated a series of Hindu conferences in Karnataka to raise awareness among the population as a whole, including religious figures, of the problems facing Hinduism.[47] At the beginning of 1982, the campaign was brought to Tamil Nadu when a

---

[45] *RSS resolves*, op. cit., p. 106.

[46] Quoted in H.V. Seshadri, *Warning of Meenakshipuram*, Bangalore: Jagarana Prakashan, 1981, pp. 27-8.

[47] H.V. Seshadri (ed.), *RSS: a vision in action*, Bangalore: Jagarana Prakashan, 1988, p. 82.

Hindu Conference was held in Kanyakumari; and in April that year, the VHP in Kerala organised a Provincial Hindu Conference at Trivandrum which was well attended, especially by *sadhus*.[48] In April 1983 Vishvesh Tirth was the inspiration behind a Hindu Samajotsav (Festival of Hindu Society) at Mangalore.[49] Jammu and Kashmir, where a Hindu Conference was held in 1981, and the North-East came immediately after the South (where seven Hindu Conferences were held in 1982) in the order of priority.[50] In the first half of February 1982 similar programmes were organised in Maharashtra. This phenomenon also spread to the Hindi-speaking North: Hindu Conferences were organised at Patna in November, then at Mathura and Muzaffarnagar (Uttar Pradesh) during the first quarter of 1983.

The objective on every occasion was to call for solidarity among Hindus in facing up to the challenge of Muslim proselytisation. This involved an increased involvement of prominent religious figures in an effort to bring about an 'awakening of the people' ('Jana Jagaran' in the current terminology, which tended to replace the former key-phrase 'Hindu Sangathan' in RSS discourse).

Activists, sadhus and patrons.   An important result of the Jana Jagaran movement was the welcoming into the VHP of *sadhus* who were concerned by the 'threats' posed to Hinduism. Two contrasting examples illustrate this significant trend. Paramahans Vamdeo abandoned his solitary life and became an active VHP member after reading a news item about Muslim proselytism.[51] Another prominent new recruit to the VHP was the Mahant Avaidyanath who in the 1970s had succeeded his *guru* Digvijay Nath as leader of the Nath sect of Gorakhpur. Like the latter he had been a campaigner in the Hindu Mahasabha – on whose ticket he had been elected as an MLA in 1962, 1967, 1974 and 1977 and as an MP in 1970. He had also served as head of the Bharat Sadhu Samaj in the area.[52]

The RSS was highly visible in the Jana Jagaran movement from the outset. Evidence of its revived militancy was also to be seen in the two unprecedentedly large camps[53] which it organised in Bangalore in January

[48] *Organiser*, 18 April 1982, p. 2.

[49] Ibid., 10 April 1983, p. 9.

[50] Ibid., 11 March 1982, p. 16.

[51] *Statesman*, 1 Oct. 1991.

[52] *Tenth Lok Sabha Who's who*, New Delhi: Lok Sabha Secretariat, 1992, p. 43, and *Who's who in UP Legislative Assembly 1962-1967*, Lucknow: UP Legislative Assembly Secretariat, 1963, p. 10.

[53] More than 21,000 *swayamsevaks* met in Bangalore (*Organiser*, Republic Day Special, 1982, p. 13).

1982 and at Poona a year later, and by its efforts to increase the number of *shakhas*, which in 1985 reached a total of 20,000.[54] But its chosen agent in this enterprise remained the VHP. In 1982 the latter acquired a new General Secretary, Har Mohan Lal, a former diamond merchant who had joined the RSS in 1945 in Agra. Before being seconded to the VHP by the mother organisation he had been the *sanghchalak* for the RSS unit in Agra and then Jaipur.[55] At the same time, Ashok Singhal, who had formerly been an RSS *pracharak* in Kanpur and *prant pracharak* for the Delhi region between 1977 and 1982, became Joint General Secretary of the VHP. Singhal succeeded to the post of General Secretary on the death of Har Mohan Lal in April 1986. At that time the post of Joint General Secretary passed to Acharya Giriraj Kishore. A *swayamsevak* since 1940 and a *pracharak* since 1943, Kishore had been appointed Organising Secretary of the ABVP in 1960 and of the Rajasthan unit of the Jana Sangh in 1971.[56] In addition to their commitment to the RSS, these men worked under the patronage of RSS veterans (like Hans Raj Gupta, who was a vice-president, and Ram Narain Shastri, who represented the movement at Indore) and leading figures who – apart from the Maharana of Udaipur, the president since 1968, and Vijaye Raje Scindia, an active 'trustee' – were mostly Marwari industrialists (Vishnu Hari Dalmia, S.B. Somayya and G.H. Singhania were vice-presidents or 'trustees') or reputable lawyers (S.N. Katju, the son of K.N. Katju – a former Congress Union Minister and Chief Minister – and retired judge of the Allahabad High Court became president of the VHP in the late 1980s). Here was to be found the tripartite alliance which the leadership team had established in the 1960s, bringing together *swayamsevaks*, notables and men of religion. The last-named were to become the object of special attention at the beginning of the 1980s. The organisers were indeed concerned to *institutionalise* the collaboration between Hindu nationalist activists and religious leaders, and, under the pressure of circumstances, this for the first time took on a significant character.

The emergence of a Hindu ecclesiastical structure (1982-4)?　In 1982 the VHP formed a Central Margdarshak Mandal (a central circle of spiritual guides – *margdarshak* meaning 'those who show the way') whose members were to 'direct and guide the religious ceremonies, morals and ethics of Hindu society'.[57] The members in question, of whom

54　Ibid., 10 Nov. 1985.
55　Ibid., 13 April 1986, p. 2 and Acharya Giriraj Kishore, 'Shri Har Mohan Lalji' in *Shraddhanjali Smarika*, op. cit., p. 33 (Hindi).
56　Interview with Acharya Giriraj Kishore, 11 Feb. 1994, New Delhi.
57　Vishwa Hindu Parishad, *The Hindu awakening – Retrospect and promise*, New Delhi [n.d.], p. 28.

there were thirty-nine, represented different sects of Hinduism but they were still less active than the 'modern *gurus*', as we shall see below. Alongside this authority, rather like an 'executive committee', the VHP founded a Sadhu Sansad (parliament of *sadhus*) whose seventeen *sadhus* were to enable the '*shakti* [power] of the *sadhus* to play an enlarged role in the activities of nation-building'.[58]

These institutions evolved over time: the Central Margdarshak Mandal, strengthened by achieving the status of a permanent institution, came to have 200 members, who were to gather twice a year with the function of 'advising the VHP in socio-religious domains'.[59] In 1984 the Sadhu Sansad became a Dharma Sansad (Parliament of the Hindu religion) with hundreds, even thousands, of participants. It met at very irregular intervals to deliberate on 'vital problems'. The idea of a Hindu parliament gained strength through the 1980s according to the strategy of emulation.[60] The best way of resisting 'aggression' from other religions was by adopting the characteristics which endowed them with strength, above all their centralised structure. The perceived threat from Christianity, Islam and even Sikhism, whose ecclesiastical hierarchies were playing an increasingly public role, probably explains the Hindu nationalists' desire to create an equivalent institution for Hinduism.

The Christian churches lobbied vigorously during the debate on the Freedom of Religion Bill in 1978-9. Soon afterwards the Catholic priesthood started to expand rapidly: the annual growth rate of ordinations rose from an average of 6% in the 1970s, to about 22% in 1980-1 (in 1981 the total number of priests was 11,880).[61] The Hindu nationalists naturally viewed this phenomenon with unease, especially when the Pope visited India in 1986.[62]

The situation in the Punjab also seemed to have a similar influence because of the involvement of the Sikh ecclesiastical hierarchy. The Akalis had endowed the Sikh community with a centralised structure in 1925 with the Shiromani Gurudwara Prabandhak Committee (SGPC), to which the British had agreed to delegate the management of the *gurudwaras* (Sikh temples). But before 1925 Sikhism already had an ecclesiastical hierarchy, namely the guardians of the sacred Book, the *Adi Granth*, and holders of temporal power whose seat, the Akal Takht, was in the

58   Ibid., pp. 30-1.
59   Interview with Acharya Giriraj Kishore, 10 Oct. 1991, New Delhi.
60   Some readers of *Organiser* also proposed their own projects (*Organiser*, 28 Sept. 1986, p. 5, and 16 Nov. 1986, p. 12).
61   P.M. Mathew, 'Politics of "peace" and "secularism" ', *EPW*, 10 May 1986, pp. 817-18.
62   S.R. Goel, 'The Pope's empire in India – A state within a state', *Organiser*, 2 Feb. 1986, pp. 817-18.

Golden Temple of Amritsar. In the 1980s the High Priests supported Sikh separatism with growing zeal, to the point where they pronounced in favour of Khalistan (Land of the Pure) in 1987.[63] These developments only hardened the determination of the Hindu nationalists to protect their community by providing it with a similarly coherent structure.[64] The goal of creating structures for Hindu religious leaders was not confined to Delhi, for the VHP worked to elaborate its network at the local level too, as the case of Madhya Pradesh testifies.

The development of the VHP network at the local level

The VHP's basic unit – similar to that of the RSS and the BJP but called *upkhand* – corresponded to an area with 2,000 inhabitants; then came the *kanda*, with 20,000, the *prakhand*, with 100,000, the district, the division and finally the state. In 1982, 150 *pracharaks* were provided by the RSS, but the VHP also undertook to train its own *dharma pracharaks*, and in July 1982 about 100 of these were 'initiated' by the leaders of the seven *akharas* of Hardwar.[65] They operated in particular at the district, divisional and state 'levels where VHP cadres sought to bring together religious leaders to form district, divisional and state Margdarshak Mandals.

The example of Madhya Bharat suggests that at every level the vital element in this enterprise consisted of RSS-trained activists receiving the patronage of notables and the help of *sadhus* as in the high command of the VHP in Delhi. The VHP in the Madhya Bharat region (its headquarters were at Indore) did not truly come into existence until the organisation was reinvigorated at the beginning of the 1980s. In 1983 Hukum Chand Savala – the son of a Jain grain merchant in Bhanpura who had joined the RSS as a youth in 1965 – became the VHP's *sangathan mantri* in that town and later became *prant sangathan mantri* for Madhya Bharat.[66] The VHP's general secretary for the region was none other than Gulab Chand Khandelwal, brother of Pyarelal Khandelwal, a *pracharak* who had become a *sangathan mantri* first in the Jana Sangh and later in the BJP. Having joined the RSS as a student at Indore in 1939, he too was representative of the merchant caste intelligentsia which had provided

[63] *Hindustan Times*, 11 Sept. 19487, p. 1.

[64] A writer sympathetic to militant Hindu themes, Arun Shourie, emphasised that when faced with Sikh separatism the Hindus would be forced to conclude 'that they too must have a central authority, their own Akal Thakt, that they too must have their full-time functionaries paid for by their SGPC who can double up for politics' (*Religion in politics*, New Delhi: Roli Books International, 1987, p. 133).

[65] *Organiser*, 28 Nov. 1982, p. 11 and 1 Aug. 1982, p. 1.

[66] Interview with H.C. Savala, 14 Oct. 1991, Bhopal.

many of the important figures in the Hindu nationalist movement of that region. Before joining the VHP full-time in the mid-1970s, he had been a partner in the family shop, now largely devoted to electronic goods, in the bazaar of Bhopal's old town.[67]

At the national level, most of the presidents of the regional and local units were merchants. In the early 1980s the regional presidency of the VHP was conferred on a Maheshwari industrialist based at Indore, Bhagwan Das Toshniwal,[68] while the presidency of the Bhopal branch went to Amerchand Ajmera, a Jain businessman who had formerly been a Hindu Mahasabha member.[69] These activists and notables had retained, or in some cases acquired, the active support of the region's religious leaders and *sadhus*. Thus the first guiding spirit of the Margdarshak Mandal of Madhya Bharat was Swami Prakashananda, a *pracharak* who had renounced the world and founded an *ashram* in Sonkatch (Dewas district);[70] the second, from 1988 onwards, was the successor to Satyamitranand Giri as head of the *pith* of Bhanpura, the Shankaracharya Divyanand Tirth. The *pith* had been discredited by the resignation of Satyamitranand, but Divyanand turned out to be as much an absentee as his predecessor; in the first three years of his appointment he spent only two weeks in a virtually deserted *pith*.[71] This suggested that in taking up this responsibility, Divyanand had probably sought a title which would allow him to occupy the rostrum in Hindu movements like the VHP, which in turn needed the support of such religious leaders. Divyanand proved his worth as a recruit due to the prestige of his ochre robe and his talents as a propagandist who could draw large audiences.

During the 1980s, the leaders of the VHP demonstrated their capacity to develop branches of the organisation at the local level in Madhya Bharat. By the end of the decade, VHP committees had been established in all but fifty of the 192 *prakhands* (equivalent to *tehsils*).[72]

[67] Interview with G.C. Khandelwal.

[68] Interestingly, B.D. Toshniwal, who patronised the VHP just as he would have done any Hindu institution, is not fully aware of its programme. By contrast his brother is one of the RSS-trained national vice-presidents of the VHP (interview with B.D. Toshniwal, 27 Aug. 1992, Indore).

[69] Interview with A. Ajmera, 13 Nov. 1990, Bhopal.

[70] *Shraddhanjali Smarika*, op. cit., p. 51.

[71] Interview with Abhousanand Sarasvati (secretary to Divyanand), 16 Oct. 1991, Bhanpura.

[72] *Shraddhanjali Smarika*, op. cit., p 132. In 1991, H.C. Savala claimed that VHP committees had been established in all but fifteen of the newly re-designed 211 *prakhands*. Those without committees were mainly located in Betul district and the *tehsil* of Harda (interview). The VHP achieved this increase in the density of its local network on the same triple social base of *swayamsevak*, notables and *sadhus*, as the example of Shivpuri demonstrates.

The VHP had been established in Shivpuri in the late 1960s but then had stagnated till the early 1980s.[73] Its reactivation came about in 1983 when a former district judge, V.D. Saxena, who had had links with the RSS in his youth, took advantage of his retirement to patronise the movement as president of the district VHP. He was assisted, from 1987, by a Brahmin who owned a clinic and acted as general secretary of the district VHP. At the same time Saxena won the support of *sadhus* who had set up *ashrams* in the region. He commented: 'All the *sadhus* and *sants* are working for the VHP. If they are not enrolled as members, they give lectures and they participate in all the activities of the VHP. [...] Whenever we need them, we call them.'[74]

The novelty of the VHP's recruitment strategy lay in the attachment of religious who till then had remained more on the periphery of the movement. The network thus established paved the way for the first Dharma Sansad to be held in Delhi on 7-8 April 1984, at which 528 religious figures were present, representing various streams of Hinduism – in the broad sense as understood by Hindu nationalists.[75]

The increasing involvement of a particular religious network

The notion of a 'religious network' arose not only from the recruitment of *sadhus* by VHP branches but also from the way in which the influence of the heads of sects was channelled. These heads of sects could in fact claim the allegiance of disciples, both lay and committed to a life of renunciation, and of the superiors of smaller monasteries or the priests of their temples.[76] Such a rallying of figures who usually guarded their independence jealously was doubtless partly a result of the decline in their status in modern India, and a downplaying of the value of ascetic discipline which accompanied the attenuation of sects as institutions. Robert Gross observed in 1979 that

the current generation of *sadhus* are generally less motivated to adhere to the strict regulations of ascetic ritual practice, social isolation, and rejection of worldly life.

---

[73] Before 1983, Babulal Sharma was the VHP president in Shivpuri district but there was no other office-holder.

[74] Interview with V.D. Saxena, 18 Nov. 1990, Shivpuri. For details, see C. Jaffrelot, 'La Vishva Hindu Parishad – structures et stratégies', *Purushartha*, 17 (1994), pp. 185-6.

[75] *Hindu Vishwa – Vishwa Hindu Parishad Silver Jubilee Special Issue*, Aug. 1990, p. 15.

[76] In the latter case a clientelistic relationship tended to become established, as the case of the *Shankaracharya* of Kanchi suggests. The network of temples and monasteries linked to the *Shankaracharya* of Kanchi was concentrated largely in the South but also had units in New Delhi, Ahmedabad and Ratlam (M. Mines and V. Gourishankar, 'Leadership and individuality in South Asia: the case of the South Indian Big-man', *Journal of Asian Studies*, 49, 4 (1990), p. 770).

[...] Many *sadhus* have loosened their affiliation to a sectarian grouping and have struck out on their own as independent entrepreneurial religious preachers and *gurus* with their own following and support network.[77]

The religious leaders who were the victims of this process – as in the case of founders of *ashrams* which had no historical legitimacy, some of whom had hitherto belonged to the VHP – found that the organisation offered some of them a useful platform from which they evolved, with the movement, into entrepreneurs of a political character.[78] The religious figures who preserved their prestige, for example as heads of historic sects, could not easily oppose the VHP as an institution active in the service of Hinduism. The only way out for those unwilling to sacrifice their independence to the VHP or who rejected its views, often consisted in presenting a programme very similar to that of the organisation. Thus even when they did not belong to the VHP, many *sadhus* nevertheless sought to present a united front in order to influence the course of social and political life.

Several *Shankaracharyas* illustrate the two cases in point. Swaroopanand Saraswati's situation was the most secure of them all, since he had been in charge of not only the *math* of Badrinath, as of right, since 1973[79] but also of the *math* of Dwarka, since 1982, as the result of the wish expressed by its previous *Shankaracharya* just before his death. Even though he took part in political movements – notably as president of the Ram Rajya Parishad in the 1950s – he kept himself at a distance from the VHP.[80] By contrast, Swami Vasudevanand, the *Shankaracharya* of Jyotish *pith*, who had claimed that it was *his* right to have charge of Badrinath but whose case had been dismissed by the High Court with a consequent loss of his legitimacy, was closer to the VHP. The intermediate positions were held by the *Shankaracharyas* of Sringeri, Puri and Kanchi, all of whom, at the beginning of the 1980s, had been in office for several decades. The first of these, being head of the most prestigious *math* of all, was content merely to give his blessing to the Hindu nationalists. The second, a dedicated activist who had been involved in the cow protection movement in 1966-7, undertook his own mobilisation yet without openly dissociating himself from the VHP, whose views after all he largely shared. This attitude was more clearly manifested by Jayendra Saraswati at Kanchi.

---

[77] R.L. Gross, 'Hindu asceticism: a study of the sadhus of North India', unpubl. Ph.D. thesis, University of California, Berkeley, vol. 2, op. cit., p. 624.

[78] The novelty here was in the notion of enterprise, because where *sadhus* had taken on a political role hitherto. it had been mainly as counsellors to those in power.

[79] *Organiser*, 27 June 1982.

[80] *India Today*, 31 July 1993, p. 62.

What was exceptional in this case was the designation by a living incumbent of his successor. In 1954, Chandrashekharandra Saraswati, who had been in office since 1908, appointed Jayendra Saraswati to take charge alongside him. The delicate position in which the latter thus found himself possibly gave him the incentive to pursue a public career in order to raise his status. For example, in response to the conversions at Meenakshipuram, he financed one of the two vehicles with which the VHP toured Tamil Nadu bearing an image which all castes were called upon to revere together as a mark of unity.[81] He then took part in a similar operation organised by the VHP, known as the *Ekatmata Yatra* (see below).[82] It seems that he appointed his own successor in 1983 to free himself for a series of journeys aimed at identifying potential agents for his planned regeneration of Hinduism. Thus he twice visited the *Shankaracharya* of Ratlam, who appreciated the interest shown in him by such an important figure. His *math*, without the patronage of the princely family to which it owed its origin, was now without funds or disciples. Undoubtedly it was because of the contact with Jayendra Saraswati that the *Shankaracharya* of Ratlam also conceived his project of a Hindu parliament, at the same time as the VHP was entertaining a similar notion.[83] Jayendra Saraswati kept in touch with the VHP and was willing to attend its ceremonies, but his activism tailed off towards the end of the 1980s, by which time Chandrashekharandra had recalled him to his duties as an ascetic.

Overall, the Hindu nationalist movement made a major advance in the early 1980s by mobilising religious figures within structures which were intended to assume the role of a Hindu ecclesiastical authority. The VHP fell a long way short of having rallied enough leading personalities to give the impression of being a federation of all the Hindu sects, but it applied itself to achieve this aim. It had already emerged that VHP organisers with a RSS background had succeeded in overcoming the rivalry between certain leaders of sects and their claims to precedence over one another, so that in the VHP all were considered as equal members of a single body. Even though the two movements do not look alike, the VHP probably has closer links with the RSS than do any of the latter's affiliates. The religious leaders of the VHP and the *pracharaks* were in fact regarded by other cadres as embodying a single sociological type: that of the renouncer, as the following appreciation of Ashok Singhal by a VHP official in charge of overseas activities attests:

---

[81] *Organiser*, 27 June 1982, p. 14.

[82] Ibid., 8 Jan. 1984, p. 4.

[83] Interview with Shankaracharya Sacchidananda Sarasvati Bharti, 2 Dec. 1990, Ratlam. See also his article 'A model Hindu Parliament', *Organiser*, 14 Oct. 1990, p. 2.

He wears white clothes [and not saffron] but he is a *sannyasin*. He is a first class engineer, he has a degree from the BHU, a top institution, but he never entered in that profession; he has not married. He is not a householder and he is devoting his entire life for the service of Hindu Dharma. Like him there are hundreds of workers of VHP and RSS who are not married, who devote their entire life for the service of Hindu society. They are not in Bhagwa [saffron] dress but they are like *sadhus*.[84]

All the same, Swami Chinmayananda was in the habit of saying to RSS members that there was 'virtually no difference between *swayamsevak* and *sannyasin*, except that one is saffron-clothed while the other 's in white'.[85] It is of course useful to bear in mind that the religious figures in question were becoming increasingly ideologically minded.

To sum up, the early 1980s were marked by the rallying of a growing number of religious leaders around VHP structures which had been established in emulation of those of the 'threatening Others'. In the 1920s and 1960s a similar process had given birth respectively to the RSS and the VHP. In the 1980s the VHP associated itself with a new religious network that strengthened the legitimacy of the Hindu nationalist movement and above all provided it with an additional instrument of national mobilisation. As in the 1960s, the phase which followed that of strategic emulation, in which this new network had taken shape, was to be ethno-religious mobilisation.

The attempt at Hindu mobilisation

(Re)conversions, the welfarist tactic and temple-building

At first, the figures of religious authority were the agents of a new wave of conversions or reconversions to Hinduism. According to the VHP, the number of reconversions reached 22,200 in 1981-2 of whom 13,000 were Rajput Muslims from Rajasthan. In the other states the (re)conversions were of Christians who were of either Scheduled Caste or tribal origin: 2,000 in Andhra Pradesh, 1,588 in Western Uttar Pradesh, 1,557 in Bihar and 1,450 in Karnataka, out of a total of 8,279.[86]

The effort to obliterate caste distinctions also intensified after the Meenakshipuram conversions. At the Hindu Solidarity Conference, held

---

[84] Interview, 8 Nov. 1990, New Delhi.

[85] *Organiser*, 11 Feb. 1979.

[86] VHP, *The Hindu awakening*, op. cit., p. 21. However, one could not arrive at the same figures on the basis of the descriptions of collective conversions published by the *Organiser*, in which the numbers were rarely in the thousands or even hundreds (15 Jan. 1984, 18 Oct. 1981, p. 14, and 18 Nov. 1981, p. 16), except in the case of the Rajputs (28 Nov. 1982, p. 4).

there on 15 July 1981, religious leaders organised a *homa* (a form of Vedic sacrifice) ceremony open to all and a *bhojanam* (banquet) at which they shared a meal with 2,000 Harijans.[87] Such ceremonies shared common elements with those which had been used in South India in 1981 during the conversion of Scheduled Caste members to Islam when, after the recital of the *Kalima* (declaring belief in one God and in His messenger Mohammad), those who had been converted took part in a common service and then had a meal together.[88]

The 1981 conversions also induced the Hindu nationalists to step up their tactic of social welfare. With the experience it had acquired in helping tribals, the VHP diversified its activity so that 867 schools were opened in 1983, of which 374 were Bal Samksar Kendras (centres for training children) with the explicit purpose of 'shaping the character of the younger generation in childhood'. (There were already in existence 700 of these institutions and 178 secondary schools awarding diplomas in Hindu culture.)[89] Another feature of the strategy of good works was to build temples, about 100 being planned for Tamil Nadu alone, mainly in Scheduled Caste areas.[90]

The VHP's temples were conceived as centres for Hindu socialisation. In the same manner as those built in the 1920s and 1930s by the Birlas, they included an educative element.[91] Above all they were meant to encourage meetings in which caste differences were removed, like the *Hindu Rashtra Mandir* envisaged by Shraddhananda. In this way they corresponded to the same logic of 'strategic emulation' since it was intended to replicate in this institution the collective character of Muslim worship in the mosque. The VHP experimented with a variant on this strategy in Assam where temples were built with 'a big compound or hall as per local requirements where all religious, cultural and social ceremonies and functions take place. Thus they are the centre of all activity of the community.'[92]

This socio-cultural work was only the first step in the strategy of the post-1970s VHP. To realise the objective set forth by Deoras at the Allahabad Conference in 1979 – the creation of a Hindu political con-

---

[87] *Indian Express*, 16 July 1981. As a variant of such practices, in 1983 the *mahants* taking part in the *Dharma Sammelan* at Amritsar deliberately passed through the Scheduled Castes quarters (H.V. Seshadri, 'The Hindu Renaissance – A brief survey of the Hindu response to the major internal and external challenges facing the Hindu society', *Manthan*, 5, 1 [May 1983], p. 117).

[88] A.M. Mujahid, *Conversion to Islam*, op. cit., p. 58.

[89] Ibid., p. 116, and VHP, *The Hindu awakening*, op. cit., p. 14.

[90] *Thousands of hands join in the service of the poor* (undated VHP pamphlet).

[91] The temples of Tamil Nadu thus had to 'educate villagers in various aspects of the Hindu Dharma' (*Organiser*, 8 Dec. 1985, p. 8).

[92] Ibid., 12 Feb. 1984, p. 1.

sciousness destined to be translated into a Hindu vote – it had to resort to instrumentalist practices.

The Ekatmata Yatra – or the shaping of an ideological devotionalism

The VHP's first campaign, in November 1983, was the *Ekatmata Yatra* (literally, pilgrimage of one-soulness). Three processions, journeying from Kathmandu in Nepal to Rameshwaram in Tamil Nadu, from Gangasagar in Bengal to Somnath in Gujarat, and from Hardwar in Uttar Pradesh to Kanyakumari in Tamil Nadu – joined on the way by 69 other columns setting off from starting-points in the interior – distributed water from the Ganges (at 50 centilitres for 10 rupees) and refilled their tanks with holy water either at temples on the way or from other sacred rivers en route. This mingling was intended to symbolise Hindu unity, and all the processions converged on Nagpur – centre of the RSS and of India – before setting off on their own again.[93] Those who worked out the detailed implementation of this operation clearly played on the Hindus' perception of their territory as being ultimately associated with rivers and other places of pilgrimage, as the programme published in the *Organiser* shows:

When the yatras reach their destination at Rameshwaram and Somnath, the khumba [jars] will contain water from all the sacred places, namely the four Dhams [the most revered places of pilgrimage being Badrinath, Puri, Rameshwaram and Dwarka], the twelve Jyotirlingam [natural stalagmites considered as *lingams* of Shiva] ... and hundreds of sacred rivers, lakes and wells.[94]

Besides this appropriation of the sacred geography of Hinduism,[95] the *Ekatmata Yatra* utilised two very tangible symbols: images representing the Ganges and Mother India in the form of divinities, which the processions transported under canopies. Swami Chinmayananda and Acharya Giriraj Kishore, who was the senior VHP official in charge of this programme, indicated that these figures had been very carefully selected.[96] In fact the

---

[93] S. Hayat, 'Hindu revivalism: genesis and implications', *Regional studies*, 2, 4 (autumn 1984), p. 64.

[94] *Organiser*, 23 Oct. 1983, p. 15.

[95] The term is not overstated since this was a deliberate action, as is made clear in the analysis by H.V. Seshadri of the use of ritual practices in a political liturgy: 'The countless spots of pilgrimages, temples and ashram, which have been till now looked upon mainly as symbols of our Punya Bhoomi – a holy land – have now acquired a new and vital emphasis; they are symbols of a common Matru Bhoomi [motherland] as well' (ibid., 15 Jan. 1984, p. 7)

[96] Ibid., 13 Nov. 1983, pp. 1–13, and interview with Acharya Giriraj Kishore, 10 Oct. 1991, New Delhi.

yatra used symbols very judiciously. The Ganges, like the cow, is one of those rare symbols venerated by all Hindus, who never fail to take home a little of its water after they have been on a pilgrimage to its banks.[97] The Ganges, being identified with the figure of Mother India (Bharat Mata), became a symbol of national unity. As the movement was intended to transcend caste and sect, the VHP associated the members of Scheduled Castes with it by giving them the task of carrying the holy water along with notable members of the Sikh and Jain communities.[98]

The *Ekatmata Yatra* marked a shift in the Hindu nationalist strategy of ethno-religious mobilisation. Till then, the only symbol that had been manipulated for political purposes was the cow. However the cow protection movements of 1952 and 1966-7 had been much less sophisticated affairs. The demonstrations and petitions had been organised along classic lines. The *Ekatmata Yatra* introduced a new ideological devotionalism: its formal appearance – as well as its name – were intended to present it as a religious pilgrimage or procession; its deities – Ganga and Bharat Mata – were expected to arouse religious veneration. And because the two idols were installed on a sort of *rath* (processional chariot), this enabled devotees to worship them and honour them with offerings. The VHP also exploited important characteristics of *bhakti* rituals, imparting them with a fresh ideological meaning so that a Hindu nationalist devotionalism would take shape. As Neeladri Bhattacharya indicates, the VHP 'invented new rituals' which, in contrast with the traditional ones associated with particular castes and sects, were intended to 'transcend these differences and build a larger "Hindu" unity'.[99]

In terms of mobilisation, the movement scored a considerable success.[100] According to Har Mohan Lal, 312 *yatras* rather than the 90 anticipated, and 4,323 meetings rather than the 1,800 scheduled, were organised – affecting 531 of the 534 districts of the entire country.[101] In the three days *en route* between Kathmandu and Rameshwaram, 6,000 images of Bharat Mata (costing a half-rupee each) and 70,000 bottles of

---

[97] In addition the form of the *yatra* was generally familiar, because certain *sadhus* make a pilgrimage which consists of taking water from the source of Ganges, at Gangotri in the Himalayas, and pouring it over the *lingam* of Rameshwaram, in the extreme south of the country (R.L. Gross, *Hindu asceticism*, vol. 1, op. cit., p. 188). The *Ekatmata Yatra* played on the territorial aspects of these pilgrimages in such a way as to both amplify and alter its own meaning.

[98] *India Today*, 30 Nov. 1983, p. 34.

[99] N. Bhattacharya, 'Myth, history and the politics of Ramjanmabhumi' in S. Gopal (ed.), *Anatomy of a confrontation*, op. cit., p. 130.

[100] *Organiser*, 27 Nov. 1983, p. 13.

[101] Ibid., 12 Feb. 1984, p. 6.

water were sold. The money collected resulted in a large profit over the 6 million rupees spent.[102] The receptivity of the people the procession encountered was probably due to religious sentiment as well as to the emergence of a Hindu feeling of vulnerability and its correlative reactions. The popularity of the *Ekatmata Yatra* was greatest in areas of inter-communal tension: in Punjab (the crowd in Amritsar was especially large), throughout all the North East (but most of all in Assam), but also in Uttar Pradesh (in Bahraich, Moradabad, etc.), thus tending to confirm the existence of a feeling of insecurity among Hindus, which would find expression in demonstrations of solidarity.[103]

The success of the strategy of Hindu mobilisation will be examined in chapter 12, but for the moment we shall concentrate on its mechanisms. The role of religious leaders was symbolised by the near total unanimity of 85 *margdarshaks* blessing the *Ekatmata Yatra* at a gathering held in May 1983 on the initiative of the VHP. The *Shankaracharyas* of Dwarka (who expressed disapproval) and of Puri (who made no statement) were the only important religious figures who were absent. As well as this patronage, the public speeches of religious leaders, or more often their disciples, and preachers like Chinmayananda, drew greater crowds than RSS volunteers could have done. Yet the RSS, being in charge of organisation, was no less indispensable to the success of the enterprise. There were allegedly 50,000 *swayamsevaks* looking after logistics, keeping order and ensuring the punctuality of the *yatras*.

Such a massive RSS presence reflected the *political* Hindu nationalist spirit of the operation. Even though the enterprise had been mounted without the cooperation of any political party – Mahant Avaidyanath criticised all politicians without exception, from Indira Gandhi to Vajpayee[104] – it was none the less part and parcel of the effort to construct a 'Hindu vote' which could pressurise the government, of whatever hue, to defend the interests of the majority community. This aim became clearer in the movement, initiated in 1984, to bring about the return to the Hindus of Ramjanmabhoomi (the birthplace of Ram at Ayodhya).

---

[102] *Dharm Marg*, 2 (3), Oct., 1984, p. 40.

[103] A journalist noted that: 'It may still be premature to attribute the popularity of the yatras to any kind of Hindu backlash, but the VHP is surely cashing in on the new Muslim militancy, the recent marks of affluence seen in the Muslim areas of Uttar Pradesh as a result of the Gulf boom and remittance economy, the new mosques springing up almost daily .... (*India Today*, 30 Nov. 1983, p. 36).

[104] Ibid.

The revival of the Ayodhya issue

As an instrument of popular mobilisation this issue, forgotten since 1950, was as powerful as it had ever been. In 1984 the first Dharma Sansad unanimously adopted a resolution demanding the 'liberation' of the site at Ayodhya.[105] In May and June, the VHP established a militant wing, the Bajrang Dal,[106] under the leadership of Vinay Katiyar, who had been organisational secretary of the ABVP from 1970-4 and an RSS *pracharak* since 1980.[107] The organisation spread throughout the whole of Uttar Pradesh, where it allegedly recruited 100,000 members. The Bajrang Dal did not claim to be as highly disciplined as the RSS; the young Hindus who belonged to it were not required to attend daily sessions in the *shakhas*, but had to go to training camps where they were taught, above all, 'how to be bold'.[108] As a main strike force the Bajrang Dal was at first used by the VHP on the pretext of 'liberating' the Ram temple. At that stage, however, the movement was not a manifestly aggressive one. Like the *Ekatmata Yatra*, it was concerned to reawaken a certain form of ideological devotion.

On 27 July 1984, a Sri Ramjanmabhoomi Mukti Yagna Samiti (Committee of sacrifice to liberate Ram's birthplace) was founded under the leadership of the Mahant Avaidyanath. On 25 September, it launched a procession which set off from Sitarmahi in Bihar with the mission of 'liberating' the temple of Ayodhya. The procession was largely ideological in character since its focal point was a lorry bearing large statues of Ram and his wife Sita beneath a banner displaying the slogan 'Bharat Mata ki Jai' (Hail to Mother India). As Peter van der Veer indicates: 'It was clearly not the intention to take the mosque by storm. It remained a religious procession with Hindu nationalist slogans.'[109] The march reached its destination on 7 October. Its impact derived, once again, from the diversity of the sects represented in it since 'Vishnuites, Shivaites and Tantrists who have a long history of violent competition were peacefully gathered under the banner of a goddess not worshipped by any of them: Bharat Mata, Mother India' and 'sadhus from all parts of the country had come to take part in the liberation movement.'[110] As in the 1983 movement, these *sadhus*, beginning with the Mahant Avaidyanath, preached

---

[105] *Organiser*, 22 April 1984, p. 1-2.

[106] *Hindu Vishva*, 21 (7), March 1986, p. 30. The epithet *'bajrang'* (strong and sturdy) is associated with the name of Hanuman (the monkey god who led Ram's armies into battle) to emphasise his power.

[107] *Tenth Lok Sabha Who's who*, op. cit., p. 332.

[108] Interview with Acharya Giriraj Kishore, 10 Oct. 1991, New Delhi.

[109] P. van der Veer, 'God must be "liberated"!', op. cit., p. 291.

[110] Ibid., p. 299.

sermons that were more or less explicit political orations since '[t]he audience was asked repeatedly to give their vote only to those parties which explicitly promised to give the Hindus their sacred places back'.[111]

After halting at Ayodhya, the procession set off again to present a petition to the state government in Lucknow where it seems to have had greater success than at Ayodhya, drawing a crowd of between 5-7,000 followers.[112] Then it left for Delhi, where it should have arrived in December, shortly before the election scheduled for January 1985. But in the meantime the assassination of Indira Gandhi had completely transformed the political situation.

The Hindu nationalist campaigns of the early 1980s were primarily the outcome of a change of strategy launched by the RSS in a favourable context. However this context partly resulted from the action of certain Congressmen who were more or less in open rebellion against their party orthodoxies.

The contribution of ex-Congressmen

In September 1981, in reaction to the Meenakshipuram conversions, Dr Karan Singh, the Maharajah of Jammu and Kashmir and a former minister in Indira Gandhi's administration, who had been elected to the Lok Sabha in 1980 as a candidate of Congress (U) – the successor to Congress (R) – founded the Virat Hindu Samaj.[113] He explained his decision as follows:

The Virat Hindu Samaj, basically, was envisaged as a social reform organisation. The real, proximate cause was the conversions of Meenakshipuram. [...] I tried to put the emphasis on looking inwards. Why is it that people convert? Is it that the Harijans still feel discriminated against? The Hindu opinion was divided, even before independence into two streams, one is the RSS *parivar* [family], the other may be called the Congress *parivar*. The latter never call themselves Hindus but they are also good Hindus as anybody else. In a way the Virat Hindu Samaj was a sort of an attempt to bridge. I, having been in the Congress all my life, felt that there were people who may be turned off, who may not go to the RSS *parivar* but who would come here.[114]

Karan Singh became president of the Virat Hindu Samaj; its officers were Hans Raj Gupta and O.P. Tyagi (vice presidents), V.H. Dalmia

---

[111] Ibid.

[112] Ibid., p. 291, and K. Nayar, 'Perception of secularism', *Tribune*, 1 Nov. 1991.

[113] *Organiser*, 13 Sept. 1981, and *Dharma Marg*, 1, 1 (April 1983), p. 9. The English edition of this journal, founded by Karan Singh, was supported by Swami Chinmayanand and Satyamitranand Giri (ibid., pp. 2-3).

[114] Interview with Dr Karan Singh, 9 Feb. 1994, New Delhi.

(treasurer) and A. Singhal (General Secretary).[115] The organisation held numerous Virat Hindu Sammelans in Delhi, Mathura, Patna and Jodhpur with the participation of Congressmen and VHP leaders. In October 1981, Karan Singh presided over a Sammelan in Delhi which attracted tens if not hundreds of thousands of followers, and during which slogans against untouchability alternated with those denouncing the influence of money from the Gulf and the absence of a uniform civil code.[116] In November 1982, a Sammelan was organised in Patna by Shankar Dayal Singh, a Congress MP; the Maharajah of Jodhpur was one of those who attended it. However, there was no real rapprochement between Karan Singh and the 'Sangh parivar'. Karan Singh was not inclined to an activist approach. His concern to defend Hinduism reflected the influence that the ideas of Aurobindo – the subject of his doctoral dissertation – and other leaders of socio-religious reform movements, such as Vivekananda, exerted on him.[117]

Other Congressmen who were being marginalised contributed more directly to the militant Hindu movement in the 1980s through the issue of Ayodhya. Dau Dayal Khanna, an octogenarian who had been a member of several Congress governments in Uttar Pradesh,[118] was in fact the first to lay before the VHP the plan to build a campaign around Ram's birthplace.[119] He had written to Indira Gandhi in May 1983 demanding the restoration of temples in Ayodhya, Varanasi and Mathura, to no avail; the *Organiser* then took up the theme.[120] According to K.R. Malkani:

The Ayodhya movement was conceived as a people movement at a meeting in Muzaffarnagar, U.P., in 1983. Among those present were Prof. Rajendra Singh, RSS leader, and Shri Gulzarilal Nanda, former Union Home Minister. Shri Daudayal Khanna, former U.P. Congress minister, mooted the subject. Shri

[115] Virat Hindu Samaj, *Memorandum of association – rules and regulations*, New Delhi, 1982, p. 3.

[116] *Organiser*, 18 Oct. 1981, pp. 1 and 5. Karan Singh presided over another Virat Hindu Sammelan at Patna in 1982 (ibid., 21 Nov. 1982, p. 5).

[117] Karan Singh's approach is well illustrated in his *Essays on Hinduism*, Delhi: Ratna Sagar, 1987.

[118] Khanna was elected to the State assembly in 1937, 1945, 1952 and 1962 (*Who's who in UP Legislative Assembly 1962-1967*, op. cit., p. 99). He was Minister for Care Development and Health in 1962-7 and Minister for Food and Civil Supplies in 1969-70. He had been a member of the AICC before 1970. (*India who's who – 1970*, New Delhi: INFA, 1970, p. 244).

[119] Interview with Acharya Giriraj Kishore, 10 Oct. 1991, New Delhi.

[120] *Organiser*, 25 Sept. 1983. At first this suggestion aroused some doubts among the Hindu nationalists, some of whom feared intercommunal violence (ibid., 27 Nov. 1983). The special issue of *Organiser* for Divali devoted half a page to Ayodhya, but did not mention the existence of a Ram temple except as heresay, and in the course of a single paragraph (ibid., Deepavali special, 1983, p. 27).

Nanda, while not saying anything directly about Ayodhya, said that everything conducive to national honour and national self-confidence should be done.[121]

In 1983, Nanda founded the Shri Ram Janmotsav Samiti (Society for celebrating Ram's birthday) and used the occasion of the feast of Ram Navami to hold a meeting in Delhi bringing together many Hindu organisations, including the RSS.[122] One year later Nanda made the celebration of this feast the occasion, simultaneously with the VHP, to demand the return of Ram's birthplace to the Hindus – at a ceremony at which Karan Singh, Dau Dayal Khanna and Ashok Singhal were present.[123] Nanda, who had joined the VHP in late 1982,[124] was probably seeking to challenge it on a popular theme, but he was anyway a prestigious recruit for the VHP. It appeared from these events that the RSS was benefiting, once again in the context of a reawakened sense of Hindu vulnerability, from the support of Congressmen as it had from that of 'Patelites' or other 'Hindu traditionalists' in the past.[125]

As we have seen, news of the conversions to Islam in South India, alleged external support for the Muslim community, and the Shah Bano affair were among the key factors which intensified a sense of vulnerability among some Hindus. The Hindu nationalist organisations were therefore able to return to the strategy of stigmatisation and emulation of the 'threatening Other'. In particular, the VHP found that it could attract religious leaders and *sadhus* and encourage them to accept ecclesiastical structures which, it was hoped, would provide Hinduism with an integrated organisation. The RSS also favoured the reorganisation of the VHP in this way. Even though the RSS was still intent on spreading its network of *shakhas* throughout India in order to carry out its programme of character-building, it was also much more interested in party politics than it had been in earlier decades. Its main objective, through the relaunch of the VHP, was to accumulate a substantial Hindu vote by the use of

---

[121] K.R. Malkani, *The politics of Ayodhya and Hindu-Muslim relations*, Delhi: Har-Anand, 1993, p. 12. A similar version is to be found in *BJP's White Paper on Ayodhya and the Rama temple movement*, New Delhi: BJP, 1993, p. 31.

[122] *Organiser*, 1 May 1983, p. 3.

[123] Ibid., 29 April 1984, p. 10.

[124] Ibid., 9 Jan. 1983, p. 13.

[125] Moreover while some Congress (I) veterans like its president K. Tripathi and two ex-ministers, R. Venkataraman and N.D. Tiwari, opposed the *Ekatmata Yatra*, other Congressmen took part in it as they had done in many Virat Hindu Sammelans. Moreover plans for the *Yatra* were presented to the President of the Republic, Giani Zail Singh, and thus made semi-official. (ibid., 13 Nov. 1983, p. 1; Deepavali special 1983, 11 Dec. 1983, p. 8; 3 April 1983, p. 9).

Hindu nationalist appeals and to build up a large body of activists; it was for this reason that it supported the formation of the Bajrang Dal, even though it possessed neither the discipline nor the long-term aims of its own *swayamsevaks*.

The 'Sangh parivar' succeeded in attracting considerable popular support through its application of the strategy of ethno-religious mobilisation partly because the strategy itself had been carefully designed and partly because of changing circumstances. In fact we have to go back to the late 1940s and the 1920s to find a similar feeling of insecurity on the part of certain parts of the Hindu community. Second, the pool of specialist activists available for Hindu nationalist agitational campaigns had been greatly increased by the success of the VHP in recruiting large numbers of *sadhus*, who had hitherto remained unorganised, and forming them into a more or less integrated network. Third, and most importantly, the governments of the day no longer insisted that the principles of secularism should be rigorously upheld, and Congressmen or ex-Congressmen legitimised styles of public discourse promoting Hindu symbols and collective interests. Hindu nationalists now felt less inhibited by the threat of the Centre's repression and the dominant political repertoire of the time.

The attainment of the objective set forth by Deoras in 1979 – the creation of a Hindu vote – was meanwhile hindered by the discordant attitude of the BJP. The VHP's actions would bring results only very slowly since the organisation did not have the political structure in place to harvest the fruits of its campaigns: it could not put up candidates who would be able to carry its message into the electoral arena. To overcome this obstacle, the RSS decided to enter politics in some states where the BJP had not become well established, namely Tamil Nadu and Kerala. In both, its involvement in elections was organised through Hindu Munnani (Hindu Fronts) – a veritable innovation in RSS tactics.

In Kerala, the Hindu Front was the direct outcome of the Hindu Conference of April 1982 which had set itself up as a movement for the protection of Hindus against Muslims (who accounted for 21.25% of the population in the state) and Christians (20.56%). As these communities tended to be favoured by the Communist government,[126] the theme of Hinduism in danger was more credible here than elsewhere in the South. The RSS thus set up the Hindu Front with the aim, according to a Hindu

---

[126] Thus in 1983 the authorities granted a hectare of forest land to some Christians to build a church where a cross that had allegedly belonged to St Thomas had been discovered; and in 1984 the government agreed to a proposal from the Muslim League, which was a member of the ruling coalition, to allow public pensions for Muslim clergy after retirement. Both these decisions prompted a strong reaction among the Hindu nationalists (ibid., 31 July 1983, p.5).

nationalist insider, of 'building a Hindu vote and thus to check the appeasement policy of major political parties [mainly the Congress (I) and the CPI (M) in Kerala] towards the Muslims and the Christians.'[127] This innovation produced some results in the Lok Sabha election of December 1984, when the Hindu Front took 2.15% of the vote as againt 1.76% for the BJP (which contested one seat). In Tamil Nadu, the Hindu Munnani had been launched by one of the RSS's organisers;[128] it succeeded in winning a by-election in Kanyakumari district soon after the 1984 general election.

But the BJP could not be ignored, especially in the North. In the second half of the 1980s, the RSS demanded that the BJP rally to Hindu nationalist themes and renounce its tactic of openness. The BJP's change of direction would be helped by the pursuit of tendencies which had originated in the early 1980: the parameters influencing the working-out of the strategy of ethno-religious mobilisation had evolved in a way that was unprecedentedly favourable to it.

[127] K. Jayaprasad, *Impact of Hindu nationalism*, op. cit., p. 264.
[128] Interview with K. Jana Krishnamurthy, 22 Feb. 1995, New Delhi.

11

THE MAKING OF A HINDU VOTE?

The elections of 1984 marked a serious reverse for the BJP. Five years later, however, it won 85 seats in the Lok Sabha – a change in fortune which can be accounted for within the terms of our model.

The political context – the most important of our variables – was to prove more favourable to the Hindu nationalists than had previously been the case, as was shown by the unprecedented communalisation of politics by the Congress government from 1986 onwards, and by the increased willingness of the main opposition front, led by V.P. Singh, to come to terms with the BJP in the months leading up to the Lok Sabha elections of 1989. Thanks to this change in circumstances the BJP was able to return to the mixed strategy which the Jana Sangh had employed in the late 1960s, when the party had combined electoral alliances with an exploitation of religious grievances such as opposition to cow-slaughter; similarly, in 1989, the BJP forged electoral alliances with mainstream opposition parties while at the same time associating itself with the campaign to build a Hindu temple in Ayodhya.

The BJP's instrumentalist campaigns – usually combined with populist agitations – largely owed their success to the VHP's expanding network of *sadhus* and to the local Sangathanist workers whose chosen strategy – namely one of uncompromising Hindu nationalism – was gradually adopted by the national leadership.

The communalisation of politics

In the second half of the 1980s, the central Congress government showed an increasing willingness to take sides in disputes within and between religious communities. Earlier in the decade it had been accused of supporting extremist groups in the Punjab, but it now appeared to be granting favours or privileges to certain groups with the result that the state no longer seemed to be above the religious divisions in society. A particularly significant issue was raised in early 1986 when a District and Sessions Judge in Faizabad ordered that the Uttar Pradesh government should unlock the gates of the Babri Masjid/Ramjanmabhoomi temple thus enabling devotees to offer *darshan* and *puja* in the disputed structure. Both the UP state Congress government and the central Congress government took no action to reverse this decision, thereby strengthening the impression that the power of the state could no longer be relied upon to defend secularism and that the margin of manoeuvre for Hindu nationalist organisations had been broadened. Shortly afterwards Rajiv Gandhi's government came forward with the Muslim Women (Protection of Rights on Divorce) Bill, which showed a surprising readiness to conciliate orthodox Muslim opinion.

Yet only a year earlier, the Congress appeared to have regained the dominant position in party politics which had enabled Nehru to implement his secularist policies in the 1950s. The victories which Congress (I) had scored in the elections of 1984 and 1985 had stopped the VHP in its tracks, and it did not renew its mobilisation campaign over the Ram temple till the end of 1985, in parallel to the Muslim mobilisation during the 'Shah Bano affair'.

On 31 October, the VHP organised, at Udipi, a second Dharma Sansad in which 831 *sadhus* took part.[1] A *satyagraha* was announced for 9 March – the beginning of the Shivratri festival – if the temple had not by then been opened to worshippers. As a preliminary, several *Ram Janaki Raths* (processions of chariots in honour of Ram and his wife Sita, also known as Janaki) toured Uttar Pradesh and Bihar, starting from twenty-five selected sites, during November and December 1985.

The pressure exerted by the campaign was not great, hence no one could predict how big the *satyagraha* would turn out to be. However the government chose to yield, at least in part, to Hindu nationalist demands. On 25 January 1986, a lawyer from Ayodhya, U.M. Pandey, who was not even a party to the civil suits filed in the 1950s, which were still pending, lodged an application with the local magistrate (*munsif*) for the gates of the Babri Masjid to be unlocked so that there would be no restrictions on the celebration of *puja* (ritual worship) and *darshan*.[2] The *munsif* refused to hear this application in the absence of the court record, which rested with the High Court. On 31 January an appeal was made to the District and Session Judge of Faizabad, who ordered on 1 February that the mosque should be unlocked.[3]

Forty minutes later, the padlocks which barred access to the mosque were taken off on the order of the District Magistrate. A television crew from the national network, Doordarshan, was already on the spot as was

---

[1] *Hindu Vishwa*, Aug. 1990, op. cit., p. 56.

[2] K. Prasad, *Report of the inquiry commission*, op. cit., p. 107.

[3] A.G. Noorani, 'Legal aspects of the issue' in S. Gopal (ed.), *Anatomy of a confrontation*, op. cit., p. 58.

a crowd of VHP supporters – which tends to confirm the general assumption that the authorities had planned to make this an 'event'.[4] In fact there had been negotiations in December between the VHP and the District Magistrate and the Chief Minister of Uttar Pradesh, Vir Bahadur Singh. The very fact that the appeal of 31 January had been considered as admissible, whereas the applicant had no *locus standi* and the matter was pending at higher levels in the judiciary, attests to the political nature of the decision of 1 February. One of Rajiv Gandhi's advisers, Arun Nehru, summed up the situation clearly three years later: 'In early 1986 the Muslim Women's Bill was passed to play the Muslim card; and then came the decision on Ayodhya to play the Hindu card. It was supposed to be [a] package deal.'[5]

After the locks were removed the authorities swiftly returned the case of the mosque/temple to the courts, in the hope of hushing up the matter after this concession – which would merely have permitted Hindus to worship the idol of Ram inside the mosque. But soon after the Hindu nationalists claimed the right to build a temple on the site, and the RSS identified the issue as an opportunity to work for a new mobilisation of the Hindus. A resolution by the ABPS in March 1986 expressed the wish that 'all our common people too should have the opportunity of suitably participating in this holy endeavour'.[6]

The RSS had seen how the Centre had yielded to one of the Hindu nationalists' demands, and this development probably gave fresh impetus to its agitation. The pro-Hindu position, previously marginalised by the politics of secularism, now enjoyed a new legitimacy. The other major factor which made the subsequent strategy of ethno-religious mobilisation effective was the extension and increasing strength of the religious network of the VHP.

Avoiding the dangers of 1967: the strength of the religious network

In 1967 the cow protection movement suffered – in the view of its organisers, who had hoped that it would yield political gains – from the spirit of independence shown by certain *sadhus*, who were not prepared to renounce their personal ambition. The agitation for the Ram temple exposed its organisers in the VHP to the same risks, since many of the religious leaders tried to appropriate aspects of it for their own benefit.

---

[4] S. Mustafa, 'Uttar Pradesh government took sides in Ayodhya dispute' in A.A. Engineer (ed.), *Babri Masjid-Ram Janmabhoomi controversy*, op. cit., p. 117.

[5] *Statesman* (Delhi), 17 Aug. 1989.

[6] *Organiser*, 30 March 1986, p. 6.

But this danger was for the most part avoided. While the *Shankaracharyas* of Puri, Kanchi (Jayendra Sarasvati) and Dwarka-Badrinath kept in the background, this was doubtless because they did not take well to the subordinate role which the VHP allotted them within the movement, which they served mainly as guarantors of its moral superiority. Jayendra Sarasvati even proposed that the agitation should be suspended after the removal of the locks, which had, in his eyes, given the VHP what it had been seeking.[7] If the desire to be regarded as the highest authority of Hinduism partly explains such detachment, it also obliged the *Shankaracharyas* not to remain entirely apart from it, and none of them dissociated themselves from the movement, which they supported intermittently.[8] Having not so much recruited as neutralised these religious figures, the VHP successfully consolidated its religious network.

On 3 February 1986 a large Sant Sammelan, held at the bidding of the Ram Janmabhoomi Mukti Yagna Samiti, set up a Ram Janmabhoomi Trust which called on the government to transfer the property rights of the Ayodhya site so that the 'biggest temple in the world' could be built there.[9] The chairmanship of the trust, with which Vijaya Raje Scindia and a number of Marwaris (G.P. Birla, G.H. Singhania, K.N. Modi, R.N. Goenka) were associated, was conferred unanimously on Ramanandacharya Shri Shivaramacharya, head of the Ramanandis of Varanasi, who enjoyed respect throughout Vaishnavite circles and beyond.[10] The consolidation of this religious network can be partly explained by the Muslim reaction to the unlocking of the Ayodhya mosque.

On 3 February 1986 a writ had been filed by a Muslim from Ayodhya, Mohammed Hashim, in the Lucknow bench of the Allahabad High Court against the unlocking of the Babri Masjid. On 5 February the Babri Masjid Action Committee (BMAC) was set up by a number of Muslim leaders, including Syed Shahabuddin and Imam Bukhari. It organised *satyagrahas* in Uttar Pradesh in April 1986, then in Delhi in August, seeking a return to the *status quo ante* at Ayodhya.[11] On 30 March 1987 a *satyagraha* in

---

[7] *Hindu Vishva*, 21, 7 (March 1986), pp. 18-20.

[8] Ibid., 22, 8 (April 1987), p. 63, and 22, 1 (Sept. 1989), p. 5.

[9] This – like its supposed predecessor – would have seven storeys and cost 250 million rupees.

[10] This decision was taken in the presence, among others, of the *Shankaracharya* of Jyotish *pith* (*Hindu Vishva*, 21, 7 (March 1986). pp. 9-12).

[11] An All India Babri Masjid Conference was held in Delhi on 22 December to demand that serious negotiations be held between the Home Ministry and the VHP. It threatened that, if they failed, there would be a call for a boycott of Republic Day on 26 January 1987, a *bandh* (large strike) on 1 February, a *satyagraha* on 30 March, and a march on Ayodhya. Shahabuddin abandoned the boycott of Republic Day, which would have appeared to have separatist connotations – already denounced by the VHP – but it stuck to the idea of a *satyagraha* (A.G. Noorani, 'The Babari Masjid Case', *EPW*, 17 Jan.

New Delhi brought together half a million people according to some estimates. A year later, the BMAC announced that a march on Ayodhya would take place on 14 October 1988. The VHP responded by organising at Ayodhya a *Shri Ram Maha Yagna* (Great sacrifice to the God Ram) lasting for five days from 11 October. The growing tension in the state set off riots at Aligarh, Muzaffarnagar and Faizabad which prompted Buta Singh, the Home Minister, to press for the march to be suspended. This was agreed to in exchange for a promise to lay the whole question before the High Court in Allahabad. This 'backing down' – attributed to Shahabuddin – caused a split. The 'radicals' remained in the BMAC behind Imam Bukhari while the 'moderates', represented by Shahabuddin, formed the Babri Masjid Coordination Committee (BMCC).[12]

This was also a defeat for the Hindu nationalists, because going back to the courts postponed the resolution of the dispute and revealed a desire by the authorities not to alienate Muslim leaders. But the measures taken. in reaction to the Muslim protest movement sustained the mobilisation of the VHP. The organisation held a third Dharma Sansad in Allahabad in February 1989, which was notable for its extremely militant tone and attracted a large number of *sadhus* who were there to attend the Kumbh Mela. This time Jayendra Saraswati was present, as also was the Devrah Baba, the most revered hermit of Vrindavan, who agreed to speak from the VHP rostrum.[13]

The two main resolutions, passed before a crowd of some 50,000 pilgrims, concerned the 'Hinduisation of public life' (to be achieved by only electing politicians who were favourable to Hindus) and the building of the Ram temple. A model of the temple was produced and, at the same time, the steps which were necessary to bring it into being were explained. The funds for its construction would be collected from door to door, and each donor would receive a certificate in exchange for a standard donation of 1.25 rupees per family. The collections would be accompanied by processions in which *puja* would be offered to bricks inscribed with the name of Ram (*Ram Shilas*), which would be used in the building of the temple. These Ram Shila processions would converge on Ayodhya in time

---

1987, p. 71).

[12] *Times of India*, 12 Dec. 1988.

[13] He said: 'Protecting this temple [which was yet to be built] of Ram is holy work. You protect your religion and it protects you. My platform from which I give my blessing every day is the platform of the Vishwa Hindu Parishad. They have my blessings. I want everyone to cooperate with their work.' (M. Tully, *No full stops in India*, New Delhi: Penguin, 1992, p. 100). The way Devrah Baba, despite his reluctance, was asked to speak on the VHP platform, is revealing of the instrumentalisation of religious figures who rallied round the movement.

for building to begin on 9 November, a date said by astrologers to be particularly auspicious.

These two resolutions potentially set the terms for the campaign for the coming general election, due to take place in early 1990 at the latest. From the start of the election campaign, the moral guarantee and support which the religious figures provided was to be exploited politically. If the VHP and, behind the scenes, the RSS were busying themselves creating a Hindu electorate, it became all the more necessary for this electorate to be turned into a reliable party.

During the winter of 1987-8, Deoras expressed his scepticism of the opposition's ability to offer a viable alternative to Congress (I). And because he regarded real co-operation as difficult to achieve, he declared his readiness to support Congress (I) 'in a good cause'.[14] The idea that only Congress (I) could govern India remained the RSS's official position in 1988.[15] There was probably a threefold explanation for this: first, the resentment caused by the dilution of Hindu nationalist ideology in the BJP; second, the conviction that the opposition parties could only give the country a weak government (as in 1977-80); and third, the pro-Hindu evolution of Congress (I) in 1986-8. However, the third factor, and then the first, were to be modified in late 1988 and early 1989.

Buta Singh's negotiating tactics with the BMAC and the VHP during 1988 suggested that the government was playing for time – in order to avoid a conflict which could only be resolved by alienating part of the 'losing' community – since the decision to leave the solution of legal disputes over Ayodhya to the courts seemed to be aimed at postponing a resolution of the conflict. For the Hindu nationalists, who maintained that no earthly authority could rule on the question of Ram's birthplace, this was merely further evidence of the dependence of Congress (I) on the Muslim electorate and of its reluctance to promote Hindu interests.

At the same time the BJP resolutely changed its line back to one of strong Hindu nationalism, thus allowing the RSS to consider giving its exclusive support to the party over which it was gaining more and more influence. This change of direction ended by making the BJP the designated beneficiary of the 'Hindu revival'. From now on the strategy of ethno-religious mobilisation would prove effective in making electoral gains.

The BJP between integration and mobilisation: the success of a mixed strategy

The defeat of the BJP in the 1984 and 1985 elections had already led to

[14] *Statesman* (Delhi), 1 Jan. 1988, and *Times of India*, 19 Jan. 1988.
[15] Ibid., 14 March 1988, and *Hindustan Times*, 7 April 1988.

the tactic of openness adopted in 1980 being questioned. Its National Executive, meeting in mid-March 1985 with Vajpayee in the chair, set up a working group to investigate, through interviews with party activists, the causes of the defeat and prepare a five-year plan of action. This revealed the strength of RSS culture among party cadres.

The reinstatement of the Sangathanists

The 'grass-roots' in fact disapproved of the quest for alliances, which suggested that the party was ill-equipped to make the most of its chances alone.[16] On the basis of this enquiry, the working group proposed a plan which rehabilitated the basic characteristics of the Jana Sangh: the appointment of a single General Secretary at the national level and in each state, and of an organising secretary with responsibility for each district – a role strongly reminiscent of the *sangathan mantri*. The General Secretaries were to become national secretaries in charge either of a particular portfolio or of a geographical area.

The working group's report was presented to the National Executive on 20 July 1985, and the leading figures in the party generally agreed to its recommendations. Advani became the party's sole General Secretary, which recalled the Jana Sangh's practice of having only one such office-holder. And like Upadhyaya in the 1950s and 1960s, he was seen to have the confidence of the RSS; in May 1986, he became party president. Advani appointed three veteran RSS men to the posts of General Secretary: K.N. Sahni (a member of the RSS since the 1940s and a *pracharak* in Kashmir before Partition and in Punjab – his home state – between 1949 and 1953);[17] M.M. Joshi (a lecturer in physics at the University of Allahabad and a *pracharak* who had been elected to the Lok Sabha for the first and only time in 1977); and Krishna Lal Sharma (a member of the RSS since 1942 and a *pracharak* from 1946 onwards). The vice presidential functions remained, but alongside S. Bakht and Vijaya Raje Scindia others with an RSS background were appointed, such as K. Thakre and S.S. Bhandari who, following the working group's recom-

---

16 BJP, *Working group report*, New Delhi: BJP Central Office, 1985, and interview with K.L. Sharma (coordinator of this working group). Where symbols were concerned, the activists were in favour of a return to Upadhyaya's slogan, 'Integral Humanism', which by implication condemned the Gandhian Socialism imposed by the party leaders in 1980. Integral Humanism was at once accepted in July 1985 as the party's fundamental philosophy, along with a resolution on economic policy reflecting a 'Gandhian approach'. In October 1985 the National Council ratified this change after a debate lasting several hours, at the end of which Gandhian Socialism was none the less maintained. At the end of 1986, Integral Humanism was written into the party's constitution.

17 Interview with K.N. Sahni, 11 Aug. 1992, New Delhi.

mendations, undertook tours in order to build up the membership, the structure of the party, and grassroots ideological training through study camps.[18] In 1988 the representation of the RSS in the top levels of the BJP was bolstered by the appointment of K.N. Govindacharya to the new post of political secretary of the BJP President.

Meanwhile Advani's speeches were becoming more militant in tone. In his address to the 8th plenary session of the BJP in May 1986, he called for a ban on cow slaughter, a uniform civil code and the abrogation of article 370 of the Constitution,[19] thus returning to issues which had been exploited by the Jana Sangh but which the BJP had at first neglected. In January 1987, in an address to the BJP's National Council in Vijayawada, he referred ominously to the 'dangers of minorityism' and 'pseudo-secularism' in an obvious allusion to the Congress government's concern to protect certain interests of the minorities, as exemplified in the Shah Bano affair.[20] At the National Executive meeting in April 1987, K.L. Sharma and Y. Rajpal presented two reports, respectively on 'Implementation of action plan' and 'Election strategy', which both argued that the BJP should contest the next elections on its own.[21] The leadership of the party was at last evolving the line demanded by the grassroots, and it is evident that this shift in strategy was a reflection not of a change of balance between contending groups within the leadership but of sustained pressure from the party's local cadres.[22]

Although many press reports suggested that the replacement of Vajpayee by Advani represented the eclipse of a liberal tendency by one which was more hard-line and militant, the reality was much more complex. The two leaders differed from each other in some respects but they did not represent opposed groups or even ideological tendencies. (Interestingly, the expression 'pseudo-secularism' was first used by Vajpayee as early as 1969.)[23] Advani and Vajpayee had worked together within the Jana Sangh and subsequently within the BJP without serious disagreement. As the first president of the BJP, Vajpayee had been responsible for the tactic of openness and the emphasis on 'Gandhian

---

[18] BJP, *National executive meeting*, July 24-6, 1987 (New Delhi), p. 29.

[19] *L.K. Advani presidential address*, 8th plenary session (New Delhi), 9 May 1986, p. 5, p. 6 and p. 9.

[20] *L.K. Advani presidential address*, 9th National Council session (Vijayawada), 2-4 Jan. 1987, pp. 8-9.

[21] BJP, *National executive meeting*, April 17-19, 1987 (Rohtak).

[22] In its plea, Rajpal referred to the local cadres in revealing terms: 'The grim reality is that there is no alternative to fighting alone if we want to perform our duty towards the nation, to our party and to our workers' (ibid., p. 31).

[23] A.B. Vajpayee, 'The bane of pseudo-secularism', in S.S. Bhandari (ed.), *Jana Sangh souvenir*, op. cit., pp. 55-8.

socialism' but Advani – then General Secretary – had also favoured this approach. The discussions which led to the BJP's change of strategy had actually begun in 1985, under Vajpayee's presidency. What lay behind this strategic reorientation were the setbacks which the BJP had suffered in the party's local cadres to reaffirm the Sangathanist style of party organisation and activity. Once more, the main division within the BJP was not vertical but horizontal.

This development allowed for an understanding between the BJP and the RSS, whose leaders might not have put direct pressure on the party but had let it be known that they disapproved of its conduct. From mid-1985 the party's leading figures once again participated in the annual Pratinidhi Sabha (Representative assembly) that brings together the all-India leaders of the affiliates of the RSS in Nagpur,[24] while BJP cadres participated in the coordination committees (*Samanvaya Samitis*) in which the other affiliates of the RSS had been represented since 1977 at the state level and to which they had never before been invited.[25] This reintegration into the body of the 'RSS complex', on the model of the relations which had existed in the Jana Sangh phase, was illustrated in October 1987 by a five-day meeting at Nagpur to review the questions of leaders of the RSS (Deoras, Seshadri, Rajendra Singh and Yadav Rao Joshi), the BMS (Thengadi and M. Mehta), the Deendayal Research Institute (Deshmukh and Malkani), the ABVP (A. Modak), the VHP (Singhal) and the BJP (Vajpayee and Advani). The theme was eminently political since one of the meeting's conclusions was that:

The political perversion of pampering and aggravating the 'minority complex' threatening the very fabric of nation's unity and its ethos, can be cured only by an enlightened Hindu electorate.[26]

Clearly the BJP had a leading role to play. This development helped to remobilise the energies of the party's activists but once again high-

---

24 K. Chandra, 'Inside the Bharatiya Janata Party: political actors and ideological choices', paper presented at the annual conference of the Association for Asian Studies (Boston, MA, 24-26 March, 1994), p. 60.

25 W. Andersen and S. Damle, *The brotherhood in saffron*, op. cit., p. 143.

26 *Organiser*, 29 Nov. 1987, p. 6. Shortly before this, Seshadri had reaffirmed the RSS's objective of seeking actively to build up a 'Hindu vote bank': 'The Muslim leadership till today have had the final laugh with the trump card of block votes in their hands. But now an entirely new and unexpected factor has emerged on the electoral front and that is the '*Brahmastra*' [an invincible or divine weapon] of Hindu vote. [...] Evidently time is ripe on the political front for rousing the Hindu society to call the secular bluff of the so-called secular parties on the one hand and that of the so-called minority pressure groups on the other (ibid., 19 July 1987, p. 9).

lighted the persistent dilemma of choosing between fidelity to RSS culture on the one hand, with the attendant risk that the BJP would again become isolated, and, on the other hand, of diluting Hindu nationalist identity, which would alienate the party from the RSS, as had happened in the recent past. In a sense, it was a question of combining the strategies of integration and of ethno-religious mobilisation within a new 'mixed strategy'. The BJP was helped in this undertaking by the attitude of the other opposition parties.

An accommodating 'legitimate opposition'

The approach of the elections was probably the principal factor that led the BJP's leaders to reject a return to the spirit of the Jana Sangh for fear of narrowing the party's base and appearing too radical to its potential allies. At the National Council meeting in January 1988, Vajpayee made the most of the fact that 15 of the party's 17 candidates elected to the Vidhan Sabha in Haryana in 1987 had won thanks to the electoral alliance with the Lok Dal of Devi Lal.[27] He was opposed by proponents of a reinvigorated Hindu nationalism who were represented principally by recruits from the ranks of *sangathan mantris*, like K. Thakre, and by party dignitaries close to the VHP, like Rajmata Scindia. Finally a compromise solution was reached which combined both the instrumentalist strategy and populist agitation: there would be campaigns to liberate the Ramjanmabhoomi in the most suitable areas along with a national movement to improve the lot of the peasants.[28] By following these two paths simultaneously, the party sought to draw closer to the RSS without becoming alienated from its potential allies.

The opposition's most effective politician was Vishwanath Pratap Singh, a former minister in Rajiv Gandhi's government who resigned in 1987 and then mounted a campaign against the Prime Minister, who was accused of corruption in the Bofors affair.[29] Singh's new party, the Janata Dal (People's Party), was intended to become the rallying-point of a coalition which would overturn Congress. It included the Jan Morcha – V.P. Singh's original party, run by Congressmen who had followed him into opposition – and the main factions of the Lok Dal (those of Devi Lal and Ajit Singh, the son of Charan Singh). In 1987 V.P. Singh described the Communists as 'natural allies' but in September that year Devi Lal,

---

[27] *Statesman* (Delhi), 4 Jan. 1988.

[28] Ibid., 5 Jan 1988.

[29] It was alleged that substantial bribes were paid to close associates of Rajiv Gandhi, in 1986, by the Swedish arms manufacturer Bofors, in order to obtain a contract for the sale of artillery to the Indian army.

who had become Chief Minister of Haryana with BJP support, called a meeting that was intended to seal the unity of all the opposition parties. The BJP was invited, and attended in the hope of being able to become integrated with the new alternative politics now being germinated.[30] As a result, the Communists boycotted the meeting and more or less demanded that V.P. Singh choose between them and the BJP.

The only way out for the BJP, which could not risk complete isolation in the aftermath of its 1984 electoral debacle, was to prove to V.P. Singh how strong it was, and to do so by means of actions free of any communalist connotations. This was probably why, far from respecting the compromise reached by the National Council in January 1988 (which was already unravelling), the party concentrated on socio-economic themes at the expense of ethno-religious mobilisation. The cancellation of debts owed by peasants to public authorities and cooperatives was given the highest priority.[31]

Meanwhile in August 1988 the BJP was excluded from negotiations held to discuss the formation of a National Front, which in October finally comprised the Janata Dal and four regional parties. At a gathering in Ahmedabad the BJP announced, to the satisfaction of the RSS, that it would fight the election alone.[32] For tactical reasons the National Front did not really change its attitude till the turn of 1988-9 when the BJP scored an unquestionable success in local elections in Uttar Pradesh. The party set about making these elections into an event of national importance. Both Advani and Vajpayee had taken part in the campaign and only the BJP put up candidates on its own ticket, while other groups supported independent candidates.[33] Its agitation on behalf of peasants undoubtedly contributed to its success, and furthermore demonstrated to V.P. Singh how indispensable the BJP was as an electoral ally. In fact Uttar Pradesh was where the Janata Dal hoped to score its greatest number of victories in the coming general elections (as the most populous state in the Union, it provided 85 of the 543 seats in the Lok Sabha).[34]

---

[30] BJP, *Resolutions adopted at the plenary session*, 8-10 April 1988 (Agra), p. 18.

[31] Ibid., pp. 9-11. In Uttar Pradesh the BJP abandoned an agitation for the 'liberation of the Ram temple' – from which its regional leader, Kalyan Singh, had expected to boost his popularity – to concentrate on the 'defence of the peasants'.

[32] *Organiser*, 23 Oct. 1988, p. 1. Deoras had declared shortly before that the RSS felt itself closer to the BJP than to any other party. Thus *Organiser*'s front-page headline was 'RSS-Chief backs BJP' (16 Oct. 1988).

[33] S. Nihal Singh, *Count down to elections*, New Delhi: Allied Publishers, 1989, pp. 125 and 196. The BJP won 120 of the 404 seats on the municipal corporations of the six biggest towns in the state. It increased the number of its representatives from 28 to 94 in district capitals and to 75 against 27 for Congress (I) in the municipal councils of the smaller towns (*India Today*, 15 Feb. 1989, pp. 51-2).

[34] In an interview published in 1989 Advani showed that he was fully aware of the impact

In May 1989, V.P. Singh began negotiations with the BJP which concluded positively in the sharing-out of seats in North India.[35] Then in June the BJP took a further step towards joining the mainstream opposition by taking part in the mass resignation of all opposition deputies in protest at Rajiv Gandhi's implication in the Bofors affair. Among the CPI (M) leaders, E.M.S. Namboodiripad was opposed to this kind of cooperation with the BJP but Jyoti Basu, Chief Minister of West Bengal, went along with it.[36] With this movement, driven along by V.P. Singh, the Communists seized on a chance to implant themselves outside their strongholds in Bengal and Kerala and overturn Congress (I) at the Centre. Thus V.P. Singh persuaded the Communists to accept the company of the BJP, notably on a 'Save India Day' (9 August) and during the Bharat Bandh (All India Strike) of 30 August which really launched the election campaign.

On 25 October, negotiations concerning seat adjustments were held between the BJP and the Janata Dal.[37] The number of constituencies where the risk of confrontation between the two parties was staved off finally reached 350, out of a total of 543, the BJP contesting 226. In the Hindi-speaking north, the Janata Dal and the BJP fought each other in

---

of the local elections in Uttar Pradesh: 'The feeling had taken roots in the party that VP [Singh] doesn't like us but wants to use us. But he must realise that even in the regions and areas of his interest we cannot be brushed aside. We are there' (ibid., p. 37). Soon after the Uttar Pradesh elections Advani's tone became more explicit. After once again recalling the success of the BJP in the municipal elections in Uttar Pradesh, he commented: 'In more than 425 Lok Sabha seats of this country the Communist Parties just do not matter. It is surprising that nevertheless they keep trying to dictate to other parties what they should do or not do. It is high time the Communist bluff is called' (BJP, *National Executive Meeting*, 3-5 March 1989, Udaipur, p. 3).

35   *India Today*, 30 June 1989, p. 18.

36   Ibid., 15 Aug. 1989, p. 18.

37   According to L.K. Advani, V.P. Singh had a survey conducted in Uttar Pradesh which showed that if the Janata Dal and the BJP did not have a seat adjustment the Congress (I) would win in a majority of the constituencies. Advani has also claimed that he met with V.P. Singh and Bhaurao Deoras after the Bombay session of the BJP in September 1989 and that he told Singh: 'If the Congress is ousted, you are going to be the Prime Minister because yours will be the largest party and mine will be the second party. If there is no adjustment between us, may be mine will be the largest party and yours would be then the second party and Congress would get   clear majority. [...] It is to you to make a decision but if you think that we will change our stand on Ayodhya, on Article 370 or on the uniform civil code issue, or on the Urdu issue, you are mistaken. [...] We have already made an adjustment with the Shiv Sena. [see below]. It may not suit you but it is done.' (Interview with L. K. Advani, 11 Feb. 1994, New Delhi). Although I have not been able to cross-check this account with other testimony the terms of Advani's description of this exchange of views can be taken as evidence of his concern to ensure that the pursuit of a strategy of integration with the opposition did not oblige the BJP to dilute its Hindu nationalist identity.

only 39 seats out of 216 – 18 in Uttar Pradesh, 8 in Bihar, 5 in Rajasthan, 4 in Madhya Pradesh, and one each in Himachal Pradesh, Delhi and Chandigarh. Paul Brass has emphasised that in Uttar Pradesh the BJP 'depended heavily for its victories upon the absence of the Janata Dal';[38] it won 5 seats in the 10 constituencies where it had a pact, and only 2 in the 17 where the two parties were opposing each other. As well as its 'mechanical' advantage, the pact was also of value in that it allowed the BJP to feature in an alternative coalition to Congress (I) and profit from the wave of hostility to the government fostered by V.P. Singh's campaigns against corruption in the highest echelons of the state.

The mainstream opposition finally set aside the secularist principles which its leader V.P. Singh stood for in order to benefit from – or at least not be harmed by – the strength of the BJP. Before making the pact V.P. Singh had demanded that the BJP clarify its position on the issue of Ayodhya, but when the party evaded this injunction, the only sanction that V.P. Singh imposed was his refusal to take part in joint election meetings.[39] The BJP barely protested; whereas in the 1970s the Hindu nationalists wished to be publicly associated with 'JP' in order to gain a new respectability and thus soften its Hindu communalist image, in 1989 the party was now fundamentally Hindu nationalist in orientation. This strategy of the BJP, combining a desire for integration in the legitimate opposition and efforts to mobilise militant Hinduism, reproduced the situation of 1967, when the Jana Sangh first became an electoral force to be reckoned with. This return to the political culture of the Jana Sangh was done discreetly so as not to jeopardise an electoral pact now regarded as essential after the disaster of 1984. However, once the principle of the pact had been agreed, the BJP, far from energetically seeking integration within the opposition, set out to make electoral capital from the 'Hindu revival'.

The BJP is won over to the strategy of ethno-religious mobilisation

At first the BJP's reaffirmation of its Hindu militancy was not expressed in the public arena but only internally. Apparently the party needed to give a guarantee of good conduct to the RSS, which was seeking a political arm, without endangering its relationship with the rest of the opposition. For three years it had been putting down roots in the Hindu nationalist

---

[38] P. Brass, 'Caste, class and community in the ninth general elections for the Lok Sabha in Uttar Pradesh' in H.A. Gould and S. Ganguly (eds), *India Votes*, Boulder, CO: Westview Press, 1993 p. 109.

[39] *Indian Express*, 14 Nov. 1989, p. 6.

camp, and this was confirmed during celebrations commemorating the 100th anniversary of the birth of Hedgewar, which lasted from the autumn of 1988 till 6 April 1989. When inaugurating the celebrations in Bombay on 29 September 1988, Advani declared: 'We will march ahead in cooperation with those who support the cause [of Ram] and without bothering about the opposition from some quarters.'[40]

A division of labour then took shape between Advani and Vajpayee, who presented a more moderate face of Hindu nationalism. Invited by Buta Singh to a meeting of the National Integration Council in May 1989, the latter proposed a compromise whereby both Hindus and Muslims would be encouraged to build their own places of worship on a site big enough to make such cohabitation feasible. Furthermore, he denied that the BJP was rejecting in advance any judicial settlement, while nevertheless acknowledging that it would be difficult to gain acceptance for this.[41] But in June the National Council of Palampur (in Himachal Pradesh) voted for the following resolution:

> The BJP holds that the nature of this controversy is such that it just cannot be sorted out by a court of law. [...] The BJP calls upon the Rajiv Government to adopt the same positive approach in respect of Ayodhya that the Nehru government did with respect to Somnath. The sentiments of the people must be respected, and Ram Janmasthan [Ram's birthplace] handed over to the Hindus – if possible through a negotiated settlement, or else, by legislation. Litigation certainly is no answer.[42]

For Advani the Palampur session was 'a milestone' because the BJP's alliance with the Shiv Sena and the party's position on the Ayodhya affair were 'finalised' there.[43] Regarding the Ayodhya affair, for the BJP the decision would find expression in an alignment of the positions of the RSS and the VHP. At the same time the RSS – in the person of K.C. Sudarshan, its chief ideologue (*baudhik pramukh*) – congratulated itself on having gained the upper hand in the BJP, which it regarded, in the long term, as an alternative to the Congress (I).[44]

At the top level of the party the political exploitation of the Ayodhya issue was always done discreetly, essentially to avoid upsetting its new allies. Except for its preamble, the party's election manifesto did not

---

40 *Organiser*, 30 Oct. 1988, p. 13. Shortly before Advani declared at the BJP's annual meeting that the 'Constitution makers never intended a secular state to mean either an irreligious state or a state that would disown the nation's ancient heritage only because it was Hindu' (*Presidential address – Fourth plenary session*, Agra, 8 April 1988, p. 18).

41 *Hindustan Times*, 16 and 17 May 1989.

42 BJP, *National Executive Meeting – Resolutions*, 9-11 June, 1989 (Palampur), pp. 14-17.

43 Interview with L.K. Advani.

44 *India Today*, 30 June 1989, p. 41.

contain a single word about Ayodhya. It was regionally and locally that the instrumentalist strategy based on the manipulation of Hindu symbols was most obviously put into effect.

The 1989 election campaign: populism, 'political *bhakti*' and riots

The creation of an issue like the Babri Masjid/Ramjanmabhoomi would have been of little benefit to the BJP had it not been brought to the attention of the greatest possible number of people, and shrewdly dramatised. This was the task of the Hindu nationalist networks.

The RSS itself was in the vanguard. Deoras, whom Advani claimed as early as 1988 that he consulted 'often',[45] seemed to be playing an active role in the BJP's election campaign.[46] This re-establishment of the link between the BJP and the RSS was all the more important because the network of *swayamsevaks* was expanding. The centenary of Hedgewar in 1988 had been the occasion for a huge campaign which, according to the *Organiser*, enabled 250,000 villages – almost half of the total for the entire country – to be penetrated.[47] This effort helped to increase the number of *swayamsevaks* to 1.8 million (against 1 million in 1979), distributed between 25,000 *shakhas* in 18,890 different localities.[48]

The VHP network operated in symbiosis with the RSS. In May, June and July 1989, Moropant Pingle, a veteran *pracharak* based in Nagpur and the link man between the RSS and the VHP (of which he was a mere 'trustee', however), toured the entire country, meeting 3,820 VHP conveners who were to coordinate the *Ram Shila Pujans* at the *tehsil* level.[49] Subsequently the logistical arrangements for transporting bricks to Ayodhya were supervised by RSS leaders like H.V. Seshadri, who posted himself at the strategic crossroads of Lucknow.[50] The official union of the VHP with the BJP only came about later, but for a long while there were already unmistakable organic links between the two organisations at the local level, where the triple network of the RSS, the VHP and the BJP worked with ever-increasing vigour as the election approached.

[45] *Statesman* (Delhi), 4 Jan. 1988.

[46] In October 1989, for example, Deoras, Vajpayee, Advani and some leaders of the VHP held a meeting in Ahmedabad (*Dainik Bhaskar*, 22 Oct. 1989).

[47] *Organiser*, 9 July 1989, p. 14.

[48] *India Today*, 30 June 1989, pp. 40-3. In 1987 Rajendra Singh, in his report, had put the figure at only 20,000 *shakhas*, of which 17,000 were in rural areas.

[49] A. Singhal, *Report on Sri Ram Janmabhoomi in meeting of the governing council held in Ayodhya on 26.1.1990*, VHP, n.p., n.d., p. 2.

[50] *Times of India*, 6 Nov. 1989, p. 6.

A superimposition of strategies: the case of Madhya Pradesh

The BJP's election campaign in Madhya Pradesh in 1989 combined a strategy of communal mobilisation with one of integration which took the form of a search for electoral allies. It also displayed the party's perennial populist tactic.

The chosen agent of this last ploy was the Bharatiya Janata Yuva Morcha (BJYM – Youth front of the Indian people), whose former vice-president, Dhyanendra Singh, stated unhesitatingly that this was a branch of the RSS.[51] In the autumn of 1988, the BJYM launched a state-wide agitation aimed at middle class youths on the theme of the 'right to work'. This involved dropping English as an obligatory subject in examinations for entry to certain levels of the administration. The extent of the movement recalled the density of the BJYM network. It drew its inspiration from the *Ekatmata Yatra*, using fire instead of water. Torchlit processions set off from the towns of Morena, Sidhi, Raigarh, Raipur and Jhabua, covering some 30 km. a day and meetings were organised in the towns through which they passed. At the end of a month-long campaign, in which the 'Torch of the Revolution' (*Kranti Mashal*) had criss-crossed Madhya Pradesh, thousands of people converged on Bhopal where the leading figures of the BJP (including Patwa) presided over the final meeting; then, according to some estimates, 25,000-40,000 people courted arrest by storming the Vidhan Sabha.[52]

Meanwhile, the main target, in socio-economic terms, of the BJP's election programme was the small peasantry. In 1986 the party entrusted Pyarelal Khandelwal with responsibility for a *Gram Raj Abhiyan* (Campaign for village autonomy) whose main theme was the abolition of peasant indebtedness. Informal committees were established by sympathisers at the local level to sustain the agitation.[53] From June 1989, the party demanded the cancellation of debts (*Rin Mukti*)[54] with a series of *dharnas* (sit-ins) at the administrative offices of the *tehsils*. The size of the *Gram Raj Abhiyan* was due to the militant network that the BJP was able to mobilise; Khandelwal claims that 2,000 activists took part, which enabled the party to reach 40,000 of the 70,000 villages of Madhya Pradesh.

In the summer of 1989 the BJP's efforts at mobilising the peasantry

---

[51] Interview with Dhyanendra Singh, 27 Nov. 1989, Gwalior.

[52] Interview with V. Dixit, General Secretary of the BJYM in Madhya Pradesh, 12 Nov. 1990, Bhopal; *Madhya Pradesh Chronicle*, 10 Oct. 1988; *Free Press Journal*, 8 Oct. 1988; and *Move On*, 25 Oct. 1988.

[53] Interview with P. Khandelwal and K. Thakre, *Madhya Pradesh mein Bhajpa ki vijay-yatra*, BJP, Bhopal, 1993, p. 40.

[54] *India Week*, 16 June 1989, p. 11.

around economic themes were coupled with the movement for the Ram temple. This penetrated the villages mostly through the network of the VHP.

The VHP's plan consisted in mobilising some 1,200 religious leaders to bless the *Ram Shilas* packages (usually donated by local industrialists) and organising processions in every *upkhand* (an administrative area occupied by 2,000 people), during which they would be venerated.[55] These *Ram Shila Pujans* involved individual contributions of 1.25 rupees which it was hoped would raise the 250 million rupees that were needed to 'rebuild' the temple at Ayodhya. They would also make it possible to tap a 'Hindu vote', even in the remotest villages, by associating the BJP with this ritual process. The movement took on a systematic character, 300,000 *Ram Shila Pujans* yielding 83 million rupees.[56] These figures (provided by the VHP) are probably inflated; the Home Ministry estimated that there had been 200,000 *Ram Shila Pujans*.[57]

The movement did very well in Madhya Pradesh, including the central and eastern regions: 3,000 ceremonies were held in Raipur and Bastar divisions where 400,000 rupees (60,000 in Raipur town alone) were allegedly collected. At Sagar 5,000 devotees marched in a procession which took the form of a *Shabhyatra* (a form of ritual pilgrimage), before depositing the bricks in one of the local temples. In Hoshangabad district there were 400 *Ram Shila Pujans* (between 43 and 75 in each *tehsil*).[58] Madhya Bharat remained the stronghold of Hindu nationalism in this respect too. There had already been 10,000 *Ram Shila Pujans* at the beginning of October in twenty-three districts, with 10 million rupees being collected.[59] The campaign was especially successful in Raigarh district, where donations totalling 300,000 rupees were raised. In a village called Piploda, which was so remote that it did not even have electricity, the VHP obtained about 100 rupees.[60] The coordinator of these ceremonies throughout the district and beyond was none other than the BJP's local Lok Sabha candidate, Pyarelal Khandelwal, who admitted to calculating that his participation in the *Ram Shila Pujan* would assure him a 'bonus' of 10% more votes in the constituency.

The results of research conducted in Shivpuri district enable one to analyse in greater detail the political instrumentalisation of an ostensibly religious ritual, namely the *Ram Shila Pujan*. The local VHP branch –

[55] *Organiser*, 20 Aug. 1989, pp. 16-17, and *Hindu Vishwa*, Aug. 1990, p. 60.
[56] Ibid., p. 63.
[57] *Hindustan Times*, 16 Nov. 1989.
[58] *Madhya Pradesh Chronicle*, 11 Nov. 1989, p. 5.
[59] *Times of India*, 7 Oct. 1989, p. 6.
[60] *Dainik Bhaskar*, 13 Nov. 1989, p. 1.

launched in 1983 by V.D. Saxena – organised one of these rituals in every *upkhand*, and on each occasion local *sadhus* came to preside over the ceremony.[61] Local BJP leaders were usually associated with these events even when not responsible for organising them. This was the case with Vinod Garg, a *swayamsevak* and the BJP chairman in Shivpuri town, who had the bricks collected in the district deposited in a temple whose trust was presided over by his brother, a vegetable oil manufacturer.[62] The 'family priest' also played a part in the ceremonies. Thus the Garg family were projected as patrons and protectors of Hinduism. Vinod Garg brought the movement to the villages of the district; he claimed to have organised 585 *Ram Shila Pujans* and collected 190,000 rupees.[63] According to these figures, it appears that more than one *Ram Shila Pujan* was held in each village *panchayat*, but that the inhabitants, who numbered 865, 930 in the district, donated less than an average of 1.25 rupees each. The case of Piparsod, a large village 17 km. from Shivpuri where 4,500 rupees were collected but the inhabitants numbered only 2,500, appears atypical in this respect but all the more interesting for that.[64]

The village had shown little enthusiasm for the installation of a RSS *shakha*, despite its inhabitants' unwavering support for Hindu nationalist parties, from the Hindu Mahasabha to the BJP. In the mid-1980s, a *pracharak* had to abandon its operations after several weeks notwithstanding the efforts of local activists. One of these explained the reverse by the fact that peasants are too divided and do not have time for an RSS training.[65] Here one notes the *shakha* system's relative lack of adaptability in the village world where work completely dominates men's lives and factional rivalries are not uncommon. In Piparsod two dominant castes vied for pre-eminence.[66] The Brahmins were the first prominent Hindu nationalists to emerge in the villages, and the Kirars, a caste of farmers classified as Other Backward Classes, undoubtedly decided that this was a good enough reason to keep their distance from the movement. Thus the RSS was dominated by Brahmins who had been attracted to it during their studies at Shivpuri.

Shiv Narayan Sharma, the son of a schoolmaster, had become aware

---

[61] Interview with V.D. Saxena.

[62] Interview with the Garg brothers, 18 and 20 Nov. 1989, Shivpuri.

[63] Interview with V. Garg, 27 Nov. 1990, Shivpuri.

[64] I am grateful to Jean-Luc Chambard for this information and for his invitation to visit Piparsod in the autumn of 1990.

[65] Interview with Shiv Narayan Sharma, 28 Nov. 1990, Piparsod. An external witness was to support this analysis, citing the heavy workload of the peasants, and the jealousies and even factional tensions that turned the villagers away from the *shakha* (interview with Sarvan, 27 Oct. 1991, Piparsod).

[66] J.L. Chambard, *Atlas d'un village indien*, op. cit., p. 18.

of the RSS and joined the Jana Sangh during his studies at Shivpuri.[67] He had then come into contact with Vinod Garg, who in the 1980s asked him to promote the 'Sangh parivar''s programmes. In 1989 Sharma took charge of the *Ram Shila Pujan*, which entailed a procession through Piparsod, much like the traditional processions which symbolised the unity of the village.[68] Vinod Garg took part in this ceremony as well. Thus the Hindu nationalist movement infiltrated Piparsod, albeit in an attenuated form compared to the installation of a *shakha*, but still with the potential to be effective politically. The electoral impact of this instrumentalisation of a religious issue was the result, above all, of politicians associating themselves with ceremonies perceived as sacred, and being conducted by personages venerated in Hinduism. Here, the network of *sadhus* was a crucial agent in such manipulation.

The same device was employed at Bhopal, where the local VHP and RSS organised a two-day *Akhand Ramayana Yagya* (a ceremony involving the uninterrupted recitation of the *Ramayana*). This was at the moment of the *shilanyas* (foundation-stone laying ceremony) at Ayodhya (see below). Bhopalis were called on to stop work for two days.[69] On 10 November most shops stayed closed, and thousands of people gathered for the finale of the *Akhand Ramayana Yagya* and then the *Mahayagya*, which a local priest performed between the hours of 8 a.m. and 6 p.m. This ritual began with 250 women singing 'Ram Janam' hymns (in honour of Ram's birth); then five couples presented *ahuti* (a sacrificial offering) before being joined by hundreds of devotees who chanted the *gayantri mantra* as they cast flower petals and valuable objects into a fire. A sum of about 11,000 rupees was contributed at the spot where the *Yagya* took place. Divyanand Tirth, *Shankaracharya* of the Bhanpura *pith*, then arrived to carry out the *navgrah pujan* (the *puja* of the nine planets, which was due to be held on that day). He garlanded a portrait of Ram, performed the *arti* (evening *puja*), in the same place as the *Akhand Ramayana Yagya*, and then a *Ram Shila Pujan* before declaring a *dharma sabha* (religious assembly) open at the same time as he unfurled the saffron flag marked with 'Om'. The religious ceremony quickly took a political turn, as a VHP speaker criticised the government for its opposition to the building of a temple at Ayodhya. Babulal Gaur, L.N. Sharma and Sushil Chandra Verma, a BJP candidate for Bhopal, were seated alongside the religious leaders. After the *dharma sabha*, at 1.35 p.m. (the precise moment when the *shilanyas* was taking place at Ayodhya), all the devotees were asked

---

[67] In the mid-1980s, by which time he had established himself in the clothing business and owned some land, he became the local BJP secretary (interview with S.N. Sharma, 26 Oct. 1991, Piparsod).

[68] J.L. Chambard, *Atlas d'un village indien*, op. cit., p. 17.

[69] *Dainik Bhaskar*, 22 Nov. 1989, p. 3.

to turn towards the north-east, facing Ayodhya, to carry out the *puchpan-jali* (a floral offering) by drawing from the five hundredweight of flowers that had been put at their disposal.[70]

There were numerous constituencies in Madhya Pradesh where candidates openly exploited religious themes for political purposes, usually by taking part in *Ram Shila Pujans*. In the contest for Khajuraho, for example, the BJP candidate, Uma Bharti, was presented to the voters as a *sadhvi* (a women who has renounced the world). She had joined the VHP in 1969, at the age of 8, after Vijaya Raje Scindia had heard her making religious speeches at Damoh.[71] In 1977 she had taken the vow of celibacy (but had still not taken the vow of *sanyas* by 1989). She joined the BJP during the 1984 election, contested the Khajuraho seat but was defeated. Uma Bharti owed her prestige to her religious status, to her ability to hold discourses on Hindu culture since she was a child, and to her familiarity with one of the most popular texts of North Indian Hinduism, the *Ramcharitmanas* (the version of the *Ramayana* by Tulsi Das).[72] Thus her electoral speeches contained several references to this very popular work. By 1989 the VHP was anxious to record her oratory, which appealed very strongly to Hindu feelings, on audio cassettes. This particular case illustrates how, since the mid-1980s, the political situation had become permeated with Hindu sentiment: in 1989 Uma Bharti won the seat by a big margin (see below) whereas in 1984 she had had little success when addressing the Khajuraho electorate.

Ram as a national hero for the 'angry Hindu'

As applied in the 1989 election campaign, the Hindu nationalist strategy of mobilisation involved not only the continued use of traditional religious symbols but also the introduction of fresh elements, such as newly invented rituals and new versions of old myths. On the surface it appeared as though this strategy entailed an appeal to religious sentiment which was similar to the 'nationalist devotionalism' of the *Ekatmata Yatra*, because of the emphasis given to the worship of Ram in the rituals of the *Ram Shila Pujans* and their associated iconography. Several of these images focussed on the vulnerable and innocent child Ram, who served as an object of intense and uncomplicated religious emotion.

---

[70] Ibid., 11 Nov. 1989, p. 3 and *Madhya Pradesh Chronicle*, 11 Nov. 1989, p. 9.

[71] She had then taken the girl to Gwalior where VHP leaders were impressed by her oratorical gifts and hence asked her to join their organisation (interview with U. Bharti, New Delhi, 12 Feb. 1994). For more biographical information see A. Basu, 'Feminism inverted: the real women and gendered imagery of Hindu nationalism', *Bulletin of concerned Asian scholars*, 25 (4), Oct.-Dec. 1993, pp. 25-37.

[72] *Dainik Bhaskar*, 22 Nov. 1989, p. 8.

Although Ram had been associated with Vaishnavism and in the epic of the *Ramayana* was depicted as a northern king, the VHP had concentrated on presenting him as a hero of significance to Hindus of all sects[73] and as the ruler of the whole of India, in command of a kingdom that was an historic reality and not simply the ideal polity (*Ram Rajya*) which for Gandhi had been a sort of utopia.

The receptiveness of the public[74] to this manipulation of the symbol of Ram had undoubtedly been heightened by the broadcasting of the *Ramayana* on national television in 78 weekly episodes in 1987 and 1988. The dramatic popularity of the serials among viewers indicated how highly esteemed was Ram, especially in North India.[75] In certain cases, watching the weekly episodes was considered as an act of devotion. Some Hindus, responding to the image of Ram on screen as if they were receiving *darshan* from god, greeted him by performing *pujas* before the television set.[76] Following the *Ramayana*, the *Mahabharata* was shown in 91 episodes; its success led in turn to all activity being suspended on Sunday mornings when the broadcast was taking place – the average audience was estimated at 91 % of those owning TV sets.[77]

These adaptations of the sacred epics tended to create a *national* Hinduism. Analysing 'the Ramayana syndrome', Romila Thapar emphasised that the TV serial was essentially based on the *Ramacharitmanas* of Tulsi Das[78] although there are 'many Ramayanas', some of which contradict each other.[79] By ignoring the other versions of the *Ramayana* and substituting a national for a large variety of regional and local versions, Doordarshan tended to standardise the epic. Thus, the broadcasting of the *Ramayana* and the *Mahabharata*, as Lloyd Rudolph has suggested, was 'playing a leading role in creating a national Hindu identity, a form of group consciousness that has not hitherto existed.'[80]

---

[73]   This manipulation was facilitated because the *Ramayana* had become a kind of reference text for all Hindus, 'the Fifth Veda', which Lutgendorf defines as 'the text we actually know and love' (*The life of a text*, op.cit., p. 439).

[74]   While it is easier to use such a general term at this stage, we shall be more specific, distinguishing different categories among the Hindu public, in the following chapter.

[75]   A village like Piparsod, which had 70 TV sets among 2,500 inhabitants, regularly welcomed people from neighbouring villages for the broadcast of the *Ramayana* on Sunday morning.

[76]   P. Richman indicates also that some viewers 'bathed before watching' and 'garlanded the set like a shrine' ('Introduction: the diversity of the Ramayana tradition' in P. Richman, ed., *Many Ramayanas – The diversity of a narrative tradition in South Asia*, Delhi: Oxford University Press, 1992, p. 3).

[77]   *India Today*, 31 Jan. 1990, p. 54.

[78]   R. Thapar 'The Ramayana syndrome', *Seminar*, 353, Jan. 1989, p. 74.

[79]   See, on this point, P. Richman (ed.), *Many Ramayanas*, op. cit.

[80]   L.I. Rudolph, 'The media and cultural politics' in S.K. Mitra and J. Chiriyankandath

The popularisation of the *Ramayana* through television[81] prepared the public for the Hindu nationalist venture of presenting Ram as both an historic hero and the supreme deity of Hinduism.

VHP propaganda displayed a clear duality in this respect. It projected Ram as the symbol of Hinduism's toleration inasmuch as he stood for a religion which could accommodate all beliefs. This liberal disposition reflected one aspect of the myth as codified in the *Ramcharitmanas*, the *udarta* of Ram (his generosity as well as his greatness of character), but this trait was used in order to demonstrate the all-encompassing nature of Hinduism and, within Hinduism, of Ram. A large sample of persons sympathetic to the Hindu nationalist movement were interviewed by Pradip Kumar Datta in Ayodhya in 1990-1. He concluded that 'Ram embodied not only toleration, but was in fact co-extensive with all beliefs, for he was immanent in everyone.'[82] This view implied that, more than any other god, Ram epitomised Hinduism. Moreover, as Datta emphasises, 'by equating Ram with the distinctive religion of Hinduism, the VHP opens the possibility of orienting the object of devotion to the particular collectivity called Hindus.'[83] Indeed, the new cult of Ram cannot be separated from Hindu militancy.

While the ethno-religious mobilisation of the Hindu nationalist movement during the 1989 election campaign displayed some features of the 'nationalist devotionalism' initiated by the *Ekatmata Yatra*, more aggressive discourses and icons also appeared around that time. Anuradha Kapur has demonstrated that this iconography was not in keeping with the traditional image of Ram. In the *Ramcharitmanas*, even though he is the lord of the universe, Ram is *udar* and conspicuously lacks in masculine assertiveness.[84] He was rarely portrayed using his bow, for Hanuman provided him with the coercive force he needed. In the late 1980s,

---

(eds), *Electoral politics in India*, New Delhi: Segment Books, 1992, p. 92.

[81] This popularisation resulted from the decision, first to broadcast the Hindu epics on national television at all, and then to extend the *Ramayana* series from 52 to 78 episodes. These decisions can be traced back to the erosion of secularism within the Congress party (N. Nugent, 'Rajiv Gandhi and the Congress party-The road to defeat' in ibid., p. 46). R. Sagar, producer of the *Ramayana*, stated at a ceremony in his honour presided over by Swami Vishvesh Tirth: 'Sri Rajiv Gandhi had always wanted a programme based on "Ramayan" to be made. The bureaucracy as usual did not show any interest in it and tried to create all sorts of difficulties. But when the Prime Minister spoke in its favour, the wheels started moving. Indeed the Minister of State for Broadcasting [...] backed the project with all his strength after his mother saw a cassette' (*Organiser*, 20 Nov. 1987, p. 12). See also M. Tully, *No full stops in India*, op. cit., p. 146.

[82] P.K. Datta, 'VHP's Ram: the Hindutva movement in Ayodhya' in G. Pandey (ed.), *Hindus and others*, op. cit., p. 47.

[83] Ibid., p. 50.

[84] A. Kapur, 'Deity to crusader: the changing iconography of Ram' in ibid., p. 76.

Ram came to be represented otherwise. During the 1989 election campaign, large advertising hoardings displayed Ram as a symbol of strength and power.[85] The usual image was that of a muscular Ram drawing his bow; he was often juxtaposed with the model of the temple that the VHP were planning to build in Ayodhya (see p. 393). As A. Kapur points out:

This Ram, the adult male, resembles the figures from a Hollywood 'epic'. And thus Ram becomes a warrior, not easily distinguished from other warriors: Ben Hur, El Cid, or to take Indian examples, an Arjun or a Bhima. Like them he fights for possession, control, status, which translates into a different language of rights as well. The sort of musculature, strength, and sportive manliness that have been the usual attributes of Hanuman have now been transferred to this Ram.[86]

This reinterpretation of a mythological character was clearly intended to express the spirit of the Jana Jagaran movement. Hindus, who were always being described in VHP publications as too tolerant and passive, were thus invited to prepare themselves to meet the challenges which confronted them; the example of the strong, aggressive Ram was intended to illustrate the style of forceful action which would be required. In other words, Ram was cast in the role of the 'angry Hindu'.[87] In 1988 the publication department of the RSS reprinted as a pamphlet an article from the *Organiser* entitled 'Angry Hindu'. The following excerpts reflect the overall philosophy of the Jana Jagaran movement:

Yes for too long I have suffered affronts in silence. [...] My number have dwindled. As a result, my adored motherland has been torn asunder. I have been deprived of my age-old rights over my own hearths and homes. Afghanistan, N.W.F.P., Sindh, Baluchisthan, half of Punjab, half of Bengal and a third of Kashmir – all these have been usurped from me. [...] My temples have been desecrated, destroyed. Their sacred stones are being trampled under the aggressor's feet. My gods are crying. They are demanding of me for reinstatement in all their original glory. [...] You get my vote but you pamper those who attack me. [...] For you, our national life minus every bit of Hindu is secularism. In short, you want me to cease to be myself. [...] Even the Haj pilgrims are subsidised from my money. [...] For so long – for too long – I was lost in a deep coma. [...] Now I have begun to see, I have begun to hear, I have begun to understand, and I have begun to feel – what tragedies have overtaken me for my centuries-old blunder. Hereafter I will sleep no more. I will not remain dumb; I will speak out. [...] I will not run away from

---

[85] I observed these boards in Madhya Pradesh, Rajasthan and Delhi but I presume it was an all India phenomenon.

[86] A. Kapur, 'Deity to crusader', op. cit., p. 105.

[87] Interestingly, some of the Hindu nationalist sympathisers whom P.K. Datta interviewed in Ayodhya considered that 'his *krodhit mudra* [aspect of anger, antagonism] ... complemented his *udarta*' (P.K. Datta, 'VHP's Ram', op. cit., p. 50).

challenge; I will face them. [...] Really speaking, I am more angry about myself than about others.[88]

This statement – forming part of a well orchestrated propaganda campaign – reflects the belief within the RSS hierarchy in the 1980s that Hindus had to be made aware of their vulnerability and of the need to act aggressively in defence of their religion. The reinterpretation of the mythological Ram must be analysed in this context. The 'new' Ram is presented as the leading figure of the 'Hindu backlash'; Hindus should identify with him in order to gain strength and courage; they used to 'run away' but now they must overcome their inferiority complex with the help of Ram. The reinterpretation of the traditional Ram was therefore expected to unveil (in fact create) a new kind of political Hinduism and to some extent this is what happened. As Kapur has suggested: 'The new images of Ram have altered the meanings of Ram *bhakti* and, as a consequence, of popular Hinduism as well.'[89] In fact, the Ramjanmabhoomi movement marked the emergence of an aggressive 'political *bhakti*', representing a shift in emphasis compared to the 'nationalist devotionalism' of the *Ekatmata Yatra*.

This manipulation of the symbol of Ram during the 1989 election campaign cannot be separated from the invention of new aggressive rituals which created the context for a wave of communal riots. In practice, Hindu processions in the form of shows of strength usually provoked an outbreak of rioting.

Processions, communitas and riots as an all-India phenomenon

Religious processions have always created circumstances in which communal riots are likely to occur.[90] Sandria Freitag has given a convincing sociological account of this phenomenon:

Though each group of participants [in a procession] might remain distinct from its neighbors, they shared involvement in the same observance for the same ostensible object. Community connections must have been felt at their most tangible and concrete, fostered by these very specific influences which were physical, spatial and temporal in nature. As long as the impact of all these influences still operated, the overarching nature of group identification based on religious community appeared utterly convincing. Threats to community values

---

[88] *Organiser*, 14 Feb. 1988, anonymous article published in the form of a pamphlet with the same title: *Angry Hindu! Yes, why not?*, New Delhi: Suruchi Prakashan, 1988.

[89] A. Kapur, 'Deity to crusader', op. cit. p. 74.

[90] For an historical discussion of this phenomenon, see C. Jaffrelot, 'Processions hindoues, stratégies politiques et émeutes entre hindous et musulmans', op. cit.

Poster showing (*left*) a model of the proposed temple on the site of the Babri Masjid in Ayodhya and (*right*) Ram. *Picture courtesy of Penguin India.*

during these occasions of integrative collective activities could prompt immediate and vehement responses.[91]

This analysis employs the notion of 'communitas' proposed by Turner as a means of designating the circumstances – such as processions or pilgrimages – in which a social structure becomes an 'undifferentiated whole'.[92] While all societies are necessarily heterogeneous, this approach appears to be particularly relevant in the case of Hindu society where the caste system presupposes a status-based hierarchy. In this context, religious processions are usually one of the very few circumstances in which different castes are involved in a common activity. Even though these processions are often strictly ordered, their form creates the impression that all those who participate are also members of a relatively homogeneous collectivity.

Hindu leaders logically tried to appropriate this traditional institution as a means of creating a Hindu front which would transcend caste differences.[93] But this unification process had an aggressive dimension,[94] a phenomenon well illustrated by the procession of *Ram Shilas* which led to many riots during the 1989 election campaign, and especially to the worst of all, in Bhagalpur.

When the procession left the town on 24 October 1989 it had been a relatively small affair but it quickly attracted a large number of participants, between 1,000 and 3,000, according to some estimates.[95] Others joined along the way, swelling the numbers to about 10,000 people. Slogans were chanted, a favourite being *'Hindi, Hindu, Hindusthan, Mullah bhago [go to] Pakistan'*.[96] When the procession approached the Muslim *mohalla* of Chattarpur, about 300 people came out to block the route. The District Magistrate tried to arrange a compromise but the

---

[91]   S. Freitag, *Collective action and community*, op. cit., p. 138.

[92]   V. Turner, *Dramas, fields and metaphors: symbolic actions in human society*, Ithaca, NY: Cornell University Press, 1974, p. 237. Elsewhere, Turner defines the 'communitas' as an unmediated 'relationship between concrete, historical, idiosyncratic individuals' (*The ritual process*, Chicago: Aldine, 1969, p. 131).

[93]   The reinterpretation of the Ganesh festival initiated by Tilak is probably the first instance of such an ideological appropriation (see N.G. Jog, *Lokamanya Bal Gangadhar Tilak*, New Delhi: Government of India, 1979, p. 44-5).

[94]   Applying a psychological method of enquiry which seems complementary to S. Freitag's sociological approach, S. Kakar suggests that transcending individuality by merging into a group is 'the primary motivational factor in both religious assembly and violent mob' because these forms of social action 'suspend judgement and reality-testing' (S. Kakar, 'Some unconscious aspects of ethnic violence in India' in V. Das, ed., *Mirrors of violence*, op. cit., p. 143).

[95]   *India Week*, 3 Nov. 1989, p. 2 and *Times of India*, 4 Nov. 1989, p. 1.

[96]   I. Bharti, 'Bhagalpur riots and Bihar government', *EPW*, 2 Dec. 1989, p. 2643.

marchers insisted on going ahead. One of the demonstrators recalled subsequently:

There seemed to be some sort of madness in the procession and [in] Mahadev Singh [who was leading it]. It was as if everyone believed that it would be a great victory for Hinduism if the procession passed through Chattarpur. The crowd seemed to be intoxicated with its power and was shouting anti-Muslim slogans with fervour.[97]

The riot which followed was the most violent of several which occurred in 1989, and illustrates how the process of forming an aggressive 'communitas' can provide a context for instigating violence for political ends. While this kind of procession is bound to arouse 'some sort of madness' among participants who may not necessarily belong to communal organisations, the leaders of such groups can obviously manipulate the symbolism and rituals of these marches to provoke riots. Once a riot has broken out, its course and form is influenced by several other factors, such as the existence of local personal and group rivalries and the presence of criminal elements, but the fact remains that an aggressive procession is one of the most potent means of heightening communal tension and precipitating violence. If an electoral contest is being held at the same time, riots can serve to polarise local people on communal lines and thus create a ready-made Hindu constituency for the BJP.[98] This hypothesis has been developed by Paul Brass in connection with the riots which took place during the 1991 election campaign. Activists from different political parties acknowledged that 'the fomenting of violence both to win votes and to ward off defeat by arousing communal sympathies and animosities is part of the standard repertoire of contemporary political practices in north India politics'.[99]

In 1989 the *Ram Shila Pujans* were undoubtedly 'rituals of confrontation' as well as 'rituals of mobilization',[100] These processions, and others sponsored by the Hindu nationalist movement, were the catalyst for a wave of riots throughout India from September 1989 onward. In the past, communal riots had been largely local phenomena. At worst, they acquired a regional dimension when news about the initial violence, often distorted by the spread of rumours, produced secondary

---

[97] Cited in *India Week*, 3 Nov. 1989, p. 3.

[98] Thus there is a political rationale behind such violence, even though the most active participants might not be ideologically minded but merely thugs who are recruited for the processions or lumpen elements attracted by the prospect of looting.

[99] P. Brass, 'The rise of the BJP and the future of party politics in Uttar Pradesh' in H. Gould and S. Ganguly (eds), *India votes*, op. cit., p. 274.

[100] These expressions are borrowed from N. Bhattacharya, 'Myth, history and the politics of Ramjanmabhumi', op. cit., p. 130.

reactions. It was unusual for riots to occur within the same region over a short space of time given the absence of a simultaneous causal factor. In 1989, however, the VHP's ability to control the initiation and conduct of numerous aggressive *Ram Shila* processions throughout India provided the main condition for the outbreak in different locations of communal riots and acts of violence during the election campaign.

The organisational reach of the VHP was indicated by the dissemination of standardised propaganda through pre-recorded audio-cassettes which could be broadcast publicly via loud-speakers. Here again devotionalism was combined with militancy. Some songs drew their inspiration from *bhajans* (devotional hymns) and/or Hindi film songs, but the tapes which attracted most attention were those of speeches by outspoken Hindu nationalist orators. Among the latter, Sadhvi Rithambara, a saffron-clad member of the Central Margdarshak Mandal of the VHP, was the most aggressive.[101] The following passage is from a pre-recorded message which was relayed on the occasion of the *Ram Shila Pujans*:

> The blood of foreigners, of traitors who do not pay tribute to the ancestors, will flow. [...] *Ram Shilas* will be the protectors of the Hindu culture. [...] The foreign conspiracy will not succeed any more. The *Ram Shilas* will mean death for those who call mother India a witch.[102]

The first riot in the 1989 cycle of communal violence took place in Rajasthan, at Kota, a frontier district adjacent to Madhya Bharat. After 33 years of intercommunal harmony, rioting broke out there on 14 September 1989, causing 15 deaths and Rs 7.5 million worth of damage. As in 1956, when last there had been violence in the town, the immediate cause of the riot was the festival of Anant Chaturdeshi, in honour of Vishnu; but this time the procession, in which BJP members were alleged to have taken part, carried firearms and swords and chanted anti-Muslim slogans as they passed through the Muslim old town. This provoked stone-throwing, providing Hindu activists with the pretext for their assault, in which 187 shops were burnt out.[103] While this phenomenon suggests that such

---

[101] A disciple of Swami Parmanand, a member of the Central Margdarshak Mandal whose ashram is in Hardwar, Sadhvi Rithambara took an active part in the VHP from 1986 onwards (*Times of India*, 19 July 1992, p. 13). For excerpts of her speeches and an analysis of them by S. Kakar, see 'Hindutva harangue', ibid.

[102] Cassette marked 'VHP-New Delhi' and entitled *Ram Shila Puja* (Hindi). A recorded speech, attributed to Uma Bharti, contained the following: 'When ten Bajrangdalis will sit on the chest of every Ali, then only will one know that this country belongs to Lord Ram' (cited in A. Nandy, S. Trivedy, S. Mayaram and A. Yagnik, *Creating a nationality – Ramjanmabhumi movement and the fear of the self*, Delhi: Oxford University Press, 1995, p. 53.)

[103] *Hindustan Times*, 17 Sept. 1989, p. 1, and 20 Sept. 1989, p. 10-11.

pre-meditated violence also had a socio-economic dimension, in so far as 70% of the Muslim families in Kota (9% of the population) had one of their number working in the Gulf and thus contributing to local investment, such micro-sociological factors counted for less in the violence than the national context,[104] as was confirmed by other riots in Rajasthan.

These were mostly provoked by *Ram Shila Pujans*, when Hindu activists resorted to violence against the police in order to carry out their procession in the face of an administrative prohibition[105] or when VHP marches were attacked, as on 6 October in the Shastri quarter of Jaipur, where one of the slogans being chanted was 'There are two places for Muslims, Pakistan or the graveyard'.[106] At the end of 1989 Rajasthan's tally of communal violence rose, with 15 clashes and 19 deaths from 14 September onwards, compared with a previous annual average of 2 clashes and 3 deaths.[107] Similar developments took place in most of the northern states in October 1989.

In Khargone (Madhya Pradesh) the *Ram Shila* procession had to pass by the mosque in the town centre. Just as it arrived there a bomb exploded, causing the death of an activist before setting off a riot in which two Muslims were killed.[108] At the same time a riot, following a similar pattern, broke out at Mhow, on the outskirts of Indore, leaving 42 people injured. At Indore a 4 km.-long procession of 25,000 people, prominent among whom were 50 *akharas* armed with swords, set out on 23 September to coincide with the *Ram Shila Pujan*. This unprecedently large show of force, punctuated by the chanting of the VHP's traditional slogans, in a town which had experienced no intercommunal violence since 1969 with the exception of anti-Sikh riots in 1984, was seen as a provocation by Muslims, who announced that they would hold a procession on 14 October, the day of *Id-e-Milad* (the anniversary of the Prophet's birth).[109] The Hindu nationalists then called on the population to observe a 'people's curfew'.[110] The procession on 14 October brought out 30,000 people. There were three bomb explosions, which caused little injury but were immediately followed by looting throughout the town, an indication that the riot – which claimed between 23 and 40 lives, according to

---

[104] A.A. Engineer recognised this ('Kota: Another case of planned violence?', *EPW*, 9 Dec. 1989, p. 2703).

[105] *Indian Express*, 12 Oct. 1989, p. 1.

[106] *Indian Week*, 19 Oct. 1989, p. 5.

[107] *Frontline*, 28 Nov. 1989, pp. 30-1.

[108] *Madhya Pradesh Chronicle*, 1 and 2 Oct. 1989, p. 1.

[109] A.A. Engineer, 'Communal frenzy at Indore', *EPW*, 4 Nov. 1989, p. 2468.

[110] *Frontline*, 28 Dec. 1989, p. 25.

different estimates – had been planned in advance.[111] All observers were agreed that its legacy was deep inter-communal division. On 7 November the *Sri Ram Shila Rath*, the cart carrying consecrated bricks from Jhabua to Ayodhya, received an enthusiastic welcome from thousands of people along the way, who threw flowers in its path.[112]

Outside the compact area formed by east Rajasthan and Madhya Bharat, the greatest number of riots broke out in Uttar Pradesh, Gujarat and Bihar, where the violence in Bhagalpur alone was officially stated to have claimed 538 victims, but unofficially around 1,000.[113] The *Ram Shila Pujans* and cycle of rioting in late 1989 marked the climax of the strategy of ethno-religious mobilisation in which the 'Hindu vote' was pursued through associating BJP candidates with prominent religious figures in *Ram Shila Pujans* and by organising processions to strengthen Hindu collective consciousness, irrespective of whether they provoked violence. Out of 88 constituencies won by the BJP in the 1989 election, 47 were in areas where there had been rioting during the autumn, thus confirming that 'an atmosphere of communal polarisation contributed to the strength of the party's showing'.[114]

The first months of the 1989 election campaign saw at the local level the implementation of an aggressive strategy of Hindu nationalist mobilisation whose scope was determined by the prevailing political situation and by Hindu nationalist networks made up of activists and religious figures. This conjunction of forces was embodied in the *shilanyas* as the election approached.

The shilanyas

In the run-up to the *shilanyas* one finds a further erosion of the politics of secularism. This process had accelerated in September 1989 when the Congress government of Uttar Pradesh introduced a bill seeking to declare Urdu an official language in certain areas of the state. The timing of the decision suggested a concern to improve the image of Congress (I) in the eyes of the Muslims, who felt they had been betrayed by their erstwhile protector since 1986.

At the same time, however, Congress (I) was in the process of affirming a Hindu identity. Rajiv Gandhi began his election campaign at Faizabad

---

[111] *Indian Express*, 15 Oct. 1989, p. 1.

[112] *Dainik Bhaskar*, 9 Nov. 1989, p. 6.

[113] G. Pandey, 'In defence of the fragment – Writing about Hindu-Muslim riots in India today', *EPW*, March 1991, p. 561, and *India Today*, 15 March 1992, pp. 34-5.

[114] J. Chiriyankandath, 'Tricolour and saffron: Congress and the new-Hindu challenge' in S.K. Mitra and J. Chiriyankandath (eds), *Electoral politics in India*, op. cit., p. 69.

because, in his own words, it was 'the land of Ram, this holy land'.[115] Notwithstanding this speech, the government played the 'Hindu card' in the Ayodhya affair.

Even though the court at Allahabad had decided, in a provisional judgement, in favour of maintaining the *status quo* at Ayodhya, a decisive meeting was held in Lucknow on 27 September, convened by the Chief Minister of Uttar Pradesh, Narayan Datt Tiwari, between Buta Singh, Ashok Singhal, Dau Dayal Khanna, Nritya Gopal Das and Avaidyanath. This concluded by authorising the *shilanyas* in exchange for a promise by the VHP to respect property rights as required by the court judgement.[116] But on 2 November, with complete impunity, some *pandits* from Varanasi and members of the Bajrang Dal marked out a site for the *shilanyas* on a disputed plot in front of the mosque The *shilanyas* took place on 9 November 1989, and in an election address at Nagpur Rajiv Gandhi expressed satisfaction at the peaceful fashion in which the ceremony had taken place.[117]

This challenge to secularism was only in part the outcome of a tactical attempt to win Hindu votes; essentially it was a policy formed under pressure from the VHP's activists and *sadhus*. In fact the VHP threatened to mobilise the latter against the government if it put obstacles in the way of its plans. According to Ashok Singhal, this would at first take the form of a *satyagraha* by 'thousands of *sadhus* and holy men'[118] if the *shilanyas* were impeded. It seems that this last threat aroused residual traces of resistance on the part of the government. On 8 November N.D. Tiwari and Buta Singh tried to 'persuade Singhal and Avaidyanath to delay the *shilanyas* – and then apparently capitulated under the threat of a *satyagraha* by activists and *sadhus* who were already assembled in readiness at Ayodhya for this eventuality.[119]

Thus the political authorities, under pressure, had allowed the *shilanyas* to take place, the ceremony serving as the occasion for a new manipulation of symbols and invention of rituals. Here the principal

---

[115] Quoted in P. Brass, 'Caste, class and community in the ninth general elections for the Lok Sabha in Uttar Pradesh', op. cit., p. 119.

[116] 'Agreement between the Chief Minister of Uttar Pradesh and the VHP, September 1989' in *White Paper on Ayodhya*, Government of India, Feb. 1993, p. 42, and *Hindu Vishwa*, Aug. 1990, p. 58.

[117] *Indian Express*, 10 Nov. 1989, p. 9. On this point his biographer, Nicholas Nugent, concludes: 'The only positive thing that can be said about Rajiv's role in the Ayodhya dispute is that he turned down a suggestion that he himself lay the temple's foundation stone, a suggestion that reportedly emanated from his own Home Minister, Buta Singh' (N. Nugent, *Rajiv Gandhi: son of a dynasty*, London: BBC Books, 1990, p. 195).

[118] *Hindustan Times*, 4 Aug. 1989 and 6 Oct. 1989, p. 5; *Times of India*, 28 Oct. 1989, p. 6, and *Statesman* (Delhi), 8 Nov. 1989, p. 1.

[119] Shukla, 'Shilanyas, a thrill', *Hindu Vishwa*, Aug. 1990, p. 65.

symbol was the heap of 167,063 *Ram Shilas* collected throughout India and in the Hindu diaspora which had then been transported to Ayodhya. The ritual sought to combine with the sacred procedures several symbols of national unity, which thereby became sanctified. Jars filled with water from all the country's sacred rivers were brought forward after the beginning of the *havan* (Vedic sacrifice) and before the ground had been broken; the first five bricks, as prescribed by the 'Hindu scriptures', were mixed with other materials, brought from 'the four corners of India'; and finally the cement fixing the first 'stone' was buried under earth brought from each of the (unidentified) sacred sites of India.[120] The crowd received the *shilanyas* as a rite, and the earth dug out of the hole was distributed as *prasad* or used to imprint a *tilak* on the foreheads of those present. Some prostrated themselves before the *Singhdwara* (lion gate of the mosque site), which was seen as the entrance to the body of the future temple.[121] The site of the *shilanyas* became an object of veneration, on which gifts accumulated. The crowd was swollen by 25,000 pilgrims who had come for the annual *parikrama,*[122] and this atmosphere naturally increased the propensity to devotion. But this sense of deliberate programming, which led the VHP systematically to combine *Dharma Sansad* with *Magh Melas,* and *Ram Shila Pujans* with processions in honour of Dasahara, was an integral part of the instrumental campaign. Beyond the crowd at Ayodhya, the VHP sought to mobilise all Hindus around the *shilanyas* by fusing symbols with Hindu nationalist connotations and procedures of sacred origin. The *modus operandi* consisted of organising throughout India simultaneous *Mahayagyas,* analogous to the *shilanyas,* and of calling on all Hindus to face Ayodhya to make the flower offering (*pushpanjali*) at 1.35 p.m. on Friday, 10 November – the moment when the stone was being laid.[123] Similarly, at the time of the *Kar Seva* of 1992, Hindus were invited to assemble in a temple and pray together on 6 December. This attitude accorded perfectly with the strategy of emulation since these rituals, consciously or not, probably borrowed from Islam one of its cohesive elements, the veneration of Mecca and prayers addressed in its direction. Also, the synchronisation of all these rituals across India corresponded to Benedict Anderson's very exact definition of the nation as

---

[120] *Hindustan Times,* 12 Nov. 1989, p. 23.

[121] *Indian Express,* 10 Nov. 1989, pp. 1-9.

[122] This pilgrimage consisted of connecting the temples of the Ayodhya and Faizabad region. The *shilanyas* took place at exactly the same time as the *Panch Kosi Parikrama* which involved making a circuit of 16 km. round Ayodhya five times.

[123] *Indian Express,* 10 Nov. 1989, p. 9. This effort to invent collective rituals inspired by the conduct of Christian and Muslim religious assemblies could already be seen at Hindu conferences, where those attending voted for resolutions by reciting together '*Om*' (*Organiser,* 18 April 1982, p. 2).

an 'imagined community', a notion referred to above in connection with the *shakhas* of the RSS.

In fact the *shilanyas* reflected the long-term desire of the Hindu nationalist movement to provide Hinduism with a physical centre which could be used to reinforce its cohesion. Parallel to the building of an ecclesiastical structure, Hindu nationalist leaders apparently aspired to create a geographic and historic Hindu heartland on the pattern of the 'Semitic religions'. Thus, following the demolition of the Babri Masjid, Acharya Dharmendra of the VHP spoke of making Ayodhya the Vatican of the Hindus by removing all Muslims from the town.[124] And in January 1993, Rajendra Singh claimed that Ayodhya, Mathura and Varanasi represented for the Hindus what Mecca and Medina represented for the Muslims.[125] In their attempt to endow Hinduism with a geographical and historical centre, the leaders of the RSS and its affiliates proceeded as they had done with the myth of Ram, when they presented him as an historical and national hero. In such propaganda Ayodhya is identified as Hinduism's most important historical site.

In the late 1980s many pamphlets were published regarding the history of Ayodhya but all were broadly similar in outline. Pandey and Bhattacharya, who studied five of them, found that they all contained the following basic story: Ram is said to have been born in Ayodhya in the *Treta Yuga*. The town went into decline when he moved his capital to Saketa. Knowledge of the location of the Ramjanmabhoomi was then lost. King Vikramaditya, after miraculously rediscovering the site, built a temple which remained intact despite the decline of the surrounding city. It was later destroyed by Babur who constructed a mosque in its place. Subsequently Hindus made repeated but unsuccessful efforts to recover control of the site. In 1949, the appearance of the idol of Ram is seen as an appeal by the deity 'to remind the Hindus of the sacred history of the place and their duty to liberate it'.[126]

This narrative depicts Ayodhya as the most sacred site of Hinduism.[127] One of the stories studied by Bhattacharya even claims that Ayodhya existed before the creation of the physical world; it was the place where

---

[124] P. Dutta and S. Sarkar, 'Manufacturing hatred: the image of the Muslim in the Ramjanmabhumi movement' in M. Arslan and J. Rajan (eds), *Communalism in India: challenge and response*, Delhi: Manohar, 1994, p. 83.

[125] Interview in *Frontline*, 15 Jan. 1993, reproduced in R. Singh, *Ayodhya episode, a turning point*, New Delhi: Suruchi Prakashan, 1993, pp. 23-4.

[126] N. Bhattacharya, 'Myth, history and the politics of the Ramjanmabhumi', op. cit., p. 132.

[127] Pandey comments that 'the eighty-four pillars [of the mosque described in many accounts as coming from the 'original' Ram temple] stand for much more than a town called Ayodhya: they stand for the Ram Janmabhumi for Hinduism, for the Hindu spirit and culture, the Hindu people, the nation'('The new Hindu history', *South Asia*, 17, 1994, p. 108).

Manu stood when he created the cosmos.[128] Since then Hindus have been involved in a long struggle for the recovery of Ram Janmasthan. One of the pamphlets published by the VHP claims that:

A long history of 77 wars for prevention of fully demolishing the temple and obstruct the completion of mosque thereon is evident, out of which 5 were at the time of Babar, 10 Humayun, 20 Akbar, 30 Aurangzeb, 5 Nawab Sahadat Ali, 3 Nasiruddin Haider, 2 Wajid Ali Shah and 2 under the British rule. The sacrifices in these struggles prevented erection of minarets and pond for Wazu and proper arrangements of offering Namaz and also kept intact the 14 pillars of the temple on which idols of Hindu gods and goddesses are still alive.[129]

This kind of discourse is supposed to present two sorts of historical evidence. On the one hand the temple is said still to be there, the mosque having been barely completed; on the other hand, the struggle for its reconstruction is depicted as one which has been going on since the time of Babur, which means that Hindus have been aware of the religious importance of the site for a very long time. In the 19 pages of Lodha's pamphlet the 77 – or, alternatively, 76 – struggles are mentioned 6 times.[130] These repetitions were also evident in the leaders' speeches.

For the RSS and its affiliates, the rewriting of the history of Ayodhya was entirely consistent with the parallel effort to reinterpret the myth of Ram as a supreme hero. Some Hindus exposed to this message eventually imbibed it. One of P. K. Datta's interviewees in Ayodhya considered that 'since all Hinduism emanated from Ram, his birthplace was a common source of origin: it was therefore everything for the

---

[128] N. Bhattacharya, 'Myth, history and the politics of the Ramjanmabhumi', op. cit., p. 134.

[129] G. Lodha, *How long Shri Ram will be insulted in Ayodhya?*, VHP, n.p. and n.d. (the content of the text suggests that it was published in late 1989), p. 8.

[130] The fictive basis of this 'history' hardly needs to be stressed. As indicated in chapter 2, historically there were few struggles in Ayodhya and at most they involved only local people and/or certain ascetic orders. It could not be otherwise because the prevalent sentiment, unlike the Hindu nationalist claim, was based on local and sectarian identities.

The pamphlets produced by the VHP in the late 1980s and early 1990s were not entirely novel. Most of their material had been taken from earlier accounts which had been in circulation for some time in Ayodhya. In a booklet published posthumously in 1977, Ramgopal Pandey described the legend of the site in familiar terms: he presents a detailed description of the original temple, relates the 76 wars which had been fought between Hindus and Muslims and even suggests that the builder of the Babri Masjid considered the Ramjanmabhoomi to be a minor Mecca (Khurd Makka) because of the Muslim prophets who were said to have been born there. The first line of the introductory 'poem' of his narrative says: 'Will [*sic* – We'll] take revenge of barbaric acts of Baber.[...]' It is likely that Ramgopal Pandey was associated with Baba Ram Lakhan Sharan, who was responsible for organising the incessant chanting of *kirtans* at the Ramjanmabhoomi since 1949. R.G. Pandey, *Shri Ram Janma Bhumi Romantic (Adventurous) History*, Ayodhya: Mani Ram Printing Press, 1977).

Hindus'.[131] Datta went on to argue that 'through the Ramjanmabhoomi movement, the VHP has been able to locate the universal self in a particular, originative space. Reintegration with the self then means a quest to recover one's manifest inheritance.'[132]

The *shilanyas* was certainly seen by Hindu nationalist leaders and sympathisers as the first step along this road. It is in this context that Hindus all over India were asked to stand facing in the direction of Ayodhya at the same time, while performing *pushpanjali*. And the effect of the *shilanyas*, the culminating ritual at Ayodhya, was heightened not only by the large numbers of activists and ordinary pilgrims who took part in the ceremony but also by the deliberate attention given to the bricks, the *Ram Shilas*, which had been transported to the site and were identified by the fact that their widely scattered places of origin were written on them. In one sense, the bricks were used to signify the huge dimensions of the collectivity which, although consisting not of a concentrated mass but of a myriad of towns and small village communities, had acted in the same way at the same time to produce these concrete manifestations of its common will.

The rituals at Ayodhya were organised to express the geographical and social solidarity of Hindus, and the VHP made a point of having a representative of the Scheduled Castes, who happened to be one of the officers of its Bihar branch, present to join with *sadhus* and others in the actual ceremony of laying the foundation stone of the temple.

The 1989 electoral campaign of the RSS-VHP-BJP combination has a dual significance. First, the invention of new rituals, the reinterpretation of the myth of Ram, the claim that Ayodhya was in some sense the centre of Hinduism, and the increased readiness to foment communal rioting represented what appeared to be a long-term policy of redefining the culture of the Hindus and their relationship with other communities. In immediate electoral terms, these techniques were partly responsible for the BJP's success, other factors being the loss of respect for Congress (I), notably as a consequence of the Bofors affair, the BJP's use of populist appeals to gather support on socio-economic issues and the seat-sharing agreement between the BJP and the Janata Dal. Second, the greater reliance on Hindu nationalism was a major explanation for the large gains in support which the BJP made between the 1984-5 and 1989 elections. As a result the Sangathanist workers were back in the forefront, as we shall see in our review of the BJP's performance in the elections of 1989-90 in Madhya Pradesh.

---

[131] Cited in P.K. Datta, 'VHP's Ram', op. cit., p. 49.
[132] Ibid., p. 50.

The BJP's victory in Madhya Pradesh: the activists in the forefront

The 1989 election allowed the BJP to improve its representation throughout North India and in Maharashtra, where its association with the Shiv Sena (an organisation which was formed in the 1960s to defend 'Maharashtrian sons of the soil' against immigrants from the Dravidian South, and which had turned increasingly towards militant Hinduism)[133] helped it to obtain 23.7% of the vote. In the states of the Gangetic plain, from Haryana to Bihar, the Hindu nationalists remained in a weak position compared with the Congress (I) and Janata Dal (see Appendix D, p. 554).

The situation was evidently much more favourable in Gujarat (where all 12 candidates were successful), in Rajasthan, Himachal Pradesh and Madhya Pradesh, where it won respectively 13 seats out of 25, 3 out of 4 and 27 out of 40. In the latter state, a number of factors contributed to their success. First, the Congress (I) was badly riven by factionalism. Regional leaders – Arjun Singh, Motilal Vora, the then Chief Minister, Madhav Rao Scindia and the Shukla brothers – failed to work together during the election campaign. In certain constituencies, the party's prospects were hindered by such rivalries. Second, the electoral pact concluded between the Janata Dal and the BJP enabled the latter to contest 28 seats directly against Congress.[134] Lastly, and most importantly, the campaigns waged by the activist network in the name of Ram and of 'the people' were probably the principal reasons for the BJP's success in Madhya Pradesh. This at least is powerfully suggested by the 'Sangathanist' profile of the party members elected in the Lok Sabha in 1989 and the Vidhan Sabha in 1990.

In 1989 the BJP put up several candidates, corresponding to its strategy of co-option, such as Narsingh Rao Dixit (Bhind), a veteran Congressman who had been a minister in the 1950s, and above all S.C. Verma. The latter, a former member of the Indian Administrative Service (IAS), had been Chief Secretary of the state's administration between 1963 and 1988, and as such undoubtedly enjoyed great prestige among the 200,000 civil servants of the Kayasth caste (his own) at Bhopal, where the BJP nominated him as its candidate.[135] These nominations clearly pursued the logic of expansion in 'clusters', following which notables and politicians with personal power-bases who had hitherto been outside the party – Dixit

---

[133] See D. Gupta, *Nativism in a metropolis: The Shiv Sena in Bombay*, Delhi: Manohar, 1982.

[134] By 'direct' contests are meant situations where Congress (I) and the BJP found themselves in a straight fight, without a Janata Dal candidate in the lists. However, this did not exclude the presence of candidates from the minor parties.

[135] *Tenth Lok Sabha Who's who*, op. cit., p. 828.

and Verma joined it in October 1989 – were given the task of representing the BJP.[136]

This case in point, however, was an exception in 1989, since most of the notables and princes nominated by the party were also militant Hindu nationalists, as is borne out by the three representatives of the princely élite of the BJP in Madhya Pradesh – Vijaya Raje Scindia (Guna), Dilip Singh Judeo (Janjgir) and the Maharajah of Panna who, at the age of 75, now confined his activity to the patronage of the VHP in his district; his son Lokendra Singh succeeded him as MP for Damoh in 1989.[137] These were the only members of aristocratic families whom the BJP put up at the 1989 elections, while Congress nominated eight.[138] However, except for Madhav Rao Scindia, who remained invincible in Gwalior, all were defeated.

In most instances these 'super notables' of the Congress (I) came to grief when faced by the BJP's plebeian activists. The majority of the BJP's victorious candidates were RSS members, among them veterans such as P. Khandelwal, S. Jatiya, P.C. Verma, L.N. Pandey, Baburao Paranjpe, R.L. Savala and Sukhendra Singh. The BJP deliberately put up a majority of its candidates from the ranks of Hindu nationalist activists – in conformity with the conviction expressed by S. Patwa, president of the party in Madhya Pradesh: 'The "key voters" like the heads of various communities in villages or the zamindars, etc. who were able to influence the voting trend, had now become redundant [...].'[139]

This development was symbolised by the election of Uma Bharti at Khajuraho and Prahlad Singh Patel in Seoni. In 1984 Uma Bharti had won only 30.81% of the vote, but in 1989 she doubled her tally, a performance unrivalled by any other candidate. Without doubt, as a Lodhi, Uma Bharti was successful in projecting herself as a representative of the Backward Castes, but her election speeches were firmly anchored to militant Hindu themes, which clearly were now better vote-winners than five years earlier. Patel became MP for Seoni in 1989 when he was just twenty-nine. Up till that point he had been active in students' unions and worked as a General Secretary of the state Yuva Morcha since 1986.[140] According to the electoral pact between the BJP and the Janata Dal, the Seoni seat

---

[136] *Dainik Bhaskar*, 28 Oct. 1989, p. 1, and 14 Nov. 1989, p. 3.

[137] Interview with Lokendra Singh, 19 Nov. 1990, New Delhi.

[138] Madhav Rao Scindia at Gwalior, his aide Mahendra Singh of the Kalukheda family at Guna, the Maharajah of Datia at Bhind, the wife of the Maharajah of Rewa, Vijay Pratap Singh at Surguja, a female descendant of the royal family of Sarangarh at Raigarh, a scion of the Khairagarh family at Rajnandgaon, and Digvijay Singh of the princedom of Raghogar at Rajgarh.

[139] *Madhya Pradesh Chronicle*, 28 Oct. 1989, p. 1.

[140] *Ninth Lok Sabha Who's who*, op. cit., p. 317.

should have been contested by the latter party's candidate. However Patel refused to withdraw because he considered that the constituency needed a 'dashing leader'. He was therefore expelled from the BJP but five days after his election victory was readmitted to the party. Retrospectively, he attributed his success to his participation in movements such as *Kranti Mashal* and *Ram Shila Pujans* and to his aggressive (*akramak*) election campaign. This militant canvassing enabled him to win over a large number of youths, either as active supporters or merely voters.[141] Generally speaking, most of the broadening of the BJP's base – which could be deduced from its electoral successes – resulted from the growing appeal of aggressive Hindu nationalist catch-words, a fact which emerges even more clearly from the sociological background of those elected to the Vidhan Sabha in 1990.

The BJP, which had an electoral pact with the Janata Dal, put up 268 candidates and faced Congress (I) in straight contests in the 205 constituencies which the Janata Dal did not contest.[142] Of its MLA candidates 219 were elected. Their bio-data reveals an exceptionally clear picture of the sociology of its local cadres. The most remarkable feature was the massive presence of acknowledged *swayamsevaks* (44) and members of organisations affiliated to the RSS – the BMS, the VKA, the old Jana Sangh, the BJP and the BJYM (137). Those elected on the BJP ticket were also remarkable for their comparative youth and the fact that they were members of the urban middle class. This type of party-member was already heavily represented among the *candidates* put up by the BJP, 26.5% of whom were aged under 35, against 22.3% for Congress (I); only 2.24% were over 60 (Congress (I), 9.12%).[143] Almost 15% of BJP candidates were in occupations connected to trade (Congress (I), 6.92%). Admittedly 56.72% of its candidates described themselves as agriculturalists (which was already 10% less than in Congress (I)) but among the 219 BJP MLAs the level of education was compatible with a purely agricultural background in only 61 cases. More often than not one found members of liberal professions, merchants or political activists who had acquired some land. The typical profile of the BJP candidate, and hence of the person elected, was of a young Hindu nationalist activist, generally born and bred in a town, relatively well educated and following a career in the professions or in trade.

[141] Interview with P.S. Patel, 21 Aug. 1992, Bhopal.

[142] The Janata Dal and the BJP contested the same seat in only 63 constituencies. In 1985, competition from the Janata Party and/or the BLD had deprived the BJP of 12 victories (estimate based on *Madhya Pradesh Vidhan Sabha General Elections – 1985: Analytical Tables*, Bhopal: Chief Electoral Officer, Madhya Pradesh, n.d., roneo, pp. 70-90).

[143] Chief Electoral Officer of Madhya Pradesh, *Vidhan Sabha General Elections – 1990 Analytical Tables*, Bhopal: 1990, p. 55 (roneo).

Since the principal ideological motive for their success was the campaign for the Ram temple, which was the work of young local cadres, one could conclude that the growth of the BJP's grassroots base was linked to the spread of a certain Hindu nationalist sentiment. But the BJP's party-building strategy also contributed to its success in 1990.

In certain areas the BJP presence was still based largely on rural notables. In the region of Gwalior, it is possible to detect a kind of equilibrium between 'activists' and 'notables'. Rajmata Scindia could still procure the election of certain close associates, like J.P. Verma (at Pohri) – who had followed her out of Congress in 1967 and had kept his distance from the 'Hindu revival' movements[144] – and her own brother, Dhyanendra Singh (at Morar), who admitted to not knowing much about the notion of *Hindu Rashtra*.[145] But such candidates were a vanishing breed compared with the pure activists with RSS backgrounds. A comparable case in point was to be found in Vindhya Pradesh, where the son of the Maharajah of Panna admitted that it was hard to find BJP candidates from beyond the party's ranks.[146] In fact a majority of successful candidates in the region were from the RSS or 'fronts' of the BJP, although there remained a powerful minority of notables.

In Malwa, the only prince nominated by the BJP – Yuvraj Tukojirao Panwar, the scion of one of the Dewas states – was also an activist involved in party work (he had become president of the district unit of the BJYM in 1985). His profile recalls that of Dilip Singh Judeo even though his Hindu nationalist credentials need to be confirmed: he became an MLA for the first time in 1990, and at the very young age of 27.[147]

The situation was very different in areas where the BJP won a very large number of seats for the first time, such as Chhattisgarh and Mahakoshal. In the former, the largest group of MLAs consisted of local notables – 9 *panchs* or *sarpanchs* and 10 members of the Janapada Panchayat or of municipal councils – slightly more than all the Hindu nationalist activists. This result is typical of 'cluster' implantation techniques in an area where the party had not previously gained a foothold in any systematic way. In these cases the activists, in varying proportions, sought the patronage of local notables and even 'super-notables' such as princes. In Surguja district, where Larang Sai (elected to the Lok Sabha in 1989) had worked for a long time among the tribals, the activist network was sufficiently well entrenched for three of the party's five elected members to be BJP cadres.

---

[144] Interview with J.P. Verma, 27 Nov. 1990, Shivpuri.

[145] Interview with Dhyanendra Singh, 27 Nov. 1989, Gwalior.

[146] Interview with Lokendra Singh, 19 Nov. 1990, New Delhi.

[147] *Madhya Pradesh Vidhan Sabha sadasya-parichay*, Bhopal: Madhya Pradesh Vidhan Sabha sachivalay, 1991, p. 120.

In Raigarh district, among the five elected MLAs, one was a VKA activist from Jashpur and the other four were *sarpanchs* or Janapada chairmen with links to Dilip Singh Judeo. The districts of Janjgir, Bilaspur, Sarangarh, Mahasamund and Bastar have the same sociological profile. Only Durg, Rajnandgaon and Kanker cannot be analysed in these terms because of the BJP's persistent weakness. But in Durg district, which is among those where the BJP is least deeply implanted,[148] it gained new urban pockets of influence like Bhilai.[149] This phenomenon remained more or less secondary compared with the weight of notables in the region's 'clusters'.

This implantation in 'clusters' was also found in the districts of Mahakoshal, where there was a balance between activists and notables among the MLAs. In Balaghat district, the BJP remained electorally weak, but in Mandla, Shahdol, Jabalpur, Narsimhapur, Seoni, Chhindwara, Hoshangabad, Sagar and Betul a high proportion (between one-third and half) of the BJP's successful candidates met the criterion of rural notability, or even urban notability in middle-sized towns. These individuals, each with a personal power-base, served as bridgeheads for the Hindu nationalist activists who constitute the 'hard core' of 'clusters' made up in this way. The difference between the districts in western and eastern Mahakoshal lies in the level of BJP successes, which rises steadily from east to west; as one approaches Malwa, one is in a region where the party won in almost every constituency in 1990.

Malwa, with Bhopal and Vidisha inside its borders, remains by and large the bastion of the BJP: here the party captured 66 out of 79 seats. Almost five-sixths of these MLAs whose careers are known can be categorised as Hindu nationalist activists (47, as against 14 notables). Some districts, such as Ujjain and Mandsaur, have five or six MLAs with RSS backgrounds. Throughout this region, the occupational roles associated with notability are often grafted onto an initial Hindu nationalist commitment.[150]

---

[148]   Interview with N.P. Gupta.

[149]   This industrial centre with a population of 500,000 has been called a 'mini-India' because it has attracted workers from all over the country. It was penetrated by the BMS in 1965 (*Organiser*, 3 May 1965). However this labour union implantation brought no political gains till 1990. The Congress (I) and Communist candidates beat the BJP candidate for the MLA seat in both the 1980 and 1985 elections. In 1990, Prem Prakash Pandey, a former leader of the ABVP and the BJYM who had joined the BMS in 1982 on finding employment in the Bhilai Steel Plant as an assistant chemist, won the MLA seat for the BJP. A factor in this success consisted of the innumerable demonstrations organised by the BMS on behalf of the public sector workers, whom the Communist trade unionists had somewhat neglected (interview with P.P. Pandey, 12 Oct. 1990, Bhopal). Just as in other towns in Chhattisgarh like Raipur, Bhilai was in the process of generating MLAs whose election was due to their socio-political work as Sangathanist activists.

[150]   In Bareli, Shamshabad, Barwaha, Dharampuri, Suwasra and Neemuch, the

The chief virtue of this strategy of 'notabilisation' is that it enables the party to dispense with the support of traditional notables and, by taking their place in the local seats of power, to remove a source of eventual competition. In its principles, this course of action corresponds with the demands of the Sangathanist model. The essential point is to minimise any compromise with the social world of the caste as an interest group, and of the faction, so as to promote a unified Hindu world, bound by the same ideology. In this respect, in the context of the Bofors affair and the opposition's crusade against corruption, some BJP activists benefited from a 'clean' image. At Shivpuri, Sushil Bahadur Asthana, who won re-election as the local MLA in 1990, illustrates this phenomenon well. Despite his caste (Kayasth) and urban background (he was a civil servant who later went into business), he enjoyed great prestige in certain rural milieux, as illustrated by the testimonies of peasants in Piparsod:

In the Congress, dubious people are found; in the BJP there are only Hindus, people who are simple and humble [*sadharan*]. Go anyday to the leader Sushil, he will at once make you sit beside him with great attention. And he will come with you, whatever your problems. [...] He is a pure man, and very austere; he is a noble soul [*devta admi*].[151]

These qualities – which were to be greatly tarnished by the BJP's years in office – have already been found in descriptions by activists of K. Thakre and A. Singhal. Such charisma comes from personal virtues cultivated in public, but also from social work – indispensable in the Sangathanist model – which these *swayamsevaks* are called on to perform.

Thus the BJP's electoral advance in Madhya Pradesh in 1989 and 1990 resulted, at one and the same time, from the instrumentalisation of the symbol of Ram, the support of notables (which proved particularly useful for the party's eastward expansion), the party's populist propaganda on socio-economic issues and long-term work by the Sangathanist network in an effort to win over constituencies. The strategies of Sangathanism and ethno-religious mobilisation were pursued in parallel. The activist network, long hostile to the strategy of integration, was well poised effectively to manipulate Hindu symbols in even the remotest villages. Moreover, a wave of sympathy in favour of the Hindu nationalists was

---

swayamsevaks who have become MLAs have often been previously elected to village *panchayats* or *Janapadpanchayats*, following a logic of 'notabilisation' initiated several decades earlier.

[151] Interview, 28 Nov. 1990, Piparsod. Another peasant supporter of Asthana in the same village declared: 'He neither takes nor gives money. He is not corrupt, at least it is what people say. So, for us, he is good. When there is some problem to sort out, he comes immediately. If there is a problem at the police station, we call him and it is settled immediately (interview, 26 Oct. 1991, Piparsod).'

necessary if the party was to dispense with notables and put up pure activists at the elections. In 1990 this policy enabled the BJP to capture two-thirds of the seats in the Vidhan Sabha and thus govern alone, a much stronger position than that enjoyed by the Jana Sangh in the coalition government of 1967-9 and by the Jana Sangh component of the Janata government of 1977-80.

By the late 1980s the Hindu nationalists were in a position to combine the strategies which most appealed to them. First, they had scope to pursue the strategy of identity-building by playing upon the sense of Hindu vulnerability while stigmatising their opponents and emulating those aspects of their beliefs and behaviour which were believed to be a source of strength. Second, the BJP adopted a mixed strategy of achieving integration within the political mainstream, mainly by means of electoral pacts, while maintaining its right to mobilise the Hindu community through ethno-religious appeals. Finally, at the local level the Sangathanists used their network to promote a style of Hindu activism which conformed to their political culture.

Two processes governed the emergence and scope of a new wave of Hindu nationalism. The first was the strengthening and extension of the network of personnel within the movement; many religious figures offered their services at this time and more RSS activists were drawn into its organisation. The second, and most important process was the tendency of the political establishment to place less stress on secularism and to tolerate the use of religious symbols and themes for propaganda purposes: the accommodating character of the legitimate opposition enabled the BJP to re-activate its mixed strategy of the 1960s and the secular approach of Congress had now been called into question. In conjunction with the lobbying of Hindu traditionalists such as G. Nanda or D.D. Khanna, Congress itself was now 'communalising' politics.

This combination of strategies and variables boosted the unprecedented electoral progress of the Hindu nationalists. Not only did the BJP obtain control of three state governments in North India (Madhya Pradesh, Rajasthan and Himachal Pradesh), but with 85 seats in the Lok Sabha it became the principal ally of V.P. Singh. His Janata Dal, with 141 seats, formed a minority government with BJP support and that of the Communists, with their 52 seats.

Part V. THE EARLY 1990s: HOW TO CONQUER AND RETAIN POWER

12

MAKING A BID FOR POWER: THE SCOPE AND LIMITATIONS OF THE HINDU MOBILISATION

This chapter differs conceptually from those that have preceded it. Up till now we have focussed on the way in which Hindu nationalist strategies were either implemented or frustrated by a limited number of variables. In Chapter 11 we reached a turning-point given that, for the first time, a strategy of ethno-religious mobilisation appeared to have been implemented on a large scale. This trend will be analysed further below, in particular to explain how the BJP shifted from a 'mixed strategy' to one based exclusively on ethno-religious mobilisation. However we shall now focus on the nature of the impact of the militant Hindu mobilisation orchestrated by the RSS-VHP-BJP combination rather than the conditions affecting its implementation.

In 1989 the only important remnant of the moderate strategy of the BJP was its association with allies of the legitimate opposition. But the RSS and VHP were unconcerned by the constraints implied by such a position and the BJP withdrew its support from the V.P. Singh government less than one year after the general election. The pretext for the decision was the arrest of Advani at the end of his *Rath Yatra*, a movement which was largely a reaction to the Prime Minister's decision to implement the Mandal Commission report. As far as its traditional social base was concerned, these events were reason enough for the BJP's decision to end its support for the ruling coalition and associate itself closely with the campaign for a Ram temple at Ayodhya.

The electoral progress of the BJP at the general election in May-June

411

1991 was predicated on these two factors, Mandir (temple) and Mandal. First, the Ayodhya agitation provided it with a means of widening its electoral base, although the motivation of 'mobilised Hindus' was not always religiosity or a new ethno-religious consciousness. Determining the motivation of those who join a mass movement is often a very difficult task. Nor can we simply assume that the manipulation of religious symbols and themes has a direct and one-way effect upon behaviour, as a purely instrumentalist approach would imply. Although leaders may think they know which appeals will bring people onto the street, the ways in which individuals interpret appeals and form their own understanding of events must be taken into account. In other words, the members of processions and crowds must be granted some degree of moral autonomy. Second, the BJP's measured opposition to the recommendations of the Mandal Commission brought it further support from the upper castes. On the other hand the low castes often remained indifferent or hostile to the its propaganda. Thus the party's expansion must be qualified from a sociological point of view.

It must also be qualified in geographical terms, since the BJP had not yet emerged as a fully nation-wide party. While it has developed pockets of influence in the South and in the East, its strongholds are still to be found in the Hindi belt. Yet even here it met with unexpected reverses in 1991.

Mandir versus Mandal: Hindu mobilisation and caste conflict

Soon after the formation of V.P. Singh's National Front Coalition government, for which the BJP and the Left Front Parties had promised conditional support, the VHP re-launched the Ramjanmabhoomi movement. Some BJP leaders were at first a little reluctant to endorse this move but the party was soon to lend massive support to, and eventually lead the agitation after the Prime Minister decided to implement the Mandal Commission report. This served to deepen the association between the party and the agenda of the VHP and marked a shift from a mixed strategy to one of undiluted ethno-religious mobilisation.

From the mixed strategy to ethno-religious mobilisation pure and simple

The BJP, the VHP and V.P. Singh.   In late January 1990, the VHP organised a meeting of the Margdarshak Mandal where the decision was taken that construction of the temple would begin at Ayodhya on 14 February. This, of course, necessitated the removal of the mosque; hence

Ashok Singhal called upon Muslims to find an alternative site for it.[1] He also called on every Hindu family to help towards the building of the temple by sending at least one family member to Ayodhya. This latest mobilisation worked against rather than in favour of the BJP's electoral tactics since the announcement threatened to jeopardise the conclusion of an electoral pact with the Janata Dal before the Vidhan Sabha elections scheduled for February 1990 in many North Indian states. Both parties finally arrived at a seat adjustment (see below), but it also risked making the Hindu nationalists appear indifferent to more vital issues: the early part of 1990 was dominated by renewed activism among Kashmiri militants which aroused fear of armed conflict with Pakistan. Thus Vajpayee called on the VHP to postpone its programme in deference to national priorities.[2] The Prime Minister followed suit, asking the VHP for a four month cooling-off period in which he would try to resolve the dispute. Finally, the VHP accepted the postponement on 9 February, thus defusing the crisis.[3]

In June 1990, at the end of the four-month period of grace conceded by V.P. Singh, during which no progress was made in negotiations between the Muslims and the VHP, the latter announced a Sant Sammelan at Hardwar. On this occasion a Sri Ram Kar Seva Samiti (Committee for construction of the temple in the service of Lord Ram) was set up, with the Shankaracharya of Jyotish *Pith*, Swami Vasudevanand, at its head. Its objective was to start the work on 30 October 1990. The plan had the blessing of many religious figures, including the *Shankaracharyas* of Kanchi, Sringeri and Puri.[4]

Meanwhile, the BJP was more and more inclined to distance itself from V.P. Singh. BJP leaders were particularly irritated by the refusal of V.P. Singh to grant statehood to Delhi – a city the party was confident of winning once elections were organised – and by his policy in Jammu and Kashmir, where the situation had deteriorated in 1990.[5] Not only had the BJP's plan for managing the Kashmir problem – to seal the border with Pakistan, which was allegedly training the separatists, and repeal Article

---

[1]   *Times of India*, 27 Jan. 1990.

[2]   *About Us*. 7,3 (3 Feb. 1990). p.1.

[3]   This was the context in which the Shankaracharya Swaroopanand Sarasvati chose to announce that he would organise his own *shilanyas* on 27 April, that of the VHP being valueless (*Times of India*, 20 Feb. 1990). This move, which was supported by certain Congressmen, notably in Gujarat (*India Speaks*, 3, 19, 8 May 1990, p. 29), could have undermined the allegiance of *sadhus* to the VHP. Eventually, the *Shankaracharya* was arrested by the police in Uttar Pradesh on 30 April as he was approaching Ayodhya. His supporters, who themselves courted arrest, numbered no more than 120. He had failed to short-circuit the VHP.

[4]   *Statesman* (Delhi), 27 June 1990.

[5]   Interview with L.K. Advani.

370 of the Constitution, denounced as an encouragement to separation[6] –
been ignored, but in May the Prime Minister had recalled the governor of
Jammu and Kashmir, Jagmohan, in whom the BJP had confidence. This
was followed by the resignation of K.N. Sahni from the consultative
committee that had been set up by the government to deal with the
Kashmir problem. Finally, on the expiry of the four month period of grace
agreed to by the VHP, the BJP's leadership reproached V.P. Singh for
having made no 'serious, sincere and honest [effort] to resolve the
problem' of Ayodhya.[7]

However, the party could not withdraw its support from the Prime
Minister without appearing to betray the anti-Congress mandate given by
the electorate in late 1989 and thus aid the rehabilitation of Congress (I)
at its own expense. Instead the BJP waited for the first outbreak of
factionalism between V.P. Singh and the vice Prime Minister, Devi Lal.

Devi Lal provoked his own dismissal from the government at the
beginning of August 1990 and undertook to mobilise not only his Jat base
but also backward caste peasants in support of his bid for the leadership
of the Janata Dal. On 7 August, without giving the BJP and the Communists any advance warning, V.P. Singh announced that the recommendations of the Mandal Commission report – that 27% of posts in the
central administration and public corporations be reserved for Other
Backward Classes (OBCs) – would be implemented.[8] With this measure
he could be sure of undermining Devi Lal's rural base and of fomenting
caste divisions in the Hindu community from which the BJP was attempting to build up a vote bank. The VHP had just gathered together 5,000
sadhus at Vrindavan to announce that thousands of *kar sevaks* would
depart for Ayodhya from September onwards.[9] V.P. Singh's action was
naturally not unconnected with this threat since it served also as a
diversionary manoeuvre.

Hindu nationalist reactions to the Mandal report.   The RSS reacted
strongly to what it considered an attempt to exacerbate the internal

---

[6]   BJP, *Resolution – National Executive Meeting*, 6-8 April 1990 (Calcutta), p. 9. At the
same time the RSS was campaigning for the elimination of cross-border terrorist camps
(*Indian Express*, 20 March 1990, p. 7, and *Organiser*, 20 May 1990, p. 9).

[7]   *Statesman* (Delhi), 9 June 1990.

[8]   The Mandal Commission, named after its president, B.P. Mandal, had been appointed
in 1978 to determine the criteria for defining the socially and educationally backward
classes and to recommend steps to be taken for their advancement. The recommendations
of its report, submitted in 1980, had been shelved by successive governments probably
in order to avoid arousing inter-caste tensions.

[9]   *Indian Express*, 2 Aug. 1990.

divisions of the 'Hindu nation'. The front page of the *Organiser* of 26 August 1990, entitled 'Raja's caste war', is highly revealing in this respect :

V.P. Singh threatens to achieve in one year what the British could not do in their 150 year long alien rule. [...] He wants to undo the great task of uniting Hindu society from the days of Vivekananda, Dayanand Saraswati, Mahatma Gandhi and Dr. Hedgewar. [...] What V.P. Singh through Mandalisation of the society intends to achieve is a division of Hindus on forward, backward and Harijan lines.[10]

In fact, the *Organiser* criticised the policy of reservations in itself : 'The havoc the politics of reservation is playing with the social fabric is unimaginable. It provides a premium for mediocrity, encourages brain-drain and sharpens caste-divide.'[11] The 'social fabric' is regarded here as in need of preservation from the state's intervention with the implicit assumption that society was in theory – if not in practice – harmonious. In the view of the *Organiser* the campaign for the Ram temple revealed this almost tangible unity: 'The dynamics of the abhiyan [campaign] was such that for the first time it transcended caste and class barriers and forced Hindu society to think and act as one.'[12]

The BJP could not condemn V.P. Singh's project without the risk of alienating the OBCs, who comprise 52% of the Indian population, but to *endorse* it would compromise its traditional support among the upper castes, since the administration had always been one of their private domains. Above all, it would imply acceptance of internal divisions among Hindus. The party reacted to V.P. Singh's decision by expressing its approval of quotas based on economic criteria rather than on caste,[13] and by throwing its whole weight behind the campaign planned by the VHP for September and October. On 12 September, Advani announced his decision to undertake a *Rath Yatra* from 25 September till 30 October 'to mobilise public opinion and solicit its support'.[14] Advani had apparently been thinking about this kind of movement for several months.[15] However, he admitted that the 'Mandal affair' created a favourable context:

The Mandal episode certainly put pressure on me particularly in my constituency,

---

[10] *Organiser*, 26 Aug. 1990 p. 1.

[11] Ibid., p. 15.

[12] Ibid., p. 1.

[13] Interview with L.K. Advani in *Hindustan Times* (Sunday supplement), 23 Sept. 1990, p. 2, and *About Us*, 7, 17 (3 Sept. 1990), pp. 6-7.

[14] Ibid., p. 2.

[15] In June, when asked by the editor of *Panchjanya* what would be the attitude of the BJP towards the VHP's *Kar Seva* he had answered that the Ayodhya affair was likely to precipitate the 'greatest mass movement' of Indian history (cited in *BJP's White Paper on Ayodhya*, op. cit., p. 40).

New Delhi, where these self-immolations [of students – see below] had taken place. Parents used to come to my place, daily: 'Why are you supporting this government? Withdraw your support!' I felt that withdrawing our support on the issue of Mandal would be of an enormous benefit to the government. I said 'I agree with you that the government is behaving very badly but we'll take action at the appropriate time.'[16]

The relaunching of the Ramjanmabhoomi movement in the framework of the *Kar Seva* offerred the right opportunity for action since it enabled the BJP to distance itself from V.P. Singh on issues other than the Mandal report itself, which had proved a popular measure among the OBCs. Thus the VHP and the BJP collaborated in organising the *Rath Yatra*.[17]

It seemed that a change in strategy had begun in which the BJP would be presented as the immediate political alternative, as was confirmed by the party's announcement on 20 September that it would fight the next elections on its own. It also boycotted the meeting on 21 September of the National Integration Council set up to deal with the Ayodhya problem.[18]

The Rath Yatra: a national procession and a demonstration of strength.
The *Rath Yatra* marked a clear shift from a 'mixed strategy' to an instrumentalist one of ethno-religious mobilisation. Advani travelled 10,000 km. in a vehicle designed to represent an epic chariot and decorated with the electoral symbols of the BJP (a lotus) and the Hindu *Om*. He left Somnath on 25 September and planned to cross eight states before reaching Ayodhya on 30 October in order to inaugurate the *Kar Seva*. He was accompanied by activists clad in saffron or dressed to resemble the monkey's head of Hanuman, and loud-speakers were used to relay his speeches and militant religious songs. The number of people exposed to this 'message' ran to hundreds of thousands. In Gujarat, for instance, 600 villages were visited and 50 meetings held within the space of a few days.[19] Demonstrations of religious fervour and of militancy became mingled: women performed the *ras* (a dance peculiar to Krishna

---

[16] Interview with Advani. On 20 September Advani and Madan Lal Khurana were attacked by students when they tried to enter the burns ward of Safdarjung hospital where Rajiv Goswami, a student of Delhi University, had just been admitted with 55% burns (*Hindustan Times*, 21 Sept. 1990).

[17] The meeting of all the BJP's MLAs and MPs, held at Bhopal on 14-16 September, was an occasion for emphasising the party's differences with V.P. Singh, but also for holding several closed sessions between Ashok Singhal and Pramod Mahajan, the BJP's chief officer in Bombay who was responsible for organising the *Rath Yatra* (*National Mail*, 16 Sept. 1990, pp. 1-6).

[18] *Indian Express*, 21 and 22 Sept. 1990.

[19] Ibid., 30 Sept. 1990.

and his *gopis* or milkmaids); at Ahmedabad a young member of the Bajrang Dal applied to Advani's forehead a *tilak* from his own blood; and at Jeptur (near Rajkot) about a hundred more offered him a jar full of their own blood. In Bombay Advani took part in nine meetings, some in the company of Bal Thackeray, the chief of the Shiv Sena. The next stage of the journey took him to Nasik, where he was given a warm welcome.[20] From here the procession went to Hyderabad, a deliberate diversion bearing witness to the party's desire to penetrate South India. Then it returned north to Madhya Pradesh. At Chhindwara he was welcomed by a crowd of 15,000 among whom was Patwa, the state Chief Minister.[21] Its journey from here to Jabalpur revealed its capacity to mobilise in an area where the BJP had established its network only recently.[22] Advani's *Rath Yatra* later visited Indore and Mandsaur, and then, in Rajasthan, Udaipur, Beawar, Ajmer and Jaipur. The caravan then moved on to Khetri and Rohtak in Haryana.[23] In Delhi, where Advani was escorted by the leaders of the VHP, badges bearing the slogan. 'Vote BJP' made their appearance.[24]

The *modus operandi* of the *Rath Yatra* reiterated and combined the main features of the *Ekatmata Yatra* and the *Ram Shila Pujans*. First, it was intended to foster the same feeling of 'communitas' as the *Ram Shila Pujans*. *Rath Yatra* means literally 'chariot procession' and the name was deliberately chosen to evoke comparisons with Hindu religious processions. As in any procession with at least a formal religious appearance, the *Rath Yatra* was expected to strengthen Hindu solidarity, which the RSS and its affiliates defined in ethno-nationalist terms. Second, like the *Ekatmata Yatra*, the *Rath Yatra* was supposed to give this 'communitas' feeling an all-India dimension. This ambition was realised not only through the geographical scope of the movement, but also thanks to the megaphone of the national and regional press. The *Rath Yatra* introduced

---

[20] Ibid., 3 Oct. 1990.

[21] *National Mail*, 7 Oct. 1990.

[22] The *National Mail*, which is not known in Madhya Pradesh for its Hindu nationalist sympathies, commented on the event as follows: 'Massive crowds turned up at all the places including hamlets and villages to give a warm and vociferous welcome to the Rath Yatra. The people defied the torrential rains and eagerly awaited the arrival of Advani. On both sides of the road thick crowds were standing cheering the Yatra. Many people had come with Trishuls and reverentially bowed before the Yatra. Slogans were raised expressing their full support to the building of the Ram temple' (ibid., 8 Oct. 1990).

[23] In this state the *Indian Express* commented upon the *Rath Yatra* as follows: 'At every village all along his route [...] crowds ranging from hundreds to thousands turned out to see him. In the towns, they clambered on to roofs to catch a glimpse of the bespectacled man on the "Rath". In villages, they perched on trees, conches blew and brightly decked women performed repeated "arti"' (ibid., 14 Oct. 1990).

[24] Ibid., 15 Oct. 1990.

a new kind of national procession with ethno-religious undertones into the repertoire of the instrumentalist strategy.

The movement also marked the culmination of the strategy of ethno-religious mobilisation. For the first time, a political leader used propaganda of an overtly Hindu nationalist character throughout eight of India's states. This innovation was made possible thanks to the political situation, which continued to work in favour of the Hindu nationalists. The Congress (I), which was in power in Maharashtra and Karnataka, did not intervene in the *Rath Yatra* even though Rajiv Gandhi had made a nationwide tour to promote communal harmony. The party could not bring itself to practise what it preached. The temptation for the Congress (I) not to oppose – or even to ride – the 'Hindu wave' could not fail to put it at odds with its professed identity, and to draw it into an unequal contest with the BJP on the battleground of Hindu nationalism.[25] On the other hand V.P. Singh, who was anxious not to lose the parliamentary support of the BJP, tried to negotiate with the Hindu nationalist forces till the last possible moment. Advani's *Rath Yatra* reached Delhi after having demonstrated the mobilisation capacities of the Hindu nationalists. Then V.P. Singh tried in vain to outflank them by instigating negotiations between Jayendra Saraswati and Imam Bukhari or Ali Mian (the leader of the Nadwat ul Ulema). The Prime Minister called a meeting of all political parties – which was boycotted by the BJP – which pronounced in favour of respecting the *status quo* at Ayodhya. However the decision had little impact on the wider political situation and did not deflect the Hindu nationalists from pursuing their Ayodhya strategy. On 17 October Advani announced that the BJP would withdraw its support from V.P. Singh's government if the latter placed a prohibition on the building of the temple, and suggested that early elections be held.[26] V.P. Singh then tried to work out a compromise solution in collaboration with Vajpayee, though without success.[27] Having failed in his negotiations, V.P. Singh opted for firm action

---

[25]   On this point see a penetrating editorial by P. Bidwai, 'Passivity is no strategy – Congress must correct course', *Times of India*, 25 Oct. 1990.

[26]   *Indian Express*, 14, 17 and 18 Oct. 1990.

[27]   This was a matter of the state acquiring portions of the Ayodhya site so as to assign those which were not subject to a claim to the Ram Janmabhoomi Yagya Samiti, so that the building of the temple could begin on 30 October. Meanwhile, those parts that were disputed would be subject to a judgement of the High Court. On 20 October, after meeting Muslim representatives, V.P. Singh cancelled the order whereby the state would have been able to acquire land at the Ayodhya site. However this climb-down was probably the result as much of Muslim pressure (which had included the threat by Imam Bukhari to hold a Bharat *bhand* on 30 October) as that of the VHP, which rejected the agreement. The BJP itself saw in this no more than a 'very small advance', and claimed the *garbhagriha* (holy of holies), which would have implied a threat to the integrity of the mosque. This refusal to compromise is at the heart of the strategy of ethno-religious

and authorised another Janata Dal leader, Laloo Prasad Yadav, the Chief Minister of Bihar, where the *Rath Yatra* was taking place, to arrest Advani on 23 October. The agitation then entered a more violent phase.

Another wave of communal riots. From 29 September the VHP, in conformity with its programme of 1 June, began to organise *Ram Jyoti Yatras* (processions bearing the light of Ram). Using a flame brought from Ayodhya, the aim was to light torches in Mathura, Varanasi and thence in every district, thus symbolising the awakening of the devotees of Ram. The campaign was to take the form of a month of local torch processions which would then coincide with celebrations for the feast of Diwali, when every house would be lit by candles.[28]

These processions were monitored by the police and some were even banned in a large number of districts of Uttar Pradesh.[29] The militants resisted such pressure, as at Colonel Ganj (Gonda district, adjoining Faizabad district), where the *Ram Jyoti Yatra* supporters forcibly intruded upon the annual *Durga Puja* despite efforts by the police to stop them.[30] When slogans in support of the Ram temple were shouted, Muslims responded by throwing stones and petrol bombs. The riot spread to Scheduled Castes areas, and then to neighbouring villages – the death toll was around 100.[31] In Rajasthan, riots were also provoked by the holding of *Ram Jyoti Yatras*[32] and by processions for the birth anniversary of the Prophet Muhammed. One can identify clear parallels in the pattern of communal violence which erupted in the wake of the *Ram Shila Pujans* and that related to the *Ram Jyoti Yatras*. However the latter were even more widely spread throughout the country.

The southward expansion of this pattern of communal violence is well illustrated by events in Karnataka. At Channapatna, some 70 km. southwest of Bangalore, the *Ram Jyoti Yatra* passed off without incident, with a strong police escort, but five days later the local procession in honour of Muhammed was attacked – the official death-toll was 17, of whom 13 were Muslims.[33] At Davangere, a riot broke out after the *Ram Jyoti Yatra*, consisting of 15-20,000 'devotees', entered the Muslim quarter despite being forbidden to do so by the police.

---

mobilisation since its activists have an interest in prolonging the struggle and so hardening the sense of Hindu nationalist identity.

[28] Interview with Acharya Giriraj Kishore, 8 Nov. 1990, New Delhi.

[29] *Indian Express*, 30 Sept. and 15 Oct. 1990.

[30] Ibid., 3 Oct. 1990.

[31] *Frontline*, 27 Oct. 1990, pp. 32-3.

[32] *Indian Express*, 6 Oct. 1990, and *Madhya Pradesh Chronicle*, 4 Oct. 1990.

[33] *Frontline*, 27 Oct. 1990, p. 11.

The violence which followed Advani's arrest affected most of the country. His detention on 23 October also led to the BJP's decision to withdraw support from V.P. Singh's minority government, which then faced the prospect of defeat in the Lok Sabha. The BJP also launched a *Bharat bandh*, a national protest movement. This soon sparked off anti-Muslim violence, notably in commercial districts where Muslims refused to close their shops and businesses. On 24 and 25 October the official death toll in communal riots was 61 (including 30 in Rajasthan, 5 in Karnataka, 2 in West Bengal and one in Andhra Pradesh). In Gujarat violence was widespread; communal riots erupted in 26 different localities, leading to about 100 fatalities between September 1 and November 20, 1990.[34] All the while, the militant Hindu nationalist network pursued its programme of *Kar Seva* despite the mass preventive arrests ordered by the Uttar Pradesh state government.

The Kar Seva and the creation of a cult of martyrdom.   About 15,000 *kar sevaks* were taken into custody on 20 October[35] and another 15,000, led by a large number of BJP MLAs and MPs, including Rajmata Scindia, were arrested when they crossed the state border from Madhya Pradesh on 28 October.[36] The VHP's leading religious figures were closely involved in the campaign; on 28 October, according to press reports, Swami Vasudevanand courted arrest with 3,000 supporters at Lucknow, where he was leading a 50,000 strong procession.[37]

The total number of people arrested in Uttar Pradesh before 30 October was around 150,000.[38] The numbers would have been higher had not the Janata Dal government of Bihar and the CPI (M) government of West Bengal made their own preventive arrests (2,000 in Bihar[39]) and deployed peace-keeping forces to seal the borders of Uttar Pradesh. In addition to stopping all trains, the security forces drove back the majority of the militants from Madhya Pradesh or those passing through the state, for whom 60 buses had been provided.[40]

[34] G. Shah , 'Tenth Lok Sabha elections – BJP's victory in Gujarat', *EPW*, 21 Dec. 1991, p. 2924.

[35] *Frontline*, 27 Oct. 1990, p. 11.

[36] *National Mail*, 29 and 30 October 1990, p. 1. On 29 October, 1,000 volunteers from Delhi courted arrest while crossing the state border into Uttar Pradesh.

[37] Ibid., 29 Oct. 1990, p. 9.

[38] *Indian Express*, 1 Nov. 1990.

[39] *National Mail*, 29 Oct. 1990, p. 1.

[40] Interview with B.L. Tiwari (organising secretary of the Shri Ram Kar Seva Samiti in Bhopal district, 12 Nov. 1990, Bhopal). For example, 10,000 people were turned back by police firing when they tried to pull down the wall built to bar their progress to Jhansi (*National Mail*, 30 Oct. 1990, pp. 17-20.)

Despite these elaborate arrangements, thousands of people succeeded in converging on Ayodhya to launch the *Kar Seva* planned for 30 October. Many militants had begun to infiltrate into Uttar Pradesh since mid-October and mingled with local villagers to escape the vigilance of the security forces.[41] The latter had often helped the militants by acting in a conciliatory way – especially the PAC (Provincial Armed Constabulary) of Uttar Pradesh. At dawn on 30 October, about 40,000 *kar sevaks* arrived at the entrance to the bridge leading to the old town of Ayodhya. The police were forced on to the defensive by the ever-growing crowd of militants, who were galvanised by the appearance of Ashok Singhal and S.C. Dixit, vice-president of the VHP and a former Director-General of police in Uttar Pradesh, who doubtless had sympathisers among the police force. A *naga sadhu* seized control of a police bus to breach the front ranks of the security cordon. About mid-day, the gate to the Babri Masjid/Ramjanmabhoomi was forced open, doubtless under pressure, allowing dozens of *kar sevaks* to enter the precinct. They began to attack the mosque and a saffron flag was placed on one of its domes. Because of the poor performance of police commanders, control of operations passed to the Border Security Force.[42]

According to the authorities six people were killed that day, whereas the VHP claimed the number was fifty. The *kar sevaks*, who had been driven back a long way from the mosque, decided to return to the offensive the following day. This time the police used tear-gas, though without effect, the dense crowd advancing slowly through the alleys of the town, braving *lathi* blows. They were unarmed, though they were soon receiving support from local residents who bombarded the police with missiles.[43] Armed police posted on terraces and roofs around the disputed structure opened fire. The VHP claimed that it identified 59 victims while the official death-toll was put at 15.[44] However some Hindi newspapers in Uttar Pradesh made sensational claims, namely that 100 *kar sevaks* had been shot.[45]

For many Hindus the shooting of *kar sevaks* was to have a profound psychological effect. The feeling of Hindu vulnerability had now been

[41] Interview with M. Moonje, the VHP *Sangathan Mantri* for Mahakoshal.

[42] A *kar sevak* from Bhopal commented: 'The PAC and the CRPF, they have a soft corner for the *kar sevaks*. And they try to cooperate with us. They try to disobey orders of firing. Indo-Tibetan force [BSF] and Tamil Nadu force *in donon ne firing ki* [both opened fire]' (interview with the General Secretary of the BJYM of Madhya Pradesh).

[43] See the video news magazine 'Newstrack' (Nov. 1990).

[44] On December 27 the Prime Minister, Chandra Shekhar maintained that only 15 *kar sevaks* were killed in police firing in Ayodhya on October 30 and November 2 (*Statesman* (Delhi) 21 Feb. 1991).

[45] *Probe*, Dec. 1990, p. 7.

transformed into exasperation against the political authorities, which were seen as inexplicably reluctant or at least inefficient in making Muslims see reason. Anger was channelled against Muslims themselves, even though most of them kept a low profile during the episode. The association in people's minds of the government of Uttar Pradesh with the Muslims was evident in the way the Janata Dal Chief Minister, Mulayam Singh Yadav was described as 'Mullah Yadav'. Outbreaks of anti-Muslim violence occurred on 30 October[46] which were often justified by the need to avenge martyrs of the *Kar Seva*.[47] And 'Hindu martyrdom' provided the RSS-VHP-BJP combination with a new theme in the following months.[48] In record time the studios of J.K. Jain (a BJP parliamentarian; see below) produced a video cassette which dwelt on the police repression and its bloody aftermath. This suggests that plans for capitalising on the propaganda value of the events at Ayodhya had been made well in advance.[49] Clandestine sales of this cassette, which actually took place through BJP party offices, quickly ran into thousands.[50] But in addition to the media, the VHP set about exploiting the *Kar Seva* episode through two other movements.

First, the remains of the martyrs of Ayodhya were paraded throughout India in *Asthi Kalash Yatras*, consisting of 22 processions carrying their ashes and bones in urns. Each VHP branch had to pass through as many *tehsils* as possible in vehicles equipped with the usual loudspeakers before handing over the urn to its counterpart in a neighbouring district. In Shivpuri district, the operation lasted three days, from 29 November to 2

---

[46] 14 people were killed on 30 October (including 7 at Baroda, 3 at Ahmedabad and 2 at Indore), 39 on 1 November (20 in Uttar Pradesh), 53 on 2 November and 16 on 5 November (9 in Uttar Pradesh and 3 in Bihar). More than thirty towns in Uttar Pradesh, mostly in the west of the state, were placed under curfew in the first week of November.

[47] In Bijnor one of the worst riots, in which 48 people died on 30 October, stemmed from a victory procession celebrating the assault on the Babri Masjid. However, the Jefferys point out: 'The success of the BJP strategy – drawing activists from all over north India into the attempt to reach Ayodhya – and the aggressive response of the UP government combined to create a highly volatile situation in Bijnor' (Roger and Patricia Jeffery, 'The Bijnor riots, October 1990 – Collapse of a mythical special relationship?', *EPW*, 5 March 1994; p. 556).

[48] The BJP accordingly fostered this feeling. On 9 and 10 November, the National Council, after comparing the 'massacre' to the one at Jallianwala Bagh in 1919, adopted the following resolution: The National Council 'bows its head in tearful homage to the sacred memory of the Martyrs of Ayodhya. [...] The blood of the Ram-Bhaktas [devotees of Ram] shall not go in vain. [...] The BJP rededicates itself to the sacred task of rebuilding the Ram Janma Mandir at Ram Janmasthan and initiating the movement for establishment of Ram Rajya' (*About Us*, 7, 22 [18 Nov. 1990], p. 8).

[49] VHP, *'Pran Jau, paru bachanu na jai'*, New Delhi: J.K Jain Studios, 1990.

[50] In addition to the 100,000 Hindi video tapes which were sold, one must also consider the copies that were illegally pirated (*Economic Times*, 23 Nov. 1990, p. 1).

December. It 'enabled contact to be maintained with the population', in the words of V.D. Saxena, who described how the VHP's network maintained a latent mobilisation.[51] In Uttar Pradesh these processions formed the backdrop to further rioting, particularly in Agra.[52]

At the same time, the VHP in each state organised ceremonies at which *kar sevaks* who had reached Ayodhya were honoured. Such celebrations were held in Madhya Pradesh. One which took place in Bhopal was patronised by K. Joshi and the Shankaracharya of Bhanpura who, by sharing a dais, suggested that there was no longer any formal separation between the political and religious wings of the Hindu nationalist movement.[53] Moreover, the Shankaracharya's speech, which was punctuated by religious references, was overtly political. He referred pointedly to the situation in Jammu and Kashmir, and suggested that the disturbances in the Vale could be brought under control if the activists there were treated as the *kar sevaks* had been in Ayodhya. However, the main object of such meetings was to reward local *kar sevaks* and honour those who had died in Ayodhya. The latter were presented as martyrs of a cause for which many had already given their lives. In fact, the mythology of the Ramjanmabhoomi movement was already invested with the theme of martyrdom, as indicated by its constant reference to the 77 battles fought in Ayodhya throughout history. A commonplace slogan of the VHP before 1990 was *'Ayodhya ke shahidon* (ironically a Persian word) *ko bhulo mat!'* (Do not forget the martyrs of Ayodhya!). In November 1990 at Bhopal this chant was repeated and adapted as *'Ayodhya ke shahidon ko zindabad!'* (Victory to the martyrs of Ayodhya!). Unusually, perhaps, the names of individual martyrs were not incorporated in such slogans.[54] Through this peculiar martyrology the VHP probably tried to substantiate its theory about the continuity of the struggle in Ayodhya.

As far as the honoured *kar sevaks* of Bhopal are concerned, they were naturally presented as heroes. One after another they were presented with a medal by the Shankaracharya, whose feet they touched as a mark of respect. The most warmly applauded of all was a Muslim man. However, a number of youths who claimed to have taken part in the *Kar Seva* lost all self-control when they realised that they were not on the list of those to be rewarded. They literally besieged the rostrum. None of the leaders seated on the dais could calm them down except the Shankaracharya, whose hold on the crowd, massed at the front of the platform, was far

---

[51] Interview with V.D. Saxena, 27 Nov. 1990, Shivpuri.

[52] *Statesman* (Delhi), 14 and 18 Dec. 1990.

[53] Observations made in Bhopal, 15 Nov. 1990.

[54] This anonymity has been noticed by P. K. Datta in his account of a pamphlet published by the VHP, *Amar shahid: kar sevakon ka ilihas*, (Our martyrs for ever: the story of the *kar sevaks*), (P. K. Datta. 'VHP's Ram', op. cit., p. 62).

greater than that of any others on the rostrum. This episode not only reinforced the role of religious leaders in the Hindu nationalist mobilisation but also suggested that the BJP might one day become dependent on them, and that the indiscipline of the young, when galvanised by aggressive slogans, might hinder party strategy.

An expanding base, but why?

As indicated in Chapters 2 and 11, our instrumentalist approach would remain incomplete and unsatisfactory if it merely considered the 'masses' as comprising undifferentiated, passive elements. It would be simplistic to assume that people mobilised only for the emotional reasons intended by the Hindu nationalists. Probably the most relevant insight of 'subaltern studies' historiography in this respect was to question the easy assumption that in modern India 'masses' have mobilised in the ways expected of them by the élites who needed their support.[55] On the other hand, it is difficult to investigate the motives of individuals in this regard. This section is thus only an overview of some important trends.

Religiosity and even ethno-religious consciousness were not the only forces impelling the mobilisation of key groups during the *Rath Yatra* and *Kar Seva* movements of 1990. Devotion to Ram and concern for the 'martyrs of Ayodhya' were certainly important factors in the case of villagers and of some women. But other women participated in order to assert their position in the public sphere, while urban youths, who played a highly significant role, were motivated largely by a militant reinterpretation of the character of Ram, an emphasis on activism for its own sake, and by hostility to the policy of implementing the job reservations scheme recommended by the Mandal Commission.

[55] Subaltern studies historian address the issue of ethno-religious mobilisation in an interesting fashion. Ranajit Guha criticized the general 'disdain for the political consciousness of the peasant masses when it is mediated by religiosity' (The prose of counter-insurgency' in R. Guha (ed.), *Subaltern Studies II*, Delhi: Oxford University Press, 1983, p. 35). He adds: 'In operative terms, this means denying a will to the masses of the rebels themselves and representing them merely as instruments of some other will' (ibid., p. 38). In the same collection of essays, Pandey gives an interesting account of the backward castes' mobilisation in the framework of the cow protection movement initiated by the Arya Samaj in 1893 and relaunched in the first decade of the century, from time to time, in the Bhojpuri region. He points to the involvement of Ahirs (Yadavs), who found in this movement a means of Sanskritisation: ' I would suggest that we have evidence here of a relatively independent force that added a good deal of power to cow-protection activities in the Bhojpuri region – marginally 'clean' castes who aspired to full 'cleanness' by emphasising the purity of their faith and the strictness of ritual adherence to it on the issue of cow-slaughter' ('Rallying round the cow' in ibid., p. 104). Pandey also mentions that backward caste people had been drawn into Hindu-Muslim riots 'by the prospect of loot' (ibid., p. 105), rather than by xenophobia.

The Ramjanmabhoomi movement enabled the Hindu nationalists to penetrate villages more efficiently than ever before. While the turning point in this respect was probably the *Ram Shila Pujans*, subsequent developments affected rural north India as well. In the case of Piparsod, our test-case village in Shivpuri district, the *Kar Seva* also made an impact. First, four villagers left for Ayodhya after being enrolled by V. Garg, who had coordinated part of the movement in Shivpuri district. Two of these *kar sevaks* were Brahmins who had been involved in the Hindu nationalist movement for some time whereas the other two were new recruits, one from the Scheduled Castes (a *chowkidar*, watchman) the other a Kirar (Other Backward Class). The latter explained that he took part in the *Kar Seva* in order to build the temple (*mandir ka nirman ke lye*). He wanted to go to Ayodhya for 'Bhagwan Ram', and added that he did not support the BJP as such but sympathised with its commitment to build a Ram temple at Ayodhya. He might abandon the party if it betrayed this cause.[56]

None of the four *kar sevaks* reached Ayodhya. Like most of the others, they were stopped as they tried to enter Uttar Pradesh, in their case at Jhansi. However they were arrested for a short while and thus on their return to the village recounted their experience of police repression. Most importantly, the villagers learnt of the 'martyrs of Ayodhya' via the Hindi press and, more dramatically, through the medium of video. In 1990, and more frequently during the 1991 campaign, video-vans toured Madhya Pradesh. Among the tapes shown was that of the *Kar Seva* filmed by J.K. Jain's studio. This exposure to propaganda largely explains the rumours about the death toll in the *Kar Seva* 'repression', some villagers maintaining that thousands of Hindus had met their deaths at Ayodhya.

It is impossible to make generalisations on the basis of these testimonies. What they suggest is that when villagers who had not yet become involved in the Hindu nationalist movement were attracted to it, this was mainly due to emotional motivation – either out of devotion to Ram or anger at the events of October-November 1990. Because of the religious or ethno-religious feelings from which their motivation stemmed, these new supporters of the BJP did not necessarily develop an anti-Muslim bias; they wanted the temple to be built, but often protested that they did not want the mosque to be demolished.[57] In his study of village politics in eastern Uttar Pradesh, G.K. Lieten shows that in mid-1990 around half of the OBC leaders he interviewed agreed that a temple should be built in Ayodhya, but only if it did not lead to communal

---

[56] Interview, 26 Oct. 1991, Piparsod.

[57] In Piparsod, hostility towards the village's few Muslim families was latent; in the 1980s the Panchayat had refused to pay for the construction of a platform from which the *muezzin* could call the prayer. However, these feelings were never translated into moves which excluded Muslims from the local circle of sociability.

tension, a reservation very few Brahmins and Banyas expressed. These OBCs can only envisage the building of the temple alongside the mosque, because they contend that 'holy places cannot be demolished'.[58]

The fact that the Hindu nationalist movement continued to rely to a large extent on religious emotions is one important reason why it remains hard to apply the concept of fascism to the 'Sangh parivar', even though its constituent organisations evolved political practices closer to this form of authoritarianism (see below).

Women played their part in the *Rath Yatra*, many of them donating their *mangalsutras* (sacred marriage necklace) in the name of Ram.[59] Subsequently reporters noticed that women often outnumbered men at BJP meetings, especially in Uttar Pradesh. Journalists explained this phenomenon in terms of the religiosity of Hindu women who wanted a Ram temple built in Ayodhya and thus reacted strongly against the crack down on the *kar sevaks*.[60] Religiosity is certainly an important factor here – the use of the Ram *lalla* (infant Ram) image by the VHP proved very appealing to mothers and probably had already made a profound impact, as Tanika Sarkar suggests.[61] However, many of the women who participated in the *Kar Seva* did so for other reasons. The VHP claimed that 20,000 of the *kar sevaks* involved in the events of October 1990 were female.[62] Sarkar argues that this was a new development since, up to mid-1990, women only featured in the movement's propaganda as mothers. This was the role which the Rashtrasevika Samiti constantly praised as being the most valuable for women to perform.[63] It appears that younger members of the organisation exerted pressure on the high command to allow them a more active role in the Ramjanmabhoomi agitation. In this context, a women's branch parallel to the Bajrang Dal, the Durga Vahini, was established. In the case of these women and more especially of the female *kar sevaks*, religiosity was probably not the only reason for their involvement.

Sarkar suggests convincingly that the Rashtrasevika Samiti 'does enable a specific and socially crucial group of middle class women in moving out of their homebound existence, to reclaim public spaces and

58 G.K. Lieten, 'On casteism and communalism in Uttar Pradesh', *EPW*, 29, 14 (1994), p. 781.

59 *Times of India*, 18 May 1991.

60 *Statesman* (Delhi), 18 and 19 May 1991.

61 T. Sarkar, 'Women's agency within authoritarian communalism: the Rashtrasevika Samiti and Ramjanmabhoomi' in G. Pandey (ed.), *Hindus and others*, op.cit., p. 24.

62 Ibid., p. 27.

63 Ibid., pp. 28-9. The Rashtrasevika Samiti, established in 1936, is an organisation parallel to the RSS and clearly conservative in outlook in so far as the status of women is concerned.

even to acquire a political identity, and gives them access to serious intellectual cogitation'.[64] Paola Bacchetta's study of a Sevika from a middle class Gujarati family illustrates this point.[65] Amrita Basu develops a similar argument in her discussion of Sadhvi Rithambara and Uma Bharti:

It may be liberating for women, who are continuously enjoined to be decorous, to be praised for their good citizenship when they deliver loud, angry, and coarse public speeches. [...] In public speeches, their use of vulgar expression and their ability to address men with familiarity and condescension transgress traditional gender roles and expresses both their anger and their power.[66]

This analysis also applies to a certain extent to the *Kar Seva* since participation in this movement helped women to acquire a political identity. One way of substantiating this assessment is to study how the Hindu nationalist leadership, an overwhelmingly male-dominated group, considered the role of women in the *Kar Seva*. P. K. Datta points out that stories were being written about 'Uma Bharti's escape from the window of the Circuit house where she was detained, and how she cut her hair to escape detection'.[67] This suggests that a new status as activists and even heroes was accorded to women by the Hindu nationalist leadership, a development confirmed at the local level by evidence collected in Madhya Pradesh. For example, there was one woman among the *kar sevaks* who were awarded medals in Bhopal in November 1990.[68] The *sangathan mantri* of the VHP for Mahakoshal, M. Moonje, related a revealing story about the involvement of women in the *Kar Seva*. While entering Uttar Pradesh clandestinely with other *kar sevaks*, he met a group of women who, according to him, came from a village, were uneducated and between 35-40 years old. The youngest asked him, in a forthright manner, for directions to join the *parikrama* (pilgrimage to Ayodhya). They met again later, and the same young woman told Moonje that they had not come for the *parikrama* but for *Kar Seva*, and that they had been fired on. She reportedly said: 'when blood appeared, we cleaned it because it was ours, and now we have to go back because our children wait for us'.[69]

---

[64] Ibid., p. 43.

[65] According to P. Bacchetta, this person 'was attempting to create for herself a new structural position to occupy: that of a perpetually single but tough and respected woman who would impose herself in the public space without definite sexual, gender, or (Indian) regional connotations' ('All our goddesses are armed: religion, resistance and revenge in the life of a militant Hindu nationalist woman', *Bulletin of Concerned Asian Scholars*, 25 (4), Oct.-Dec. 1993, p. 43).

[66] A. Basu, 'Feminism inverted', op. cit., p. 29.

[67] P. K. Datta, 'VHP's Ram', op. cit., p. 62.

[68] *Dainik Jagaran* (Hindi), 16 Nov. 1990, p. 10.

[69] Interview with M. Moonje, 12 Oct. 1991, Bhopal.

The accuracy of many aspects of the story if of course doubtful, but most important for our purpose is the way Moonje narrated it. It reveals that the ideal woman, from the Hindu nationalists' point of view, is now not only maternal and discreet, but also resolute in her dedication to the cause. In this context male Hindu nationalist cadres seem to be prepared to recognise a public role for women. Some women took part in the *Kar Seva* in order to take advantage of this opportunity and not merely on account of their religious devotion. However, social and psychological motivations – often of a different kind – were probably more important in the case of the male *kar sevaks* and, more generally speaking, of the urban youth who supported the agitation.

The *Kar Seva* episode illustrates how the Ayodhya issue appealed to large sections of the Hindu youth. As was obvious in the audiovisual reports, while some of those taking part were men of mature years and some – though few – were clearly from villages, most *kar sevaks* were recruited from among urban youths – as indicated by their style of dress. Their involvement resulted from many factors, most of which were not directly related to religious motives.

As one would expect, these young men invoked their devotion to Ram. The wounded *kar sevaks* who gave their testimonies in the hospital at Faizabad to *Rashtradharma* (a Hindi monthly published by the RSS) insisted that they had been motivated by religion. They regretted that they were unable to fulfill their vow of building the temple and emphasised their determination to come back in order to do so, even if badly wounded.[70] Some of them belonged to teams of *kar sevaks* led by *sadhus* from their home towns. However, more clearly than any kind of religiosity, their narrative reveals a taste for adventure: they dwell on the difficulties encountered in reaching Ayodhya secretly and the risks they undertook. For them, as in the case of most of the *kar sevaks* interviewed by the author in Madhya Pradesh, participation in the *Kar Seva* was primarily a contest against the forces of law and order, and highly demanding in physical terms.

These testimonies are congruent with the version of Ram which the RSS and its affiliates were keen to project. In this image of the muscular warrior-god the *kar sevaks* found a heroic figure whom they wished to emulate and with whom they could identify. It is significant that the Ram of the Hindu nationalists shares many things in common with stereotypical heroes of Hindi popular cinema. For urban youths, these films often provide role models which enable them to sublimate their daily lives. Most of the time, such youths are unemployed and to a large extent devoid of self-esteem.[71]

---

[70]   *Rashtradharma* (Hindi), Jan. 1991 pp. 26-36.

[71]   This is based on interviews with members of the Bajrang Dal in Bhopal where most of

Taking part in the movement launched by the Hindu nationalists in the name of Ram enabled them to associate with an idealised, virile and moral figure. To some extent it provided their life with meaning. Interestingly, in December 1992, during the second *Kar Seva*, Uma Bharti exhorted Hindu youths to change their life of mediocrity.[72]

The sociology and psychology of the *kar sevaks* and, more precisely, the Bajrang Dal are very similar to the concerns the Shiv Sena had been representing for many years. According to Gérard Heuzé, this organisation 'arose directly from urban unemployment'.[73] In his study of the Shiv Sainiks of Chhattisgarh, Heuzé shows that most of them are poorly educated young people – they generally lack fluency in the English language – who are unemployed or who regard their job as unsatisfactory; in fact frustration is their common denominator. Their addiction to films stems largely from the need to forget what they perceive as their miserable condition and acquire a positive identity by associating themselves with, and emulating fictional characters. Some of them, Heuzé points out, long 'to be the hero of a Bombay film in which violence leads to justice'.[74] They are keen to fight Muslims in order to assert themselves, to prove their strength. Moreover they echo all the usual negative stereotypes of Muslims (polygamy leading to rapid population increase, sympathy for Pakistan, etc.). Such a psychological profile appears to be common to most of the young *kar sevaks* who went to Ayodhya in order to test themselves, physically and morally, in the name of the sacred cause of Ram.

These young men are not interested in doctrinal rigour or discipline. Moreover, the organisations where they are found in great numbers, the Shiv Sena and the Bajrang Dal, are known for their loose structures. While the Shiv Sainiks often openly despise the RSS (which is seen as a staid and old-fashioned body) the Bajrang Dalis, probably because they are exposed to the influence of *pracharaks*, generally express respect for the 'Sangh'. However, they are generally unwilling to follow its discipline. Till 1993 the Bajrang Dal did not even have a uniform; its members were recognised merely because they often wore a saffron headband bearing the word 'Ram'. The Ramjanmabhoomi movement provided the members of the Bajrang Dal and the Shiv Sena with a highly appealing cause and a kind of shared political idiom – if not ideology – which coalesced in 1990 after the *Kar Seva*. Religious belief is less important as a unifying

---

the Bajrang Dalis whom the present author met were idle or involved in the lottery business (observations made in Aug. 1992).

[72] A *kar sevak* from Andhra Pradesh, an unemployed graduate, admitted that 'she had made a lot of sense'. He said he had come here to build the temple at the cost of his own life if necessary (*Times of India*, 5 Dec. 1992).

[73] G. Heuzé, 'Shiv Sena and "National" Hinduism', *EPW*, 3 Oct. 1992, p. 2189.

[74] Ibid., p. 2191.

factor than the sentiment of having taking part in the same 'epics' sanctified by the 'martyr of brothers'; if not based on religiosity, this 'culture' developed in conformity with the ethno-religious propaganda of the Hindu nationalist organisations.

Another important common denominator of the *kar sevaks* (from the Bajrang Dal and the Shiv Sena) lay in their social background. In Maharashtra, Shiv Sainiks are traditionally recruited among the middle castes – predominantly Marathas – and the middle classses.[75] Those studied by Heuzé in Chhattisgarh were from high castes and most had been involved in the anti-Mandal agitation before taking part in the *Kar Seva*.

The youths who took part in the Ramjanmabhoomi agitation in 1990 often belonged to the upper castes. A majority of the 21 'martyrs' of the *Kar Seva* claimed by *Rashtradharma* had Brahmin and Banya names and among the wounded *kar sevaks* interviewed by the paper three had well-known backward caste names, five were Brahmins, one a Kayasth and one a Banya.[76] Similarly, among the twelve *kar sevaks* who were honoured at Bhopal in November 1990, besides one Yadav (OBC) and one Muslim there were two Jains, one Kayasth, one Banya and one Brahmin.[77] This over-representation of the upper castes has to be understood in relation to the Mandal report protests.

In August and September 1990, in reaction to V.P. Singh's announcement that the report's recommendations would be implemented, thousands of young people from the upper and intermediate castes and lower middle class families, mostly students, took to the streets out of fear that the new quotas would reduce their career prospects in the public sector, and probably also because these reservations questioned the 'social order'. Hundreds were arrested in the course of road blockades and other violent protests and a number of demonstrators committed suicide by self-immolation in the weeks preceding the *Kar Seva*. In many cases, the same young people took part in both agitations,[78] some of whom were attracted to the Ayodhya agitation through having participated in the anti-reservation campaign, because the latter had created an atmosphere conducive to mobilisation and sacrifice, but, most importantly, because

---

[75] M.F. Katzenstein, *Ethnicity and equality – the Shiv Sena and preferential policies in Bombay*, Ithaca NY: Cornell University Press, 1979, pp. 69-75.

[76] *Rashtradharma* (Hindi), Jan. 1991, p. 18.

[77] *Dainik Jagaran* (Hindi), 16 Nov. 1990, p.10.

[78] Interviews with BJYM activists from Madhya Pradesh testify to this. S. Mayaram observed a similar situation in Rajasthan ('Communal violence in Jaipur', *EPW*, 13-20 Nov. 1993, p. 2530). See also the situation in Gujarat as analysed in chapter 4, entitled 'Hindutva as a savarna Purana', by A. Nandy, S. Trivedy, S. Mayaram and A. Yagnik, (*Creating a nationality*, op. cit.)

the Hindu nationalist organisations were opposed to caste-based reservations.

As early as August 1990 the BJP declared its preference for quotas defined by economic criteria. The *Organiser* denounced the very principle of reservations by saying that it 'provides a premium of mediocrity'. Other BJP leaders repeated such declarations at the local level. One of their number, J.K. Jain, who had held a seat in the Rajya Sabha since March 1990, began a fast over the issue.[79] Not surprisingly this move was criticised by the party high command and Jain had to fall in line with the BJP's official policy.[80] The party then shrewdly eluded the debate on reservations by launching its counter-offensive in the shape of the *Rath Yatra*.

Hindu nationalists leaders and organs (such as the *Organiser*) presented the Ayodhya movement as the means of uniting all Hindus in such a way as to defuse the OBCs' demands. By trying to make the OBCs regard themselves as Hindus first and foremost the RSS combine could preserve the social *status quo*. This strategy naturally attracted additional support to the *Rath Yatra* and later the *Kar Seva* from upper caste Hindus who felt threatened by the reservations policy. To a certain extent, the *kar sevaks* from high caste families whose socio-economic status was precarious represented the modern equivalents of the downwardly mobile Maharashtrian Brahmins who, as Ashis Nandy has shown, joined the Hindu Mahasabha and the RSS in the 1920s, '30s and '40s in order to counter the challenge to the social order presented by the mass politics of Gandhi.

To sum up, it appears that there was a coalescence of 'Hindu feeling', to a greater or lesser degree, in various parts of India. However there was a wide variety of motives driving those who participated in the *Rath Yatra* and *Kar Seva*, ranging from religiosity to upper caste activism. We must now turn to those elements of the modern middle class which did not on the whole play an active role in the Hindu nationalist mobilisations of 1990 but rallied to the BJP in large numbers. For such people religious factors apparently played a minor role compared to their opposition to the reservations policy and commitment to a more disciplined (or even authoritarian) form of politics and the clean image of the BJP.

---

[79] Originally a medical practitioner, J.K. Jain later became president of Jain Medical Centre, Medical Computer, Medical Television, Jain Studios and Video on Wheels and the International Federation for Family Health. His career illustrates the emerging modern entrepreneurial face of the Hindu nationalist movement (Parliament of India, *Rajya Sabha Who's Who*, New Delhi: Rajya Sabha Secretariat, 1990, p. 122.)

[80] *National Mail*, 5 Sept. 1990.

The affinities between the new élite and the BJP: the impact of social and economic change

In the late 1980s and early 1990s the BJP began to attract increasing support from the modern upper middle class, a group that had expanded since the mid-1980s because of the policy of economic liberalisation pursued by Rajiv Gandhi's government. This policy, which stressed the benefits of rapid modernisation and gave more legitimacy to the capitalist ethic, also changed this class's outlook. Its system of values was based – in theory at least – on merit gained through hard work and thus its members showed little concern for the social needs of the lower classes and were antagonistic to the very principle of reservations. As early as 1988, Rajni Kothari highlighted the affinities which exist between this mentality and Hindu nationalism:

The new elite that has emerged and follows those in command in the global framework no longer tries to keep up the socialist rhetoric but is following the capitalist path. They, in fact, bluntly say that those millions of people who are left out are in fact a drag. They are the source of continuous demand, continuous noise. [...] This includes the poor, the under- privileged communities in the ethnic sense, the tribals, the dalits, the former untouchables and it includes the religious minorities.[81]

Muslims figure predominantly here, not only because they are over-represented in the lower strata of Indian society but also because they form one of the country's biggest minorities. And besides poverty, diversity is what the new élite dislikes most, again because it hinders the development of 'a strong India, economically as well as militarily; hence one can observe a perspective in which the upper strata of Hindu society are being pushed more and more to a majority chauvinist model for the control of the State'.[82]

One finds other affinities between the urban middle class and the BJP in so far as attitudes towards authority are concerned. In 1993, an opinion poll conducted by MARG (a sample of 1,715 adults in Bombay, Delhi, Calcutta, Madras and Bangalore, many of whom were probably from the middle class) revealed that 58% of interviewees agreed with the following proposition: 'If the country is to progress it needs a dictator.'[83] This trend became increasingly apparent in 1990-1 at a time when the BJP reaffirmed its faith in a presidential form of government intended to guarantee a stronger Centre,[84] and can probably be traced to the impact of the

[81]   R. Kothari, 'Class and communalism in India', *EPW*, 3 Dec., 1988, p. 2591.

[82]   Ibid., p. 2592.

[83]   *Sunday*, 9 Jan. 1994, p. 59.

[84]   *Statesman* (Delhi), 16 Jan. 1991 and 2 Feb. 1991.

reservations issue. As a result, the BJP began to garner additional support not only from its traditional base in the trading castes – who had become more powerful in the wake of economic liberalisation – but also from executives, ex-servicemen and former administrative cadres.

A brief survey by *India Today* revealed that the growth in popularity of the BJP among business executives was chiefly motivated by the desire to improve the country's fortunes. One such businessman commented: 'We have reached rock-bottom in world stature, economically, in every way. If the BJP is an alternative to a better end then so be it.'[85] Another considered that 'the rest have monkeyed around with the economy and with law and order for so long.' The BJP attracted support by default because the Congress (I) was deeply unpopular. Moreover the BJP probably won over former Congress (I) supporters all the more easily because it appeared to be the sole proponent of a political project – the building of a strong India – which had been established and assiduously promoted by Indira Gandhi. In the 1970s she partly succeeded in marginalising the Jana Sangh on account of her militant nationalism and because she was identified with authority and power. By the early 1990s, in the mind of many Indians, the Congress (I) had lost this mantle. The image of the party in power was further damaged because of its perceived corruption and inefficiency. Its capacity to respond to the successive demands of different elements within Indian society, which had long enabled Congress to project itself as the party of consensus, had become a handicap in the minds of many in the modern middle class, who thought it led to inconsistency and demagogy. In this context factionalism, which had helped Congress to adapt to the emerging sectional demands of Indian society, now rendered it impotent. In contrast, the BJP appeared to be a more coherent party and was therefore better placed to manage India's affairs efficiently. Such attitudes, with occasional qualifications, were common to members of the upper middle classes other than the executives interviewed by *India Today*, e.g. ex-servicemen and former administrative cadres who supported the BJP in the early 1990s.

A substantial number of retired military officers joined the BJP in 1991. Up till then, Jaswant Singh, a retired major from an aristocratic background in Rajasthan who was a member of the Rajya Sabha between 1980 and 1989 and of the Lok Sabha from 1989 onwards, had been almost their only representative. Suddenly, former members of the armed services, most of whom had been high-ranking officers, began to enter the party; among those who joined in 1991 were 2 Air Marshals, 6 Lieutenant-Generals, 4 Major-Generals, 4 Brigadiers, 1 Air Commodore, 4 Colonels, 1 Lieutenant-Colonel, 2 Wing Commanders, 2 Majors, 3 Captains, 1

---

[85] Cited in *India Today*, 15 May 1991, p. 19.

Squadron Leader and 1 Flying Officer.[86] Along with these servicemen, at least one retired Inspector-General of police and 2 retired Director-Generals of police joined the ranks of the party. The latter had already forged close links with the RSS: B.P. Singhal was the brother of Ashok Singhal and Shrish Chandra Dixit had joined the VHP after retiring in 1984.[87] In fact, a number of servicemen who had gone over to the BJP since the late 1980s had been involved with the RSS combine for some time. Capt. Jagat Vir Singh Drona, who had unsuccessfully contested the Kanpur seat in 1989 on a BJP ticket, had been a member of the RSS since he was 12 and became a *sanghchalak* on leaving the Army.[88]

Militant Hinduism was not predominant among the motives of most of the ex-army men who joined the BJP. Maj.-Gen. B.C. Khanduri, who was elected MP for Pauri Garhwal in 1991, even expressed mixed feelings about the *Rath Yatra*.[89] Besides the fact that the BJP stood for better pensions for soldiers, the most common explanations of the party's success in attracting their support were its discipline and stand for a strong India, which entails an aggressive defence of its frontier, especially in Kashmir.[90]

Bhuwan Chandra Khanduri, a nephew of the late Congress leader H.N. Bahuguna, had been approached by M.M. Joshi in mid-March 1991 and was the first general to join the BJP, in April, a few weeks before the elections. He explained his decision in the following terms:

One motivation was based on nationalistic feelings. I was quite sad of the turn of events in the country, the way politicians were concentrating on selfish motives rather than national interest. When I retired in October 1990 there was a feeling of distress and disgust. And the BJP was a party with a nationalist approach, disciplined in its behaviour and with certain clear-cut policy parameters.[91]

One of the retired Lieutenant-Generals approved openly of the BJP's demand for the abrogation of Article 370.[92] Former servicemen also felt aggrieved with Congress (I) over the way it dealt with the purchase of military equipment in the 'Bofors affair'. In the view of some of them, the episode suggested that the ruling party might subordinate the country's defence's interests to questions of finance.[93] The reputation for integrity claimed by the BJP was thus another factor in its favour.

[86] *Statesman* (Delhi), 9 July 1991, and *Times of India*, 30 May 1991.
[87] *Organiser*, 28 April 1991, p. 5, and *Times of India*, 22 July 1991.
[88] He was elected MP for Kanpur in 1991 (ibid.,12 July 1991).
[89] Ibid., 2 July 1991.
[90] Ibid., 30 May 1991.
[91] Interview with B.C. Khanduri, Paris, 23 March 1994.
[92] *Organiser*, 28 April 1991, p. 5.
[93] I. Malhotra, 'Political Commentary – Khaki to saffron via khadi', *Statesman* (Delhi), 23 May 1991.

This factor might also explain the adherence to the BJP of some ex-IAS cadres, a body usually known for its relative probity. Among the more prominent figures here was T.N. Chaturvedi, a former Controller and Auditor General.[94] From the Indian Foreign Service Brajesh Mishra, the son of D.P. Mishra, joined the BJP and was appointed to its National Executive. As far as these former administrators are concerned, opposition to the implementation of the Mandal Commission report yet again contributed to their decision to enter politics, not least because a high percentage of the sons and daughters of IAS cadres try to join the central administrative services. Moreover T.N. Chaturvedi expressed concern regarding the implementation of the Mandal report because he considered that the quotas meant for the Scheduled Castes and Scheduled Tribes failed to achieve their objective. He also felt it 'important to ensure that caste divisions are not accentuated.'[95]

Thus, as we have seen, the BJP expanded its base among the middle class in two directions in the late 1980s and early 1990s. Its primary source of support had formerly been found among the high castes from the urban 'middle world' – shopkeepers, lawyers and white-collar workers of intermediate rank. At the time of writing, the BJP has made inroads among the lower middle classes – especially students or unemployed youths – and the new élite. These two poles of the middle class often shared a common high caste background and an antipathy towards the Mandal Commission report and its implementation. However they have little in common beyond this and one might envisage tensions developing between them. In particular, at a later stage the upper middle class, which is strongly attached to law and order, may resent the disturbances orchestrated by the militant youth wing of the Hindu nationalists in the context of the Ram movement.

The main point, for our purpose, which emerges from this overview of the social base of the Hindu nationalist movement is that many of its supporters were motivated not by religious or ethno-religious themes but by social factors, especially fear of the rise of the OBCs. This diversity of motives was a potential source of weakness for the RSS and its affiliates. The apparent advantage of the strategy of ethno-religious mobilisation lies in the fact that it relies on emotions which transcend differences in social status and even political opinion. However, this state of affairs also meant that the RSS and its affiliates were dependent on an emotional wave which could not be sustained indefinitely. Indeed, in 1990-1, the BJP

---

94 *Organiser*, 28 April 1991, pp. 5-14, and 12 May 1991, p. 6, and interview with T.N. Chaturvedi, 22 Feb. 1995, New Delhi.

95 Cited in *Organiser*, 28 April 1991, p. 14.

seemed anxious to translate this mobilisation into votes as quickly as possible. Yet the mid-term Lok Sabha elections of May-June 1991 enabled the BJP to make significant gains without expanding decisively beyond the Hindi belt, and its success was due nearly as much to social reasons as to a classic Hindu mobilisation.

The 1991 elections

The origins of the crisis which led to the dissolution of the Lok Sabha and to the 1991 elections can be traced back to the events of November 1990, when V.P. Singh, already lacking the parliamentary support of the BJP, was further weakened by a split in his party, with the formation of the Janata Dal (S) (S for Socialist); consequently, on 7 November his government lost a vote of confidence in the Lok Sabha. Following the resignation of V.P. Singh, Chandra Shekhar, the leader of the JD(S), was able to form another minority government, which held office with the support of Congress (I). However, on 6 March 1991 Chandra Shekhar resigned after the Congress (I) withdrew its support and on the 13th the Union President dissolved the Lok Sabha so that fresh elections, from which Rajiv Gandhi hoped to gain a decisive advantage, could be held in May. The BJP launched an aggressive campaign and tried to wrest electoral benefit from the Ayodhya affair.

An aggressive electoral campaign.

The BJP changed its president in February 1991, Advani having completed more than the two 2 year terms allowed by the party constitution because of exceptional circumstances. He was replaced by Murli Manohar Joshi, one of the party's General Secretaries,[96] who led the BJP in an electoral campaign which was radical in tone.

The launching of the Hindu nationalist campaign in fact took place on a VHP platform, one indication of its religious nature and of its stridency. During the winter of 1990-1, Chandra Shekhar had persuaded the VHP and the BMAC to exchange evidence substantiating their claims to the Babri Masjid. After three rounds of talks the VHP accused the BMAC of adopting 'dilatory tactics' and decided to 'resume mass action'.[97] A month

---

[96] While studying at Allahabad University, he had been taught physics by Rajendra Singh who went on to become General Secretary of the RSS. After he in turn became a teacher of physics in the same university, Joshi remained close to the RSS. He stood for election only once, his primary role being that of an ideologue (*Times of India*, 15 Dec. 1991). For a short biographical sketch see *Sixth Lok Sabha Who's Who*, op. cit., p. 252.

[97] *Organiser*, 17 Feb. 1991.

earlier, when the VHP had announced plans for a *gherao* of Parliament House on April 4, Singhal had declared:

At least 10 million Ram Bhaktas, including saints, *sadhus, dharmacharyas* and *shankaracharyas* will reach the national capital to see to it that Government, which is the biggest obstacle in the construction of Shri Ram Temple at Ayodhya, either surrenders or collapses.[98]

The dissolution of the Lok Sabha, according to the *Organiser*, called into question the desirability of holding the rally but eventually 'the decision to stick to the plan was taken on the occasion of the meeting of the Akhil Bharatiya Pratinidhi Sabha of [...] the RSS at Nagpur where top leaders of all sister organisations met to take stock of the situation'.[99]

This decision, and the way it was implemented, were consistent with the aggressive posture which the Hindu nationalist organisations had adopted in their bid for power. Such developments suggest that the Hindu nationalist movement was developing authoritarian features. Since the mid-1960s and especially after Deoras became its *sarsanghchalak* in 1973, the RSS had become far more interested in gaining power. However, the demonstrations of 1991 differed in important respects from those which had been launched on other occasions. For example, whereas at the time of the 1966 campaign against cow slaughter the aim of the 'Sangh parivar' had been to force MPs to adopt a particular measure, in 1991 Ashok Singhal was speaking as if he wanted to push through a vote of no-confidence in the government and that the judgement of the crowds in the street was preferable to that of the electorate. When a similar policy had been adopted by the 'JP movement' in the 1970s, the RSS had agreed to pursue non-violent methods, whereas in 1991 Ashok Singhal declared that since the politicians had refused to understand the language of persuasion, the VHP had decided to talk to them in the 'language of strength'.[100]

The rally brought together between 1 and 3 million people, according to various estimates, some of whom came from very distant, often rural, areas.[101] Seated next to each other on the platform were leaders of the BJP (Advani, Vajpayee, Joshi), the RSS (Sudarshan), the VHP (Singhal, Dalmia) and religious figures (Uma Bharti, Sadhvi Rithambara, Mahant Avaidyanath). The BJP was obviously not the sole master of its electoral campaign, although the party tried to avoid being identified with the issue of Ayodhya alone.

In 1991 the BJP repeatedly underlined its 'high integrity, consistent

[98] Cited in *Statesman* (Delhi), 17 Jan. 1991.

[99] *Organiser*, 31 March 1991, p. 16.

[100] *Statesman* (Delhi), 5 April 1991.

[101] See the interviews by a reporter from the *Statesman* (Delhi), 5 April 1991.

ideology, internal discipline and stability, mature leadership, and a dedicated cadre to do them all',[102] which, it claimed, contrasted with those of
the other parties. It also tried to satisfy the expectations of various social
groups. Its slogans were 'let's go for Ram Rajya', and *'Ram'* (freedom
from fear), *'Roti'* (bread – freedom from want) and *'Insaaf'* (justice –
freedom from discrimination). The first expression attempted to appropriate a Gandhian theme; the second referred to the Hindu feeling of
vulnerability, as exemplified in BJP leaflets :

Ever since we earned our freedom, we have been living in fear of losing it. Fear
of separatism, fear of terrorism, fear of exploitation, fear of losing one's cultural
identity.

'Freedom from discrimination' referred to so-called special treatment
in favour of the minorities – which was also described as 'pseudo-
secularism' and 'minorityism' – and to the issue of reservations:

If Congress used minorityism to divide us, their worthy successors chose casteism
to tear us apart. Turning Indians against Indians. Brothers against brothers.[103]

Certain themes of the BJP campaign in the English language press were
framed so as to echo the anxieties of high caste and middle class Hindus.
An advertisement published in the *Times of India* under the slogan
'Freedom of want' was aimed specificlly at the expectations of the
middle class:

The BJP shall liberate the economy from clutches of the bureaucracy so that
individual initiative can spearhead production.[104]

As in 1989, the campaign addressed topics other than mobilisation
around religion, although Ayodhya was clearly its central preoccupation.

The BJP as a national party?

After the elections of May-June 1991, the Congress (I) regained a relative
majority, thanks in part to a wave of sympathy following the assassination

[102] BJP advertisement published in the *Times of India* (4 May 1991).

[103] BJP advertisement published in the *National Mail* (6 May 1991).

[104] *Times of India*, 6 April 1991. This slogan took up the presidential address given by M.
M. Joshi a few months earlier: 'I would wish that the economy of the country is freed
from those constraints that kill industriousness, promote corruption, make
industrialisation more expensive and decrease production. Only the restraint required for
social justice is justifiable. Excellence in trade and commerce should be publicly
honoured and Indian industrialists encouraged to come forward as first-rate
manufacturers on the international level' (*Presidential address by Dr Murli Manohar
Joshi at the 5th National Convention-Jaipur 1 February 1991*, New Delhi: BJP Central
Office, 1991, p. 21).

of Rajiv Gandhi in between the two dates scheduled for voting. The BJP progressed from 85 to 120 seats and from 11.36% to 20.08% of the valid votes. At an all-India level the party benefited from the fact that since 1989 40 million 18-21 year olds, among whom the BJP was relatively popular, were now enfranchised. However the situation differed greatly from one state to another, as the adjoining map shows on p. 440. The strength of the BJP is still concentrated in the Hindi belt, with the exception of Gujarat. The party remains very weak in the South – except in Karnataka – and in the East and North-East. In order to provide an overview of the all-India position of the BJP, we shall look beyond the situation in our test-case of Madhya Pradesh by relying on specialist studies of other areas.

The Hindu nationalist parties have always been a marginal force in South India. Even in 1989 the BJP did not manage to poll 5% of the valid votes in any of the four states. In Chapter 1, the fact that South India was unreceptive to Hindu nationalism was partly explained by the fact that this ideology was too closely associated with the Sanskritised culture of North India, by the smaller proportion of upper castes beyond the Hindi belt and by the greater integration of the local Muslim community. Things have changed with time. On the one hand, South India witnessed a new Islam in the 1980s as indicated by the conversions of Meenakshipuram and the increasing number of Muslims working in the Arab world. On the other hand, the Hindu nationalists gave up the idea of establishing Hindi as the only national language and have tended to replace its Sanskritised Brahminical ideology by a sort of nationalist devotionalism in the framework of their agitation in the name of Ram. These adjustments and the simultaneous development of the RSS, especially in Kerala, partly explain the electoral growth of the BJP in 1991. However, the party remained marginal except in Karnataka where its success seems to be attributable largely to factors other than Hindu nationalism.

In Kerala and Tamil Nadu the BJP failed to make a breakthrough. In Kerala, where the Jana Sangh and its successors have never won a single seat in elections to the state assembly or the Lok Sabha, the BJP polled 4.61 % of the vote. As James Manor points out, its 'extreme weakness was apparent from its decision to revert to its 1989 role as covert supporter of the Congress (I) against the Communist Party of India (Marxist)'.[105] The position of the BJP in Tamil Nadu was even worse; it received only 1.65% of the total vote. In Andhra Pradesh, the party polled 9.63%, a

---

[105] J. Manor, 'BJP in South India: 1991 General Election', *EPW*, 13 June 1992, p. 1267. The BJP, which had received one million votes in the District Council elections held in December 1991, polled only 675,000 votes in the general election probably because many of its sympathisers preferred to support the Congress (I) as the only serious rival to the Communists (*India Today*, 31 Oct., 1991 p. 20).

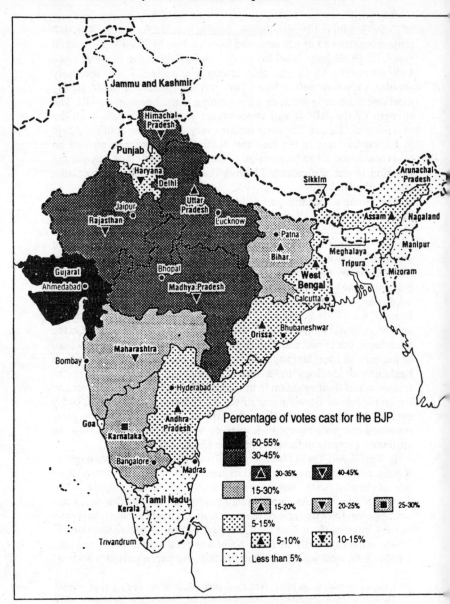

VOTES WON BY THE B.J.P. IN THE NATIONAL LOK SABHA
ELECTION, 1991 (BY STATE)

substantial improvement over the 1.97% it gained in 1989. But much of that increase was accounted for by its showing in Hyderabad and Secunderabad and by the fact that it contested 41 seats instead of 2 in 1989 when it reached an electoral agreement with the Telugu Desam Party.[106]

North of Andhra Pradesh, in the Eastern states of Orissa, West Bengal and Assam, the BJP made inroads but its score remained around 10% of the valid votes. In West Bengal, even through it did not win a single seat, the party progressed from 1.67 to 11.67%.[107] It received heavy support among the non-Bengali community of Calcutta, where businessmen from the Hindi belt, Marwaris and Gujaratis, traditionally opposed the CPI(M). According to press reports, 'every Maruti car in the Burra Bazar area sported a "Jai Shri Ram" sticker'.[108] However it is undeniable that Bengali voters in Calcutta were also attracted to the BJP.[109]

In West Bengal the rise of the party was not predicated on the exploitation of the Ayodhya issue partly because, as Sumit Ganguly points out, 'owing to the particular translation of the Ram myth into Bengali, he is not considered to be particularly God-like' and the Krishna cult that had developed in Bengal was 'opposed to one centered around Ram'.[110] The BJP's propaganda focussed instead on the issue of illegal, predominantly Muslim, immigration from Bangladesh. This tactic was especially successful in border districts and among those who had been displaced at Partition. One particularly emotive question asked by BJP activists was: 'Do you want to become refugees for the second time in your life because of Bangladeshi infiltrators?'.[111] It must be emphasised that the activist network of the RSS combine in West Bengal had been in place for many years. According to the *Organiser*, in 1992 there were 1,500 *shakhas* and 225 *pracharaks* in the state and 116 full time VHP workers.[112] In Assam too the BJP concentrated more on the immigration issue during the election campaign.[113] Nine of the ten Assembly seats it won and its two Lok Sabha seats were in the Bengali dominated Barak valley in southern Assam. Despite remarkable progress in West Bengal and Assam, the BJP remained weak in the East, the North-East and in most of the Southern states in 1991.

[106] J. Manor, 'BJP in South India', op. cit., p. 1268.

[107] For a statistical overview, see A. Roy, 'BJP's rise as a mass force', *EPW*, 29 June 1991, p. 1592.

[108] *Times of India*, 10 Feb. 1993; see also *Statesman* (Delhi), 13 May 1991.

[109] For a constituency-wide analysis of the election in the city, see A. Mitra, 'BJP in West Bengal-End of political polarization', in ibid., 9 Aug. 1991.

[110] S. Ganguly, 'The salience of national issues in the tenth general election in West Bengal' in H. Gould and S. Ganguly (eds), *India votes*, op. cit., p. 433.

[111] *Statesman* (Delhi), 13 May 1991, p. 9.

[112] *Organiser*, 1 March 1992, p. 9.

[113] *Statesman* (Delhi), 13 May, 1991.

If we now turn to the states where it performed better, it becomes useful to differentiate the states where it was in office from the rest. In the latter category, the BJP's best performance was in Gujarat where the party won 50.37% of the valid votes and 20 seats out of 25. In this state, the Ayodhya issue seemed to have been more important than elsewere. In his account of the 1991 elections in Gujarat, Ghanshyam Shah mentions Hindu religious feelings as a factor in the BJP's success. The way *kathakars* (religious story-tellers of the *Ramayana*) such as Morari Bapu, who sided with the BJP, attracted 'a cross-section of society both in urban and rural areas'[114] was revealing in this respect. The popularity of Deepika Chikhalia and Arvind Trivedi, who had, respectively, played Sita and Ravana in the television serialisation of the *Ramayana* and who were both elected as MPs, illustrates the same phenomenon.

However, social factors also help to account for the BJP's rise. Shah points out that: 'The growth of the middle class in Gujarat has been disproportionate to the economic growth of the state. This has resulted in a steep increase in the number of educated unemployment and consequent expansion of the lumpen element in urban areas.'[115] The BJP were quick to exploit this phenomenon; as early as 1990 its election manifesto contained a demand that Gujaratis be given preference in public undertakings and government departments. It also promised an allowance for educated unemployed youth.

Social factors were even more in evidence in the states where the decision to implement the Mandal Commission recommendations had a bigger impact, such as Karnataka and Uttar Pradesh. In 1991 Karnataka saw the most dramatic improvement in the BJP's showing anywhere in India, the party receiving 28.78% of the vote as against 2.55% in 1989 and 4.7% in 1984. Scrutinising the five constituencies where its candidates won seats, however, Manor emphasises the importance of local factors and the 'belief among many Lingayats and Vokkaligas that both the Congress (I) and the Janata Dal had abandoned them in favour of the "backward classes"'.[116] These two dominant landed 'jati'-clusters were not considered as Other Backward Classes in the Mandal report; the Janata Dal, therefore, alienated them because of its commitment to the OBCs and the Congress (I) did likewise by nominating a larger number of Backward Caste candidates than usual.

Many disgruntled Lingayats and Vokkaligas felt forced to seek an alternative to the two main parties, and there was only one place to turn – the BJP, which carefully nominated many members of these groups for parliament. It was this,

[114] G. Shah, 'Tenth Lok Sabha elections-BJP's victory in Gujarat', op. cit., p. 2922.

[115] Ibid., p. 2921.

[116] J. Manor, 'BJP in South India', op. cit., p. 1270.

rather than a widespread commitment to the Hindu nationalist ideals of the BJP, that mainly accounts for its increase in popular support at this election.[117]

In Uttar Pradesh, the 'Mandal effect' was even more in evidence. Here, the BJP won 51 of the 85 Lok Sabha seats and 211 of the 425 Vidhan Sabha seats, which enabled it to form a government even though it received less than one-third of the valid vote. That such a modest share of the vote yielded so many seats is accounted for by the large number of parties in the field. In many constituencies, there was a four-way fight: besides the Congress (I) and the BJP, there were now two parties in the fray representing primarily the Backward Castes, the Janata Dal and the Samajwadi Janata Party (SJP), born of the Janata Dal (Socialist). The JD won 25.3% of the valid votes while the SJP received 13.1%. Had this schism not split the OBC vote, the BJP would have won only 39 Lok Sabha seats according to Brass's estimates.[118]

Nearly all the victories of the JD (22) and the SJP (4) occurred in the western and eastern parts of the state where there are the greatest concentrations of OBCs. Obviously, the latter appreciated the way the two parties supported the implementation of the Mandal report. By contrast, the bulk of BJP voters were to be found among Brahmins, Rajputs, Banyas and Bhumihars.[119] The shift in allegiance of large numbers of Brahmins from the Congress (I) to the BJP was an important factor in the latter's success.[120] Among the explanations of such disaffection were the indifferent performance of the Congress (I), its efforts to woo the Muslim community and the rapid decline of the party's organisation at the local and state level. This was the result partly of factionalism and partly of the lack of strong leaders. Men such as N.D. Tiwari were ageing. The Ayodhya issue also strongly motivated the vote of the upper castes, especially after the aborted *Kar Seva* of October-November 1990 which created much resentment against Mulayam Singh Yadav, the then Janata Dal Chief Minister. Once again, however, a more important factor was the high proportion of upper castes voting for the BJP because of 'anti-Mandal sentiment'. Harold Gould argues that the BJP's 'ethnoreligious

---

[117] Ibid., p. 1271. Moreover, except in Mangalore, the RSS-VHP-BJP cadres were not present in force and the latter had to nominate new recruits, often ex-Congressmen, such as the son of the last Maharajah of Mysore, S.N. Wodiyar, who lost in the capital of the former princely state.

[118] P. Brass, 'The rise of the BJP and the future of party politics in Uttar Pradesh' in H. Gould and S. Ganguly (eds), *India votes*, op. cit., p. 281.

[119] Ibid., p. 266 and H. Gould, 'Mandal, Mandir and Dalits: melding class with ethnoreligious conflict in India's tenth general election', ibid., p. 303.

[120] This trend has been noticed by many observers in Uttar Pradesh (see, for instance, *Times of India*, 15 June 1991). Brahmins represented 9.2% of the population in the United Provinces in 1931.

strategy' was an 'implicit class strategy',[121] and Paul Brass contends that the upper caste vote for the BJP has 'not been *for* the BJP but was "anti-Mandal"'.[122]

While the BJP benefited from the anti-reservation sentiment of the dominant groups in Uttar Pradesh and Karnataka, where they represent a high proportion of the population, the party suffered from its opposition to the recommendations of the Mandal report in states where OBCs were more numerous and have acquired a certain class consciousness. Here the BJP failed to make a breakthrough. In Bihar, it won only 5 seats – 3 less than in 1989 – as against 28 for the Janata Dal. The reservations controversy had consequences even inside the state party unit since it was an important factor in the split, just before the 1991 elections, of 13 MLAs – most of whom belonged to the OBCs and the Scheduled Castes – who formed the Sampurna Kranti Dal (Party for total revolution).[123] In 1991, the ticket was given to a majority of Upper Caste candidates (21 against 17 Backward Castes),[124] a decision which proved to be counter-productive in a state where OBCs form a majority (50.7% of the total population according to the 1931 census).

In Haryana, a state whose hinterland is largely dominated by the Jats – a farming caste which forms one-fourth of the population – the BJP did not win a single seat and polled only 10.17% of the total vote. Here, the Hindu nationalist parties never succeeded in attracting much support from the rural population; its pockets of influence were concentrated in towns where displaced persons from Punjab – about one-fifth of the total population – formed its main base. However, in 1989 and 1991 these 'Punjabis' were more inclined to vote in favour of the Congress (I).[125]

In Maharashtra also the BJP-Shiv Sena combine experienced a setback on account of the strength of the Congress (I), ably managed by Sharad Pawar, and of the OBC vote. In the 1980s, the association of the BJP and the Shiv Sena worked in each other's favour. The former attracted more upper caste, middle class Hindus while the latter had many OBCs among its cadres.[126] In 1989, this alliance helped the BJP to win 10 Lok Sabha

[121] H. Gould, Mandal, Mandir and Dalits', op. cit., p. 298.

[122] P. Brass, 'The rise of the BJP', op. cit., p. 266. Brass points out that 'Anti-Mandal sentiments reflects deep-seated concerns on the part of the upper-caste groups about the growing threat to their economic and political power from the middle castes in virtually all districts of the state.' (Ibid).

[123] *National Mail*, 7 Jan. 1991, and *Statesman* (Delhi), 12 May 1991.

[124] *Times of India*, 24 Apr. 1991, p. 9.

[125] P. Wallace, 'The regionalization of Indian electoral politics 1989-90: Punjab and Haryana' and 'India's 1991 elections: regional factors in Haryana and Punjab' in H. Gould and S. Ganguly (eds), *India votes*, op. cit., pp. 150 and 408.

[126] R. Sardesai, 'The complementarity of Ram and Shivaji', *Times of India*, 27 July 1991.

seats with 23.72% of the valid votes. However, in 1990, Bal Thackeray 'launched an intemperate outburst against the Mandal report despite the party's new found base being the OBCs'.[127] This policy further alienated the organised farmer groups, such as the Shetkari Sanghatana, which had already refused to endorse Hindu nationalist candidates in 1989, much to the chagrin of the BJP and the Shiv Sena.[128] The anti-Mandal propaganda of the BJP-Shiv Sena alliance was a factor in the former's reversal of fortunes (it won 5 Lok Sabha seats and 20.20% of the valid votes).[129]

This overview of the BJP's performance in the 1991 general election suggests that the rise of the party must be qualified on several grounds. First, despite remarkable progress in states such as Karnataka, Assam and West Bengal, the BJP remained weak in the South and in the East. It is more a 'mega-regional' party, to use H. Gould's expression,[130] than a fully national one. Second, even though the ethno-religious mobilisation engendered by the Ramjanmabhoomi campaign made a great impact in states such as Uttar Pradesh and Karnataka, anti-Mandal sentiment was obviously an important factor in the upper castes' decision to vote for the BJP. The mirror image of this development was the fact that, despite the Ram temple agitation, the party experienced setbacks largely because of the mobilisation of the OBCs about the reservation issue, especially in Bihar. Thus, in geographical as well as in social terms, in 1991 the BJP had not yet reached a stage where it could be considered as a truly national party.

The reverses suffered by the BJP in several states went largely unnoticed in the wake of the 1991 elections. However, these setbacks occurred not only in Bihar and Maharashtra but also in the three states where the BJP had held power since March 1990: Himachal Pradesh, Rajasthan and Madhya Pradesh. The party's losses in these states suggest that evaluating its overall rise must be done with no little caution. They point to the fact that, as in the case of most other parties, the BJP could not but be affected by the exercise of power. This phenomenon is especially clear in the case of Madhya Pradesh, where the setback to the BJP was the most pronounced.

---

[127] R. Sardesai, 'Cracks in the Shiv Sena', ibid., 18 Dec. 1991.

[128] H.W. Blair, 'Local support bases and the ninth general elections in Bihar and Maharashtra' in H. Gould and S. Ganguly (eds), *India votes*, op. cit., p. 57.

[129] A few months later it was also the root cause of the defection of C. Bhujbal, an OBC who had been an influential lieutenant of Bal Thackeray (*Frontline*, 27 March 1992, p. 39).

[130] H. Gould, 'Patterns of political mobilization in the parliamentary and assembly elections of 1989 and 1990' in H. Gould and S. Ganguly (eds), *India votes*, op. cit., p. 22.

The cost of being in power

The BJP met with a severe reverse in Madhya Pradesh, where it retained only 12 seats (compared with 27 for Congress), all of which – with the exception of nearby Damoh – were in its stronghold of Madhya Bharat. This loss of seats was accompanied by an increase in votes (41.88%, compared to 39.66% in 1989) because the party put up candidates in 40 constituencies, compared with only 33 in 1989. Thus the tenth general election represented, at one and the same time, a consolidation of a two-party system in which the BJP was the main rival to the Congress (I) (which won 45.34% of the valid votes) and a major reverse for the BJP, coming slightly more than one year after the formation of the Patwa government. The latter development was symptomatic of the increasing tendency of voters to lash out against incumbent politicians.[131]

The BJP also experienced a setback in the two other states where it was in power, Rajasthan and Himachal Pradesh, and for similar reasons. In the former the party won 12 seats against 13 in 1989 despite a dramatic growth in terms of valid votes (from 29.64 % to 40.88%). In 1991 it contested all 25 constituencies while two years earlier the seat adjustment with the Janata Dal had reduced the number of constituencies in which it could put up candidates to 17, hence the apparent upswing in its support. In Himachal Pradesh the BJP won 2 seats against 3 in 1989 and received 42.79% of the valid votes against 45.25% two years earlier, even though it constested as many seats (4). The evolution of the BJP in these three states suggests that it is subject, though to a lesser extent, to the same evils of poor performance, internal dissension and corruption as other parties. We shall examine this trend in Chapter 14 in our analysis of the Vidhan Sabha elections of 1993, when the effects of local issues can better be taken into account.

In 1990-1 the BJP shifted from a mixed strategy to a purely instrumentalist one and intensified this strategy of ethno-religious mobilisation in a bid to capture power at the Centre as well as in the states where elections had been scheduled. This policy succeeded to some degree: it became the second largest force in the Lok Sabha and formed the government in Uttar Pradesh. However it did not enable the BJP to spread its influence very deeply in the South and in the East. In addition it met with setbacks of varying severity in the three states where it had been in office since 1990.

[131] Gould points out: 'While predominantly illiterate, they [the Indian voters] nevertheless seem to pay close attention to performance and very frequently assert their conclusions with regard to this quality regardless of how massively they have been bombarded by propaganda and machine-generated pressures' (ibid., p. 18).

Finally, and most importantly, it should be stressed that the motives of those who took part in the Hindu nationalist agitations ranged from religiosity to 'anti-Mandal' hostility. Village-based participants were probably motivated more by devotion to Ram, which did not necessarily imply anti-Muslim sentiment or ethno-religious xenophobia. Others were driven in part by their search for a new political identity. The scope of the Hindu nationalist mobilisation was also to some extent determined by caste. The BJP's opposition to positive discrimination through caste-based job reservations won it votes among the upper castes but reduced its appeal to members of the OBCs.

Paul Brass wrote that 'the social base for the BJP to strengthen further its position in U.P. simply does not exist'[132] since the upper castes only form one-fifth of the population in the state. Such a conclusion, however, is probably too radical. It implies that the low castes have acquired such a strong class consciousness that they are bound to vote together for non-BJP parties. Such a statement is partly contradicted by Brass himself since he noticed that substantial numbers of Lodhis, Kurmis and Gadarias voted for the BJP in 1991.[133] Moreover, prominent cadres of the Hindu nationalist movement in Uttar Pradesh belong to such castes (Katiyar, the then leader of the Bajrang Dal, is a Kurmi, for example) and the BJP, in a shrewd move, nominated a Lodhi, Kalyan Singh, as Chief Minister of Uttar Pradesh in 1991. However the party certainly needs to expand its base among the low castes to sustain its growth.

The strategy of ethno-religious mobilisation which largely under-pinned the electoral growth of the BJP in 1991 presented obvious dangers and even contradictions. A correlation can be established between the rise of the BJP vote and an increase in Hindu-Muslim riots, as testified by the table and diagram in Appendixes A and B, pp. 552-3. Between January and June 1991, just before the elections, there were 13 major riots claiming 135 lives (89 people were killed in Uttar Pradesh).[134] The map on p. 551 can be compared to that of the BJP vote in 1991. Although Bihar witnessed the largest number of people killed in riots in 1986-90, many of them in the violence at Bhagalpur in 1989 – this did not lead to a massive surge in support for the BJP. However many other states where the BJP performed creditably – Gujarat, Uttar Pradesh, Karnataka and Rajasthan – did experience an increase in communal riots. In Andhra Pradesh, where the rise in communal violence does not appear to have translated into electoral gains for the BJP, the high number of fatalities

---

[132] P. Brass, 'The rise of the BJP', op. cit., p. 264.

[133] Ibid., p. 268.

[134] Written answer of M.M. Jacob, Minister of State for Home Affairs, before the Rajya Sabha cited in *National Mail*, 18 July 1991 and *Frontline*, 26 Nov. 1991, p. 123.

was largely due to the unprecedented riot in Hyderabad, which accounted for 120 deaths in late 1990. Manor points out that these events go some way to explain why the two constituencies in which the BJP did best in Andhra Pradesh in 1991 were Hyderabad and nearby Secunderabad, whose seat it won.[135]

This violence precipitated a polarisation which was associated with a concentration of voting for the BJP in areas affected by rioting, especially among Scheduled Caste voters. Since the latter often lived cheek by jowl with Muslims, communal violence had an immediate impact that often led them to adopt a more aggressively 'Hindu' posture. Extreme forms of ethno-religious mobilisation thus present the BJP with a means of widening its social base.[136] However, communal violence is very volatile and jeopardises a strategy of ethno-religious mobilisation once it has reached a certain intensity. If the rioting spreads in such as way as to challenge the law and order situation, the initiators of the strategy of Hindu mobilisation, the RSS and its affiliates, run the risk of losing their credibility and being sidelined by uncontrollable elements. This contradiction, which is inherent in the strategy of ethno-religious mobilisation, was experienced by the Hindu nationalist movement in 1992 and 1993.

---

[135] J. Manor, 'BJP in the South', op. cit., p. 1268.

[136] Moreover, as Brass points out in the case of Uttar Pradesh, the unleashing of communal violence would 'very likely produce a full-scale Hindu consolidation, but at the cost of the disintegration of U.P. into a state of civil war comparable to that in Punjab, Assam, or Sri Lanka' (P. Brass, 'The rise of the BJP', op. cit., p. 279).

13

THE PARADOX OF THE
RAMJANMABHOOMI MOVEMENT

In the early 1990s the BJP encountered many difficulties in maintaining its integrity as a political party and especially in presenting itself as a party of government because it was closely identified with the Hindu mobilisation. Having gained power in several important states, the BJP had every reason to reduce its reliance upon its ethno-religious strategy, but the VHP and the Bajrang Dal were still insisting that the construction of the Ram temple in Ayodhya should remain on the party's political agenda. The division of labour between the VHP and the BJP became increasingly unstable as their priorities diverged: the BJP had derived electoral dividends from ethno-religious mobilisation but in the process became dependent on new groups – the *sadhus* and the activists of the Bajrang Dal and the VHP – which were likely to resort to extreme methods, as the demolition of the Babri Masjid testified.

The other actors in the political arena then retook the initiative: the Congress(I) government combined strong anti-communal measures that the breach of law justified with a search for a compromise likely to marginalise the Hindu nationalists without transforming them into martyrs.

Problems of division of labour

In 1991, after the BJP had become the second largest party in the Lok Sabha and formed the government in Uttar Pradesh, it seemed anxious not to be perceived as a 'single issue party' and to fulfil its commitment to discipline by avoiding large-scale riots in the states where it held office. Most of the BJP leaders did not want to be identified with the Ayodhya issue because it was important for the party – as well as for the RSS and its affiliates – to project a Hindu *nationalist* image and not to become involved in an essentially religious controversy. Soon after his *Rath Yatra* Advani had insisted that he was a political, not a religious leader and that the same distinction applied to the BJP;[1] and in the preparation for the *Kar Seva*, Singhal had emphasised the nationalist rather than the religious objects of the Ramjanmabhoomi movement.[2] Herein lies a major paradox of the strategy of ethno-religious mobilisation: it resorts to religious symbols but the political leaders involved in it must preserve their image as statesmen (or would be statesmen) and not appear to depend on religious figures or the more militant activists.

The BJP's difficulties as a nationalist and a government party

In order to strengthen its 'nationalist' image, the BJP decided, as early as February 1991, at the convention where M.M. Joshi became party president, to arrange a march to Srinagar where a symbolic hoisting of the Indian flag was to take place.[3] A variant of the *Rath Yatra*, which had relied more on religious emotion, this *Ekta Yatra* (Pilgrimage of Unity) was led by M.M. Joshi himself. It spanned 15,000 km., from Kanyakumari to Kashmir, passed through fourteen states, and was intended to make the country's territorial integrity the party's new and most important policy issue. In Tamil Nadu, from where it departed on 11 December 1991, and then in Kerala, in Karnataka and in Andhra Pradesh, the *Yatra* attracted substantial crowds.[4] It proved less successful in Maharashtra[5] but was well received in Madhya Pradesh and Uttar Pradesh where the state party machines lent their support.[6] Religious figures were by and large kept at a distance as the BJP was trying to project a purely nationalist image.

The *Ekta Yatra* ended in anti-climax. The procession was halted in Jammu because of the risk of an attack by Kashmiri militants and a meagre contingent of 67 BJP workers was flown to Srinagar courtesy of the Indian Air Force. Joshi hoisted the flag in a brief ceremony that was ridiculed by the press.[7] Even RSS cadres expressed their disappointment at what had turned out to be a fiasco.[8] The *Ekta Yatra* had certainly not had an impact comparable to Advani's *Rath Yatra*.

The VHP, meanwhile, concentrated on the Ayodhya issue. Since the Uttar Pradesh state government was now in the hands of the BJP, the VHP expected that the Chief Minister, Kalyan Singh, would fulfil his party's commitment to build the Ram temple. In July 1991, it demanded that the

[1] *Times of India*, 25 Dec. 1990.
[2] *Organiser*, 20 May 1990, p. 13.
[3] *National Mail*, 9 Feb. 1991. It was postponed soon afterwards because of the general election.
[4] *Times of India*, 12, 13, 16 and 20 Dec. 1990.
[5] *India Today*, 31 Jan. 1992, p. 44.
[6] *National Mail*, 31 Dec. 1991; *Times of India*, 12 and 13 Jan. 1992.
[7] See, for instance, *India Today*, 15 Feb. 1992.
[8] *Times of India*, 1 Feb. 1992.

legal and other obstacles in the way of temple construction should be removed before 18 November. However taking action would have exposed the state government to retaliatory measures from the Centre and to large-scale communal violence.[9]

In the monsoon parliamentary session, the central government introduced a Places of Worship (Special Provisions) Bill which proposed that the location of places of worship should be those which obtained on 15 August 1947. The Babri Masjid/ Ramjanmabhoomi was excluded from the scope of the act, ostensibly because it was the subject of litigation. This act was indicative of a certain determination which might lead the Centre to retaliate – if necessary through the imposition of President's rule – were the Uttar Pradesh government to flout the orders of the Supreme Court with respect to Ayodhya. Such a decision would have prevented the BJP from using the state machinery for its own purposes. In addition, any move on the Ram temple was likely to provoke a new wave of communal riots in the state – because of Hindu victory processions or Muslim demonstrations of anger. This would have been all the more damaging to the BJP as it had promised during its campaign to keep Uttar Pradesh free from riots. Furthermore, the core of its support, namely members of the middle class who wished to see a strong government in which the maintainance of law and order was a priority (one of Kalyan Singh's electoral platforms had been a promise to crack down on underworld gangs), could not be expected to look kindly on a renewal of disorder in the state.

Thus, the Uttar Pradesh BJP was confronted with a serious dilemma: it was keen to exert power in the most orderly way possible, while at the same time the very forces to which it was heavily indebted for gaining power put pressure on the government so that it would adopt a more confrontational posture. The compromise solution worked out by Kalyan Singh in September 1991 consisted in acquiring 2.77 acres of land adjoining the Babri Masjid under the pretext of developing a tourist complex and providing amenities for pilgrims. Of this plot 2.04 acres were acquired from the VHP, which allegedly 'had earlier acquired it by purchase or gift from the previous owners'.[10] The ultimate aim was probably to include the mosque in the land acquired and to build a temple.[11] However this acquisition was challenged in writs in the Allahabad High Court and the Supreme Court.

---

9   On that point, see 'Rhetoric and reality', *EPW*, 2 Nov. 1991.

10   *BJP's White Paper on Ayodhya and the Rama Temple Movement*, New Delhi: BJP, 1993, p. 96.

11   It is explicitly stated in the *BJP's White Paper on Ayodhya and the Rama Temple Movement* that the 'U.P. government acquired 2.77 acres of land adjoining the structure for temple construction' (ibid., p. 43).

Soon after the notification was issued, on 7 and 10 October, the VHP began to prepare the 2.77 acre site by levelling the ground and acquiring adjoining houses and temples whose *mahants* were sometimes evicted by means of intimidation.[12] On 18 October, the VHP invited *kar sevaks* to Ayodhya to begin construction of the temple;[13] but on the 25th of that month the High Court, while allowing the state government to take possession of the 2.77 acres, restrained it from erecting any permanent structure.

On 29 October, the RSS and the VHP organised in Ayodhya a *Bajrang Rudra Yajna* which was intended to honour the *kar sevaks* who had died the previous year. Observers noticed that a number of *sadhus* and activists had become impatient with the government of Uttar Pradesh. Some speakers even 'made clear that if the BJP dragged its feet over the construction of the temple, its government in the state would be pulled down'.[14] On 31 October young activists clambered onto the domes of the Babri Masjid to hoist the saffron flag, damaging the outer wall of the building. The VHP's leaders urged these activists to exercise restraint and assured them that the BJP was committed to the Ram temple[15] – a stance that is indicative of the difficulties encountered by the VHP's leaders in keeping its activists under control. Revealingly, a day after Kalyan Singh had condemned those who had hoisted saffron flags atop the Babri Masjid, leading VHP *sadhus* defended the action.[16]

The RSS cadres heading the VHP were themselves eager to 'resume' the *Kar Seva*.[17] On 9 July 1992, *kar sevaks* and *sadhus* began to build a

---

[12]   The Sankat Mochan temple, the major portion of the Sakshi Gopal temple, Sumitra Bhawan, Lomas Ashram and Gopal Bhawan were demolished. In several cases, such as that of the priest of the Sakshi Temple, it was alleged that coercion was used to acquire these buildings (K. Prasad, *Report of the inquiry commitssion*, op. cit., p. 72). On this point see the testimony of Baba Lal Das, who had been appointed by the court as chief priest of the Ramjanmabhoomi Mandir (in the Babri Masjid) and whom the government of Kalyan Singh illegally removed on 1 March 1992 because he had criticised the Ayodhya movement (*Manushi*, no. 79, Nov.-Dec. 1993, pp. 2-21). Baba Lal Das was mysteriously murdered on November 16, 1993.

[13]   On 21 October, a ceremony was performed on the site of the second pillar of the main entrance (*Times of India*, 22 Oct.1991).

[14]   A. Nandy, S. Trivedy, S. Mayaram and Y. Yagnik, *Creating a nationality: Ramjanmabhumi movement and the fear of the self*, op.cit., p. 160.

[15]   *Times of India*, 27 Oct. 1991; *Sunday*, 10 Nov. 1991, pp. 35-6.

[16]   Ibid., 3 Nov. 1991. On 2 Jan., Kalyan Singh denied permission to religious leaders to hoist the red flag of Hanuman on the mosque (*Times of India*, 26 Jan. 1992).

[17]   *Times of India*, 23 March 1992. Soon after the completion of the *Ekta Yatra*, the VHP announced a definite timetable for construction. The plan of this construction, designed by C.B. Sompura, whose family firm of architects has built many temples, including that in Somnath, reproduced the 1989 model but a Lakshman temple was added to the right of the disputed structure.

concrete platform, in contravention of the order issued by the High Court and reiterated on 15 November 1991 by the Supreme Court. On 11 July 1992 the latter made an order so as 'no permanent structure would be or is being or intended to be put on the acquired land'.[18] At that juncture the Prime Minister received a delegation of six religious leaders from the VHP. He asked them to abandon the *Kar Seva* and, as indicated in his statement in Parliament, to give him three to four months to revive the efforts initiated by the previous governments to bring about 'a negotiated settlement'.[19] The resumption of talks between the VHP and the BMAC brought no results. The BMAC contested the government's acquisition of the 2.77 acres on the ground that parts of the plot formed a graveyard, while the VHP naturally supported the move. The issue was thus referred to the High Court. The talks broke down when the VHP announced, in late October, that the construction of the temple would resume on 6 December. This was another example of the VHP taking action while paying little or no attention to the priorities of the BJP.

On 27 November, the Supreme Court prohibited the resumption of the *Kar Seva* by directing the Uttar Pradesh government to provide assurances that it would not allow it to take place. Kalyan Singh answered positively and a compromise solution was finally worked out whereby a 'symbolic *Kar Seva*' would be held, consisting of a congregation performing rituals on the undisputed parcels of land. On 24 November 1992, 195 companies of the central government para-military forces (such as CRPF troops) were moved to Ayodhya and Faizabad. Kalyan Singh protested, but S. B. Chavan, the Union Home Minister, drew his attention to 'the constitutional and legal right of the Union Government to station or deploy in certain situations its forces in the country whenever called for' and to the threat represented by the gathering of so many *kar sevaks*.[20] As early as 27 November, over 10,000 *kar sevaks* from different parts of the country had already reached Ayodhya. Their number steadily increased so that by 5

---

[18] On 15 July the High Court of Allahabad issued an order in the same direction. For the texts of these orders see O. Chinappa Reddy, D. A. Desai and D. S. Tewatia, *Citizens' Tribunal on Ayodhya: Judgement and recommendations*, New Delhi: Secretariat of the citizen's tribunal on Ayodhya, 1993, pp. 18- 19.

[19] 'Prime Minister's statement in Parliament 27.07.92' in *White Paper on Ayodhya*, op. cit., p. 81. In this statement Narasimha Rao declared: 'The Congress is for the construction of the Temple without dismantling the mosque.'

[20] Cited in O. Chinappa Reddy et al., *Citizens' Tribunal on Ayodhya*, op. cit., p. 35. Chavan probably referred, here, to Article 355 of the Constitution : 'It shall be the duty of the Union to protect every State against external aggression and internal disturbance and to ensure that the government of every State is carried on in accordance with the provisions of this Constitution.' For more details see 'Gist of correspondence between the Ministry of Home Affairs and the Government of U.P. on RJB-BM issue' in *White Paper on Ayodhya*, op. cit., pp. 61-76.

December they were about 150,000.[21] Such a massive mobilisation apparently took Hindu nationalist leaders by surprise and they asked local units of the RSS and its affiliates to stop *kar sevaks* from coming to Ayodhya.[22]

In the last days of November BJP leaders began to take an active role in the movement. The *BJP's White Paper on Ayodhya* suggests that the party's leaders, and especially Kalyan Singh, were hoping that the High Court would issue an order allowing the resumption of the *Kar Seva* on the 2.77 acre plot. The government of Uttar Pradesh wanted to delink the *Kar Seva* from the dispute about the Babri Masjid/Ramjanmabhoomi. It hoped that in a first phase the construction of the temple could take place on the 2.77 acres and in a second an attempt would be made to reach agreement concerning the disputed structure:

This was possible because the architectural plan and engineering charts showed that it would take not less than two to two and half years for the construction on the adjoining site [the 2.77 acres] to be completed, and this time lag could be used to decide the fate of the structure by negotiation, and judicial adjudication or opinion, or by legislation.[23]

From 8 November till 5 December Hindu nationalist leaders apparently asked Union Ministers and the Prime Minister, Narasimha Rao, to approach the High Court and the Supreme Court to expedite the judgement on the 2.77 acre plot, in the hope that the government of Uttar Pradesh or the previous owner, the VHP, would be recognised as proprietors of at least 2.04 acres so that they could begin the *Kar Seva* there.[24] At that stage 'the party decided to send Shri L.K. Advani and Shri M.M. Joshi on a *yatra* to explain the position of the party and its government to the people and to participate in the *Kar Seva*'.[25] Joshi left from Mathura and Advani from Varanasi and between them they toured 28 districts of Uttar Pradesh. Advani made many speeches which revealed his determination to have a temple built at the site of the holy of holies where the images stood.[26] On

21 O. Chinappa Reddy et al., *Citizens' Tribunal on Ayodhya*, op. cit. p. 31. The BJP's estimate was only 75,000 (BJP's *White Paper on Ayodhya*, op. cit., p. 129), the same as the government's (*White paper on Ayodhya*, op. cit., p. 5.)

22 K. Prasad, *Report of the inquiry commission*, op. cit., p. 45. Such commands were issued in Bhopal and justified by the difficulties the RSS and its affiliates encountered in Ayodhya in accommodating all the *kar sevaks* (interview with B.D. Gadhge, a local Bajrang Dal leadr, 19 Feb. 1994, Bhopa).

23 *BJP's white paper on Ayodhya*, op. cit., p. 95.

24 Ibid., pp. 124-5. The judgement came on 11 December and denied any title of ownership to the government of Uttar Pradesh or the VHP (see below).

25 Ibid., p. 128.

26 See O. Chinappa Reddy *et al., Citizen's Tribunal on Ayodhya*, op. cit. p.29.

6 December Joshi and Advani were present at the 'symbolic *Kar Seva*' along with many other RSS and VHP leaders.

6 December 1992. At about 11 a.m., as people gathered before the platform adjacent to the disputed area to listen to speeches, *kar sevaks* breached the cordon formed by RSS volunteers, entered the disputed area and began stoning the mosque as well as the police guarding it. Then they used ropes to clamber on to the domes and set about dismantling them with iron rods. Journalists who took pictures were attacked. The PAC, which was stationed in the immediate vicinity of the Babri Masjid, failed to intervene and the CRPF (which was originally stationed inside, though without firearms) quickly left the scene. At about 12.45 p.m. the idols, collection boxes, and the portraits of Ram, of K.K. Nair and of Guru Datt Singh were carried from the building. The left dome caved in at 2.55 p.m., the right collapsed at 4.35 p.m. and the central one fifteen minutes later. Even before that, Muslims were attacked in Ayodhya town and many houses whose inhabitants had fled were set ablaze. After the demolition of the Babri Masjid and the clearing of the site on which it had stood, the *kar sevaks* constructed a temporary temple in which images were placed.

The recurring question in the aftermath of the demolition was: had it been planned in advance? The BJP, whose *White Paper* did not give any description of the demolition, claimed that it had not:

The demolition of the disputed structure was an uncontrolled and, in fact, uncontrollable upsurge of spontaneous nature which was provoked only by the callousness of the Government in dealing with the Ayodhya issue without understanding the sensitive nature of the issue.[27]

RSS leaders argued that the indiscipline of the *kar sevaks* proved that the affair had not been premeditated because it did not comply with the traditions of *swayamsevaks* who, they claimed, had tried to contain the hotheads. Deoras attributed the demolition to outside elements.[28]

Many clues suggest that the demolition had been the result of careful preparation; one group of activists was seen rehearsing on the 5th what was accomplished on the 6th.[29] The members of this special team wore yellow headbands, different from the saffron ones of the Bajrang Dalis.[30] Second, the *kar sevaks* carried with them ropes, pickaxes, shovels and hammers, implements which were not necessary for a 'symbolic *Kar Seva*'. One question remains, however: were all the leaders aware of the

---

[27] *BJP's White Paper on Ayodhya,* op. cit., p. 131.

[28] *Times of India,* 8 Dec. 1992, p. 5.

[29] O. Chinappa Reddy *et al., Citizens' Tribunal on Ayodhya,* op. cit., pp. 36-8 and K. Prasad, *Report of the inquiry commision,* op. cit., p. 57.

[30] They are in evidence in the issues of 'Newstrack' and 'Eyewitness' of January 1993.

plan ?[31] The question is especially important in the case of the leaders of the BJP, given their sober and responsible image. Advani, like the other leaders on the platform, asked the *kar sevaks* not to climb on the domes. According to certain journalists he appeared to be distressed when the demolition began.[32] One of them considered that 'L.K. Advani certainly may not have known the plans to tell you'.[33] He immediately resigned from the post of leader of the opposition, as Kalyan Singh resigned from the Chief Ministership, in order to show that he felt moral responsibility for what had happened.

It is difficult to assess the reactions of the various leaders to the onset of the demolition, all the more so given that parallel to their calls to the *kar sevaks* to stop, recorded speeches by Sadhvi Rithambara and Uma Bharti heightened the excitement of the participants. Some of these calls to moderation might well have been simply for the record. This hypothesis is supported by the fact that in the afternoon Sadhvi Rithambara and others used the microphone to exhort the *kar sevaks*[34] while many other leaders were seen congratulating themselves on what was happening.

According to the 'Citizens' Tribunal on Ayodhya' the demolition was pre-planned and finalised at a meeting held on 5 December 1992 and

[31]   Many journalists present at Ayodhya on that day underlined that most of the personalities on the platform – Singhal, Seshadri, Advani, Vijaya Raje Scindia, Uma Bharti etc. – tried to call back the *kar sevaks* when they penetrated the disputed area. However Uma Bharti exhorted them in ambiguous terms: 'don't climb on top of the dome; it is not the time. You might get hurt, we have a plan, follow our plan' (cited in O. Chinappa Reddy *et al.*, *Citizens' Tribunal on Ayodhya*, op. cit., p. 46). Such words may indicate that the *kar sevaks* were simply admonished for acting too quickly rather than for setting out to demolish the disputed structure. This argument is substantiated by the testimonies of certain *kar sevaks*. One of them said to a journalist interviewed by the 'Citizens' Tribunal on Ayodhya' that he belonged to a team which had rehearsed a plan. He was supposed to climb on the top of the dome at 11.35 a.m. but he decided to climb up at 11.15 because the slogans and the music had stirred him to a state of frenzy (ibid., p. 51).

[32]   Later on he said '[...] December 6 [1992] turned out to be one of the most depressing days in my life. Of course, most others there were ecstatic with joy, a mood I just could not share. [...] Firstly, I felt sad the December 6 happenings had impaired the reputation of the BJP and the RSS as organisations capable of enforcing discipline. [...] Secondly, I felt sad that a meticulously drawn up plan of action where under the UP Government was steadily marching forward towards discharging its mandate regarding temple construction, without violating any law or discharging any court order, had gone awry. [...] The third and most important reason for my unhappiness that day was that, in my perception, the day's incidents would affect the BJP's overall image (not electoral prospects) adversely, and, to that extent, our cause would suffer a temporary setback' (*Indian Express*, 27 Dec. 1992).

[33]   Cited in O. Chinappa Reddy *et al.*, *Citizens' Tribunal on Ayodhya*, op. cit., p. 51.

[34]   While dancing she sang: '*Ek dhakka aur do, Babri masjid tor do*' (Give one more push, destroy the Babri Masjid) (cited in K. Prasad, *Report of the Inquiry Commission*, op. cit., p. 26.)

attended by Advani, Joshi, Seshadri, Katiyar, Vijaya Raje Scindia, Uma Bharti, Sadhvi Rithambara, K.S. Sudarshan and others. For the members of this tribunal, however, 'it is possible that some netas [leaders][...] had no knowledge until the 5th December of the precise manner in which the object of the conspiracy was to be achieved.'[35] The plan was perhaps elaborated within the RSS-VHP combination and BJP leaders (such as Advani, who did not seem to be aware of it in detail) were informed later on. Other BJP leaders, such as Vajpayee, who were not present at Ayodhya on 6 December and who stated the following day that the demolition was the 'worse miscalculation' ever made by his party, might even have been unaware of the plan altogether or were informed about it only at the last moment.

The demolition of the Babri Masjid, whether or not it was a concerted or even a unanimous decision, completely transformed the terms of the strategy of ethno-religious mobilisation that the RSS-VHP-BJP combination had been pursuing for almost a decade. Up till then it had channelled the anti-Muslim sentiment of Hindus towards the mosque as a symbol of their former 'humiliating domination' and simultaneously exploited their feelings of devotion for Ram. The combine's agitation was systematically intensified in the run up to the polls so that the BJP could thereby increase its electoral support. By and large this instrumentalist strategy was developed within the constitutional framework: judicial orders were not radically infringed before 1992 and if the communal riots – which were a tacit element of this strategy – were especially violent at the time of election campaigns, they never prevented elections from being conducted. From the early 1980s the Hindu nationalists were gradually providing a focus for anti-Muslim sentiment and building up an emotional wave in the name of Ram. This process contributed steadily to the consolidation of their position. The situation was considerably altered by the demolition of the Babri Masjid.

Hindu nationalist leaders who wanted to eliminate the Babri Masjid for ideological reasons might have thought that its demolition would serve two purposes. First, it would show to their followers (especially those within the VHP who had become impatient with the vacillation of Kalyan Singh) that they had not contributed to the electoral success of the BJP in Uttar Pradesh in vain. Second, the demolition could enable Hindus to regain their supposedly wounded self-esteem: a sign of humiliation, a relic of Muslim historical domination, had been brushed aside. As far as future plans were concerned, the mosques of Mathura and Varanasi could be targetted for the same reason and, in any case, the demolition of the Babri Masjid cleared the way for the long-term construction of a great Ram

---

[35] O Chinappa Reddy *et al.*, *Citizens' Tribunal on Ayodhya*, op. cit., p. 68.

temple. These same Hindu nationalist leaders probably regarded it as a new symbol which could be manipulated in the years to come in the context of a strategy of ethno-religious mobilisation.

In the short term the Hindu nationalist movement probably gained in popularity because of the demolition of the mosque (see below). However, this event revealed two contradictions of the instrumentalist strategy. While the demolition was in one sense the logical conclusion of the Ayodhya movement, it deprived the RSS-VHP-BJP combine of a powerful symbol. As the results of the 1993 election were to show, it was easier to mobilise Hindus *against* the Babri Masjid than *for* anything else (see chapter 14). Second, the demolition of the Babri Masjid demonstrated that the Hindu nationalist movement was largely dominated by the VHP activists, *sadhus*, Bajrang Dalis and other *kar sevaks*. Whether the demolition had been pre-planned or not, these actors were recognised as having more weight in the RSS-VHP-BJP combination than had been generally thought to be the case. They were responsible for the demolition and most of the communal violences which followed, and had been directed by, or ignored orders from their organisational leaders in setting their own objectives. For the BJP, one of the obvious dangers of the strategy of ethno-religious mobilisation was that it entailed a reliance on activists who were literally out of control. The wave of riots which followed the demolition of the mosque indicated just how violent these activists could be.

The unleashing of communal violence

Film of the demolition of the Babri Masjid was shown repeatedly by the BBC on its satellite news bulletins, and coverage of the event served to intensify Muslim despair and anger. In many places these feelings were a factor in a new wave of riots but in other areas communal disturbances stemmed mainly from Hindu victory parades.

Rioting broke out immediately in Bombay and continued into January 1993. The causes of the riots were discussed in unofficial reports, from which the following picture emerges. As in other Indian cities and towns the situation was already tense before the demolition because of the mobilisation of Hindu nationalist activists en route to Ayodhya or supporting the *Kar Seva*.[36] The violence began on 7 December after Muslim youths put up placards condemning the demolition of the mosque,

---

[36] In November, for instance, in Byculla-Mazgaon BJP leaders headed a procession whose slogan was '*jo humse takrayega, woh mitti mein mil jayega*' (those who oppose us will be reduced to dust) (Justice S.M. Daud and Justice H. Suresh, *The people's verdict – An inquiry into the Dec '92 and Jan '93 riots in Bombay*, Bombay: Indian People's Human Rights Commission, 1993, p. 33).

demanded that shopkeepers observe a *bandh* and even demonstrated in the street.[37] The targets of the demonstrators were mainly policemen – who were perceived as symbols of the state which had allowed the demolition to occur[38] – and Hindu temples. On 7 and 8 December, according to the Ekta Samiti report, three temples were damaged.[39] Riots were also sparked off by the victory processions organised by Hindu leaders to celebrate the demolition of the Babri Masjid. In Dharavi – supposedly the largest slum in Asia – such a demonstration was conducted by a Shiv Sena leader as early as 6 December. One of the slogans uttered was that the proper place for Muslims was either Pakistan or the cemetary (*kabristan*). Muslims led a retaliatory procession on the following day with similar, provocative slogans. A riot ensued.[40]

However, a couple of days after the first acts of violence 'the police literally took over the riots':[41] it became less a case of Hindu-Muslim conflict than Muslims against the police or vice-versa. Of 202 casualties – the official toll – 132 died in police firing and 51 in mob violence, of which 98 and 32, respectively, were Muslims.[42] The riots, which lasted till 16 December, revealed the depth of the communal bias of the police as well as its lack of preparedness.

The instigators of many acts of violence were Hindu activists. On Friday 11 December, the curfew was relaxed so that Muslims could take part in *namaz*. Immediately, Shiv Sena leaders, who had long objected to the inconvenience created by Muslims praying outside the mosque – sometimes in the streets – and to the nuisance caused by their loudspeakers, criticised the move and demanded the same rights for Hindus willing to attend *arti*.[43] Their demand was accepted by the administration. The *Maha artis* imitated the collective and large-scale character of the *namaz* with the declared aim of demonstrating against it in the logic of a strategy of stigmatisation and emulation.[44] *Maha artis* are

---

[37] Ibid., pp. 48, 65 and 66.

[38] The first casualty of the riots, moreover, as early as the evening of 6 December, was a constable.

[39] A.A. Engineer, 'Bombay Shames India' in *Bombay's shame: A report on Bombay riots*, Bombay: Ekta Samiti, 1993, pp. 6 and p. 15. Ekta Samiti, formed in 1987 after the Meerut riot , produced a detailed report which is congruent to the one by the IPHRC.

[40] S.M. Daud and H. Suresh, *The people's verdict*, op. cit., p. 37 and p. 99.

[41] Ibid., p. 100

[42] These figures were announced by the police commissioner. According to *the Times of India*, the real toll was 227 (D. Padgaonkar, ed., *When Bombay burned*, New Delhi: UBSPD, 1993, p. xvi).

[43] J. Masselos, 'The Bombay riots of January 1993: the politics of urban conflagration', *South Asia*, 17 (1994), p. 84.

[44] C. Fernandez and N. Fernandes, 'The winter of discontent' in D. Padgaonkar, *When Bombay burned*, op. cit., p. 37 and 'A city at war with itself' in ibid., p. 44.

traditionally performed on festivals or other special occasions and *arti* is performed twice a day, usually in the morning and evening, in all Hindu temples. The ceremony within which Hindus offer *puja* usually lasts about half an hour. In mid-December 1992, the Shiv Sena and members of the RSS-VHP-BJP combination initiated in Bombay, Poona and other places in Maharashtra a programme reinterpreting this ritual: *Maha artis* lasted for one or two hours and brought together hundreds or even thousands of people. Between 26 December 1992 and 5 February 1993, 498 *Maha artis* took place, of which 172 were attended by 1,500 persons or more.[45] After the evening programme came to an end, many of the *Maha artis* were followed by attacks on Muslim properties.

In many instances, the rioting has been described by S.M. Daud and H. Suresh as a pure and simple attack on Muslims by Shiv Sainiks.[46] BJP local leaders or members of other affiliates of the RSS were also involved in rioting.[47] The close links between Hindu nationalists and the police partly explain the scope and duration of the riot, which lasted till 22 January.[48] Moreover Shiv Sena cadres were unable to control their members, a problem inherent in the movement's loose structure.[49]

In the second phase of Bombay riots, in January 1993, 458 persons died, according to official sources, of whom 288 were Muslims and 170 Hindus.[50] Thousands of people fled from Bombay, most of them Muslims from North India. Others tended to gather together in neighborhoods where they formed the majority community. This process of ghettoisation became the most extreme form of communal polarisation.

Besides Bombay – which had the highest death toll – communal violence broke out in other parts of India too. The second worse affected city was Surat, where the official death toll was put at about 200.[51] In the Hindi-belt Bhopal, where 139 people died, fared worst of all. The riot was sparked off in the old town, where Muslims are concentrated, by victory

[45] These figures were released by the government and cited in A.A. Engineer, 'Bombay shames India – Phase II' in *Bombay's shame*, op. cit., p. 16.

[46] S.M. Daud and H. Suresh mention such a scenario in eight neighborhoods, at least (*The people's verdict*, op. cit., pp. 11, 13, 19, 53, 61, 63 and 72).

[47] See, for instance, ibid., p. 43.

[48] Ibid., p. 46.

[49] Violence continued even afer Thackeray wrote in the Shiv Sena newspaper *Samna* that a 'lesson' having been taught, peace should be restored (R. Sardesai, 'The great betrayal', in D. Padgaonkar (ed.), *When Bombay burned*, op. cit., p. 200).

[50] Out of those killed, 133 died in police firing, 259 in mob violence and 66 in arson (A.A. Engineer, 'Bombay shames India – Phase II', op.cit., p. 22). *The Times of India*'s estimate puts the toll at 557.

[51] J. Breman, 'Anti-Muslim pogrom in Surat', *EPW*, 17 April 1993, pp. 737-41; S. Chandra, 'Of communal consciousness and communal violence' in ibid., 4 Sept. 1993, pp. 1883-7, and P. Sheth, 'Degeneration of a city' in ibid., 30 Jan. 1993, pp. 151-2.

processions celebrating the mosque's demolition but also and more decisively by the BBC's reports of the destruction. On the morning of 7 December bands of Muslim youths attacked government buildings and Hindus in Jehangirabad, in the old town, notably with a view to enforcing a *bandh*.[52] Arif Aqueel, the Muslim MLA of Bhopal North (a constituency where Muslims constitute about 40-45 % of the population) was arrested on the night of 7 December possibly as a precautionary measure but more probably because of his protest against the demolition of the Babri Masjid.[53] Till the afternoon of the 8th 'it was Muslims, in the age group of 15-25 who took over the streets'.[54] Hindus took the lead in instigating riots from then onwards. Their actions were sparked off in part by rumours and false or sensational information published in the Hindi press. *Nav Bharat* and *Jan Charcha*, two local newspapers, wrongly announced that girls' hostels had been attacked. *Dainik Bhaskar*, one of the largest Hindi newspapers in Madhya Pradesh, described how people were burned alive in a locality where Hindus were known to be in a minority; it referred to the gang rape of a woman whose breast was said to have been severed; and the newspaper also published reports on how train passengers under attack were protected by *kar sevaks* returning from Ayodhya – which suggests that the target of the rioters were Hindus.[55] Such press reports provoked further outbreaks of violence.

Hindu nationalist activists played a prominent role in the riots from 8 December onwards. First, Bajrang Dalis took to arms. One of the young men in charge of the Bajrang Dal office in Bhopal spontaneously declared that he had taken an active part in the riot.[56]

We received the order from the Sangh parivar not to go to Ayodhya [on 6 December 1992] because there was the premonition [*purvabhas*] that fight might happen here [in Bhopal]. Therefore, a few people stayed here in alert. [...] We took part in the riot. Muslim people killed policemen and looted the people. Therefore we took part [in the riot] and then scared Muslims away.

The district collector declared that riots and attempted arson were pre-planned in at least two localities, Govindpura (in the BHEL area) and Piplani.[57]

---

[52] *Statesman* (Delhi), 9 Dec. 1992, *National Mail* (Bhopal), 8 Dec. 1992 and *Bhopal riot: A report*, Bhopal and Delhi: Sanskritik Morcha and PUDR, 1993, p. 4. The following account draws primarily on this source.

[53] *National Mail*, 15 Dec. 1992.

[54] *Bhopal riot – A report*, op. cit., p. 6.

[55] *Dainik Bhaskar* (Hindi), 7 and 8 Dec. 1992.

[56] Interview in Bhopal, 19 Feb. 1994.

[57] *National Mail*, 15 Dec. 1992. The premeditated nature of the violence was attested by one of the techniques the rioters used to create panic and provoke aggression. At night

Kar sevaks returning from Ayodhya by train were not allowed to alight at Bhopal station because of the riot, but got out at Habibganj station, near the BHEL complex where some of them had been accommodated. Violence, which had already spread to New Bhopal the previous day, reached the BHEL township on 9 December. Nearly seventy BHEL dwellings belonging to Muslim factory workers were completely looted.[58] But the riot also affected the dwellings of Muslims who had settled in the slums which had grown up within the BHEL compound.

The BJP state government in Madhya Pradesh showed little urgency in containing the rioting or caring for the victims, while rioters from the Bajrang Dal had almost become accustomed to receiving government protection.[59] On 9 December, the state unit of the party organised a *bandh* in protest against the arrest of Hindu nationalist leaders in the aftermath of the demolition of the mosque (see below). On the same day, Babulal Gaur, the BJP MLA for Govindpura, was deputed by the state cabinet to the railway station to receive *kar sevaks* coming back from Uttar Pradesh, an action which was unlikely to moderate Hindu militancy while violence raged.[60] Soon after the riot ended, Gaur staged a demonstration before a police control room in protest against the arrest of Hindus who were accused of arson, looting and even killing in his constituency.[61] Far from moderating their expression of communal feeling, local BJP leaders tended to exploit and aggravate still further the Hindu-Muslim polarisa-

---

cars were parked in sensitive localities and played at full blast cassette recordings of slogans and the noise of crowds. This made local residents think that mobs had arrived (*Bhopal riots – A report*, op. cit., p. 11). In Acharya Narendra Dev Nagar (located right next to BHEL), on December 8, a dozen dwellings were set on fire and after a short while a group of men armed with firearms arrived by lorry (*National Mail*, 26 Dec. 1992). Some survivors were even able to identify their assailants as being from the Bajrang Dal. In Indira Nagar, on 8 December, Bajrang Dal activists, accompanied by policemen, raided the colony and 400 huts were razed (ibid., 19 Dec. 1992). The *Statesman* correspondent who camped in the riot-hit area wrote on 9 December that 'while in the last two days the minorities had gained, today it was the turn of the Hindus (led by the Bajrang Dal and the VHP). With saffron headgear and orange "tikas" to make identification easy they stormed the Muslim pockets accompanied by the local police (strangely the Army was nowhere in sight)' (*Statesman* [Delhi], 10 Dec. 1992). The army was called in as early as the evening of the 7th because the police were not up to the task and, moreover, were displaying communal bias (*National Mail*, 16 Dec. 1992). However, there were only two columns available in Bhopal and soldiers had to be sent from Sagar on 8 December.

58   Ibid., 25 Dec. 1992.
59   A female BJP member of the Municipal Corporation, who had returned from Ayodhya on the night of the 8th along with other *kar sevaks*, were even named by the victims as having participated in the riot (*Bhopal riots – A report*, op. cit., p. 41).
60   *National Mail*, 10 Dec. 1992.
61   Ibid., 26 Dec. 1992.

tion.[62] The Bhopal rioting lasted a whole week and 16,895 people (one-third of them Hindus) were forced to find shelter in 31 refugee camps.[63] Riots occurred in other places in Madhya Pradesh – notably in Ujjain – but none of them were of the same intensity.

In the nation as a whole, between 6 and 13 December 1992, communal riots officially claimed some 1,200 lives. Maharashtra, which includes Bombay, suffered worse, with 259 deaths; then came Gujarat with 246, Uttar Pradesh with 201 and Madhya Pradesh with 161 fatalities. Elsewhere in the Hindi belt, Delhi and Rajasthan were badly hit (15 and 48 dead respectively) whereas Bihar remained relatively free of violence (24 dead), an achievement often attributed in the media to the way the Chief Minister, Laloo Prasad Yadav, demanded that the District Magistrates and chiefs of police act decisively. However, in 1992 even more than in 1989-1990, communal riots touched states which had been relatively free of this form of violence till then:73 people died in Karnataka, 35 in West Bengal and about 100 in Assam where districts with the largest number of Muslim immigrants were the worse affected. The other southern states escaped comparatively lightly (12 people were killed in Kerala and Andhra Pradesh and 2 in Tamil Nadu).[64]

From the *Ekta Yatra* to the demolition of the Babri Masjid, the events of 1991-2 illustrate the difficulties the BJP faced in its attempt to influence the Hindu nationalist agenda. While its national leadership was anxious to emphasise national integrity and the claim to be the party of law and order, such plans were undermined by *sadhus*, members of the Bajrang Dal and more generally *kar sevaks*, who appeared to be beyond the party's control. Such considerations prompted Ashis Nandy to argue convincingly that 'the BJP *as a political party* has emerged, however strange this might sound, weaker from the events of 6 December.' We shall return

---

62 Communal leaders even tried to sustain the Hindu-Muslim polarisation after the rioting came to an end. On 27 December, a newly constituted Hindu-Muslim Ekta Samiti (Committee for Hindu-Muslim unity), which brought together Hindu and Muslim leaders, some of them to the Congress (I), announced that Muslims would launch a *Kar Seva* to repair a Durga Temple on Berasia Road which had been damaged during the riot. Meanwhile the Muslim community collected money for this purpose (ibid., 28 Dec. 1992). The Hindu Ekta Manch, an organisation linked to the RSS, immediately objected, claiming that, before launching such a *Kar Seva*, the damaged idol of the temple had to be immersed in water and the whole temple purified in a special ritual called *subh muhurat* (ibid., 29 Dec. 1992). This argument enabled the Hindu Ekta Manch to delay the *Kar Seva*.

63 Ibid., 27 Dec. 1992. According to a survey conducted in 18 of these camps, 47 % of the 7,684 people surveyed were from poor labouring families (*Bhopal riot – a report*, op. cit., p. 12.)

64 There were no casualties in Punjab and Haryana. *See Frontline* (1 Jan. 1993, pp. 105-9), *Sunday* (20 Dec. 1992, pp. 28-9 and 52-6, and 27 Dec. 1992, pp. 48-50) and *India Today* (31 Dec. 1992, pp. 40-3).

to this point in studying the BJP's search for an alternative strategy; but before that we must consider another parameter of our model, the political context. The way Hindu militants overstepped the mark damaged their credibility and enabled the Centre to act against them in a justified manner, even though the repression was mitigated by a search for a compromise.

The reaction of the central government: an ambivalent tactic

On 9 December, Narasimha Rao declared that the Babri Masjid would be rebuilt on the very same site. Soon afterwards, his government announced carefully prepared measures to control the Hindu nationalist movement; it now appeared determined to deal decisively with the Ayodhya affair. However, this new approach was soon hindered by judicial rulings, and the Centre also decided to moderate its position, probably because of the unwillingness of some sections of the Hindu public to countenance a firm response. Even so, the Centre's policy, ostensibly inspired by secular principles, did produce some positive results.

A limited crackdown

On the evening of 6 December 1992 President's rule was imposed in Uttar Pradesh shortly after Kalyan Singh resigned his post as Chief Minister. Three days after the demolition of the mosque, L.K. Advani, M.M. Joshi, Uma Bharti, Sadhvi Rithambara, Ashok Singhal and Vinay Katiyar were arrested on charges of inciting communal violence. The following day, the RSS, the VHP, the Bajrang Dal, the Jamaat-e-Islami and the Islamic Sevak Sangh (a newly-founded association based in Kerala) were banned. As in the initial stages of the Emergency in 1975, Muslim organisations were also subjected to central control although Hindu nationalist ones were naturally the main target. Their offices were sealed and all activity – for instance the meeting of RSS *shakhas* – was prohibited. The two common grounds for the banning of the RSS, the VHP and the Bajrang Dal were the participation of their members in the demolition of the Babri Masjid and their incitement of communal antagonism. The notification issued against the RSS added that it was intent on asserting 'that members of certain religious communities have alien religions and cannot, therefore, be considered nationals of India'.[66] The notification issued against the Bajrang Dal added that its training methods made it 'likely that the participants in such activity will use criminal force of violence against

---

[65] A. Nandy, 'Three propositions', *Seminar*, no. 402, Feb. 1993, p. 16.

[66] See the notifications in *White Paper on Ayodhya*, op. cit., p. 115.

other religious communities.'[67] On 15 December 1992, the BJP governments in Madhya Pradesh, Rajasthan and Himachal Pradesh were dismissed on the charge that 'the Government of the State could not be carried on in accordance with the provisions of the Constitution.'[68] The state assemblies were dissolved and President's rule was imposed in each of the states concerned.

Within Narasimha Rao's government, the main advocate of a repressive policy was Arjun Singh (the Minister for Human Resources and Development). He probably tried to project himself as a strong defender of secularism because such a reputation was likely to work to his advantage in any future bid for the post of Prime Minister. In contrast, since becoming Prime Minister in 1991, Narasimha Rao was apparently inclined to avoid a confrontation with the Hindu nationalists. He probably considered that strong repressive measures would help them to present themselves as 'martyrs' and that, ultimately, the support which they had attracted would diminish. Even after the demolition of the Babri Masjid, the government's policy toward the RSS-BJP-VHP combination oscillated between firmness and conciliation.

The crackdown introduced after the Ayodhya incident was soon relaxed. The seven leaders confined in the aftermath of the demolition were freed on January 10, 1993, while only a relatively small number of people were taken into custody under the Unlawful Activities (Prevention) Act following the banning of the five communal organisations. In Uttar Pradesh, about 1,500 were being held in jail on 15 December, most of them from the RSS, the VHP and the Bajrang Dal.[69] In Madhya Pradesh, nearly 1,000 members of these organisations were taken into custody.[70] In other states, there were far fewer arrests. Probably no more than 3,500-4,000[71] Hindu nationalist activists went to jail. Key cadres had gone into hiding (often outside the Hindi belt – in West Bengal or Tamil Nadu, for instance)[72] but in any case the government was unwilling to keep people behind bars for long.

The government's policy was certainly hampered by the verdicts of the courts. The first major judicial decisions were rendered in Madhya Pradesh. On 16 December, the full bench of the High Court of Jabalpur admitted a writ by Jagdish Jain, a veteran RSS leader and businessman

---

[67]   Ibid., p. 117.
[68]   Ibid., p. 35.
[69]   *Pioneer*, 15 Dec. 1992.
[70]   *National Mail*, 19 Dec. 1992.
[71]   According to press reports, the number of activists of all the banned organisations up to December 17 was 4,735 (*National Mail*, 20 Dec. 1992).
[72]   H.V. Seshadri, K.C. Sudarshan and D. Thengadi evaded arrest, for instance (*Statesman* (Delhi), 16 Dec. 1992 and *Sunday*, 27 Dec. 1992, pp. 28-35).

from Raipur, challenging the central government's notification banning the five organisations and granted an interim stay.[73] A few days later, the High Court ordered that the RSS offices in Indore and Jabalpur be opened.[74] Meanwhile, the Chief Justice ordered the release of several RSS leaders.[75] On April 2, 1993, the High Court overturned the imposition of President's Rule in Madhya Pradesh and ordered the restoration of the Vidhan Sabha. The central government appealed before the Supreme Court and President's Rule remained in force.

The ban imposed on the Hindu nationalist organisations was covered by the Unlawful Activities (Prevention) Act, 1967, which requires that notification should be confirmed by a Tribunal headed by a High Court judge. Justice P.K. Bahri of Delhi High Court was appointed in this capacity, and on 4 June 1993 he upheld the ban on the VHP for a statutory period of two years because of the inflammatory nature of some of its members' speeches but cancelled those against the RSS and the Bajrang Dal. The judge considered 'that it was not in contemplation of either the leaders of the three associations or the authorities that harm would be caused to the disputed structure during the *Kar Seva* permitted by the Hon'ble Supreme Court on December 6, 1992.'[76] The Judge paid little attention to the other grounds for banning the RSS and Bajrang Dal. The judicial process therefore affected the impact of the repressive measures enforced by the Centre.

However, the government vacillated between a firm policy and one of conciliation even before the court rulings. This attitude was suggested by the way it dealt with the disputed site in Ayodhya after the demolition of the mosque. The Centre did not prevent the *Kar Sevaks* from building a makeslift temple, because they 'were in a defiant mood'. The police intervened on the night of 7-8 December 1992 only to avoid 'large-scale use of force and violence'.[77] The ambiguities of the Union government were also evident in its treatment of the question of whether devotees could offer *darshan* of the images which had been installed in the temporary shelter on the Babri Masjid/Ramjanmabhoomi site. Towards the end of December 1992, *sadhus* began a fast in Ayodhya to protest against the refusal of the authorities to permit *darshan* of the images. The district administration at first allowed devotees to offer prayers at the

[73]   *National Mail*, 18 Dec. 1992.

[74]   Ibid., 25 Dec. 1992.

[75]   *Ibid.*, 20 Dec. 1992. This attitude possibly reflects certain sympathies among the judiciary in Madhya Pradesh. For instance, the State Advocate-General resigned his post in protest at the dismissal of the BJP government (ibid., 17 Dec. 1992).

[76]   Cited in A.G. Noorani, 'A touch of gloss – Bahri report: bizzare conclusions', *Frontline*, 10 Sept. 1993, p. 111.

[77]   *White paper on Ayodhya*, op. cit., p. 34.

disputed site and then withdrew its permission. Eventually, the Lucknow Bench of the Allahabad High Court ruled that *darshan* should be permitted on the ground that Ram was a 'Constitutional entity and a reality of our national culture and fabric'.[78] Immediately large numbers of devotees converged on Ayodhya. Once again, a judicial decision had impeded the government's policy. It was now much more difficult to rebuild the Babri Masjid – as Narasimha Rao had promised – given that a makeshift temple had been allowed to function on the site. Although the government could have challenged the High Court ruling before the Supreme Court, it did not seem inclined to do so. Press reports even claimed that the decision of the district administration had been approved – or even suggested – by the Centre, which, under President's Rule, virtually ran the state.[79]

This interpretation is consistent with the limited scope of the arrests and the slow pace of the investigation into the events of 6 December. Despite – and before – unfavourable judicial rulings, the Centre could have detained a much larger number of Hindu nationalist activists – and for a longer period – had it wanted to do so. But as early as late December 1992, the will to do so seemed to be lacking. On 13 December 1992 the Central Bureau of Investigation (CBI) was entrusted with the task of investigating the demolition of the Babri Masjid, but it was not allocated the staff it needed till the following May. Finally it filed a charge sheet against forty Hindu nationalists (including Advani, Kalyan Singh and Thackeray) on 5 October 1993.

The government's hesitation was probably founded on their suspicion that large sectors of public opinion would disapprove of a strong clampdown against the Hindu nationalist movement. A nationwide opinion poll conducted by MARG between 17 and 23 December and published in *India Today* indicated that 53.3% of those interviewed disapproved of the decision to rebuild the mosque, 55.2% approved of the dismissal of the government of Uttar Pradesh, but only 37.1% as far as the other states were concerned (30.4% in North India against 50.6% in South India). Respectively 48 and 49.9% approved of the arrest of the BJP's leaders and of the banning of communal organisations but, again, support was much weaker in the North (38.7% and 44.3%) than in the South (70.9% and 69.3%).[80] New Delhi probably realised that Hindu feelings were such that in North India, where the Congress (I) had already lost much of its influence, the post-demolition policy might be counter-productive. The decision to allow *darshan* in the makeshift temple and the near suspension

[78] This plea was based on the fact that a sketch of Ram appeared in one of the copies of the Constitution signed by the members of the Constituent Assembly in 1949 (S. Muralidharan, 'Darshan Force – Legitimising a trespass', *Frontline*, 23 Jan. 1993, p. 20).
[79] Ibid.
[80] *India Today*, 15 Jan. 1993.

of repressive measures against the Hindu nationalists must be seen in this perspective: the risk of antagonising the majority community and casting Hindu nationalist leaders in the role of martyrs was too great.

Narasimha Rao's response to the demolition of the disputed structure, therefore, cannot be compared to that of Nehru's after Gandhi's assassination. Nor does it compare with the steps which Mrs Gandhi took to ban communal organisations at the onset of the Emergency. The Hindu nationalist movement had become too strong and too popular in many quarters, so the Prime Minister opted for a longer term strategy combining firmness with conciliation. The central government was however willing to act decisively when Hindu nationalist organisations resorted to street agitation while the bans against them were still in force. On 25 February 1993, the BJP organised a demonstration in Delhi protesting against the bans and calling for a mid-term Lok Sabha poll as well as for elections in the four states where BJP governments had been dismissed. Many party workers were put into preventive detention in their home states (about 4,500 in Delhi, 2,500 in Madhya Pradesh, 3,750 in Maharashtra, etc., according to official sources)[81] and, more importantly, the police dealt severely with the demonstrators: they lobbed teargas shells into the processions, made several *lathi* charges and occasionally used water cannon and stun-grenades. The government took such firm action because it regarded the demonstration as a provocation. This hard-line response apparently had a demoralising effect on BJP activists.[82] In combination with its policy of selective repression the Narasimha Rao government set in train a longer term plan to bring the Ayodhya affair to a satisfactory conclusion.

In quest of a compromise at Ayodhya

On 11 December 1992, the Lucknow Bench of the Allahabad High Court gave its long-awaited decision concerning the 2.77 acres of land adjoining the Babri Masjid/Ramjanmabhoomi whose acquisition by the Kalyan Singh government in 1991 had been challenged by Muslim associations. The acquisition was cancelled, and on several grounds, the principal one being that, since the notified area belonged to the Sunni Central Waqf Board, and included a Muslim graveyard, such properties could not be acquired under the Land Acquisition Act.

On 27 December, the central government issued an ordinance for the acquisition of all the disputed areas in Ayodhya. The Presidential Or-

---

[81] *Statesman* (Delhi), 24 and 27 Feb. 1993. The BJP claimed higher figures, between 16,000 and 30,000.

[82] 78. M. Jain, 'BJP workers low on morale', *Statesman* (Delhi), 5 March 1993.

dinance, issued on 7 January 1993, was confirmed on 24 March, by the passing of a bill. The Centre thereby acquired 67.7 acres and provided that the land would be made available to two trusts which would construct a Ram temple and a mosque respectively.[83] On 27 December 1992 the government had also requested the President to seek, under article 143(1), the opinion of the Supreme Court on the question of 'Whether a Hindu temple or any Hindu religious structure existed prior to the construction of the Ram-Janma Bhumi-Babri Masjid (including the premises of the inner and outer courtyards of such structure) in the area on which the structure stood?'[84] Once again, the Supreme Court's terms of reference were suggestive of a pro-Hindu bias.

These initiatives also revealed that Narasimha Rao's government was trying to defer its immediate reaction while working towards a final agreement. First it had referred a group of contentious issues, including those which concerned the history of the site, to the Supreme Court, in an obvious attempt to buy time and avoid a confrontation. Second, it began to search for a compromise by keeping the Hindu nationalist fold at bay: the envisaged Hindu trust was supposed to supplant the one set up by the VHP to build the temple. Thus the government set out to co-opt allegedly apolitical religious figures in order to challenge the VHP's claim to represent 'the Hindus';[85] for this purpose it turned to two contrasting figures, Chandra Swami and Swaroopanand Saraswati.

Chandra Swami had begun his public career as a Youth Congress leader in Hyderabad but had subsequently taken part in the anti-cow slaughter agitation of 1966-7. After 1972, he acquired a reputation as a Tantrik *guru* and later reportedly established close links with Adnan Khashoggi, who was reputed to be an international arms dealer. In 1988 Chandra Swami was arrested on a charge of fraud and then released. He had nevertheless established close relations with many politicians who now regarded him as their *guru*.[86] Narasimha Rao, whom Swami claimed

[83] This plan drew most of its inspiration from a more elaborate version of a 14-point proposal evolved the previous day by the Congress Working Committee: the temple should be constructed at the site where the *Shilanyas* took place but should not include the structure housing the images. The mosque had to be built outside the *panchkosi parikrama* (the perimeter of the most famous Ayodhya pilgrimage site). See 'The acqisition of certain area at Ayodhya ordinance, 1993', in *White Paper on Ayodhya*, op. cit., pp. 97-106.

[84] Ibid., p. 107.

[85] On 28 December 1992, twelve *mahants* from Ayodhya – including Baba Lal Das, the former priest of the Ramjanmabhoomi – met Arjun Singh to offer their services to the Centre in its efforts to evolve a compromise in Ayodhya (*National Mail*, 29 Dec. 1992).

[86] *Frontline*, 2 July 1993. The funeral of Chandra Swami's mother was attended by Narasimha Rao's son, V.C. Shukla and Kamal Nath (both Union Ministers), Chandra Shekhar, Devi Lal and many others (*Statesman* (Delhi), 21 April 1993).

as one of his disciples, apparently used him to erode the influence of the VHP among *sadhus* and stifle its ability to exploit the Ayodhya issue. In April 1993, Chandra Swami organised a gathering of 300 *sadhus* and *dharmacharyas* (including Ramanandacharya Haryacharya of Ayodhya) in Delhi which adopted one resolution urging Hindu religious figures to abjure politics and another declaring that, while a Ram temple should be built where the Babri Masjid had stood, a mosque should not be reconstructed within 5 km. of the spot.[87] However, it appears that the Centre realised the limits of Chandra Swami's appeal and decided to seek with more determination the help of the four *Shankaracharyas*.[88]

Of the four, Swaroopanand Saraswati was the most hostile to the VHP and had the greatest sympathy for the Congress (I). He certainly played a leading role in setting up a meeting between the four *Shankaracharyas*, a most unusual event. It was held on 27 June 1993 at Sringeri, a *math* whose relatively young *Shankaracharya* (he was appointed to the post in 1989), Bharathi Tirth, was eager to settle the Ayodhya affair, which he considered had become a political rather than a religious matter. Swami Nischalananda, the Puri *Shankaracharya* who had recently succeeded Niranjan Dev, took a rather different view: like his predecessor, he was more inclined to adopt a Hindu nationalist attitude and thought that *sadhus* should have a role in politics.[89] According to press reports, he was persuaded to attend the meeting by the intervention of K.C. Lenka, the Minister of State for Railways, who wields considerable influence in Puri.[90]

The programme that emerged from the meeting proved to be very similar to that which the VHP had developed. According to Swaroopanand Saraswati:

[87] Chandra Swami attracted a few religious figures such as Swami Divyanand. The Shankaracharya of Bhanpura had left the VHP in 1991 or 1992 because he disapproved of Kalyan Singh's vacillation about building the temple and probably also because this relatively disciplined organisation did not leave him enough room for manoeuvre. Divyanand, therefore, had founded a Dharma Raksha Mandal which supported Chandra Swami (ibid., 2 June 1993).

[88] In early June 1993, Chandra Swami organised a *Som Yagya* (a Vedic sacrifice) in Ayodhya in order to break the monopoly of the VHP over the site and make a show of force by attracting thousands of *sadhus*. That this venture had been patronised by the Centre was indicated by the help which Chandra Swami was given by Uttar Pradesh and central government officials. He was allowed to enter the disputed zone and the state administration was involved in preparations for the *Som Yagya*. According to press reports, the Union deputy minister of state for home affairs met the governor in relation to this matter (*Times of India*, 5 June 1993). However, the number of people taking part in the *Yagya* and those that came to see it performed was relatively small. The gathering endorsed the resolutions adopted at the April meeting and announced that similar events would be held in other parts of India.

[89] See his interview in *Frontline*, 30 July 1993, p. 28.

[90] Ibid., p. 24.

The Ram temple has to be built at the same place [where the Babri Masjid stood]. [...] The temple and the mosque may be close together, but built separately. So much so that the bells from the temple are not heard at the mosque and the *azaan* [call to the faithful] from the mosque is not heard at the temple.[91]

In the joint statement issued after their meeting the four *Shankaracharyas* called upon the central government to hand over the disputed land which it had acquired to a newly constituted, independent, apolitical, religious body which would oversee the construction of the Ram temple.[92] It was indeed the government's intention to take such a preliminary step as a means of sidelining the VHP-backed Ramjanmabhoomi Trust. The VHP protested that the Sringeri meeting had been engineered by the Centre with the intention of dividing the *sadhus* who had been united in supporting the VHP's own plans.

There is little doubt that the Sringeri meeting led to a schism between the VHP and the Akhara Parishad, a Hardwar-based institution which coordinates the work of the 13 Akhara governing bodies, each controlling an average of 100 religious bodies (such as temples, *ashrams* and *maths*).[93] In June 1993, the head of the Akhara Parishad announced that he 'fully support[ed]' the appeal issued after the Sringeri meeting and rejected the request of the Ramjanmabhoomi Trust for the nomination of two representatives of the Akhara Parishad to the Nyas Manch (a body formed in January 1993 and presided over by Swami Vamdeo).[94] The process initiated by the four *Shankaracharyas* gathered momentum when, in October 1993, they organised a convention in Fatehpur (Rajasthan) attended by a large number of *sadhus*. It was an important step towards launching a trust to build the Ram temple.[95]

The attenuation of the VHP's ability to influence *sadhus* was an important achievement. However, the *Shankaracharyas'* scheme did entail the building of the temple on the very place where the Babri Masjid had stood, and no Muslim organisation was prepared to accept such an outcome. In April 1993, the All India Muslim Personal Law Board rejected the government's proposal and directed Muslim leaders not to affiliate themselves with the trust which it wished to establish for the construction of a new mosque.[96]

---

91 Interview in ibid., p. 29.
92 Ibid, 16 July 1993.
93 Interview in ibid., 30 July 1993.
94 *Times of India*, 26 Jan. 1993.
95 Ibid., 29 Oct. 1993.
96 *Times of India*, 4 April 1993. Shahabuddin also wrote to the *shankaracharyas* to persuade them not to campaign for the building of a temple on the site where the Babri Masjid stood (*Muslim India*, no. 132, Dec. 1993).

Our study of the Centre's reaction to the demolition of the mosque suggests two conclusions. The first is that although robust speeches were made in defence of secularism, little was done to reestablish this principle as a norm of the régime. The sanctions against the Hindu nationalists were limited in scope (at least compared to what happened in 1948 and 1975), as were attempts to apply legal restrictions to the use of communal propaganda during the summer 1993. In this respect, the Congress (I) failed to receive the support it might have been entitled to expect from the parties of the legitimate opposition, and thus a secular front did not emerge. On 29 July 1993 the government introduced the Constitution (Eightieth) Amendment Bill, which was intended to separate religion from politics. Another bill, with the aim of amending the Representation of the People Act, 1951, was also announced. Both bills were intended to prevent politicians from using appeals to religious sentiment, especially during election campaigns.[97] However, consideration of these bills was deferred by the Lok Sabha on 24 August because the Congress (I) could not obtain the support of opposition parties – primarily that of the Janata Dal – to agree to the proposed changes to the law.[98] George Fernandes (Janata Dal), in a dissenting note to the Joint Committee Report, objected that no change in the law was needed; rather, a political response to the challenge of communalism had to be worked out.[99] In contrast with what happened when the RSS was first banned in the late 1940s, a strong coalition of secular forces did not materialise. While a joint vote on these bills by the 'non-communal' parties would have been 'a political rejoinder' to Hindu nationalism, the political context in 1993 was not likely to lead to the marginalisation of the Hindu nationalists.

The Centre's policy must be seen in this context. Apparently Narasimha Rao had concluded as early as 1991 that the government was not strong enough to confront Hindu nationalism in a straight fight, especially because it had to give priority to the economic reforms required to achieve the structural adjustments negotiated with the IMF in mid-1991 (see below). Thus his long-term strategy was to avoid an immediate confrontation with the Hindu nationalists but instead gradually to weaken them, first, by providing space for the *Shankaracharyas* to establish alternative plans for dealing with the problems posed by the Ayodhya affair, and, second, by allowing support for the Hindu nationalists to ebb away as the

---

[97] The text of the bill has been reproduced in S. Kashyap, *Delinking Religion and Politics*, New Delhi: Vimot, 1993, pp. 74-5.

[98] *Times of India*, 25 Aug. 1993. A two-thirds majority is required in Parliament to amend the Constitution.

[99] A. Nauriya, 'Politics of religious hate – Beyond the bills', *EPW*, 11 Sept. 1993, p. 1906. The bills were also criticised because they could be misused by the governing party in order to deregister opposition political parties.

public became preoccupied with other issues, such as socio-economic ones. Indeed, the economic liberalisation policy which had been initiated by Narasimha Rao's government was bound to reorder the priorities of the political debate.[100] Arjun Singh's more direct approach might well have been counter-productive, but his pressure for a resolute response may have served indirectly to stiffen the Prime Minister's resolve. Narasimha Rao was reportedly reluctant to dismiss the BJP governments in Madhya Pradesh, Rajasthan and Himachal Pradesh but Singh had favoured such a step. In the event, the imposition of President's rule in these states laid the groundwork for a certain electoral recovery by Congress (I) at the expense of the BJP. Thus the combination of firmness and delaying tactics did at least enable the central government to check the rise of Hindu nationalism even though it did not lead to the unequivocal restoration of secularism. The reaction of the Centre to the demolition of the Babri Masjid was a contributory factor in the BJP's change of policy. Such a change was in any case dictated by the contradictions of the strategy of ethno-religious mobilisation.

The strategy of ethno-religious mobilisation in question

In the aftermath of the mosque's demolition the Hindu nationalist movement continued to benefit from a 'Ram wave' in North India, but it soon became evident that the RSS-trained leadership risked being marginalised by actors who had come to the fore on 6 December, namely *sadhus* and *kar sevaks,* and that the unleashing of communal violence would alienate actual or potential supporters, especially after the Bombay blasts.

The MARG opinion poll already referred to showed that 52.6% of those interviewed in the North approved of the demolition – as opposed to 16.7% in the South. The survey of voting intentions revealed that a parliamentary election would have enabled the BJP to increase its representation in the Lok Sabha from 120 to 170 seats while that of the Congress (I) would have fallen from 245 to 233.[101] The pattern was one of sharp contrast, with the South rejecting Hindu nationalism on a massive scale while the North was offering it increased support.[102] These findings appeared to demonstrate the efficacy of the strategy of ethno-religious mobilisation: that by arousing Hindu feelings and inducing communal

---

[100] On Narasimha Rao's strategy, see the editorial by Harish Khare, 'Struggle over party agenda' (*Times of India,* 16 Feb. 1993).

[101] *India Today,* 15 Jan. 1993, p. 14.

[102] This North-South divide was even more apparent in the answers to the question: 'Who makes the best Prime Minister?': 17.9% and 28% of those interviewed chose Narasimha Rao respectively in the North and in the South while the proportions were 21.2% and 4.5% for Vajpayee and 10.1% and 4.5% for Advani.

violence, the electorate would become polarised to the immediate advantage of the BJP. When asked what would be the impact of the December 1992 events on the 'electoral arithmetic', K.N. Govindacharya replied:

There will be a semblance of polarisation in which the nationalists will be on one side and the pseudo-secularists will be on the other. People who believe in the concept of geo-cultural nationalism on one side and those who believe in dharmasala nationalism on the other. This polarisation will only be advantageous for us, for this is the thought process, ethos and psyche of the people. We have touched that sympathetic chord and definitely the thought process will resonate.[103]

Interestingly, this line was followed by all the BJP leaders, to varying degrees, a fact which illustrates once again the irrelevance of analysing this party in terms of ideologically differentiated factions. If this model is an accurate one, then the party would undoubtedly have lost most of its coherence after the demolition of the mosque. Y.K. Malik and V.B. Singh, for instance, argue that 'the BJP leadership can be divided into ideological factions', of which Vajpayee represents the 'moderate Hindu nationalists with libertarian emphasis' while Advani is classified as a 'Hindu nationalist'.[104] This typology is common in the Indian press but it is largely misleading – as the BJP's decision to search for a new strategy after 6 December 1992 suggests.

The resilience of BJP unity

In the aftermath of the demolition, leaders of the BJP whom the media described as 'moderates', such as Vajpayee and Jaswant Singh, expressed their reservations about the party's strategy. But it transpired that their views were not so moderate and were shared by other members of he party who were regarded as being more militant.

Soon after the demolition, Vajpayee declared that the events of 6 December had been the BJP's 'worse miscalculation'.[105] Similar statements were made by members such as Brajesh Mishra, but Vajpayee reportedly did not support his proposal to table a resolution vigorously condemning the demolition.[106] In February 1994 he claimed that 'those who divide the BJP between moderates and hardliners do not understand what the BJP is.'[107] This may be a fair comment, because the

103   Interview with K.N. Govindacharya, *National Mail*, 27 Dec. 1992, p. 4.
104   Y.K. Malik and V.B. Singh, 'Bharatiya Janata Party: An alternative to the Congress(I)?', *Asian Survey*, 32(4), April 1992, pp. 322-3.
105   See his interview in *India Abroad News Service*, 10 Dec. 1992.
106   *Pioneer*, 13 Dec. 1992, p. 1.
107   Interview with A.B. Vajpayee, 23 Feb. 1994, New Delhi.

leaders, whether 'moderate' or 'extremist', were all apparently unwilling to criticise the demolition of the mosque. Jaswant Singh, for instance, wrote in the *Organiser*:

Without doubt a wrong took place. But in this act of destruction, I do not see the kind of cataclysm that people are pointing out, or wish to draw attention to. [...] I think in a very real sense, and this might hurt many, a political era ended on 6 December. It is a great sorrow to me that this transition from the old order towards an emerging India – you can question whether the emerging India is the 'right' India or whether it ought to be moving differently – had to occur accompanied by violence. But it is without doubt a transition from the old to the new.[108]

In late December 1992, Vajpayee delivered a speech in which he declared that the Babri Masjid 'was a symbol of shame and has been erased'.[109] Such declarations require careful attention. Although there are differences in temperament and sensibility, and thus in the interpretation of events, between the various leaders of the BJP, these are of fine degree and do not justify any distinction between 'moderates' and 'hard-liners'. There exists in the party a division of labour between its leaders which enables them to attract, recruit and retain individual supporters with a variety of outlooks. Indeed, nobody left the party after 6 December, even though that day's events made some party members feel ill-at-ease.

After the events of 6 December Vajpayee even moved a no-confidence motion in the Lok Sabha on 17 December and delivered on this occasion a speech in which he said that the delay in the pronouncement of the Allahabad High Court's judgement was mainly responsible for the decision of 'a group' to demolish the disputed structure.[110] Interestingly, this argument became the BJP's official line of defence at the emergency meeting of the party's National Executive held at New Delhi on 23 and 24 December. At the same gathering an attempt was made to present the party as the victim of a government ignorant, not only of the people's will but also of democratic rules and values, as the imposition of President's rule allegedly testified.[111]

On 24 December, a 12-point 'action plan' was worked out with the aim of putting pressure on the Centre in order to precipitate mid-term elections, elections in the states formerly ruled by the BJP and a lifting of the bans on the Hindu nationalist organisations. The programme included, *inter alia*, a nationwide tour by party leaders, a petition in favour of the

[108] *Organiser*, 11 Apr. 1993.

[109] Cited in *Sunday*, 27 Dec. 1992-2 Jan. 1993.

[110] *Speeches of Shri Atal Bihari Vajpayee, Swamy Chinmayanand and Shri Lal Krishan Advani on Ayodhya issue*, New Delhi: BJP Publication, 1993.

[111] *BJP National Executive Meeting – Political Resolution*, 23-4, Dec. 1992 (New Delhi), p. 18.

building of the Ram temple and a mass demonstration in Delhi on 25 February, on the opening day of the budget session of Parliament. The BJP leadership abandoned its apologetic stance and divisions between 'moderates' and 'hard-liners' over the demolition of the Babri Masjid were nowhere to be seen. *Kar sevaks* even featured as 'honoured guests' during public meetings addressed by BJP leaders.[112] The 'action plan' was primarily the work of M.M. Joshi, the BJP President, who threatened the Centre with 'direct action' from 25 February if it did not announce elections by that date.[113]

It seems, therefore, that after the demolition the Hindu nationalist leaders were eager to pursue a militant policy, of which a large number of Hindus in North India seemed to approve. However, the atmosphere changed after the onset of communal violence and especially in the wake of the Bombay blasts.

According to reliable sources in Bhopal, the BJP commissioned a survey in Madhya Pradesh and Uttar Pradesh which revealed in March 1993 that rural-dwellers, while supporting the idea of building a temple in Ayodhya, disapproved of the demolition of a place of worship and were concerned about the use of violence to sow dissension between members of communities who had lived together in the same locality notwithstanding religious differences. Although villagers were susceptible to the appeal of the BJP's 'nationalist devotionalism', even when expressed in aggressive terms, their occasional involvement in ritual activities and processions connected with the Ramjanmabhoomi movement did not mean, as Hindu nationalists may have hoped, that they adopted anti-Muslim attitudes. In his study of village politics in Eastern Uttar Pradesh, G.K. Lieten shows that, after the demolition of the Babri Masjid, in contrast with the situation prevailing in the early 1990s, a majority of OBC and Scheduled Caste leaders pronounced against the building of a temple at Ayodhya and condemned the communal riots precipitated by the Ramjanmabhoomi movement.[114] At the village level, it was reverence for Ram rather than anti-Muslim feeling which was most in evidence. Moreover a survey conducted in Delhi and West UP revealed that only 28% of workers supported the demolition of the mosque as against 60% among white-collar occupations and 62% of traders.[115] Contrary to the hopes entertained by these organisations, the 'nationalist devotionalism' and 'political *bhakti*' of the late 1980s and early 1990s were not translated into

[112] *Times of India*, 27 Dec. 1992, p. 1.

[113] *Statesman* (Delhi), 16 Jan. 1993.

[114] 'On casteism and communalism in Uttar Pradesh', op. cit., p. 781.

[115] P.K. Chhibber and S. Misra, 'Hindus and the Babri Masjid', *Asian Survey*, 33 (7), July 1993, p. 669.

an ethnic form of political consciousness, at least among the peasants and urban workers of North India for whom survey data is available. The RSS-VHP-BJP combine used the instrumentalisation of religious symbols for political purposes, but many of its followers mobilised for religious ends and disapproved of the 1992 events.

The demolition of the mosque and the ensuing riots were also anathema to other potential or actual supporters of the BJP. The middle classes, local property owners and traders who are often affected by riots were naturally worried about the maintenance of law and order.[116] Every responsible citizen could not but be disturbed by the way in which the Ramjanmab-hoomi movement had brought about communal violence. The Bombay blasts also showed that the minoritites could retaliate in ways which harmed Hindu interests. On 12 March 1993, a dozen or so bombs exploded in Bombay, killing about 250 people and causing severe damage to symbolic targets such as the Stock Exchange. These attacks were imme-diately linked to Muslims seeking revenge for the communal riots of December 1992 and January 1993, an interpretation that was gradually substantiated by police investigations. One of the few Muslim contibutors to *Organiser* wrote with feeling about where such a chain of events might lead the country:

Although in the long run the Islamic terrorists fail to achieve their objective, the havoc they wreak on the country with their ghoulish deeds cannot be ignored. Ever since the metropolis of Bombay has suffered the worst riots and the horrifying series of blasts of March 12 the common Indian is naturally worried of the likely onset in India of destructive terrorist activities of the Muslims. [...] There is a genuine apprehension of, God forbid, the entire Muslim community in India turning to terrorism. And unfortunately even if it so happens, i. e. if 14% of the population become terrorists, it will be unbelievable that the majority of about 84% will remain imprevious to the 'vogue' of fanaticism. And if such an abominable fate overtakes us, it will be literally suicidal for the 14% minority.[117]

The writer was expressing what must have been a widespread sense of anxiety about the consequences for society of such mutual hostility while predicting how violence would become more organised and impersonal. It was impossible for potential or actual supporters of the BJP, or even its members, not to be moved by this vision of a violent future,[118] and the

---

[116] A survey conducted in early 1993 in Bombay, Calcutta, Delhi and Madras showed that only 30.1% of interviewees thought that 'Hindu nationalism' would have a 'very positive' or a 'positive' effect on the 'way of life here in India' (33.6% in Bombay and 23.2% in Delhi). Even within the categories most favourably inclined towards Hindu nationalism (businessmen and retail traders – 37.8% – and white-collar workers – 35.1% –) the level of support for this viewpoint was well below an absolute majority (*Monthly Public Opinion Surveys*, Feb.-March 1993, p. XIII).

[117] M. Hussain, 'Islamic fundamentalism overtaking India', *Organiser*, 2 May 1993.

party itself may well have been influenced by such considerations when moderating the tone of its ideological statements.

The risks in relying on sadhus and Bajrang Dalis

The wisdom of relying on ethno-religious mobilisation was called into question after 6 December because it precipitated nation-wide civil disorder and left the RSS-BJP-VHP combination dependent upon *sadhus* and Bajrang Dalis who were largely responsible for the violence. The growing capacity of the VHP, members of the Bajrang Dal and of *kar sevaks* in general to dictate the political agenda of the Hindu nationalist movement posed great problems for the RSS and its affiliates and, more especially, for the BJP. As Nandy has pointed out, the prestige of the BJP has declined while that of the VHP (which also benefited from heavy financial support from the diaspora) and even the Bajrang Dal has been enhanced:

> The RSS stalwarts may think the Dal to be a necessary evil, a collection of lumpen gangsters at the moment fighting for a good cause, but politically the Dal has arrived, at least within the parivar [i. e. the RSS 'family']. It cannot be held in leash by the BJP or the politically more alert elements within the Rashtriya Swayamsevak Sangh.[119]

Ethno-religious mobilisation had therefore resulted in a decisive (and, for the RSS and the BJP, unwelcome) shift in the balance of power within Hindu nationalist politics. The RSS and the BJP also had to reckon with a further, related problem, namely that as communal violence increased so large sections of the population affected by it – notably the business community, which had provided so much of their support and funding – might lose faith in their role as responsible political actors.

Thus the RSS-trained leaders of the VHP decided to reassert their control over the Bajrang Dal. On 11 July 1993, the Bajrang Dal became an all-India body with a more rigid organisational structure that resembled that of the RSS in several respects. Uniforms were introduced (blue shorts, white shirt and saffron scarf) and in 1993 some 350 training camps were held.[120] A handbook was published discussing the ways in which 'the

---

[118] Immediately after the bomb explosions which occurred in Bombay on 12 March 1993, an opinion poll conducted in Jaipur, Bhopal, Lucknow and Shimla between 12 and 15 March revealed that a large majority of the respondents (except in Jaipur) considered that the promulgation of President's Rule had been justified because if it had not been imposed, the law and order situation would have 'greatly deteriorated'. These towns all contained a considerable number of BJP supporters and it is significant that the measure of approval for President's Rule had increased to this extent over a period of only three or four months. (*Monthly Public Opinion Surveys*, April 1993, p. IV).

[119] A. Nandy, 'Three propositions', op. cit., p. 15.

[120] Interview with Acharya Giriraj Kishore, New Delhi, 11 Feb. 1994.

trainers should give mental and physical training to the trainees', in the preface to which Acharya Giriraj Kishore praised the resolution shown by 'the young generation' of Hindus on 6 December 1992:

This day the force of youth, rejecting the leadership, and despite the leaders' repeated prohibitions, went ahead to accomplish the task at hand – the task of wiping off this mark of dishonour.[121]

However, he went on to emphasise the need for discipline:

Be it individual or nation, society or organisation, only the one who has discipline can attain success, consciousness and excellence. Without discipline there is no success in life. Discipline comes from training and exercise. And if the disciplined are further blessed with valour, then what more could one ask for?[122]

Another major player in the strategy of ethno-religious mobilisation, the *sadhus*, having won a great deal of influence in Hindu nationalist circles, seemed willing to oppose a number of the BJP's policies and generally to take a larger role in politics than in the past. In early 1993 Swami Chinmayanand, the BJP member for the Uttar Pradesh seat of Budaun in the Lok Sabha and one of the leaders of the VHP, delivered a speech in Parliament in which he emphasised the role *sadhus* had played in the Ramjanmabhoomi movement from 1984 onwards and their participation in the demolition of the mosque:

I would like to repeat that the call for kar sevaks was given by them [*sadhus*] and not given by the Vishva Hindu Parishad, the BJP or RSS. I take the blame here and now. Till yesterday, nobody was prepared to own responsibility. Today I come forward to own the responsibility for the entire sequence of events.[123]

This expression of pride in the demolition provides a further indication of the way in which certain *sadhus* were claiming for themselves their own sphere of political action, a trend that was apparent even before 6 December 1992. First, more and more *sadhus* contested elections. In 1991, the BJP had 6 saffron-clad MPs: Swami Chinmayanda (Budaun), Mahant Avaidyanath (Gorakhpur), Uma Bharti (Khajurao), Swami Sureshanand (Jalesar), Swami Sakshiji Maharaj (Mathura) and Yoganand Saraswati (Bhind). Second, *sadhus* tried increasingly to influence purely political matters. In October 1992 Swami Vamdeo, one of the most influential members of the VHP Margdarshak Mandal, announced that the 'Sant Samiti' had set up a committee to redraft what he described as

---

[121] R.P. Sharma, *Shikshak Margdarshaka*, Delhi: Bajrang Dal, 1993, pp. 3-4. I am most grateful to Akshay Bakaya for the translation of this highly Sanskritised text.

[122] Ibid., p. 4.

[123] *Speeches of Shri Atal Bihari Vajpayee, Swami Chinmayanand and Shri Lal Krishan Advani on Ayodhya issue*, New Delhi: BJP, 1993, p. 31.

the 'anti-Hindu' Constitution. On 25 December he published a pamphlet which challenged several basic principles of the Indian Constitution, including federalism, the recognition of English as an official language and the criteria of citizenship (he argued that citizenship rights should not be bestowed automatically on all individuals who are born in India of Indian parents but only on the basis of 'loyalty and patriotism').[124] The RSS, which was in favour of evolving a 'Constitution more suited to the ethos and genius [of India]', to quote Rajendra Singh,[125] might well have agreed with such proposals but the politically inclined *sadhus* went several steps further, questioning the very notion of positive discrimination on the basis of caste and demanding for themselves greater access to political power. The RSS and more especially the BJP could not adopt such an approach without jeopardising the support they had won among the Scheduled Castes. Moreover they were loathe to increase their dependence on the authority of religious leaders, many of whom were regarded as obscurantists by modern, middle-class Hindus and even probably by many of those voting for the BJP. An Eyewitness-MARG opinion poll conducted in late 1993 in five metropolitan cities included a question comparing the public esteem of ten professions. Religious leaders ranked just above politicians – who came last.[126]

The demolition of the Babri Masjid, which in a way was the logical conclusion of the Ramjanmabhoomi movement, revealed the contradictions of the strategy of ethno-religious mobilisation. While the Hindu nationalist organisations needed the support of as many activists and *sadhus* as possible in order to campaign on their behalf and sustain an emotional wave that would be translated into ideological and electoral gains, these was always the danger that such groups might go too far. Whether or not the leaders of the VHP and RSS had conspired to demolish the mosque, the event itself and the riots that followed revealed that the Bajrang Dalis and the *sadhus* were a force to be reckoned with. The BJP realised that its association with such firebrands might tarnish its reputation and jeopardise its hold on the political initiative. The BJP was all the more inclined to reshape its strategy because Narasimha Rao's government, while not restoring secularism as a norm of the régime, nonetheless implemented repressive measures.

Thus, in 1993 the Hindu nationalists began to amend their strategy. The RSS combination as a whole faced the same problem but for the BJP,

---

[124] *Frontline*, 29 Jan. 1993, pp. 4-5.

[125] Interview given to the *Indian Express*, 14 Jan. 1993. In another interview he said that he did not 'approve of everything going into the Constitution' (*Sunday Observer*, 7 Feb. 1993).

[126] *Sunday*, 15 Jan. 1994, p. 58.

which had to contest elections in the four states in which it had been removed from power, it was more acute. Under the Constitution the imposition of President's Rule had to be followed within six months by elections, for which the BJP needed to prepare its political agenda.

14

THE B.J.P. HELD IN CHECK IN
THE HINDI BELT

The demolition of the Babri Masjid and the violence that followed in its wake did not split the BJP but instead prompted an internal debate and a search for a new strategy. The party's leaders gradually evolved a strategy of mobilisation which continued to rely on ethno-religious themes but was less dependent on the issue of Ayodhya. This shift in strategy, however, proved to be less successful than the BJP had hoped.

Another major strategy of the Hindu nationalist movement – to promote the Sangathanist pattern of implantation and party-building – proved difficult to maintain once the BJP became the governing party in several states after 1990. Conflicts over the feasibility and merits of ideal policies often arise when a party achieves power – especially when it does so on its own for the first time. In the case of the Madhya Pradesh unit of the BJP, on which we shall focus, the BJP was affected by internal troubles. These resulted not from factionalism but rather from a form of groupism which revealed that the party's Sangathanist infrastructure was in danger of breaking down.

The declining efficiency of the strategies of mobilisation and party-building and the poor performance of the BJP state governments largely explain its relative electoral setback in the Hindi belt in 1993.

A gradual shift in emphasis in the ethno-nationalist repertoire

The heavy-handed police response to the BJP's demonstration of 25 February, the escalation of violence culminating in the Bombay blasts and the fact that elections were not due to be held for some time – on 12 May 1993 President's rule was extended for a further six months in Uttar Pradesh, Madhya Pradesh, Rajasthan and Himachal Pradesh, a decision that had been widely anticipated – raised further doubts about the party's continued reliance on the strategy of mobilisation. Such a policy could not be sustained over the long term, and might prove counter-productive given the electorate's fear of violence and unrest.

The meeting of the party's National Executive Council, held in Calcutta

from 10-12 April 1993, gave the first indication that a political reorientation might take place. The first four resolutions did not mention Ayodhya
at all and were restricted to expressions of opposition to Narasimha Rao's
economic policies and references to 'infiltration from Bangladesh', the
problems of the agricultural sector and the situation in Kashmir. The plan
of action of the fifth (political) resolution no longer aimed at precipitating
elections but instead demanded that all obstacles to the building of the
Ram temple be removed and that the RSS and the VHP be unbanned; it
called also for a fight against high-level corruption[1] and the strengthening
of internal security.[2]

This more cautious policy was confirmed at the annual session of the
party in Bangalore in June. Advani was designated to succeed M.M. Joshi,
who thus became the first BJP president not to be re-elected for a second
term. But this change in personnel did not imply a break with the new
party policy. Although Advani's accession to the presidency signified a
return to a more circumspect style of action, he took care to justify the
appropriateness of the strategy of ethno-religious mobilisation and did not
portray the demolition of the mosque as an error. Indeed, he represented
the Ramjanmabhoomi movement as part of a process of national integration and development[3] and his presidential address once again stressed the
importance of the movement[4] and emphasised its non-religious and

[1] At that time, Narasimha Rao had been accused in the press of being involved in a
security-scam at the Bombay stock exchange.

[2] BJP, *National Executive Meeting – Resolutions*, 10-12 April 1993 (Calcutta).

[3] In an interview to *Organiser* in February 1993, he declared: 'I have called ... cultural
nationalism not only the substratum of India's unity but also a dynamo for the country's
progress and transformation into a modern progressive and prosperous nation. The
dynamo is missing. If, in the last 45 years we have experienced an economic set-back it
is also because of this factor. There is nothing to unite us. Secularism, Constitution,
democracy, these by themselves have not been adequate inspiration for the masses. [...]
After all the position in India six years back was that all of us accepted that the country
came face to face with a number of fissiparous tendencies exploding, like in Kashmir,
Punjab, Assam, Tamil Nadu. Casteist tensions in U[ttar] P[radesh] and Bihar grew in
such a manner as to see massacre of entire villages. The Ayodhya issue came up at that
time. We perceived that the country can be united through that movement. And Ayodhya
has really sublimated all these fissiparous tendencies' (*Organiser*, 28 Feb. 1993, p. 6).
The strategy of ethno-religious mobilisation was therefore vindicated by Advani as a
means of creating a new dynamic for India. K.N. Govindacharya shared this view,
concerned as he was with 'the task of galvanising the people, of harnessing their talents
and energies for national reconstruction' (K.N. Govindacharya, 'Future vistas' in J.
Bajaj, ed., *Ayodhya and the future of India*, Madras: Centre for Policy Studies, 1993. p.
183).

[4] He said, for instance: 'Hindutva is not the panacea for the crises that have overwhelmed
our society; but at least it establishes the moral and ethical base to cope with the assaults
with a measure of self-confidence' (*Presidential address by Shri L.K. Advani – Bharatiya
Janata Party National Council Session*, 18-20 June, 1993, Bangalore, p. 4.)

nationalist substance in terms which implicitly refuted the claims of *sadhus* to appropriate it for themselves.

The campaign to construct a Rama Temple at the birthplace of Rama in Ayodhya may have been initiated by the *sadhus*, the VHP and the RSS. The BJP extended to it its full support. The campaign became a mass movement. Now, it is not just the aspiration of any organisation or party, it is the resolve of the entire nation.[5]

Advani went on to say that the party respected the Constitution,[6] thus enabling him further to differentiate the BJP from certain *sadhus*. He even spoke out against the participation of religious leaders in political movements, but was hastily obliged to qualify his statement.[7] Advani declared that soon after Swami Vamdeo's statement on the Constitution, he protested to Ashok Singhal in order to maintain a clear distribution of roles so that *sadhus* would refrain from making political pronouncements:

The religious figures should have a moral, ethical role. For issues related to religion, I can understand their interest. As far as issues pertaining to the politics or economy of the country aré concerned, it is to the political parties to decide.[8]

Under Advani's leadership, the BJP reaffirmed its attachment to ethno-religious mobilisation but at the same time widened its terms of reference to socio-economic and national issues. In his Bangalore address he mentioned 'the Bangladesh infiltration' and the Kashmir problem, both of which were cited as evidence that India was 'being gradually encircled by a hostile Islamic fundamentalist arc'.[9] In Bangalore, similarly, the resolutions of the National Council emphasised the corruption of Congress (I), the problems of the agricultural sector and even social policy, since it was agreed that 27% of government jobs should be reserved for Other Backward Classes. However, the National Council also called for an additional 10% of jobs to be reserved for the economically deprived, regardless of caste.[10] During the election campaign, which began in the summer of 1993, the BJP continued to rely on ethno-religious mobilisation while trying to dissociate itself from the *sadhus* and enlarge its appeal by resorting to other issues.

[5] Ibid., p. 2.
[6] Ibid., p. 3.
[7] *Times of India*, 31 July 1993.
[8] Interview with L.K. Advani.
[9] *Presidential address by Shri L.K. Advani*, op. cit., p. 15.
[10] BJP, *National Executive Meeting – Resolutions*, 18- 20 June, 1993 (Bangalore), p. 21-2.

The 1993 campaign for the Assembly elections: the strategy of ethno-religious mobilisation ebbs away

Compared with 1989, 1990 and 1991, the RSS-VHP-BJP combine's strategy of ethno-religious mobilisation failed to arouse strong Hindu sentiments during the 1993 campaign. At an all-India level – the situation in the states will be considered below – this failure was attributed to two principal factors, the nature of the BJP's appeal for support and the shortcomings of the VHP's campaign. The BJP sought to adjust its appeal to its Hindu nationalist constituency by stressing the links between the external threats facing India, only to find that voters barely heeded such claims. The VHP, for its part, behaved differently from the way it had in 1989, 1990 and 1991. Moreover, because the BJP chose to rely on issues other than that of Ayodhya, it distanced itself from the VHP during the campaign. The latter had been hurt by the ban and found that its ability to coordinate the activities of religious figures was much reduced and the Ayodhya issue had lost its immediacy.

The BJP in search of an ethno-nationalist image

Compared to 1991, the BJP tried once again to tone down its religious image in order to be identified more strongly as a nationalist party. It had already moved in this direction in late 1991 when it launched the *Ekta Yatra* under its own auspices. But in 1992, mainly because of the activism of the VHP, Ayodhya again came to dominate the Hindu nationalist agenda. The tactical shift of 1993 did not imply that the BJP had given up its exploitation of the Ayodhya issue but rather that it wanted to place it within a wider ethno-nationalist campaign. Commenting upon the campaign, L.K. Advani declared:

The *sadhus* were less involved in the last election campaign than in the previous ones. It was not a decision. It was on their own because there was not such a climate as there was in 1991. [...] We did not want to create such a climate. Why should we? We always worked up an emotional mood. [...] An emotional wave was not desirable. In Bangalore session we said that Ram mandir remained an issue and that we shall not rest until it is constructed; but at the same time we emphasised' corruption, social harmony etc. [...] No party can have credibility if it is seen as a one issue party. We would like the BJP to be accepted by the people as a party which has an holistic view of the problems of the country and which is not trying to win power simply on the basis of an emotional issue.[11]

In a two-part 'statement on national issue before the electorate in the mini-general elections, November 1993' published in the *Organiser*,

---

[11] Interview with L.K. Advani.

Advani did not refer to Ayodhya even once. He identified six themes, of which only two (the poor performance of the Rao government and the corruption of the Congress (I) regime) were not directly related to the question of nationalism. He focussed first on so-called international Muslim terrorism and with reference to the Bombay bombings stressed that 'the initial findings point to the existence of the same international terrorist network within India that has been responsible for outrages in countries such as Algeria, Egypt and the U.S.A.'[12] Second, he dwelt on Kashmiri separatism and the support he claimed it receives from Pakistan and pan-Islamic forces. He denounced 'the ethnic cleansing [a term borrowed from the war in the former Yugoslavia] of Hindus from the Kashmir Valley' and the way the government was 'overwhelmed by a mood of dithering and defeatism'.[13] Third, the BJP tried to whip up hostility towards Bangladeshi migrants. Advani highlighted 'the sinister dimension of [the] organized infiltration from Bangladesh':

The infiltrators are being used by pan-Islamic forces to create a Muslim zone across the Bangladesh border, and there are suggestions of a demand for an independent Islamic Bangalbhoomi. Steadily and silently, a fifth column is being created out of our very doorstep.[14]

These themes were used to reactivate a Hindu feeling of vulnerability during the election campaign. In fact, the party's election manifesto drew heavily on Advani's statement (the extracts quoted above were incorporated without alteration).[15] The other principal theme of his statement was the bill introduced by the government in order to separate religion from politics.

Advani protested that *dharma* was the essence of India and the bill was 'a crude attempt, bordering on the sinister, to take the soul out of the nation.'[16] As in earlier campaigns, so on this occasion the BJP appealed to Hindu nationalist sentiment as a means of creating a wave of support in its favour. In order to achieve such a mobilisation, the party relied heavily on the use of video films. According to *India Today*, about 2.3

---

[12] L.K. Advani, 'Onwards to Ramrajya', *Organiser*, 7 Nov. 1993, p. 11.

[13] This theme gained in importance after Kashmiri militants took control of the Hazratbal mosque – the most important shrine in Kashmir, said to contain a hair of the Prophet. The Indian army besieged the mosque for 34 days during the election campaign. Eventually, negotiations bore fruit and the militants surrendered. However the Hindu nationalists criticised the very fact that Narasimha Rao had entered into negotiations at all. Advani declared, for instance, that the way the Congress (I) government dealt with the issue showed its 'weak, vascillating, dithering and indecisive' nature (*Times of India*, 4 Nov. 1993, p. 5).

[14] L.K. Advani, 'Onwards to Ramrajya', op. cit., p. 11.

[15] Bharatiya Janata Party, *Onwards to Ramrajya*, op. cit.

[16] L.K. Advani, 'Cultural rootlessness', *Organiser*, 10 Oct. 1993, p. 19.

million rupees were spent for this purpose, mostly at Jain Studios. Some 125 video *raths* (trucks equipped with projectors and screens) were pressed into service.[17] They showed films of police firing on *kar sevaks* in Ayodhya in 1990 but also new ones produced for the campaign: images of the Bombay bomb blasts and of Narasimha Rao allegedly receiving bundles of rupee notes, were among the most popular.[18]

In addition to the medium of video, the BJP mass contact campaign again concentrated on the use of *yatras* to mobilise opposition to the bill intended to separate religion from politics. On 1 September 1993, the BJP announced that four *Janadesh Yatras* (Journeys to meet the people of the country) were to take place from 11 September 1993. One procession, leaving from Mangalore, was led by Advani; another, led by M.M. Joshi, left from Porbandar (Gujarat); a third, under Kalyan Singh's auspices, left from Calcutta; while a fourth, headed by Shekhawat, started out from Jammu. All four converged on Bhopal on 25 September after following complicated routes which enabled them to cross as many states as possible. The numerous meetings organised along the way consisted mainly of speeches attacking the bill. Their reception was uneven. The final rally in Bhopal on 25 September was a success[19] but the public response was much less enthusiastic than it had been during the *Rath Yatra* of 1990. For one thing, the appeal of the *Janadesh Yatras* was restricted by the abstract character of the speeches about *dharma*. M.M. Joshi, for instance, repeatedly argued in an abstruse manner for the separation of *adharma* rather than *dharma* from politics.[20]

Compared to the 1989, 1990 and 1991 election campaigns, the BJP's effort in the 1993 poll was low key and concentrated instead on issues of current interest that had an ethno-nationalist overtone rather than on the question of Ayodhya. Some party activists tried to exploit the issue at the local level but this turned out to be a delicate enterprise.

The difficulty of exploiting the Ayodhya issue

The weakening of the VHP. In contrast with 1989, 1990 and 1991, when the BJP election campaign was launched in close association with the VHP, in 1993 the two did not cooperate to the same extent. The VHP was hampered by the government's ban on its activities. Although this was not

---

[17] *India Today*, 15 Nov. 1993.

[18] See, for instance, 'Himalavar Khabardar – Hindusthan hai, teyar', J.K. Jain, New Delhi, 1993.

[19] *Times of India*, 21 Sept. 1993; *Statesman* (Delhi), 19 Sept. 1993; and *Times of India*, 26 Sept. 1993.

[20] *Organiser*, 19 Sept. 1993, p. 19.

strictly enforced (as early as March 1993 its Delhi office was re-opened because of a judicial decision in its favour) it had to proceed with caution given that any display of militancy could lead to the imposition of further restrictions and because it no longer had free access to its bank account.[21] Both factors explain the relative decline in activity at the VHP's head-quarters.[22]

The government's policy also had the indirect effect of dissuading *sadhus* from working with the VHP. A number of sadhus were concerned that their religious institutions might have to forfeit some of their property were they to be associated with a banned organisation. The BJP govern-ment of Uttar Pradesh had also aroused the ire of *sadhus* by implementing legislation in 1991-2 aimed at controlling the expenditure of temples.[23] In addition the four *Shankaracharyas'* support for the Ayodhya issue had attracted *sadhus* who were previously associated with the VHP. Ashok Singhal wrote to the former to express approval of their plan for the Ram temple and to ask what they meant by their reference to the 'apolitical religious leaders' who were expected to head the trust which would direct the construction of the temple. Swami Nischalananda alone responded, assuring Singhal that his views and those of the VHP were one and the same.[24] The Margdarshak Mandal held a meeting in mid-October in Nagpur and 'decided to persuade the *Shankaracharyas* of Sringeri and Kanchi not to join the government-sponsored trust'. It also urged the gathering 'not to bother about [the] property [which they might lose].'[25] However, some religious congregations' – especially the *akharas* in Haridwar – no longer backed the VHP as strongly as they had before.[26]

This attenuation of the VHP goes some way to explain the difficulties it faced in launching a new mobilisation. In June it announced that it was seeking the transfer of all the land acquired by the government in Ayodhya to the Ramjanmabhoomi Nyas. The statement was endorsed at the Nagpur meeting in October but the timing altered: although the campaign was still due to begin on the 24th, which was the day of Dasahara, it was now proposed that there would be a demonstration in Ayodhya; as it turned

21   According to Acharya Giriraj Kishore this financial constraint was the main effect of the ban (interview on 11 Feb. 1994, New Delhi).

22   One of the joint secretaries of the VHP working there declared that the activities of the organisation were 'dislocated' (interview, 12 Feb. 1994, New Delhi). Kishore emphasised that while the leaders of the VHP did not launch an agitation they spent 1993 strengthening their organisation (1,404 workshops were held all over Indian in 1993, according to him).

23   *Hindustan Times*, 30 Oct. 1993, p. 11.

24   *Organiser*, 19 Sept. 1993, p. 18.

25   Ibid., 24 Oct. 1992.

26   *Frontline*. 22 Oct. 1993. p. 29.

out, *sadhus* were asked to 'go round the states where polling [was] to be held in November to campaign against the Congress'.[27]

The indirect nature of the support given by the VHP to the BJP was possibly due as much to its reluctance to be associated with the latter as to the concern of the 'banned VHP' not to irritate the government by its activism. In Madhya Pradesh the leader of the VHP unit in Shivpuri district commented on the 1993 election campaign as follows:

There were some differences in the high commands of the BJP and the VHP. VHP and RSS are purely Hindu minded and pro-Hindu bodies while the BJP, being a political body, certain Muslims are also members of it; so their perspectives are to some extent different from our outlook. They don't want to give the impression to the public that they are anti-Muslim. Due to that difference, the high command did not ask any support from the VHP or the RSS in these elections. It has affected the results. We were not so active as we were in 1989, 1990 and 1991. Then we toured the whole countryside. But this time we were just sitting at home or doing local canvasing, that's all.[28]

This suggests that the lack of close co-operation between the BJP and the VHP at the local level was common knowledge, even though this informant was prepared to attribute the rift to the BJP's apparent attempt to recruit Muslim members, which was certainly not the principal explanation. In fact the VHP did not even implement the limited agenda which had been set out at Nagpur. The *Ramjanmabhoomi bachao* (Save Ram's birthplace) agitation was postponed till 15 November, lasted only a fortnight and had little impact.[29] Organisational factors cannot in themselves explain this poor response; the Ayodhya issue appeared to have lost some of its appeal.

Ayodhya: an issue on the wane?   While the demolition of the Babri Masjid and the ensuing violence probably led BJP voters to distance themselves from Hindu nationalism, it is just as likely that many Hindu nationalist symphathisers dissociated themselves from the RSS-VHP-BJP combination because the object of their hatred had disappeared.

For many Hindus, the Babri Masjid embodied the stigma of an historical Muslim domination. They were persuaded that it had to be demolished and it was relatively easy to mobilise them for this purpose.[30] Ethno-

---

[27] The *Organiser* report added: 'The sants will not appeal to the voters to vote BJP but, explained Shri Ashok Singhal, General Secretary of the banned VHP, it meant that. They could ask people to vote against the Congress. People are wise enough to understand, as the BJP Governments were dismissed on the temple issue.' (*Organiser*, 24 Oct. 1993.)

[28] Interview on 13 Feb. 1994, Shivpuri.

[29] *Times of India*, 2 Nov. 1993.

[30] In Bijnor, the Jefferys noticed that 'The tussle over Ayodhya is, in large part, seen locally as a matter of izzat; if the temple is built, Hindus across North India will feel a sense of

religious mobilisations always function negatively, against a scapegoat or any other kind of enemy. After the destruction of the mosque, many supporters of the Ayodhya agitation probably took the view that Muslims had been taught the lesson they deserved and that their goal had been achieved. The 'constructive' aspect – the building of a Ram temple – was not an immediate concern. The same break in motivation may also have affected members of the BJP, the VHP and the RSS. One leader of the VHP in Shivpuri explains the absence of any large-scale agitation in 1993 in such terms:

There was no need for any campaign in 1993. The Indians, the Hindus were angry because of the mosque, and we have demolished the mosque. We have demolished the mosque! [laughs] Next time we will start a campaign again if something has to be done. Now the question is about Mathura or Varanasi but it will come after a long period. For the time being the question remains whether the temple can be constructed at the same place or not. The matter is lying with the Supreme Court. Let the Supreme Court decide. We are also waiting. If it is not in our favour we will start a campaign.[31]

This VHP cadre, in common with other Hindu activists, regarded the campaign as almost closed. His next goal would be not the construction of the Ram Mandir but the demolition of another mosque. Interestingly, after the demolition of the Babri Masjid, Hindu nationalist leaders and sympathisers no longer referred to it as 'the disputed structure' but as 'the mosque' because this was in fact how they perceived it. For instance Arun Shourie declared:

It is better that we call the structure a mosque. If people want to believe that a mosque has been pulled down, well a mosque has been pulled down. So I will not keep referring to 'the structure which some people call a mosque'.[32]

The goal of destroying the Babri Masjid was far more appealing than that of constructing the temple, thus explaining the difficulty of mobilising Hindus – and even supporters of the VHP – in the name of Ram after its demolition.

What we see here is further evidence of the contradiction inherent in

---

pride, a previous wrong will have been redressed and their izzat will be enhanced; while the mosque stands, Muslims can feel they still have some izzat left.' (Roger and Patricia Jeffery, 'The Bijnor Riots', op. cit, p. 556.)

[31]   Interview, 13 Feb. 1994, Shivpuri.

[32]   A. Shourie, 'The buckling state' in J. Bajaj (ed.), *Ayodhya and the future of India,* op. cit, p. 47. Moreover, as Pandey has shown, the Hindu nationalist history of Ayodhya 'is not about the *construction* of the Ram Janmabhumi temple. It is about its *destruction.* To that extent it is a history, not of the temple, but of the mosque built upon its ruins – not of the greatness of "the Hindu" but of the evilness of "the Muslim"' ('The new Hindu history', op. cit., p. 108)

the strategy of ethno-religious mobilisation. The Ayodhya movement relied on the manipulation of symbols and stereotypes – such as the dominating Muslim – by an activist network of *sadhus* and Bajrang Dalis. As we tried to show in Chapter 13, this brought with it the unwelcome result that the Hindu nationalists lost control of these activists. Moreover, the demolition of the Babri Masjid deprived the RSS-VHP-BJP combine of the very focus of anger and resentment that it needed continually to foster in order to keep the movement in full spate. Thus in 1993 the BJP decided to focus on issues that would help it to recover its former respectability and strengthen its nationalist image; but it also realised that the Ayodhya policy had largely run its course. However, this shift in emphasis was partly due to the changing political context.

The Congress (I)'s electoral strategy and the difficulty of the BJP in evolving an economic programme

The appeal of Ayodhya was also weakened by the electoral strategy of the ruling party. First, the Prime Minister repeated the promise he had made on 15 August 1993 that a temple and a mosque would be built in Ayodhya. This announcement to some extent deprived the BJP of a vital propaganda weapon. Narasimha Rao rarely mentioned Ayodhya in the campaign but concentrated instead on socio-economic issues.[33] In so doing, he put the problem of development centre stage in public debate. In his speeches the Prime Minister contrasted the allegedly poor performance of the four BJP state governments with the success of the Centre's new economic policy.

In the past the Jana Sangh had suffered greatly from the shortcomings of its economic programme – which was confined largely to the theme of decentralisation – in comparison with the policies of Nehru and later Indira Gandhi. The Hindu nationalist movement, finding itself on the defensive, therefore propounded counter-proposals (namely populist measures or others directed against state control of the economy) which served to divert the Jana Sangh towards forms of mobilisation other than the ethno-religious. A similar response was to some extent initiated by Narasimha Rao.

The high level of India's foreign debt led his government to adopt in 1991 a new policy based on further liberalisation and far greater openness to foreign investment. This sea-change in Indian economic strategy en-

---

[33] During a meeting in Uttar Pradesh, for instance, he said of the Ayodhya issue: 'Forget about it. This is no longer important. It is now time to move ahead and think of development.' He then focussed on the BJP government's neglect of socio-economic issues and promised that, if voted to power, the Congress (I) would implement various rural development schemes (*Times of India*, 16 Nov. 1993).

gendered a debate in which the weaknesses and contradictions of the BJP's economic programme became evident. As was obvious from its election manifesto and campaign in 1991, one of the party's principal concerns was to advocate economic liberalisation, a policy popular with its business and middle-class bases of support. In April 1993, Jaswant Singh even declared at the National Conference of the Confederation of Indian Industry that 'the BJP would welcome foreign capital in all spheres of national endeavour'.[34]

However liberalisation was criticised by the BMS (which organised demonstrations against what it regarded as the anti-labour policies of Narasimha Rao's government)[35] and the RSS, whose executive committee, the ABKM, expressed 'its deep concern at throwing open the door for foreigners and multinational companies in the name of economic liberalisation'.[36] The RSS then launched a Swadeshi Jagaran Manch (Forum for the awakening of economic self-sufficiency), which was close to the BMS line and claimed to be in tune with Gandhian economic thinking.[37] The programme of the Manch was endorsed by religious leaders associated with the VHP.[38] Its first meeting brought together nearly 600 delegates from the executive committees of nearly all the affiliates of the RSS and was marked by the inevitable dissensions between advocates of liberalisation, who were mostly BJP representatives, and proponents of *Swadeshi*.[39]

The economic debate within the Hindu nationalist movement was reflected in the shift of emphasis in the series of resolutions passed by the BJP on this issue. In August 1992 the party's National Executive declared that the BJP stood for 'liberalisation with self-reliance, or to stress the *Swadeshi* angle, self-reliance with liberalisation'.[40] In April 1993, the idea of delinking internal liberalisation and the integration of India with the global market emerged[41] and became the official policy of the BJP before the 1993 elections:

The BJP has long been an advocate of decentralisation and deregulation but it has

---

[34] *BJP meets Indian industry*, New Delhi: BJP, 1993, p. 9.

[35] *Statesman* (Delhi), 21 April 1993.

[36] *Organiser*, 4 July 1993, p. 9.

[37] Ibid., 26 Sept. 1993.

[38] See Thengadi's speech to religious figures in ibid., 26 Sept. 1993, p. 16.

[39] *Times of India*, 1 Sept. 1993, and P. Bidwai, 'Discord in the "parivar" – BJP has a "swadeshi" problem', ibid., 10 Sept. 1993, p. 8. See the resolutions passed at the end of this meeting in the BMS monthly, *Vishwakarma Sanket*, 1 (12), Oct. 1993, pp. 6-8.

[40] BJP, *National Executive Meeting – Resolutions*, 22-4 August 1992 (Bhopal), p. 19.

[41] BJP, *National Executive Meeting – Resolutions*, 10-12 April 1993 (Calcutta), pp. 8-9.

always maintained that internal liberalisation should precede, not follow, the mad rush towards globalisation.[42]

These resolutions reflected ambiguities within the Hindu nationalist movement. They even suggested a certain lack of coherence which might have worried the business followers of the BJP upon whom the party was increasingly dependent, politically and financially.[43]

To sum up, the 1993 election campaign was not as dominated by communal issues as had been previous ones. For the first time since 1989, the canvassing period passed off without massive riots. In fact, the only Hindu-Muslim violence took place in Kanpur, in mid-November, when there was only one fatality. Nor was the clash blamed on Hindu activists alone: it resulted from a procession by the BSP and Samajwadi Party who had raised provocative slogans to which BJP supporters reacted violently. Despite the Bombay riots of January, the number of victims of communalism dropped in 1993 to the level of the early 1980s (see Appendixes A and B, pp. 551-2). For the first time in many years, violence did not contribute to a polarisation of the electorate along communal lines.

With a reduction in communal tension came an increased focus on social issues such as the growing political consciousness of the Other Backward Classes. This was a factor of crucial importance working against the BJP, but not the only one. In most of the five states which went to the polls in 1993, the party suffered from having exercised power; it was often punished for its poor performance and perceived lack of internal discipline – a development also attributable to its period in office. This trend was particularly evident in Madhya Pradesh.

---

[42] BJP, *Onwards to Ramrajya – A statement on National Issues Before the Electorate in the Mini- General Elections*, New Delhi, 1993, p. 9. A member of the National Executive and the economic team of the BJP elaborates on this issue in the following terms: 'Liberalisation and Swadeshi are not contradictory. Right from the Jana Sangh years we have been in favour of liberalisation in terms of deregulation of the control system, licences and also privatisation of the public sector except in the strategic fields. We want to dismantle the entire control system which is too bureaucratised. The investments will not take off so long as the bureaucracy is not cleared, trusted. The bureaucracy must only give guidelines like the police on the traffic roads. Only in the case of external liberalisation we have some reservations. In high tech areas and in the areas where foreigners can help us to manufacture items for exportations, we are inclined to open the country. But in the realm of consumer goods we have reservations for the time being. [...] If we give full freedom to the investors, it is in the consumer goods that they will find the best opportunities because we have an unexploited middle class market. We must prevent investments from these areas and divert them to other areas in which we are more interested' (interview with J. Shettigar, 11 Feb. 1994, New Delhi).

[43] R. Sardesai, 'Banking on the BJP', *Times of India*, 29 Aug. 1993.

The test of power: Madhya Pradesh

The decline of the Sangathanist pattern

As we showed in Chapter 3 with reference to Madhya Pradesh, one of the traditional assets of the Sangathanist pattern of party-building lay in its dual power structure. This was based on organisational leaders (*sangathan mantris*) and elected, more public figures. The former are not expected to face the electorate[44] or assume ministerial responsibilities but to devote themselves exclusively to organisational work. In Madhya Pradesh, after Patwa had formed his government in 1990, this arrangement was consolidated by the establishment of an unofficial working group which was separate from the formal institutions of power but intended to oversee the conduct of ministers. The key member of this 'core group' was K. Thakre. Usually the Chief Minister also took part in the meeting to enable party organisers 'to know what are his constraints'.[45]

This arrangement contributed to the cohesion of the party in power and exemplified the ability of *sangathan mantris* to contain rivalries among the office-holders involved in electoral and ministerial politics. The efficiency of this dual structure was affected by the accession to power. While the BJP had claimed, with some justification until that time, that it differed from other parties in its unity and relative absence of internal conflict, direct involvement in the government of the state stimulated the development of rivalries just as in most other parties. The Madhya Pradesh BJP was to suffer from internal dissensions on a scale seen nowhere else except perhaps Bihar. In the event its divisions proved to be different in form from those of Congress (I) and similar parties.

Patwa, Sakhlecha and Joshi as faction leaders?   Tensions had emerged between Patwa, Sakhlecha and Kailash Joshi in the late 1970s while the Janata Party was in office. The rivalry between K. Joshi and V.K. Sakhlecha came to a head when the former had to resign as Chief Minister and was succeeded by the latter in January 1978. Sakhlecha later took exception to his replacement, in January 1980, by Patwa, who had kept

---

[44] K. Thakre stood only twice in Khandwa – the first time during a critical by-election in 1979 which the Janata Party needed to win. N.P. Gupta contested a seat in 1952, 1977 and 1980 and P. Khandelwal in 1989 and 1991. This tactic of standing aside from electoral policies perpetuated the policy of Upadhyaya, who contested a by-election only once.

[45] Interview with K. Thakre, 11 Aug. 1992, New Delhi. The RSS was also interested in exercising its influence on the government, one of its channels being the newspaper *Swadesh*. As early as July 1990 the paper's editor criticised the ostentatious manner in which Patwa had commemorated the anniversary of his father's death – a function to which V.P. Singh had been invited (*India Today*, 31 July 1990, p. 14).

aloof from the two previous governments. The antagonism between Sakhlecha and Patwa – who had originally worked together in Mandsaur district – worsened after cases of corruption were registered against them in 1982 and 1984 respectively.[46] In 1984 Sakhlecha was suspended from membership of the party for having infringed its disciplinary code. He complained that the BJP had not defended him against the charges of corruption levelled by the Congress (I),[47] and then set up his own party at the time of the 1985 elections, for which he had not been nominated by the BJP. An underlying cause of this state of affairs was the rivalry between him and Patwa. In 1980 Patwa had become opposition leader in the Vidhan Sabha and then, in 1985, he succeeded Joshi as president of the BJP in the state, while Sakhlecha resented the fact that he had no post in the party apparatus. When, in 1985, Sakhlecha's new party put up candidates in many constituencies in Malwa,[48] it did not win a single seat, since activists were accustomed to the exercise of discipline by the established organisation and accepted control by *sangathan mantris*. They were therefore not disposed to follow a party leader involved in electoral politics who chose to chart an independent course.

The failure of Sakhlecha in his efforts to persuade his followers to desert the BJP is indicative of two things. The first is a lack of charisma, which is common to the majority of BJP leaders involved in electoral politics. Most of them have imbued in the RSS a sense of discipline and submission to the authority of the organisation which persists when they work under *sangathan mantris* and thus inhibits their personality. Then there is the fact that the Jana Sangh's and later the BJP's party-building methods, which were derived from the RSS, deliberately minimise the role of the individual. Besides Vajpayee and, lately, Advani at the top, Shekhawat is the only charismatic state leader the Jana Sangh and the BJP has ever had. In Madhya Pradesh no figure could match him, and in fact the most popular crowd-pullers are women, namely Vijaya Raje Scindia and Uma Bharti.

Second, Sakhlecha's failure to form his own party exemplifies the ineffectiveness of attempts by an individual leader to build up a personal following in a party like the BJP, one with an internal culture founded on a disciplined acceptance of established doctrines and the authority of *sangathan mantris*. In this respect, the internecine conflicts in Madhya Pradesh do not fulfil one of the main criteria Bruce Graham mentions in his analysis of factionalism. According to him, this process

---

[46] It seemed that the background to these charges was partly rooted in their rivalry (*Statesman* (Delhi), 7 Nov. 1982, p. 7, and 14 Nov. 1984, p. 6).

[47] Interview with Sakhlecha.

[48] Patwa preferred to stand in Bhojpur, near Bhopal, in addition to Manasa (Mandsaur district) where Sakhlecha's party might erode his base.

[...]depends above all on personal commitment, and for this reason recruitment to a faction takes the form of a series of one-to-one engagements between individuals: in its simplest form, therefore, a faction consists of a leader and a diversity of followers, each of whom has formed a vertical tie with him and offers him personal loyalty in return for some specific promise of future recompense.[49]

Most studies of the Congress party specify the importance of leader-follower relations in limiting the scope of organisational discipline and the consequent propensity of the party to split into groups associated with leading personalities.[50] This factionalism is based on a clientelist kind of relationship which is inherent in the 'aggregative' party-building pattern discussed in Chapter 3. Since this party-building technique relies on co-opting notables and politicians who command a support base – and who have often been targetted because of their control of a 'vote bank' – it is only to be expected that they maintain their personal network, try to expand it and even use it in their fight for power within the party.

This criterion of factionalism – the vertical allegiance between a patron and clients – is not really fulfilled in the case of the BJP in Madhya Pradesh. While leaders such as Sakhlecha and Joshi tried to win over the largest number of followers by means of their personal contacts,[51] building a network of followers presented an almost impossible task given that *sangathan mantris* can hinder the development of a clientelist system between the party's leaders and potential clients. Eventually, in 1989, Sakhlecha applied for, and was granted, readmission to the BJP;[52] Joshi followed a similar path.

In March 1990 Joshi had refused to join Patwa's government in order, he said, to take care of the party's organisation.[53] In fact his disappointment at failing to become Chief Minister was manifested when he stayed away from Patwa's swearing-in ceremony. Eight months later, however, he accepted the post of Minister of Industry and Energy. The primary motive underlying Joshi's and Sakhlecha's decision to 'return to the ranks' was probably a negative one. They realised that outside the party or on its fringes they were losing influence, since most of their strength had derived not so much from their personal appeal or following, but rather from a Sangathanist network of activists who were now likely to

---

[49] B.D. Graham, *Representation and party politics*, Oxford: Blackwell, 1993, p. 156.

[50] See, for instance, Paul Brass, 'Factionalism in the Congress party in Uttar Pradesh', reprinted in P. Brass, *Caste, Faction and Party in Indian Politics*, Delhi: Chanakya, 1984, pp. 143-4.

[51] In 1992, the author was interviewing the BJP MP for Shajapur when Sakhlecha came to pay his condolences after the death of the MP's father...and to talk politics.

[52] In December 1990 he was appointed to the BJP National Council.

[53] *Dainik Bhaskar*, 6 March 1990, pp. 1 and 3.

become indifferent or even hostile to their ambitions. However both of them decided to fight Patwa from within the party.

In 1990 Sakhlecha, who was denied a party ticket to contest the Vidhan Sabha election, went on the offensive to stand for the party presidency in Madhya Pradesh against Lakhiram Aggarwal, the 'official' candidate supported by Patwa and Thakre. He received 68 votes from local delegates as against 123 for Aggarwal (there were 132 abstentions),[54] an outcome which indicated that although Sakhlecha could count on about one-quarter of the votes in such a forum, he had nothing like the level of support needed to obtain a predominant position in the party.[55] In 1993, Joshi succeeded Sakhlecha as Patwa's main rival for the party leadership in the elections which had been initiated in late 1992 (as provided for by the regular schedule) but delayed by six months after the events of December 1992. Aggarwal was again in the fray with the support of Patwa and Thakre. He polled 224 votes while Joshi won the support of 98 delegates.[56] Aggarwal retained Joshi but dropped Sakhlecha, who was evidently thought to represent the greater threat.

At first sight, the rivalry between Patwa, Sakhlecha and Joshi appears to resemble a factional struggle. However, as we have seen, the jockeying for power between leaders of the Madhya Pradesh BJP was successfully contained and ultimately controlled by the *sangathan mantri* system. It was that system which began to fracture in mid-1991 and a new pattern of conflict, which we shall term 'groupism', emerged in the Madhya Pradesh BJP.

The development of groupism.   Some of the experienced *sangathan mantris*, such as N.P. Gupta and P. Khandelwal, greatly resented the defence of Patwa by Thakre after the setback the BJP suffered in the 1991 parliamentary elections, when its number of MPs fell from 27 to 12. The obstinacy of Thakre in supporting Patwa, even after the 1991 reverse and against the wishes of senior colleagues, is all the more puzzling given that he used to hold N.P. Gupta in high esteem.[57] The most likely explanation lies in his special relationship with Patwa: as a *pracharak* he had initiated him into the RSS forty-five years earlier. In 1994 Patwa revealed the following, which suggests why he was the ideal Chief Minister from Thakre's point of view:

I never decided for myself. Right from 1957 it was always the party's decision,

---

[54] *National Mail*, 31 Dec. 1990, p. 1.

[55] Text of Footnote

[56] *Statesman* (Delhi), 30 May 1993.

[57] In 1989 he dwelt on the role of Gadre and Gupta as 'the main builders of the Jana Sangh in Madhya Pradesh' (interview in Bhopal on 23 Nov. 1989).

mainly Thakreji's. I left it to them, to decide for me, what should I do. [...] Thakre was my source of inspiration after Guruji [Golwalkar] and Deendayal Upadhyaya. They influenced me all.[58]

Another prominent *sangathan mantri* who had been deeply influenced by Thakre and who supported Patwa was Kailash Sarang. A former RSS *pracharak*, he had run the Bhopal office of the Jana Sangh between 1960 and 1977 and then rose to become General Secretary of the Janata Dal in Madhya Pradesh and later General Secretary and Treasurer of the state BJP. He had been appointed Vice President of the BJP in Madhya Pradesh by Aggarwal in 1991. Sarang dismissed the attitude of Gupta and Khandelwal by saying that they 'wanted more power'. He lamented that 'RSS *pracharaks* of our BJP became indisciplined'.[59]

Indeed, the confrontation between Gupta and Khandelwal on the one hand and Thakre and Sarang on the other hand indicated that the equilibrium of the whole 'Sangathanist' system was in jeopardy. Till then, *sangathan mantris* had worked together as organisers and arbitrators in the case of disputes. They were supposed to deliberate and then adopt a common position bearing in mind the interest of the party. In this scheme of things Thakre had been *primus inter pares*. Now, however, he began to act more independently and backed Patwa fully. Eventually, the 'core group' which he headed became a sort of closed group comprising S. Patwa, Vijaya Raje Scindia, S. Angre, K. Sarang and L. Aggarwal. After the 1991 elections Khandelwal and Gupta, who considered that they had been sidelined, complained to the party's national leadership in revealing terms:

It is for the first time in 40 years that we have gone to Delhi and complained to the top leadership of the BJP and the RSS regarding our internal matters. [...] so long we have been living like a family with Mr Thakre as the elder brother. But there is a limit to tolerating the whims of someone. [...] We cannot be mute spectators if someone destroys the work of our lifetime.[60]

Naturally, the RSS – which continuously stresses the importance of organisational integrity – was sensitive to Khandelwal's and Gupta's plea. Its mouthpiece, the *Organiser*, commented soon after the 1991 election:

Shri Patwa must realise that there is something seriously wrong with his functioning. For one thing, his failure to set up a machinery to remove public grievances and a channel to route requests from party cadres, is too glaring to miss anyone's notice.[61]

---

[58] Interview with S. Patwa, 17 Feb. 1994, Bhopal.
[59] Interview with K. Sarang, 16 Feb. 1994, Bhopal.
[60] Cited in the *Times of India*, 23 Sept. 1991, p. 4.
[61] *Organiser*, 14 July 1991, p. 9.

BJP leaders now felt free to criticise Patwa. S. Bakht told him that he did 'not know the art of governance'.[62] A managing committee was formed to conduct a fortnightly review of the functioning of the state government.[63] Yet the impact of the dissidents' complaints to the party's national headquarters was moderated by the fact that members of the ruling group were well entrenched there: Thakre had been appointed one of the all-India secretaries of the BJP in 1980 and later one of its Vice Presidents in 1986 before becoming one of its General Secretaries in 1988. These responsibilities meant that he was spending a lot of time in Delhi. Moreover Vijaya Raje Scindia was one of the BJP's Vice Presidents; she also became head of the 'managing committee' in Bhopal.

Dissidents were therefore at the mercy of the ruling group. In 1993 Gupta launched a petition urging party members to elect Kailash Joshi as party president. After the 1993 party elections, not only Sakhlecha but also Khandelwal and Gupta were dropped by Aggarwal from the newly constituted 110-strong executive committee.[64] Nor was Gupta reappointed to the post of party state vice-president.

At this point the national leadership of the BJP chose to redress the balance between the contending groups. The first step was to appoint Joshi to head the BJP Kisan Morcha at the national level; the second, and most important, was to remove Thakre from his commanding position in the Madhya Pradesh party and place him in charge of the national party organisation. S.S. Bhandari was appointed to replace him. Simultaneously, P. Khandelwal was transferred to Haryana.[65]

To sum up, the divisions which appeared within the Madhya Pradesh BJP in the early 1990s were not comparable to those which were typical of Congress factionalism. The politicians who appeared to resemble faction leaders were not the important personalities: Patwa was largely a creature of Thakre and Sarang while Sakhlecha and Joshi lacked the status of Gupta and Khandelwal. These two had sufficient prestige and authority to engineer central intervention against Thakre's attempt to concentrate power in his group. They were frustrated and wished to exert more power behind the scenes but did not press for office as faction leaders usually do. Their concern for the way Patwa's policies jeopardised the future of the party to which they had dedicated their life was probably another motivation. In fact they promoted a form of groupism by allying and supporting Joshi against the ruling group. This groupism was more important – as its impact on the national leadership, which removed

[62] *National Mail*, 1 July 191, p. 1.
[63] *Times of India*, 25 Sept. 1991.
[64] Ibid., 10 June 1993.
[65] Ibid., 9 July 1993.

Thakre, testifies – than the action of would be faction leaders such as Joshi and Sakhlecha.

The nature of these dissensions suggests that, in contrast with the 'aggregative' parties, the BJP is not susceptible to breakdown along factional lines. The failure of Sakhlecha's attempt at forming his own party illustrates this point. In addition, it is unlikely that a large number of *sangathan mantris* would support this kind of secession because they are committed to the organisation and all their legitimacy derives from the way they serve it. However, the groupism which developed from 1991 onwards in the Madhya Pradesh BJP suggests that the cohesion of *sangathan mantris* can be severely eroded. Such divisions might stem from rivalries for power or concerns for the future of the organisation. Both are often intermingled, since personal rivalries are legitimised in the name of the organisation and the protection of the organisation justifies gaining control of the leadership.

These developments relate to a more general source of instability which is common to any party, namely, the growth of dissent about the uses of power, a process which can be especially damaging in the case of a cadre-based party like the BJP.

Indiscipline among party workers. After the formation of the government, those party leaders who became ministers changed their mode of political behaviour. Frequently, on account of their new roles and responsibilities as well as their access to new channels of authority, they became cut off from the activist network. The feeling of being neglected by ministers, and especially by Patwa, accounted for many of the party workers' criticisms of the latter after the Lok Sabha election in 1991.[66] Even before then such considerations led some of them not to 'do their job whole-heartedly'[67] during the 1991 election campaign, while other activists, aggrieved by the attitude of their leaders, decided against canvassing, notably in Jabalpur.[68]

---

[66] *National Mail*, 20, 21 and 29 July 1991. An interesting example of conflict between local activists and party leaders turned MPs or ministers took place in the heartland of the BJP, in Indore-Mhow. The Indore district BJP vice-president and Mhow city BJP president, along with a large number of activists, left the party because they resented the haughty attitude of Bherulal Patidar (the Panchayat minister who started out as a local MLA in Mhow) and Sumitra Mahajan, the Indore MP whom they accused of never bothering about her party workers except when election campaigns were underway (ibid., 8 April 1991). Similar rifts arose between local leaders and the Parliamentary Secretary, H.P. Garg, in Rajgarh. K. Joshi and the BJP MP from Bhopal, S.C. Verma, attributed the 1991 setback to the failure to encourage party workers about the need for a closer rapport with the people at the grassroots (ibid., 20 June 1991).

[67] Ibid., 23 June 1991.

[68] Ibid., 16 May 1991 and interview with B. Paranjpe. After the 1991 elections the General

The impossibility of fulfilling expectations the BJP had helped to arouse while in opposition, particularly regarding unemployment, also annoyed local activists. Some party workers regretted the limitations on the loan-waiving campaign (see below). In the Vidhan Sabha, back-benchers from the ruling party were quick to arraign senior ministers for the paucity of teachers or the shortage of *tendu* leaves for *bidi* workers.[69]

In any party activists are swift to criticise leaders who they feel are betraying the party programme for which they campaigned while in opposition. However, the alacrity with which BJP organisers and MLAs questioned the government's policy reveals much about their political culture: activists of the Hindu nationalist parties were all the more likely to oppose the government – even their own – because they had made many promises during the election campaign and had developed an activist political culture in their long opposition to the 'Congress régime'. From their point of view, the claim that financial and administrative constraints were limiting the scope for reform were not valid arguments.

A commonplace criticism related to the neglect shown by the Bhopal government toward the zones newly conquered by the BJP. In the Vidhan Sabha, Jayshree Banerjee, from Mahakoshal, complained that Patwa always thought first of Madhya Bharat[70] and Larang Sai, from Chhattis-garh, accused Patwa's government of exploiting the tribals. The Chief Minister responded forcefully and Larang Sai was suspended from primary membership of the party. This punishment of a senior party leader who had served in government at the Centre during the Janata period caused a furore, and was eventually revoked.

With a view to restoring party discipline, a three-day training camp was held in the summer of 1992 to 'acquaint the participants – Members of the Parliament and the Legislative Assembly – with the role of MLAs of the ruling party'.[71] But it failed to have any effect, partly because the ruling group, far from correcting its course, continued to react strongly to its critics. Patwa, in particular, displayed authoritarian tendencies. Dis-satisfaction with the party leadership continued to grow, and in September 1992 a petition directed against Patwa gained momentum and drew support from 71 MLAs. The initiative for this move was attributed to Virendra Pandey, a member of the state executive committee and an associate of Sakhlecha. But most MLAs involved did not acknowledge

---

Secretary of the BJP of Khandwa district demanded the resignation of Patwa and L. Aggarwal because of their 'utter neglect' of party workers, induction of 'inefficient' people in the state cabinet, besides 'promoting opportunists' in the party (ibid., 20 June 1991).

[69] Ibid., 18 Feb. 1992 and 13 March 1992.

[70] Ibid., 17 March 1992.

[71] Ibid., 14 June 1992.

allegiance to Sakhlecha; they mainly directed their anger towards the ruling group on account of its poor performance and unwillingness to listen to party workers.[72] As a result of this protest, Pandey was suspended from primary membership. A few weeks later, the state government was dismissed in the aftermath of the demolition of the Babri Masjid.

Dissensions and the 1993 elections.   In September 1992, when elections were announced by the Election Commission in Madhya Pradesh as well as in the three other states whose governments had been removed from office in December 1992, the BJP high command decided that Thakre should return to Bhopal for the election campaign because his local knowledge exceeded that of Bhopal for the election campaign because his local knowledge exceeded that of Bhandari. This enabled the ruling group to have the upper hand in the selection of candidates.[73]

The party chose not to renominate 56 former MLAs including some of those who had signed the petition criticising Patwa, those whose popularity had waned (notably because of corruption charges) and others who were simply dropped in favour of candidates sponsored by the RSS. As a result, about a dozen influential dissidents who were disappointed over the denial of tickets or angered by the issuing of tickets to candidates they disapproved of, decided to stand against official candidates.

For instance in Susner (Shajapur district), Haribhau Joshi, who had won the seat on four previous occasions, was denied the ticket because of his hostility to the dominant group. He contested as an independent and deprived the BJP of the seat.[74] Such indiscipline was without precedent in the Madhya Pradesh BJP.

Besides the rebel candidates, the attitude of the party activists must be taken into account. Sometime they refused to canvass for the official candidate because they disliked him – notably in the cases of ministers

[72]   Among the complaints three must be cited: 'The party high command has formed district: advisory committees but MLAs in the region hardly have any say in those committees;' 'It is difficult for us [MLAs] to face the people,since many of their demands are pending with the ministers who are just seating [sic] on files; 'Earlier we knew that there was at least one leader who was above petty differences [K. Thakre]. Sadly we cannot say the same anymore'. (*Statesman* (Delhi), 28 Sept. 1992).

[73]   Sakhlecha, for instance, was once again denied a ticket from his traditional constituency of Jawad. Instead, the State BJP leadership nominated Ram Lal Patidar – who had lost in 1985 when Sakhlecha, who contested as an independent, came second behind the Congress (I). In 1993 the seat again went to the latter. Sakhlecha probably sabotaged the chances of the BJP candidate.

[74]   In Jagdalpur (Bastar district), Dineshkumar Kashyap, the outgoing MLA and son of Baliram Kashyap, the Tribal Welfare Minister, was refused the nomination. He contested as an independent and the Congress (I) won the seat. In Narsingarh and in Manasa the renomination of the out going MLAs led dissidents to stand against BJP candidates (on a Shiv Sena ticket and as an independent respectively); in both cases they prevented the BJP from winning

whose behaviour they resented – and, in some instances, activists sabotaged the elections.[75] The MLA for Shivpuri admits that party cadres who were angry with ministers decided not to work for them during the election campaign.[76] In one instance at least, the choice of the official candidate led local party workers to seek an alternative nominee. In Burhanpur (Khandwa district), where Muslims number some 53,000 people (out of a total of 122,000), the BJP nominated its only Muslim candidate, Abdul Rab; in response, local party workers persuaded Swami Umesh Muni – a *sadhu* from the Vishwa Hindu Parishad – to file his nomination as an independent and he went on to win the seat.

This novel outbreak of indiscipline within the BJP's ranks in Madhya Pradesh was all the more damaging because its Sangathanist strategy meant that it relied more heavily than others on a network of party workers. Such dissent was occasionally manipulated by state leaders but more often than not took the form of a rebellion by party workers.

The inability of the party's MLAs to remain incorruptible was another reason for the weakening of the Sangathanist strategy and hence for the setback suffered by the BJP in Madhya Pradesh. One of the pillars of Sangathanist party-building is the personal prestige of Hindu nationalist cadres, which was often a reflection of their personal integrity and dedication to the cause if not to the people. These characteristics were inherited from the highly disciplined nature of the RSS, but they began to be dissipated after the BJP gained control of Madhya Pradesh.

In Shivpuri district there have been dramatic developments; two and a half years after the coming to power of the BJP, one leader of the district unit of the VHP considered that of five MLAs in Shivpuri district, three were more or less corrupt. This is the usual outcome of gaining access to power and in this case may be regarded also as a 'rational reaction'. Since the government was unable to fulfil the promises made to the voters, some MLAs became sceptical about their prospects of re-election and prepared themselves accordingly. Thus the electoral asset that was the BJP's reputation for integrity was soon diminished after the party came to power.

In addition to the decline of the Sangathanist party-building strategy,

---

[75] In Chhindwara, the local party activists strongly objected to the replacement of Chanderbhan Chandhury (Public Works Minister) by an RSS-backed candidate who in the event was defeated at the polls. In Narsimhapur, the replacement of Uttam Lunawat (the outgoing MLA) by Kailash Soni, the BJP district President, caused a similar reaction – and the same result. In Itarsi, the replacement of Sita Sharam Sharma, the outgoing MLA, by Dushyant Gaur led to similar protests. Party workers also strongly resented the choice of the party nominee in Sarangpur.

[76] Interview with Devendra Jain, 13 Feb. 1994, Shivpuri.

while in office the BJP failed to cater to the interests of the principal sectors of society.

The poor performance and 'pro-rich' image of the Patwa government

The poor performance of the Patwa government – one of the dissidents' grievances – largely accounts for the BJP's electoral setbacks in the 1991 and 1993 polls.

The issue of loan-waiving.   In 1992, Patwa claimed that Rs 71.5 million of accumulated debt had been waived, freeing 3.2 million farmers from the onerous burden of owing money.[77] Implicitly, however, he admitted that not all the indebted peasants could benefit from the scheme. Thakre claimed that the government was prevented from doing more because it had not received sufficient financial aid from the Centre.[78] Thus, while the dues of farmers who had taken loans of up to 10,000 Rs were waived as early as 1991, the remainder were not covered by the scheme.[79] Obviously the BJP had overestimated the state's ability to make financial concessions and failed to foresee the divisive effect of the loan-waiving scheme. The government only waived the loans of those who had not paid off *any* of their debt while those who had been repaying their loans were expected to continue doing so. Current borrowers started defaulting on their payments and another scheme had to be launched under which agriculturalists who had paid half of their short-term loans were provided debt relief on the remainder. Because of these various programmes, banks faced increasing difficulties in recovering bad debts and refused to approve new credits, which in turn obliged farmers to become more dependent on money-lenders. The failure to honour their original promises eroded the credibility of the BJP in rural Madhya Pradesh during the 1993 elections.[80]

---

[77]   *Times of India*, 5 March 1992.

[78]   K. Thakre, 'Madhya Pradesh mein bhajpa sarkar', op. cit, p. 3.

[79]   See the interview with Patwa in the *National Mail*, 5 March 1991.

[80]   Some agriculturalists could not benefit from the loan waiving scheme because they were not recognised as the legal owners of the land they were cultivating. In Dhar district, many tribals therefore found themselves excluded from the scheme (*Statesman* [Delhi], 3 April 1991). In Sagar district the failure on the part of the Patwa government to waive the peasants' loans was a prominent issue during the 1993 election campaign (ibid., 15 Nov. 1993). In Mandsaur district, small cultivators resented the fact that they were still being made to pay penal interest on the loans taken from the cooperative banks despite the BJP's assurance during the 1990 election that they would not have to do so (ibid., 24 Nov. 1993).

The alienation of the tribals.   The policy of the BJP government towards the harvesters of *tendu* leaves clearly had an averse effect. *Tendu* leaves are used in the making of *bidi* cigarettes, and two-thirds of the leaves come from the forests of Madhya Pradesh. They are harvested by tribals and the industry provides work for about one million people during the harvest season. When he was Chief Minister Arjun Singh had introduced a cooperativisation scheme which enabled the workers to earn better wages (in 1989 their piece work rate was raised to Rs 15 per thousand leaves, as against Rs 8 previously).[81] The state government, to which the cooperatives sold the leaves, made large profits from the industry. In 1990, the BJP government handed over the post-plucking operations to private traders who were also allowed to collect *tendu* leaves. Patwa apparently 'bowed to the *tendu* lobby',[82] which was represented by L. Aggarwal in the state BJP unit. Less than six months later Patwa had to reverse the policy because these same traders, who resolutely opposed even a partial cooperativisation, quoted very low purchase prices and acquired the best leaves, leading to a massive loss of Rs 20 million to the state. The image of the BJP among the tribals was thus severely damaged. Possibly as a means of compensation, the Patwa government decided to give *patta* (certificates of ownership) to tribals who had encroached on forest areas and converted the land to agriculture. The Chief Minister also announced in 1991 a collective insurance scheme for *tendu* gatherers but, at the same time, refused to pay them the bonus for the 1989 season which they should have received in 1990, according to Arjun Singh who continued to campaign for the restoration of his scheme.[83] The fact that the *tendu* gatherers were each given a bonus of about 1,000 Rs in certain districts during the period of President's Rule was even more damaging for the BJP since this policy was attributed to the Congress (I). In addition to its ill-conceived policy regarding the harvest of *tendu* leaves, the BJP government interfered with the tribals' recognised right to produce up to 5 litres of alcohol for their domestic consumption. According to new legislation, only traders were allowed to provide alcohol, a move much resented by the tribals.[84] Again, the BJP government seemed to have favoured the Banyas or merchants of Madhya Pradesh.

Thus it was hardly surprising that the tribal areas rejected the BJP at the polls. In 1990, the party won 54 out of 75 seats reserved for the

---

[81] *Statesman* (Delhi), 17 Jan. 1991.

[82] N.K. Singh, 'A new leaf', *India Today*, 15 Feb. 1991, p. 58.

[83] *Times of India*, 15 Feb. 1991 and 21 Oct. 1991.

[84] This fact is admitted or claimed from different quarters (interview with K. Thakre, 15 Feb. 1994, Bhopal, and Suraj Bhanu Solanki, a tribal MP from Dhar elected on a Congress (I) ticket, 20 March 1994, Paris).

Scheduled Tribes; in 1993 it secured only 16. Five of these were in Raigarh district, where the result may have reflected the increasing intervention of the Vanavasi Kalyan Ashram, whose members, with the help of Dilip Singh Judeo, intensified their attempts to reconvert Christian tribals in 1992-3.[85] By contrast, in the 1993 poll the Congress (I) won in 60 constituencies where the tribals account for more than 30% of the population (out of 84 such constituencies).[86]

Taking all this into account, the Patwa government had not proved to be a success. It showed little concern for the poor and even appeared to be 'pro-rich'. This image was all the more damaging and in stark contrast to the leadership of the Madhya Pradesh Congress (I), which, as much as Narasimha Rao had done at the national level, highlighted socio-economic issues. In the 1993 campaign Arjun Singh and Madhav Rao Scindia canvassed on the theme 'Vikas or Vinash' (development or destruction – of the Babri Masjid as well as of the economy). Madhav Rao Scindia, who canvassed actively in Gwalior, succeeded in pinning down the BJP to the issue of development. He was described by his supporters as '*Vikas ke masiha*' (the messiah of development).[87] During his tour of Madhya Pradesh, the Prime Minister also concentrated on socio-economic issues. In Bastar, he condemned the 'anti-development trend' in BJP policy and drew attention to the lack of water and electricity in many areas.[88] The Congress (I) also tried to cash in on the growing political consciousness of the Other Backward Classes.

The OBC vote and the question of reservations.   In 1990 the reservation policy controversy was an issue of secondary importance during the election campaign in Madhya Pradesh. V.P. Singh's announcement about the Mandal Commission report failed to provoke a mobilisation of the OBCs from which the BJP might have suffered electorally. For one thing the Janata Dal was weak (it did not win a single seat in 1991); for another, the OBCs had little tradition of organisation, except in certain border districts where such influences had spread from Uttar Pradesh. Undoubtedly their fragmentation stunted feelings of caste solidarity, as evident from Table 1 (p. 133). In 1931, with the exception of the Ahirs (or Yadavs) in Chhattisgarh and Vindhya Pradesh, none of the Backward Castes represented more than 5% of the population of any one of the four

---

[85]   Over two years four reconversion programmes were organised – in the last of which, on 29 October 1993, according to *Organiser*, 4,253 Christianised Tribals 'returned' to Hinduism (*Organiser*, 9 Jan. 1994).

[86]   I am grateful to Yogendra Yadav for providing me with these figures from the CSDS Data Unit.

[87]   *Times of India*, 26 Nov. 1993.

[88]   Ibid., 25 Nov. 1993.

sub-regions of Madhya Pradesh. Accordingly, in 1984 this state had the lowest proportion of MPs from the Backward Castes of any in India, namely 5%.[89] An 'OBC vote' was observable only in some northern districts adjacent to Uttar Pradesh where in 1991 the Bahujan Samaj Party (Party of the masses – lit. 'of the many') won one seat in Rewa. However, even in this area, the BJP tended to develop pockets of influence among the Backward Castes. This was achieved by establishing a 'Kisan Morcha' (Peasants' front) and 'Pichre Varg Morcha' (Front of the Backward Castes),[90] a strategy that was to prove electorally successful in the northern districts of the state. Besides Uma Bharti (a Lodhi active in the state BJP Kisan Morcha, of which she was vice-president), who was reelected as the MP for Khajuraho, R.K. Kusmariya – a Kurmi and former Jana Sanghi from Damoh who was president of the Kisan Morcha – was elected MP for Damoh in 1991.[91]

The situation changed in 1993 because of the growing political consciousness of the OBCs in the state and the efforts of the Congress (I) to project itself as the guardian of the backward castes. It demanded the implementation of the recommendations made by the Mahajan Commission, named after Ramji Mahajan, a former state minister who in 1981 had been asked by Arjun Singh's government to identify the needs of the OBCs in the state. Madhya Pradesh was then the only large state, apart from West Bengal, 'which ha[d] never prepared a list of OBCs or taken any separate action for their uplifment' [sic].[92] The Mahajan Commission report had been submitted in 1983. It identified 80 OBCs (of which 24 were Muslim) that together represented 48.08% of the state's population. The report recommended the reservation of 35% of posts in the state administration for the OBCs.[93] The Arjun Singh government had implemented one recommendation for the provision of quotas for OBCs in technical colleges and for the granting of scholarships but the former decision was contested in the courts, which issued a stay order.[94]

In late 1992, Mahajan challenged Patwa to an open debate on his

---

[89]   F. Frankel and M.S.A. Rao (eds), *Dominance and state power in India*, vol. 1, op. cit., p. 423.

[90]   The latter was set up under the chairmanship of Babulal Bhanpur, a member of the Kushwaha *jati*. He once worked in a Bhopal textile mill and joined the RSS in 1946 and then the Jana Sangh in 1952. He was also the co-founder of the BMS (interview with Babulal Bhanpur, 13 Nov. 1990, Bhopal).

[91]   Parliament of India, Tenth Lok Sabha Who's Who, op. cit., p. 377.

[92]   *Report of the Backward Classes Commission*, New Delhi: Government of India, 1980. First Part, p. 11.

[93]   *Madhya Pradesh Rajya Picchra Varg Ayog – Antim Prativedan*, Bhopal: Government of Madhya Pradesh, 1983 p. 461.

report.[95] During the 1993 election campaign, Madhav Rao Scindia and Arjun Singh demanded its implementation and the Congress (I) took full credit for having given effect to the Mandal report. It is significant in this regard that Sita Ram Kesri, the Union Minister for Welfare who had applied the Supreme Court's decision in favour of the Mandal report, was invited to canvass in Madhya Pradesh.[96] The party thus made a deliberate appeal to low caste support. This was an astute move. First, there was no strong opponent projecting a similar image: the Janata Dal was weaker in Madhya Pradesh than in the adjoining states of the Hindi belt and the Bahujan Samaj Party was still relatively unknown there. Second, although OBCs were less organised in Madhya Pradesh than in Bihar or Uttar Pradesh, their level of political awareness had risen in the wake of the 'Mandal affair'. The Congress (I) both stimulated this emerging consciousness and drew electoral dividends from it: in late 1991, the Sahu[97] Samaj of Bhopal district held a convention at which the Union Minister of State for Finance, S. Potolukhe, declared that the Sahu Samaj was in favour of the full implementation of the Mandal Commission report.[98] In early 1992, the 9th annual conference of Raipur district Sahu Sangh was inaugurated by the Minister of State for Cooperation, Kriparam Sahu, who stressed 'the need for tightening the grip of Sahu community on politics' and declared that the number of MPs and MLAs from the community should be increased.[99] Besides the Sahus, the Kurmis – a peasant caste representing 2.6% of the state's population – also became better organised in the early 1990s, especially during the election campaigns. In November 1993, the Kurmis of Hoshangabad division held a big convention and pressed for candidates from their community to be given due priority in the allocation of tickets.[100]

The growing political awareness of the OBCs benefited the Congress (I) because it had already shown that it was sympathetic to their cause. The Congress (I) included in its list of candidates a record number of tickets (70) for members of the OBCs. Scheduled Tribes and Scheduled Castes were

---

[95] *Statesman* (Delhi), 1 Dec. 1992.

[96] See, for instance, his speech in Gwalior (*Times of India*, 27 Sept. 1993). He came to Bhopal in early October for a two day seminar on 'liberation and rehabilitation of scavengers'. He then pointed out that 'the Union Government's decision to give 27% reservation for the socially backward classes was yet another hint of the revolution taking place in the country for social justice' (*National Mail*, 3 October 1993.)

[97] Sahus are oil pressers; they represent 4.2% of the state population according to the 1931 Census.

[98] *National Mail*, 23 Dec. 1991.

[99] Ibid., 5 Jan. 1992.

[100] Ibid., 19 Nov. 1993.

given their due share – respectively 74 and 45 tickets. Brahmins were alloted 55, Rajputs 37, Banyas 22 and Kayasths 4. Candidates from the minority communities – Muslims, Christians and Sikhs – numbered 13.[101] During the campaign Arjun Singh let it be known that, were the Congress (I) to win power again, it would not appoint an upper caste Chief Minister.

The Congress (I)'s appeal to the OBCs was an additional blow to the BJP since Patwa continued to oppose the Mahajan Commission's recommendations for the state.[102] The BJP, however, nominated almost as many OBC candidates as the Congress (I) in 1993. Of the 317 candidates whose caste or tribe or community can be identified, besides 44 Scheduled Castes and 75 Scheduled Tribes, we find 53 Brahmins, 27 Rajputs, 33 Banyas, 11 Jains, 2 Khattris, 3 Kayasths, 2 Jats – considered as OBCs in the Mahajan report –, 1 Maratha, 1 Muslim and 65 OBCs. But the BJP did not present its OBC nominees as Backward Caste leaders. This was due largely to Hindu nationalist ideology: the insistence of the RSS and its offshoots on the desirability of emphasising the Hindu sense of belonging to an organic community, the 'Hindu nation' (*rashtra*), rather than to particular castes. Second, many low caste BJP members have joined the Hindu nationalist movement under the logic of Sanskritisation whereby they seek to emulate high caste patterns of behaviour rather than showing pride in their lowly origins. According to Uma Bharti, the acceptance of such an outlook has given the OBCs of the BJP a 'Brahmin's mentality'.[103]

Indeed, interviews with BJP leaders from OBCs revealed a certain reluctance to present themselves as low caste leaders. Babulal Gaur said that he was an Ahir and not a Yadav, the term often used by the most politically conscious members of this caste in the Hindi belt. He also stressed the special relationship that this caste of herdsmen entertained with Krishna – the cowherd deity – whereas Vaishnavaite folkore is not valued by the politically conscious 'Yadav'. Another BJP leader from a low caste, Bherulal Patidar (MLA from Mhow and Panchayat Minister in Patwa's government) was reluctant to admit that he was a Kurmi; he preferred to present himself as a Patel, a name he associated with Gujarat's dominant caste.[104]

In fact BJP leaders from the low castes attract little support from voters of the same social milieu. While the proportion of OBC candidates fielded by the BJP for the assembly elections increased, the proportion of the party's MLAs from these castes fell from 27.2% in 1985 to 18.4% in 1993.

---

[101] *Hindustan Times*, 4 Nov. 1993.

[102] *Times of India*, 26 Oct. 1993.

[103] Interview with U. Bharti.

[104] Interview with Bherulal Patidar, Bhopal, 17 Feb. 1994.

Simultaneously, the share of upper caste MLAs was increasing slightly at 36.8% (see Appendix H, p. 559).

The BJP in Madhya Pradesh remained identified with the upper castes because the latter retained a tight hold on the party apparatus both at the local and state levels. In 1990, out of 39 presidents of BJP district units, 27 belonged to the upper castes, 9 to the OBCs, 1 to the Scheduled Castes and 1 to the Scheduled Tribes. The over-representation of the upper castes is even more significant at the state level since, in 1991-3, out of 100 members of the state executive 60 were from the upper castes and only 13 from the OBCs.

The 1993 elections in Madhya Pradesh: the BJP sustains damage

In the 1993 state elections in Madhya Pradesh the BJP suffered a serious defeat; it won only 117 of the 320 seats compared to the 219 which it had gained in 1990. A comparison between the two polls has to take account of the fact that the party contested only 269 constituencies in 1990 (when it was in alliance with Janata Dal) but nominated candidates from all 320 seats in 1993, thus accounting for the slight increase in its share of the valid votes, from 38.8% to 39%. In those seats which it contested on both occasions its percentage share fell by 6 to 8 points.[105] In 1993 the Congress (I) won 177 seats, an absolute majority, the BSP, 11 and the Janata Dal 2.

The BJP was most resilient in its traditional strongholds of Malwa and Bhopal. In Malwa it retained three-quarters of the 50 seats it had won in 1990, which meant that it still had a majority (34 out of 63). In contrast, the party suffered a severe setback in Mahakoshal: its 1990 tally of 61 constituencies out of 72 fell to 23. There were also disappointing results for the BJP in the Gwalior area and Vindhya Pradesh. In the first region, in 1990, the BJP had won three-quarters of the seats, of which it retained only half in 1993; in Vindhya Pradesh, where it had won fewer that half of the seats (17 out of 44), the number fell by 50% in 1993. In the same year Vindhya Pradesh was the only area where the BJP won a smaller number of seats than in 1985.[106] Lastly, in Chhattisgarh, the party's results in 1993 were worse than in Malwa and Bhopal but better than in all the other regions. The performance of the BJP in 1993 was quite unexpected given that it had made inroads in this Congress stronghold only recently. In 1985, for the first time, the BJP won more than 10 seats in Chhattisgarh.

---

[105] Y. Yadav, 'Political change in North India – Interpreting Assembly election results', *EPW*, 18 Dec. 1993, p. 2772.

[106] Since the late 1980s, the main leader of the BJP in this region has been Uma Bharti. Because of her involvement in the Ayodhya movement, she could not visit her constituency between her election in 1991 and the 1993 election campaign (interview with U. Bharti).

In 1990, it triumphed in 51 constituencies (less than in Mahakoshal) but in 1993 it repeated this performance in three-fifths of them, giving it one-third of the seats. This result is all the more surprising given the BJP's precipitate decline in popularity in the tribal belt in 1993 since 34 of the 75 seats reserved for the Scheduled Tribes are situated in Chhattisgarh. These statistics suggest that the BJP proved relatively resilient on account of its much stronger showing in urban constituencies where there were fewer tribal voters.

The BJP becomes ever more urban.   The CSDS Data Unit's statistics for the 1993 Madhya Pradesh assembly elections show that of the 17 seats defined as 'urban', the BJP won 11 (with an average of 45.8% of the valid votes) against 6 for the Congress (I), which polled ten points fewer (34.6%). The party was already well established in cities like Bhopal and Ujjain. In most other cities where it won all the seats in 1993 – Raipur, Jabalpur, Indore – it was either already in command or a strong contender for power in 1990. In fact, the turning point in these three former Congress strongholds was in 1989 when the BJP won the three Lok Sabha seats with comfortable margins. What was new in 1993, however, was the fact that the BJP continued to make progress and bucked the general trend. In 12 of the 17 constituencies of the five cities where the BJP won all the seats – Bhopal, Indore, Ujjain, Jabalpur and Raipur – the party gained more than 50% of the valid votes. Among the urban constituencies that the BJP won for the first time, Jabalpur Cantonment deserves special mention since it had been held till recently by Chandra Mohan, the grandson of Seth Govind Das. By contrast, the BJP's winning candidate was contesting it for the first time.[107]

The urban success of the BJP was symptomatic of the implantation by the RSS and its affiliates of a dense network of activists and of the latter's propagation of Hindu nationalism and a social welfare tactic. The evolution of the political culture of the middle class and the communal polarisation of the cities must also be taken into account, issues that we shall examine using Bhopal as an example.

Bhopal: the making of a stronghold.   As evident from previous chapters, the BJP had made its presence felt in Bhopal relatively late, in part because of the large numbers of Muslims in the old town and the presence of Communist activists in working-class areas. Bhopal, from this point of view, is all the more interesting as it has experienced the second highest

---

[107] A businessman by occupation, he considers that his victory was chiefly due to his daily contact with the people, especially in terms of social work (interview with Ishwar Das Rohani, 16 Feb. 1994, Bhopal).

rate of growth (after Satna) of the class 1 cities (those with more than 100,000 inhabitants) of Madhya Pradesh over the last two decades, 74.35% between 1971 and 1981 and 58.51% between 1981 and 1991.[108] This growth is partly explained by the migration to the city of villagers or workers from other states who were attracted by the prospect of employment. Despite the constant expansion of the working class areas, from 1974 onwards Babulal Gaur was installed as the official representative in the constituency of Govindpura – which contained most of Bhopal's heavy industry – largely because the BJP made a special effort to adapt to this changing context, as exemplified in Bharat Heavy Electricals Ltd (BHEL), the town's largest industrial complex, which has 18,000 employees, of whom 13,000 are manual labourers.

Given the large numbers of unemployed migrants who arrived at the BHEL works – 3-4,000 from Kerala, 2,000 from Tamil Nadu, and 3-4,000 from Maharashtra – many of them could not find employment and lived in slums, earning a pittance as casual workers. This influx was naturally a challenge for the BJP, which risked losing Govindpura if the migrants voted against it – hence the problem was tackled in depth under the guidance of Giriraj Kishore, a former aide of Babulal Gaur. A foreman at BHEL since 1960, he had developed the BMS, set up *shakhas*[109] and augmented these networks by initiating a new social welfare tactic. In 1980 the Madhya Pradesh BJP founded a Jhuggi Jhonpri Mahasangh (JJM – Hut dwellers' association – *jhuggi jhonpris* are the huts found in the slums), of which Giriraj Kishore was appointed General Secretary. He set the organisation two objectives, the first of which was alleviating the living conditions of the most deprived. In one slum, occupied by Biharis and hemmed in close to the railway line, Kishore's team worked successfully for the allocation of a larger site and had wells dug. The JJM tried to find work for migrants in the administration and also provided a volunteer doctor who lived in the slum and treated patients free of charge.[110] The other aspect of Kishore's work was truly Hindu, namely of organising the festivals in the Hindu calender celebrated in BHEL, including all the regional variants, e.g. the Maharashtrian feast in honour of Ganesh and the Bengalis' Durga Puja. Giriraj Kishore even supported, with the same end in view, a Hindu Ekta Manch (Tribune of Hindu unity) to support a number of these festivals. The JJM also coordinated a fund-raising drive to build a temple dedicated to Vishvakarma, a mythological figure who as the architect and builder of the world was the

---

[108] *Census of India 1991 – Madhya Pradesh, Provisional population totals*, Bhopal: 1991, p. 71.

[109] Interview with Giriraj Kishore, 13 Nov. 1990, Bhopal.

[110] Observations made in 1990.

workers' patron. This was hardly a wise move, since the BMS had long been trying to popularise the observance of a day in honour of Vishvakarma (represented as a symbol of class unity for economic advancement) to compete with the Communists' observance of May Day.[111] This social welfare tactic, with its strong ideological connotations, served the electoral interests of the BJP. Babulal Gaur won his seat in the 1993 election by an unprecedented margin with 69% of the valid votes.

The second factor which the BJP exploited in Bhopal in the late 1980s and early 1990s was the growing intensity of urban communalism. Less than one year later, memories of the December 1992 riot were still fresh and these partly account for the BJP's success, especially in the constituency of Bhopal North, which it had never previously won. In 1990 its candidate, Ramesh Sharma, had lost against an independent, Arif Aqueel, who had received the support of most Muslim voters (the Congress candidate had polled only 8% on that occasion). The BJP could not escape the fact that Muslims accounted for 40-45% of voters in the constituency and thus any Hindu nationalist candidate faced severe problems in winning the seat, one which had always been held by Muslim MLAs. In 1993, Sharma received 50.34% of the votes, Aqueel – on a Janata Dal ticket – 43.47% and the Congress candidate – also a Muslim – 5.26%. Thus even if the Congress (I) and the Janata Dal had not divided the Muslim vote, the BJP would still have prevailed. This example illustrates the relevance for the BJP of a strategy of communal polarisation: since Muslims are seldom in a majority, when the BJP builds a large Hindu 'vote bank', it can win. Ramesh Sharma considered that his victory was due to the riot and more especially to the votes of Hindu women who, having been frightened by the violence or having suffered from it, went in large numbers to the polling stations.[112] The turnout was very high indeed, 76.26% as against 62.07% in 1990.

The impact of such communal polarisation can be observed in other urban constituencies, such as Burhanpur, a town with a 22% Muslim population, where the winning candidate was a VHP *sadhu*. Given this context, the fact that the BJP won in 8 of the 12 constituencies where Muslims accounted for more than 20% of the population – all of them urban – now seems less puzzling. Interestingly enough, for the first time

---

[111] See my 'Note sur un syndicat nationaliste hindou', art. cit.

[112] 'The poll percentage among women increased because last year there was a riot. During the riot people suffered a lot. And those who provoked the riot where from a certain community [sampraday] therefore, people were angry. Logically society thought "We are strong, if we all vote, we'll win"' (interview with R. Sharma, 19 Feb. 1994, Bhopal). A video film made by Sharma's sympathisers shows that he fully exploited Hindu feelings: one of his canvassing techniques consisted in visiting all the temples of his constituency surrounded by supporters shouting 'Jai Shri Ram'

since Independence no Muslim was elected to the Madhya Pradesh Vidhan Sabha, largely because of the increase in urban communal tension.

Commenting upon the success of the BJP in the cities of Madhya Pradesh, a journalist suggested that it confirmed the communal bias of the middle class.[113] This proposition requires some clarification. First, the middle class was certainly not the only source of urban support for the BJP, otherwise it would have lost; and second, the urban middle class did not vote so preponderantly for the BJP on account of communal issues alone. Other strands of the BJP's political platform attracted the middle class, among which the culture of discipline and a discreet but determined opposition to the policies of positive discrimination in favour of the OBCs were the most important.

As far as the question of discipline is concerned, many middle class voters apparently supported what became known as the 'anti-encroachment drive' launched by the Patwa government in 1991. Its aim was to demolish illegal constructions – most of which were slum dwellings – in the name of urban rationalisation and beautification. By mid-1992, almost 100,000 such 'encroachments' had been removed in 45 towns. As a result 16,000 slum-dwellers had to be resettled.[114] In Indore, the anti-encroachment drive was prosecuted with particular vigour in Bombay Bazar, a Muslim-dominated locality.[115] However, the encroachers were provided with more generous resettlement conditions than in Bhopal.[116] This authoritarian policy responded to the concerns of the Hindu middle class for a more disciplined approach to urban life.

Bhopal also offers a relevant illustration of the BJP's popularity among the high caste urban upper middle class. Bhopal South, even though it comprises parts of the old Muslim town and sectors of the industrial area, is essentially a middle-class constituency. The BJP MLA for the area since 1990, Sailendra Pradhan, is an engineer whose family owns a farm and a cement factory. He belongs to the Rotary Club and since 1988 has presided over a Ramcharitmanas Samiti which patronises the recitation of religious texts, especially during Dasahara. He thus exemplifies the desire of members of the wealthy middle class to combine modernity with an interest in its cultural inheritance. The concept of Hindu nationalism is compatible with the aspiration of such people to be both respectful of tradition and modern in their outlook, because it provides them with access to a consistent reinterpretation of a valued tradition.[117] Pradhan

---

[113] *Times of India*, 2 Dec. 1993, p. 1.

[114] Ibid., 14 Feb. 1991.

[115] Ibid., 7 May 1991.

[116] *Indian Express*, 21 Nov. 1993.

[117] This hypothesis needs further evaluation and might form a very fruitful research topic

claims to receive support from fellow engineers, Kayasths (of which he is one) who are numerous in this administrative city (the MP for Bhopal, also a Kayasth, is a former IAS officer), long-term residents of Bhopal who knew his father and grandfather, Rotarians, and groups of businessmen and their employees.[118] Moreover the attractiveness to the middle class of the BJP certainly increased after the 'Mandal affair' .

The BJP in Uttar Pradesh, Himachal Pradesh, Rajasthan and Delhi

Some of the reasons for the BJP's setback in Madhya Pradesh are also to be found in other states which went to the polls in 1993. In Uttar Pradesh, the BJP's reverse came about because of the electorate's polarisation along caste lines. The party's seats fell from 211 to 177 but its share of valid votes rose from 31.6 to 33.4% (for the same number of candidates). It would probably have won a majority of seats if its opponents' supporters had split their votes, as in 1991, between Congress (I), Janata Dal, the Samajwadi Party and the Bahujan Samaj Party. However, the latter two parties formed an alliance in 1993 which polled very strongly among the OBCs, the Scheduled Castes and the Muslims, who had been drawn to Mulayam Singh Yadav following the demolition of the Babri Masjid[119] and saw in the SP-BSP alliance the best means of defeating the BJP. The SP and BSP together won 28.7% of the votes and 176 seats. Thanks to the support of 28 Congress (I) MLAs and of 27 MLAs from the Janata Dal, Yadav was able to form a government.

The BJP had lost ground in every region of the state except Central UP and Western UP, in which it made a net gain of 16 seats. As in 1991, the party obtained substantial support from the Jats, a numerous and influential caste in the area between Meerut and Agra which used to support the faction of the Janata Dal led by Ajit Singh, the son of Charan Singh. Here the Jats transferred some of their support to the BJP probably on account of the Janata Dal's support for the Mandal Report, from which they could derive no benefit given that they were not classified as OBCs.

The BJP also received some support from OBCs; according to the *India Today*-MARG exit poll, 63% of upper caste interviewees voted for the BJP as did 28% of OBCs (compared to 36% and 33% for the SP and BSP respectively).[120] Thus although the party's strongest base remains the

for anthropologists.

[118] Interview with S. Pradhan, 16 Feb., 1994, Bhopal.

[119] Many Muslims accused the Congress (I) of having allowed the mosque's demolition to go ahead and hence distanced themselves from the party.

[120] Cited in Y. Yadav, 'Political change in North India', op. cit., p. 2273.

upper castes, it might still win support among lower castes such as the Lodhis and the Kurmis who show some reluctance to vote along with the Yadavs. The BJP benefited from these inter-caste rivalries but also from its skill at masking its upper-caste pedigree. In addition to projecting Kalyan Singh as its candidate for the post of Chief Minister, in its election manifesto the party promised to implement a quota of 27% of state government posts for OBCs and 10% for poor members of the upper castes. The SP-BSP's election manifesto promised to do likewise.[121] Kalyan Singh argued for the inclusion of a large number of OBC candidates in the BJP list of nominees but upper caste BJP leaders and the party high command seemed to be reluctant to condone any move likely to alienate their traditional base. Eventually an even balance of representation from almost all segments of society – albeit not the minorities – was established.[122] The BJP raised the number of OBC candidates on its list from 93 in 1991 to 97 in 1993 (compared to 105 on the Janata Dal, 103 on the SP-BSP and 74 on the Congress (I) lists respectively).[123] Nevertheless, the BJP remains associated with the upper castes in the mind of many OBCs. G.K. Lieten's research in rural eastern Uttar Pradesh in the early 1990s revealed that 'Since the BJP from the very onset was perceived as a party of "bhadralok" and "Lalaji's" (Brahmins and traders), it failed to reach the downtrodden villagers'[124] while many OBCs regard the manipulation of the Ramjanmabhoomi issue as 'a means of evoking loyalties against the dangers of a civic emancipatory process'.[125]

Besides sections of the OBCs, the BJP partly alienated another social category which previously supported it: urban youths. While educated high caste youths played a major role in the Ramjanmabhoomi movement, they largely deserted the BJP in 1993 because of the disappointing performance of Kalyan Singh's government and the Anti-copying Act – which allowed the police to enter campuses in order to prosecute students accused of cheating in exams. Mulayam Singh Yadav achieved some popularity among students by his campaign promise to scrap the Act.[126] The student union elections in universities in Uttar Pradesh in March 1993 revealed how quickly the Hindu nationalist movement was losing ground: the ABVP recorded humiliating defeats in the universities of Allahabad,

---

[121] *Indian Express*, 8 Oct. 1993 and 27 Oct. 1993.

[122] *Statesman* (Delhi), 21 Oct. 1993.

[123] *India Today*, 15 Nov. 1993.

[124] 'On casteism and communalism in Uttar Pradesh', op. cit., p. 779.

[125] G.K. Lieten, 'Of sharecroppers and scared croppers in Easter UP', 13th European conference on modern South Asian studies (Toulouse, 31 Aug-3 Sept., 1994), p. 17.

[126] *Times of India*, 13 and 15 Nov. 1993.

Lucknow, Kumaon, in the Benares Hindu University and the Aligarh Muslim University.[127]

In Himachal Pradesh, the BJP was literally routed, again largely because of the mobilisation of the masses against 'anti-people decisions'.[128] The party's total number of seats fell from 46 to 8 while the Congress (I) increased its tally from 9 to 52 in a house of 68. Here the 'Rama wave' had receded completely (only 11% of those interviewed by MARG mentioned Ram and religion as the main factors influencing their vote).[129] The outcome of the poll was above all a severe indictment of the performance of the government of Shanta Kumar, who lost his own seat.[130] The BJP had alienated government employees when Kumar enforced the 'no work – no pay' principle and crushed their protest against it (11 employees were dismissed for striking), a serious blow to its popularity in a state where government employees represent approximately a quarter of all voters. Another interest group, the apple-growers, strongly disapproved of the government's decision to withdraw subsidies and price support. The claim that the government was élitist was given substance when Shanta Kumar challenged the Mandal report in the Supreme Court, a move which prompted many OBCs to transfer their allegiance to the Congress (I).

Divisions within the party were exacerbated by the policies of Shanta Kumar. The non-implementation of reservation quotas for Scheduled Castes and Scheduled Tribes caused resentment, and just after the 1991 elections the state party vice-president and the Panchayat Minister, both of whom belonged to the Scheduled Castes, resigned their posts.[131] Besides such low caste dissidence, factional rivalries have been prominent ever since the party assumed power. Jagdev Chand, the party's second in command, had been vying for the post of Chief Minister, to which end he initiated a petition against Shanta Kumar, who retaliated by depriving him of the important portfolio of Public Works and allotting him that of Revenue instead.[132] All the ministers in Shanta Kumar's government were defeated, except Jagdev Chand, and six of the eight successful BJP candidates were newcomers, which testifies to the unpopularity of the outgoing regime.

[127] K. Chaitanya, 'Ideology returns to the campus', *EPW*, June 12, 1993, p. 1215.

[128] Shanta Kumar admitted after the elections: 'We have been punished for certain perceived anti-people decisions' (cited in *India Today*, 15 Dec. 1993, p. 36).

[129] Ibid., 30 Nov. 1993, p. 22.

[130] However, the MARG opinion poll reveals that Shanta Kumar remained the favoured Chief Minister of 42% of the interviewees – possibly because there were no other good candidates for the post, at least on the BJP side (ibid.).

[131] *National Mail*, 6 July 1991.

[132] *Times of India*, 28 Aug. 1992.

Rajasthan was the only state where the BJP strengthened its position in terms of seats as well as valid votes between the elections of 1990 and 1993. It won 95 seats (as opposed to 85 in 1990) and 38.7% of the valid votes (as against 25.5% in 1990). However, in contrast to 1990, when it was allied to the Janata Dal, the party contested almost all of the state's 200 seats in 1993 (as opposed to 132 in 1990); this goes some way to explain its upsurge in support.

Rajasthan was the only state where the BJP regained power for positive reasons (the main 'negative' reason being the indiscipline within the Congress (I)).[133] First, the personality of Shekhawat must be highlighted. He was put forward as the BJP candidate for the post of Chief Minister with the approval of most party workers; many candidates benefited from the personal popularity he had acquired after more than four decades in Rajasthan politics. Compared to other former BJP Chief Ministers – e.g. Patwa and Shanta Kumar – Shekhawat was recognised as a political leader of consequence, and as one who was pragmatic and responsive to the people. The pre-election opinion poll conducted by MARG revealed that 44% of interviewees in Rajasthan favoured Shekhawat as their candidate for Chief Minister.[134]

Second, Shekhawat also enhanced the BJP's appeal to uncommitted voters because he did not hesitate to challenge the RSS line, to nominate former Janata Dal or Congress (I) members as BJP candidates[135] and to take the caste composition of each constituency into account when allocating tickets. While the Congress (I) attracted many Jat leaders, the BJP chiefly fielded Rajputs but was willing to put forward Jats, Gujars and other candidates where this caste-based strategy increased their chances of success in certain seats.[136]

Third, while the 'RSS lobby' headed by Lalit Kishore Chaturvedi, one of the former ministers, criticised Shekhawat's pragmatism and especially the nomination of candidates who were not committed to Hindu nationalism, such dissenting voices barely affected the party's coherence.[137] Fourth,

---

[133] The nomination of many candidates whose only asset was their relationship with Congress leaders in Delhi – such as in the case of relatives of Union Ministers – was an important factor in the unprecedented number of rebel candidates.

[134] *India Today*, 30 Nov. p. 19.

[135] Ibid., 15 Nov. 1993. Of the 24 MLAs of the Janata Dal (D) – a group led by Digvijay Singh which seceded from the JD in 1990 to support the Shekhawat government – 14 joined the BJP after the dismissal of the Shekhawat government (while others joined the Congress (I) or returned to the JD). All 14 were given tickets from their constituencies (*Times of India*, 29 Oct. 1993).

[136] However, the BJP was especially successful in the towns and cities: it won 12 urban constituencies out of 14 and secured over 50% votes in this category of seats (Y. Yadav, 'Political change in North India', op. cit., p. 2769).

[137] R. Jenkins, 'Where the BJP survived – Rajasthan Assembly Elections, 1993', *EPW*, 12

Shekhawat's performance was also relatively sound. The Chief Minister 'ran a substantially less corrupt administration than the Congress government' and his economic policy, combining subsidies to industry and some protection to agriculturalists, was well received.[138] Finally, Rajasthan was probably the state where the Hindu nationalist propaganda of the early 1990s had been imbued most deeply. According to Jenkins, the BJP succeeded in fostering the emergence of a regional version of Hindutva by capitalising on the importance of Rajput Hinduism in the state:

So instead of stressing the destruction of the Ram mandir [sic], Shekhawat has played on the cultural sensibilities of the Rajasthan electorate to transform that basis of rajput Hinduism into a movement for a sort of 'rajput Hindutva'.[139]

Shekhawat, as a member of a non-aristocratic segment of the Rajput community, was ideally placed for this kind of manipulation.

In Delhi, the BJP's situation was different from that in the other states of the Hindi belt where elections were held in 1993 because here the party had been in opposition and did not have the problem of explaining its role in government. In fact, no elections had been held in Delhi since 1983, when the Congress (I) had taken control. The Union Territory was administered by the Centre when the term of the Municipal Corporation and Metropolitan Council expired. In 1993, Delhi had been given some of the attributes of a state – a Vidhan Sabha and a Chief Minister – which required elections. With a share of the vote of 43.5%, the BJP won an overwhelming majority of 49 seats out of 70 in the newly-established Vidhan Sabha. As pointed out by Y. Yadav, the BJP did well 'in all sections of the society: it has won 10 out of the 15 rural seats, 20 out of the 30 seats dominated by unauthorised colonies, eight out of the 13 reserved seats, and three out of the five seats dominated by the Sikhs.'[140]

The Sikhs seized the opportunity to punish the Congress (I) for the 1984 riots of which they had been the victims and were wooed by BJP promises to prosecute those responsible for instigating them. The middle class was probably drawn to the BJP by its measured stand against reservations. Generally speaking, many Delhi voters rejected the Congress (I) because of the way the Centre had managed local affairs: power cuts, water shortages and traffic jams had affected everybody. Thus, the BJP was enthusiastically voted into power in a state which it had not previously governed.

March 1994, pp. 635-41. The following paragraphs draws on this article.

[138] Ibid., pp. 638-9.

[139] Ibid., p. 641.

[140] Y. Yadav, 'Political change in North India', op. cit., p. 2768.

However, the MARG opinion poll revealed that for BJP supporters, Ayodhya and religion had been the main election issue, which tends to confirm the continuing influence of communal factors in urban areas.[141] The BJP also owed its success to factional infighting within the Congress (I) and the Janata Dal's ability to cut into the Congress (I) vote in the rural constituencies of Outer Delhi.

The reverses which the BJP suffered in the Vidhan Sabha elections of 1993 in Madhya Pradesh, Uttar Pradesh and Himachal Pradesh must be balanced against the gains which it made in Rajasthan and Delhi. On the debit side of the account, the results in the former group of states confirm the two internal contradictions of the strategy of ethno-religious mobilisation mentioned earlier in our study. The Babri Masjid's demolition was the logical culmination of the RSS's campaign but it deprived the RSS and its affiliates of the immediate subject of a highly focussed mass movement. The second was that the strategy of ethno-religious mobilisation enabled *sadhus* and young Hindus, notably those from the Bajrang Dal, to assert themselves as political actors beyond the control of the RSS and the BJP. Their violent methods damaged the credibility of the Hindu nationalist party, which in turn led the BJP to distance itself from the VHP.

The Sangathanist party-building pattern was also affected, at least in Madhya Pradesh, during the early 1990s. Even though the party did not suffer from the usual form of factionalism, the exercise of power precipitated a new kind of groupism in its top echelons, in which the cohesiveness of *sangathan mantris* broke down and there emerged an unprecedented level of indiscipline among local cadres.

As far as the political context is concerned, the Congress (I) now regards the BJP as its principal opponent in the Hindu belt, and has sought to exploit the BJP's weaknesses. The sanctions against the BJP, the VHP and the RSS following the demolition of the Babri Masjid were applied firmly but not with so much force as to earn public sympathy for the Hindu nationalists. Second, Congress leaders were adept at placing issues of economic development at the centre of the election campaign while playing down the importance of communal issues.

The mobilisation of the OBCs in the wake of the Mandal affair and the accession to power of the BJP in some states where it experienced electoral reverses suggest that we should broaden our framework and include factors other than our set of strategies and variables. One overarching problem has been that, except in Rajasthan, the BJP has not performed well as a party of government and has been unable to avoid

---

[141] *India Today*, 30 Nov. 1993, p. 19.

internal power struggles. K.N. Govindacharya did not disguise the poor record of BJP governments:

> To be better and different in the matter of governance, we need to do much more both at the level of ideas and at the level of implementation. What we can, however, claim is that we are aware of the need and alive to the situation, and we admit the lacunae and the handicaps.[142]

Partly as a result of some of the policies adopted by its state governments, the BJP also suffered from its upper-caste image at a time when tribals and members of the OBCs and of the Scheduled Castes were becoming very aware of their status and its effect on job reservations.

On the positive side of its account, the BJP could congratulate itself on its increasing appeal to urban-dwellers, especially the upper-caste middle class, and on the fact that despite its losses it remained the biggest party, in terms of votes as well as the share of valid votes in the five states taken together: it polled about 36% – as opposed to 28% for the Congress (I) – and won 446 seats – against 347 for the Congress (I). According to Y. Yadav, 'the trend indicates the possibility of the emergence of the BJP as the successor to the Congress'.[143] This hypothesis is certainly supported by the decline of the Congress (I), at least in terms of organisation, in Uttar Pradesh and Rajasthan. However, the fact remains that the BJP lost ground in its main stronghold – the Hindi belt.

---

[142] K.N. Govindacharya, 'Future vistas', op. cit., p. 204.

[143] Y. Yadav, 'Political change in North India', op. cit., p. 2773.

CONCLUSION

Our review of the history of the Hindu nationalist movement has been designed to explain the strategies which its proponents have variously evolved and implemented. In defining these strategies as ideal types we have assumed that each contained its own logical requirements and conditioned patterns of action.

In the first part of the book two strategic combinations were identified, one 'militant', the other 'moderate'. The first allied ideological identity-building (achieved by stigmatising and emulating 'Others' who allegedly posed a threat) with 'Sangathanism' – the penetration of Indian society by a network of activists – and ethno-religious mobilisation.

The strategy of stigmatisation and emulation of 'threatening Others' is based on a feeling of vulnerability born of a largely imaginary threat posed by 'aliens', principally Muslims and Christians. This strategy is the cornerstone of the Hindu nationalist movement; it was the first to be formulated, and sustains its ideology.

In the first chapter Hindu nationalism was characterised as an ideological ethnic movement of the upper castes. Indeed its ideology was originally evolved by high-caste socio-religious reformers anxious to preserve a Hindu culture and order by imitating some of the more robust features of the West and the otherwise stigmatised 'Semitic religions'. However, the upper-caste overtone largely contradicted the nationalist mission of the Hindu militant organisations as codified by Savarkar and later Golwalkar. The Sangathanist *modus operandi* was first developed by the RSS in order to communicate its doctrine to the largest number of people. Indeed the RSS was originally conceived as a kind of nationalist sect, a model and vanguard of the *Hindu Rashtra* which relied on a framework of dedicated and even ascetic cadres whose mission was the conversion of society as a whole. To this end the RSS developed a strategy of social welfare which became part of Sangathanism. The Jana Sangh adopted a similar pattern of party-building in the 1950s since its organisation relied primarily on a hierarchy of RSS trained-cadres. A network of *sangathan mantris* was in charge of implanting party branches at the local level, as evident from the case of Madhya Pradesh, while at the head of the Jana Sangh was a clearly demarcated élite whose leadership culture was collegiate rather than of

522

an adverserial or debating style. But Sangathanist techniques did not enable the Hindu nationalist movement quickly to expand its base. Ethnoreligious mobilisation thus appeared the most relevant strategy. This instrumentalist strategy consisted in manipulating symbols of Hindu identity which often had anti-Muslim connotations (such as the cow, presented as a victim of Islamic ritual sacrifices, or Ram 'imprisoned' in the Babri Masjid) in order to bring Hindus on to the streets *en masse*. The three strategies continued to be used in combination especially after the RSS entered the political arena through the Jana Sangh.

The 'moderate' combination united three elements which appeared perfectly to balance the three components of its 'militant' counterpart. At the ideological level it implied a mere 'Hindu traditionalism' which was less aggressively xenophobic, especially against Muslims, than Hindu nationalism. In terms of mobilisation or simply gathering support, it was concerned to gain acceptance in mainstream politics through an emphasis on socio-economic issues and the pragmatic search for alliances with the parties of the 'legitimate opposition'. Finally, for local implantation this combination used an 'aggregative' strategy of party-building relying more on the recruitment of non-ideological but influential politicians and particularly of local notables. The two sets of strategies are presented here as ideal types, but in practice they overlapped. Indeed the RSS and its affiliates were ultimately to employ elements of both strategies, largely because the constraints of the political system obliged the Hindu nationalist movement to shift from a militant to a moderate combination.

While the Jana Sangh's founder, S.P. Mookerjee, was inclined at the outset to develop the party along 'moderate' lines, the RSS-trained leaders who took control of the Jana Sangh in the mid-1950s chose militancy as their preferred option. However the Jana Sangh found it hard to attract a substantial following. First, Hindu nationalist ideology could only gain unqualified support in a situation where the 'Other' (Muslim and Christian) was *subjectively perceived* as posing a threat sufficiently serious to create an inferiority complex among sections of the majority community. After Partition, and especially after 1950, the conditions for a similar feeling of vulnerability did not occur again till the 1980s. Second, the investment in time required by Sangathanist techniques proved ill-suited to the needs of political parties, which are dictated by short-term electoral considerations. Third, the Sangathanist network was hardly in a position to activate a strategy of ethno-religious mobilisation, which, as was to become clear, was governed by two variables: the political context and, to a lesser degree, the support of religious leaders. On the one hand, politics until the 1960s was largely identified with the 'Congress system' in which Hindu traditionalist elements tended at the local level to appropriate the Hindu nationalists' propaganda themes, while the Congress leadership at the Centre displayed a vigilant secularism which, along with socio-economic development, became one of the legitimate norms of the Indian régime. Secularism and development were also valued as such by the most important non-Congress political forces – the leftist parties forming the core of the 'legitimate opposition'. On the other hand, while a religious network proved a useful ally that could be relied on to manipulate Hindu symbols, most of the few religious figures involved in politics sided with the Ram Rajya Parishad, the Hindu Mahasabha or the Congress.

These constraints led the Jana Sangh, in the late 1950s and early 1960s, to challenge the doctrinal purity of the 'militant' model in favour of a hybrid strategy which had many features of the 'moderate' combination. It embarked on a plan to develop its base by co-opting notables to serve as election candidates in the hope of building up pockets of electoral strength or 'clusters' whose core comprised RSS-trained party workers while the periphery consisted of notables, a process discernible in Madhya Pradesh, especially in Mandsaur district. The Jana Sangh also forged pragmatic alliances not only with the Swatantra Party but also with the Socialists and in its programmes emphasised socio-economic themes such as opposition to a state-controlled economy. This development did not involve a radical departure from its past practices. The RSS and its affiliates had always been hostile to an omnipresent state since what came first in their endeavour of nation-building was society. Moreover, the 'cluster' technique enabled RSS cadres at the local level to keep control of the party – something of prime importance to the local party workers who were vigilant in preventing any dilution of the Jana Sangh's Hindu nationalist identity. The persistent tensions between the all-India leaders and the local Sangathanist network over the question of integration within the 'legitimate political system' suggested that the true division of the Jana Sangh, because of its specific party-building pattern, was not vertical, of the factional type, but horizontal, separating the leaders from the local organisers.

In 1964 the RSS played a leading role in founding the VHP, whose centralised and integrated structure indicated an effort to match Christian and other styles of ecclesiastical organisation in line with the strategy of stigmatisation and emulation. Soon afterwards the mixed strategy was implemented in the 1967 election campaign. This consisted in forging electoral alliances with mainstream opposition parties while at the same time launching an ethno-religious mobilisation campaign. In 1966-7, the Jana Sangh negotiated seat adjustments with the opposition parties while at the same time participating in an instrumentalist agitation over the issue of cow protection. At that time the legitimate opposition, in its search for an anti-Congress coalition, was not deterred by the Jana Sangh's communalism, an attitude that signifies probably the first erosion of secularism as a norm of Indian politics. This highly significant political development enabled the Jana Sangh to integrate itself with mainstream politics without renouncing its Hindu nationalist identity. While its mixed strategy played an important role in the party's electoral advance in 1967, such success remained very limited. The cow protection movement had been checked partly by the independent action of numerous *sadhus* who were not well integrated into the VHP's network and by the central government's firm policy of upholding secularism.

In the late 1960s local Jana Sangh cadres protested against the dilution of the party's identity implied by the participation of some of its state leaders in coalition governments, especially those in which Communist ministers also took part. In shaping the party's strategy, the national leaders had to take account of the views of those workers who were part of the Sangathanist network and who would resist any attempt to moderate the party's Hindu nationalism. This difference of outlook was more important than any other within the leadership itself. At the same time, however, the Jana Sangh's leaders had to form a judgement of the likely effectiveness of Mrs Gandhi's use of social and economic slogans to build up support for Congress (R). In the end they opted for a style of populism which would be acceptable both to the party activists and to the leaders who wanted the Jana Sangh to remain within the bounds of mainstream politics and fight Congress on the ground it had chosen. In order to compete with Indira Gandhi, whose appeal to the masses was based on her *'Garabi Hatao!'* slogan, the Jana Sangh thus concentrated on a populist socio-economic programme. As in the 1950s, when Nehru's central planning tempted the Hindu nationalists to launch a propaganda campaign against state control of the economy, so Indira Gandhi's populism in the early 1970s persuaded the Jana Sangh to focus on economic issues and play down its lingering interest in ethno-religious mobilisation. However, this decision also revealed a number of contradictions. As far as party-building was concerned, during elections it exploited the local influence of the growing number of princely candidates who were attracted to its ranks – as the cases of Madhya Pradesh and, to a lesser extent, Rajasthan make clear. At the same time it was able to join the 'legitimate opposition' in the Grand Alliance of 1971 dominated by the Congress(O). The combination of populism and the recourse to princes and conservative allies quickly proved unworkable when confronted by Indira Gandhi who, in addition to greater effectiveness in her 'appeal to the masses', achieved an unassailable reputation for patriotism after the defeat of Pakistan in the war of 1971. This deprived the Hindu nationalists of their claim to be the best custodians of the country's security.

In the mid-1970s the Sangathanist technique prevailed *vis-à-vis* the

notabilisation of the party, after Balasaheb Deoras, who was more interested in politics than Golwalkar, became *sarsanghchalak*. This was
augmented in the course of the 'JP movement' and the Emergency
imposed by Mrs Gandhi when RSS-trained activists acquired a new
prestige and legitimacy. Involvement in the Janata Party brought the
former Jana Sanghis into a political culture based on Gandhian notions of
social reform and decentralisation which echoed aspects of the RSS's
ideology and finally integrated the ex-Jana Sangh leaders in mainstream
politics – even giving them access to power at the Centre. However, a
contradiction appeared between the efforts of these leaders to merge with
the Hindu traditionalist wing of conservative Gandhians in the Janata
Party, such as Morarji Desai, and the renewed assertiveness of local and
state cadres who remained attached to its Hindu nationalist identity. The
uncompromising behaviour of ex-Jana Sangh leaders – in Madhya
Pradesh for instance – and the involvement of RSS members of the Janata
Party in Hindu-Muslim riots – which led to a wave of anti-communal
protest, even among the partners of the ex-Jana Sanghis in the ruling
coalition, epitomised this contradiction; it reflected the long-standing
tension between the Jana Sangh leadership's pursuit of a strategy of
moderation and the political culture and *modus operandi* of its local
cadres, whose activities served to constrain the party's strategy nationally.
Notwithstanding this inner-party contradiction, the immediate obstacle to
integration lay in the political arena, the most important variable of our
model. Charan Singh's faction of the Janata Party denounced the former
Jana Sangh's association with the RSS and its departure, at least at the
local level, from secularism in order to weaken the position of Morarji
Desai. Disturbed by the growing strength of the Hindu nationalist activist
network and the reluctance of former Jana Sanghis to move towards
reforms that would favour the OBCs, ex-BLD leaders and socialists joined
hands in the battle for secularism, which the Congress opposition continued to represent as a normative rule of Indian politics; the resulting
tension was one of the factors which lead to the break-up of the Janata
Party in 1980.

In 1980, therefore, the Hindu nationalists had reached deadlock: they
had tried unsuccessfully to develop a militant strategy and then to become
integrated in mainstream politics. At that time the newly-founded BJP
tried to pursue a 'moderate' strategy while the RSS, which now considered
such an approach irrelevant, evolved a strategy of ethno-religious
mobilisation the main agency of which was the VHP. Its aim – an overtly
political one – was the creation of a Hindu vote bank. The 1980s saw a
gradual return by the BJP to the combination of 'militant' strategies. These
could now be implemented more efficiently as a result of the awakening
of a Hindu sense of vulnerability, the communalisation of politics under

the auspices of the Congress (I) and the rallying of a large number of *sadhus* to the VHP.

Hindu nationalist identity found itself reinvigorated through the reactivation of a vulnerability complex among many Hindus that was sparked off by conversions to Islam in 1981 and sustained by the Shah Bano affair. Thus militant Hindu identity was once again refashioned through a strategy of stigmatisation and emulation of 'threatening Others'. This phenomenon took the particular form of rallying more *sadhus* to the restructured VHP, which thereafter could command a relatively disciplined religious network. These were significant changes in the strategy of ethno-religious mobilisation, not least because the other variable conditioning the operation of this strategy – the political context – was being transformed too. The Congress (I) government now appeared willing to adhere less firmly to its secularist principles; it had given way to orthodox Muslim opinion in its handling of the Shah Bano affair, it had condoned the decision to unseal the disputed structure in Ayodhya, and it had allowed the *shilanyas* ceremony to go ahead. The Congress no longer had either the will or the means to uphold secular ideals. In the 1950s and '60s, local Congressmen did not hesitate to use communal appeals while the central leadership maintained a secular profile. However, in the 1980s it was the central government which resorted to a communalised form of politics which gave much more prominence to the alleged rights of religious groups, with the result that debate about ethnic questions became commonplace. To some extent the Hindu nationalist discourse was legitimised. In addition, the mainstream opposition, though antagonised by the revival of Hindu militancy, agreed to form an anti-Congress (I) alliance with the BJP in the late 1980s. The BJP was thus presented with ideal conditions for the launch of a 'mixed strategy' in which instrumentalism was centred on manipulation of the symbol of Ramjanmabhoomi. The trajectory of Hindu nationalism up to the 1980s can be summarised in the table overleaf, where the variables are printed in bold letters below the strategies they influence and the synthesis between two strategies are italicised.

The fifth part of this book, devoted to the early 1990s, studies new problems in the framework of the original model. Hindus for the first time mobilised massively behind the RSS-VHP-BJP combination. We analysed in Chapter 12 not only the instrumentalist strategy and the parameters on which it depended, but also its impact on Indian society. The Ramjanmabhoomi movement enabled the Hindu nationalists, chiefly through the VHP, to play down its élitist, Brahminical image in favour of a nationalist devotionalism borrowing from *bhakti* forms of worship. The mobilisation was far from universal – southern and eastern India were

MILITANT COMBINATION	STRATEGIES	MODERATE COMBINATION
	1. Identity-building	
Stigmatisation and emulation of 'threatening others'		Hindu traditionalism (defence of cultural symbols)
Hindu feeling of vulnerability		
	2. Implantation	
Sangathanism (including welfare tactics)	*'Cluster technique'* *'Ideologisation of princes'*	Co-option of politicians, notables and princes
		Attitude of the Sangathanist network and the RSS
	3. Mobilisation of support	
Ethno-religious mobilisation	*Mixed strategy*	Electoral alliances; propaganda on patriotic and socio-economic themes
Political context, religious network		**Attitude of the Sangathanist network and the RSS**

little affected – and those who mobilised appeared to have differing motives. While devotion to Ram was an important motivation for certain groups, especially in villages and among women, for many young Hindus the Ramjanmabhoomi movement primarily offered an opportunity to improve their self-esteem and assert themselves, *inter alia*, through anti-Muslim activities and even rioting. Sociological factors also played a part: in 1991 the BJP kept up its momentum by combining ethno-religious mobilisation with appeals to sectional interests. Indeed the party received support from many members of the upper castes who felt threatened by the implementation of the Mandal Commission report.

Another limitation of ethno-religious mobilisation is its reliance on emotions which often cover a number of different and even contradictory motives. The reliance of the RSS and its affiliates on *sadhus* and activists of the Bajrang Dal type is a case in point. The BJP needed the latter to agitate in the street and the former to endow the Ayodhya movement with religious legitimacy, but both groups proved uncontrollable. Their impact on the Ramjanmabhoomi movement was bound to alienate Hindus who had been attracted by the devotional forms of the movement and the middle classes who supported the BJP on account of its opposition to the reservation policy and because the party stood for a strong, united India in which order prevailed.

In Chapter 14, the model is further elaborated with the emergence of an additional variable, the exercise of power. In Madhya Pradesh, Himachal Pradesh and Uttar Pradesh the BJP's record in government was unimpressive; it had projected itself while in opposition as a party of probity but once in power found this reputation hard to live up to. While the poor performance of the BJP governments in 1990-2 partly accounts for its electoral setback, this reverse can also be explained in the framework of our model since the Sangathanist strategy of party-building was affected by the accession to power, as the development of dissension within the Madhya Pradesh BJP shows.

The Hindu nationalist leaders realised that two important strategies of the 'militant' combination –Sangathanism and ethno-religious mobilisation – were facing severe constraints. The BJP responded by appearing less militant and dissociating itself from the VHP, which had been weakened by the ban and the ebbing of emotions after the demolition of the mosque, which it had previously portrayed as a symbol of 'Hindu humiliation'. Lastly, the BJP's decline in the Hindi belt was largely due to its inability to attract many voters from the OBCs or counter the parties promoting the interests of those castes.

The strategy based on the stigmatisation and emulation of the Other made little impact on the backward castes and Scheduled Castes, mainly because it relied on a high-caste view of society, a reinterpreted High Tradition which ignored the concerns of the disadvantaged. The RSS and its affiliates expanded their base in the late 1980s and early 1990s because they appealed to religious feelings that transcended caste but especially because they were increasingly supported by the upper castes. However, this arrangement did not enable it to remain in power in a state like Uttar Pradesh, as the rise of the SP and BSP testifies.

In the short run, one might wonder whether the BJP is likely to become the alternative to the Congress (I), which it claims to be. Despite some progress in the south and in the east in the 1990s, the BJP is still less 'a national party' than the Congress (I); similarly, the Hindu nationalist party is still under-represented in large sections of society: not only in the religious minorities, the Scheduled Castes and Scheduled Tribes but also, to a lesser extent, the Other Backward Classes – at least in the Hindi belt. Yet, the decline of the Congress (I), in terms of popularity as well as organisation, might well enable the BJP to make progress in future general elections. In a way, this achievement would be 'by default'.

However, focussing only on the near future may cloud our judgement somewhat because trends other than overtly political ones may prove in the long term to be of greater importance. Even though the RSS has become more involved in power politics since the 1970s, it has constantly pursued the goal of penetrating Indian society with the aim of converting it to its ideology. The network of *shakhas* continues to be the cornerstone of this policy. Not only did the number of *shakhas* triple between 1977 and 1994, from 10,000 to 30,288,[1] but one must also take into account

1   This is the number of localities where the RSS functions. However, many cities comprise

those who have been exposed to the RSS's message in their youth and later left the organisation. More important, perhaps, the *shakha* network has been supplemented by others.

The RSS has had to adjust to changes in Indian society whereby the prestige of asceticism and discipline has declined. RSS leaders admit the increasing difficulty of persuading young men to embrace the career of *pracharak*'s (and the lifetime of personal sacrifice this involves) or even to gather together *swayamsevaks* for *shakhas* because of the alternative attractions of television or evening classes.[2] The Bajrang Dal reflects this trend since it has a loose structure in which personal discipline is not so highly valued. The RSS has adjusted to social change in India by developing its tactic of social welfare, by improving its position in the media and by expanding its network of schools.

The tactic of social welfare is a feature of the Sangthanist method of implantation and has been developed by most affiliates of the RSS – e.g. the BMS and the BJP. However the main agency for social work in the RSS combination is Seva Bharti (Service of India), which was founded in 1979. This organisation provides free medical assistance (in Delhi it runs an ambulance service in slum areas) and very low-cost education for the poor. In Delhi 129 Bal and Balika Kendras (educational centres) provide an elementary education for 19,304 children.[3] The social welfare tactic of the RSS obviously benefited from the weakness of the public sector in fields such as health and education, a situation exacerbated in the early 1990s as pressure to reduce India's budget deficit led to a squeeze on public expenditure. Moreover, the central government relies increasingly on voluntary associations to implement social welfare; in 1991 it awarded a 'certificate of merit' and Rs 50,000 to Seva Bharti, which the Delhi Development Authority also provided with office space.[4]

While Hedgewar intended the RSS to work silently if not secretly to spread its influence, the organisation has of late increasingly turned to the media.[5] Newspapers and a newsagency were launched from the 1940s onwards in many regional languages and in a large number of towns; in 1983, twenty-eight local or national papers produced by Hindu nationalist presses were catalogued by the Deendayal Research Institute.[6] More

several branches (called *upshakhas*, sub-branches), which numbered 42,682 in March 1994 (*Times of India*, 20 March 1994).

2   Interviews in Delhi in October 1991 and in Madhya Pradesh in August 1992 (notably with a *pracharak* from Indore).

3   *Introduction–Seva Bharti,* roneoed document, p. 2 and interview with Vishwamitra Pushkarma, Vice-President of Seva Bharti, 12 Aug. 1992, Delhi.

4   Y. Ghinurie, 'Altruistic expansion', *India Today*, 31 July, 1992, p. 27 and C. Jaffrelot, 'Oeuvres pies et rationalité économique en Inde' in J.F. Bayart (ed.), *La réinvention du capitalisme*, Paris: Karthala, 1994, pp. 145-74.

5   See W. Andersen and S. Damle, *The brotherhood in saffron*, op. cit., pp. 115-16.

6   *Panchjanya, Rashtradharma, Deshbhakt, Himalay* and *Swadesh Dainik* were published

recently Hindu nationalists have made extensive use of audiovisual technology. They began exploiting the potential of video, and Jain Studios later launched a satellite channel broadcasting 'religious, moral and spiritual programmes'.[7] These media disseminate Hindu nationalist propaganda discreetly and effectively.

The expansion of the RSS educational sector was also a shrewd move given the growing demand for education and the reluctance of some citizens to rely on the ill-managed and underfunded public system. Vidya Bharti ('Indian knowledge'), the RSS affiliate and umbrella body which runs the Saraswati Shishu Mandirs, was responsible for managing 700 such schools in 1977, the year of its foundation.[8] By the early 1990s the organisation had 5,000 schools (1,325 of which were in Uttar Pradesh and about 1,000 in Madhya Pradesh) with 1.2 million pupils enrolled and 40,000 teachers employed.[9] Shishu Mandirs are increasingly running classes aimed at the poor.[10]

While the BJP does not appear to be in a position to capture power at the Centre, the ideas spread by the *shakhas*, by RSS-affiliated unions such as the BMS and the ABVP, and by Seva Bharti, Vidya Bharti and the Hindu nationalist media constantly strengthen the influence of the RSS

---

in Lucknow, *Uthan* at Kanpur, *Chetna* at Varanasi, *Janata* at Meerut, *Pracharak* at Bulanshahar, *Akhand Bharat* at Dehra Dun, *Sangathan*, *Organiser* and *Bharat Varsh* at Delhi, *Pravartak* at Patna, *Swastika* at Calcutta, *Shankhnad* at Gauhati, *Sudershan* at Gwalior, *Ushakal* at Jabalpur, *Rashtra Bhakti* and *Yugadharma* at Nagpur, *Sudershan* at Akola, *Bharat* and *Ekta* at Poona, *Vivek* at Bombay, *Kranti* at Jaipur and *Naneri* at Madras (*Organiser* 24 July 1983, p. 10). This list is incomplete since many states are not mentioned. Among well-known titles not listed are *Tarun Bharat* (Nagpur), *Manthan* (Delhi), *Swadesh* (Bhopal, Indore and Gwalior) and *Move on* (Bhopal).

7 *Times of India*, 6 Sept. 1993. Interestingly, the four hours of religious programmes were followed by 'programmes on sex education'. 'Just as the spiritual programmes are for the elderly, the films are for our adult viewers', commented J.K. Jain (ibid., 13 Nov. 1994).

8 *Organiser*, 19 Nov. 1978, p. 1. The network of Shishu Mandirs was especially dense in Uttar Pradesh where the scheme was first implemented. In 1972 there were 5,000 pupils enrolled in the Shishu Mandirs of this state (ibid., 25 March 1972, p. 15).

9 N. Khanna, 'Education: the RSS way', *Sunday*, 1 Dec. 1991, pp. 22-3. See also T. Sarkar, 'Educating the children of the Hindu Rashtra: note on the RSS schools', *South Asia Bulletin*, 14 (2), 1994, pp. 10-15.

10 In our test-village of Piparsod in Madhya Pradesh, such a school was set up in 1991. The registration fees – 300 rupees per child per year – enabled low-caste children to enrol. The teachers are volunteers deputed by the RSS who are prepared to work for low salaries. They impart a Hindu nationalist-oriented education with Sanskritised overtones (classes open with a prayer in Sanskrit). In 1992 the teachers were able to use the school premises to hold daily *shakhas* which had been the aim of the district *pracharak* since the building's inception (interviews with Vivek Joshi, *pracharak* of Shivpuri district, 27 October 1991, Piparsod, and with M. L. Pandey, one of the teachers,17 Aug. 1992, Piparsod). The success of the school, which attracted about 50 pupils, was due largely to the anxiety of poor families to have their children educated in a village which, despite its 2,500 inhabitants, had no school.

combination. This trend, if sustained, will help the latter to crystallise a Hindu nationalist identity which in the long term could challenge the durability of India's multicultural society.

EPILOGUE

From mid-1993 onwards, the BJP seemed fully aware that the Hindutva tide, which flowed so strongly in 1990-1, was receding and that the electorate's preoccupations were increasingly social and economic. The opposition which the BJP faces in the Hindi heartland is becoming more diverse, more oriented to the concerns of the backward and the lower castes, and much less predictable than was the case in the 1980s. Its last opportunity to build up its strength outside North India before the general election due in 1996 was provided by a sequence of state elections which occurred in late 1994 and early 1995, notably in Andhra Pradesh, Karnataka, Gujarat, Maharashtra, Orissa and Bihar. In this epilogue we shall consider how it adjusted its strategies to deal with this opportunity and position itself for the impending national elections.

After the 1993 state elections the BJP continued to rely less on a strategy of ethno-religious mobilisation and more on a pragmatic response – combining a new interest in the OBC vote and strong elements of populism – to the electoral situation, as if it had decided that Hindu nationalist ideology alone would no longer ensure its further expansion. The shift in approach had been initiated after 6 December 1992 as the party had sought to switch attention away from the aim of building a temple dedicated to Ram and towards general ethno-nationalist issues associated with hostility towards Muslims and Bangladeshi immigrants or alleged threats to the nation's integrity. After 1993 the BJP gave more prominence to social and economic issues, such as those affecting the conditions of the OBCs, and did so in a populist style reminiscent of that which the Jana Sangh had assumed in the early 1970s and the BJP in the early 1980s.

This particular pattern provides a further example of the oscillation between extreme and moderate strategies which has always characterised the political and social activities of Hindu nationalist organisations. Just as the Jana Sangh shifted the emphasis in the late 1960s from an ethno-religious mobilisation associated with the cow protection movement to the socio-economic populism which it employed against Mrs Gandhi's Congress (R), so in the mid-1990s the BJP adjusted to the changing context by professing its interest in the concrete social and economic demands of particular sections of the electorate. However, this trend may meet with the disapproval of the RSS and the VHP, which have held to the unqualified doctrines of Hindu nationalism and may attack the new realism of the BJP, as they did in the early 1980s.

Can the Hindu nationalists cater for the socio-economic interests of the OBCs?

The 1993 election results prompted the BJP's leaders to promote a larger number of OBCs in the party apparatus. In Uttar Pradesh six of the fifteen senior positions in the BJP state executive went to members of the OBCs, the other places going to two Brahmins, one Kayasth, one Jat, and one member of the Schedules Castes.[1] In Madhya Pradesh, the BJP parliamentary group chose as its leader Vikram Verma, a Jat, rather than the outgoing Chief Minister, Sunderlal Patwa, and Verma thus became Leader of the Opposition in the Legislative Assembly; it also appointed Babulal Gaur, an Ahir, as its Chief Whip and nominated Bherulal Patidar, a Kurmi, as its candidate for the post of Deputy Speaker of the assembly (he was duly elected to the post). At the national level, Uma Bharti (a Lodhi) was asked to head the Bharatiya Janata Yuva Morcha, the party's youth organisation. Before her appointment, she had argued:

We should change the image of the party as a party of those who sit and smoke in air-conditioned rooms. This may hurt some but we should go ahead with it. We have to go to the grassroots, to the Dalits. The party has become complacent after the Ram Janmabhoomi movement. Kanshi Ram has woken us up.[2]

The main advocate of the incorporation of more low caste members at all levels of the party apparatus was K.N. Govindacharya, one of the BJP's general secretaries; he called the policy 'social engineering'. However the strategy was opposed by some of his colleagues and by RSS leaders who objected in principle to any artificial transformation of the social order – generally seen as potentially harmonious – and did not wish to use caste criteria for appointments in response to the pressures exerted by the Mandal Commission. Sunder Singh Bhandari, one of the BJP's vice-presidents, declared: 'We will keep social equilibrium in mind. It is an expansion programme and there is no question of being lopsided.'[3] More importantly, the General Secretary of the RSS, H.V. Seshadri, reacted to the SP-BSP propaganda in terms which showed that the organisation was not prepared to allow the BJP to appeal to notions of caste identity as a means of gathering support:

[1] *Times of India*, 4 July 1994.
[2] Cited in ibid., 26 Dec. 1993.
[3] Ibid.

Social justice can be rendered to the weaker sections of society only when the entire society is imbued with the spirit of oneness and internal harmony. Society is like a living body and its weak limbs get strengthened by the entire body coming to its aid in every possible manner. And this becomes possible when the life-force of the body remains active and powerful. The fire-force in the case of society is its vibrant awareness of its abiding oneness. That alone will result in a spirit of harmony among all its sections and ensuring the equality, dignity, security and justice, especially to its weaker parts. And this precisely is the path the Sangh has been pursuing through its shakha technique of social reorganisation for the past 68 years.[4]

Such a discourse did indeed echo the organicist conceptions expounded by Golwalkar. If the Hindu nationalist movement complies with them and ignores caste, it is bound to remain an upper caste movement. It will alienate low caste members whose ideas of social advancement are more egalitarian and who do not set great store by the Sanskritisation which might have been favoured by an earlier generation.

There is an obvious tension between the strong reservation expressed by RSS leaders towards quotas for the OBCs and the more pragmatic attitude of the BJP. For example the party displayed a shrewd ambivalence during the 'Uttarakhand affair' of summer 1994. This hill area of northwest Uttar Pradesh, comprising eight districts of the regions of Garhwal (Tehri, Puari, Uttarkashi, Chamoli, Dehra Dun) and Kumaon (Nainital, Almora and Pithorgarh), was the setting for an agitation against the 27% reservation scheme implemented by Mulayam Singh Yadav's government, the demonstrators arguing that OBCs constituted only 2% of the local population whereas the upper castes represented 60%. The protestors opposed the reservation of 27% of administrative posts for OBCs, which they argued would favour people living in lowland UP and revive the latent movement for a separate state of Uttarakhand. The BJP, whose government had made a similar demand to the Centre in 1991 while it was in power in Uttar Pradesh, launched an Uttaranchal Pradesh Sangharah Samiti headed by its MP for Pauri Garhwal, B.C. Khanduri, and joined

---

[4]   *Organiser*, 19 Dec. 1993, p. 17. RSS leaders strongly criticised the programme of the SP and the BSP, From their point of view, the interests of the low castes were not distinct from those of the nation as a whole. Seshadri expounded their position in revealing terms:

'...in any confrontation with the rest of the society, the weaker sections always stand to lose. It is only with the goodwill and cooperation of the entire society that they can get the necessary opportunities to raise themselves up. The very concept of social justice implies recognition of equality, dignity and opportunity in every sphere of national life by the entire society. And this is possible only when the society becomes imbued with the spirit of oneness and harmony among all sections just as a weak limb can get strengthened only when the entire bodily life-force is quite active and ensures that the entire body goes out to continuously nurture that limb. This is exactly how the Hindutva life-force works in case of our society' (*Organiser*, 5 Dec. 1993, p. 7).

the protest,[5] which met harsh counter-measures by the authorities. Interestingly, while the protest had an anti-lower caste overtone[6] the party tried to lend it an exclusively regional meaning and refused to pronounce against reservations. Kalyan Singh declared: 'The main issue is that of a separate state, not reservations.'[7] Subsequently, the 1994-5 state elections revealed that the BJP was anxious to nominate an OBC candidate wherever the arithmetic of the constituency made this choice relevant. If the selection of OBCs as candidates remains haphazard and does not lead to a systematic policy of recruiting them in due proportion into the higher echelons of the party, at the national as well as the state levels, the BJP may continue to be handicapped by the upper-caste image which has restricted its expansion in the past. In Madhya Pradesh, out of 117 members in 1994, the State BJP Executive Committee was composed of 74 persons from upper and intermediate castes (as against 68 out of 100 in the Committee designated in 1991), only 22 OBCs (as against 13), 9 Scheduled Tribes members (as against 8), 7 Scheduled Castes members (as against 6) and 5 persons from religious minorities (unchanged in comparison to 1991).[8] In addition, the high-ranking posts were often monopolised by upper-caste party men.

The BJP emphasises socio-economic rather than ethno-religious issues

The first meeting of the BJP's National Executive to be held after the 1993 elections, in March 1994, brought the party's strategic re-orientation to its logical conclusion. In his opening remarks, L.K. Advani reaffirmed his faith in Hindu nationalism:

Hindutva is not a slogan for us. It is the Bharatiya Janata party's ideological mascot, the most distinctive feature of its identity and approach. It has been the hall mark of the party well before Ayodhya and will continue to be so even after a magnificent Rama Temple at the birth place of Rama in Ayodhya becomes a fact of life.[9]

However, having paid lip service to this cause, Advani then invited the National Executive to deal mainly with economic issues: indeed, the first

---

5   Interview with B.C. Khanduri, 22 Feb. 1995. New Delhi, and *Organiser*, 18 Dec. 1994. p. 17.
6   B. Dogra, 'Uttarakhand: pawns in a chess game', EPW, 10 Dec. 1994. p. 3130.
7   Interview in *Organiser*, 6 Nov. 1994, p. 13.
8   *Madhya Pradesh karyasamiti sadasyon ke nam eren pare, varsh 1994-1995* (Hindi, duplicated).
9   BJP, *Resolutions adopted at the National Executive Meeting at Hyderabad and Opening Remarks of Shri L.K. Advani, National President*, 20, 21 and 22 March, 1994, Hyderabad. p. 2.

resolution passed by this body was devoted to the budget, which had just been passed. The government's economic policy was arraigned because it hit the 'common man' – a phrase reminiscent of the Jana Sangh in the 1970s and repeated in each of the first four paragraphs of the resolution – not only in terms of inflation but also of jobs: the opening of India to foreign firms would expose small-scale industries to unfair competition and precipitate a rise in unemployment:

It is they [the foreigners] who stand to benefit the most from the budget, not the common man, neither the farmer nor the factory workers, who will now have to fight with their back to the wall to protect their livelihood from government-sponsored foreign invasion and continuing stagnation of agriculture.[10]

The National Executive recommended the abolition of 'preferential treatment to multinationals *vis-à-vis* domestic industries, investment etc.', 'complete ban on the entry of multinationals into consumer goods sector', 'strict enforcement of reservation policies of small-scale and cottage industries' and lambasted the reduction of customs duties on foreign capital goods and machinery – suggesting that if it were to take power it would restore some of the protectionist measures which the Centre had abolished in the name of liberalisation.[11] As early as December 1993, the BJP National Executive passed a resolution against the GATT treaty that Narasimha Rao had just approved;[12] even Jaswant Singh, who used to be a staunch advocate of the opening of Indian economy, argued in the Rajya Sabha that 'internal liberalisation must precede external liberalisation and the sequencing of the measures that you do or the fine tuning of these measures must take care of the internal or indigenous industry before you permit the global competition in a full-fledged form to be present in the country.'[13]

The BJP's opposition to 'globalisation' was strongly reaffirmed by the

---

10 Ibid., p. 6.
11 Ibid., pp. 7-8.
12 The National Executive then resorted to anti-imperialist rhetoric: 'We had demanded fair trade, not free trade, but what we have got instead are unfairest of trading arrangements in which the rich countries have used their economic and political muscle to ride roughshod over the interests of poor countries and which will keep the Indian consumer as well as the Indian producer perpetually at the receiving end of powerful multinational corporations. The third world is once again under the threat of a new type of colonial aggression.'(National Executive Committee Resolution on the GATT Treaty', BJP, *The GATT treaty – a total surrender*, New Delhi: BJP, n.d., p. 9).
13 Jaswant Singh, 'The GATT Treaty: Compromise of National Interests', ibid., p. 24. See also the speech delivered in the Rajya Sabha on 6 Dec. 1993 by M.M. Joshi, reproduced as *Dunkel Draft – a surrender of Economic Sovereignty*, New Delhi: BJP, 1994, p. 12. On these questions, see S. Lakha,'The Bharatiya Janata Party and globalisation of the Indian economy', *South Asia*, 17 (1994), pp. 213-29.

National Executive at its June 1994 meeting.[14] On this occasion too
Advani attempted to combine two levels of discourse: he stressed the
importance of 'Hindutva' as 'the cementing force that keeps the nation
together'[15] while the main part of his speech was devoted to developing
the economic thesis that India should reject globalisation:

> What India needs is the reverse, the activation of the foundation of India by mainly
> Indian solutions as supplemented by ideas that might improve the Indian solutions.
> Here the Indian is the core and the Western is the additive; the modern supplements
> the traditional. [...].The primary emphasis today is on urban-industry and attention
> to agriculture is secondary. This approach will have to yield to rural-agricultural
> and agro-industries combination becoming the primary area of emphasis.[16]

Thus in 1994 the BJP continued to invoke the spirit of ethno-
nationalism while placing more and more emphasis on socio-economic
issues. The latter approach complied with traditional themes of Hindu
nationalism such as the promotion of cottage industries and agriculture in
a 'Gandhian' perspective. But this preoccupation with the ideas of
economic nationalism has occurred only recently – even in the early
1990s they did not figure prominently in the party's literature. How can
this change in attitude be explained? First, the adoption of the *Swadeshi*
theme has enabled the BJP to return once more to the kind of economic
nationalism favoured by the RSS; secondly, opposition to trade liberalisation has enabled the BJP to align itself with social groups which have
become increasingly critical of the government's economic policies. This
trend became more pronounced during the 'Bharat Parikrama' which L.K.
Advani launched in July 1994 from Varanasi and entailed a tour by twenty
senior BJP leaders of the nation's 450 districts by mid-September. While
the Ayodhya issue figured prominently in Advani's early campaign
speeches, it quickly receded into the background.[17] On 17 July the BJP
President even stated that if Narasimha Rao declared 'that the Ram
Mandir would be constructed at the place where the deity of Ram Lala
was placed at present, then he would use his good offices to make the
"Sangh parivar" agree that they should not object to its construction either
by Shankaracharyas or by any other agency.'[18] This announcement was

---

14 The resolution on the economic situation stipulated: 'The BJP is not against the entry
    of foreign capital and technology in hi-tech areas. Even here, however, it should not be
    to the exclusion of Indian companies' and it recommended 'a *Swadeshi* model based on
    Gandhiji's Ram Rajya and Deen Dayalji's Integral Humanism' (BJP, *Resolutions
    adopted by the National Council at Vadodra*, 10, 11 and 12 June 1994, pp. 18 and 23).
15 *Presidential address by Shri L.K. Advani, BJP National Council session, 10-12 June
    1994, Varodra, Gujarat* (New Delhi: BJP, n.d., p. 22).
16 Ibid., p. 14.
17 *Times of India*, 16, 18 and 19 July 1994.
18 Ibid. 17 July 1994, p. 1.

not well received by the leaders of the VHP, who considered that they had a natural right to build the Ram temple.[19]

Advani distanced himself further from the VHP by asserting that the dismantling of the Gyanvapi Mosque, allegedly built on the site of a Shiva Mandir in Varanasi (see below), was 'not on the BJP's agenda.'[20] In August 1994, BJP leaders stayed away from the national conclave of the ex-VHP, designated as the Hindu Sangam, held in Ahmedabad.[21] In September the BJP concluded its Bharat Parikrama by releasing in Patna, in the context of a pre-election meeting of its National Executive, 'A charge sheet against the Congress government' in which its demands were listed in order of significance: the first was 'Your money is not safe' (regarding inflation and corruption); the second 'Your life is not safe' (regarding a growing sense of insecurity and threat of terrorism); and the third 'Nation's sovereignty is not safe' (the Kashmir and Ayodhya issues appeared at this stage).[22] This programme was on a par with the priorities which had been established by the RSS during its ABPS meeting in July, '*Swadeshi* and *suraksha* [security]'.[23] The BJP's increasing reliance on socio-economic and populist issues was reaffirmed in the election campaigns that took place in several important states from November 1994 to March 1995.

Populism and the 1994-5 state elections

In Karnataka in late 1994 the BJP state unit published a 41-page election manifesto that was highly revealing of the party's efforts to project a populist and pragmatic image.[24] Its four chapter headings were 'Priority to agriculture, irrigation and electricity', 'Special schemes for employment opportunities to youth', 'Establishment of social justice and amity' and 'Integrated schemes for Scheduled groups and women welfare.'[25] The remainder of the document contained a detailed list of promises to almost very section of society. The only non-socio-economic issues highlighted were 'Security for the day to day life of the people', corruption, prohibi-

---

[19] Ibid., 16 July 1994.

[20] Ibid., 19 July 1994.

[21] Ibid., 7 Aug. 1995.

[22] BJP, *A charge sheet against the Congress government led by Shri P.V. Narasimha Rao*, BJP, 1994, n.p.

[23] *Times of India*, 13 July 1994.

[24] I am most grateful to James Manor for providing me with this document.

[25] V.S. Acharya (convenor, election manifesto committee), *We have a right for stable, clean and people's government – BJP determined to make it: Assembly elections 1994, to the great people of Karnataka, BJP's assurance*, Bangalore: BJP unit of Karnataka, 1994, p. 1.

tion of cow-slaughter, 'National integrity' – but Kannada was to be given 'priority in all spheres', including administration, a far cry from the slogan of 'one country, one language' which the Hindu nationalists had once used in their campaign for Hindi. During the campaign the BJP raised other regional issues, namely that Karnataka's 300,000 fishermen were adversely affected by the policy of allowing big trawlers, from India and abroad, to fish in deep waters.[26]

It should be noted, however, that neither the Jana Sangh nor the BJP has ever focussed exclusively on socio-economic issues during election campaigns. Even when party leaders make a conscious attempt to play down the party's attachment to Hindu nationalism, they retain some freedom to exploit local grievances in which relations between Hindus and Muslims are an issue. The Karnataka campaign of 1994 was no exception. In Hubli, the BJP relaunched an old controversy in order to polarise the electorate along communal lines. Here the BJP had already canvassed for the national flag to be hoisted in the Idgah Maidan, which was controlled by the Anjuman-e-Islami.[27] On 26 January 1992, while M.M. Joshi unfurled the national flag in Srinagar, the Karnataka unit of the BJP managed to do the same in Hubli. A similar attempt was launched on 15 August 1992 but aborted; and on 15 August 1994, at the beginning of the election campaign, another attempt was made: some activists again succeeded in hoisting the flag inside the Idgah Maidan but the police killed six people in firing officially aimed at avoiding a communal provocation. Some commentators argued that the Congress government had reacted so forcefully in order to prove to the Muslims before the elections that it was protecting them.[28] The BJP exploited the incident, depicting those who had been killed as martyrs, much as it had done after the 1990 *Kar Seva.*[29] The ensuing polarisation of the local electorate along communal lines paid dividends: in November, the BJP won all 3 seats in the Hubli-Dharwad Corporation area.[30]

---

[26] Interview with J. Shettigar, 22 Feb. 1995. L.K. Advani also used this argument (*Times of India*, 18 Feb. 1994).

[27] On this issue see A. Pinto, 'Hoisting national flag at Idgah Maidan', *EPW*, 4 Feb. 1995, pp. 246-7, and J. Assayag, 'Violence de l'histoire, histoires de violence – frontières, 'communalisme' et mémoire en Inde du sud (Karnataka)', *Annales*, no. 6, 1994, p. 1298.

[28] Engineer, A.A., 'Communalism and communal violence in 1994', *EPW*, 4 Feb. 1994, p. 250. This hypothesis can be substantiated in view of the subsequent 'Urdu bulletin affair': in early October, the Bangalore branch of the state-controlled television channel launched a news bulletin in Urdu which was probably intended to win the support of the Muslim community before the elections. This decision provoked a communal riot in which about 30 people died.

[29] This attempt is especially evident from the copiously illustrated publication entitled, *Hubli, paradox and challenges* (Mangalore: Jnanabharathi Prakashana, 1994, 31 pp.). I am also grateful to James Manor for providing me with this booklet.

However in Karnataka as a whole, the BJP's share of valid votes dropped from 28.8% in 1991 (when it was leading in 59 Assembly segments) to 16.97%, as against 27.34% to the Congress (I) and 33.49% to the Janata Dal – which won 115 seats. As James Manor explains, the BJP won more seats than the Congress (I) – 40 as against 36 – because its votes were concentrated in particular areas, notably in Dakshina, Kannada and Shimoga districts.[31] In Andhra Pradesh, the other southern state which went to the polls in November 1994, the BJP suffered a more serious setback: it won only 2 seats as against 5 in 1989. The perennial obstacles in the way of the BJP's penetration of South India – which seriously hinders its chances of gaining power at the Centre – is reminiscent of certain factors already observed in Uttar Pradesh and Madhya Pradesh in 1993, such as the party's inability to significantly broaden its social basis and maintain internal discipline.

In Karnataka an opinion poll commissioned by *India Today* from MARG revealed that the BJP was especially popular among the small Brahmin community, 39% of whom favoured the party.[32] It also attracted the support of the Lingayats, the community of its leader, B.S. Yediyurappa, from which the party recruited 86 of its 224 candidates (as against 43 in the Congress (I)'s ranks).[33] Yet in many districts where the Lingayats were the dominant force the BJP did not do well.[34]

The modest performance of the BJP in Karnataka can also be attributed to its difficulty in containing dissension. As in Madhya Pradesh, the party was weakened by groupism resulting from the 'reactions for and against the leadership which packs the organisation with its loyalists'.[35] This phenomenon was manifested, according to Manor, during the ticket distribution process. This alienated many activists whose meritorious leaders were denied nominations. As a result, party discipline was further eroded by the lack of responsiveness of the state leadership to the network of activists, which had formerly been one of the BJP's assets.

In fact, the BJP came second in the only southern state where it had made some inroads, Karnataka, because it benefited from a negative vote: the opinion poll commissioned by *Frontline* from CMS showed that the electorate's main concerns were infighting in the ruling party, corruption and price rises. Interestingly, communalism was not mentioned as a

---

[30] The local correspondent of *Organiser* commented that 'Hubli constituency was a good example of the community-wise division of votes' (*Organiser*, 1 Jan. 1995, p. 13).

[31] J. Manor, 'Still a marginal force: the Bharatiya Janata Party in Karnataka, 1991 and 1994', in P. Oldenburg (ed.) (forthcoming).

[32] *India Today*, 15 Dec. 1995, p. 25.

[33] Ibid., 30 Nov. 1995, p. 26 and interview with J. Shettigar, 22 Feb. 1995, New Delhi.

[34] J. Manor, 'Still a marginal force', op.cit.

[35] Ibid.

preponderant factor, 28.5% of interviewees being unaware of even the Hubli incident, for instance.[36]

The contrast between the emphasis on socio-economic issues in the BJP's election manifesto in Karnataka and the persistence of an ethno-religious strategy – as reflected in the Hubli affair – probably reflects the division of labour between leaders charged with projecting a respectable image for Hindu nationalism and local activists whose ends justify all kinds of means. It is interesting to note that the use of demonstrations and violence to polarise the electorate along communal lines remained marginal in 1994-5; in keeping with the trend initiated in mid-1993, there were very few communal riots in 1994, even in the states going to the polls. There was only one incident in Maharashtra in 1994-5 before the state elections, two in Gujarat, one in Andhra Pradesh and three in Karnataka, the latter being by far the most seriously affected, where 38 lives were lost.[37] The BJP was obviously trying to attract additional voters by relying on themes and methods unrelated to Hindu nationalism, as the 1995 state elections testified.

In Gujarat the reimposition of the ban on the VHP by the central government proved particularly unpopular.[38] More importantly, it convinced *sadhus* to 'run a parallel campaign' in Maharashtra and, especially, Gujarat in February 1995.[39] Here, Sadhvi Rithambara and other *sadhus* attracted large crowds to meetings protesting against the ban and the 'anti-Hindu' attitude of the Congress (I) as a whole.[40] This movement certainly helped the BJP but it was the only element reminiscent of the election campaigns of the late 1980s and early 1990s. In fact, opinion polls conducted before the 1995 elections in Gujarat and Maharashtra revealed that the BJP was benefiting mainly from the failure of the Congress (I) to deal with corruption, prevent price increases and curb factionalism.[41] The BJP was systematically viewed in Gujarat as 'the best party for honest administration', 'best party to contain price rise' and 'best party for communal harmony'.[42] Among those interviewed 40% even chose the

---

[36] *Frontline*, 2 Dec. 1995, p. 11.

[37] A.A. Engineer, 'Communalism and communal violence', op.cit., pp. 249-50.

[38] Hence the decision of the RSS to exploit the situation by launching an agitation on this apparently un-planned theme.

[39] This decision was made at the Allahabad Virat Sant Sammelan (*Organiser*, 12 Feb. 1995, p. 7).

[40] *Times of India*, 3 Feb. 1995 and *India Today*, 28 Feb. 1995, p. 92. A. Ganguli stresses that the ex- VHP 'warned against the possible islamisation of the country...' (A. Ganguli, 'Echoes of Godse – VHP's "election" campaign', *Times of India*, 13 Feb. 1995, p. 12).

[41] A.B. Vajpayee admitted that there had not been any pro-BJP wave in Gujarat (Ibid, 14 March 1995).

[42] For details, see *India Today*, 28 Feb. 1995, pp. 86-7 and 15 March 1995, pp. 50-6 and

BJP for 'improving law and order'. In both states Hindu nationalists toned down their ideology in order to emphasise their sense of discipline, 'clean image' and populist promises: in Gujarat, the BJP announced that wheat would sell for Rs 2 per kg. if the party came to power.[43] In Maharashtra, the Shiv Sena and the BJP, which had forged an alliance, promised to freeze the prices of five basic commodities.[44]

In Gujarat, the BJP won 121 seats out of 182, as against 45 secured by Congress (I); in 1990 the BJP, then allied to the Janata Dal, won only 67 seats. In Maharashtra, the BJP won 65 seats and the Shiv Sena 73 (which gave a total of 138 seats for the alliance as against 94 in 1990). The Congress (I) was reduced to 80 seats, compared to the 141 it had held in 1990. The legislative group of the BJP-Shiv Sena combine was 7 seats below an absolute majority (145) but the alliance was able to obtain the support of enough independent MLAs to form a government. In Orissa, where elections were held at about the same time, the BJP did not make a breakthrough: it won only 9 seats. In Bihar, the BJP won 41 seats compared to the Janata Dal's 260, which represented a tiny advance on 1990 (39 seats), when it had benefited from its alliance with the Janata Dal. Nevertheless, the decline of the Congress (I) enabled the BJP to become the second largest party in the state (in terms of seats rather than valid votes), as in Karnataka.

The BJP's stagnation in Bihar reflected the social profile of its electorate. It remained relatively unattractive to OBCs – especially to the Yadavs who form such an influential group in Bihar – and the Scheduled Castes.[45] According to a survey conducted by the Bihar Study Group at CSDS, only 13.7% of the 'backward castes' voted for the BJP (as against the identical figure for Congress and 49.8% for the Janata Dal).[46] Among the 40 MLAs from the BJP, 21 were OBCs, 5 from the Scheduled Castes, 4 from the Scheduled Tribes and only 10 from the upper castes, but the low caste candidates might well have been elected by a majority of upper caste voters.[47] In Maharashtra and Gujarat, respectively 64 and 59% of

---

Frontline, 10 Feb. 1995, p. 28, 24 Feb. 1995, p. 11 and 10 March 1995, p. 9.

[43] The election manifesto of the Gujarat BJP contained no less than 101 promises, ranging from the waiving away of bank loans for tribals worth Rs 10,000 to the complete exemption of fertilizers, seeds and insecticides from sales tax (*Madhya Pradesh Chronicle*, 9 Feb. 1995).

[44] *India Today*, 31 Jan. 1995, p. 45.

[45] While, according to a MARG opinion poll 55.2% of the Yadavs and 20.7% of the other OBCs voted for the Janata Dal, the BJP attracted respectively 2.6 and 16.6% of these groups. The BJP nominated 118 candidates from the upper castes (as against 28 on the Janata Dal's list), and 121 from the OBCs, as against 147 (ibid., 15 March 1995, p. 61 and p. 83).

[46] *Frontline*, 2 June 1995, p. 101.

[47] Ibid., 30 Apr. 1995, p. 14.

Brahmins voted for the Hindu nationalists. The BJP and Shiv Sena meanwhile consolidated their position in a decisive sector of society, the intermediate castes, who were not classified as OBCs in the Mandal Commission Report or regarded as being among the 'twice born'. Like the Jats in Uttar Pradesh, the Patidars in Gujarat (62%) and the Marathas in Maharashtra (36%) opted in large numbers for the BJP and the BJP-Shiv Sena combination.[48] According to a poll published by *Frontline*, the proportion of OBCs among the BJP-Shiv Sena electorate amounted to 25.5% of the total as against 19.5% in the Congress (I). Thus, the appeal of the Hindu nationalist combine to non-élite groups is far from negligible. This is in sharp contrast to the Untouchables, who contributed only marginally to the BJP-Shiv Sena's vote.[49]

To sum up, the Hindu nationalist parties, whose rise had been halted in 1993, fared better in the 1995 state elections. While they did not improve their position in Karnataka, Andhra Pradesh, Orissa and Bihar, they made remarkable progress in India's two most economically developed states, Gujarat and Maharashtra. But this success was not based on an ethno-religious mobilisation, the BJP having given priority to socio-economic, security and corruption questions. This canvassing technique drew heavily upon the strategic reorientation initiated in 1993. To what factors should we attribute this change?

The state, the judiciary and the Hindu nationalists

On previous occasions the shift in the balance of Hindu nationalist appeals from ethno-religious to socio-economic issues coincided with periods in which the Centre reaffirmed its attachment to secularist norms. A similar coincidence was not so apparent in 1994 and 1995.

The attitude of the Union government towards Ayodhya remained ambivalent. The original two-year ban on the VHP expired on 9 December 1994 but a further ban for the same period was promulgated on 14 January 1995 on the grounds that the organisation was still engaged in communal activities.[50] Yet the government was evidently not prepared either to leave the Ayodhya dispute to wither away or restore the situation which had obtained before the destruction of the mosque; instead, in 1994 it estab-

---

[48] Ibid., 31 Jan. 1995, pp. 50-61. On Maharashtra see T. Hansen, 'The Maratha'isation of Hindutva: Shiv Sena and BJP in rural Maharashtra', paper given at the 13th European Conference of South Studies, 31 Aug.-4 Sept., Toulouse (France).

[49] *Frontline*, 21 Apr. 1995, p. 36.

[50] At the first major meeting organised by the VHP after the ban on its activities expired, the Virat Hindu Sangam, held in Lucknow on 25 December, the movement announced that it would launch a new campaign to construct temples at Ayodhya, Varanasi and Mathura (*Organiser*, 8 Jan. 1995, p. 13).

lished a Hindu trust with the goal of constructing a Ram temple at Ayodhya.[51] It was known as the Ramlaya Trust, but the four *Shankaracharyas* who led it found it hard (mainly because of resistance from the VHP) to recruit the 21 trustees which were required. Of the 9 trustees whose names had been registered up to January 1995, Vishvesh Tirth was the only well-known religious figure who deserted the VHP for the trust.[52] Moreover, the support extended by the Congress(I) to set up the Ramlaya Trust helped the Hindu nationalists keep the Ayodhya issue on the national agenda.

The judiciary, despite lapses, remained the most reliable agency in the defence of secularism. On 24 October 1994, the Supreme Court delivered its judgement on the Presidential reference (concerning the existence of a Hindu temple before the Babri Masjid) and the Acquisition of Certain Areas at Ayodhya Act, 1993. The majority decision said that 'the reference made under article 143(1) of the Constitution is superfluous and unnecessary and does not require to be answered.'[53] In a dissenting note the minority bench – two of the five judges – propounded a more fundamental reason for rejecting the Presidential reference: it considered that the wording favoured the Hindu community and was therefore opposed to secularism and unconstitutional. Second, the majority judgement upheld the sections of the Act dealing with the acquisition of the disputed 67 acres of land in Ayodhya, empowering the government to delegate a trust to manage the property and enabling Hindus to worship in the makeshift temple. This decision was based on the concept of 'comparative user', the Muslims being described as praying less often than Hindus in the disputed structure before its demolition. This argument was open to question because, as Rajeev Dhavan has pointed out, 'If the Muslims had not prayed there since 1949, it was because they were prohibited from doing so by interlocutory restraint orders'.[54] The minority judges, moreover, wanted to strike down the Act, considering that to 'condone the acquisition of a place of worship under these circumstances [was...]to efface the principles of secularism from the Constitution.'[55] But the majority struck down as 'unconstitutional' section 4(3) of the Act which abated any pending 'suit, appeal or other proceeding'. Thus the proceedings pending in the Allahabad High Court were revived and the question of whether Muslims had the right to worship in the disputed area will now

---

[51] V. Ramakrishnan, 'To build a temple – The trust vs the Nyas', *Frontline*, 9 Sept. 1994, pp. 20-7.

[52] *Organiser*, 4 Sept. 1994.

[53] *Times of India*, 25 Oct. 1994, p. 1.

[54] R. Dhavan, 'The Ayodhya judgement – Encoding secularism in the Law', *EPW*, 26 Nov. 1994, p. 3036.

[55] Cited in ibid.

be decided on the completion of these pending suits. The Supreme Court thus thwarted the Hindu Trust's plan to start building a temple in Ayodhya before the completion of the judicial process. In addition, the Court held that Kalyan Singh, by allowing a concrete platform to be built, was guilty of violating his assurance that no permanent structure would be erected on the disputed 2.77 acres on the Babri Masjid-Ramjanmabhoomi site. The former Chief Minister was sentenced to one day's imprisonment and fined Rs 2,000.[56]

The courts also upheld the principles of secularism in the regulation of election campaigns. In the early 1990s, High Court judges were presented with claims that the use of religious themes by candidates violated the relevant articles or rules of the Representation of the People Act prohibiting appeals to religious sentiment for electoral purposes. They acted decisively in several cases; in Maharashtra, for instance, between 1990 and 1995 the Bombay High Court set aside the election of 6 MLAs from the Shiv Sena and 3 MLAs from the BJP as well as of one BJP MP.[57] This judicial constraint was augmented by the Chief Election Commissioner, T.N. Seshan, who argued forcefully that the use of religious and communal themes was illegal in an election campaign. These warnings apparently exerted a moderating influence on the 1994-5 election campaigns, during which no communal riot took place.[58] In Gujarat, fear of Election Commission sanctions was mentioned by senior Hindu nationalist leaders in explaining why the VHP kept its distance from the BJP during the campaign.[59]

While the judiciary and Election Commission might have influenced the strategy of the Hindu nationalists, the BJP's decision to focus on socio-economic issues and distance itself from communal themes probably reflects the judgement of its own leaders that voters were more likely to respond to such issues. Indeed, the BJP lost a great deal of popularity in 1993 through its association with the Ayodhya movement, while the 1994-5 opinion polls revealed that the party was back in tune with public sentiment in exposing Congress(I)'s various shortcomings. A prominent member of the BJP's National Executive justified the 'new' approach quite unambiguously:

[56] *Times of India*, 27 and 28 Oct. 1994.

[57] At the time of writing a case is pending against at least one Shiv Sena MP, Moreshwar Save (*Times of India*, 16 Apr. 1994 and *India Today*, 31 Jan. 1995, p. 15. However, the Bombay High Court dismissed a writ petition aiming at prosecuting Bal Thackeray for his articles during the riots of January 1993 (P. Bidwai, 'Ayodhya and rule of law', *Times of India*, 6 Oct. 1994.

[58] Ibid.

[59] *Madhya Pradesh Chronicle*, 8 Feb. 1995.

Apart from emotional issues people are interested in issues directly related to their day-to-day life; we did not pay enough attention [in Karnataka] to farmers' problems and shortage of water. Emotional issues can only attract people when the stomach is full. [...] A dynamic party has to follow the dynamic of society. Unless we are able to feel the pulse of society then we cannot succeed. That was our failure in Andhra. Rama Rao promised 2 Rs kg. of rice and prohibition, which have reached fifty per cent of the voters, that is women who suffer from the rise of food prices and drunkenness of men.[60]

This kind of populist discourse, reminiscent of that employed by the Jana Sangh in the early 1970s and the BJP in the early 1980s, suggests that the BJP's leaders are aware that Hindu nationalism, as an ideology, cannot on its own help them to win power; they have to be alive to the people's expectations. This pragmatic approach is unlikely to please the RSS and especially the VHP whose leaders remain attached to their original doctrine and *modus operandi*.

Will tensions emerge in the 'Sangh parivar'?

While it was certainly affected by the ban, the VHP was not irrevocably damaged between 1992 and 1995. For one thing the measure was not strictly enforced (the VHP continued to function under the name of Hindu Sangam); for another, many religious leaders remained in its fold. The Ramlaya Trust attracted some individuals, such as Vishvesh Tirth, but of the nine trustees originally contacted at its inception in October 1994, Hari Acharya and Purushottam Acharya, both of whom were former members of the VHP, turned out to be unreliable recruits when the Trust was officially registered in December 1994.[61] Moreover the *Shankaracharya* of Puri remained close to the VHP and thus deplored the reimposition of the ban on the organisation.[62] The Ramlaya Trust doubtless exerted a major constraint on the VHP because the organisation could not afford to antagonise the *Shankaracharyas*, who commanded general respect. The organisation even met eminent members of the Ramlaya Trust in order to reach a compromise: some VHP leaders, such as Swami Vamdeo, said they were willing to allow the Trust to build the temple, provided the construction took place where the idols stood and according to the plan worked out by the VHP.[63] While the VHP may content itself with exerting pressure from behind the scenes in the case of Ayodhya and let the Ramlaya Trust play the leading role, the Hindu nationalist organisation

---

[60] Interview, 22 Feb. 1995, New Delhi.

[61] *Frontline*, 30 Dec. 1994, p. 25.

[62] *National Mail*, 20 Jan. 1995.

[63] *Frontline*, 30 Dec. 1994, p. 24 and *Madhya Pradesh Chronicle*, 14 Feb. 1995.

may well concentrate on the 'liberation' of the Kashi Vishwanath temple
at Varanasi. The original temple was probably built, adjacent to the
mosque, around 490 AD, before being destroyed by Muslim rulers,
re-built in 1585 and replaced by a mosque under the auspices of
Aurangzeb in 1669. The present temple, which is adjaccent to the mosque,
was built in 1777 by the heir of the princely family of Indore.

On 31 January 1995 the VHP organised a Sant Sammelan in Allahabad
at the time of the Ardh Kumbh Mela. It then announced the launch of a
campaign to rebuild the Kashi Vishwanath temple on its original site at
the time of Shivratri. Indeed, on 26 February, the date of the festival,
25,000 VHP activists gathered at Varanasi to launch the movement
formally. The VHP's joint General Secretary, Acharya Giriraj Kishore,
then demanded that 'the government transfer the disputed religious structures of Varanasi and Mathura to the Hindus before the movement takes
an aggressive turn'.[64] A month earlier, he had declared at Allahabad:
'Politics is no longer taboo for *sadhus* and *sants*.'[65] This aspect of the
VHP's programme had already been suggested at the VHP meeting in
Lucknow in December 1994 when the organisation had passed a purely
political resolution demanding a separate state in Uttarakhand.[66]

This development is congruent with the RSS's strategy. During his
all-India tour in early 1995, Rajendra Singh reaffirmed the apolitical status
of the RSS but stressed that 'if the situation demanded, it would not
hesitate to plunge into politics'.[67] More importantly, he emphasised that
'Only the reconstruction of the Kashi, Mathura and Ayodhya shrines
would bring harmony between Hindus and minorities.'[68] Besides the
themes of economic nationalism and national security developed by the
RSS, the rest of its programme remained couched in terms of militant
Hinduism. While the first objectives were mainly the responsibility of the
BJP, the VHP was charged with the second. This duality may become a
problem for the BJP. Although the party's leaders stressed that 'Varanasi
and Mathura are not on the BJP's agenda'[69] and tried to project a moderate

---

[64] Cited in *Hindustan Times*, 26 Feb. 1995. Soon after the VHP formed a Kashi Vishwanath
Gyanvapi Mandir Jeernodhar Samiti which was entrusted with the charge of taking out
Rath Yatras aimed at mobilising people on this new theme, during the first week of June
1995 (*Organiser*, 9 Apr. 1995, p. 16).

[65] Cited in *India Today*, 28 Feb. 1995, p. 29.

[66] *Organiser*, 8 Jan. 1995, p. 13.

[67] *Hindustan Times*, 11 Feb. 1995. This speech, made in Kerala was qualified in Bhopal
where Rajendra Singh declared that though the 'liberation' of the Kashi and Mathura
temples was not on the RSS's agenda at present, it could be included in it 'in the future'
(*National Mail*, 5 March 1995).

[68] Ibid.

[69] See, for instance, the policy articulated by Vajpayee soon after Shivratri (*Hindustan
Times*, 1 March 1995).

image at the National Executive meeting held in Goa in April 1995,[70] they may come under pressure from the RSS and VHP to adopt these objectives as well. In the mid-1980s, the Ayodhya issue was not on the BJP's agenda although it became part of its election manifesto in 1989.[71] This kind of tension is inherent in the structure of the 'Sangh parivar' and partly explains some of the re-orientations of the Jana Sangh and the BJP: in the early 1960s, early 1970s and early 1980s the Jana Sangh's leaders and later the BJP's leaders developed pragmatic – even populist, in socio-economic terms – programmes which were not contrary to the legitimate norms of politics. It was a phenomenon which reflected their belief that Hindu nationalism on its own was not enough to win elections. But they were confronted by the doctrinal rigidity of the party cadres, the RSS and the VHP whose attitudes eventually led the BJP's leaders to fall in line and even contribute substantially to Hindu nationalist propaganda (as Advani's *Rath Yatra* testifies). The BJP's leaders were not just responding to pressure from the RSS and VHP; they realised that moderate strategies had failed, and thus turned to a more radical programme in the late 1980s and early 1990s.

In the early 1990s, the BJP's leadership became convinced of the efficacy of the strategy of ethno-religious mobilisation up to 1992-3, when its limitations became apparent, namely that the party risked being over-ruled, politically, by uncontrollable militants and *sadhus* and the strategy was proving counter-productive when it resulted in major breaches of law and order. Hence the subsequent re-orientation in favour of a more populist approach. Whether the BJP will be able to maintain this line remains to be seen. If it does, it will indicate that a new populist cycle has begun.

---

[70] In his opening remarks, Advani even appealed to party activists to work among all sections of society,including minorities (*Times of India*, 8 Apr. 1995).

[71] L.K. Advani argues, in this respect, that the Babri Masjid-Ramjanmabhoomi offerred a particular case since it was 'not at all a functioning mosque' but 'a de facto temple' (see the interview with Advani in *India Today*, 15 Apr. 1995, p. 65). In this the BJP President made it clear that moderation and an emphasis on socio-economic and law and order issues was the only strategy likely to win his party power at the Centre: 'Whatever our adversaries might have been able to convince them, we will act in a truly secular and constitutional way. Everyone, including the so-called minorities will be free to exercise their fundamental rights regarding freedom to worship. Over and above that, there will be a complete guarantee of security, equality and social justice. If our governments in the states succeed in doing that, we will win their confidence and the Congress(I) and other pseudo-secular forces will be exposed.'

February 1996

In the final Assembly elections before the April 1996 general election the BJP further distanced itself (compared with 1993) from ethno-religious issues and based its propaganda on socio-economic themes with a populist overtone. This strategy is reminiscent of previous similar attempts by the Jana Sangh and the BJP. It might well be criticised, as were these previous attempts, by the RSS and the VHP which may try to turn the BJP back towards the ethno-religious repertoire. More immediately, this strategy may not be sufficient to beat the Congress (I). While voters may still be wooed by populist discourses at a time when the government's economic policy is making life harder for the majority, this asset may not compensate for other factors. First, the BJP still has difficulties in expanding its base among the OBCs, the Scheduled Castes and the Scheduled Tribes and in broadening its influence in the South and the East, as the 1994-5 elections testify. Second, the growth of the party may be hampered by increasing dissension within the state units of the BJP. This phenomenon largely results from the exercise of power (as in Madhya Pradesh) or from the hope of exercising it (as in Karnataka). The further it progresses along the road to power, the harder it becomes for the BJP to remain united.

AFTERWORD

The first edition of this book was published just before the 1996 parliamentary elections in which the BJP gained sufficient seats to become the largest party in the Lok Sabha, though still short of an absolute majority in that house (160 seats out of 543). Its increase in strength was partly due to the continuing shift of the BJP from its traditional strategy of ethno-religious mobilisation towards a strategy based on moderation where communal relations were concerned, populist appeals for support for its economic and social policies, attacks on corruption and claims that it would foster law and order. Its willingness to reduce its emphasis on Hindu nationalism helped it to form links with regional parties which had become wary of joining with the Congress or with the Third Front alliance. Immediately after the elections the BJP was able to form a coalition government headed by Atal Bihari Vajpayee, but its parliamentary base was weak, and it was forced to resign after only 13 days in office.

Two years later, in the 1998 parliamentary elections, the BJP made further gains. It won 178 of the 543 elective seats in the Lok Sabha and attracted 25.5% of the valid votes (compared with 20.7% in 1996). In regional terms, it had consolidated its position in the Hindi belt (where it obtained 119 seats as against 114 in 1996), increased its representation in the South from 6 seats to 20 and won 8 seats in the East. The other 31 came mainly from Gujarat (19) and Maharashtra (where the BJP could retain only 4 of its 18 seats). Outside the North, it had benefitted considerably from the support of its regional allies, such as the AIADMK in Tamil Nadu, the Akali Dal in Punjab, the Trinamool Congress in West Bengal, the Biju Janata Dal in Orissa, the Samta Party in Bihar and the Lok Shakti in Karnataka[1]. Thus strengthened, the BJP worked with its

[1] For more details, see T. Blom Hansen and C. Jaffrelot (eds.), *The BJP and the*

provincial allies to form a coalition government. In doing so, it dropped the most controversial proposals from its election manifesto, such as those for building a Ram mandir at Ayodhya, for abrogating Article 370 of the Constitution (providing for the special status of Jammu and Kashmir) and for establishing a uniform civil code. The National Agenda for Governance which it negotiated with its partners highlighted issues of national security and social and economic policy. The government formed on the basis of this programme was again headed by Vajpayee, but it included a high proportion of non-BJP members despite the BJP's dominance of the parliamentary alliance[2]. In some ways, the BJP appeared to have adopted the role of the post-independence Congress Party by providing a relatively neutral pivot around which other groups could arrange themselves.

The position of the BJP in Indian politics resembles the Congress one in other ways. It is now more a national party in geographical and social terms. It has established itself more strongly outside the Hindi belt, in Karnataka and Andhra Pradesh in particular, and it has broadened its social base, even to the point of attracting large numbers of OBC voters (although it is still shunned by the Scheduled Caste electorate). On the debit side, like the old-style Congress, it has now to countenance factional conflict within its state units and it is open to accusations of corruption. It had also permitted its state units to strike deals with defectors as a means of taking power: in Uttar Pradesh, for example, the state BJP leader, Kalyan Singh, became Chief Minister of the State in late 1997 after winning the support of dissidents who had broken away from the Congress and the BSP. Its reputation as a clean and disciplined party has been tarnished to some extent and, as a party of government, it has shown that it is by no means a party with such a difference—contrary to its election slogan. In the state elections of November 1988 it suffered from the disadvantage of being the party in office at the centre and in several of the northern states and was blamed by the voters for rising food prices, with the result that it was dislodged from government in both Rajasthan and Delhi and failed to defeat the Congress in Madhya Pradesh[3].

However, it would be a mistake to assume on this evidence that the BJP has changed its nature fundamentally. It still has close affinities with other units of the Sangh Parivar, and is still willing to use its grip on power to promote Hindu nationalist policies. For example, the Union Minister for Human Resource Development, Murli Manohar Joshi, is concerned

---

Compulsions of Politics in India, Delhi, Oxford University Press, 1998.

[2] While it accounted for 70% of the coalition in Parliament, the BJP accepted to get only 56% of the portfolios in the first Vajpayee government.

[3] In Rajasthan the BJP could retain only 33 of its 95 seats, in Delhi, 15 of its 49 seats and in Madhya Pradesh it could only add to 2 seats its 117 seats.

to 'Hinduise' the educational system, which is consistent with the long-term aim of the RSS to change the outlook of Indians through the medium of schooling. The atomic device tests carried out by India in May 1988 were equally in line with the military strategy favoured by Hindu nationalists, although they were also welcomed by others of the BJP's coalition partners.

The future development of the BJP will be influenced by a number of factors, such as its judgement of its electoral prospects and the pressure exerted upon it by other units of the Sangh Parivar. The RSS and the VHP may resign themselves to accepting that the strategy of moderation and regional alliances is the only means of gaining office and to gradually implementing their educational and social policies. On the contrary, they may take the view that the evidence of factionalism and allegations of corruption will ultimately undermine the party's reputation for discipline and puritanism and, having taken such a view, they may either distance themselves from the BJP (as they did in the early 1980s) or force it to change its political style even if this were to result in a lower profile so far as power politics is concerned. In either case, the BJP would be forced to make a choice between bending to pressure from the RSS and the VHP and striking out on its own in order to maintain its strategy of moderation.

A reversion to a new form of the old strategy of ethno-religious mobilisation, may become more attractive to some of the BJP's leaders if the party continues to be blamed for unpopular government policies and if the Congress re-establishes itself as a coherent and attractive alternative to the BJP-led coalition at the centre.

APPENDICES

A

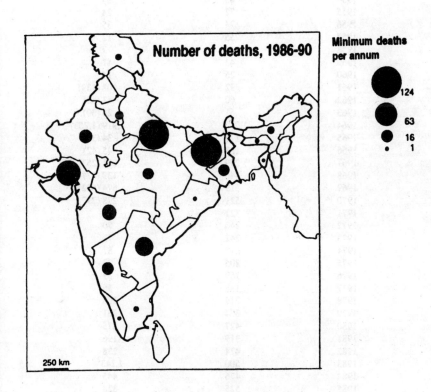

VICTIMS OF HINDU-MUSLIM RIOTS, 1986-90

B

HINDU-MUSLIM RIOTS AND RESULTING VICTIMS, 1954-93

	No. of riots	No. of casualties
1954	83	34
1955	72	24
1956	74	35
1957	55	12
1958	41	7
1959	42	41
1960	26	14
1961	92	108 (139)
1962	60	43 (42)
1963	61	26 (30)
1964	1,070	1,919 (1,703)[1]
1965	173	34 (30)
1966	133	45 (42)
1967	209	251 (253)
1968	346	133 (87)
1969	519	674 (572)
1970	521	298 (297)
1971	321	103
1972	240	70
1973	242	72
1974	248	87
1975	205	33
1976	169	39
1977	188	36
1978	219	108
1979	304	261
1980	427	375
1981	319	196
1982	474	238
1983	500	1,143[2]
1984	476	445
1985	525	328
1986	764	418
1987	711	383
1988	611	223
1989	706	1,155[4]
1990	1,404	1,248[4]
1991	905	474[5]
1992	1,991	1,640[5]
1993	?	558[3]

These official figures under-estimate the actual number of casualties but it is not possible to say to what extent.

556

Notes:

[1] This figure is due to an exceptionally high death toll of 985 in Orissa.

[2] This high figure is due to the anti-Bangladeshi riots in Assam.

[3] Out of 558 casualties, 557 died in January during the second phase of the Bombay riot following the demolition of the mosque.

[4] Communication from the Minister of State for Home before the Rajya Sabha (*National Mail*, 18 July 1991).

[5] *Muslim India*, no. 134 (Feb. 1994).

Sources:

P. Brass, *The Politics of India since Independence*, Cambridge University Press, 1990, p. 168.

For the figures in brackets, see G. Krishna, 'Communal violence in India', *EPW*, 12 Jan. 1985, p. 71.

The figures in italics have been released in Parliament by the government and reproduced in *India Today*, 15 Oct. 1990, p. 24, and 15 Jan. 1991, p. 26, and in *Muslim India*, nos 81, 103 and 108 (Sept. 1989, July and Dec. 1991), pp. 419, 323 and 557.

C

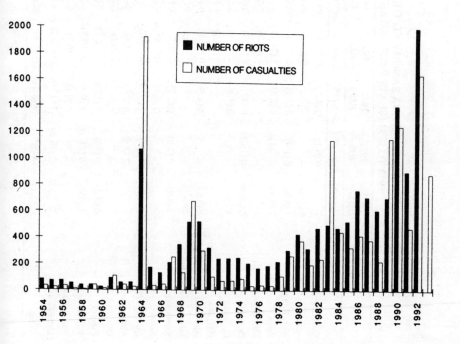

D

PERFORMANCE OF THE JANA SANGH AND THE B.J.P. IN LOK SABHA ELECTIONS, 1952 TO 1991 (SEATS WON AND SHARE OF VALID VOTES)

	1952 BJS	1957 BJS	1962 BJS	1967 BJS	1971 BJS	1977 JP	1980 JP	1984 BJP	1989 BJP	1991 BJP
	Seats (%)	Seats (%)	Seats (%)	Seats (%)	Seats (%)	Seats (%)	Seats (%)	Seats (%)	Seats (%)	Seats (%)
Andhra Pradesh	–	0 (0.1)	0 (1.2)	0 (1.4)	0 (1.6)	1 (32.3)	0 (15.2)	1 (2.2)	0 (2)	1 (9.6)
Assam	0 (3.6)	–	–	0 (5.5)	0 (2.5)	3 (35.8)	0 (8.0)	0 (0.4)	No election	2 (8.6)
West Bengal	2 (5.9)	0 (1.4)	0 (1.1)	0 (1.4)	0 (0.9)	15 (21.5)	0 (4.5)	0 (0.4)	0 (1.7)	0 (11.7)
Bihar	0 (0.04)	0 (0.1)	0 (2.3)	1 (11.1)	2 (12.1)	52 (65.0)	8 (23.6)	0 (6.9)	8 (11.7)	5 (15.9)
Chandigarh	–	–	–	1 (48.7)	0 (23.3)	1 (66.1)	0 (9.3)	0 (5.6)	–	–
Delhi	0 (25.9)	0 (19.7)	0 (32.7)	6 (46.7)	0 (29.6)	7 (68.2)	1 (37.9)	0 (18.8)	4 (26.2)	5 (40.2)
Gujarat	–	–	0 (1.4)	–	0 (2.2)	16 (49.5)	1 (36.9)	1 (18.6)	12 (30.5)	20 (50.4)
Haryana	–	–	–	1 (19.9)	1 (11.2)	10 (70.4)	1 (28.1)	0 (7.5)	0 (8.3)	0 (10.2)
Himachal Pradesh	0 (10.7)	–	0 (4.5)	0 (19.1)	0 (10.6)	4 (57.2)	0 (36.4)	0 (23.3)	3 (45.3)	2 (42.8)
Jammu and Kashmir	–	–	–	0 (20.3)	0 (12.2)	0 (8.2)	0 (8.6)	0 (1.7)	0 (7.2)	No election
Karnataka	0 (4.2)	0 (2.5)	0 (2.7)	0 (2.3)	0 (1.9)	2 (39.9)	1 (22.9)	0 (4.7)	0 (2.6)	4 (28.8)
Kerala	–	–	0 (0.7)	0 (1.4)	0 (1.4)	0 (7.2)	0 (6.7)	0 (1.8)	0 (4.5)	0 (4.6)
Madhya Pradesh	0 (4.9)	0 (14)	3 (17.9)	10 (29.6)	11 (33.6)	37 (57.9)	4 (31.3)	0 (30.0)	27 (39.7)	12 (41.9)
Maharashtra	–	2 (3.4)	0 (4.4)	0 (7.4)	0 (5.2)	19 (31.4)	8 (20.4)	0 (10.1)	10 (23.7)	5 (20.2)
Orissa	–	–	–	0 (0.6)	0 (0.2)	15 (51.8)	0 (14.1)	0 (1.2)	0 (1.3)	0 (9.5)
Punjab	0 (5.6)	0 (16)	3 (15.2)	1 (12.5)	0 (4.5)	3 (12.5)	0 (10.0)	0 (3.4)	0 (4.3)	No election
Rajasthan	1 (3)	0 (11.1)	1 (9.3)	3 (10.3)	4 (12.4)	24 (65.2	4 (31.7)	0 (23.7)	13 (29.6)	12 (40.9)
Tamil Nadu	–	–	0 (0.1)	0 (0.2)	0 (0.1)	–	0 (8.0)	0 (0.1)	0 (0.3)	0 (1.6)
Uttar Pradesh	0 (7.3)	2 (14.8)	7 (17.6)	12 (22.2)	4 (12.3)	85 (68.1)	3 (22.6)	0 (6.4)	8 (7.6)	50 (32.8)
Total	3 (3.1)	4 (5.9)	14 (6.4)	35 (9.4)	22 (7.4)	294 (41.3)	31 (19)	2 (7.4)	85 (11.4)	119 (20.1)

E

PERFORMANCE OF THE JANA SANGH AND THE B.J.P. IN VIDHAN SABHA ELECTIONS, 1952 TO 1993-5 (SEATS WON AND SHARE OF VALID VOTES)

States	1952
Ajmer	3 (11.95)
Assam	0 (0.29)
West Bengal	9 (5.58)
Bhopal	0 (4.92)
Bihar	0 (1.18)
Bombay	0 (0.04)
Coorg	
Delhi	5 (21.89)
Himachal Pradesh	0 (3.35)
Hyderabad	0 (0.04)
Madhya Bharat	4 (9.74)
Madhya Pradesh	0 (3.59)
Madras	0 (0.04)
Mysore	0 (2.26)
Orissa	
PEPSU	2 (3.32)
Punjab	0 (5.56)
Rajasthan	8 (5.93)
Saurashtra	0 (0.46)
Travancore Cochin	
Uttar Pradesh	2 (6.43)
Vindhya Pradesh	2 (9.88)

States	1957	1962	1967	1968-9	1972-4	1980-3	1984-7	1989-91	1993-5
Andhra Pradesh	0 (0.11)	0 (1.04)	3 (2.11)		0 (1.87)	3 (2.8)	8 (1.6)	5 (1.7)	2 (3.8)
Assam	0 (0.98)	0 (0.45)	0 (1.84)		0 (0.27)		0 (0.1)	10	
West Bengal		0 (0.45)	1 (1.53)	0 (0.89)	0 (0.26)	0 (1.71)	0 (1.71)	0 (10)	
Bihar	0 (1.19)	3 (2.77)	26 (10.42)	34 (15.63)	26 (11.37)	21 (8.44)	16 (7.5)	39 (11)	41 (13.1)
Delhi									49 (43.5)
Gujarat	0 (0.55)	0 (1.33)	1 (1.88)		3 (8.29)	9 (14.2)	11 (14.9)	67 (26.7)	121 (42.5)
Haryana	4 (12.02)	4 (13.46)	12 (14.39)	7 (18.45)	2 (6.54)	6 (7.7)	17 (9.7)	6 (10.1)	
Himachal Pradesh			7 (13.87)		5 (7.76)	29 (35.15)	7 (30.6) 2	46 (42.7)	8 (35.6)
Jammu and Kashmir	5 (24.63)	3 (17.47)	3 (16.45)		3 (10.03)	0 (3.2)	2 (3.7)	0 (4.1)	
Karnataka	0 (1.34)	0 (2.27)	4 (2.82)		0 (4.25)	18 (7.8)	0 (6.5)	0 (4.7)	40 (16.9)
Kerala	0 (0.06)	0 (0.52)	0 (0.85)			0 (2.75)			
Madhya Pradesh	10 (9.88)	41 (16.66)	78 (28.2)		48 (28.72)	60 (30.34)	58 (32.4)	219 (38.8)	117 (39)
Maharashtra	4 (2.01)	0 (5.0)	4 (8.18)		5 (6.44)	14 (9.17)	16 (7.26)	42 (14.6)	138 (29.4)[1]
Orissa			0 (0.54)			0 (1.42)	1 (2.6)	2 (3.9)	9 (7.9)
Punjab	5 (7.47)	4 (7.59)	9 (9.84)	8 (9.01)	0 (4.95)	1 (6.43)	4 (3.84)	6	
Rajasthan	6 (5.42)	15 (9.15)	22 (11.69)		8 (12.04)	32 (18.6)	39 (21.2)	85 (25.2)	95 (38.4)
Tamil Nadu		0 (0.08)	0 (0)			0 (0.06)	0 (0.2)	0	
Uttar Pradesh	17 (9.77)	49 (16.46)	98 (21.67)	49 (17.93)	61 (17.12)	11 (10.62)	16 (9.9)	57 (12.6)[2] 211 (31.6)[2]	177 (33.4)

[1] BJP-Shiv Sena alliance [2] In 1990. [3] In 1991

F

NOTABLES AND ACTIVISTS AMONG MADHYA PRADESH B.J.S. AND B.J.P. MLAs BY REGION, 1957-90

	1957	1962	1967	1972	1977	1980	1985	1990
% of valid votes	9.9	16.7	28.3	28.5	47.3[1]	30.3	32.5	39.7
Total no. of seats (seats won)	288 (10)	288 (41)	296 (77)	296 (50)	320 (231)[1]-128[2]	320 (60)	320 (58)	320 (219)
GWALIOR AREA (districts: Morena, Bhind, Gwalior, Datia, Shivpuri, Guna, Vidisha)								
Seats (seats won)	35 (0)	35 (0)	35 (19)	35 (21)	39 (39)[1]-20[2]	39 (11)	39 (9)	39 (29)
Notables[3]	-	-	10	13	2[2]	4	3	11
Activists[3]	-	-	7	5[2]	13[2][2]	7[2]	4[1]	14[4]
MALWA AREA (districts: Raigarh, Shajapur, Ujjain, Indore, Dewas, Khargone, Dhar, Jhabua, Ratlam, Mandsaur)								
Seats (seats won)	56 (8)	56 (26)	58 (27)	58 (6)	63 (55)[1]-40[2]	63 (23)	63 (8)	63 (50)
Notables	2	8	6	3	3[2]	4	3	13
Activists	5[1]	15 (6)	11 (4)	3[1]	26[2] [7]	17[5]	4[3]	33 [9]
BHOPAL AREA (districts: Sehore, Bhopal, Raisen)								
Seats (seats won)	9 (0)	9 (0)	11 (7)	11 (2)	12 (8)[1]-6[2]	12 (7)	12 (5)	12 (11)
Notables	-	-	2	-	0[2]	-	1	1
Activists	-	-	2	2	5[2]	4[1]	4	7[1]
VINDHYA PRADESH (districts: Tikamgarh, Chhatarpur, Panna, Satna, Rewa, Sindhi, Shahdol)								
Seats (seats won)	37 (2)	37 (5)	38 (1)	38 (4)	40 (33)[1]-15[2]	40 (2)	40 (8)	40 (18)
Notables	-	2	-	2	3[2]	1	5	7
Activists	2	2	1	2	7[2]	0	2	10

CHHATTISGARH (districts: Surguja, Raigarh, Bilaspur, Raipur, Bastar Durg, Rajnandgaon)

Seats (seats won)	81 (10)	81 (5)	84 (9)	84 (10)	90 (54)[1]-22[2]	90 (6)	90 (13)	90 (51)
Notables	–	1	5	1	5[2]	2	7	19
Activists	–	2 [1]	1	1	9[2] [3]	2	3 [1]	16 [4]

MAHAKOSHAL (districts: Narsimhapur, Balaghat, Mandla, Jabalpur, Chhindwara, Hoshangabad, Betul, Khandwa, Sagar, Damoh, Seoni)

Seats (seats won)	70 (0)	70 (5)	70 (14)	70 (7)	76 (42)[1]-25[2]	76 (11)	76 (15)	76 (60)
Notables	–	–	4	2	5[2]	4	8	25
Activists	–	1	5 [1]	3	15[2] [1]	6 [2]	3	20

[1] Figures of the Janata Party

[2] Figures of ex-Jan Sangh members elected as Janata Party candidates.

'Notables' are leading citizens without formal ideological commitment to Hindu nationalism and especially rural leaders elected as members of Gram Panchayats, Janapada Sabhas, Zila Parishads or of the boards of cooperative institutions, marketing societies and Mandi committees. In urban contexts, this term refers also to members of municipal councils, merchants or prestigious advocates.

'Activists' implies an ideological commitment testified by fidelity to the same party over a long period and an active involvement in at least one of the branches of the 'RSS complex' other than the BJP. 'Activists' who become notabilised through their elections or appointments to influential posts are indicated square brackets.

Sources: Election results published by the Madhya Pradesh Chief Electoral Officer (Bhopal) and Madhya Pradesh Vidhan Sabha sadasyon ka sankshipt parichay, Bhopal, 1961, 1964, 1970, 1972, 1977, 1980, 1985 and 1991.

G

OCCUPATIONS OF MADHYA PRADESH B.J.S. AND B.J.P. MLAs 1957-90

	1957	1962	1967	1972	1977	1980	1985	1990
Agriculturalists[1]	2	15	12	14	23	21	27	99
Merchants, industrialists	4	7	8	6	12	11	10	29
Lawyers	1	2	8	9	22	14	6	37
Medical practitioners	–	3	3	1	9	3	2	12
Teachers	–	–	1	6	7	1	1	6
Clerks, executives	–	1	6	1	4	2	3	9
Workers, craftsmen	–	6	2	1	3	2	2	5
Social workers	1	1	1	2	9	1	1	5
Pujaris, Sadhus	–	1	1	–	1	–	–	–
Journalists	–	1	1	1	–	–	2	1

[1] The figures in this category must be considered as approximate because 'agriculturalists' seem to designate cultivators as well as landowners. The biographical data do not permit differentiation of the intermediate status, even though education led me to reclassify some individuals (e.g. an 'agriculturalist' with an LLB has been considered a 'lawyer'). This table remains relevant for visualising the balance between MLAs from a rural background and the other. As far as politicians are concerned, they have been classified according to their original professions.

Sources: As for App. F.

CASTE-AND COMMUNITY-BASED DISTRIBUTION OF JANA SANGH AND B.J.P. MLAs IN MADHYA PRADESH, 1952-93 (% in brackets, except on the last line)

Caste groups and communities	1952	1957	1962	1967	1972	1977	1980	1985	1990	1993
Upper castes										
Brahmin	2 (40)	3 (30)	11 (29.7)	31 (42.5)	25 (49)	57 (48.3)	18 (32.7)	19 (34.5)	71 (32.5)	42 (36.8)
Rajput	2 (40)	1 (10)	7 (18.9)	14 (19.1)	7 (13.7)	32 (27.1)	8 (14.5)	11 (20)	31 (14.2)	22 (19.2)
Kayasth		1 (10)	3 (8.1)	7 (9.5)	10 (19.6)	8 (6.7)	3 (5.4)	4 (7.2)	17 (7.8)	10 (8.7)
Banya				4 (5.4)	4 (7.8)	4 (3.3)	1 (1.8)		3 (1.3)	1 (0.9)
Khattri		1 (10)	1 (2.7)	5 (6.8)	4 (7.8)	10 (8.4)	4 (7.2)	4 (7.2)	16 (7.3)	7 (6.3)
Sindhi				1 (1.3)		2 (1.7)	1 (1.8)		1 (0.4)	1 (0.9)
Intermediate castes			2 (5.4)			2 (1.7)	1 (1.8)			1 (0.8)
Maratha		2 (20)	2 (5.4)			2 (1.7)	1 (1.8)	1 (1.8)		1 (0.8)
Other backward classes			3 (8.1)	9 (12.3)	8 (15.6)	11 (9.1)	10 (16.2)	15 (27.2)	48 (21.7)	21 (18.4)
Jat						1 (0.8)	1 (1.8)	1 (1.8)	1 (0.4)	1 (0.9)
Yadav				2 (2.7)	1 (1.9)	1 (0.8)	1 (1.8)		5 (2.3)	3 (2.7)
Kurmi		1 (10)	2 (2.7)	2 (2.7)	1 (1.9)	3 (2.5)	2 (3.6)	3 (5.4)	8 (3.6)	3 (2.7)
Teli			2 (2.7)	1 (1.3)	1 (1.9)		1 (1.8)	3 (5.4)	5 (2.3)	1 (0.9)
Kira			1 (1.3)		1 (1.9)	2 (1.7)	1 (1.8)		4 (1.8)	2 (1.8)
Panwar					1 (1.9)	1 (0.8)	3 (5.4)		5 (2.3)	2 (1.8)
Gujjar			1 (2.7)	2 (2.7)	2 (3.9)		1 (1.8)		3 (1.3)	
Raghuwanshi			1 (1.3)	1 (1.3)					1 (0.4)	
Pokhal										
Others					1 (1.9)	3 (2.5)		8 (14.5)	16 (7.3)	9 (8.1)
Scheduled castes	1 (20)	1 (10)	2 (5.4)	16 (21.9)	8 (15.6)	20 (16.9)	12 (21.8)	7 (12.7)	36 (16.5)	27 (23.6)
Scheduled tribes		1 (10)	9 (24.3)	13 (17.8)	11 (21.5)	17 (14.4)	10 (18)	10 (18.1)	53 (24.3)	16 (14)
Jains	2 (40)	4 (40)	3 (8.1)	4 (5.4)	10 (8.4)	10 (8.4)	4 (7.2)	3 (5.4)	8 (3.6)	7 (6.1)
Muslims						1 (0.8)		1 (1.8)	2 (0.9)	
Sikhs									1 (0.4)	
Total	5 (6)	10 (10)	37 (41)	73 (78)	51 (51)[1]	118 (128)	55 (60)	55 (58)	218 (219)	114 (117)

[1] The Jana Sangh won only 48 seats in 1972, but the party succeeded in winning three more in subsequent by-elections.

NB. We have not been able to identify the caste of some MLAs; the last line indicates the total number of those whose caste was known and the total of MLAs in parenthesis.

J

MADHYA PRADESH VIDHAN SABHA ELECTION
RESULTS, 1952-1993

VOTES FOR THE JANA SANGH AND HINDU MAHASABHA IN THE VIDHAN
SABHA ELECTIONS OF 1952 IN CENTRAL INDIA
(PROJECTED AS FOR THE BOUNDARIES OF MADHYA PRADESH)

*Note All the following maps show the Lok Sabha constituency boundaries introduced in
1977.*

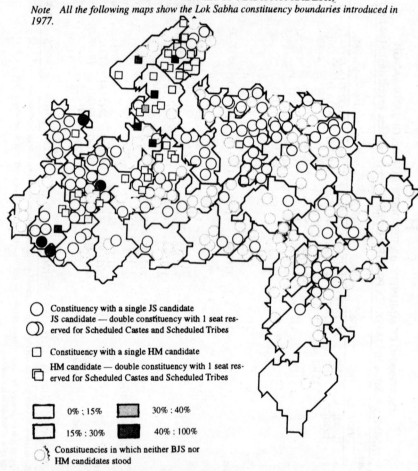

○ Constituency with a single JS candidate
◑ JS candidate — double constituency with 1 seat reserved for Scheduled Castes and Scheduled Tribes

□ Constituency with a single HM candidate
▣ HM candidate — double constituency with 1 seat reserved for Scheduled Castes and Scheduled Tribes

0% : 15%	30% : 40%
15% : 30%	40% : 100%

Constituencies in which neither BJS nor HM candidates stood

Source: *Report on the First General Elections in India, 1951-1952*, vol. II
(Statistical), New Delhi: Election Commission, n.d.

564

VOTES FOR THE JANA SANGH AND HINDU MAHASABHA IN THE VIDHAN
SABHA ELECTIONS OF 1957 IN MADHYA PRADESH

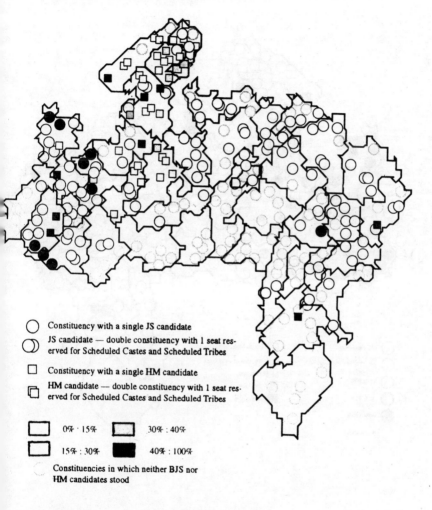

○ Constituency with a single JS candidate

◖ JS candidate — double constituency with 1 seat reserved for Scheduled Castes and Scheduled Tribes

□ Constituency with a single HM candidate

▣ HM candidate — double constituency with 1 seat reserved for Scheduled Castes and Scheduled Tribes

0% : 15%		30% : 40%
15% : 30%		40% : 100%

Constituencies in which neither BJS nor
HM candidates stood

Source: *Madhya Pradesh Vidhan Sabha General Elections — 1957-1980: Results and
Statistical Data* , Bhopal: Chief Electoral Officer of Madhya Pradesh, 1980

VOTES FOR THE JANA SANGH AND HINDU MAHASABHA
IN THE VIDHAN SABHA ELECTIONS OF 1962 IN MADHYA PRADESH

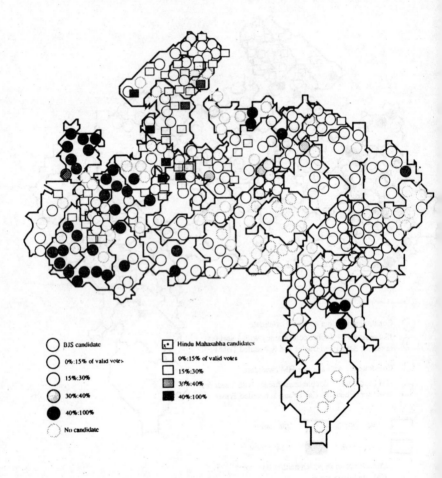

BJS candidate   Hindu Mahasabha candidates

0%:15% of valid votes   0%:15% of valid votes

15%:30%   15%:30%

30%:40%   30%:40%

40%:100%   40%:100%

No candidate

Source: *Madhya Pradesh Vidhan Sabha General Elections — 1957-1980: Results and
Statistical Data* , Bhopal: Chief Electoral Officer of Madhya Pradesh, 1980

VOTES FOR THE JANA SANGH AND CANDIDATES BACKED BY
THE SCINDIAS IN THE VIDHAN SABHA ELECTIONS OF 1967 IN
MADHYA PRADESH

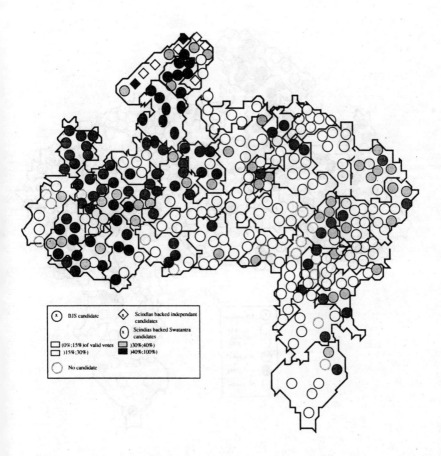

Source: *Madhya Pradesh Vidhan Sabha General Elections — 1985 Analytical tables*
Bhopal, Chief Electoral Officer of Madhya Pradesh, 1980

**VOTES FOR THE JANA SANGH IN THE VIDHAN
SABHA ELECTIONS OF 1972 IN MADHYA PRADESH**

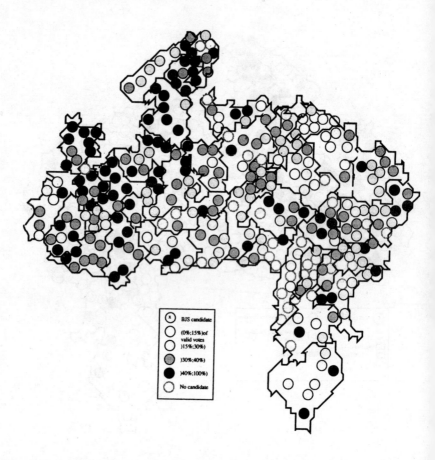

Source: *Madhya Pradesh Vidhan Sabha General Elections — 1957-1980: Results and
Statistical Data*, Bhopal: Chief Electoral Officer of Madhya Pradesh, 1980

VOTES FOR THE BJP IN THE VIDHAN
SABHA ELECTIONS OF 1980 IN MADHYA PRADESH

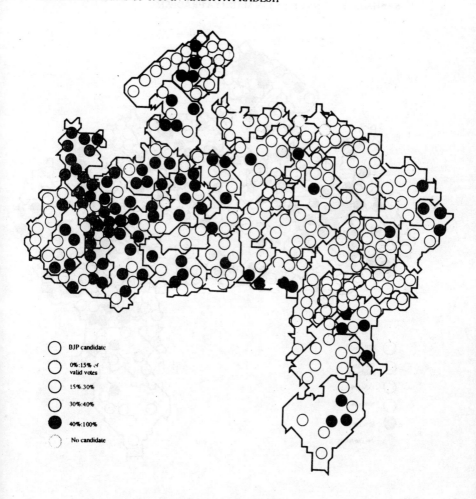

Source: *Madhya Pradesh Vidhan Sabha General Elections 1957-1980 Results and Statistical Data*. Bhopal: Chief Electoral Officer of Madhya Pradesh, 1980.

**VOTES FOR THE BJP IN THE VIDHAN
SABHA ELECTIONS OF 1985 IN MADHYA PRADESH**

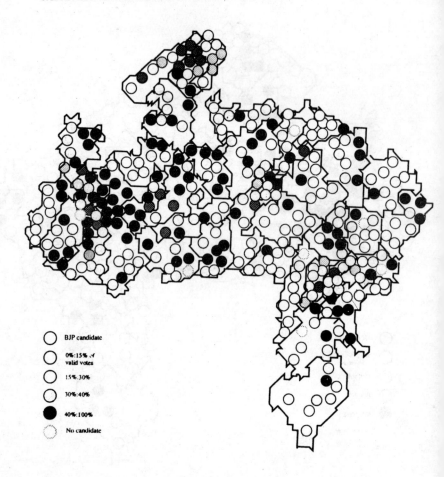

Source: *Madhya Pradesh Vidhan Sabha General Elections   1957-1980 Results and
Statistical Data*. Bhopal: Chief Electoral Officer of Madhya Pradesh. 1980

VOTES FOR THE BJP IN THE VIDHAN
SABHA ELECTIONS OF 1990 IN MADHYA PRADESH

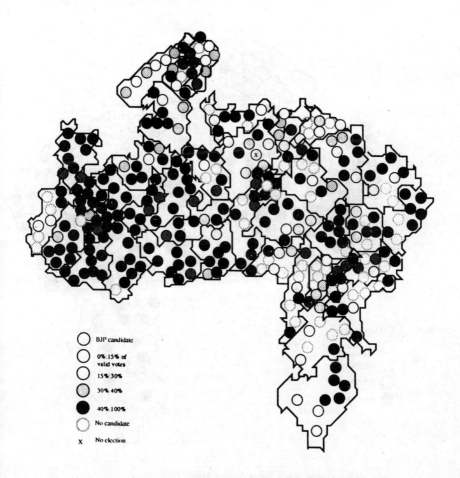

Source: *Madhya Pradesh Vidhan Sabha Nirvachan*, Bhopal, 1990.

VOTES FOR THE BJP IN THE VIDHAN
SABHA ELECTIONS OF 1993 IN MADHYA PRADESH

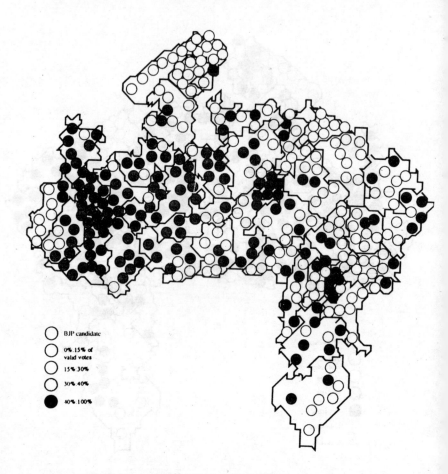

Source: *Madhya Pradesh Vidhan Vyapak Parinam*, Bhopal, 1993.

SELECT BIBLIOGRAPHY

Official archives

Consulted at the India Office Library and Records, London
Political (Confidential) Proceedings and Home Department Political Files
Public and Judicial Department Files

Consulted at the National Archives of India, New Delhi
Home Political Department
Proceedings of Ministry of Home Affairs

Consulted at the Madhya Pradesh State Archives, Bhopal
Gwalior State Papers
Madhya Bharat Cabinet
Madhya Bharat Rajpramukh

Private papers, archives of political parties and interview transcriptions

Private papers consulted at the National Archives of India, New Delhi
> N.B. Khare

Private papers consulted at the Nehru Memorial Museum and Library, New Delhi
> M.G. Chitnavis
> S.P. Mookerjee
> B.S. Moonje
> V.D. Savarkar
> K.R. Malkani

Interview transcriptions consulted at the Nehru Memorial Museum and Library
> N.B. Khare
> M.C. Sharma

Archives of political parties consulted at the Nehru Memorial Museum and Library
> Hindu Mahasabha (the files classified with the letter 'C' concern the national
> affairs of the party and those classified 'P' the provincial branches)
> Madhya Pradesh Congress Committee.

Unpublished works

Dissertations

Davey, H.T., 'The transformation of an ideological movement into an aggregative party: a case study of the Bharatiya Jana Sangh', Ph.D., University of California, Los Angeles, 1969

Gross, R.L., 'Hindu asceticism: a study of the *sadhu* of North India', 2 vols, Ph.D., University of California, Berkeley, 1979

Jayaprasad, K., 'Impact of Hindu nationalism on Kerala society and politics – a study of the RSS', Ph.D., Trivandrum University, 1989

Congress papers and 'grey literature'

Curran, J.A., 'Militant Hinduism in Indian politics – A study of the RSS', Institute of Pacific Relations, 1951, duplicated.

Graham, B., 'The challenge of Hindu nationalism: The BJP in contemporary Indian politics', *Hull Papers in Politics*, 40, Oct. 1987

Sen, I., 'Women and proselytisation: A case study of Christian missionary and Hindu revivalist attitudes towards women in Raigarh district of Madhya Pradesh' (paper presented to World Sociology Congress, Madrid, July 1990)

Chiriyankandath, J., 'Hindu nationalism and Indian regional political culture: a study of Kerala', Paper prepared for the European Consortium for Political Research Workshop on 'Political culture and religion in the Third World', Bordeaux, 27 April-2 May 1995.

Hansen, T.B., 'The Maratha'isation of Hindutva: Shiv Sena and BJP in rural Maharashtra', Paper prepared for the 13th European Conference of South Asian Studies, Toulouse, 31 Aug.-4 Sept. 1994.

Books

Advani, L.K., *The people betrayed*, Delhi: Vision Books, 1979.

———, *A prisoner's scrap book*, New Delhi: Arnold-Heinemann, 1978.

Andersen, W., and S.D. Damle, *The brotherhood in saffron: The Rashtriya Swayamsevak Sangh and Hindu revivalism*, New Delhi: Vistaar Publications, 1987.

Anderson, B., *Imagined communities: Reflections on the origin and spread of nationalism*, London: Verso, 1983.

Ashfaq Ali, Syed, *Bhopal past and present*, Bhopal, 1984.

Bailey, F.G., *Stratagems and spoils: A social anthropology of politics*, Oxford: Blackwell, 1969.

Baker, D.E.U., *Changing political leadership in an Indian province: The Central Provinces and Berar, 1919-1939*, Delhi: Oxford University Press, 1979.

Basu, T., P. Datta, S. Sarkar, T. Sarkar and S. Sen, *Khaki shorts, saffron flags*, New Delhi: Orient Longman, 1993.

Baxter, C., *A biography of an Indian political party – Jana Sangh*, Bombay: Oxford University Press, 1971.

Brass, P., *Language, religion and politics in North India*, Cambridge University Press, 1974.

Burger, A.S., *Opposition in a dominant party system*, Berkeley: University of California Press, 1969.

Chambard, J.L., *Atlas d'un village indien*, Paris: EHESS, 1980.

Das, D. (ed.), *Sardar Patel's correspondence, 1945-1950*, Ahmedabad: Navajivan Trust, 1973.

Deshmukh, N., *RSS: Victim of slander*, New Delhi: Vision Books, 1979.

Deshpande, B.V., and S.R. Ramaswamy, *Dr Hedgewar the epoch maker*, Bangalore: Sahitya Sindhu, 1981.

Dhooria, R.L., *I was a swayamsevak*, New Delhi: Sampradayikta Virodhi Committee (n.d.).

Dumont, L., *Homo hierarchicus*, Paris: Gallimard, 1966.

Frankel, F., *India's political economy 1947-1977*, Princeton University Press.

Frankel, F. and M.S.A. Rao (eds), *Dominance and state power in modern India: Decline of a social order*, 2 vols., New Delhi: Oxford University Press, 1989 and 1990.

Golwalkar, M.S., *We, or our nationhood defined*, Nagpur: Bharat Prakashan, 1939.

———, *Bunch of thoughts*, Bangalore: Jagarana Prakashan, 1966.

Gopal, S., *Jawaharlal Nehru: A biography*, London: Jonathan Cape, 1984.

——— (ed.), *Anatomy of a confrontation – The Babri Masjid Ramjanmabhumi issue*, New Delhi: Viking, 1990.

Goyal, D.R., *Rashtriya Swayamsevak Sangh*, New Delhi: Radha Krishna Prakashan, 1979.

Graham, B., *Hindu nationalism and Indian politics: The origins and development of the Bharatiya Jana Sangh*, Cambridge University Press, 1990.

Gupta, N.L.(ed.), *Nehru on communalism*, New Delhi: Sampradayikta Virodhi Committee, 1965.

Halbfass, W., *India and Europe: An essay in understanding*, Albany, NY: State University of New York Press, 1988.

Jones, K., *Arya Dharm: Hindu Consciousness in 19th century Punjab*, Berkeley: University of California Press, 1976.

Lal Chand, *Self-abnegation in politics*, Lahore: The Central Yuvak Sabha, 1938.

Madhok, B., *RSS and politics*, New Delhi: Hindu World Publications, 1986.

Malkani, K.R., *The RSS story*, New Delhi: Impex India, 1980.

Mishra, D.N., *RSS: Myth and reality*, New Delhi: Vikas, 1980.

Nandy, A., Trivedy, S., Mayaram, S., and Yagnik, A., *Creating a nationality – the Ramjanmabhumi movement and fear of the self*, Delhi: Oxford University Press, 1995.

Pandey, G. (ed.), *Hindus and others: The question of identity in India today*, New Delhi: Viking, 1993.

Prakash, I., *A review of the history and work of the Hindu Mahasabha and the Hindu Sangathan movement*, New Delhi: Akhil Cheratiya Hindu Mahasabha, 1938.

Puri, G., *Bharatiya Jana Sangh: Organisation and ideology*, New Delhi: Sterling, 1980.

Report of the Commission of Inquiry into the conspiracy to murder Mahatma Gandhi, 2 vols, Delhi: Government of India, 1969.

Savarkar, V.D., *Hindutva: Who is a Hindu?*, Bombay: S.S. Savarkar, 1969.
Scindia, Vijaya Raje, with M. Malgonkar, *Princess: The autobiography of the Dowager Maharani of Gwalior*, New Delhi: Times Books International, 1985.
Shraddhananda, *Hindu Sangathan: Saviour of the dying race*, Delhi: Arjun Press, 1926.
Smith, A.D., *Theories of nationalism*, London: Duckworth, 1971.
Smith, D.E., *India as a secular state*, Princeton University Press, 1963.
[anon.] *The Rashtriya Swayam Sevak Sangh*, Lahore: Government Printing, 1948.
Turner, V., *The ritual process*, Chicago: Aldine: 1969.
Upadhyaya, D., *Integral humanism*, New Delhi: Bharatiya Jana Sangh, 1965.
van der Veer, P., *Religious nationalism – Hindus and Muslims in India*, Berkeley: University of California Press, 1994.

Contributions to books

Brass, P., 'Elite groups, symbol manipulation and ethnic identity among the Muslims of South Asia' in D. Taylor and M. Yapp (eds), *Political identity in South Asia*, London: Curzon Press, 1979.
Gold, D., 'Organized Hinduisms: from Vedic truth to Hindu nation', in M.E. Martin and R. Scott Appleby (eds), *Fundamentalisms observed*, University of Chicago Press, 1991.
Graham, B., 'Syama Prasad Mookerjee and the communalist alternative' in D.A. Low (ed.), *Soundings in modern South Asian history*, Berkeley: University of California Press, 1968.
———, 'The Congress and Hindu nationalism' in D.A. Low (ed.), *The Indian National Congress*, Delhi: Oxford University Press, 1988.
———, 'The Prime Minister and the Hindu right' in J. Manor (ed.), *Nehru to the nineties*, London: Hurst, 1994.
Jaffrelot, C., 'Les modèles explicatifs de l'émergence des nations et du nationalisme. Revue critique' in G. Delannoi and P.A. Taguieff (eds), *Théories du nationalisme*, Paris: Kimé, 1991.
———, 'The BJP in Madhya Pradesh: networks, strategies and power', in G. Pandey (ed.), *Hindus and others – The question of identity in India today*, New Delhi: Viking, 1993.
———, 'Oeuvres pies et rationalité économique en Inde', in J.-F. Bayart (ed.), *La réinvention du capitalisme*, Paris: Karthala, 1994.
———, 'The idea of the Hindu race in the writings of Hindu nationalist ideologues in the 1920s and 1930s: a concept between two cultures' in P. Robb (ed.), *The concept of race in South Asia*, Delhi: Oxford University Press, 1995.
Plamenatz, J., 'Two types of nationalism' in E. Kamenka (ed.), *Nationalism: The nature and evolution of an idea*, London: Edward Arnold, 1973.
Rudolph, L.I., and S.H. Rudolph, 'Rethinking secularism: Genesis and implications of the next text-book controversy, 1977-79' in L.I. Rudolph and S.M. Rudolph (eds), *Cultural policy in India*, Delhi: Chanakya, 1984.
'The communal problem in India', *South Asia Bulletin*, 14 (1 and 2), 1994.
van der Veer, Peter, 'Hindu nationalism and the discourse of modernity: the

Vishva Hindu Parishad' in M. Marty and R. Scott Applebly (eds), *Accounting for fundamentalisms*, University of Chicago Press, 1993.
Wilcox, W., 'Madhya Pradesh' in M. Weiner (ed.), *State politics in India*, Princeton University Press, 1968.

Special Issues

'After Ayodhya', *South Asia*, vol. 17, 1994.
'BJP', *Seminar*, no. 417, May 1994
'Women and religious nationalism in India', *Bulletin of Concerned Asia Scholars* 25 (4), 1994.
'South Asia: responses to the Ayodhya crisis', *Asian Survey*, 33 (7), July 1993.

Articles

Andersen, W., 'The Rashtriya Swayamsevak Sangh, I: Early Concerns', *Economic and Political Weekly* (hereafter *EPW*), 11 March 1972.
———, 'The Rashtriya Swayamsevak Sangh, III: Participation in Politics, *EPW*, 25 March 1972.
Basu, A., 'Feminism inverted: the real women and gendered imagery of Hindu nationalism', *Bulletin of Concerned Asian Scholars*, 25(4), Oct.-Dec. 1993.
Bourdieu, P., 'La représentation politique – éléments pour une théorie du champ politique', *Actes de la Recherche en Sciences Sociales*, 36-7 (Feb.-March 1981).
Brass, P.R., 'Coalition politics in North India', *American Political Science Review*, 62, 4 (Dec. 1968).
Fox, R.G., 'Gandhian socialism and Hindu nationalism: Cultural domination in the world system', *Journal of Commonwealth and Comparative Politics* (hereafter *JCCP*), 25, 3 (Nov. 1987).
Freitag, S., 'Sacred symbols as mobilizing ideology: The North Indian search for a "Hindu" community', *Comparative Studies of Society and History*, 22, 4 (1980).
Frykenberg, R.E., 'The concept of "Majority" as a Devilish Force in the Politics of Modern Asia', *JCCP*, 15, 3 (Nov. 1987).
Gaborieau, M., 'Hiérarchie sociale et mouvements de réforme chez les musulmans de sous-continent indien', *Social Compass*, 33, 2-3 (1986).
———, 'From Al-Beruni to Jinnah – Indian ritual and ideology of the Hindu-Muslim confrontation in South Asia', *The Anthropologist*, 1, 3 (Jan. 1985).
Gold, D., 'Organized Hinduisms: from Vedic truth to Hindu nation' in M. E. Marty and R. Scott Appleby (eds), *Fundamentalisms observed*, The University of Chicago Press, 1991.
Graham, B., 'The Jana Sangh and Party Alliances: 1967-70', *South Asian Review*, 4, 1 (Oct. 1970).
Jaffrelot, C., 'L'émergence des nationalisme en Inde – Perspectives théoriques', *Revue Française de Science Politique* (hereafter *RFSP*), 38, 4 (Aug. 1988).
———, 'La place de l'Etat dans l'ideologie nationale hindoue. Eléments pour l'étude de "l"invention de la tradition politique" ', *RFSP*, 39, 6 (Dec. 1989).

————, 'Note sur un syndicat nationaliste hindou. Le travail et les travailleurs dans l'idéologie et les stratégies du Bharatiya Mazdoor Sangh', *Purushartha*, 14 (1991).

————, 'Les émeutes entre hindous et musulmans: Essai de hiérarchisation des facteurs culturels, économiques et politiques', *Cultures et conflits*, 5 (Spring 1992).

————, 'Hindu nationalism: strategic syncretism in ideology building', *EPW*, 20 March 1993.

————, 'Processions hindoues, stratégies politiques et emeutes entre hindous et musulmans', *Purushartha*, 16 (1993).

————, 'Les (re)conversions à l'hindouisme (1885-1990). Politisation et diffusion d'une "invention de la tradition" ', *Archives de Sciences Sociales des Religions*, no 87, (July-Sept. 1994).

————, 'La Vishva Hindu Parishad – structures et stratégies', *Purushartha*, 17 (1994).

————, 'The genesis and development of Hindu nationalism in the Punjab: from the Arya Samaj to the Hindu Sabha (1875-1910)', *The Indo-British Review*, 21 (1).

Jhari, K.D., 'Revealing details of *pracharak*'s life', *Secular Democracy*, June 1970.

————, 'I was a swayamsevak – II', *Secular Democracy*, 1970.

————, 'Creating the urge to kill', *Secular Democracy*, July 1970.

Kothari, R., 'The Congress "System" in India', *Asian Survey*, 4, 12 (Dec. 1964).

————, 'Tradition and modernity revisited', *Government and opposition*, Summer 1968.

Thapar, R., 'Syndicated Moksha?', *Seminar*, Sept. 1985.

————, 'Imagined Religious Communities? Ancient History and the Modern Search for a Hindu Identity', *Modern Asian Studies*, 23, 2 (1989).

van der Veer, P., ' "God must be liberated!" A Hindu liberation movement in Ayodhya', *Modern Asian Studies*, 21, 1 (1987).

Newspapers and journals

Mahratta (Poona, 1920-5)
Hindu Outlook (Delhi, 1938-57)
Statesman (Calcutta, 1946)
Organiser (Delhi, 1947-)
Hitavada (Nagpur, 1947-57)
Economic and Political Weekly (Bombay, 1948)
Seminar (Delhi, 1957-90)
Madhya Pradesh Chronicle (Bhopal, 1963-93)
Motherland (Delhi, 1971-5)
Statesman (Delhi, 1977-)
Hindu Vishva (Allahabad, 1982-93)
India Today (New Delhi, 1987)
Dainik Bhaskar (Bhopal, 1988-90)
India Week (1989-90)

National Mail (Bhopal, 1990-)
About Us (Internal bulletin of the BJP – 1990-2)

Certain periodicals cited in the notes are not included in this list because articles from them were consulted in the press clippings files at Sapru House (Delhi).

Election documents concerning Madhya Pradesh

Election results

Chief Electoral Officer Madhya Pradesh, *Vidhan Sabha General Elections 1957-1980 – Results and statistical data* (parts I, & II), Bhopal: Government Central Press, 1980.

Chief Electoral Officer Madhya Pradesh, *Lok Sabha General Elections 1980 – Analytical Tables*, Bhopal, 1980.

Chief Electoral Officer Madhya Pradesh, *Lok Sabha General Elections 1985 – Analytical Tables*, Bhopal, 1985.

Chief Electoral Officer Madhya Pradesh, *Lok Sabha General Elections 1989 – Analytical Tables*, Bhopal, 1989.

Chief Electoral Officer Madhya Pradesh, *Vidhan Sabha General Elections 1990 – Analytical Tables*, Bhopal, 1990.

Chief Electoral Officer Madhya Pradesh, *Vidhan Sabha vyapak nirvachan 1993 parinam*, Bhopal, 1993 (Hindi).

Biographical notes on those elected to the Madhya Pradesh Vidhan Sabha (Hindi):

Madhya Pradesh Vidhan Sabha sadasyon ka sankshipt parishay 1957, Bhopal: Madhya Pradesh sabha sachivalay, 1961.

Madhya Pradesh Vidhan Sabha sadasyon ka sankshipt parishay 1962, Bhopal: Madhya Pradesh sabha sachivalay, 1964.

Madhya Pradesh Vidhan Sabha sadasyon ka sankshipt parishay 1967, Bhopal: Madhya Pradesh sabha sachivalay, 1970.

Madhya Pradesh Vidhan Sabha sadasyon ka sankshipt parishay 1972, Bhopal: Madhya Pradesh sabha sachivalay, 1972.

Madhya Pradesh Vidhan Sabha sadasyon ka sankshipt parishay 1977, Bhopal: Madhya Pradesh sabha sachivalay, 1977.

Madhya Pradesh Vidhan Sabha sadasyon ka sankshipt parishay 1980, Bhopal: Madhya Pradesh sabha sachivalay, 1980.

Madhya Pradesh Vidhan Sabha sadasyon ka sankshipt parishay 1985, Bhopal: Madhya Pradesh sabha sachivalay, 1985.

Madhya Pradesh Vidhan Sabha sadasya-parichay 1990, Bhopal: Madhya Pradesh Vidhan Sabha sachivalay, 1991.

INDEX

Advani, Lal Krishan: reasons for joining RSS, 72; expels Madhok as Jana Sangh's president, 236; early career and closeness to RSS, 237; on decentralisation, 262 (fn); supports the 'JP movement', 266; addresses Jana Sangh session of 1975, 272; detained in Bangalore during the Emergency, 277-9; favours amalgamation of opposition parties in 1976, 280; canvassed in 1977 on theme of decentralisation, 284; Minister of Information and Broadcasting, 285; affinities with Desai, 286; as mediator between Janata Party factions, 292; as BJP's vice-president and later general secretary, 316; criticises Muslim Women (Protection of Rights) Bill, 346; BJP's General Secretary and then President, 376; increasing militancy, 377; relations with Vajpayee, 377; negotiates 1989 seat adjustment with V.P. Singh, 382 (fn); supports Ayodhya movement, 383; consults Deoras, 383; and anti-Mandal demonstrations, 415-16; and Rath Yatra, 416-20; negotiates with V.P. Singh during *Rath Yatra*, 418; claims he is not a religious leader, 449; tours Uttar Pradesh before 6 December 1992, 454; and demolition of Babri Masjid, 455-7; arrested in December 1992, 464; charge-sheet filed by the CBI, 467; re-elected BJP president, 483; change in political discourse, 484-6; and 1993 election campaign,

486-7 *Janadesh Yatras*, 487; shift from ethno-religious nationalism to economic nationalism and populism, 536-8; denies BJP's interest in the sites of Varanasi and Mathura, 549
Acharya Giriraj Kishore, 43, 351, 360, 479, 548
Aggarwal, Lakhi Ram, 323, 498-9
Ajit Singh, 378
Akhand Bharat/Hindustan: theme supported by K.M. Munshi, 85; article of the Hindu Mahasabha's programme, 108
Ajmera, Amar Chand, 354
akhara (gymnasium), 35-6
Akhil Bharatiya Vidyarthi Parishad (ABVP): foundation of 1948, 126; and Jabalpur communal riot (1961), 165-6; and Aligarh communal riot (1961), 167; strike in 1973, 254 (fn); Gujarat student agitation of 1973, 258; and 'JP movement', 258-60; growth in late 1970s, 302
Aligarh Muslim University, 167, 286 (fn), 333-4
Ali Mian, 418
All India Muslim Personal Law Board, 334-5
Alwar, Maharajah of, 81
Ambedkar, Dr, 21
Aney, M.S., 53
Angre, Chandrojirao, 109-10
Angre, Sambhajirao, 109, 218-19, 247
Anjuman-e-Taraqqi-e-Urdu, 160
anuloma (marriage), 21, 28
Anushilan Samiti, 33-4
Apte, Babasaheb, 41 (fn), 42, 47, 65-6, 68

READ MORE IN PENGUIN

In every corner of the world, on every subject under the sun. Penguin represents quality and variety—the very best in publishing today.

For complete information about books available from Penguin—including Puffin, Penguin Classics and Arkana—and how to order them, write to us at the appropriate address below. Please note that for copyright reasons the selection of books varies from country to country.

In India: Please write to *Penguin Books India Pvt. Ltd. 11, Community Centre, Panchsheel Park, New Delhi, 110017*

In the United Kingdom: Please write to *Dept JC, Penguin Books Ltd. Bath Road, Harmondsworth, West Drayton, Middlesex, UB7 ODA, UK*

In the United States: Please write to *Penguin Putnam Inc., 375 Hudson Street, New York, NY 10014*

In Canada: Please write to *Penguin Books Canada Ltd. 10 Alcorn Avenue, Suite 300; Toronto, Ontario M4V 3B2*

In Australia: Please write to *Penguin Books Australia Ltd. 487, Maroondah Highway, Ring Wood, Victoria 3134*

In New Zealand: Please write to *Penguin Books (NZ) Ltd. Private Bag, Takapuna, Auckland 9*

In the Netherlands: Please write to *Penguin Books Netherlands B.V., Keizersgracht 231 NL-1016 DV Amsterdam*

In Germany: Please write to *Penguin Books Deutschland GmbH, Metzlerstrasse 26, 60595 Frankfurt am Main, Germany*

In Spain: Please write to *Penguin Books S.A., Bravo Murillo, 19-I'B, E-28015 Madrid Spain*

In Italy: Please write to *Penguin Italia s.r.l., Via Felice Casati 20, I-20104 Milano*

In France: Please write to *Penguin France S.A., 17 rue Lejeune, F-31000 Toulouse*

In Japan: Please write to *Penguin Books Japan, Ishikiribashi Building, 2-5-4 Suido, Tokyo 112*

In Greece: Please write to *Penguin Hellas Ltd, dimocritou 3, GR-106 71 Athens*

In South Africa: Please write to *Longman Penguin Books Southern Africa (Pty) Ltd, Private Bag X08, Bertsham 2013*